Encyclopedia of
HOMELESSNESS

Encyclopedia of HOMELESSNESS

VOLUME 1

Editor
David Levinson
Berkshire Publishing Group

A Berkshire Reference Work

A SAGE Reference Publication

SAGE Publications
Thousand Oaks ▪ London

For information:

Sage Publications, Inc.
2455 Teller Road
Thousand Oaks, California 91320
E-mail: order@sagepub.com

Sage Publications Ltd.
1 Oliver's Yard
55 City Road
London EC1Y 1SP
United Kingdom

Sage Publications India Pvt. Ltd.
B-42 Panchsheel Enclave
Post Box 4109
New Delhi 110017 India

Printed in the United States of America

Library of Congress Cataloging-in-Publication Data

Main entry under title:
    Encyclopedia of homelessness / David Levinson, editor.
        v. cm.
    A Berkshire Reference Work.
    A Sage Reference Publication.
    Includes bibliographical references and index.
    ISBN 0-7619-2751-4 (cloth)

    1. Homelessness--Encyclopedias. I. Levinson, David, 1947-

HV4493.E53 2004
362.5'0973'03--dc22

2004009279

04 05 06 07 10 9 8 7 6 5 4 3 2 1

Berkshire Publishing Staff		Sage Publications Staff	
Project Director:	David Levinson	*Publisher:*	Rolf A. Janke
Project Coordinators:	Marcy Ross and George Woodward	*Editorial Assistant:*	Sara Tauber
		Production Editor:	Diana E. Axelsen
Copy Editors:	Martha Keskinen, Mike Nichols, Carol Parikh, Mark Siemens, and Daniel Spinella	*Production Assistant:*	Patricia Zeman
		Typesetter/Designer:	Tim Giesen/Straight Line Design
		Indexer:	Mary Mortensen
Information Management and Programming:	Deborah Dillon and Trevor Young	*Cover Designer:*	Ravi Balasuriya
Editorial Assistant:	Emily A. Colangelo	*Production Artist:*	Michelle Lee Kenny

Contents

List of Entries, vii

Reader's Guide, xi

List of Sidebars, xiii

List of Historical Documents, xiv

Contributors, xv

Introduction, xxi

Acknowledgments, xxv

About the Editors, xxvii

Entries

VOLUME I: A–O
1–434

VOLUME II: P–Z
435–626

Appendix 1: Bibliography of Autobiographical and
Fictional Accounts of Homelessness, 627

Appendix 2: Filmography of American Narrative
and Documentary Films on Homelessness, 631

Appendix 3: Directory of Street Newspapers, 635

Appendix 4: Documentary History of Homelessness, 639

Appendix 5: Master Bibliography of Publications on Homelessness, 765

Index, 823

List of Entries

Abeyance Theory
Africa.
   See Egypt; Homelessness,
   International Perspectives on;
   Housing and Homelessness in
   Developing Nations; Nairobi;
   Nigeria; South Africa; Zimbabwe
African-Americans
Alcohol and Drugs
Almshouses.
   See Poorhouses; Workhouses
American Bar Association
   Commission on Homelessness
   and Poverty
Asia
   See Australia; Calcutta;
   Homelessness, International
   Perspectives on; Housing and
   Homelessness in Developing
   Nations; India; Indonesia; Japan;
   Mumbai (Bombay); Sydney;
   Tokyo
Assertive Community Treatment
   (ACT)
Association of Gospel Rescue
   Missions
Associations and Organizations
   See American Bar Association
   Commission on Homelessness
   and Poverty; Association of
   Gospel Rescue Missions;
   Corporation for Supportive
   Housing; Council of State
   Community Development
   Agencies; European Network for
   Housing Research; FEANTSA;
   Goodwill Industries International;
   Homeless Assistance Services and

Networks; Homeless
International; "Housing First"
Approach; International Network
of Street Newspapers;
International Union of Tenants;
National Alliance to End
Homelessness; National
Association of State Housing
Agencies; National Center on
Family Homelessness; National
Coalition for the Homeless;
National Resource Center on
Homelessness and Mental Illness;
Salvation Army; UN-HABITAT;
Urban Institute; Wilder Research
Center
Australia
Autobiography and Memoir,
   Contemporary Homeless

Bangladesh
Bombay
   See Mumbai
Boston
Bowery, The
Brazil

Calcutta
Canada
Case Management
Causes of Homelessness: Overview
Chicago Skid Row
Child Care
Child Support
Children
   See Child Care; Child Support;
   Children, Education of; Children,
   Impact of Homelessness on;

Families; Foster Care; Parenting;
   Youth, Homeless
Children, Education of
Children, Impact of Homelessness on
Cinema
   See Appendix 2: Filmography of
   American Narrative and
   Documentary Films on
   Homelessness; Images of the
   Homeless in Contemporary
   Documentary Film; Images of the
   Homeless in Narrative Film,
   History of
Continuum of Care
Copenhagen
Corporation for Supportive Housing
Cost-Effectiveness Analysis
Criminal Activity and Policing
Cuba

Dallas
Deindustrialization
Deinstitutionalization
Denmark
Disorders and Health Problems:
   Overview

Egypt
Encampments, Urban
Epidemiology
Ethnography
European Network for Housing
   Research

Fair Housing Laws
Families
Family Separations and Reunifications
FEANTSA
Food Programs

Foster Care
France

Gentrification
Germany
Goodwill Industries International
Great Depression

Harm Reduction
Health Care
Hidden Homelessness
History of Homelessness
    See Appendix 4: Documentary
    History of Homelessness;
    Bowery, The; Chicago Skid Row;
    Deindustrialization; Great
    Depression; Hobo and Tramp
    Culture and History; Literature,
    Hobo and Tramp; Missions;
    Poorhouses; Skid Row Culture
    and History; Workhouses
HIV and AIDS
Homeless Assistance Services and
    Networks
Homeless Court Program
Homeless International
Homeless Organizing
Homeless Populations
    See African-Americans; Children;
    Epidemiology; Families;
    Homelessness, Definitions and
    Estimates of; Homelessness,
    Patterns of; Homelessness, Rural;
    Homelessness, Suburban;
    Latino(a)s; Older Homeless
    Persons; Street Youth; Veterans;
    Women; Youth, Homeless
Homelessness, Course of
Homelessness, Definitions and
    Estimates of
Homelessness, International
    Perspectives on
Homelessness, Patterns of
Homelessness, Rural
Homelessness, Suburban
Homelessness, Urban
    See Appendix 4: Documentary
    History of Homelessness;
    Bowery, The; Calcutta; Chicago
    Skid Row; Copenhagen; Dallas;
    Houston; London; Los Angeles;
    Madrid; Minneapolis and
    St. Paul; Montreal; Mumbai;

Nairobi; New York City; Paris;
    Philadelphia; St. Louis; Sydney;
    Tokyo; Toronto; Washington, D.C.
Housing
    See Appendix 4: Documentary
    History of Homelessness;
    Corporation for Supportive
    Housing; European Network for
    Housing Research; Fair Housing
    Laws; Foster Care; Hidden
    Homelessness; Housing and
    Homelessness in Developing
    Nations; Housing, Affordable;
    Housing, Transitional; "Housing
    First" Approach; International
    Union of Tenants; Interventions,
    Housing; Low-Income Housing
    Development; Missions;
    Municipal Lodging Houses;
    National Alliance of State Housing
    Agencies; Right to Shelter; Self-
    Help Housing; Shelters; Single-
    Room Occupancy Hotels; Survival
    Strategies; Workhouses
Housing, Affordable
Housing, Transitional
Housing and Homelessness in
    Developing Nations
"Housing First" Approach
Houston
Hunger and Nutrition

Images of Homelessness in
    Contemporary Documentary Film
Images of Homelessness in Narrative
    Film, History of
Images of Homelessness in
    Nineteenth- and Twentieth-
    Century America
Images of Homelessness in the
    Media
Indonesia
International Network of Street
    Newspapers
International Union of Tenants
Interventions, Clinical
Interventions, Housing
Italy

Japan

Latin America
    See Brazil; Cuba; Homelessness,

International Perspectives on;
    Housing and Homelessness in
    Developing Nations; Latino(a)s
Latino(a)s
Legal Advocacy
Legislation, Programs, and Policies,
    U.S. Federal
Libraries: Issues in Serving the
    Homeless
Liminality
Literature on Homelessness
    See Appendix 1: Bibliography of
    Autobiographical and Fictional
    Accounts of Homelessness;
    Appendix 4: Documentary
    History of Homelessness;
    Autobiography and Memoir,
    Contemporary Homeless; Images
    of Homelessness in Nineteenth-
    and Twentieth-Century American
    Literature; Literature, Hobo and
    Tramp; Media
Literature, Hobo and Tramp
London
Los Angeles
Low-Income Housing

Marginality
Media
    See Appendix 3: Directory of
    Street Newspapers; Images of
    Homelessness in the Media;
    Photography; Public Opinion;
    Street Newspapers
Men
    See Bowery, The; Chicago Skid
    Row; Great Depression;
    Literature, Hobo and Tramp; Skid
    Row Culture and History;
    Veterans
Mental Health System
Mental Illness and Health
Minneapolis and St. Paul
Mobility
Montreal
Mumbai (Bombay)
Municipal Lodging Houses

Nairobi
National Alliance to End
    Homelessness
National Center on Family
    Homelessness

National Coalition for the Homeless
National Resource Center on
   Homelessness and Mental Illness
Netherlands
New York City
Nigeria

Older Homeless Persons
Outreach

Panhandling
Parenting
Paris
Philadelphia
Photography
Poorhouses
Poverty
   See American Bar Association
   Commission on Homelessness
   and Poverty; Causes of
   Homelessness: Overview;
   Gentrification; Great Depression;
   Hidden Homelessness; Hunger
   and Nutrition; Panhandling;
   Poorhouses; Prevention of
   Homelessness: Overview; Social
   Welfare Policy and Income
   Maintenance; Soup Kitchens;
   Vagrancy; Workhouses
Prevention of Homelessness:
   Overview
Program Evaluation Research

Prostitution
Public Opinion

Religion
   See Appendix 4: Documentary
   History of Homelessness;
   Association of Gospel Rescue
   Missions; Goodwill Industries
   International; Missions; Salvation
   Army
Research on Homelessness:
   Overview
Russia

Safe Havens
Salvation Army
Self-Help Housing
Service Integration
Service Utilization Research
Shelters
Single-Room Occupancy Hotels
Skid Row Culture and History
Social Support
Social Welfare Policy and Income
   Maintenance
Soup Kitchens
South Africa
Spain
St. Louis
Street Life
   See Panhandling; Street Youth and
   Violence; Stressful Life Events;

Survival Strategies; Work on the
   Streets
Street Newspapers
Street Youth and Violence
Stressful Life Events
Survival Strategies
Sweden
Sydney

Tokyo
Toronto
Trauma and Victimization

UN-HABITAT
United Kingdom
United Kingdom, Rural
Urban Institute

Vagrancy
Veterans

Washington, D.C.
Wilder Research Center
Women
Work on the Streets
Workhouses

Youth, Homeless

Zimbabwe

Reader's Guide

This list is provided to assist readers in locating entries on related topics. It classifies entries into fourteen general categories: Causes; Cities; Demography and Characteristics; Health Issues; History; Housing; Legal Issues, Advocacy, and Policy; Lifestyle Issues; Organizations; Perceptions of Homelessness; Populations; Research; Service Systems and Settings; and World Perspectives and Issues. Some entry titles appear in more than one category.

CAUSES

Abeyance Theory
Causes of Homelessness: Overview
Deindustrialization
Deinstitutionalization
Gentrification
Housing and Homelessness in
    Developing Nations
Housing, Affordable
Liminality
Marginality
Social Welfare Policy and Income
    Maintenance
Stressful Life Events
Trauma and Victimization

CITIES

Boston
Bowery, The
Calcutta
Chicago Skid Row
Copenhagen
Dallas
Houston
London
Los Angeles
Minneapolis and St. Paul
Montreal
Mumbai (Bombay)
Nairobi
New York City
Paris
Philadelphia

St. Louis
Sydney
Tokyo
Toronto
Washington, D.C.

DEMOGRAPHY AND CHARACTERISTICS

Hidden Homelessness
Homelessness, Course of
Homelessness, Definitions and
    Estimates of
Homelessness, Patterns of
Homelessness, Rural
Homelessness, Suburban

HEALTH ISSUES

Alcohol and Drugs
Children, Impact of Homelessness on
Disorders and Health Problems:
    Overview
Food Programs
Health Care
HIV and AIDS
Hunger and Nutrition
Interventions, Clinical
Mental Health System
Mental Illness and Health

HISTORY

Appendix 4: Documentary History of
    Homelessness

Bowery, The
Chicago Skid Row
Great Depression
Literature, Hobo and Tramp
Municipal Lodging Houses
Poorhouses
Skid Row Culture and History
Workhouses

HOUSING

Fair Housing Laws
Housing and Homelessness in
    Developing Nations
Housing, Affordable
Housing, Transitional
"Housing First" Approach
Safe Havens
Self-Help Housing
Shelters
Single-Room Occupancy Hotels

LEGAL ISSUES, ADVOCACY, AND POLICY

Fair Housing Laws
Homeless Court Program
Homeless Organizing
Legal Advocacy
Legislation, Programs, and Policies,
    U.S. Federal
Prevention of Homelessness:
    Overview
Vagrancy

LIFESTYLE ISSUES

Appendix 3: Directory of Street
  Newspapers
Child Care
Child Support
Criminal Activity and Policing
Encampments, Urban
Libraries: Issues in Serving the
  Homeless
Mobility
Panhandling
Parenting
Prostitution
Shelters
Single-Room Occupancy Hotels
Soup Kitchens
Social Support
Street Newspapers
Survival Strategies
Work on the Streets

ORGANIZATIONS

American Bar Association
  Commission on Homelessness and
  Poverty
Association of Gospel Rescue
  Missions
Corporation for Supportive Housing
European Network for Housing
  Research
FEANTSA
Goodwill Industries International
Homeless International
International Network of Street
  Newspapers
International Union of Tenants
National Alliance to End
  Homelessness
National Center on Family
  Homelessness
National Coalition for the Homeless
National Resource Center on
  Homelessness and Mental Illness
Salvation Army
UN-HABITAT
Urban Institute
Wilder Research Center

PERCEPTIONS OF
HOMELESSNESS

Appendix 1: Bibliography of
  Autobiographical and Fictional
  Accounts of Homelessness

Appendix 2: Filmography of American
  Narrative and Documentary Films
  on Homelessness
Autobiography and Memoir,
  Contemporary Homelessness
Images of Homelessness in
  Contemporary Documentary Film
Images of Homelessness in Narrative
  Film, History of
Images of Homelessness in
  Nineteenth- and Twentieth-
  Century America
Images of Homelessness in the Media
Literature, Hobo and Tramp
Photography
Public Opinion

POPULATIONS

African-Americans
Families
Latino(a)s
Older Homeless Persons
Street Youth and Violence
Veterans
Women
Youth, Homeless

RESEARCH

Appendix 5: Master Bibliography of
  Publications on Homelessness
Cost-Effectiveness Analysis
Epidemiology
Ethnography
Program Evaluation Research
Research on Homelessness: Overview
Service Utilization Research

SERVICE SYSTEMS
AND SETTINGS

Assertive Community Treatment
  (ACT)
Case Management
Children, Education of
Continuum of Care
Family Separations and
  Reunifications
Food Programs
Foster Care
Harm Reduction
Health Care
Homeless Assistance Services and
  Networks

Housing, Transitional
"Housing First" Approach
Interventions, Clinical
Interventions, Housing
Mental Health System
Outreach
Poorhouses
Safe Havens
Self-Help Housing
Service Integration
Shelters
Single-Room Occupancy Hotels
Soup Kitchens
Work on the Streets
Workhouses

WORLD PERSPECTIVES
AND ISSUES

Australia
Bangladesh
Brazil
Calcutta
Canada
Copenhagen
Cuba
Denmark
Egypt
France
Germany
Homelessness, International
  Perspectives on
Housing and Homelessness in
  Developing Nations
Indonesia
Italy
Japan
London
Montreal
Mumbai (Bombay)
Nairobi
Netherlands
Nigeria
Paris
Russia
South Africa
Spain
Sweden
Sydney
Tokyo
Toronto
United Kingdom
United Kingdom, Rural
Zimbabwe

List of Sidebars

Alcohol and Drugs
A "Healing Place" for Recovery   10
Australia
Selection from Australia's *Working towards a National Homelessness Strategy*   22
Autobiography and Memoir, Contemporary Homeless
Excerpts from Four Autobiographical Stories of Homelessness   24
Bowery, The
Unexpected Attention for the Bowery   33
Brazil
A Street Child in Porto Alegre, Brazil   36
Children, Education of
The McKinney-Vento Homeless Assistance Act, Subtitle VII-B   73
Continuum of Care
Integrating Group Homes into Neighborhoods   81
Health Care
An Excerpt from *Down and Out in London and Paris,* by George Orwell   195
Foreign-Trained MDs Give Vital Service to Poor   199
Homelessness, International Perspectives on
A Green Statement on Homelessness   243
Housing and Homelessness in Developing Nations
Rita: A Case Study   276
Legal Advocacy
Privacy Rights versus Homeless Surveillance   337
Libraries: Issues in Serving the Homeless
America's Libraries and the Homeless   349
Literature, Hobo and Tramp
Catching Your First Train   357
London
Applying to Be Registered as Homeless   361
An Encounter with a Homeless Girl in Central London, circa 1990   362

Minneapolis and St. Paul
A Twin Cities Success Story   388
New York City
Housing Works: A Unique Service Provider   419
Older Homeless Persons
A Dying Neighborhood Turns Around   429
Paris
Maigret and the Homeless   443
Public Opinion
"You Get Thirty Days!"   471
A Wary Welcome   472
Street Newspapers
Homeless Journalists Hone Their Reporting Skills   537
The Big Issue of Britain   538
Survival Strategies
Finding a New Life in the Circus   552
Toronto
A Healthier Homeless Life in Toronto   564
United Kingdom
British Prime Minister Margaret Thatcher on Entitlements   577
Washington, D.C.
Safe Haven for Refugee Families in Washington, D.C.   595
Women
Homeless Women Become Self-Advocates   600
Workhouses
Selection from *The Warden,* by Anthony Trollope   610
Youth, Homeless
Selections from *Oliver Twist:* Oliver Twist Escapes to London   618

List of Historical Documents

The following documents appear in Appendix 4, Documentary History of Homelessness, in Volume II.

Document 1 *640*
Biblical Passages Relevant to Homelessness

Document 2 *647*
Chaucer, Geoffrey, "The Begging Friar and the Pardoner," from *Canterbury Tales*

Document 3 *647*
Luther, Martin, Three Classification Schemes (1500, 1561, 1627)

Document 4 *651*
Harman, Thomas, "A Caveat or Warening for Commen Corsetors, vulgarely called Vagabones"

Document 5 *653*
An Act for the Relief of the Poor, Anno xliii. Reginæ ELIZABETHÆ. CAP. II. (1601)

Document 6 *658*
"The Cunning Northern Beggar"

Document 7 *660*
Chambers, James, "The Poor Poetaster" from *The Political Works of James Chambers, Itinerant Poet, With the Life of the Author*

Document 8 *662*
The Poor Law Amendment Act of 1834—An Act for the Amendment and better Administration of the Laws relating to the Poor in England and Wales

Document 9 *692*
Mayhew, Henry, *Labour and the London Poor; A Cyclopædia of the Condition and Earnings of Those That Will Work, Those That Cannot Work, and Those That Will Not Work*

Document 10 *696*
Riis, Jacob, *How the Other Half Lives*

Document 11 *699*
Booth, Charles, *Life and Labour of the People in London*

Document 12 *711*
Higgs, Mary, *Glimpses into the Abyss*

Document 13 *716*
Rice, Stuart A., " The Homeless"

Document 14 *723*
Stiff, Dean (Nels Anderson), *The Milk And Honey Route*

Document 15 *730*
Gibbs, Philip, *England Speaks*

Document 16 *736*
Benson, Ben, "How to go to California without a Dollar"

Document 17 *738*
Camp La Guardia News

Document 18 *740*
United States Fair Housing Act. Sec. 800. [42 U.S.C. 3601 note]

Document 19 *747*
Summary of the Stewart B. McKinney Homeless Assistance Act [U.S. Public Law 100–77, 42 U.S.C. 119]

Document 20 *752*
European Social Charter (1966)

Document 21 *755*
Istanbul Declaration on Human Settlements of 1996

Document 22 *757*
Resolutions of the United Nations Housing Rights Programme (April–May 2003)
Women's equal ownership, access to and control over land and the equal rights to own property and to adequate housing *757*
Adequate housing as a component of the right to an adequate standard of living *760*
Global campaigns on secure tenure and urban governance *762*

Document 23 *763*
U. S. Conference of Mayors, Resolution No. 22, Endorsing Ten-Year Planning Process to End Chronic Homelessness (2003)

Contributors

Acevedo, Gregory
Temple University
Latino(a)s

Ahmed, Sawssan R.
Wayne State University
African-Americans
Egypt

Allen, Michael
Bazelon Center for Mental Health Law
Fair Housing Laws

Amer, Mona
University of Toledo
Egypt

Anderson, Isobel
University of Stirling
Cuba
United Kingdom

Arangua, Lisa
University of California, Los Angeles
Disorders and Health Problems:
Overview
Service Utilization

Aron, Laudan
The Urban Institute
Homelessness, Rural

Banks, Steven
Legal Aid Society of New York
Legal Advocacy

Barber, Charles
Moodus, Connecticut
Literature, Hobo and Tramp

Baron, Stephen W.
Queen's University
Street Youth and Violence

Barrow, Susan M.
New York State Psychiatric Institute
Family Separations and
Reunifications
Housing, Transitional
Women

Bassuk, Ellen
Harvard Medical School / National
Center on Family Homelessness
Families
Trauma and Victimization

Baumohl, Jim
Bryn Mawr College
Abeyance Theory
Deinstitutionalization
Liminality
Panhandling
Social Welfare Policy and Income
Maintenance

Berg, Steve
National Alliance to End Homelessness
Legislation, Programs, and Poli-
cies, U.S. Federal

Binder, Steve
San Diego, California
Homeless Court Program

Borchert, James
Cleveland State University
Deindustrialization

Goodwill Industries International
Goodwill Industries International

Breakey, William R.
Johns Hopkins University School of
Medicine
Interventions, Clinical
Mental Illness and Health

Bridgman, Rae
University of Manitoba
Homelessnes, International Per
spectives on
Safe Havens
Self-Help Housing

Buck, David S.
Baylor College of Medicine
Houston

Buck, Philip O.
Wayne State University
Images of Homelessness in the
Media

Buckner, John C.
Harvard Medical School
Children, Impact of
Homelessness on
Epidemiology

Burt, Martha
Urban Institute
Continuum of Care
Homeless Assistance Services and
Networks
Homelessness, Definitions and
Estimates of

Busch-Geertsema, Volker
GISS Bremen
Germany

Calsyn, Robert J.
University of Missouri , St. Louis
Social Support

Chase, Richard
Wilder Research Center
Wilder Research Center

Christensen, Michael
Drew University
Calcutta

Christian, Julie
University of Birmingham
London
United Kingdom

Cloke, Paul
University of Bristol
United Kingdom, Rural

Clower, Terry L.
University of North Texas
Dallas

Cohen, Carl I.
SUNY Downstate Medical Center
Older Homeless Persons

Colangelo, Emily A.
Berkshire Publishing Group
Association of Gospel Rescue
Missions
European Network for Housing
Research
Homeless International
International Network of Street
Newspapers
International Union of Tenants
National Alliance to End
Homelessness
National Center on Family
Homelessness
National Coalition for the
Homeless
Salvation Army
UN-HABITAT
Urban Institute

Cousineau, Michael R.
University of Southern California
Encampments, Urban

Covell, Nancy
University of Connecticut
Cost-Effectiveness Analysis

Crannell, Linda M.
www.poorhousestory.com
Poorhouses

Crowley, Sheila
National Low Income Housing
Coalition
Low-Income Housing

Curtis, Karen A.
University of Delaware
Food Programs

Daly, Gerald
York University
Canada

Davidson, Amy
AIDS Housing of Washington
HIV and AIDS

DePastino, Todd
Waynesburg College
Great Depression

DeVerteuil, Geoffrey
University of Manitoba
Mobility

Doorn, Lia van
Nederlands Instituut voor Zorg en
Welzijn (NIZW)
Netherlands

Erickson, Victoria Lee
Drew University
Hidden Homelessness

Firdion, Jean-Marie
Institut National d' Études
Démographiques
Foster Care
France
Paris

Fischer, Pamela J.
Substance Abuse and Mental Health
Services Administration
Criminal Activity and Policing

Fischer, Sean N.
New York University
New York City
Research on Homelessness:
Overview

Forney, Jason
Oakland University
Prostitution

Frisman, Linda
University of Connecticut
Cost-Effectiveness Analysis

Fujimura, Clementine
U.S. Naval Academy
Russia

Gaetz, Stephen
York University
Work on the Streets

Gelberg, Lillian
UCLA Center for Health Policy
Research
Disorders and Health Problems:
Overview

Ghafur, Shayer
Bangladesh University of Engineering
and Technology
Bangladesh

Gillis, Laura
Health Care for the Homeless, Inc.
Interventions, Clinical

Glasser, Irene
Community Renewal Team, Inc.
Alcohol and Drugs
Homelessness, International
Perspectives on
Soup Kitchens

Grzyb, Amanda F.
University of Western Ontario
Appendix 2: Filmography of Amer-
ican Narrative and Documen-
tary Films on Homelessness
Autobiography and Memoir,
Contemporary Homeless
Images of Homelessness in Con-
temporary Documentary Film
Images of Homelessness in Narra-
tive Film, History of
Images of Homelessness in
Nineteenth- and Twentieth-
Century American Literature

Heinz, Teresa L.
Indiana University
Street Newspapers

Hess, Nancy Owens
Holderness, New Hampshire
Child Care

Higginbotham, Peter
Oxford University
Workhouses

Hikida, Lyn
Corporation for Supportive Housing
Corporation for Supportive Housing

Hoburg, Robin
University of Connecticut
Cost-Effectiveness Analysis

Hoch, Charles
University of Illinois at Chicago
Chicago Skid Row
Single-Room Occupancy Hotels

Holter, Mark
University of Michigan
Mental Health System

Holupka, C. Scott
Vanderbilt Institute for Public Policy
Studies
Interventions, Housing

Hopper, Kim
Nathan Kline Institute
Abeyance Theory
Ethnography
Liminality
Municipal Lodging Houses
Shelters

Horton-Newell, Amy E.
American Bar Association
American Bar Association
Commission on Homelessness
and Poverty

Hurtubise, Roch
Université de Sherbrooke
Montreal

Hwang, Stephen W.
St. Michael's Hospital,
University of Toronto
Toronto

Janisse, Heather C.
Wayne State University
Homelessness, Patterns of

Javits, Carla
Corporation for Supportive Housing
Corporation for Supportive Housing

Johnsen, Matthew
University of Massachusetts Medical
School
Service Utilization Research

Kamete, Amin Y.
University of Zimbabwe
Zimbabwe

Kasprow, Wesley
Yale University
Veterans

Kim, Myoung
Mathematica Policy Research
Hunger and Nutrition

Koegel, Paul
RAND
Causes of Homelessness:
Overview
Ethnography
Homelessness, Course of
Houston

Leufgen, Jillianne
University of California, Irvine
Survival Strategies

Levinson, David
Berkshire Publishing Group
Bowery, The

Lewis, Dan
Northwestern University
Homelessness, Suburban

Linares, Esperanza
CARITAS ESPA—OLA
Spain

Lombardo, Sylvie
Oakland University
Prostitution

Loschiavo dos Santos, Maria Cecília
University of São Paulo
Brazil

Lovell, Anne
Université Toulouse le Mirail
Marginality

MacManus, Donal
FEANTSA
FEANTSA

Marpsat, Maryse
Institut National d' Études
Démographiques
France
Paris

Marr, Matthew
University of California, Los Angeles
Japan
Tokyo

McIntosh, Greg
Canberra, Australia
Australia
Sydney

Milbourne, Paul
Cardiff University
United Kingdom, Rural

Morse, Gary
Community Alternatives
Case Management
St. Louis

Mowbray, Carol
University of Michigan
Mental Health System

Munoz, Manuel
Universidad Complutense de Madrid
Stressful Life Events

Nelson, Bruce
Northwestern University
Homelessness, Suburban

O'Callaghan, Seana
Nathan Kline Institute
Harm Reduction

O'Connell, James
Boston Health Care for the Homeless
Program
Boston
Health Care

O'Grady, Bill
University of Guelph
Work on the Streets

Olufemi, Olusola
Memorial University, Newfoundland
Nigeria
South Africa

Owen, Greg
Wilder Research Center
Minneapolis and St. Paul
Wilder Research Center

Panadero, Sonia
Madrid, Spain
  Stressful Life Events

Piening, Suzanne
National Center on Family
  Homelessness
  Trauma and Victimization

Price, Jillian M.
National Resource Center
  on Homelessness and
  Mental Illness
  *National Resource Center
    on Homelessness and
    Mental Illness*

Rafferty, Yvonne
Pace University
  Children, Education of

Rahardjo, Tjahjono
Soegijapranata Catholic University
  Indonesia

Robertson, Marjorie
Public Health Institute
  Youth, Homeless

Rog, Debra J.
Vanderbilt University
  *Interventions, Housing
  Program Evaluation Research*

Roman, Nan
National Alliance to End
  Homelessness
  *Legislation, Programs, and Poli-
    cies, U.S. Federal*

Rosenheck, Robert A.
Yale School of Medicine
  *Assertive Community Treatment
    (ACT)*
  Veterans

Rosenthal, Rob
Wesleyan University
  Homeless Organizing

Ross, Marcy
Berkshire Publishing Group
  Philadelphia
  Washington, D.C.

Rowe, Michael
Yale University
  Service Integration

Roy, Shirley
Université du Québec à Montréal
  Montreal

Sahlin, Ingrid
Goteborg University
  Sweden

Salter, Charles A.
Library Consultant
  *Libraries: Issues in Serving the
    Homeless*

Salter, Jeffrey L.
Shreve Memorial Library
  *Libraries: Issues in Serving the
    Homeless*

Schneider, John C.
Tufts University
  Skid Row Culture and History

Schulz, Dorothy Moses
John Jay College of Criminal Justice
  Vagrancy

Seibyl, Catherine
Yale University School of Medicine
  Veterans

Sharma, Kalpana
The Hindu
  Mumbai (Bombay)

Shinn, Marybeth
New York University
  Families
  *Prevention of Homelessness:
    Overview*
  *Research on Homelessness:
    Overview*

Snow, David A.
University of California, Irvine
  Survival Strategies

Speak, Suzanne
University of Newcastle upon Tyne
  *Housing and Homelessnes in
    Developing Nations*

Spinnewijn, Freek
FEANTSA
  FEANTSA

Stax, Tobias Børner B.
Danish National Institute of

Social Research
  Copenhagen
  Denmark

Sullivan, Mary
Worcester Family Health Center
  Service Utilization

Swain, Stacy E.
Boston Health Care for the
  Homeless Program
  Boston

Tepper, Paul
The Weingart Center
  Los Angeles

Thomas, Susan
Hollins University
  Child Support

Tipple, Graham
University of Newcastle upon Tyne
  *Housing and Homelessness in
    Developing Nations*

Tompsett, Carolyn J.
Wayne State University
  Public Opinion

Toro, Paul A.
Wayne State University
  African-Americans
  Egypt
  Homelessness, Patterns of
  *Images of Homelessness in the
    Media*
  Public Opinion

Torquati, Julia C.
University of Nebraska, Lincoln
  Parenting

Tosi, Antonio
Polytechnic of Milan
  Italy

Tsemberis, Sam
Pathways to Housing, Inc.
  Harm Reduction
  "Housing First" Approach

Vazquez, Carmelo
Universidad Complutense de Madrid
  Stressful Life Events

Wamiti, Maurice
Nairobi, Kenya
Nairobi

Weinreb, Linda
University of Massachusetts Medical
    School
*Disorders and Health Problems:
    Overview*

Weinstein, Bernard L.
University of North Texas
Dallas

Weitzman, Beth C.
New York University
New York City

Williams, Brett
American University
Gentrification

Williams, Francine
Policy Research Associates, Inc.
*National Resource Center on
    Homelessness and Mental
    Illness*

Winarski, James T.
Advocates for Human Potential, Inc.
Outreach

Wolf, Judith
Netherlands Institute of Mental Health
    and Addiction
Netherlands

Yochelson, Bonnie
New York Historical Society
Photography

Ziebarth, Ann C.
University of Minnesota
Housing, Affordable

Zywiak, William H.
Decision Sciences Institute
Alcohol and Drugs

Introduction

There is nothing new about homelessness. There have been homeless people for some 10,000 years—from the time when humans built their first permanent homes in the first towns of the Fertile Crescent. The historical record, novels and poems, and sacred texts tell us the stories of beggars, wandering ascetics, penniless friars, displaced peasants, lost soldiers, street youths, vagrants, new arrivals in the city, and displaced workers.

Homelessness has changed over the years. In the United States, during the late nineteenth century, it was hoboes and tramps who drew the attention of the public, the police, and then the social reformers of the Progressive Era. From the 1920s through the Great Depression, attention shifted to the skid rows, home to transient workers and retired single men. The decline of skid rows in the 1970s was followed by a new era of homelessness with many formerly institutionalized people—who had untreated or poorly treated emotional disorders—winding up on the streets of America. In the 1980s, the nature of homelessness changed again. Growing economic inequality, racism, a permanent decrease in the number of well-paid unskilled jobs, and a lack of affordable housing combined to make several million people—many of them African-American women and their children—homeless on America's streets, in shelters, in motels, and in substandard and temporary apartments. This pattern continues in 2004.

Homelessness is not just a U.S. problem, although when viewed cross-culturally, it becomes a more complex issue. In many developed nations, homeless families, many of them immigrants, are the major issue. In the developing nations of Asia, Africa, and Latin America, the homeless are often women and their children, youths, and migrants from rural areas who have come to cities looking for work and opportunity. The emergence of many cities in developing nations as major regional or global commercial centers has made the problem even worse, by increasing the appeal of cities as employment centers to the rural poor while at the same time providing less and less affordable housing and support services for immigrants.

The goal of the *Encyclopedia of Homelessness* is to summarize our knowledge of homelessness. This includes describing the patterns of homelessness in the past, focusing on the recent and current situation in the United States, and sampling homelessness around the world. Entries cover causes; history; legal issues, advocacy, and policy; legislation and programs; lifestyle and health problems; organizations; research; services and service settings; size and perceptions; subpopulations and lifestyles; and world issues and perspectives. Descriptive articles cover homelessness today in eight major American cities and more than thirty cities and nations around the world. These entries allow for quick and easy comparisons.

Homelessness is one of the least understood social issues. The public image of homelessness and public perceptions of the nature and causes of homelessness have little relation to the reality of the situation. Most Americans have little or no contact with homeless people. Encounters on the street are quick and awkward and immediately pushed out of one's consciousness. I vividly remember that when I was doing anthropological research posing as a panhandler near the Bowery in the early 1970s, passersby simply did not seem to know that I existed. In that guise, I had no place and therefore no existence in their social and physical world. This avoidance of the homeless has made it easy for misconceptions to develop and persist—misconceptions that are routinely reinforced by the depictions of the homeless by the news media, on television, and in film.

Homelessness in the United States has changed dramatically since my research in 1971 on the transition of skid rows like the Bowery. This was a time when skid row was just about gone, and a few years before the homeless population went from being single, old men to younger men, the deinstitutionalized mentally ill, and the working poor who could not find affordable housing. Still, there are commonalities from the past to the present, including health problems, violence, inadequate housing, lack of jobs, difficulties with law enforcement, and a continuing avoidance of homeless people by most of American society. At the same time, as this encyclopedia shows, there are solutions and potential solutions at hand, and our understanding of homelessness in its various forms is more complete and more policy-directed than in the past.

Despite the changing nature of homelessness, when I tell people about this encyclopedia, they are usually surprised to hear that it is not mainly about drunken old men on the Bowery. They are even more surprised to hear that it contains much about families and children, African-American women in the United States and other Western nations, street children, and immigrant families in Asia, Africa, and Latin America. And, they think the homeless is an issue only in poor neighborhoods in large cities. Sure, they know about Construct, Inc,. in our small town of Great Barrington, Massachusetts, and its annual Walk for the Homeless, but they never realized that their donations actually help provide food and shelter for homeless people in our affluent community. They are also unaware that the rapidly rising housing prices in response to the housing boom created by well-off second-home owners and retirees has produced an affordable housing crisis and more homelessness in the rural Berkshires of western Massachusetts.

A major purpose of this encyclopedia is to correct these false images and misconceptions and beliefs from the past by providing readers with a comprehensive, accurate, and up-to-date description of homelessness in the twenty-first century.

AUDIENCE

As a topic of considerable current urgency, with a rich history and drawing the attention of experts from different disciplines and perspectives, the *Encyclopedia of Homelessness* meets the needs of a broad audience. This includes sociologists, anthropologists, economists, historians, and other social scientists; social policy analysts and planners who develop control and prevention programs; program administrators; physicians, social workers and lawyers who provide advocacy and services; journalists; and students in high school through graduate school in history, social studies, and the social sciences.

SCOPE AND BREADTH

Homelessness is a complex topic, and experts have yet to agree on a single definition or criterion to measure homelessness (see entry on Homelessness, Definitions and Estimates of). To some extent, this is because the nature and severity of homelessness as a social issue has changed over time, has varied over place, and has been studied or dealt with by different groups of experts. Homelessness has been a topic of interest for religious organizations, journalists, social reformers, public policy analysts, filmmakers, photographers, poets, novelists, songwriters, anthropologists, sociologists, psychologists, historians, geographers, physicians, government officials, law enforcements agents, attorneys, and social workers.

The contributors to this work come from many of these disciplines and several others, and they bring different perspectives to homelessness. These varying perspectives are apparent in many of the more focused entries, while a broader, interdisciplinary perspective defines the more general overview entries on topics such as prevention, health, and services.

The issue of homelessness cannot be addressed apart from the related issue of housing. This is true everywhere today, but especially so outside the United States where homelessness is often defined as a lack of housing or suitable housing. In the Western world, it is clear that a lack of affordable housing is one the leading contributing causes to homelessness today, and solving homeless will require providing affordable housing for all.

Global coverage is a hallmark of Berkshire Publishing encyclopedias, and this one is no different. Two general overviews—Homelessness, International Perspectives on, and Housing and Homelessness in Developing Nations—address the major patterns and issues of homelessness. These are supplemented by several dozen focused entries on international organizations and homelessness in a sample of nations and cities. In addition, information on homelessness beyond the United States is provided in each of the five appendixes.

The entries cover the following eleven general topics.

Homelessness in the United States

These entries examine the nature of homelessness in the United States in the late twentieth and early twenty-first centuries. Covered are the number of homeless, characteristics of homeless populations, subgroups, lifestyles and lifestyle issues, and perceptions of the homeless.

Homelessness in U.S. History

These entries cover homelessness in the past including hobo, tramp, and skid row culture, with an emphasis on social history and within the context of key events and processes in American history.

Research on Homelessness

Studying homelessness is not easy, and multi-method approaches often produce more trustworthy and richer conclusions than do single-method approaches such as a questionnaire. These entries cover research strategies and methods used in studying homelessness. The strategies and methods are defined and described, and much space is given to their role and contribution to our understanding of homelessness.

Causes of Homelessness

These entries cover the factors and processes that are commonly cited as leading causes of homelessness.

The editors recognize that homelessness has multiple causes, which may vary over time, place, and form of homelessness. The entries define and describe causal factors or processes, review evidence relating them to homelessness, and discuss controversies and implications for preventing homelessness.

Health Issues

The homeless experience high levels of social, emotional, and physical problems. These entries define and describe these problems, discuss their effects on the homeless, and review the causes of the problems and efforts to eliminate or treat them.

Organizations

For many centuries, there have been organizations whose missions and activities have an impact on homelessness. The number of such organizations today, their missions, and the issues they address are broader than ever. More than a dozen organizations are covered here, with an emphasis on the issues they address and the services and programs they provide. Inclusion here is not meant to imply that these are the "most important" organizations. While we do include major organizations, the goal is also to include a sampling of organizations that deal with a wide range of issues.

Cities and Nations

These entries provide summaries of the nature of homelessness in a sample of nations and cities around the world. The entries define homelessness in the national or urban setting being discussed, describe the key features of the homeless population, review causes, and discuss prevention and service initiatives.

Services and Service Settings

These entries concern service approaches and programs designed to alleviate problems experienced by the homeless and to prevent homelessness. Different approaches and programs aimed at different populations (families, children, men, etc.) are covered, their rationales explained, and research on their effectiveness reviewed.

Housing

As discussed above, housing issues and homelessness are interrelated. These entries focus on housing and its relationship to homelessness, various types of housing and housing programs, and legal and economic issues that influence the interaction between housing and homelessness.

Legal Issues, Advocacy, and Policy

These entries concern policies and initiatives meant to prevent homelessness or to protect or improve the lives of the homeless. The entries define and describe the particular policies and initiatives, and trace their development. Key people and organizations are identified and discussed.

Legislation and Programs

Entries in this category concern the relationship between homelessness and the federal, state, or local governments. The entries cover particular laws and programs and trace their development. Key people and organizations are identified and their roles discussed.

ILLUSTRATIVE MATERIAL AND APPENDIXES

In addition to the entries, the encyclopedia contains sidebars of additional and primary source material, photos and illustrations, and five appendixes. The appendixes are particularly important because they provide additional information that makes this encyclopedia a rich resource on homelessness. In compiling the appendixes, we sought to add material that is not readily or meaningfully available elsewhere and to direct readers to other important resources. The appendixes are:

1. Bibliography of Autobiographical and Fictional Accounts of Homelessness
2. Filmography of American Narrative and Documentary Films about Homelessness
3. Directory of Street Newspapers
4. Documentary History of Homelessness
5. Master Bibliography of Publications on Homelessness

Finally, it needs be mentioned that several navigational aids are provided for users including blind entries, cross-references to entries, a list of entries, a reader's guide to the content, a list of contributors, and a detailed index in Volume II.

Acknowledgments

In some ways, this project was a natural for both Berkshire Publishing and Sage given my research on homelessness, Berkshire's interest in pressing global issues, and Sage's role as a leading publisher of books and journals in the social and policy sciences. I want to especially thank Sage VP Blaise Simqu for his strong backing for the project and Rolf Janke of Sage Reference for suggesting it and shepherding it through the acquisitions process.

As far as research and planning go, homelessness is a relatively small field of inquiry. Most people active in the field know each other's work, and most know and have worked with one another. There is much collaboration, mutual respect, and sharing of one's work. Given this culture of homelessness studies, it was easy to form an editorial board composed of nearly all the leading researchers in the field. Once we talked to a few potential editorial board members, they began talking to each other and then others and in some sense formed the board almost by themselves. The few who could not find time to serve on the editorial board did make time to write an entry or two.

Once the editorial board was formed, the editors quickly and with much cooperation revised the preliminary entry list into the final one and recommended people (including themselves) to write the entries. As the project moved forward, they also helped revise and streamline the list. I also want to acknowledge the efforts of the contributors—several of whom were willing to write more than one article, some who also helped find other contributors, and some outside the United States who worked hard to make our coverage as global as possible.

In-house, George Woodward, the project's initial coordinator, played the lead role in getting the project moving. When he moved west, his place was filled ably by Marcy Ross, who took the project to completion and also managed the editorial process as she does for all our projects. Last, I need to thank our in-house photographer, Karen Christensen, who supplied photos taken in the United States, England, Italy, and Greece.

—*David Levinson*

About the Editors

GENERAL EDITOR

David Levinson, Ph.D., is a cultural anthropologist and president of the Berkshire Publishing Group. Prior to founding BPG in 1996 with Karen Christensen, he was at the Human Relations Area Files at Yale University. He has a B.A. in psychology (Montclair State University), an M.P.A. (Wagner School, New York University), and a Ph.D. in anthropology (SUNY/Buffalo). He conducted ethnographic research on the Bowery and in Newark, New Jersey, in 1971–1972 and 1984 and a survey of homelessness in U.S. cities in 1972. The results of this research were published in *Urban Anthropology* and the *International Journal of Social Psychiatry* and reported elsewhere. Other research has been on family relationships, the treatment of alcoholism, ethnic relations, and social theory. He is the author of *Family Violence in Cross-Cultural Perspective* (Sage 1989) and *Religion: A Cross-Cultural Dictionary* (1995) and the editor or coeditor of several major multi-volume academic encyclopedias, including the *Encyclopedia of Marriage and Family* (1995), *Encyclopedia of Crime and Punishment* (Sage 2002), and the *Encyclopedia of Community* (Sage 2003). His books and reference works have won numerous awards including *Choice* best academic and best reference, *Booklist* editor's choice, *Library Journal* best reference, and RUSA best reference.

EDITORIAL BOARD

Susan Barrow, Ph.D, is an anthropologist who works as a research scientist at the New York State Psychi-

atric Institute. She received her doctorate from Brandeis University and has spent the last twenty-five years researching the circumstances of homelessness in the urban United States. Her studies have combined survey techniques and other quantitative methods with ethnographic approaches to documenting both the experiences of people who are homeless and the shelters, outreach, social service, and mental health programs that they encounter. Her first research on homelessness focused on street outreach programs and other emerging models of service delivery developed in response to the homelessness crisis in New York City. Since then, she has conducted studies in shelters for unaccompanied men and women, drop-in centers, transitional housing sites, and an array of supported and supportive housing programs for formerly homeless adults in New York and several other U.S. cities. Her current work focuses on kin networks and parent-child separations in homeless families.

Ellen Bassuk, M.D., is cofounder and president of the National Center on Family Homelessness, a nonprofit organization that conducts research, policy analysis, program development and support, and public education on issues pertaining to homelessness and extreme poverty, and related social services. She received her degree in medicine from the Tufts Medical School. Her research interests and writings focus on the risks of family homelessness; the impact of homelessness on the mental and physical health of women and their children; the relationship among mental illness, substance abuse, family violence, and social support in poor families; and the impact of welfare reform on low-income families. She served as director of Psychiatric Emergency Services at the Beth Israel Hospital, is a board-certified psychiatrist, and holds an academic appointment as Associate Professor of Psychiatry at Harvard Medical School. She has received many research grants, has served on national and regional health policy committees, and has held numerous consultancies. She is the former editor of the *American Journal of Orthopsychiatry*. She has received numerous awards and honors in recognition of her work, including the Outstanding Psychiatric Award from the Massachusetts Psychiatric Society, the Sanctity of Life Award from Brandeis University, and an honorary degree, Doctor of Public Service, from Northeastern University.

Jim Baumohl, Ph.D., is Professor of Social Work and Social Research at Bryn Mawr College in Bryn Mawr, Pennsylvania. He is also director of the Ph.D. program in the School of Social Work and Social Research. He earned undergraduate, M.S.W., and Ph.D. degrees from the University of California, Berkeley, and before turning to full-time academic employment in 1986, he held jobs as a street worker, a shelter director, a tenant organizer, and a wine merchant, among others. Prior to joining the Bryn Mawr faculty in 1990, he taught at McGill University in Montreal, Quebec. Since 1973, he has written extensively about homelessness, welfare policy, and the history of alcohol and drug treatment and control policy. He is the editor of *Homelessness in America* (1996), a benefit book for the National Coalition for the Homeless, and an editor of the interdisciplinary and international quarterly, *Contemporary Drug Problems*. He teaches courses on social welfare history and policy, social theory, addiction, and disability.

Martha Burt, Ph.D, is the director of the Social Services Research Program at the Urban Institute. She received her Ph.D. in sociology in 1972, from the University of Wisconsin–Madison. Since then she has been involved in research and evaluation pertaining to a wide variety of populations and issues. She recently completed her third book on homelessness, *Helping America's Homeless: Emergency Shelter or Affordable Housing?* (2001), based on analyses and interpretation of the National Survey of Homeless Assistance Providers and Clients. She is also the author of the federal report of the same survey, *Homelessness Programs and the People They Serve* (1999). She has just finished a project for the Department of Housing and Urban Development, assessing continuums of care throughout the country (*Evaluating Continuums of Care for Homeless People, 2002*), and projects on the effects of health insurance on homeless people's receipt of health care and on the homeless service system in the District of Columbia. She is working on a project on the role of supportive services in maintaining chronically homeless people in housing. Her work on homelessness began in 1983 with an examination of the administrative structure of the first two waves of FEMA's Emergency Food and Shelter Program. In 1987, she directed the first national survey of homeless individuals. That study focused on soup kitchen and shelter users in cities with a population of more than 100,000 and is reported in *America's Homeless: Numbers, Characteristics, and the Programs That Serve Them* (1989). In 1992, she published *Over the Edge: The Growth of Homelessness in the 1980s,* which analyzes why homelessness became a major social problem in that decade. Also in 1992 (and again in 1994), she compiled *Practical Methods for Counting Homeless People: A Manual for State and Local Jurisdictions,* which has been widely disseminated and used. She has presented papers at a number of European conferences on homelessness, and continues to be involved in research and policy work on homelessness and residential instability.

Robert Drake, M.D., is the Andrew Thomson Jr. Professor of Psychiatry and Community and Family Medicine at Dartmouth Medical School and director of the New Hampshire–Dartmouth Psychiatric Research Center. He was educated at Princeton, Duke, and Harvard Universities. In addition to working actively as a clinician in community mental health centers for the past twenty years, he has been developing and evaluating innovative community programs for persons with severe mental disorders. He is well known for his work in co-occurring substance use disorder and severe mental illness. Some of his recent work has focused on vocational rehabilitation. He is the author of more than 200 publications, which cover diverse aspects of adjustment and quality of life among persons with severe mental disorders and those in their support systems.

Irene Glasser, Ph.D., is a senior planning/research analyst with the Community Renewal Team, Inc., in Hartford, Connecticut, which is the oldest community action agency in continual existence in the United States. She received her Ph.D. in anthropology and her M.S.W. from the University of Connecticut. Her research specialties include homelessness, treatment outcome research for the addictions, cross-national comparisons of urban poverty, the history of single-room occupancy hotels, and mothers in prison. She was a professor in anthropology at Eastern Connecticut State University, where she directed the Canadian Studies Program. She completed the Research Fellowship at the Center for Alcohol and Addiction Studies at Brown University and is now a training faculty for the Center. She has published widely on topics of urban poverty and homelessness. In all of her work, she integrates qualitative and quantitative methods of research, placing the data in the broadest historical, social, and cultural context.

Kim Hopper, Ph.D., is a medical anthropologist who works as a research scientist at the Nathan S. Kline Institute for Psychiatric Research, where he codirects the Center for the Study of Issues in Public Mental Health. He is also Associate Professor at the Mailman School of Public Health, Columbia University. Since 1979, he has done ethnographic and historical research on psychiatric care and on homelessness, chiefly in New York City. Active in homeless advocacy efforts since 1980, he is a cofounder of both the National Coalition for the Homeless and the New York Coalition for the Homeless. He is the author of *Reckoning With Homelessness* (2003), as well as the coeditor of the upcoming *Recovery from Schizophrenia: An International Perspective.*

Paul Koegel, Ph.D., is a medical and urban anthropologist who serves as associate director of RAND Health, a $45 million program of health services research at the RAND Corporation. His research has focused primarily on the adaptation of marginal populations to contemporary urban settings and how the

systems of care that are mandated to assist them either facilitate or hinder that adaptation. Throughout his twenty-five-year research career, he has addressed questions related to these issues with regard to several populations, including adults with mental retardation, homeless individuals, adults with serious mental illness, and substance abusers. He has done so using multiple methods, including the qualitative methods associated with anthropology, epidemiological methods, evaluation techniques, and health services methods and perspectives. His intimate knowledge of and experience with each of these paradigms has enabled him to effectively triangulate multiple methods in his research and has made him an attractive collaborator for quantitatively oriented investigators eager to blend qualitative methods into their research efforts. His work on homelessness, mental illness, and substance abuse has involved international collaborations.

Kenneth L. Kusmer, Ph.D., is Professor of History at Temple University, where he teaches American social history, African-American history, and recent American history. A graduate of Oberlin College, he received an M.A. from Kent State University, where he studied with August Meier, and a Ph.D. in history from the University of Chicago, where he studied with Neil Harris, John Hope Franklin, and John Coatsworth. He is the author of *A Ghetto Takes Shape: Black Cleveland, 1870–1930* (1978), and *Down and Out, On the Road: The Homeless in American History* (2001), the first scholarly history of homelessness (and the response to the homeless) that covers the entire span of American history from the colonial period to the present. He also edited *Black Communities and Urban Development in America, 1720–1990* (1991). He has published more than twenty-five scholarly articles and fifty book reviews on a wide range of topics in American social, ethnic, and African-American history, and has lectured extensively throughout the United States and Western Europe. He has taught at Temple University since 1976 and has also been a visiting professor at the University of Pennsylvania. In 1987–1988, he held the Bancroft Chair in American History at the University of Goettingen, Germany, and, during the spring semester, 2001, he was Senior Fulbright Lecturer at the University of Genoa, Italy.

Gretchen Noll is deputy director of programs at the National Network for Youth and oversees the day-to-day operations of the Network's HIV prevention portfolio. As deputy director of one of the nation's leading HIV prevention initiatives for youth in high-risk situations, she has designed and implemented many capacity-building projects for youth workers, teachers, health department personnel, and community leaders. She often consults for foundations, national organizations, government, and community-based organizations on a broad range of issues, including adolescent sexual health, youth development, the specialized needs of runaway and homeless youth and sexual minority youth, service standards, and the professional development of youth workers. She has broad experience in working with community-based agencies to plan programs and develop policy and has worked with runaway and homeless youth service providers, domestic violence professionals, and educators.

Debra J. Rog, Ph.D., is a Senior Research Associate with Vanderbilt University's Institute for Public Policy Studies and has been the director of the Washington office of the Center for Mental Health Policy since 1990. She received her Ph.D. in social psychology from Vanderbilt University and has more than 20 years of experience designing and implementing evaluation and applied research studies in a range of settings involving issues of mental health, poverty, homelessness, and housing and services for vulnerable populations. Just prior to joining VIPPS, she served as the associate director in the NIMH Office of Programs for the Homeless Mentally Ill on a three-year Special Expert appointment, where she developed the first research and multi-site evaluation initiatives for programs serving homeless persons with severe mental illness funded under the Stewart B. McKinney Act. Currently, she is the principal investigator of a Coordinating Center for the Center for Mental Services' Housing Initiative for Persons with Serious Mental Illness; a Coordinating Center for the Centers for Mental Health Services; Substance Abuse Treatment's Homeless Families Initiative; and two foundation-funded, cross-site evaluations of local collaboratives focused on violence prevention. She has been coeditor of the *Applied Social Research Methods Series* since 1980, a series that has produced over fifty volumes on both quantitative and qualitative research topics. She is also the coeditor of the *Handbook of Applied Social Research Methods* (1997) and a coauthor of *Applied Research Design* (1993).

Marybeth Shinn, Ph.D, is Professor of Psychology at New York University. She was president of the Society for Community Research and Action in 1990–1991, and received that organization's Award for Distinguished Contributions to Theory and Research in 1996. She and her colleagues have conducted numerous studies of homelessness in New York, including both surveys and evaluations of intervention programs. Other research interests include welfare reform, community contexts of human welfare, social policy, and social intervention. She has authored numerous articles on these topics, which have appeared in such journals as the *American Journal of Public Health,* the *Annual Review of Psychology,* and the *Handbook of Community Psychology.* In addition, she has served as associate editor for the *American Journal of Community Psychology* (1986–1988, 1993–1997).

A

▣ ABEYANCE THEORY

Since the sixteenth century—roughly the end of feudalism and emergence of capitalism in Europe—modern societies have had to deal with the problem of people whose basic needs are met neither by market forces (employment) nor by kinship (informal support). In the late nineteenth and early twentieth centuries, taking care of abandoned mothers and assisting returning soldiers became the founding tasks of the welfare state. But social alternatives were invented to accommodate excess populations well before then. *Abeyance,* a term borrowed from historical sociology, refers to solutions to this long-standing problem of a mismatch between productive positions available in a society and numbers of potential claimants of those positions.

The alternatives devised to absorb surplus people and neutralize the potential mischief of idle hands were varied. They included state-sponsored projects (frontier settlements, public works, compulsory education), breakaway religious orders (the Franciscans, wandering clerics, the Beguines), and countercultural movements (alternative communities). All of these provided sustenance and industry—that is, they furnished the functional equivalents of work—and, if necessary, lodging. And they did so for people

who would otherwise have posed a substantial burden to kin or may have threatened social order.

As social inventions, abeyance mechanisms are full-service operations. They address not only where people will spend the night, but also what they will do when the sun comes up. Shelter is only part of the equation. To be part of abeyance is to be subject to the social contract of general reciprocity and the social control of organized work, including performing jobs that require no special talent. During the Great Depression, this could mean building roads, cutting trails, or doing construction. More recently, "workfare" programs, making no pretense of training participants for gainful employment elsewhere, have put public assistance recipients to work picking up litter or filing paperwork. But the "make work" practice is an old one. In the Middle Ages, monks could be hired to perform surrogate penances for busy sinners who could afford their catered services.

Public shelter, however, falls short of such provisions. Specifically, overnight lodging fails to meet the usual requirement of surrogate labor, while performing the "integration and surveillance" role that theorists usually expect of abeyance mechanisms. Such lodging fulfill the warehouse function but fail to put their charges to productive work. At best, then, shelters are partial abeyance mechanisms and

1

for that reason are subject to distinctive problems of demoralization.

ABEYANCE AND THE PROBLEM OF HOMELESSNESS

An abeyance perspective serves to reframe the problem of homelessness. History suggests that short of mass incarceration or a police state, means (formal or informal) will invariably be found to support redundant populations without overt repression. Whether this will mean a haphazard mix of market and state forces (as was true in traditional skid rows), recourse to religious agencies (charitable missions with an avowed interest in moral reformation), or formal bureaucracies of relief will depend on a host of local and temporal contingencies. The durable question is how people with insufficient resources to purchase housing on the market, who are unable or disinclined to turn to friends or family, will be accommodated—and under what circumstances the terms of their accommodation will include public shelter. This question and its answer not only resituate shelter as part of larger social mechanisms but also may throw into relief historical developments whose "reabsorptive" capacity preempted homelessness and made shelters unnecessary. Two examples are illustrative.

Historically, the last two prolonged periods of redundancy and homelessness this country experienced, the Progressive Era (1890–1915) and the Great Depression (1929–1941), were solved by the domestic mobilization for world war. Mass homelessness resurfaced in the wake of demobilization after World War I and likely would have done so again in the late 1940s but for Congressional passage of the G.I. Bill. Photos from the latter period show armories being put to use as the functional equivalent of dormitories for ex-service men—not layabouts in warehouse shelters—who were now newly enrolled students or freshly hired workers. And land giveaways and other concessions have long been used by governments to stave off the potential trouble posed by returning soldiers, such as those who made up the core of the "tramp problem" in the 1870s.

The second example is cross-cultural in nature. Because abeyance mechanisms must be assessed in relation to local economies and social formations, similar cultural practices should not be mistaken for solutions to similar problems. Throughout Latin America, illegal "land invasions" in rural areas and, more recently, takeovers of abandoned urban properties are providing housing for a low-waged proletariat. Although technically illegal, these takeovers function as informal, state-sanctioned abeyance mechanisms by increasing the "social wage." In the United States, where the economics of both wage-labor and state subsidies differ markedly, their counterparts—rough-hewn shanty settlements found in some cities—provide shelter for the street-dwelling homeless, not the working poor. At the same time, turning a blind official eye to housing codes may count as abeyance in intent. Locally, lax enforcement of occupancy standards, even in public housing, betray official understanding that what the market fails to ensure by the usual rules may need to be supplied by bending them. Culture also plays a role in shaping how abeyance mechanisms operate. Closely documented studies of the practice of "doubling up" (living with family or friends) in U.S. cities show that both its meaning and utility vary markedly across ethnic groups in housing-strapped areas.

RETHINKING HOMELESSNESS

Reframing homelessness as part of the standing problem of redundant people lacking sufficient resources (money or kin) to manage subsistence on their own also invites us to rethink the social response to homelessness. It may make better sense to consider "regular access to a conventional dwelling" (sociologist Peter Rossi's formula for what homeless people lack) as something more akin to work than residence. Homelessness could then be analyzed in ways analogous to those used by economists in measuring "regular access to a conventional job." Just as the official "unemployment" rate is understood to be but a weak index of the true extent of joblessness, so are "literal" homeless rates (people on the street or in shelters) poor indicators of genuine residential instability. Students of homelessness must learn to take account of the "absorptive" capacities of institutions not designed for the homeless and of informal practices (such as doubling up) in the same way that labor economists have learned to examine alternative "employments" in military service, prisons, hospitals, and the informal economy. This will also mean tracking the institutional hybrids other than shelters—functional equivalents of yesterday's almshouses, bridewells, asylums, workhouses, city homes, and police stations—that are pressed into service to lodge the otherwise homeless poor.

—*Kim Hopper and Jim Baumohl*

Further Reading

Hopper, K., & Baumohl, J. (1994). Held in abeyance. *American Behavioral Scientist 37*, 522–552.

Jusserand, J. J. (1920). *English wayfaring as a way of life in the Middle Ages* (rev. ed.). London: Ernest Benn.

Mizruchi, E. (1987). *Regulating society*. Chicago: University of Chicago Press.

Modell, J. (1989). *Into one's own: From youth to adulthood in the United States, 1920–1975*. Berkeley: University of California Press.

Ringenbach, P. T. (1973). *Tramps and reformers, 1873–1916*. Westport, CT: Greenwood.

Rossi, P. H. (1986). *Down and out in America*. Chicago: University of Chicago Press.

Waddell, H. (1961). *The wandering scholars*. New York: Doubleday. (Originally published 1927)

▣ AFRICA

See Egypt; Homelessness, International Perspectives on; Housing and Homelessness in Developing Nations; Nairobi; Nigeria; South Africa; Zimbabwe

▣ AFRICAN-AMERICANS

The old stereotype of a homeless person in America was a solitary middle-aged white male alcoholic. Although this may have described a majority of homeless people before the 1980s, the current homeless population in the United States is younger, includes a large number of families composed mostly of women and their children, is much poorer, and is much more ethnically diverse. African-Americans are overrepresented in all subgroups of homeless people, including adults, families, and adolescents.

Those who identify themselves as African-Americans represent 12 percent of the U.S. population and 50 percent of the U.S. homeless population. In some U.S. cities, African-Americans make up an even larger proportion of the homeless population. For example, in Buffalo, New York, African-Americans constitute 68 percent of homeless adults and in Detroit, Michigan, African-Americans make up 85 percent of the homeless population. African-Americans appear to be most heavily overrepresented among homeless adults and families.

EXPLAINING THE OVERREPRESENTATION

The surge of homelessness that began in the 1980s has been attributed to an increase in the number of poor people, a lack of affordable housing, and the loss of well-paying unskilled jobs. Additional historic and structural factors include racism, discrimination, and a lack of access to higher education. Research suggests that African-Americans are more likely to become homeless as a result of external factors like chronic and pervasive poverty than European-Americans, who are more likely to experience homelessness due to internal factors like mental illness, family dysfunction, and substance abuse.

Poverty

Homelessness can be seen as the by-product of a rise in the number of people experiencing poverty and an increase in the disparity between the rich and the poor. In fact, many scholars view homelessness simply as an extreme form of poverty. Research suggests that the current homeless population is suffering from more extreme poverty than the homeless population before the 1980s, whose income was three times higher than the income of the current homeless. Some studies have found that the problems of homeless people differ only slightly from the problems of the very poor. For example, some have found that rates of mental illness are much higher in both homeless and

A mother and her child get ready to leave their temporary apartment in New York City at 6:30 a.m. for work and school.
Source: Mark Peterson/Corbis; used with permission.

matched housed poor individuals (similar to the homeless in terms of age, gender, ethnicity, and/or neighborhood income). Because of the overrepresentation of African-Americans among poor persons in the United States, poverty can be viewed as an important cause of the overrepresentation of African-Americans among the homeless. Roughly 25 percent of African-Americans in the United States live in poverty. In addition, whereas 20 percent of U.S. children live below the poverty line, 50 percent of ethnic minority children live below the poverty line.

Factors that might be driving the increase in the number of poor persons, as well as the increase in the number of poor African-Americans, include welfare reform, gentrification, and a lack of well-paying unskilled jobs. In recent years, "welfare reform" has resulted in a reduction in the services provided to those who are poor. African-Americans appear to be faring worse than other ethnic groups on many factors directly related to poverty, including education, unemployment rates, and the availability of transferable job skills.

Change in Economic Structure

The change in the economic structure of America worsened the already grave situation of America's poor. The move from factory jobs to service-oriented jobs has decreased the availability of employment for workers who do not have transferable job skills (skills acquired during life activities that are transferable and applicable to other occupations) and who may be less educated. Historically, African-Americans have disproportionately relied on blue-collar manufacturing positions. This can be seen in the auto industry in Detroit, where many African-Americans have traditionally been employed. In addition, entry-level jobs are moving away from the inner city, where many African-Americans reside, and into the mostly European-American suburbs, making it difficult for African-Americans to obtain and maintain employment.

Affordable Housing

Homelessness is directly related to the availability of low-rent housing. Whereas the need for affordable housing has increased, the availability of low-rent housing and government-subsidized housing has decreased. This lack of affordable housing, especially in some of the major U.S. cities where there are high concentrations of African-Americans, has also been suggested as an explanation for the overrepresentation of African-Americans in the homeless population. The process of gentrification, in which low-income neighborhoods are reclaimed by developers, has also resulted in higher housing costs in many urban areas. Urban renewal programs have occurred in cities where African-Americans are highly concentrated, including Chicago, Illinois, Washington, D.C., and Los Angeles, California.

Discrimination and Racism

Several factors directly related to the minority status of African-Americans in the United States also contribute to homelessness. Discrimination in the workplace makes it more difficult to obtain well-paying jobs and often leads to the acceptance of lower wages for the same work. For example, African-Americans with some college education have a higher rate of unemployment than European-Americans with less than a high school diploma. In addition, there is a clear difference in the types of jobs African-Americans are likely to hold. African-Americans are overrepresented in low-paying service jobs and underrepresented in higher-paying professional and managerial positions.

Discrimination in housing practices makes it difficult for African-Americans to find affordable housing. Many landlords are more inclined to rent to European-Americans than to African-Americans, and sellers and mortgage companies are less likely to provide loans or sell homes to African-Americans. These discriminatory practices, especially common in neighborhoods where European-Americans predominate, can result from blatant racism but can also reflect more subtle forms of prejudice. These factors contribute to African-Americans accepting less satisfactory terms when choosing to rent or buy a home and make them more likely to live in segregated inner-city neighborhoods where economic growth is declining and where there are often poor-quality school districts and more violence. Discrimination in the labor and housing markets puts African-Americans in a perilous situation. Such discrimination requires them to possess superior academic credentials and experience in order to achieve parity with European-Americans.

DIFFERENCES BETWEEN AFRICAN-AMERICAN AND EUROPEAN-AMERICAN HOMELESS POPULATIONS

Some researchers have suggested that the factors that contribute to poverty and homelessness are different for African-Americans than for European-Americans, but few studies have attempted to document the differences. However, understanding the different paths to homelessness could help guide policy initiatives.

Demographic Differences

Some studies have found distinct differences between homeless individuals who are African-American and those who are European-American. In a 1994 study comparing European-American and non-European-American (mostly African-American)

homeless adults, European-American participants were older and more likely to be married than their African-American counterparts (North and Smith, 1994). Homeless women were more likely to be members of an ethnic minority, especially African-American. This was especially so for homeless women with children. European-Americans were more likely to be divorced or widowed. In addition, African-American women were more likely to be mothers and more likely to have children under fifteen years old in their physical custody than European-American women.

Economic Differences

African-American and European-American homeless people have different employment and financial experiences, too. Homeless African-American men are more likely to be employed than European-American homeless men, although they report having lower incomes from their employment. European-American men are more likely to have quit their jobs and more likely to list psychiatric problems as having contributed to their unemployment. In addition, it appears that the time gap between an individual's last steady job and the onset of a spell of homelessness is longer for African-Americans than for European-Americans. This suggests that African-Americans are able to avoid homelessness for a longer time on little or no income.

African-American homeless women depend more on welfare benefits than European-American homeless women do. African-American homeless women often cite poverty as the reason for their homelessness, while European-American homeless women are more likely to cite a traumatic event such as domestic violence or mental illness as the cause. A study of homeless African-American women with families found that more than half of these women were receiving public assistance and almost a fifth were employed. This research suggests that although African-American homeless women may be receiving monetary help through employment or public assistance, this monetary help is not sufficient to provide shelter for these women and their children.

HISTORY OF HOMELESSNESS

There appears to be a difference in the duration and frequency of incidence of homelessness between European-Americans and African-Americans. European-Americans who are homeless report more episodes of homelessness than do African-Americans. European-American homeless women also report more time being homeless and more time living on the streets than do African-American homeless women. Homelessness for African-Americans seems to be episodic, while for European-Americans, homelessness may represent more complex personal and social problems.

Familial Factors

African-American homeless adults are more likely than their European-American counterparts to report having stayed most of the past year with their families. A European-American homeless individual is more likely to report having been physically abused as a child, and a European-American woman is more likely to report having been sexually abused. In a study of homeless adolescents, European-American adolescents reported coming from families that were more dysfunctional than those of their African-American peers. European-American adolescents were also more likely to have experienced a family characterized by verbal and physical aggression, conflict, and a lack of cohesion. It appears that the African-American homeless may have more contact with their families than the European-American homeless do and may have come from more functional families.

Psychological Difficulties and Treatment

Research also suggests that ethnic differences exist in mental health and substance abuse problems among homeless individuals. European-American homeless individuals are more likely to report a history of psychological difficulties and to report that these difficulties contributed to their homelessness. Looking at a lifetime prevalence of substance abuse disorders, one study found that European-American homeless men report higher rates of both alcohol and drug abuse problems than their African-American counterparts.

Studies have also found that European-American homeless women exhibit higher rates of psychological disorders than African-American homeless women. Additionally, African-American women report less use of both inpatient and outpatient care; unlike European-American women, they also report that they wanted but were unable to obtain psychological care.

PUBLIC POLICY

Public policy and economic changes that affect the poor and those living in the inner city disproportionately affect African-Americans because they are more likely to be poor and more likely to live in the inner city. The causes of homelessness are different for African-Americans than for European-Americans. Family dysfunction, physical and sexual abuse, and mental illness appear to be the most important causes of European-American homelessness. Factors related to poverty and discrimination appear to explain the overrepresentation of African-Americans among the homeless. An awareness of these differences can help guide public policy initiatives that aim to reduce the disparity between African-American and European-American rates of homelessness.

—*Sawssan R. Ahmed and Paul A. Toro*

Further Reading

Atlas, J., & Shoshkes, E. (1996). Saving affordable housing: What community groups can do & what government should do? *Shelterforce, 18*(6).

Baker, S. G. (1994). Gender, ethnicity, and homelessness: Accounting for demographic diversity on the streets. *American Behavioral Scientist, 37*(4), 476–504.

Bukowski, P. A., & Toro, P. A. (1995, August). *Gender and racial differences on psychosocial factors among homeless youth.* Paper presented at the 103rd annual convention of the American Psychological Association, New York, NY.

Burt, M., Aron, L. Y., Lee, E., & Valente, J. (2001). *Helping America's homeless: Emergency shelter or affordable housing?* Washington, DC: The Urban Institute Press.

Cohen, E. L. (1999). *Pathways to homelessness: An exploration of ethnic differences in homeless mothers.* Unpublished master's thesis, Wayne State University, Detroit, MI.

Gilliam, A. (1992). Homeless women with children. In R. L. Braithwaite & S. E. Taylor (Eds.), *Health issues in the black community* (pp. 147–163). San Francisco: Jossey-Bass.

Molina, E. (2000). Informal non-kin networks among homeless Latino and African-American men. *American Behavioral Scientist, 43*(4), 663–685.

North, C. S., & Smith, E. M. (1994). Comparison of European-American and nonwhite homeless men and women. *Social Work, 39*(6), 639–647.

Rossi, P. H. (1990). The old homeless and the new homelessness in historical perspective. *American Psychologist, 45*(8), 954–959.

Toro, P. A. (1998). Homelessness. In A. S. Bellack & M. Hersen (Eds.), *Comprehensive clinical psychology: Applications in diverse populations* (pp. 119–135). New York: Pergamon.

Toro, P. A., Wolfe, S. M., Bellavia, C. W., Thomas, D. M., Rowland, L. L., Daeschler, C. V., & McCaskill, P. A. (1999). Obtaining representative samples of homeless persons: A two-city study. *Journal of Community Psychology, 27*(2), 157–177.

United States Census Bureau. (1999). *Census Bureau facts for features: African-American History month: February 1–28.* Retrieved April 23, 2003, from www.census.gov/Press-Release/www/1999

U.S. Conference of Mayors. (1999). *A status report on hunger and homelessness in America's cities.* Washington, DC: Author.

United States Department of Health and Human Services, Office of the Surgeon General. (n.d.). *Culture, race, and ethnicity: A supplement to mental health: A report of the Surgeon General.* Retrieved April 23, 2003, from http://www.surgeongeneral.gov/library/mentalhealth/cre/fact1.asp

Whaley, A. L. (2002). Demographic and clinical correlates of homelessness among African-Americans with severe mental illness. *Community Mental Health Journal, 38*(4), 327–338.

ALCOHOL AND DRUGS

Our understanding of the creation of homelessness is grounded in the ecological model, which views homelessness as a result of the interplay between personal factors, such as alcohol abuse, drug abuse, and/or mental illness, and structural factors, such as the scarcity of affordable housing, economic restructuring to a low-wage service economy, and the reduction in financial assistance. The ecological model integrates issues of individual vulnerabilities within the broadest cultural and societal landscapes. It recognizes that important housing niches in U.S. cities have been eliminated, and that those who are most vulnerable, including those with alcohol and drug abuse problems, are pushed into homelessness. The ecological model avoids the victim-blaming trap of viewing people's alcohol and/or drug abuse as causing their homelessness.

While the relationship between alcohol/drug abuse and homelessness is best understood in a larger context, so strong is the link historically between alcoholism and homelessness that in some parts the two words are one and the same. For example, in Finland, until recently, the word for "homeless" and "alcoholic" was *puliukko,* which is derived from the words *ukko* (old man) and *puli* (varnish or lacquer, used as a particularly cheap and dangerous source of alcohol) (Glasser, 1994). In Quebec, Canada, one of the words for homeless was *robineux,* which is a French adaptation of the English word "rubbing" (as in rubbing alcohol, again a cheap and dangerous source of alcohol) (Glasser, Fournier, and Costopoulos, 1999).

HOMELESS, SKID ROW, AND ALCOHOL

The classic case of homelessness is the solitary drinking man. He was viewed either with fear and revulsion (his lack of connection to kith and kin appeared to be linked to a lack of both control and a sense of responsibility), or he was viewed more positively as the romantic "traveling man" of Depression-era fame, who had given up his attachment to the material world of schedules and obligations (Glasser, 1994). Historically, homeless men were often assumed to be inhabitants of the skid rows of U.S. cities, neighborhoods that contained cheap lodging for transients and the marginally employed. The term comes from "skid road," a road along which logs were skidded, probably in Seattle, Washington, where cheap rooms were available to lumberjacks in the early twentieth century (Cohen and Sokolovsky, 1989). Much of the single-room occupancy (SRO) housing in skid rows was torn down in the urban renewal programs of the 1960s and 1970s and in the process of gentrification of the 1980s and 1990s.

In 1970, utilizing participant observation and methods from linguistic anthropology, James Spradley documented the broad array of adaptive strategies used by men on the streets of skid row in

Seattle, Washington. He also sought to figure out why men who spent time in the "drunk tank" of the local jails immediately returned to drinking upon their release. Spradley followed the life of skid row resident William R. Tanner, a literate man of forty-nine who was arrested for public drunkenness nine times in the course of the year and served nearly 200 days in jail on drunk charges. At the end of one of his drunk-tank sojourns, Tanner wrote a letter to Spradley, which gave him insight into the futility of the drunk tank as a cure for alcoholism as well as the title of his book, *You Owe Yourself a Drunk.* (Mr. Tanner said that after thirty days in jail, "you owe yourself a drunk.")

It is ironic that after tearing down much of the cheap housing that previously sheltered single drinking men, we now view having access to an inexpensive room with a key in a convenient location and in the company of other single men as ideal. In fact, it is the goal to which many of the most innovative supportive housing programs for the homeless now aspire. This also means that an important strategy to prevent more homelessness is to stop the demolition (or change of use) of the few remaining single-room occupancy hotels. There are some good examples of success, such as the Times Square Hotel in New York City, in which a community organization, in this case, Common Ground, was able to renovate an SRO and now offers inexpensive and accessible housing with additional supportive services for single homeless men.

PREVALENCE OF ALCOHOL AND DRUG ABUSE AMONG HOMELESS INDIVIDUALS

There is substantial evidence that alcohol and drug abuse are the most pervasive health problems of the homeless in the United States. For example, the rate of alcohol abuse has been estimated to be 58 to 68 percent for homeless men, 30 percent for homeless single women, and 10 percent for mothers in homeless families (Fischer and Breakey, 1991). Alcohol abuse rates among the homeless tend to vary by ethnicity, with the prevalence for whites (57.1 percent) being significantly higher than for nonwhites (34.2 percent) (Robertson, Koegel, and Ferguson, 1989).

An Urban Institute (1999) study of 4,207 randomly selected clients of homeless-serving agencies found the rate of reported alcohol abuse to be 38 percent within the past month, 46 percent within the past year, and 62 percent within an individual's lifetime. The lifetime reported use of drugs was 58 percent and the lifetime reported existence of mental health problems was 57 percent, with 86 percent reporting having had one of these problems during their lifetime. These rates contrast with the total U.S. population rates of 15 percent lifetime risk for alcohol dependence and the 5 percent current alcohol dependence when the DSM-IV criteria are applied (*Diagnostic and Statistical Manual of Mental Disorders,* 2000). There is an estimated lifetime heroin use of 1 percent and a lifetime cocaine use of 10 percent within the general U.S. population (*Diagnostic and Statistical Manual of Mental Disorders,* 2000).

In a study of the relationship between homelessness and alcohol and drug abuse, Johnson and Freels (1997) interviewed 303 homeless people and people at risk of becoming homeless (those living in single-room occupancy hotels) in order to disentangle the relationship between substance abuse and homelessness. They concluded that a multidirectional model is the most appropriate. Substance abuse and homelessness were posited as risk factors for one another. They found that drug use was associated with first episodes of homelessness and suggest that drugs are displacing alcohol as an important precursor to homelessness.

PATHS TO HOMELESSNESS

The relationship of alcohol and drug use to homelessness is reciprocal, in that it is very difficult for individuals with limited financial resources to remain in housing when much of their money is spent on substances, and it is difficult for individuals to focus on treatment for alcohol and drug abuse when their basic survival needs for shelter, food, and warmth are only precariously met. Once people begin to live on the street, they often spend much of their time in agencies such as shelters, soup kitchens, and day centers meeting their survival needs for food and shelter. These agencies attract large numbers of homeless individuals who abuse alcohol and drugs and could therefore serve as effective links to treatment for those clients whose lives on the street have become intolerable to them (see Glasser, 1988 and Fournier et al., 1993 on the culture of soup kitchens and day centers); unfortunately, however, they typically have limited budgets and are understaffed to treat these problems among their "guests" (the term that is often employed by soup kitchen staff). Not only are substance abuse treatment opportunities inadequate for the homeless, the homeless milieu may facilitate continued alcohol and drug consumption. For example, once on the street, drinking may provide a sense of camaraderie for individuals who have left many of their previous family and work place relationships (Spradley, 1970). In this sense, alcohol use may be seen as an adaptation to life on the streets.

THE TREATMENT OF ALCOHOL- AND DRUG-RELATED PROBLEMS IN HOMELESS PERSONS

A recent review of the literature on substance abuse treatments sponsored by the National Health Care for the Homeless Council concluded that homeless individuals pose a number of challenges to the treatment community (Zerger, 2002). The first challenge is the difficulty of engaging the homeless in treatment, given the extent of their social isolation, distrust of authorities, and immobility. A second challenge is the difficulty of retaining clients in substance abuse treatment programs; drop-out rates of two-thirds or more are common. Although there is a move toward brief interventions in the substance abuse treatment field, brief interventions have not yet been tested on the homeless.

There is an irony in the world of the services for the extremely poor in North America. On the one hand, "low-demand" (no-questions-asked) services for the poor and homeless delivered in places such as shelters, soup kitchens, and day centers attract high numbers of people, yet have few professional staff. On the other hand, treatment programs that require people to leave the homeless milieu, even programs designed specifically for the homeless, have large attrition rates before and during treatment. For exam-

The traditional image of a homeless person was a drunken man living on skid row in a major city. This photo from c. 1950 shows a drunken man on the sidewalk of the Chicago skid row.
Source: Hulton-Deutsch/Corbis; used with permission.

ple, in a study that assessed the feasibility of using the therapeutic community and community residences for the homeless mentally ill chemical abuser, there was a 58 percent attrition of previously screened and interested shelter residents before entering the treatment center. Although 23 percent of the attrition rate was due to clients being rejected from programs, most of the attrition was due to clients not showing up (Nuttbrock et al., 1998). The challenge, then, is to design programs that begin the treatment process in the settings in which the homeless already live or spend much of their time. A treatment, however, should be offered in such a way that those who do *not* desire it will not be deterred from entering the shelter, soup kitchen, or day center and inadvertently driven back to the street.

The major treatment modalities that have been tried with homeless individuals with alcohol and drug abuse, as described in the literature, are Outreach/

A "Healing Place" for Recovery

Louisville, Ky. (ANS)—Seven years ago, Andrew DeGrella lived on the streets of Louisville. He was 32, homeless, and addicted to alcohol and drugs. "I did what I had to do to take care of myself," DeGrella said. "I was stealing, robbing people, whatever I needed to do. Then I got a couple of felony drug charges and went to jail first, then the penitentiary."

When DeGrella came up for parole a year later, he had nowhere to go.

His family, from whom he had long been estranged, wanted nothing to do with him, even though his body was now physically free of the addictions.

But while in jail, DeGrella had heard about a long-term mutual self-help recovery program structured to help homeless people beat their addictions, the reason most of them had become homeless in the first place.

"About 80 percent of homeless people are addicted to drugs and/or alcohol," said Chris Fajardo, director of programs at the project called the Healing Place. "Most are in the middle to late stages of addictions and most have many other issues that need attention. Those issues aren't the cause of the addiction, they are the results."

Such issues range from health problems caused by years of drug abuse to the inability to hold a job to estrangement from friends and relatives.

The Healing Place is not a treatment center, but a peer-directed long-term recovery program. With a 62 percent success rate, it is now being duplicated across the country.

The U.S. Health Resources and Services Administration recognized the Healing Place in its 1998 Models That Work campaign, which identifies organizations across the country that have developed innovative programs for improving the delivery of primary health care services to vulnerable and underserved populations.

Since it began in 1993, 318 men and 22 women have completed the recovery program.

The center was founded by the Jefferson County Medical Society, which wanted to find a way to bring health care services to those who needed them most and yet were least likely to have the money to pay for them: the homeless.

Most homeless shelters simply provide short-term emergency shelter and immediate medical care without addressing the reasons its occupants have become homeless.

In its original life, for 20 years the Healing Place was such a shelter called the Morgan Center, founded and operated by a Catholic priest, Father John Morgan.

Fajardo said Morgan recognized that most of his occupants had substance abuse issues that had never been addressed, so he approached the Jefferson County Medical Society's Outreach Program.

The Society responded by deciding to donate a portion of its monthly dues to help fund the shelter. The recovery program itself, however, was developed by Fajardo and Healing Place executive director Jay P. Davidson.

"It's not meant to replace treatment centers or other programs that are already out there," Fajardo said. "It's meant to complement them. It's for those who need additional help."

Fajardo said a key component of the center's recovery program is Alcoholics Anonymous' 12-step program and Recovery Dynamics, developed by the Kelly Foundation of Little Rock, Ark.

Phase 1 of the program focuses on helping the client overcome the addiction and the psychological triggers that cause him or her to start using again.

Phase 2 focuses on dealing with issues that may be causes of the addiction or that have been neglected as a result of the addiction, such as employment, sexual abuse, social skills, education, vocational training, housing and health care issues.

Mike Townsend, director of the Division of Substance Abuse, Kentucky Department of Mental Health and Mental Retardation Services, said the Healing Place fills a vital niche.

"Traditional treatment centers keep someone there for 15 to 20 days," Townsend said. "After that period of time, these people are expected to follow through with a doctor's recom-

Source: "'Healing Place' Gives Late-Stage Addicts and Alcoholics Time to Recover," American News Service, September 9, 1999.

Engagement, Intensive Case Management, Post-Detoxification Shelter Stabilization, and Therapeutic Communities in Shelters. *Outreach* is a first step to making contact with people living out-of-doors and in shelters, and participating in day programs and soup kitchens. The outreach worker, who may be on foot or travel in a van, offers an individual social contact, food, referrals, and advocacy. The Park Homeless Outreach Project in New York City was one interesting example of outreach work, and it was subsequently evaluated (Ukeles Associates, 1995). During this project, teams of workers became acquainted with the homeless men and women who occupied three Manhattan parks, one of which also contained Gracie Mansion, the mayor's official residence. During the two years of the project, the outreach teams had con-

mended outpatient follow-up. They're expected to turn their life around after a lifelong process of getting to this point.

"For you and me, adhering to these recommendations wouldn't be a problem, because we have a home, car, family, job and a support network. We would easily be able to follow through on that outpatient program. For these people, it's next to impossible."

DeGrella said he was such a person when he first came to the Healing Place. "Here I was, a person with no skills to live in functional society clean and sober," he said. "I hadn't held a job in seven or eight years. I didn't know how to communicate with people clean and sober. I had the best intentions in the world to stay clean and sober, but had not developed the tools to do that."

After about 30 days at the Healing Place, he began drinking and using drugs again. "I fell back into my old ways. They put me back in detox and asked me if I wanted to try again. I said yes. This time I went about forty or fifty days and I drank again. It was the only thing I really knew how to do."

Then, DeGrello said the 12-step program took hold and "my obsession to use and drink was miraculously lifted from me. To this day, it's gone," he said. "I could have never done it by myself. I have never wanted to drink or use since. And I now have the skills I need to take care of myself physically, spiritually and emotionally."

After his sobriety date of Oct. 6, 1993, he stayed on at the Healing Place for an additional nine months. Then he was ready to move on.

DeGrella now owns a successful cleaning business and employs some clients of the Healing Place. Ironically, his primary clients are bars and taverns.

He recently added another entrepreneurial venture to his business: real estate. He bought a large house with several bedrooms to rent to other men as soon as they are ready to move out of the Healing Place.

"It's just my way of giving back to the program that helped me so much," he said. "I want to be part of that solution."

tact with 283 different individuals, and they connected 89 of them to services including detoxification, alcohol and drug treatment, entitlement programs, and temporary shelters.

In 1990, the National Institutes of Health National Institute of Alcohol Abuse and Alcoholism (NIAAA), in consultation with the National Institute of Drug Abuse (NIDA), funded fourteen demonstra-

tion projects for alcohol and drug abuse treatment for the homeless. Thirteen of the projects provided *case management* services in order to meet the primary goals, which were to reduce the consumption of alcohol and other drugs, to increase the participants' level of residential stability, and to enhance their economic and/or employment status (Perl and Jacobs, 1992). The case management model can be viewed as particularly useful for people who live in shelters and on the streets, where services are fragmented and individuals have to be continually on the move. In particular, substance abuse treatment and psychological help must be combined with helping clients meet their survival needs for food, stable housing, and employment and/or receipt of financial benefits (Stahler, 1995).

Another approach has attempted to bring the treatment of substance abuse to the homeless milieu. Portions of shelters have been transformed into *post-detoxification stabilization* programs in Boston (Argeriou and McCarty, 1993). In this way, even homeless individuals who have not yet found stable housing are able to maintain abstinence even when returning to a shelter. A similar program, the *therapeutic community (TC)*, a well-established alcohol and drug treatment approach with non-homeless people, has been modified to meet the needs of homeless individuals who abuse alcohol and drugs and who are also mentally ill (Sacks and De Leon, 1997). These modifications include more individualized, more flexible, and less intense treatments than are found in standard TC programs.

The general conclusions drawn about treatment efficacy derived from a review of ten NIAAA- and NIDA-funded treatment outcome studies of homeless individuals with alcohol and drug abuse (Stahler, 1995) were as follows:

- substance abuse treatment must go hand in hand with addressing the tangible needs of housing, income support, and employment;

- drop-out rates are very high for all treatments for the homeless, and so there is a need for flexible, "low-demand" interventions;

- clients in both treatment and control groups improved, in part because the control groups received nearly the same quantity of services as the treatment group and because many of the clients recruited had "hit bottom" and were already on the road up;

- even treatment outcomes that were positive seemed to diminish over time, suggesting the need for extended aftercare; and

- some clients (such as those with less criminal involvement) did have comparatively more positive outcomes, suggesting the importance of a more precise matching of clients with treatments.

A problem with many of the interventions shown to be effective under study conditions is that it is often difficult to deliver adequate treatment outside of research conditions. The typical low ratio of staff to clients in shelters and the need to prioritize the most pressing needs of "guests" contribute to this difficulty.

In the search for low-demand, flexible, and ongoing treatment, we have considered an adaptation of motivation interviewing (Miller and Rollnick, 2002). Motivational interviewing can be adapted to address an individual's most pressing problems, including housing and physical health as well as alcohol and drug abuse. If proven to be efficacious, motivational interviewing has an advantage in that it can be taught to the shelter, soup kitchen, and day center workers who are already situated within the homeless milieu. It would mean that in order to begin to work on their recovery, individuals would not need to leave the familiarity of their environment. It would also mean that if people did not have appropriate housing to go to after formal treatment and had to return to a shelter, there would be staff who were trained to continue to work with them in the homeless milieu. Finally, it would shift some of the responsibility for changing a homeless client's situation from the staff to the client. This shift, when combined with smaller goals of increased motivation, may decrease staff burnout and attrition and offer more hope to those who work with homeless clients.

SCREENING FOR ALCOHOL- AND DRUG-RELATED PROBLEMS

Testing is being done on a new screening measure, the AUDIT-12, that will enable shelter and day center staff to rapidly identify individuals at high risk for alcohol-

and drug-related problems and refer them to treatment (Campbell, Barrett, Cisler, Solliday-McRoy, and Melchert, 2001). The AUDIT-12 consists of five questions regarding alcohol and/or drug involvement, three questions regarding dependency, and four questions regarding harm. In their study of 771 homeless men in Milwaukee, Wisconsin, Campbell and his team found that 74 percent received scores on the AUDIT that indicated a possible problem with drugs and/or alcohol. The AUDIT-12 is currently being tested in Hartford, Connecticut, and in Rhode Island.

IMPLICATIONS

Alcohol and drug use and abuse are important factors in the lives of homeless individuals even when they are not sufficient causes for an individual's homelessness. On the other hand, as we have seen, treatment opportunities are few for homeless individuals. Given the co-occurrence of substance abuse and homelessness, the theoretical reciprocal causality of substance abuse and homelessness, and the costs to homeless individuals as well as society, it appears appropriate to increase efforts to provide substance abuse interventions to the homeless in a manner tailored to the homeless milieu. Shelters, soup kitchens, and day centers are ideal places in which to begin a process of engagement with homeless individuals who may want to address their alcohol- and drug-related problems.

—*Irene Glasser and William Zywiak*

Further Reading

American Psychiatric Association. (2000). *Diagnostic and statistical manual of mental disorders* (4th ed., revised). Washington, DC: Author.

Argeriou, M., & McCarty, D. (1993). The use of shelters as substance abuse stabilization sites. *The Journal of Mental Health Administration, 20*(2), 126–137.

Campbell, T., Barrett, D., Cisler, R. A., Solliday-McRoy, C., & Melchert, T. P. (2001). Reliability estimates of the alcohol use disorders identification test revised to include other drugs (AUDIT-12). Montreal, Canada: Research Society on Alcoholism Poster Presentation.

Cohen, C., & Sokolovsky, J. (1989). *Old men of the Bowery: Strategies for survival among the homeless.* New York: Guilford Press.

Fischer, P. J., & Breakey, W. R. (1991). The epidemiology of alcohol, drug, and mental disorders among homeless persons. *American Psychologist, 46,* 1115–1128.

Fournier, L., Mercier, C., Raynault, M., Ohayon, M., & Caulet, M. (1993). Reaching the most destitute of the homeless: When success turns to failure. *Contemporary Drug Problems, 20*(3), 415–431.

Glasser, I. (1988). *More than bread: Ethnography of a soup kitchen.* Tuscaloosa: University of Alabama Press.

Glasser, I. (1994). *Homelessness in global perspective.* New York: MacMillan.

Glasser, I., Fournier, L., & Costopoulos, A. (1999). Homelessness in Quebec City, Quebec and Hartford, Connecticut: A cross-national and cross-cultural analysis. *Urban Anthropology and Studies of Cultural Systems and World Economic Development, 28,* 141–164.

Glasser, I., & Zywiak, W. (2003). Homelessness and substance use: a tale of two cities. *Substance Use and Misuse, 38,* 553–578.

Johnson, T. (Ed). (2003). *Substance Use and Misuse, 38*(3–6). Issue devoted to substance use and misuse and homelessness.

Johnson, T., & Freels, S. (1997). Substance abuse and homelessness: Social selection or social adaptation? *Addiction, 92,* 437–445.

Joseph, H., & Paone, D. (1997). The homeless. In Lowinson, J., Ruiz, P., Millman, R. & Langrod, J. (Eds.), *Substance abuse: A comprehensive textbook* (3rd ed., pp. 733–741). Baltimore: Williams & Wilkins.

Link, B., & Phelan, J. (1995). Lifetime and five-year prevalence of homelessness in the United States. *American Journal of Orthopsychiatry, 65,* 347–354.

Miller, W., & Rollnick, S. (2002). *Motivational interviewing: Preparing people to change addictive behavior.* New York: Guilford.

National Institute on Alcohol Abuse and Alcoholism. (1995). NIAAA releases new estimates of alcohol abuse and dependence. Press Release.

Nuttbrock, L.A., Rahav, M., Rivera, J. J., et al. (1998). Outcomes of homeless mentally ill chemical abusers in community residences and a therapeutic community. *Psychiatric Services, 49*:68-76.

Perl, H. I., & Jacobs, M. L. (1992). Case management models for homeless persons with alcohol and other drug problems: An overview of the NIAAA research demonstration. *Progress and issues in case management.* (NIDA Research Monograph Series No. 127), 208–222.

Robertson, M., Koegel, P., & Ferguson, L. (1989). Alcohol use and abuse among homeless adolescents in Hollywood. *Contemporary Drug Problems, 16,* 415–452.

Sacks, S., & De Leon, G. (1997). *Modified therapeutic community for homeless MICAs (mentally ill chemical abusers): Profiles, process and outcomes.* Paper presented at the American Psychological Association annual meeting, Chicago.

Spradley, J. (1970). *You owe yourself a drunk: An ethnography of urban nomads.* Boston: Little, Brown.

Stahler, G. J. (1995). Social interventions for homeless substance abusers: Evaluating treatment outcomes. In G. J. Stahler & B. Stimmel (Eds.), *The effectiveness of social interventions for homeless substance abusers* (pp. xiii–xxiv). New York: The Haworth Medical Press.

Ukeles Associates, Inc. (1995). Evaluation of the park homeless outreach project report to the New York Community Trust. New York: Author.

Urban Institute. (1999). *Homeless programs and the people they serve.* Summary report of the national survey of homeless assistance providers and clients. Washington, DC: Author.

Wright, J. D., & Weber E. (1987). *Homelessness and health.* Washington, DC: McGraw-Hill, Healthcare Information Center.

Zerger, S. (2002). *Substance abuse treatment: What works for homeless people? A review of the literature.* Nashville, TN: National Health Care for the Homeless Council.

▣ ALMSHOUSES

See Poorhouses; Workhouses

▣ AMERICAN BAR ASSOCIATION COMMISSION ON HOMELESSNESS AND POVERTY

The board of governors of the American Bar Association (ABA) created the Commission on Homelessness and Poverty in 1991. The Commission consists of one full-time ABA staff attorney and thirteen volunteer members appointed by the ABA president, and is charged with the following tasks: (1) Educating members of the bar and the public about legal and other problems of poor and homeless people and ways in which lawyers can assist in solving or ameliorating them; (2) training lawyers in areas needed to provide pro bono legal assistance to homeless and near homeless people; (3) working with all ABA entities on issues arising in their jurisdiction that affect poor and homeless people; and (4) engaging in further activities that are necessary to fulfill these responsibilities, including working with state and federal executive branches and legislative bodies concerning matters relating to the poor and homeless.

The Commission grew from the ABA Representation of the Homeless Project, a program created by the Section of Individual Rights and Responsibilities after the ABA first adopted a policy on homelessness in 1986. That 1986 resolution expressed the ABA's support of legislation and programs that protect the rights of homeless people; it also created housing and other programs to aid homeless people in their battle for self-sufficiency and urged pro bono legal representation of homeless clients. To implement this resolution, the Representation of the Homeless Project provided technical assistance to the ABA's pro bono homeless programs, worked to educate the profession about homelessness and the needs of homeless people, and drafted policy for the ABA House of Delegates (the ABA's legislative body).

Building on the work of the Project, the ABA created the Commission on Homelessness and Poverty to demonstrate its commitment to addressing the legal needs of homeless and impoverished people. The Commission provides policy-based advocacy on behalf of homeless and impoverished people. Through the ABA Governmental Affairs Office, it lobbies Congress to develop and fund programs that will address the causes of homelessness and poverty in the United States, and to enact laws that will protect and provide for those in desperate need of assistance. The ABA presently has policies on many issues relating to homeless and impoverished people: affordable housing, public housing, public benefits, funding for service programs, voting rights for homeless people, the "digital divide," legal services, health care, and predatory lending, among others.

The Commission seeks to educate the bar and the public about homelessness and poverty and the ways in which the legal community and advocates can assist those in need. To achieve this goal, it drafts publications and conducts training sessions across the country to equip the legal community to advocate on behalf of homeless and impoverished people. It also coordinates with national, state, and local advocates and organizations to facilitate the exchange of information and resources.

One recent publication, *The Homeless Court Program: Taking the Court to the Streets,* examines San Diego's Homeless Court, a special voluntary court session convened on a monthly basis at a homeless shelter. The philosophy behind this unique and successful program, begun in the late 1980s, is rehabilitative rather than punitive—no one is taken into custody. The key players involved in the program realize that outstanding criminal warrants often preclude homeless people from accessing vital services such as employment and housing assistance, public benefits, and treatment for mental health or substance abuse problems. As such, the court seeks to address the legal problems of the homeless participants as well as linking them with appropriate services and treatment programs.

Educating Children Without Housing: A Primer on Legal Requirements and Implementation Strategies for Educators, Advocates and Policy Makers provides innovative strategies for ensuring the educational rights of homeless children and youth, as required by the McKinney-Vento Homeless Assistance Act. Published jointly with the Steering Committee on the Unmet Legal Needs of Children, the book also provides a directory of state coordinators for the education of homeless children and youth, as well as a list of homeless advocacy organizations around the country.

Representing the Poor and Homeless: Innovations in Advocacy is a compilation of articles written by law professors and advocates addressing both the causes of and solutions to homelessness. Its topics include the lawyer's role in ending homelessness, developing and locating affordable housing, addressing mental illness and substance abuse, microenterprise development, and promoting economic self-sufficiency. The book also includes directories of publications and a list of websites addressing homelessness and poverty.

NIMBY: A Primer for Lawyers and Advocates discusses the potential roadblocks that may arise when establishing a facility such as a shelter or soup kitchen in a residential area. The book addresses the issues and reaction within communities, tips on how to work with the community, the zoning process, and an overview of legal tools to combat NIMBY ("not in my backyard") attitudes and exclusionary zoning ordinances.

The Commission also administers the John J. Curtin, Jr. Justice Fund Legal Internship Program. Named for the ABA's president in 1990–1991, the program awards stipends to law students who spend the summer months working for a bar association or legal services program designed to prevent homelessness or assist homeless or indigent clients or their advocates. The program provides much-needed legal assistance to organizations serving the underrepresented and gives students direct experience in a public interest forum. Through this, it aims both to help homeless clients and to encourage legal careers that further the goals of social justice.

Further information can be found at www.abanet. org/homeless, the website of the American Bar Association Commission on Homelessness.

—*Amy E. Horton-Newell*

ASIA

See Australia; Calcutta; Homelessness, International Perspectives on; Housing and Homelessness in Developing Nations; India; Indonesia; Japan; Mumbai (Bombay); Sydney; Tokyo

ASSERTIVE COMMUNITY TREATMENT (ACT)

The Assertive Community Treatment (ACT) model of assisting people with severe mental illness was developed in the late 1970s by Leonard Stein and Mary Ann Test and their colleagues at the Mendota Mental Health Institute in Madison, Wisconsin. ACT was originally designed to prevent relapse and to foster successful adaptation to community living following discharge from the hospital. But since the 1990s, the model has been increasingly used to stabilize and improve the quality of life of mentally ill homeless clients such as those living in shelters, on the streets, or in parks or abandoned buildings.

A nonresidential program often with an openended time frame, ACT is delivered by interdisciplinary teams composed of ten to fifteen members. ACT staff may work with a client for several hours in a given day assisting with wide-ranging tasks: resolving an interpersonal crisis, searching for an apartment, shopping or cleaning house, maintaining employment, or obtaining health care services. In principle, ACT teams provide all services directly, but in practice they often make referrals to other agencies and providers, especially for services that address the diverse needs of homeless people. Staff members share responsibility for their clients and typically meet daily to review the status of their entire caseload and to plan that day's activities.

EVALUATING ACT AND ITS VARIATIONS

ACT is probably the most extensively evaluated intervention in the field of community mental health. Beginning with Stein and Test's experimental evaluation, studies have consistently shown that clients treated in ACT spend fewer days in psychiatric inpatient units than those who receive standard outpatient care, and that they are frequently more satisfied with their care. Some studies have also documented reduced symptoms, improved social functioning, and higher employment rates with ACT, but these benefits have been less consistently observed. ACT has also been the subject of several cost-effectiveness studies. Most of these have shown that the high cost of ACT services can be offset by reduced hospital utilization.

In recent years, Robert Drake and his colleagues at the Dartmouth-New Hampshire Psychiatric Research Center have further shown that if ACT teams include specialists in substance abuse treatment, outcomes can be improved for clients dually diagnosed with both psychiatric and addictive disorders. With the addition of employment specialists, a far higher percentage of clients can participate in competitive employment. As the ACT model has come into widespread use, variations have also emerged. Researchers have devised ways to measure specific programs' fidelity to ACT's operating principles, and there is some evidence that programs that do conform achieve sharper reductions in hospital use. Some experts believe that the benefits of ACT can be achieved only through strict adherence to these principles—especially low caseloads, sharing of clients by the entire team, treatment in community settings, and a long-term commitment to care. But others suggest that adherence can be relaxed to meet local circumstances without loss of effectiveness. Moreover, the boundary between ACT and other intensive or clinical case management approaches is not easy to define.

Applications of ACT for Homeless Clients

Using controlled trials, researchers have assessed various combinations of case management and housing assistance for homeless persons with severe mental illness. But only two studies have formally compared ACT with standard treatment for these groups.

ACT versus Broker Case Management: The St. Louis Study (Morse et al.). As a control group, the first published study used a broker case management intervention—a model that emphasizes linking clients to service providers. Against this model, two types of ACT program were compared: standard ACT and one with additional specially trained community workers. Clinically, the ACT clients in this St. Louis study had reduced symptoms and were more satisfied with their services than were the controls, although there were no differences in housing outcomes. A cost-effectiveness analysis showed that although the direct costs for both ACT models exceeded $9,000 per client over the eighteen-month study period, they were both also associated with substantially reduced inpatient costs. When all health care costs were considered, costs were lowest for the ACT program with community workers ($39,913 per client), highest for standard ACT ($49,510), and in the middle for brokered case management ($45,076). These results replicate findings in other seriously mentally ill populations, showing that ACT's high costs can be at least partly offset by reduced hospital use.

ACT versus Standard Care: The Baltimore Study (Lehman et al.). A second study found that ACT clients experienced greater improvements in symptoms, life satisfaction, and general health than controls, and had more days in stable housing when they received standard community services. It reported similarly high costs for ACT services ($8,244 per client per year) but also much lower psychiatric inpatient costs for ACT clients ($31,427 versus $55,946 for controls). As a result, total annual health care costs were about $16,000 lower for ACT than for controls ($50,748 versus $66,479). As in the St. Louis study, significant benefits for ACT emerged in several domains. Moreover, because of reduced inpatient service use, total costs were similar to those of controls. These data suggest that ACT may be preferable to standard care since it is both more effective and, due to reduced inpatient care, costs the same or less.

But to calculate the total cost impact of an intervention, one must consider previous levels of service use and expenses among study participants. There is much room for savings with high-cost clients, but little to save with low-cost clients. Patients in both the St. Louis and Baltimore studies had already incurred especially high inpatient costs.

To correct this skewed picture, ACT costs were also compared with those of two more typical, lower-budget programs: the Health Care for Homeless Veterans (HCHV) program run by the Department of Veteran Affairs (VA), and the Center for Mental Health Services' ACCESS program. Twelve-month cost data for both programs, adjusted for inflation, placed average annual inpatient costs at only $7,905 for HCHV and $8,346 for ACCESS, less than one-third of those in the St. Louis and Baltimore studies. Only the highest-need patients—those in the top tenth, measured by expense—approached those spending levels: $32,605 in HCHV and $25,010 in ACCESS. Thus, in these two more representative programs, inpatient costs approached those of the St. Louis and Baltimore studies for only one-tenth of the clientele—suggesting that ACT is likely to achieve cost-neutrality for only a small segment of this population, although it may achieve beneficial clinical and housing outcomes for all segments.

MODIFIED ACT PROGRAMS

Many other programs have explored the value of intensive case management models similar to ACT, sometimes explicitly linked with residential treatment or supported housing services. In a recent literature review, Morse (1999) discussed ten experimental studies of case management programs that served homeless persons with mental illness. All were either ACT programs (including the St. Louis and Baltimore studies noted above) or variants of ACT. Seven of ten studies showed fewer homeless days for those assigned to case management, while two showed significant reduction in symptoms when compared to control groups.

Outreach-Oriented Modifications

In one modified ACT approach, staff members focus on outreach and engagement with alienated homeless people who may be unwilling to seek conventional assistance. One experimental study evaluated the New York "Choices" program, which included four services: outreach and engagement, a low-demand drop-in center for daytime use, a ten-bed respite housing unit, and community-based rehabilitation. Over a two-year follow-up period, Choices clients had much greater access to basic resources such as food and shelter than did their controls. They also enjoyed improved psychiatric symptoms, higher quality of life, and a 54 percent reduction in nights sleeping on the street—almost twice the 28 percent reduction among controls.

Nonexperimental data from the Center for Mental Health Services' eighteen-site ACCESS program provide a fuller perspective on the outreach process. During its first three years, ACCESS contacted a total of 11,857 clients through outreach. Those contacted in street settings were typically the sickest and most vulnerable, but only 34 percent of them initially expressed interest in services, and only 19 percent eventually entered case management—as opposed to the 46 percent overall enrollment rate. Once enrolled, however, all clients showed fairly equal improvements in both clinical and housing domains.

Housing-Oriented Modifications

Another modified ACT approach combines intensive case management with direct housing subsidies. In the early 1990s, researchers attempted to untangle the effects of this double-stranded approach using a two-by-two study design, crossing rent subsidies with intensive case management. Indeed, the study found that subsidy recipients were more likely to be independently housed after eighteen months. But intensive case management was not associated with greater improvement than standard case management in any outcome domain. However, the findings were ambiguous for two reasons. Receipt of housing subsidies did not reduce nights of homelessness during the eighteen-month study period. Moreover, the intensive case management intervention—as actually delivered—was very similar to the standard care intervention. Thus, in spite of its intuitive appeal, it remained unclear whether linking housing subsidies directly with clinical services offers an advantage over clinical services alone.

In 1992, the Department of Housing and Urban Development joined with the VA to establish the HUD-VA Supported Housing (HUD-VASH) Program, now operating at thirty-five sites across the country. These programs combine HUD Section 8 rent subsidy vouchers with case management supervised by VA staff at a 20 to 1 ratio with clients. In an experimental evaluation at four sites, participants were randomly assigned to three groups. The first group received full HUD-VASH benefits: vouchers and intensive case management. The second received case management only, without special access to vouchers, and the third received standard VA care. Over a three-year follow-up period, HUD-VASH veterans had 16 percent more nights housed (in an apartment, room or house) than the second group and 25 percent more than the third group. (The second and third groups differed by just 7 percent on this score.) The HUD-VASH group also experienced 35 and 36 percent fewer nights homeless than each of the control groups, excluding days spent in an institution such as a hospital or jail. But the study found no significant differences between treatment groups on any measures of psychiatric or substance abuse status.

Both of these studies suggest that housing subsidies may be more important than case management in helping homeless people with mental illness to exit from homelessness—although it is also possible that the case management would have been more effective if it had adhered more closely to the ACT model.

Time-Limited ACT-like Programs

The Critical Time Intervention (CTI) approach is in many ways similar to ACT, with the major difference that it is time-limited. CTI was specifically designed in the early 1990s to help homeless mentally ill clients in a shelter-based New York day program make the transition into mainstream housing and health care services—which is, in fact, the ultimate goal of any such service program. It consists of three phases: During the accommodation phase (the first three months), CTI workers conduct home visits and link clients with providers. Next, in the tryout phase (months four through seven), clients begin to use mainstream services, while in the termination phase (months eight and nine) they further develop their resourcefulness. Over an eighteen-month follow-up period, CTI clients spent an average of thirty nights homeless compared to ninety nights for the control group (5.5 versus 16.6 percent). They also showed sharper reduction in negative psychiatric symptoms. These data suggest that, contrary to one of the basic principles of ACT, gains may be consolidated and maintained even when ACT-like services are delivered for a limited period of time.

Similarly, an eighteen-month follow-up assessment of ACCESS clients found that they can be selectively discharged or transferred from ACT to other services without compromising their progress in the mental health, substance abuse, housing, or employment arenas. In that study, 8.7 percent of the clients had participated in ACCESS for less than three months; 40.6 percent for three to ten months; 15.3% for eleven to thirteen months; and 35.3% for fourteen months or more. Mental health, substance abuse, and housing outcomes did not significantly differ between clients who had been discharged from care management at the time of follow-up as compared to those who had not yet been discharged. In fact, those who had been discharged had worked significantly *more* days than those who had not, and reported significantly less outpatient health service use.

GREATER BENEFITS, HIGHER COST

ACT has been shown in many studies to be a cost-effective approach to the treatment of non-homeless high service users with severe mental illness. This model also appears to be cost-effective when offered to homeless people with severe mental illness who already make extensive use of inpatient care—although that fraction of the homeless population is relatively small. Variations of ACT emphasizing outreach, linkage with housing subsidies, and time-limited interventions suggest that ACT and its variants can yield benefits for the wider population of homeless people with severe mental illness, but may be associated with increased costs.

—*Robert A. Rosenheck*

Further Reading

Burns, B. J., & Santos, A. B. (1995). Assertive community treatment: An update of randomized trials. *Psychiatric Services 46,* 669–675.

Dixon, L. B., Krauss, N., Lehman, A. F., & DeForge, B. R. (1995). Modifying the PACT model to serve homeless persons with severe mental illness. *Psychiatric Services, 46,* 684–688.

Herman, D., Opler, L., Felix, A., Valencia, E., Wyatt, R., & Susser, E. A. (2000). "Critical time intervention" with mentally ill homeless men: Impact on psychiatric symptoms. *Journal of Nervous and Mental Disease, 188,* 135–140.

Hurlburt, M. S., Wood, P. A., & Hough, R. L. (1996). Effects of substance abuse on housing stability of homeless mentally ill persons in supported housing. *Psychiatric Services, 47,* 731–736.

Johnsen, M., Samberg, L., Calsyn, R., Blasinsky, M., Landow, W., & Goldman, H. (1999). Case management models for persons who are homeless and mentally ill: The ACCESS demonstration project. *Community Mental Health Journal, 35*(4), 325–346.

Lam, J., & Rosenheck, R. A. (1999). Street outreach for homeless persons with serious mental illness: Is it effective? *Medical Care, 37*(9), 894–907.

Lehman, A. F., Dixon, L. B., Hoch, J. S., DeForge, B. R., Kernan, E., & Frank, R. (1999). Cost-effectiveness of Assertive Community Treatment for homeless persons with severe mental illness. *British Journal of Psychiatry, 174*(4), 346–353.

Lehman, A. F., Dixon, L. B., Kernan, E., DeForge, B. R., & Postrado, L. A. (1997). Randomized trial of Assertive Community Treatment for homeless persons with severe mental illness. *Archives of General Psychiatry, 54,* 1038–1043.

Morse, G. (1999). A review of case management for people who are homeless: Implications for practice, policy and research. In L. B. Fosburg & D. L. Dennis (Eds.), *Practical lessons: The 1998 National Symposium on Homelessness Research.* Washington, DC: U.S. Department of Housing and Urban Development, U.S. Department of Health and Human Services.

Morse, G., Calsyn, R. J., Allen, G., Templehoff, B., & Smith, R. (1992). Experimental comparison of the effects of three treatment programs for homeless mentally ill people. *Hospital and Community Psychiatry, 43,* 1005–1010.

Phillips, S. D., Burns, B. J., Edgar, E., Mueser, K. T., Linkins, K. W., Rosenheck, R. A., Drake, R. E., & Herr, E. C. M. (2001). Assertive Community Treatment: Moving an evidence-based intervention into standard practice. *Psychiatric Services, 52*(6), 771–779.

Rosenheck, R. A., & Dennis, D. (2001). Time-limited Assertive Community Treatment (ACT) for homeless persons with severe mental illness. *Archives of General Psychiatry, 58*(11), 1073–1080.

Rosenheck, R. A., Kasprow, W., Frisman, L. K., Liu-Mares, W., Dilella, D., Dausey, D., & Lin, H. (2002, June). *Integrating health care and housing supports from federal agencies: An evaluation of the HUD-VA Supported Housing Program (HUD-VASH).* West Haven, CT: Northeast Program Evaluation Center.

Rosenheck, R. A., & Neale, M. S. (1998). Cost-effectiveness of intensive psychiatric community care for high users of inpatient services. *Archives of General Psychiatry, 55,* 459–466.

Shern, D., Tsemberis, S., Anthony, W., Lovell, A. M., Richmond, L., Felton, C. J., Winarski, J., & Cohen, M. (2000). Serving street-dwelling individuals with psychiatric disabilities: Outcomes of a psychiatric rehabilitation clinical trial. *American Journal of Public Health, 90*(12), 1873–1878.

Stein, L. I., & Test, M. A. (1980). Alternative to mental hospital treatment: I. Conceptual model, treatment program, and clinical evaluation. *Archives of General Psychiatry, 37,* 392–397.

Susser, E., Valencia, E., Conover, S., Felix, A., Tsai, W., & Wyatt, R. J. (1997). Preventing recurrent homelessness among mentally ill men: A "critical time" intervention after discharge from a shelter. *American Journal of Public Health, 87*(2), 256–262.

Teague, G. B., Bond, G. R., & Drake, R. E. (1998). Program fidelity in assertive community treatment: Development and use of a measure. *American Journal of Orthopsychiatry, 68*(2), 216–232.

Wolfe, N., Helminiak, T. W., Morse, G. A., Calsyn, R. J., Klinkenberg, W. D., & Trusty, M. L. (1997). Cost-effectiveness of three approaches to case management for homeless mentally ill clients. *American Journal of Psychiatry, 154,* 341–348.

▣ ASSOCIATION OF GOSPEL RESCUE MISSIONS

Founded in 1913, the Association of Gospel Rescue Missions (AGRM)—formerly known as the International Union of Gospel Missions—is a nonprofit organization whose member missions work to provide emergency shelter, food, youth and family services, and education and job training programs. In addition, the AGRM operates rehabilitation programs for drug addicts and alcoholics, and assistance to the elderly poor and at-risk youth. The sixth largest nonprofit organization in the United States, the AGRM has a network of 294 rescue missions, which provide approximately 30 million meals and 12 million nights of lodging to needy and homeless people every year. The AGRM has more than 9,000 full-time employees and 300,000 volunteers and has over 300 affiliates in the United States, Canada, India, Australia, South America, and Africa.

As part of its mission, the AGRM takes on five major responsibilities: (1) Creating new rescue ministries; (2) promoting and emphasizing prayer and spiritual values and growth; (3) providing local ministries with education, training, consultation, conferences, conventions, and networking; (4) stressing to the church and community the importance and value of their rescue efforts; and (5) and operating over 114 Alcoholics Victorious groups, as well as Rescue College.

The AGRM and other member missions consider themselves to be an "arm of the Church," in that they work to meet the spiritual, emotional, and physical needs of people who are unable to be reached by the traditional church.

PROGRAMS

The AGRM has developed three major programs that help accomplish these goals by offering services to both those in need and those willing to help.

The Bowery Mission, founded in 1879, shown here in 2003.
Source: Karen Christensen; used with permission.

- *Job Placement Program.* The AGRM website provides a resume file for potential employees, and full-time employment opportunities with member rescue missions are posted each month both on the website and in the AGRM newsletter.

- *Alcoholics Victorious.* Founded in 1948, Alcoholics Victorious provides a support group medium for recovering alcoholics who profess a deep religious faith. Group members gather at meetings to share feelings, experiences, and goals with one another. Also included in the process of recovery are the Alcoholics Victorious Creed and the group's Twelve Steps toward recovery.

- *Rescue College.* Rescue College is an Internet-based distance-learning program that prepares men and women for an administrative career with rescue missions and other church-related organizations. The programs offered allow students to acquire either a Certificate in Rescue Ministry or a Bachelor in Rescue Ministry, which is equivalent to a four-year degree awarded at other accredited colleges and universities in the United States.

The newest project added to the AGRM's repertoire is the Program Outcomes Assessment Project, which was initiated to measure the outcomes and effectiveness of the association's various programs. This evaluation is done for two reasons—to upgrade and modify programs by identifying what does and does not work, and to use in fund-raising, public relations, and promotional efforts. Outcome indicators are used to measure the effectiveness of the associa-

tion's programs, and they serve as guidelines for whether or not an individual has successfully "graduated" from the AGRM's rehabilitation programs. The Mission Program outcomes one year after leaving the program state that in order to be considered "successfully graduated" an individual must be (1) gainfully employed or actively involved in continuing education, (2) free of primary life-controlling issues identified during the mission program, (3) in stabilized housing, (4) maintaining healthy relationships, (5) achieving financial stability, (6) content with quality of life, and (7) involved in a local church.

The Association of Gospel Rescue Missions is responsible for aiding millions of homeless people and others in need every year. In 2001 alone, the association graduated more than 12,000 homeless men and women into productive living, distributed more than 24 million pieces of clothing, and provided some 210,000 families with 735,000 items of furniture—along with offering millions of meals and nights of lodging. The AGRM welcomes both individual and organizational memberships, and those interested can learn more about the membership process at www.agrm.org.

—Emily A. Colangelo

ASSOCIATIONS AND ORGANIZATIONS

See American Bar Association Commission on Homelessness and Poverty; Association of Gospel Rescue Missions; Corporation for Supportive Housing; European Network for Housing Research; FEANTSA; Goodwill Industries International; Homeless Assistance Services and Networks; Homeless International; "Housing First" Approach; International Network of Street Newspapers; International Union of Tenants; National Alliance to End Homelessness; National Center on Family Homelessness; National Coalition for the Homeless; National Resource Center on Homelessness and Mental Illness; Salvation Army; UN-HABITAT; Urban Institute; Wilder Research Center

▣ AUSTRALIA

As generally understood in the Australian context, the term *homeless* can refer not only to those who lack "a roof over the head" but also to anyone who is inappropriately housed—or as one definition has it, "who does not have access to safe, secure and adequate housing" (Productivity Commission 2003, 71). Such inadequate housing includes not only emergency accommodation but also any housing that threatens one's economic or social support structure, compromises one's health or security, or is of unsecured tenure, with eviction an ever-present possibility. For example, an elderly non-English speaking migrant housed in an exclusively English speaking group home.

THE EXTENT OF HOMELESSNESS

Measuring the extent of homelessness in Australia is difficult, as many of the unhoused are transient and therefore hard to locate and count. Moreover, because there is no generally agreed-on methodology for assessing homelessness, estimates can vary widely. Still, useful approximations have been made based on data from two sources: the Australian Bureau of Statistics (ABS) and the Supported Accommodation Assistance Program (SAAP).

The SAAP is a joint program of the Commonwealth of Australia and its individual states and territories. Aimed at assisting people who are homeless or in danger of becoming so, it is the main government-funded program targeted to this area. Funding from the SAAP enables over 1,200 nongovernmental, community, and local government organizations to provide accommodation and other services to those in need. Data on its operations (Australian Institute of Health and Welfare 2002) show that in 2001–2002, an estimated 95,600 people received SAAP assistance in one form or another.

The ABS conducts periodic counts of Australia's population every four years. One study (Chamberlain 1999) used a "point in time" analysis and found that on ABS census night in 1996, there were an estimated 105,304 homeless people across Australia. Of this total, about 46 percent were staying with friends or relatives, 22 percent were in boarding houses, almost 20 percent were sleeping out or in improvised housing, and about 12 percent were in emergency accommodation provided under the auspices of the SAAP.

How are Australia's homeless distributed by age and gender? SAAP data also show that of the people seeking SAAP assistance in 2001–2002, one-third were lone males aged 25 and over. One-fifth were females with children. Lone females aged 25 and over comprised 15 percent. Lone individuals under 25 were split almost evenly between males, at 13 percent, and females, at 12 percent. Couples with children account for 3 percent, whereas couples with no children are 2.6 percent. Lone males with children make up 1 percent and the 'other' category is 0.9 percent of the total. (Some figures have been rounded, which accounts for the missing 7 percent.)

PREVENTION AND OTHER ASSISTANCE PROGRAMS

Governments at all levels (i.e., commonwealth, state, and local) in Australia fund and support several other programs aimed at alleviating or preventing homelessness. Complementing the SAAP, the Crisis Accommodation Program (CAP) provides capital funds to either government agencies or nongovernment bodies for the purchase of housing and shelter for people who are homeless. The Emergency Relief Program (ERP) funds various community and welfare organizations so that they can monetarily assist families and individuals in short-term financial crisis. These groups also provide substantial resources of their own for a wide range of programs and practical assistance designed to help people who are homeless or likely to become so.

Two other programs, the Commonwealth-State Housing Agreement (CSHA) and Commonwealth Rent Assistance (CRA), provide housing assistance. The CSHA is mainly concerned with providing public housing assistance, and the CRA helps renters in the private rental market through the provision of funds for rent assistance. The Commonwealth also provides a limited number of tax incentives to encourage homebuying, either for occupancy or as

Selection from Australia's *Working towards a National Homelessness Strategy*

It is not acceptable for people in Australia to be homeless. Myths that link homelessness to personal flaws or bad choices must be dispelled. Homelessness is caused by structural factors such as poverty, an inadequate supply of affordable housing and unemployment. Personal factors such as poor health and disability will increase an individual's vulnerability to homelessness insofar as they reduce their access to income, housing and employment.

People may experience family, community or social isolation as a consequence of, or a precursor to, homelessness. In addition, people who are homeless are more likely to misuse substances and have contact with the criminal justice system. Some population groups are more at risk of homelessness than others because they experience more poverty, more unemployment and more restricted access to affordable housing.

The only way to reduce homelessness is by tackling the structural factors that produce it. This will require a concerted national effort. It is with this in mind that the Commonwealth has committed itself to developing a National Homelessness Strategy focusing specifically on

1. prevention,
2. early intervention,
3. working together,
4. and crisis transition and support.

Source: *Working towards a National Homelessness Strategy.* (2001). Commonwealth Advisory Committee on Homelessness Consultation Paper. Commonwealth of Australia. Retrieved November 14, 2003, from http://www.housingjustice.org.au

rental investment properties. For example, one's principal place of residence is exempt from capital gains tax when a property is sold, thus providing an effective tax break for owner occupiers (not the landlord).

The Commonwealth government also provides a range of social security benefits—for example, disability, unemployment, and the Youth Allowance, which is generally paid to full-time students aged between 18 to 24 years and to young people aged under 21 who are looking for employment opportunities. It also provides health and other welfare benefits that in many cases help prevent homelessness.

So do other policies and programs, such as those aimed at reducing drug abuse and crime and improving family relationships. On both the state and local levels, governments run a range of homeless-specific programs; they also provide financial and other assistance to community and charitable groups working in this area.

Youth homelessness has been specifically targeted through the Commonwealth's Reconnect program. Aiming to forestall homelessness, it emphasizes early intervention strategies and encourages vulnerable young people to "reconnect" with family, education, and training.

TOWARD A NATIONAL HOMELESSNESS STRATEGY

With Australia's homelessness prevention programs spread across three levels of government, there are frequent service duplications, gaps, and debates over funding and cost shifting. In May 2000, the Commonwealth government announced its plan to develop a National Homelessness Strategy—an effort to correct the ad hoc and fragmented nature of these programs, for which Australia's federal system of government is itself partly to blame. A key aim of the strategy is to develop a national framework that will enable a more holistic, systemic approach to resolving homelessness. The strategy has focused primarily on prevention, early intervention, and crisis transition and support.

Much still needs to be done. Many people remain on long waiting lists for access to public housing. Many who are eligible for SAAP services find their needs unmet. And the private rental market seems unable to provide affordable housing to many families and individuals on low incomes or welfare support. But the National Homelessness Strategy, if fully implemented and properly resourced, may well be a key factor in helping to reduce future instances of homelessness in Australia.

—*Greg McIntosh*

See also Sydney

Further Reading
Australian Federation of Homeless Organisations. (2003).

Retrieved May 12, 2003, from http://www.afho.org.au/index.htm

Australian Institute of Health and Welfare. (2001). Services for homeless people. In *Australia's Welfare 2001* (pp. 322–362). Canberra: Australian Institute of Health and Welfare.

Australian Institute of Health and Welfare. (2002). *Homeless people in SAAP: SAAP national data collection annual report 2001–02.* Canberra: Australian Institute of Health and Welfare.

Cecily, N., & Fopp, R. (1994). *Homelessness in Australia: Causes and Consequences.* Melbourne: Australian Housing and Urban Research Institute.

Chamberlain, C. (1999). *Counting the homeless: Implications for policy development.* Canberra: Australian Bureau of Statistics.

Commonwealth Department of Family and Community Services. (2002). *National homelessness strategy.* Retrieved May 12, 2003, from http://www.facs.gov.au/internet/facsinternet.nsf/aboutfacs/programs/house-nhs_nav.htm

Council for Homeless Persons Australia. (1996, September). *National conference on homelessness.* Melbourne: Author.

Council to Homeless Persons (Victoria). *Parity (ongoing).* Retrieved July 7, 2003, from http://www.parity.infoxchange.net.au/

Council for Homeless Persons Australia. (1999). Retrieved May 12, 2003, from http://www.chpa.org.au

Productivity Commission. (2003). *Report on government services 2003* (Chapters 15 and 16). Retrieved May 12, 2003, from http://www.pc.gov.au/gsp/2003/index.html

▣ AUTOBIOGRAPHY AND MEMOIR, CONTEMPORARY HOMELESS

The emergence of the "new homeless" in the United States in the early 1980s inspired a series of homeless-authored books in the 1990s—autobiographies and memoirs that are reminiscent of Jack London's *The Road* (1907) and Tom Kromer's *Waiting for Nothing* (1935). Like their predecessors, contemporary homeless writers are usually male, and their narratives are often episodic urban stories without significant plot development or closure. The male emphasis does not adequately reflect the diversity of the contemporary homeless population, and the few autobiographies by homeless women are usually collaborative efforts, strongly indicative of community ties. Homeless writers usually empha-

size class over race, gender, and sexual orientation. Empowerment plays a significant role in the subjectivity of homeless writers, and displacement often replaces the traditional emphasis on genealogy and nation. Rather than chronicling a list of achievements, or emphasizing their relationship to family or their position within a particular ancestral line, or exploring their citizenship in a particular city or even America itself, homeless authors usually limit their narrative to the experience of homelessness, their survival strategies, and people encountered in their daily experience.

AUTOBIOGRAPHY AS EMPOWERMENT

Some of these works also belong to other subgenres of American memoir, including the conversion narrative, the testimonial, and the travel narrative. Autobiography provides a voice for an underrepresented and disenfranchised segment of the population, offering "a way of testifying to oppression and empowering the subject through their cultural inscription and recognition" (Anderson 2001, 104). Writing is an overtly social and political act for homeless authors, and the process of creating the text can be as important as the content. In *Grand Central Winter,* Lee Stringer describes his first accidental attempts at prose as a revelation: "Pretty soon I forget all about hustling and getting a hit. I'm scribbling like a maniac; heart pumping, adrenaline rushing, hands trembling" (Stringer 1998, 15). *Grand Central Winter*—like the autobiographies of Joe Homeless, Lars Eighner, Bobby Burns, Timothy F. Donohue, and the women of *I Have Arrived Before My Words*—was written while the author was homeless. Writing gave Stringer a renewed sense of purpose after more than a decade of addiction and street life, and his documentation of it was the very means by which he made the transition to permanent housing.

The act of writing the "unhoused self" also seeks to normalize the homeless experience. Unlike sensational biographies and media articles, the autobiographies serve as an antidote to dominant cultural images of the homeless as "other," images that tend to cast the homeless "in the mold of the grotesque" (Hopper 1993, 108). While the writers chronicle the pivotal

Excerpts from Four Autobiographical Stories of Homelessness

From *Travels with Lizbeth*

Day after day I could aspire, within reason, to nothing more than survival. Although planets wandered among the stars and the moon waxed and waned, the identical naked barrenness of existence was exposed to me, day in and day out. I do not think I could write a narrative that would quite capture the unrelenting ennui of homelessness, but if were to write it, no one could bear to read it. I spare myself as much as the reader in not attempting to recall so many empty hours. Every life has trivial occurrences, pointless episodes, and unresolved mysteries, but a homeless life has these and virtually nothing else.

Source: Eighner, Lars. (1993). *Travels with Lizbeth: Three years on the road and on the streets* (p. ix). New York: Fawcett Columbine.

From *Living at the Edge of the World*

When I came to I was lying on the ground, my pants were down around my ankles, the guy was gone. I tried to sit up but it hurt and my neck was so painful I could hardly move my head. There were little bloody cuts around my thighs. Maybe from his hands, his nails digging into me.

Getting up was hard because I was so trembly and my legs were tangled in my pants. When I did manage to stand and get my clothes back on they were all wet. I think I must have peed in them. They felt cold and clammy.

I couldn't go to the cops. They'd have to take me into custody because being down in the tunnels is criminal trespassing, plus legally I was a runaway. I wasn't going to spend another three days eating bologna sandwiches in Central Booking.

Source: Tina S. & Bolnick, Jamie Pastor. (2000). Living at the edge of the world: A teenager's survival in the tunnels of Grand Central Station (p. 84). New York: St. Martin's Press.

From *I Have Arrived before My Words*

I would like to help others by letting them know that, if they are still alive today and have been through pain, they are blessed. Because they have a mission in life to find happiness and peace. To find a God of their understanding and go out and enjoy their life and to take one day at a time because can't nothing change what has happened in the past. The present can be so fulfilling as it has been for me.

Also, I have written my story for my children so that they may understand why I let my family raise them. So that they wouldn't be lonely growing up. So that they can see what kind of life I had and to make their lives better.

Source: Pugh, Deborah, & Tietjen, Jeanie. (1997). *I have arrived before my words: Autobiographical writings of homeless women* (p. 49). Alexandria, VA: Charles River Press.

From *Grand Central Winter*

I start off writing about a friend of mine. Just describing his cluttered apartment. How I kind of like the clutter. How it gives the place a lived-in look. How you can just about read his life by looking around

Pretty soon I forget all about hustling and getting a hit. I'm scribbling like a maniac; heart pumping, adrenaline rushing, hands trembling. I'm so excited I almost crap on myself.

It's just like I'm taking a hit.

Before I know it, I have a whole story.

Source: Stringer, Lee. (1998). *Grand Central winter: Stories from the street* (p. 15). New York: Seven Stories Press.

events in their lives, they also reveal the banalities of daily living. Joe Homeless writes, "The time of day and day of the week were really irrelevant to me, because each day was just like every other. I spent them all looking out the window, sitting on a piece of foam rubber by the radiator" (Homeless 1994, 97). Lars Eighner concurs: "I do not think I could write a narrative that would quite capture the ennui of homelessness, but if I were to write it, no one could bear to read it" (Eighner 1993, xi).

TESTIMONY

Autobiographies of homelessness often testify to the discrimination their authors face, and to the hardships and adventures of a transient life. They tell of police sweeps, abuses by doctors, shelter life, sleeping rough, trauma, addiction, and the indifference of the public. Despite this, most male writers resist the suggestion that they are writing on behalf of others; they often set themselves apart from the greater homeless community. Lars Eighner, for example, does not characterize himself as an advocate: "I do not pretend to speak for the homeless" (Eighner 1993, x). Many authors forgo both an overview of homelessness and a chronological life history, concentrating exclusively on the individual experience of displacement. Nevertheless, they may feel a tremendous tension between their individual testimony and their obligation to serve as a witness for the rest of the homeless population. A notable exception is David Wojnarowicz's *The Waterfront Journals,* an obliquely autobiographical work of fiction. It is difficult to determine which of Wojnarowicz's monologues represent the author's experience as a homeless youth, and which are the stories of the people he met on the street.

HOMELESS WOMEN AND AUTOBIOGRAPHY

A number of biographers and ethnographers have focused on homeless women, most notably Jonathan Kozol in *Rachel and Her Children* (1988) and Elliott Liebow in *Tell Them Who I Am* (1993). The women's autobiographies that do exist are often collaborative efforts. They emphasize community and transformation, and they usually explore family relationships more deeply than male-authored narratives do. *Living at the Edge of the World,* an autobiography cowritten by Tina S. and Jamie Pastor Bolnick recounts Tina's life in the tunnels of Grand Central Station as a teenager and her descent into crack addiction. Tina's search for companionship initially attracts her to the homeless community: "Here, for the first time, I felt like I fit in" (S. and Bolnick, 2000, 24). Four years later—after being raped, incarcerated, and losing her friend to suicide—she finds a network of supportive adults who help her overcome her addiction and move into permanent housing. Tina's story is a testament to the power of these relationships.

Similarly, *I Have Arrived Before My Words* is a collaborative project that grew out of a writing workshop for homeless and incarcerated women. The workshop was initiated and led by Deborah Pugh and Jeanie Tietjen in Washington, D.C., as part of a WriterCorps arts outreach project, a collaboration between AmeriCorps and the National Endowment for the Arts. The five writers reflect upon their family histories and the factors that contributed to their displacement. They are empowered by the act of writing, and some hope to educate others. Dionne wants to write "a story so inspiring, so important to

turn peoples' lives around" (Pugh and Tietjen, 1997, 132) and Gayle wants "to help others by letting them know that, if they are still alive today and have been through pain, they are blessed" (Pugh and Tietjen 1997, 49). A number of biographers and ethnographers have focused on homeless women, most notably Jonathan Kozol in *Rachel and Her Children* (1988) and Elliott Liewbow in *Tell Them Who I Am* (1993), but autobiographies by homeless women remain scarce.

RESEARCH DIRECTIONS

There are no significant academic studies of contemporary autobiographies and memoirs of homelessness, although they are commonly reviewed in popular media. The implications of these narratives for historical record and the study of autobiography have not been fully explored. The importance of the texts—as a voice for homeless individuals, as expressions of empowerment, and as testimonies about the homeless experience—should not be overlooked.

—*Amanda F. Grzyb*

See also Appendix 1: Bibliography of Autobiographical and Fictional Accounts of Homelessness

Further Reading

Anderson, L. (2001). *Autobiography.* New York: Routledge.

Brodski, B., & Schenk, C. (Eds.). (1988). *Life/lines: Theorizing women's autobiography.* Ithaca, NY: Cornell University Press.

Burn, B. (1998*). Shelter: One man's journey from homelessness to hope.* Tucson: University of Arizona Press.

Donohue, T. E. (1996). *In the open: Diary of a homeless alcoholic.* Chicago: University of Chicago Press.

Duarte, C. (1990*). Odella: A hidden survivor.* Albuquerque: University of New Mexico Press.

Eighner, L. (1993). *Travels with Lizbeth: Three years on the road and on the streets.* New York: Fawcett Columbine.

Homeless, J. (1994). *My life on the street: Memoirs of a faceless man.* Far Hills, NJ: New Horizon Press.

Hopper, K. (1993). A poor apart: The distancing of homeless men in New York's history. In A. Mack (Ed.), *Home: A place in the world* (pp. 107–132). New York: New York University Press.

Kozol, J. (1988). *Rachel and her children: Homeless families in America.* New York: Fawcett Columbine.

Liebow, E. (1993). *Tell them who I am.* New York: Free Press.

Pugh, D., & Tietjen, J. (1997). *I have arrived before my words:*

Autobiographical writings of homeless women. Alexandria, VA: Charles River Press.

S., T., & Bolnick, J. P. (2000). *Living at the edge of the world: A teenager's survival in the tunnels of Grand Central Station.* New York: St. Martin's Press.

Stringer, L. (1998). *Grand Central winter: Stories from the street.* New York: Seven Stories Press.

Vonnegut, K., & Stringer, L. (1999). *Like shaking hands with God: A conversation about writing.* New York: Seven Stories Press.

Wojnarowicz, D. (1996*). The waterfront journals.* New York: Grove Press.

B

⊡ BANGLADESH

In a nation as socially and economically stratified as Bangladesh, homelessness has serious physical, social, and economic repercussions. The systemic issues that cause homelessness in Bangladesh stem from its large, overcrowded population, pervasive poverty, rapid urbanization, and vulnerability to natural disasters. The 2001 census counted the national population at 129.24 million. In a country of 147,570 square kilometers, this yields a population density of 876 persons per square kilometer—among the highest in the world (Bangladesh Bureau of Statistics [BBS], 2001). According to *Human Development Report 2002,* Bangladesh ranks 145th among 174 countries on the human development index, or HDI. This measure of human misery is based on per capita income, literacy rate, and longevity. Due to rapid urbanization, the capital city of Dhaka has been forecast to become the world's sixth-largest megacity in 2010, with a projected 18.4 million inhabitants (United Nations 2001, 11). A dismal nationwide shelter deficit has also greatly contributed to homelessness. This shortage was estimated in 1991 at about 3.1 million units, with about two-thirds of the deficit in rural areas and one-third in cities.

DEFINITION OF HOMELESSNESS

Homeless people in Bangladesh are often referred to as the "floating population" or "rootless people"; in urban areas, they are also called "pavement dwellers." Central to the official census definition of this floating population (in both urban and rural areas) is its rootlessness—a state that includes the vagrant, the displaced, the landless, and people exposed to the risk of total economic deprivation. The Bangladesh Bureau of Statistics (1999, 4) defined rootless people as those in any of several circumstances. First, the term encompasses landless people whose losses even include their traditional family homesteads (ancestral home) through such processes as the gradual subdivision of meager land among large family members. Second are the landless who have lost their land and homestead for political, economic, or social reasons. In the third category are abandoned women, the population affected by river erosion, and people flooded from their homes, as well as the population driven out of their own homestead areas by an unscrupulous land-grabbing "mafia." As for urban areas, the *Census of Slum Areas and Floating Population 1997* offered this definition: "Floating population are the mobile and vagrant category of rootless people who have no permanent dwelling units . . . [who] are found on the census night . . . in the rail station, launch *ghat* (terminal), bus station, *hat-bazaar* (market places), *mazar* (shrine), staircase of public/government buildings, open space, etc." (BBS, 1999, 4).

In all its various rural and urban manifestations, homelessness in Bangladesh generally means human loss in three areas (Ghafur, 2002a): "rooflessness," or loss of shelter against the elements of nature; "rootlessness," or loss of the identity, privacy, comfort, and protection enjoyed by housed people; and "resourcelessness," the erosion of one's endowment base—the resources needed to sustain life on a daily basis. Resources include a small kitchen garden in which to grow vegetables, a small pond/courtyard that is used to raise poultry and livestock, and alternative spaces that are used for home-based income generation.

RURAL HOMELESSNESS

About 76 percent of Bangladesh's population lives in rural areas, including both the landless and the rootless. Anyone who owns less than half an acre of cultivable land is considered functionally landless in Bangadesh. When poor people lack access to homestead land, two types of rural homelessness result (Rahman, 1993). "Squatter homeless" people occupy rural public land to which they have no legal right of occupancy, often building a flimsy shelter there. "Dependent homeless" people, on the other hand, take shelter on a landlord's property, or perhaps live in a corner of the landlord's own house. They are thus dependent on the charity and goodwill of solvent landlords, who in return usually demand hard labor in their domestic or agricultural work.

Rural homeless households—those with no homestead or cultivable land—are estimated at about 5 percent of all the nation's households. Poverty among the rural landless is pervasive; an estimated 66 percent of 1,013,037 landless rural households are chronically poor. Not only do their sheer numbers constitute a serious problem, these rural homeless affect the urban picture as well. A large number of this category will eventually migrate to major cities, especially Dhaka, in search of income, and will add to the existing urban homelessness there.

URBAN HOMELESSNESS

Two basic types of homelessness can be observed in major cities in Bangladesh (Ghafur, 2002b). "Extreme homelessness," the most visible, is based on the narrow physical criteria of rooflessness; it refers to situations where people live in streets or other public spaces without a permanent residence or shelter of their own. They are often called "pavement dwellers," "street dwellers," or "destitute"; all these terms imply floating status for day-to-day survival. The *Census of Slum Areas and Floating Population 1997* (BBS, 1999) estimated Dhaka's "extreme homeless" at 14,999; another 32,078 were counted in 118 other cities and towns collectively. That this estimate is very conservative is revealed by an ARISE study that found 445,226 street children in the six largest cities in Bangladesh (DSS, 2001)—75 percent of these in Dhaka alone.

"Passive homelessness," the second type, refers to those who may technically have a roof over their heads, yet suffer the loss of identity, privacy, and comfort that adequate shelter provides. Squatters living illegally in public or private land are a prime example. In several recent studies, squatters in Dhaka have been found to vary between 10 and 24 percent of the total city population. Other notable groups in this category are abandoned children and orphans, brothel-based sex workers, trafficked women and children, and housemaids and servants charged with child care in wealthy households. Passive homelessness is not a fixed state; an act of eviction by the state or a vested interest group, for example, can easily demote people from the passive to the extreme category. Under favorable conditions, created mainly by supports from nongovernmental organizations, people can also expect to rise out of this type of homelessness.

OVERCOMING HOMOGENEOUS REPRESENTATION

Access to a home offers its dwellers a setting for daily household production, family life, and social identity. Living under male-dominated gender relations, Bangladesh's poor women do not inherit paternal properties that are usually allocated to male siblings in accordance with social and religious norms. Moreover, women get a smaller share of their husband's property after they become widows. In addition, poor women are often divorced or abandoned by their husbands during economic hardship. People become homeless for a variety of reasons—poverty, patriarchy, or natural and human-made disasters—and their stories and circumstances may vary widely. Yet those who are housed tend to perceive the homeless as a homogenous group. Bangladesh's censuses, policy documents, research reports, and media tend to treat homeless people as a faceless group of "others," without making any helpful distinctions as to age, gender, or type—extreme or passive, for example. The typecasting of homeless people as "victims of their own fate" abandons them as footloose pariahs in a context where housing deficits are huge, and their chance of gaining access to meager resources remains remote.

Homeless people vary in their degrees of rooflessness, rootlessness, and resourcelessness; they differ in their access to the means of shelter, social identity, and daily subsistence. To become more effective, Bangladesh's current and future policies and actions to eradicate homelessness should overcome this tendency toward homogenous representation.

—Shayer Ghafur

Further Reading

Bangladesh Bureau of Statistics (1999). *Census of slum areas and floating population 1997.* Dhaka, Bangladesh: Author.

Bangladesh Bureau of Statistics. (2001). *Population census 2001, Preliminary report.* Dhaka, Bangladesh: Author.

Bangladesh Institute of Development Studies. (2001). *Fighting human poverty. Bangladesh human development report 2000.* Dhaka, Bangladesh: Author.

Department of Social Services. (2001). *Baseline survey of street children in six divisional cities in Bangladesh.* Appropriate Resources for Improving Street Children's Environment ARISE (BGD/97/028). Dhaka, Bangladesh: Author.

Ghafur, S. (2002a). Development begins at home: Policy implications for homelessness in cities in Bangladesh. *Proceedings of the XXX International Association for Housing Science (IAHS) World Congress on Housing, Housing Construction* (Vol. 1, pp. 363–371).

Ghafur, S. (2002b, February). *The nature, extent and eradication of homelessness in developing countries: The case of Bangladesh.* DFID funded ESCOR Project R7905. Final Report submitted to the CARDO, University of Newcastle upon Tyne, United Kingdom.

Government of Bangladesh. (1996). *Bangladesh national report on human settlements, Habitat II.* Dhaka, Bangladesh: Author.

Islam, N., et al. (1997). *Addressing the urban poverty agenda in Bangladesh: Critical issues and the 1995 survey findings.* Dhaka, Bangladesh: University Press.

Rahman, T. (1993). *The rural homelessness in Bangladesh.* Dhaka, Bangladesh: UNICEF-Bangladesh.

United Nations. (2001). *The state of the world's cities.* New York: Author.

▣ BOMBAY

See Mumbai

▣ BOSTON

Boston has a long-standing tradition of providing emergency services for homeless persons. In operation for more than thirty years, Pine Street Inn is the oldest and largest shelter for adults in New England, while Rosie's Place (opened in 1974) was the first shelter in America dedicated to serving homeless women. Only two mayors have served in City Hall during the twenty-year period of 1984–2004, Raymond Flynn and Thomas Menino. Under both administrations, the City of Boston has maintained a commitment that no homeless individual or family will be left "without a bed, without a meal, without medical care, without opportunity and hope." To meet the annual increase in demand for shelter each winter, temporary overflow shelters have been created and additional beds have been funded in permanent shelters.

SIZE AND SCOPE OF HOMELESSNESS

No research methodology has been able to accurately enumerate the homeless population. Estimating the size of this population in the United States and in any particular city has been a contentious problem, hampered by the geographic and temporal transience of homeless persons, as well as daunting logistical difficulties with sampling techniques. Nationally, numbers have ranged from 250,000 to 3 million homeless (Burt and Cohen 1989; Kuhn and

Culhane 1998) on any specific night; some estimate that 13.5 million Americans have experienced "literal" homelessness at some period in their lifetimes (Hoombs and Snyder 1982; Link et al. 1994). .

The City of Boston believes that accurate numbers are critical to a comprehensive approach to ending homelessness. Services can be better coordinated, and homeless persons can be moved beyond shelter when providers and policymakers have an integrated approach that includes street outreach, emergency shelter with food and clothing, accessible health care, transitional programs for those suffering from mental health and substance abuse issues, and most importantly, the creation and maintenance of affordable and safe housing.

While there are no comprehensive, exact numbers for the number of homeless persons in Boston during the entire year, the city's Emergency Shelter Commission conducts an annual single night census on the second Monday of December. The census began modestly in 1983, with a street count conducted by six volunteers over a two-week period. The census has grown considerably and now utilizes more than 250 volunteers, under the direction of the mayor, who gather at City Hall at 9:00 p.m. and then scour the city until 2:00 a.m. on a single night.

This annual census has served as a useful barometer for noting trends in Boston's homeless population and helping to guide both city and state policymakers. Boston's homeless population has grown by over 40 percent in the past decade, with a single night count increasing from 4,441 in 1992 to 6,210 in 2002. The number of homeless children showed the most dramatic growth, increasing over 70 percent in ten years, from 800 to 1,367. The number of women grew by almost 60 percent during the decade, from 989 in 1992 to 1,572 in 2002. While the number has risen only 25 percent in the past decade, homeless men remain the largest subgroup of Boston's homeless population. The 3,271 homeless men in the 2002 census comprised 53 percent of the total homeless population (Emergency Shelter Commission 2002).

The homeless census on December 9, 2002, conducted on a chilly and windy night with a temperature of 19° F, counted 6,210 homeless men, women, and children in Boston. This represented an increase of 3.4 percent from the total of 6,001 in 2001. The number of families in shelters, motels, and domestic violence and transitional programs was 2,328, an increase of 8.3 percent from 2,149 the previous year. Women represented the fastest growing segment of the homeless population, increasing 10 percent from 1,427 in 2001 to 1,572 in 2002 (Emergency Shelter Commission 2002).

A single night census is a "point in time" methodology and has several limitations. In particular, the number of people who are literally homeless in Boston during a year remains unknown. In addition, this strategy is unable to provide information about the city's "hidden homeless," those who are living in poverty and struggling to survive by living doubled up with family or friends.

As a complement to the single night census, the citywide Boston Health Care for the Homeless Program (BHCHP) reviewed the demographics and health care utilization patterns of the 6,311 unduplicated homeless persons who received direct health care services during the calendar year 2000. BHCHP provides health care services but does not see all homeless persons in the metropolitan area. The number of persons who experience literal homelessness during the course of a year is certainly much larger than 6,311, and the best available estimates suggest that the number of persons in Boston who suffer homelessness at some time during the year is between 12,000 and 15,000.

BHCHP had over 36,000 encounters with these 6,311 unduplicated individuals during the year. The information gleaned from these encounters helps us understand the demographics of homelessness in Boston. More men than women were served (4,269 men and 2,042 women), consistent with the demographics of the homeless populations of most cities. The age range of the BHCHP population is broad, and included over 300 children under the age of 13 and over 200 persons age 65 or older. Six hundred and twenty-eight adolescents and young adults received care, while the largest age groups included 3,231 persons from age 25 to 44 and 1,915 individuals from age 45 to 64. The demographics of the homeless population served by BHCHP reflect the population of the City of Boston as a whole, as seen in the following table:

Table 1. Ethnicity of Homeless Population Served by BHCHP

Ethnicity	No. Patients
Unknown	737
Asian	58
Black, born in U.S	1,735
Black, not born in U.S.	242
Hispanic	1,043
Native American Indian	37
Other	133
Pacific Islander	3
White, not Hispanic	2,323
Total	**6,311**

Multidisciplinary teams of doctors, nurse practitioners/physician assistants, nurses, and mental health clinicians form the critical core of the BHCHP service delivery model. These teams are firmly embedded in the mainstream of Boston's medical community and conduct primary care clinics at academic medical centers. The teams venture to over seventy community and outreach sites in the metropolitan Boston area to provide direct care services, including adult and family shelters, soup kitchens and day centers, homes for victims of domestic violence, motels and hotels, detoxification units, and methadone clinics. A racetrack team serves migrant and homeless workers who live in the barns and labor on the backstretch of two thoroughbred racetracks. A street team joins the local shelter teams, using an overnight rescue van to deliver primary and episodic care to Boston's "rough sleepers" who eschew shelters.

SERVICE DELIVERY

The Boston Public Health Commission's Homeless Services Bureau provides a continuum of services that include shelter, health care, job training, transitional housing, substance abuse counseling, and education. The nonprofit Friends of Boston's Homeless

works in partnership with the Homeless Services Bureau on a variety of programs. The Friends of Boston's Homeless services range from Project Soar, which provides supportive, transitional housing, to Project Lighthouse, an adult education and literacy program. Serving Ourselves, another Friends program, offers work experience, employment training, and job placement. The Farm at Long Island Shelter—a four-acre organic farm on Long Island in Boston Harbor—provides work experience and training in food production and culinary arts.

As noted above, medical, psychiatric, dental, and nursing care, in addition to case management and benefits assistance, are the services offered by the Boston Health Care for the Homeless Program. The program operates the Barbara McInnis House—a ninety-bed facility offering short-term medical and nursing care for homeless persons who would otherwise require costly acute care hospitalizations or endure high risk in the shelters or on the streets of Boston.

Community organizations serving specific populations include the Committee to End Elder Homelessness, which provides housing placement and support for homeless elders, and Bridge Over Troubled Waters, an agency that offers counseling, medical care, career development, and transitional living programs for runaway and homeless youth. The Paul Sullivan Housing Trust—the housing arm of the Pine Street Inn—has developed more than 300 housing units for the chronically homeless.

OVERVIEW

The 2002 annual census in Boston offered an interesting glimpse into the remarkable and often hidden burden of acute and chronic illness among the homeless population. This population lives in abject and persistent poverty, which is a powerful social determinant of poor health. As the 2002 report showed, on the night of the census, 23 individuals were in emergency departments, 184 in acute or chronic care hospitals, 292 in detoxification units, and 325 in mental health facilities. In a real sense, homelessness is a public health emergency, and the costs of homelessness to our society are indeed staggering.

—James J. O'Connell and Stacy E. Swain

Further Reading

Burt, M., & Cohen, B. (1989). *America's homeless: numbers, characteristics, and programs that serve them.* Washington, DC: Urban Institute Press.

Emergency Shelter Commission. (2002, December 9). *Homelessness in the City of Boston, winter 2002–2003: Annual census report.* Boston: Emergency Shelter Commission. Retrieved January 6, 2004, from http://www.cityofboston.gov/shelter/pdfs/report.pdf

Hoombs, M. E., & Snyder, M. (1982). *Homelessness in America: A forced march to nowhere.* Washington, DC: Community for Creative Non-Violence.

Kuhn, R., & Culhane, D. P. (1998). Applying cluster analysis to test a typology of homelessness by pattern of shelter utilization: Results from the analysis of administrative data. *American Journal of Community Psychology, 26,* 207–232.

Link, B. G., Susser, E., Stueve, A., Phelan, J., Moore, R. E., & Struening, E. (1994). Lifetime and five-year prevalence of homelessness in the United States. *American Journal of Public Health, 84,*1907–1912.

▣ BOWERY, THE

The Bowery is a major street that runs south to north for about a mile from Chatham Square to Copper Square in lower Manhattan. The major cross streets from south to north are Canal, Delancey, and Houston. One of the oldest in the nation, it is the street most associated in the public mind with homelessness, and from the late 1870s into the 1970s, it was "home" to many of the homeless in New York City. The Bowery as a skid row in the twentieth century included not just the street itself but also several side

The garden on the corner of Bowery and East Houston Street in New York City, October 2003.
Source: Karen Christensen; used with permission.

streets to the east and west, which at times housed institutions and organizations that served the homeless, such as the men's and women's municipal shelters. The Bowery's importance in the history of homelessness goes beyond its role as a major skid row. It has been a major venue for a considerable amount of research on the homelessness dating from the late 1800s and continuing into the 1990s.

HISTORY OF THE BOWERY

The Bowery (the name is derived from the Dutch word *bouwerij* meaning "farm") began as Bowery Lane, the major road out of New Amsterdam after the Dutch founded their New World colony and, beginning in 1626, granted large plots of land adjacent to the road to wealthy landowners to induce them to settle in New Amsterdam. The largest plot went to Petrus (Peter) Stuyvesant in 1651. His farm colony became known as Bowery or Stuyvesant Village. When the English displaced the Dutch and established New York in 1664, they maintained the farms and in 1673 renamed Bowery Lane the Boston Post Road, noting its role as part of the route from New York to Boston. But the name Bowery stuck, and it has been called that ever since. It remained a mainly country lane of houses, farms, and small shops for nearly 100 years. In the 1760s, the road began to attract a rougher crowd and was the site of foot racing and horse racing, dog fighting, and cock fighting.

The first major transformation began in the 1750s and continued into the next century as the large estates bordering the Bowery were subdivided and sold off, with houses and shops replacing farms. The Bowery became a major retail street, and by the early 1800s, the southern end became part of the immigrant slum centered in the Five Points. In 1826, the Bowery Theater (the largest in the nation at the time) opened, followed later by the Park and Chatham Theaters. The Bowery population shifted from the wealthy to the middle class to workers and poor European immigrants over the century and, by the 1850s, was associated in the public imagination with a working-class lifestyle and nativism, especially in regard to conflicts with recent arrivals from

Unexpected Attention for the Bowery

As the excerpt below demonstrates, urban gardening in New York City takes place in the most unlikely of spots:

Fed up with government inaction, in 1973 an impassioned artist named Liz Christy and a band of like-minded activists called the Green Guerillas began taking over abandoned lots of Manhattan's Lower East Side. Armed with bolt-cutters and pickaxes, they conceived of themselves as strike force to liberate the crumbling landscape around them. They founded their first garden on the corner of Bowery and Houston, where a few months earlier a couple of bums had been found frozen to death in a cardboard box. "You could not have picked a more unlikely place to start a garden," recalls Bull Brunson, an early Guerilla. "At the time, there were still all these men lined up along the Bowery drinking wine and panhandling. To put a garden there–in what was probably the ultimate slime spot in the city–that was unheard of." It was also, in the eyes of many bureaucrats, illegal. Although the Guerillas initially got permission to clean the lots, the City later accused them of trespassing and threatened to boot them off the land. But after a media blitz, when Christy and her compadres brought in TV cameras to show how they transformed the lot-creating soil with nothing but sifted rubble and compost-the City backed down and offered them a lease in 1974.

The Liz Christy Bowery-Houston Community Garden, as it later became known, was a lightning rod for do-it-yourself greening, inspiring passersby to create similar plots in their own neighborhoods. The Guerillas held training sessions and set up a phone line so people could call to find out where to get free plants and trees. They also lobbed "seed Green-Aids"-balloons or Christmas tree ornaments stuffed with peat moss, fertilizer, and wildflower seeds-into fenced-off lots and along highways and street meridians across the five boroughs.

Source: "Modern Research Tools Help African Americans Trace Their Roots." American News Service, August 19, 1999.

Ireland. The Bowery Boys and Gals, Mose (an urban Paul Bunyan), and gangs such as Bowery Boys and Atlantic Guards drew attention to the Bowery and beyond.

The emergence of the Bowery as a working-class enclave was accompanied by the demise of the Bowery as an up-market residential, shopping, and entertainment district. As the city expanded north, it took its wealthier residents and businesses with it. By the 1860s, the Bowery was New York's primary locale for down-market entertainment—saloons, beer gardens, amusement halls, dime museums, street vendors, and oyster houses. Its location near the harbor made it a regular stop for many sailors. By the 1880s, it had become a tourist attraction, with "uptowners" and out-of-towners eager for a look at McGuirk's Suicide Hall, Steve Brodie's saloon, fake opium dens, and political boss "Big" Tim Sullivan.

The Bowery emerged as a home for the homeless in the 1870s, as many of the post–Civil War homeless in the city found their way to the low-cost housing on the Bowery. In 1873, the YMCA opened a branch on the Bowery, the first lodging houses opened the following year, and the Bowery Mission opened in 1879. In 1878, elevated railroad tracks were erected over the sidewalks, making the street unattractive for pedestrians. In 1890, the Salvation Army opened four facilities, and by 1900, there were 100 lodging houses lining the street. The living facilities were soon neighbors to labor halls, secondhand stores, cheap restaurants, pawnshops, brothels, and saloons. In 1916, the Third Street El (elevated railroad tracks) was built over the street itself, blocking out sunlight (until removed in the early 1960s). The population was composed almost entirely of men, including those who lived there year-round, day laborers, hoboes, and tramps. The Bowery existed in the center, of but was not really part of, the crowded tenement communities of Chinatown to the south, Little Italy to the west, and New Israel to the east.

POPULATION GROWTH AND DECLINE

For the first fifty years of the twentieth century, the Bowery was a major skid row; perhaps smaller than those in Chicago, St. Louis, and San Francisco, but

The Bowery on a Sunday morning in October 2003 shows little sign of the skid row culture that defined the street for much of the twentieth century.
Source: Karen Christensen; used with permission.

better known to the public. The lodging houses, restaurants, bars, work halls, barber colleges, and secondhand clothing stores served the poor who lived there year-round and the seasonal residents. The population increased in winter and during hard economic times. Bowery institutions such as Tomato Mary's bar, Uncle Sam's Lodging House, and the *Hobo News* were known to traveling people across the nation.

Several surveys give a fair sense of the growth and decline of the Bowery's population during its skid row period:

1890s–9,000	1966–5,406
1907–25,000	1971–3,000
1914–25,000+	1979–2,000
1930–75,000	1983–3,500
1949–13,675	1987–1,000
1964–7,611	

As these figures show, the Bowery, like other skid rows across the nation, began to disappear after World War II when economic expansion, social welfare programs, and veterans' benefits reduced the number of homeless. The population was not only fewer in number but also older and getting older still and less transient. Those who left in the summer for seasonal work often went to the Catskills to work at the summer resorts. In the 1960s, the population changed further with an increase in the number of homeless African-American men and in the number of drug addicts. By the early 1970s, long-time residents were complaining that the Bowery was now too violent and unsafe.

As the population decreased, so too did the number of skid row establishments. The *Hobo News* went under in 1948 and was replaced by the short-lived *Bowery News*. All the barber colleges were gone by the early 1970s, as were most of the clothing stores and cheap restaurants. In 1973, there were 20 lodging houses and 16 bars; in 1983, 15 and 5; and in 1988, 9 and 2. By the 1990s, most signs of skid row life were gone, with the Bowery below Delancey Street being absorbed into Chinatown and the stretch north of Delancey becoming home to numerous lighting fixture stores and wholesale restaurant equipment outlets. New York still had a homeless population that numbered in the tens of thousands, but few were on the Bowery.

THE BOWERY TODAY

Nonetheless, remnants of the old Bowery remain. Several lodging houses had been converted to tourist hotels. The Pioneer, which claims to be the oldest hotel in the city, now operates as a low-budget tourist hotel. The Whitehouse, on the upper Bowery, builds on the Bowery name to attract a new clientele; according to its website (www.whitehousehotelofny.com): "Located on New York's famous Bowery, the Whitehouse was a well known 'Lodging House' providing housing accommodations to New York's working class close to 100 years ago. Today, the unique charm of the Whitehouse has been preserved to capture the 'feel' of yesteryear, but the property has been upgraded for the modern-day traveler." And the Bowery maintains its presence as an entertainment street with the Amato Opera Company, Bowery Ballroom, and the Bowery Lane Theatre.

—*David Levinson*

See also New York City; Skid Row Culture and History

Further Reading
Bahr, H. M., & Caplow, T. (1973). *Old men drunk and sober.* New York: New York University Press.
Baxter, E., & Hopper, K. (1981). *Private lives/public spaces:*

Homeless adults on the streets of New York City. New York: Community Service Society.

Bendiner, E. (1961). *The Bowery man.* New York: Thomas Nelson and Sons.

Cohen, C. I., & Sokolovsky, J. (1989). *Old men of the Bowery: Strategies for survival among the homeless.* New York: Guilford Press.

Giamo, B. (1989). *On the Bowery: Confronting homelessness in American society.* Iowa City: University of Iowa Press.

Harlow, A. F. (1931). *Old Bowery days.* New York: Appleton.

Isay, D., & Abramson, S. (2001). *Flophouse: Life on the Bowery.* New York: Random House.

Levinson, D. (1974). Skid Row in transition. *Urban Anthropology, 3*(1), 79–93.

Rice, S. A. (1918). The homeless. *Annals of the American Academy of Political Science, 77,* 140–153.

▣ BRAZIL

To understand homelessness in Brazil, one must consider some of the systemic forces behind the nation's wide social disparities. Grinding poverty and misery coexist with great industrial wealth; 20 percent of the population is extremely poor, while 1 percent is extremely wealthy. Millions of people live in unbearable conditions in cities, in high-risk areas on riverbanks, in slums, or in *favelas*—makeshift settlements on urban outskirts. Thousands of abandoned children live on the streets, public health and education provisions are grossly inadequate, and landless peasants suffer frequent violence. Homelessness is just one aspect of this broad context of poverty.

During the last twenty years, poverty levels have exploded along with the urban population. Thus, the homeless have become a dramatic feature of the Brazilian urban landscape. In major cities such as São Paulo, Belo Horizonte, Porto Alegre, Rio de Janeiro, Brasília, and Salvador, their numbers are increasing, and so is their visibility; cardboard houses, blue plastic tents, and other improvised dwellings are often found in public spaces.

The rise of homelessness in Brazil is due to a multiplicity of factors. One of the fundamental elements is the low economic growth, which has brought about a growing unemployment rate. For some, a criminal record is an ever-present obstacle to a stable job. Homelessness also results from internal migration as people move from rural areas to the main Brazilian metropolis. Family disruption and substance abuse are often linked with these factors. When such trends are compounded by personal crises, the chronically poor are often forced to move their lives to the streets. This has become their only means to material survival.

SURVIVAL STRATEGIES ON BRAZILIAN STREETS

On the streets of Brazilian cities, the homeless have developed a variety of ways to resist helplessness and attend to basic human needs. One of the most pressing daily problems, of course, is to find a place to stay, to create a makeshift habitat or sleeping arrangement that provides some sense of personal space and physical protection. The results of this creative practice are fully apparent on Brazilian streets.

Also apparent are their income-generating strategies. These vary from city to city, but the homeless recycler is a familiar figure in the urban Brazilian landscape. Rescuing discarded materials and products, the homeless recycler navigates the city daily, often pulling a wooden wagon or other cart through dense traffic, sometimes under difficult tropical weather conditions. It is very hard work. Many follow set routines and routes as they sort items and load their wagons. Their routes always lead eventually to a recycle center or cooperative. Here, the recyclers disassemble products to extract components for resale; materials are reintegrated into the productive cycle. The cooperative is a collective project managed and organized by the recyclers themselves, many of whom are no longer homeless. In fact, the cooperative represents an impressive movement of social solidarity. Throughout Brazil, there is an informal economy built on the reuse of waste, with a variety of recycling strategies used by homeless people to help generate some income.

Other survival strategies pursued by the Brazilian homeless including panhandling in public spaces, peddling small goods at street corners, loading trucks, serving as nonofficial security guards for parked cars, and many other informal, very low-paying odd jobs.

◨

A Street Child in Porto Alegre, Brazil

The life of a street child in Brazil is poignantly and painfully portrayed in this excerpt from Ideas Forum, *a UNICEF publication.*

As I crossed the main central city intersection, I noticed a crumpled and ragged figure crouching on the curb on the opposite corner. He was rubbing his eyes and spitting into the gutter. Filthy and alone, he was a candidate for abandonment to be sure!

He appeared to be about 7 years old (he was actually 11), and as I approached him, he stood up and came to see me with the sad countenance and outstretched palm of the trained street kid who learns to inspire pity if his begging is to be successful. He limped and stooped slightly to add legitimacy to his performance. Instead of paying off the boy and my conscience, I spoke a few words to him and settled on the curb myself. After carefully assessing me, he joined me.

I guess I had heard his story of Bogota, San Jose, Managua, Mexico and Lima a thousand times before—moved from the country to the city, father left, mother took up with one and then another stepfather, the latter of whom had beaten the living daylights out of him, no food at home, seven brothers and sisters (he was the oldest boy), a final fight in the slum shack of a home, tears, kicking, blood . . . and he was out! But what was little Luis Carlos doing in downtown Porto Alegre!

"I had no place to go once I left the vila [neighborhood]. Nobody gives a damn there about the son of a whore who's been booted out of the home. There are lots of us. The only person I still have in the world is my father; he'd never turn me away; he's a good guy and he works down here somewhere in one of the plants or on the docks or something."

"But your father left you and your family. How long ago was that?" I countered.

"Oh, Paizinho took off about five years ago, but he had to then. He couldn't get work and we kids were driving him crazy. But he's been back to visit us, and he's told us to look him up if ever any one of us boys gets into trouble."

Good Lord, I thought, what had I come upon—the classic collage of every little kid's life I'd ever known. I suggested we continue our talk as we moved towards a food vendor who was still open near the central park, and I asked myself why Luis Carlos had not been invited to our banquet: there had been far too much food there. Like a piranha he devoured something that resembled a cheese sandwich and a chunk of tough beef, talking all the time-about how he's gone to school but had dropped out of grade one after the third trying in order to work and look after his little brothers and sisters, how he'd been beaten up and had his quota stolen several times by the older kids of his vila, and how his mother needed an operation and was always crying, how he slept on the floor, how the roof leaked, how the house stank, etc., etc. On and on he plunged into the dark past of his 11 years on an unfriendly planet, not resentful of what life had done to him, just wishing things had been and would be better. He was going to find his father, and that would cure everything. He would never go back home to the vila—never.

Source: Tacon, Peter. (1984). "I know my father's here somewhere." *Ideas Forum 18,* 5. UNICEF.

HOMELESSNESS: SCOPE, RESEARCH, AND ACTIVISM

Homelessness issues have not received systematic attention in Brazil, despite efforts by some politicians, scholars, and activists. A fairly accurate homeless census is critically important for any nation's policymakers and homeless service planners, but Brazil lacks such nationwide data. According to the Brazilian Institute for Geography and Statistics (IBGE), the nation's entire population was counted at 169,799,170 in the year 2000. Approximately 34 percent lived below the poverty line, defined as income of less than ninety-eight *reais* a month (about US$33), according to the National Household Sample Survey (1999) and the Ministry of Social Security and Assistance (2002).

Political and religious activism on behalf of homeless people is increasing all over the country. In the absence of a national strategy, this activism has become a key factor in changing the level of public consciousness related to the homeless in Brazil. Activists confront the anti-homeless policies and attitudes around the nation, and provide information to help generate at least a minimum of planning and services to address the needs of the homeless population.

With the growing number of homeless people,

government agencies have embraced joint initiatives with universities, businesses, non-governmental agencies, and churches. Among these partnerships is the Solidarity Community Programme, which develops literacy, job training, and health programs that attempt to break the vicious cycle of poverty and homelessness.

—*Maria Cecília Loschiavo dos Santos*

A homeless Brazilian teenager and her child in Recife, Brazil, in 1992.
Source: Bill Gentile/Corbis; used with permission.

Further Reading

Bursztyn, M. (2000). *No meio da rua* [In the middle of the street]. Rio de Janeiro, Brazil: Garamond.

Santos, M. C. L. dos. (1996). *Paper or plastic: A wrapped culture by the homeless. A comparative study of materials the homeless use in São Paulo, Brazil and Los Angeles, California.* Traditional Dwellings and Settlements. Working Paper Series (Vol. 99). IASTE, *99–96*, 36–64.

Santos, M. C. L. dos. (2000). The vital package: Living on the streets in global cities: São Paulo, Los Angeles and Tokyo. *Visual Sociology, 15,* 101–118.

Santos, M. C. L. dos. (1994). *Um outro espaço* [Another space]. *Psicologia USP,* Instituto de Psicologia da Universidade de São Paulo, *5*(1–2), 145–155.

Santos, M. C. L. (1998). *Castoff/outcast: Living on the street.* In *Recycling and the creative transformation of mass-produced objects* (pp. 111–140). Los Angeles: UCLA Fowler Museum of Cultural History.

Santos, M. C. L. (1999). Discarded products, design and homeless' materials in global cities. In *City and culture: Cultural processes and urban sustainability* (pp. 261–269). Karlskrona, Sweden: Swedish Urban Environment Council.

Santos, M. C. L. (2000). *Vivendo das sobras. A cultura do desemprego e o catador de papel* [Living from leftovers: Unemployment culture and the homeless recycler]. In J. V. Muñoz (Ed.), *O catador de papel e o mundo do trabalho* (pp. 37–47). Rio de Janeiro, Brazil: Nova Pesquisa e Assessoria em Educação.

Vieira, M. et al. (1994). *População de rua, quem é, como vive, como é vista.* [Homeless population: Who it is, how it lives, how it is seen.]. São Paulo, Brazil: Hucitec.

CALCUTTA

The "homeless" of Calcutta do not necessarily think of themselves as literally homeless; their habitat is a place of belonging on a particular city street or a colony of neighbors where being poor does not necessarily mean being without a home. Given the estimate that nearly half of the population would be considered "homeless"—because they sleep on the streets or in makeshift shelters—perhaps homelessness needs to be nuanced and redefined as virtual.

CITY OF CONTRASTS

Calcutta, the capital city of West Bengal, India, is located on the east delta bank of the Hooghly River, a branch of the Ganges. The former capital of British India (1772–1912), Calcutta has the nation's largest metropolitan area, but retains its international reputation as the "problem city of the world" (Moorhouse 1974)—a microcosm of India and the Third World.

Calcutta has a growing population of over 14 million. Approximately a million of these sleep on the streets. As many as 5 million residents live in makeshift cardboard or bamboo-thatched habitats. Another 5 million are considered "slum dwellers." The remaining 3 million live relatively well in homes and apartments in Calcutta.

Paradoxically, Calcutta was once the richest and most important cities in India. A city of palaces, an intellectual, cultural, and commercial capital, Calcutta is a monument to the faded glory of the Raj, British India. From 1599, when the British established "a quiet trade" with India through the East India Company, Calcutta was considered an imperial city of the British empire. In 1912, Calcutta ceased to be the country's capital, though British fortunes could still be made for another two or three decades of political and economic domination. Even today, Calcutta has a prosperous side. Most people work to make a living. Universities educate the young. Businesses succeed. Culture inspires. Five-star hotels and restaurants exist for tourists. Calcutta has many foreign banks, several chambers of commerce, and a stock exchange. The city serves as the major educational and cultural center of India, catering to a growing cosmopolitan population.

CITY OF REFUSE

More than most urban centers, however, Calcutta has an acute housing shortage. In addition to densely populated public and private housing units, there are hundreds of *bustees,* or slums, where about one-third of the city's population lives. (*Bustees* are officially defined as "a collection of huts standing on a plot of land of at least one-sixth of an acre GAIA" [n.d.]). The majority of these huts are

Homeless people asleep in the streets of Calcutta c. 1950.
Source: Steve Prezent/Corbis; used with permission.

through the floods, up to their knees and axles in water" (Moorhouse 1974, 25). As the storms rage and the river floods, the city becomes a breeding ground for malaria and other diseases that thrive on moisture.

Begging is a way of life in Calcutta. Streams of open-handed and crying children greet visitors at Dum Dum International Airport. At a hotel, an old man with a wooden leg and downcast eyes and an outstretched bowl may approach the newly arrived. A seemingly starving young woman may thrust her crying child into a visitor's face. There are beggars who are horribly mutilated, and those who are professional and cunning, in this "city of refuse."

CITY OF JOY

Calcutta is not only a "city of refuse" but also, simultaneously, a "city of joy." Everywhere on the streets of the city, there is shocking poverty—and the extraordinary compassion of those who seek to relieve human suffering. Thousands of destitute people, many on the threshold of death, can be found near the train stations and under Howrah Bridge. "Being unwanted," said Mother Teresa, "is the greatest disease of all. This is the poverty we find around us here. The hunger is not so much for bread and rice, but to be loved, to be someone" (cited in Christensen 1988, 36). Yet, as a visitor literally steps over and round the masses in the daytime, dodging the shabby rickshaws and careless taxis that pollute the streets, amid the exotic smells and arid fumes that permeate the city, there is another reality present: what Mother Teresa and her sisters called the "city of joy." Inside the cardboard boxes and thatched huts, there are loving families who struggle together to make life meaningful, who conduct their business on the pavement, where they play and quarrel, cook and bath, shave and get their hair cut by neighbors and in the company of friends.

Hundreds of hospitals, private clinics, and free dis-

tiny, flimsy, unventilated, unfinished, single-story rooms with few sanitary facilities and little open space. In part, because of *bustees,* ecological congestion and air and water pollution remain a medical and environmental crisis in the city.

The weather in Calcutta exacerbates the poverty and disease. Though it is warm enough for the masses to sleep on the streets in winter without freezing to death, exposure to disease and unsanitary conditions continue to put millions at medical risk. The summer monsoon season lasts four months and creates a unique challenge: Huge shafts of water threaten to flood the homeless from the streets. As Geoffrey Moorhouse describes it: "Calcutta before the monsoon means being soaked with sweat after walking a slow fifty yards; it means not having an inch of dry skin except in air-conditioning." When the monsoon breaks in June, there is a torrent of water and fierce thunder. "The streets are awash, the motor traffic is stalled, the trams can no longer move and only the rickshaw-pullers keep going

pensaries serve the Calcutta region. Additionally, the Roman Catholic Order of the Missionaries of Charity, founded by Mother Teresa (recipient of the Nobel Peace Prize of 1979) in 1948, works on the streets and cares for those Jesus called "the least of these" (Matthew 25:40), namely: "the poor, the lame, the maimed, the blind" (Luke 14:21). Many who are diseased and neglected, rejected and unable to care for themselves, or simply discarded or abandoned are often rescued by a member of the order and taken to a place of refuge. Since 1948, Nirmal Hriday, alongside Kali's Temple at Kalighat, has been such a place, and now is one of several dozen homes for the dying, for lepers, or for abandoned infants. A sign at the entrance to Kalighat reads: "The greatest aim in human life is to die in peace with God." What the Missionaries of Charity try to do is simply to offer loving attention, nurturing a dying victim back to health, or helping him or her die with dignity. "We let the one who has lived like an animal die like an angel," Mother Teresa often explained (1983, 5). (For her devotion to the "poorest of the poor," Pope John Paul II beatified Mother Teresa on 19 October 2003, paving the way toward sainthood for her.)

At Howrah House, where sick and abandoned babies are cared for, volunteers hold and feed infants their breakfast of chopped-up eggs, change diapers, and walk children around the room to help them regain their strength. Despite their bloated stomachs, balding heads, and open sores from malnutrition, the children are visibly responsive to human touch. Most will recover and be adopted.

The Roman Catholic Order of the Missionaries of Charity and their international network of volunteers are the most visible among those humanitarians who care for Calcutta's destitute. Most hospitals and social institutions, already overwhelmed, do not admit those Mother Teresa called "the poorest of the poor." Even so, the Missionaries of Charity are a controversial social service agency because of their devout religious convictions, their objection to becoming a professional medical service provider with modern equipment, and their mercy and relief rather than public policy and community developmental approach to Calcutta's systemic social ills (Hitchens 1995, 38).

VIRTUAL HOMELESSNESS AND A VIRTUAL FUTURE.

Both individual compassion and corporate community development are needed in Calcutta to revitalize the city where millions are virtually homeless. Other cities in India—Mumbai (Bombay), Chennai (Madras), Bangalore, and New Delhi—have been modernized and are going "global." Calcutta, for various reasons, retains both its reputation and reality as India's nightmare city. One new global experience is the presence of a cybercafe in the immediate neighborhood where Mother Teresa's work began. Perhaps the global future of Calcutta has been entrusted to the young entrepreneurs in the neighborhood who know how to connect their impoverished urban ghetto to international culture, commerce, and virtual reality. Indeed, as globalization continues to impact the most impoverished neighborhoods of the City of Joy, the youth of these communities find themselves connected by the Internet to peers and mentors around the world with whom they have more in common than with their own indigenous culture.

—*Michael J. Christensen*

Further Reading

Christensen, M. (1988). *City streets, city people: A call to compassion.* Nashville, TN: Abingdon.

GAIA Environmental Information System. (n.d.). "Calcutta: Not the 'City of Joy'." Retrieved November 3, 2003, from www.ess.co.at/GAIA/CASES/IND/CAL/CALmain.html

Hitchens, C. (1995). *The missionary position: Mother Teresa in theory and practice.* London: Verso.

Le Joly, E. (1983). *Mother Teresa of Calcutta: A biography.* San Francisco: Harper & Row.

Moorhouse, G. (1974). *Calcutta: The city revealed.* New York: Penguin.

Mother Teresa. (1983). *Words to love by.* Notre Dame, IN: Ave Maria Press.

◉ CANADA

With a population of 30 million, Canada has 11 million households, most of which now live in urban areas: With the growth in the country's urban population, driven in good part by both internal and exter-

A protestor is carried off by police at a demonstration against home-lessness in Ottawa on 12 November 1999.
Source: Reuters NewMedia Inc./Corbis; used with permission.

nal immigration, Canadians have increasingly needed to confront their perceptions of homelessness and the country's social policies toward it. It is now accepted in principle by all levels of government and the nonprofit sector that the definition of homeless-ness should include those individuals and families who are "sleeping rough" (outside) or frequenting emergency shelters, who are doubled up with friends and relatives, or who are precariously housed, sub-ject to eviction, and thus at risk of becoming absolutely homeless. Nonetheless, public agencies, shelter providers, and nonprofit and volunteer organ-izations differ substantially on what constitutes an appropriate response to the homeless situation.

THE FACE OF HOMELESSNESS

The face of homelessness has been changing across Canada, where people without shelter have gravi-tated to the cities. Many of the native-born homeless are Aboriginals, indigenous people who have moved from reserves into cities to secure shelter and social services; they are overrepresented by a factor of ten in Canada's homeless population. The largest munic-ipalities, Montreal, Vancouver, and Toronto, receive well over half of all immigrants. As a result, half of the urban population in the largest cities is foreign-

born (Statistics Canada, 2001). In Toronto, the Mayor's Homelessness Action Task Force found that about 15 percent of people in the hostel system are immigrants or refugees (Golden et al., 1999, 19).

Most new arrivals to Canada who experience housing difficulties find support within their own ethnic affinity groups, rather than with drop-ins, hos-tels, and social housing organizations. The latter have been slowly adapting to the need for more cul-turally sensitive services. For those in need of social housing, the waiting lists are so long—often seven years or more for individuals and families—that many applicants either move to another jurisdiction or opt for illegal basement apartments or "couch-surfing." As the demand for housing has increased with the rising tide of immigrants and urban dwellers, there has been a commensurate increase in the cost of rentals. Between 1995 and 2000 in Toronto, average wages rose by 9 percent while rents increased by 29 percent.

The idea of a richly diverse multicultural society holds out the promise of inclusion and equity, but the reality for many new arrivals is lack of respect, low wages, poor working conditions, and exclusion. The housing situation for households living marginally is characterized by a growing trend of evictions, land-lord discrimination, overcrowding, and increasing evidence of an invisible homeless population that suffers from ill health, lack of access to services, and social isolation.

In Toronto, whose trends are representative of large Canadian cities, 60,000 households are on the waiting list for social housing, shelter use doubled during the 1990s, and each year more than 32,000 people resort to shelters. Most are single adults over 24, but 20 percent are young people, ages 15 to 24. The number of children in the hostel system more than tripled in the past decade, to a total of 6,000. Some are handed over to child welfare agencies by parents who cannot manage to keep the family housed together (City of Toronto, 2001). These numbers do not include all those who are doubled up, living on the edge of homelessness, or living in substandard units, or who refuse to patronize shelters because of health or safety concerns, even during the coldest weather (Golden et al., 1999).

The fastest-growing groups among homeless people are families. They now account for over 40 percent of shelter bed use, with stays averaging from one to two months, after which most move into social housing or transitional units. The average length of stay in shelters has increased because of the scarcity of affordable housing and job opportunities.

For single individuals, shelter stays are shorter, since most are forced to move on by shelter operators. The great majority of single shelter users are on a merry-go-round, moving from one shelter to another. Rates of recidivism for single individuals are very high (Daly and Ward, 2003).

RESPONSES BY GOVERNMENTS AND NONPROFITS

A distinguishing characteristic of Canada's political system is the degree to which each province, to a considerable extent, controls its own purse strings. Housing is financed principally by the federal government, but provincial authorities have some discretion in determining how those funds, as well as additional resources provided by provincial and municipal agencies, will be used. Thus cities are dependent on the largesse of both the federal and provincial governments. Unlike the United States, where property taxes represent just 21 percent of revenue, Canada's municipalities depend on property taxes for half of total revenues. Likewise, per capita municipal expenditure in Canada is less than one-half the average of that spent by U.S. cities (Federation of Canadian Municipalities, 2001). Thus, despite the fact that urban centers house a majority of the Canadian population, the fiscal limitations under which cities and towns operate severely limit their ability to finance homeless and low-income housing support.

During the 1990s, a recession in Canada was followed in mid-decade by substantial government cuts in social housing, welfare, and income security benefits, even though Canada's economy remained strong. Major structural changes were made in the allocation of public resources, with the responsibility for financing social services, housing, and public transit downloaded from provinces to municipalities.

At the same time, poverty was increasing from 15.3 percent of the population in 1990 to 16.2 percent in 1999. As real incomes declined and federal program spending fell nearly 30 percent during the decade—to 11.6 percent of gross domestic product in 2002—the costs of housing, health care, public transportation, and day care for low-income households grew. By 2002, only about 1 percent of the federal budget was allocated for social housing, an amount that represented 5 percent of total housing stock (Canadian Council on Social Development, 2002).

In response to growing political disquiet over these changes, the federal government announced an initiative at the end of 2001 to provide $680 million over five years for the provision of affordable housing, conditional on provincial matching funds. The federal budget made public in early 2003 provided additional funds for affordable housing, for a housing renovation program, and for the existing Supporting Community Partnerships Initiative to address homelessness. Provincial responses to these programs have varied. Some have responded with new initiatives, recognizing that new housing programs aimed at low-income households are less costly than the annual per capita cost of homeless shelters. Nonetheless, many housing activists remain skeptical, fearing that like so many earlier federal programs these initiatives will not actually reach the truly needy, that is, the poorer half of the renter population. The Province of Quebec (*Société d'habitation du Québec*) made major commitments: It matched the federal funds with $140 million from the province and $57 million from municipalities. Quebec also reserved 5,000 units for nonprofit and residential developers who target their projects to low- and moderate-income households. Most of the other provinces, with the exception of Ontario, the country's wealthiest jurisdiction, will be matching the federal contribution (*Housing Again Bulletin,* 2003). British Columbia, for example, committed to 1,764 units of nonprofit housing (with continuing operating subsidies for thirty-five years) for low-income households, homeless people, and those with mental and physical disabilities. Provincial housing authorities took these steps after concluding that the annual cost of emergency shelters—$30,000–$40,000 per person—significantly exceeded the costs of housing plus services for people in supportive housing—$22,000–$28,000 per year. (BC Housing, 2001).

While the federal government was essentially opting out of social housing in the mid-1990s, demand was increasing. Most of this demand was met and continues to be met not by permanent accommodations, but by emergency shelters, consisting of cots in large hostels or mats on the floors of dormitory-type settings. Those who cannot gain admittance or who are afraid to use emergency shelters sleep outside until the weather forces them to patronize "out of the cold" programs such as church basements used as drop-ins. The acute shortage of affordable housing means that people are staying longer in the shelter system because they have few alternatives.

One partial but notable exception has been the city of Montreal. Although one in four tenant households there still pays 50% or more of their incomes on rent (Schetagne, 2000), the city has achieved some success in providing affordable housing due in good part to a sympathetic provincial government and land costs that are lower than in Vancouver or Toronto. Moreover, nonprofit organizations and church-based housing groups in Quebec play very active roles and have raised the level of awareness concerning housing and homelessness issues throughout the province. Partnerships between government and private organizations have provided a substantial amount of secure, affordable housing for families, seniors, and special needs groups, who pay 25 percent of income for rent. However, these programs have not yet addressed the crucial element of funding for support services. In most Canadian cities, housing demand outstrips affordable supply and there is increased reliance on emergency shelters and such supplements as food banks and clothing/furniture depots. Recently, city authorities and nonprofit providers have increasingly encountered virulent opposition from neighborhood groups in areas near the downtown cores, who argue that hostels are unfairly concentrated in their sections of the city. In early 2003, Canada's largest and most ethnically diverse city, Toronto, enacted a by-law that mandates the equitable distribution of shelters and drop-in centers in all wards of the municipality. The question

remains, however, whether such facilities can be built in the face of "not-in-my-backyard" (NIMBY) opposition. One approach to overcoming NIMBY opposition is to locate affordable housing, such as single-occupancy residences (efficiency apartments), in commercial areas that are in close proximity to services but are not adjacent to established residential neighborhoods (Franck and Ahrentzen, 1994, 309). This strategy has been employed successfully on a number of projects in Vancouver (e.g., Portland, Sunrise, and Washington Hotels, as well as a former squat) and in Ottawa and Montreal (acquisition and renovation of rooming houses). The limitation of all of these laws and programs, however, is that they fail to address the underlying need for a long-term housing solution.

For volunteer and nonprofit groups, federal and provincial budget cuts have limited their abilities to fill the void created by the weakening of the public sector's interventions. Many organizations now spend scarce resources competing with similar organizations for a relatively small pot of federal and provincial funds. At the same time, private sector developers have shown very little interest in building low-income housing.

LESSONS LEARNED

Studies published in the 1990s and early 2000s have yielded a number of important lessons on dealing with homelessness in Canada:

> Access to affordable, appropriate, permanent housing is the most important factor in reducing the level of homelessness (Shinn, Baumohl and Hopper 2001; Mansur et al. 2002).

> Stable housing is the most important factor in improving quality of life for those who have been homeless; however, further material and non-material supports are required to avoid a return to homelessness (Wolf 2001).

> Expanding the supply of emergency shelters does not solve homelessness.

> The evidence indicates that longer-term housing and support programs have much higher rates of success than short-term, crisis response.

> The seeds of homelessness often are sown in child-

hood (Sullivan 2000); children who grew up in homeless households now constitute a second or third generation of people without adequate accommodation; homelessness, as a state of being, is becoming normalized (Sullivan 2000).

Relationship breakdowns are a key factor in homelessness; prevention of breakdowns, therefore, is important in reducing vulnerability to homelessness.

Escaping violent abuse is a frequent path to homelessness for women; therefore, it is essential to bring the supply of housing for women in these situations in line with demand (Sev'er 2002).

Assertive community outreach has proven to be cost-effective and essential in addressing the needs of those who are socially isolated. It consists of providing care for immediate needs, building trust with people who have lost faith in the social support delivery system, and connecting clients to services (Tommasello 1999).

Since mental illness and addictions are common among shelter users, training in these areas for shelter staff is essential in responding appropriately to the particular needs raised by these issues (Vamvakas and Rowe 2001).

Harm reduction approaches have proven to be effective for many homeless people with substance abuse problems.

Facilities that support community-oriented homeless programs enjoy stronger community agency relationships (McGuire et al. 2002).

Maximum involvement by users in homelessness programs increases effectiveness. Programs enjoy greater success when they emphasize democratic principles and self-determination.

A sense of self-worth and motivation to leave homelessness can be increased markedly when homeless people are treated with dignity by service providers (Miller and Keys 2001).

Programs focusing on competency in carrying out life tasks and engendering a belief in having the ability to direct one's future have been highly successful in ending homelessness among families (Gold and Hauser 1998).

SEEKING A WAY FORWARD

For most of the past decade, Canada's economy has been the most robust among G7 nations, with the federal budget in balance or a state of surplus. However, income gaps between rich and poor have widened considerably during this period. While public programs provide homeowners with considerable support, renters continue to be largely ignored by both the government and private sector developers. Wages have not kept pace with rental increases, exacerbating the difficulties low-income individuals and families face. Despite the fact that the great majority of Canadians are urban dwellers, the federal government has no agency that deals exclusively with urban issues. Its housing portfolio is handled by a minor ministry, and the great majority of taxes collected in the cities are not returned to meet urban needs. This lack of interest stands in contrast with the fact that, as local politicians and bankers are fond of observing, Canada's major urban centers are the engines that drive the nation's economy. Homelessness, along with declining urban infrastructure and a dwindling supply of affordable housing, has become a visible reminder of the challenges that Canada faces if it is to address the needs of its urban centers.

—Gerald Daly

Further Reading

BC Housing and the Ministry of Social Development and Economic Security. (2001). *Homelessness—Cause and effects.* Victoria, British Columbia: Author.

Canadian Council on Social Development (2002). *Urban poverty in Canada: A statistical profile.* Ottawa. Retrieved from http://www.ccsd.ca/factsheets/2002

City of Calgary. (2000). *Action plan—Homeless consultation.* Retrieved from http://www.gov.calgary.ab.ca

City of Edmonton. (1998). *A count of homeless persons in Edmonton.* Retrieved from http://www.gov.edmonton.ab.ca

City of Montreal. (n.d.). *Interaction, Le bulletin de la vie associative des HLM de Montreal.* Retrieved January 20, 2004, from http://www2.ville.montreal.gc.ca

City of Toronto. (2001). *The Toronto report card on homelessness.* Retrieved from http://www.city.toronto.on.ca/homelessness/homelessnessreports

City of Vancouver. (1998). *Prevention of homelessness.* Retrieved from http://www.city.vancouver.bc.ca

Community Action Plan on Homelessness Steering Committee (2000). *Halifax community action on homelessness.* Halifax, Nova Scotia, Canada: Community Action on Homelessness Steering Committee.

Daly, G. (1996). *Homeless: policies, strategies, and lives on the street.* London and New York: Routledge.

Daly, G., & Ward, J. (2003). *Homeless services review.* Retrieved January 20, 2004, from http://www.region.peel.on.ca

Edmonton Joint Planning Committee on Housing. (2000). *Edmonton Community Plan on Homelessness, 2000–2003.* Edmonton, Saskatchewan, Canada: Author.

Federation of Canadian Municipalities. (2001). Early warning: Will Canadian cities compete? http://www.nrtee.trnee.ca

Franck, K., & Ahrentzen, S. (Eds.). (1994). *New households, new housing.* New York: Van Nostrand Reinhold.

Gold, J., & Hauser, S. (1998). Homeless families: A treatment outcome study. *International Journal for the Advancement of Counselling, 20,* 87–93.

Golden, A., Currie, W., Greaves, E., & Latimer, J. (1999). *Taking responsibility for homelessness: An action plan for Toronto. Report of the Mayor's Homelessness Action Task Force.* Retrieved from http://www.city.toronto.on.ca/mayor/homelessness

Housing Again Bulletin. (2003, March 3). Retrieved from http://www.housingagain.web.net

Mansur, E., et al. (2002). Examining policies to reduce homelessness using a general equilibrium model of the housing market. *Journal of Urban Economics, 52*(2), 316–340.

McGuire, J., et al. (2002). Expanding service delivery: does it improve relationships among agencies serving homeless people with mental illness? *Administration and Policy in Mental Health, 29*(3), 243

Miller, A., & Keys, C. (2001). Understanding dignity in the lives of homeless persons. *American Journal of Community Psychology, 29*(2), 331–355.

Regional Municipality of Ottawa-Carleton. (2002). *Describing the homeless population of Ottawa-Carleton.* Retrieved January 20, 2004, from http://www.uottawa.ca/academic/socsci/crcs/homeless/index.htm

Sev'er, A. (2002). A feminist analysis of flight of abused women, plight of Canadian shelters: Another ode to homelessness. *Journal of Social Distress and the Homeless, 11*(4), 307–324.

Schetagne, S. (2000). *La pauvreté dans les agglomerations urbaines du Québec.* Ottawa, Ontario, Canada: Canadian Council on Social Development.

Shinn, M., Baumohl, J., & Hopper, K. (2001). The prevention of homelessness revisited. *Analyses of Social Issues and Public Policy, 1*(1), 95–127.

Statistics Canada. (2002). *Census of population, 2001.* Ottawa. Retrieved January 20, 2004, from http://www.statscan.ca

Sullivan, G. (2000). Pathways to homelessness among the mentally ill. *Social Psychiatry, 35,* 444–450.

TD Economics. (2002, April 22). *A choice between investing in Canada's cities or disinvesting in Canada's future.* Toronto, Ontario, Canada: TD Bank.

Tommasello, A. (1999). Effectiveness of outreach to homeless substance abusers. *Evaluation and Program Planning, 22,* 295–303.

Vamvakas, A., & M. Rowe. (2001). Mental health training in emergency homeless shelters. *Community Mental Health, 37*(3), 287–295.

Wolf, J., et al. (2001). Changes in subjective quality of life among homeless adults who obtain housing: A prospective examination. *Social Psychiatry 36,* 391–398.

◉ CASE MANAGEMENT

Since the 1980s, the case management approach has gained acceptance throughout the United States as a strategy for assisting homeless people. Service providers and researchers alike have recommended the development of such approaches, and the U.S. Congress has encouraged states to do so through legislative initiatives and appropriations. Today, case management is a key ingredient in local, state, and federal efforts to provide homeless people with needed services and resources.

Why is the case management strategy so widely advocated? In part, it reflects a trend within the entire field of health and human services during the late twentieth century—a trend that encourages a comprehensive view of each client, or case. In this model, a designated case manager first assesses a client's needs, then works to coordinate and optimize the client's services over time. But as Morse (1999, p. 7-2) has noted, there are also "several interrelated, key assumptions about the problems, causes, and solutions of homelessness" that make the case management approach especially suitable in this arena. These premises are based on several observations. First, homeless people often have serious and multiple unmet service needs. Second, the existing service system is typically fragmented, composed of various disconnected organizations. Third, clients often encounter barriers to needed services and resources. And fourth, case managers are needed to ensure access to these services in a coordinated and efficient manner.

Together, these observations point to problems in the way existing service systems are organized and operate. Indeed, some researchers and policymakers believe that case management can also serve to improve the service systems themselves. That remains debatable, but case managers certainly do, as Hopper and colleagues (1989) put it, perform service-system "microsurgery" on behalf of specific clients. A case manager may, for example, successfully intervene with public housing officials to keep a Section 8 voucher open for a client who has been temporarily hospitalized for psychiatric problems, and therefore unable to meet a deadline for moving into a new apartment.

WHAT IS CASE MANAGEMENT?

Despite its widespread use, there is often confusion and sometimes controversy about the definition and nature of case management. One federally commissioned paper on the topic deemed it "a much discussed but poorly defined concept" (National Resource Center on Homelessness and Mental Illness, 1990, p. 1). Similarly, some practitioners view the term as an imprecise catchall phrase for a variety of service activities. Since the early 1990s, however, more attention has been paid to defining the concept. In a 1991 paper, Willenbring and colleagues identified six defining primary service functions of case management programs:

1. Engage in outreach, identifying and enrolling clients for service.
2. Assess each client's individual strengths, weaknesses, and needs.
3. Develop an individualized and comprehensive service plan for each client.
4. Link, refer, or transfer clients to needed services, resources, and support systems.
5. Monitor the client's progress and ongoing needs.
6. Advocate on behalf of clients to ensure that they receive equitable and appropriate services.

They also identified several other functions offered by many, but not all, such programs:

7. Providing direct clinical services, rather than merely referring and linking clients to other service providers.
8. Providing crisis intervention assistance.
9. System advocating for system change, such as more favorable housing policies for homeless.
10. Developing needed resources such as housing or employment resources.

SERVICE CHARACTERISTICS AND VARIABLES

Despite common functions, case management programs vary considerably in operation, as documented by Willenbring and colleagues and by Morse. These programs can be characterized in terms of seven variables describing the process of service delivery.

Duration. Case management programs vary from very brief, time-limited assistance to ongoing and open-ended services.

Intensity. Programs vary widely, some providing daily assistance, others contacting clients monthly or even less frequently. Moreover, some programs have client-to-staff ratios as low as 10 to 1, while in others each staff person may serve fifty or more clients.

Focus. Programs may target a specific area of service, such as assisting individuals with housing, or they may assist with a broad, comprehensive set of needs.

Availability. Some offer services by appointment only during normal day hours; others offer extended evening and weekend hours, and even twenty-four-hour assistance as needed for crises or urgent situations.

Location. Some services are provided only in office settings, while others serve clients almost exclusively in the community on an outreach basis.

Providers. Programs vary in their staffing patterns, including paraprofessionals, professionals, or a mix of the two. Staff members may all be similarly trained—in social work, for example—or they may represent multiple disciplines.

Team. In some programs, each staff person has an individual caseload of clients; other programs take an interdisciplinary team approach with shared caseloads.

APPROACHES AND MODELS OF CASE MANAGEMENT

It is not surprising, therefore, that case management models for homeless populations vary widely as well, both in theory and practice. The research literature focuses mostly on programs for homeless people with mental health disorders, but it also considers subgroups such as single mothers and children, people with substance abuse disorders, and youths, although theory remains less developed in these areas.

Because many homeless people are wary of service providers—often as a result of illness, past traumas, or other negative experiences—the first tasks for almost any case manager are to develop trust and to nurture a positive, working relationship. A number of techniques have been developed to help in the engagement process. For example, Morse and colleagues (1996) recommended that mental health professionals build rapport with homeless clients by striking up nonthreatening conversations; by providing resources for basic needs, such as food and clothing; and by providing transportation assistance. Beyond this first step, however, programs generally follow one of several models.

Broker case management offers little if any direct clinical service to clients; the emphasis instead is on assisting homeless clients primarily through assessment, service planning, and referral and linkage to other service providers. Staff may also monitor client progress on an ongoing basis. Caseloads can be relatively high, with a single staff person assigned fifty or more clients at one time.

Intensive case management approaches, among the most widely used, have been provided to various subgroups including people with mental illness or substance abuse disorders, mothers with dependent children, and youths. In general, they are characterized by assertive and persistent outreach efforts, smaller caseloads, and active assistance and advocacy to help clients obtain a range of needed resources.

Assertive Community Treatment (ACT) is another popular approach for homeless people with severe mental illnesses. Although advocates of ACT generally avoid the label "case management," in actual practice ACT staff do often provide case management as well as mental health treatment and other services. A transdisciplinary team, including such specialists as nurses and psychiatrists, works together with a shared caseload, offering direct treatment, support, and intense levels of client contact. The model was originally developed in the early 1970s to help non-homeless people with mental illness adjust to living in the community after hospital discharge. It has been adapted for people who are both homeless and mentally ill, now placing more emphasis on outreach and engagement strategies and on assisting clients with housing and other needs.

Critical Time Intervention (CTI), another intensive model, limits case management services to a relatively brief period, for example, nine months. It is usually focused on helping mentally ill homeless clients during the "critical," or transitional, phase of moving from a shelter to housing in the community. Interventions provide practical as well as emotional support to clients during the transition, and also strengthen the links with other support systems and service providers who will continue to work with the person afterward.

Other models, less commonly provided to homeless populations, include *clinical case management,* which combines therapy with guidance and attention to psychosocial needs. In *social network case management,* interventions are designed not only to offer direct support when needed, but to help the person develop and mobilize support from families and friends. The *strengths model* emphasizes a client's strong points rather than problems. Staff members are often paraprofessionals who focus on changing the environment to meet the client's needs and goals. Widely used with non-homeless people with severe mental illness, this model has been applied more recently to serving homeless people. Another new approach is that of *consumer case management.* Under this model, consumers—individuals who have severe mental health disorders themselves and who may have also been formerly homeless—are hired as staff to provide case management to people who are currently homeless.

In addition to these specific programs, many other service providers provide some case management functions to homeless clients. Nurses, substance counselors, and even shelter staff, for example, often handle at least some of these functions, such as referral assistance for housing, in addition to their primary professional activities.

MEASURING EFFECTIVENESS

A small but growing body of research indicates that at least certain case management approaches are effective in helping homeless people improve their lives. A recent review of the research literature (Morse, 1999) documented ten scientific or experimental studies on the subject. Experimental research, which uses scientific methods (such as random assignment of clients to treatment programs), provides the clearest results. Most of these studies have found positive results for case management clients. The most common—and important—finding was that case management helps people exit homelessness and secure stable housing.

The effectiveness of ACT is notable in these experimental study results: The vast majority found that ACT clients experience better outcomes than those in more usual community services such as broker case management programs. In addition to helping to end homelessness, some ACT programs have proven effective in other areas, such as reducing clients' psychiatric symptoms.

Fewer studies have been conducted on other approaches. Still, the available literature, consisting of a few experimental studies and some less rigorous evaluation studies, yields some supportive evidence for the intensive case management approach. The results may be modest or equivocal, but they tend to suggest that such programs do help people gain housing. Other surveys indicate that the CTI approach is effective in helping people make the transition into stable housing.

As for the cost-effectiveness of case management services, the one study on this topic found that ACT was more cost-effective (as well as more effective) than the broker case management model for homeless people with severe mental illness.

Finally, it is worth noting that standard programs such as broker case management were generally found to be less effective than ACT or some other

intensive strategies. This does not necessarily mean that basic case management activities—such as referral and monitoring—have no value to homeless clients, but only that they are comparatively less effective than some other models.

The literature also contains one negative finding that may place the benefits of case management in a broader context: One study has suggested that for helping homeless people find and retain housing, Section 8 housing certificates are more effective than case management.

FUTURE DIRECTIONS

To date, most of the research assessing case management for severely mentally ill homeless people has found that ACT, and to a lesser degree intensive case management and CTI, are most effective. More work needs to be done to develop and evaluate case management models for other prevalent homeless subgroups, such as those with substance abuse disorders, families, youths, and people with both severe mental illness and co-occurring substance abuse disorders.

Another future topic relates to case management and public policy. It is clear that certain models are effective for ending homelessness, at least for some groups. However, the number of homeless people who need these services far outstrips those now being served. A continuing challenge remains: how to develop needed services in order to help large numbers of people end homelessness and become housed.

—Gary Morse

See also Assertive Community Treatment (ACT)

Further Reading

Bebout, R. R. (1993). Contextual case management: Restructuring the social support networks of seriously mentally ill adults. In M. Harris & H. C. Bergman (Eds.), *Case management for mentally ill patients: Theory and practice.* New York: Harwood Academic Publishers.

Burns, B. J., & Santos, A. B. (1995). Assertive community treatment: An update of randomized trials. *Psychiatric Services, 46*(7), 669–675.

Dennis, D. (1990). *Case management with homeless mentally ill persons.* Delmar, NY: National Resource Center on Homelessness and Mental Illness.

Dixon, L., Krauss, N., Kernan, E., Lehman, A. F., & DeForge, B. R. (1995). Modifying the PACT model for homeless persons with severe mental illness. *Psychiatric Services, 46*(7), 684–688.

Federal Task Force on Homelessness and Mental Illness. (1992). *Outcasts on Main Street: Report of the federal task force on homelessness and severe mental illness.* Washington, DC: Interagency Council for the Homeless.

Frances, A., & Goldfinger, S. (1986). "Treating" a homeless mentally ill patient who cannot be managed in the shelter system. *Hospital and Community Psychiatry, 37*(6), 577–579.

Herinckx, H. A., Kinney, R. F., Clarke, G. N., & Paulson, R. I. (1997). Assertive community treatment versus usual care in engaging and retaining clients with severe mental illness. *Psychiatric Services, 48*(10), 1297–1306.

Hopper, K., Mauch, D., & Morse, G. (1989). *The 1986–1987 NIMH-Funded CSP demonstration projects to serve homeless mentally ill persons: A preliminary assessment.* Rockville, MD: National Institute of Mental Health.

Kline, J. D. (1993). Challenges to the clinical case management of the chronic mentally ill: Emerging special populations. In M. Harris & H. C. Bergman (Eds.), *Case management for mentally ill patients: Theory and practice.* New York: Harwood Academic Publishers.

Lehman, A. F., Dixon, L. B., Kernan, E., DeForge, B. R., & Postrado, L. T. (1997). A randomized trial of assertive community treatment for homeless people with severe mental illness. *Archives of General Psychiatry, 54,* 1038–1043.

Morse, G.A. (1999). A review of case management for people who are homeless: Implications for practice, policy, and research. In Fosburg, L. G., & Dennis, D. L. (Eds.) *Practical Lessons: The 1998 National Symposium on Homelessness Research.* Delmar, NY: National Resource Center on Homelessness and Mental Illness.

Morse, G., Calsyn, R. J., Allen, G., Tempelhoff, B., & Smith, R. (1992). Experimental comparison of the effects of three treatment programs for homeless mentally ill people. *Hospital and Community Psychiatry, 43,* 1005–1010.

Morse, G. A., Calsyn, R. J., Klinkenberg, W. D., Trusty, M. L., Gerber, F., Smith, R., Tempelhoff, B., & Ahmad, L. (1997). An experimental comparison of three types of case management for homeless mentally ill persons. *Psychiatric Services, 48*(4), 497–503.

Morse, G. A., Calsyn, R. J., Miller, J., Rosenberg, P., West, L., & Gilliland, J. (1996). Outreach to homeless mentally ill people: Conceptual and clinical considerations. *Community Mental Health Journal, 32*(3), 261–274.

National Resource Center on Homelessness and Mental Illness. (1990). *Case Management with homeless mentally ill persons.* Delmar, NY: The National Resource Center on Homelessness and Mental Illness.

Phillips, S. D., Burns, B. J., Edgar, E. R., et al. (2001). Moving assertive community treatment into standard practice. *Psychiatric Services, 52,* 771–779.

Rapp, C. A. (1993). Theory principles and methods of the strengths model of case management. In M. Harris & H. C. Bergman (Eds.), *Case management for mentally ill patients: Theory and practice.* New York: Harwood Academic Publishers.

Rog, D. J. (1988). *Engaging homeless persons with mental illness into treatment.* Alexandria, VA: National Mental Health Association.

Rog, D., Andranovich, G., & Rosenblum, S. (1987). *Intensive case management for persons who are homeless and mentally ill: A review of CSP and human resource development program efforts, Vols. 1–3.* Rockville, MD: National Institute of Mental Health.

Rog, D. J., Holupka, C. S., McCombs-Thirnton, K. L., Brito, M. C., & Hambrick, R. (1996). Case management in practice: Lessons from the evaluation of the RWJ/HUD homeless families program. *Journal of Prevention and Intervention in the Community, 15*(2), 67–82.

Surles, R. W., Blanch, A. K., Shern, D. L., & Donahue, S. A. (1992, Spring). Case management as a strategy for systems change. *Health Affairs,* 151–163.

Susser, E., Valencia, E., Conover, S., Felix, A., Tsai, W., & Wyatt, R. J. (1997). Preventing recurrent homelessness among mentally ill men: A "critical time" intervention after discharge from a shelter. *American Journal of Public Health, 87*(2), 256–262.

Willenbring, M. L., Ridgely, M. S., Stinchfield, R., & Rose, M. (1991). *Application of case management in alcohol and drug dependence: Matching techniques and populations.* Rockville, MD: National Institute on Alcohol Abuse and Alcoholism.

▣ CAUSES OF HOMELESSNESS: OVERVIEW

Like the villages in the following tale, America's first response to homelessness was to mobilize and confront the threat by targeting the immediate needs of the homeless:

Early one morning, in a village located on the banks of a river, a woman walked to the river's edge and discovered, much to her horror, that the river was filled with baskets rushing downstream and that each basket held a baby. Aware of the danger the babies faced, she quickly ran back and mobilized the village's inhabitants. Everyone rushed to the river and began fishing as many babies out as they could. Many more slipped by than they were able to save, but they toiled on anyway, so consumed by their task that it never occurred to them to send someone upstream in order to find out how the babies were getting into the river in the first place.

—Anonymous

We responded to the crisis with shelters and soup kitchens, spearheaded by private charitable organizations but frequently supported by public-sector dollars. We were like the villagers in the introductory tale, although our efforts were aimed not at fishing babies out of the water but at keeping them afloat. After a time, these efforts were accompanied by more tangible efforts to bring people to dry land. Outreach and case management programs were designed to reduce barriers to health and social services, for instance. Transitional housing programs were developed to teach skills and provide support to people as they moved into their own apartments. Such efforts became increasingly sophisticated, reflecting a growing sensitivity to the continuum of care required to stabilize homeless people.

America's walk to the river's edge began in the early 1980s, when people of the United States awoke to find that masses of homeless people had appeared in their midst, seemingly overnight. Homelessness was not a new phenomenon, of course. Periods of pervasive homelessness had checkered our nation's history, most recently in a post-World War II population consisting largely of single, older, white males who inhabited the skid row neighborhoods of our largest cities, where they drew upon a network of private sector resources, including missions, cubicle flophouses, and single-room occupancy (SRO) hotels. However, the new homelessness that we awoke to was a different, far more jarring phenomenon. Whereas homeless individuals during that prior period had remained safely ghettoized in the isolated urban niches ceded to them, these new homeless people were everywhere, occupying spaces throughout the city, spilling into the suburbs, and appearing even in rural areas. Moreover, they looked different from the homeless

people we had become accustomed to. They were younger, more ethnically diverse, and more likely to include parents with dependent children. Even worse, whereas the vast majority of "homeless" individuals of decades past had been *housed,* albeit marginally, this new population was *literally* homeless, bedding down in large congregate shelters or on the streets and in other locations not meant for sleeping. More visible and far greater in number, they invaded our public consciousness and daily existences in a way that had not occurred since the Great Depression.

Yet, homelessness remained, perhaps even worsened. Although able to point to real success stories, service providers haven't stemmed the tide of homelessness for reasons that go beyond the fact that their programs are underfunded and unable to meet demand. Many of the people who graduate from their programs become homeless again. Even more disturbingly, a seemingly inexhaustible supply of new faces joins the homeless ranks. Meanwhile, early optimism on the part of the public that a solution to this distressing social problem was at hand has given way to increasingly sharp frustration over the extent to which homelessness impinges on everyday life and a growing backlash against homeless people themselves.

Given the contemporary response to contemporary homelessness, it is hard to shake the feeling that our current quandary is not all that different from the one in which our allegorical villagers found themselves. Like the villagers, we have been toiling laboriously but ineffectively to end homelessness at least in part because our preoccupation with fishing people out of a bad situation has distracted us from the more fundamental issue of how they got there in the first place. Unless we understand and address the causes of homelessness, people will continue to fall into homelessness at a faster rate than we can pull them out.

Understanding the causes of homelessness, however, is not easy, in part because the factors that explain contemporary homelessness are so complex and intertwined, but also because the concept of "cause" itself, as researchers Wright, Rubin, and Devine point out, is so ambiguous. Wright and his colleagues present the hypothetical case of a man named Bill:

> Bill is a high school dropout. Because of Bill's inadequate education, he has never held a steady job; rather, he has spent his adult lifetime doing various odd jobs, picking up temporary or seasonal work when available, hustling at other times. Because of his irregular and discontinuous employment history, Bill's routine weekly income is meager, and because his income is minimal, he is unable to afford his own apartment and lives instead with his older sister. Now, Bill drinks more than he should (this for a dozen different reasons) and because he drinks more than he should, he is frequently abusive and hard to get along with. Bill's sister is usually pretty tolerant in such matters, but because she has been having some problems at work, she comes home one Friday in a foul, ungenerous mood only to find Bill passed out on the couch. She decides that Bill's dependency and alcoholism are more than she can continue to take, and . . . Bill is asked to leave. Bill spends Saturday looking for an apartment that he can afford, but because his income is so low and because there are very few units available to someone with Bill's income, he finds nothing and heads to the local shelter for homeless people instead, whereupon Bill effectively becomes a homeless person. (Wright, Rubin, and Devine 1998, 8)

Why is Bill homeless? Wright and colleagues point out that one can generate countless sentences that begin with "Bill is homeless because . . ." and that each would be true. Bill is homeless because he drinks too much. Bill is homeless because there are so few apartments available to people with his income. Bill is homeless because there are fewer stable jobs for people with poor educations. Bill is homeless because . . . . Moreover, we can see how pairing the question, "Why is Bill homeless?" with the question, "Why are there so many people who find themselves in situations similar to Bill's?" might take us in entirely new, equally relevant directions.

Talking about causes is difficult because "cause" can refer to many things—distal (more distant, though no less important) versus proximal (more immediate) conditions, for instance, or predisposing factors versus precipitating adverse events, or individual cases versus aggregate trends. In talking

about causes, in other words, people can easily talk past each other by grabbing onto different pieces of the truth. This reality at least partially explains the sterile debate regarding the causes of homelessness that dominated much of the 1980s as people tried to come to terms with why homelessness was so evident. On one side of this debate were those people who attributed homelessness to the personal limitations of homeless people, particularly mental illness and substance abuse. Pitted against those people were those people who argued that pervasive homelessness is essentially a function of structural factors, particularly the failure of the housing market to meet the demands of a poverty population that had swelled due to a complex set of interrelated factors. Each group of people stridently rejected the claims of the other. The structuralists dismissed explanations of homelessness that cited high rates of serious mental illness and substance abuse as myths designed to medicalize a fundamentally social/economic problem. Those people espousing an individual limitations perspective, on the other hand, turned to the obvious presence of psychotic and substance-abusing homeless adults as proof that the structuralists were attempting to "normalize" homeless people as part of a bid to advance a policy agenda that had more to do with eliminating poverty than helping those who were literally homeless.

In fact, neither perspective was able to independently accommodate a growing body of evidence. Narrowly defined structuralist arguments could not satisfactorily explain the high rates of mental disorder, substance abuse, and personal problems increasingly documented among the homeless in carefully designed studies. By the same token, people who argued that individual limitations cause homelessness turned a blind eye toward a well-developed body of scholarship suggesting a close historical relationship between homelessness and broader economic conditions and ignored the changing social contexts in which poor people—including poor, non-institutionalized mentally ill and substance-abusing adults—live their lives. Moreover, these people could not explain the distinctive demographics of contemporary homelessness, which did not resemble the demographics of the broader group of those troubled by mental health and substance abuse problems but instead the demographics of those groups at greatest disadvantage in our socioeconomic system. Although acknowledging the influences of structural events such as deinstitutionalization (without necessarily recognizing their structural character), such people continued to frame their explanations of homelessness largely in terms of the limitations of *people*. They ignored one of history's clear lessons: that the lives of all people, disabled or not, are embedded in circumstances shaped as much by structural factors as personal and biographical ones and that in a permissive environment full of cheap flophouses and undemanding work, even outcasts largely remain housed.

Perhaps the biggest mistake that adherents of each of these perspectives made was thinking they were addressing the same question. In reality, they were addressing two related but different questions. The structuralists were answering the questions, "Why does pervasive homelessness exist now, and even further, why is it currently manifesting itself as 'houselessness'?" Adherents of the individual limitations argument, despite their protestations that they were dealing with the fundamental causes of homelessness, were actually answering the question, "Who is at greatest risk for homelessness?" or, put slightly differently, "Who is most vulnerable to becoming homeless?" Identifying these two perspectives as addressing different questions makes it easier to see how they may not be mutually exclusive and how they might be reconciled to tell a fuller story.

In place of these opposing perspectives has emerged a widely held, more integrative framework—a structural explanation of homelessness that gives the individual limitations argument its due. Within this framework, the answer to the questions of why homelessness exists now and why it manifests itself as houselessness draws on the structural context in which contemporary homelessness emerged. This context was defined by a complex set of interwoven demographic, social, economic, and policy trends that increasingly left poor people—particularly the impaired among them—facing a growing set of pressures that included a dearth of affordable housing, a disappearance of the housing on which the most unstable had relied, and a diminished ability to support themselves either through entitlements or conventional or makeshift labor. Households and individuals barely making do increasingly found themselves under financial and interpersonal stresses that made a bad situation worse, culminating, by the early 1980s, in the pervasive homelessness that now seems to be an enduring part of our social lives.

Who actually becomes homeless in such a structural environment is not random, of course. Given that by the early 1980s, low-cost housing had become a scarce resource, it stands to reason that the first group to fall off the housing ladder would disproportionately include those people least able to compete for housing, especially those vulnerable individuals who had traditionally relied on a type of housing that was at extremely high risk of demolition and conversion. Viewed in this context, it is not surprising to find high numbers of people with mental illness and substance abuse among contemporary homeless populations—not just any mentally ill and substance-abusing individuals, it should be noted, but rather disproportionate numbers of those who came from backgrounds of poverty and/or who had diminished support resources to fall back on. For the same reason, it is hardly surprising to find high numbers of individuals with other sorts of personal vulnerabilities and problems among the homeless. This is not to say that mental illness, substance abuse, and other individual limitations in and of themselves *cause* homelessness, as witnessed in the fact that such individuals had remained housed in prior periods when low-cost housing and day labor suited to their occasionally chaotic lives were widely available. It is to say, rather, that such factors impaired the ability of people to compete with less vulnerable individuals for the scarce resource that affordable housing had become and thus left them at much greater risk for homelessness. People with problems are disproportionately numerous among the homeless, it becomes clear, because in a housing arena characterized by fierce competition, they are more vulnerable and, as a result, less likely to prevail.

We should spell out these structural trends and personal vulnerabilities in greater detail. First, let's look at the salient factors that have created and defined the context in which pervasive homelessness has emerged and is sustained.

THE STRUCTURAL CONTEXT

Those researchers who have examined the structural underpinnings of homelessness have concentrated primarily on two sets of factors and their ultimate collision: a growing pool of vulnerable poor people and a concomitant decline in the availability of low-cost housing. As poverty rates fluctuated between the early 1970s and the late 1980s, the absolute number of poor individuals grew substantially, and their poverty deepened. Several factors contributed to these developments. For one, this period coincided exactly with a potent demographic trend—the coming of age of those people born during the "baby boom," the post-World War II birth explosion that lasted through 1964. Unfortunately, this boom coincided with a marked transformation and a restructuring of global and local economies that severely restricted opportunities for the growing numbers of unskilled laborers preparing to enter the workforce. Referred to, in its different aspects, as "globalization," "post-Fordism," and "deindustrialization," these changes involved a shift from a predominance of relatively high-paying manufacturing jobs to lower-paying, often part-time, service jobs that lacked the same level of benefits and security and to a general slowing of wage growth rates.

Ultimately, these trends created a growing pool of young workers, particularly ill-educated individuals of minority status, who were either marginally employed or chronically unemployed. Simultaneously, a series of policy changes with regard to federal entitlements steadily eroded the real dollar value of both Social Security and Aid to Families with Dependent Children (AFDC) payments and, through tightened eligibility criteria, reduced the number of people who were able to rely on the government for support. Finally, changes in policies regarding the management of two economically and socially marginal populations—deinstitutionalization in the case of the severely mentally ill and decriminalization in the case of chronic public inebriates—meant that

new groups of previously institutionalized people were swelling the ranks of the very poor. Because these latter people primarily relied on zones of tolerance characterized by SRO housing and intermittent day labor—zones of tolerance that were rapidly disappearing in response to pressures related, respectively, to gentrification and immigration—they were at particularly high risk. Gone were the safety valves that allowed this population to adapt to life on the margins, without an alternative set of mechanisms to take their place.

At the same time that the absolute number of poor people was growing, the nation's supply of low-cost rental housing was shrinking for a variety of complex reasons and was thus increasingly unable to meet burgeoning demand. This occurred not only in the stock of multi-room units typically inhabited by poor families but also and even more precipitously in the stock of SRO hotels that served as the housing of last resort for single people—including the severely mentally ill and down-and-out substance abusers—on society's margins. Thus, whereas in 1970 a substantial surplus of housing units affordable to households in the bottom quartile of income was available, by 1989, there was a deficit of 5 million units—2.8 million units for 7.8 million bottom-quartile renter households. In response, poor households began to spend more of their income on rent and to double up (move in with family or friends), leaving them more and more vulnerable to economic crisis and domestic stress and increasingly less able to support unproductive household members. The result was pervasive homelessness.

Although researchers have mobilized an enormous amount of convincing evidence to document these structural trends, researchers have had difficulty "proving" the structural argument by relating these trends directly (i.e., through mathematical modeling) to variation in homelessness over time and over region, despite necessarily crude attempts to do so. This is mostly due to the fact that precise and reliable estimates of the outcome variable—numbers of homeless people in a representative set of places at different time points—simply do not exist. Although advances in the science of enumerating homeless populations may allow more reliable estimates in the future and thus more precise modeling efforts, the absence of such data for the critical time period spanning the late 1970s to mid-1980s means that the data on observed trends and the persuasiveness of the structural argument must remain the basis on which the structural perspective's merit rests.

INDIVIDUAL VULNERABILITIES

Who is most vulnerable to homelessness in this context defined by housing scarcity? Efforts to identify the individual-level factors that place people at risk for homelessness have focused primarily on discrete and readily identifiable disorders, particularly severe mental illness and substance abuse. Such disorders *are* disproportionately present among the homeless, although perhaps not to the extent that a number of early, methodologically flawed studies first suggested. More rigorous studies have indicated that as many as one-fifth to one-quarter of the homeless have experienced severe and extremely disabling mental illnesses such as schizophrenia and the major affective disorders (clinical depression or bipolar disorder) at some point in their lives and that one-half have experienced either alcohol- or drug-use disorders. Current prevalence rates (symptoms present within a recent time frame) are substantially lower but are still disproportionately high relative to domiciled comparison groups.

As high as they are, these numbers almost certainly overestimate the prevalence of alcohol, drug, and serious mental disorders among the total population of persons who experience homelessness for a number of reasons. First, most estimates are derived from cross-sectional samples of homeless adults—that is, from samples drawn at one point in time. Such samples tend to overrepresent the chronically homeless and to underrepresent the much larger group of individuals who are homeless for much shorter periods of time. To the extent that these latter individuals are less likely to suffer from these disorders, rates of disorder among the population of different people who have experienced homelessness within longer spans of time—a year, for instance—will be lower. Second, most estimates are derived from studies consisting largely of unattached home-

less adults (i.e., those who are unmarried and without children in their care). Although this group still predominates among the homeless, to the extent that these studies underrepresent adults in homeless families—whose mental health and substance abuse profiles are far less severe—they overrepresent the prevalence of these disorders among the total homeless population. Third, these estimates are based on the prevalence of disorders among homeless *adults*. If the children currently in the care of these adults—a large number in many cities—were added to the denominator, rates would change substantially.

Even so, mental illness and substance abuse, alone or together, are undoubtedly much more common among homeless adults than domiciled adults, suggesting that these disorders do indeed contribute to vulnerability to homelessness. However, not every severely mentally ill or substance-abusing adult becomes homeless. Nor are those people who do become homeless representative of the larger population of severely mentally ill and substance-abusing adults who remain housed, as we would expect if only mental illness and substance abuse were operating. In fact, severely mentally ill and substance-abusing adults who eventually experience homelessness instead more closely resemble the profile of homeless adults who are *not* mentally ill or substance abusing. Certainly this is true demographically. Like their non-disabled homeless counterparts, they are disproportionately African-American and poor. However, other factors—factors related to biography and situational circumstances—are also at work here, sometimes singly, often in complex combinations. Some of these factors may be as, or even more, important in understanding who is vulnerable to homelessness in an environment characterized by housing scarcity.

One such set of factors pertains to the childhood experiences of homeless adults. The picture that emerges when one delves more deeply into the backgrounds of homeless adults—particularly single homeless adults—is that homeless people are no strangers to poverty, housing instability, or the host of personal problems that disproportionately besets them as adults. As children, they disproportionately experienced significant disruptions in their residential stability, for example. In Los Angeles, fully two-fifths of a probability sample of homeless adults—the Course of Homelessness baseline sample (Sullivan, Burnam, Koegel, and Hollenberg 2000)—experienced housing problems while living with their families between the ages of six and eighteen (this at a time when the low-income housing market was far more forgiving). They doubled up with other households because of difficulty paying their rent, experienced evictions, and (in much smaller numbers) experienced literal homelessness with their families before such a phenomenon became common.

The backgrounds of homeless adults also suggest serious disruptions in family stability. Surprising numbers experienced out-of-home placement as children (in foster care, juvenile hall, orphanages, and treatment facilities); estimates cluster around 20 percent but reach as high as 40 percent in some reports. These extraordinarily high rates may be tied to other indicators that suggest early family disruption in the lives of homeless adults as well—high rates of mental health, substance abuse, and physical health problems among their parents and/or other adult members of their households; physical or sexual abuse in the household; and jail time among adult household members. This is not to say, of course, that every homeless individual comes from a background in which each set of problems—residential instability, out-of-home placement, and family trouble—was apparent. However, the vast majority of the Course of Homelessness baseline sample had experienced at least one of these problems as children, and many had experienced more. Such problems, not surprisingly, are often bundled together. These childhood experiences, in turn, may be related to the long-standing observation that many homeless individuals either do not have the family and friendship ties that people rely on to buffer them from the consequences of hard times or have ties to people who are similarly stretched and are thus in no position to provide substantial support.

More immediate situational factors appear to increase an individual's vulnerability to homelessness as well. The impact of such factors was apparent in the Course of Homelessness study, which included detailed questions on events that occurred in the year before the members first became homeless. Some of these events had clear structural or policy connections. In the year before becoming homeless, for instance, half of the individuals in this sample experienced a drop in income, either because they lost a job or lost the benefits on which they had been relying. Moreover, approximately one-third experienced a major increase in expenses during that period, such as rent or health care. Other events spoke more pointedly to changing interpersonal relationships. More than two-fifths reported that they had become separated or divorced or that they had experienced a break in a relationship with someone with whom they had been close. Somewhat more than one-third had faced a situation in which someone on whom they had depended for housing, food, or money was no longer willing or able to help them. (Although not asked about in this study, an association between being pregnant or giving birth within the last year and homelessness was found in a study of homeless versus housed families on public assistance in New York City.) Still other events spoke more directly to individual disorders and their impacts. Almost half of these adults admitted that they were frequently using alcohol and drugs during the year prior to first becoming homeless. One-quarter had spent time in a hospital, jail or prison, group care, or treatment facility during that year. One-fifth acknowledged that they had experienced serious physical or mental health problems during that period. Nearly 90 percent of the sample reported at least one of these various experiences, but multiple experiences were the rule. On average, sample members reported three such experiences.

In the absence of good comparative data on people who are "vulnerable" but for the time being housed, it is impossible to say with certainty whether and how these situational precipitants—or indeed the other background factors that may make them more likely to occur—combine to put people over the edge. Identifying the real basis for vulnerability is not always straightforward. Homeless families, to take one example, have certain characteristics that would intuitively appear to confer risk—such families are almost uniformly female-headed, single-parent households, for instance—but the fact that their housed poor counterparts are equally likely to be headed by single mothers suggests otherwise. More complex statistical analyses of who ends up in family shelters in New York City, in fact, show that factors such as race, pregnancy or recent birth of a child, childhood poverty and childhood disruptions, domestic violence, and particularly *housing* conditions (that is, whether one is in one's own apartment, whether it is subsidized, and how crowded it is) are primary, not factors related to education, work history, or disorder. Similarly, multivariate analyses (i.e., analyses that examine the impact of variables while controlling for the impact of other variables) of data on homeless and vulnerable meal program users in Chicago suggest that social institutional factors such as whether people are receiving income maintenance grants when domiciled, whether they are living with others, and how high their rent is explain who is homeless—not factors related to disability. Careful comparative studies such as these add to our knowledge of the factors that actually confer vulnerability. More work along these lines is needed. Also needed are empirical studies that pinpoint the precise mechanisms through which earlier antecedents translate into later vulnerability.

When we look more deeply into the backgrounds of homeless adults—particularly single homeless adults—we see multiple events and conditions emerging at different points in their life span that potentially increase their risk for homelessness. Conceptual models designed to explain who is at highest risk for homelessness and the data on which they are based increasingly take into account these myriad factors, including those factors related to demography, diagnosis, life experiences, and current circumstances, and highlight the complex ways in which these factors are interrelated. These models emphasize that single pathways to homelessness, in which a solitary source of vulnerability acts in isolation from others to leave one at risk for homelessness, are comparatively rare. Far more frequently, characteristics, life experiences, and their consequences interact to create a particular trajectory. The cumulative burden of these problems and experiences leaves certain individuals at particularly high risk.

Structure plays a role here as well because structure creates and perpetuates vulnerability—it both directly and indirectly fosters the conditions and events that leave some people at greater risk for homelessness at the same time as it establishes the context in which pervasive homelessness is inevitable. As researchers Koegel, Burnam, and Baumohl noted, risk factors "are almost invariably bundled; very rarely does one alone cause homelessness. And the chances that one will acquire such bundles are not evenly distributed at the outset of the game. Nor do they even out over time" (Koegel, Burnam, and Baumohl 1996, 33).

AN INTEGRATED PERSPECTIVE

To explain the presence and face of homelessness, then, one must consider two sets of factors: structural factors, which set the context for pervasive homelessness; and individual vulnerabilities, which earmark those people at highest risk for homelessness within tight housing and job markets. With regard to structural factors, a complex set of changes in the housing market, in income distribution, in social policy regarding marginal populations, and in the availability of urban zones of tolerance all coalesced to set the stage for homelessness. In the case of individual vulnerabilities, a bundled set of risk factors emerging at critical points during an individual's life span compounds itself to create the kinds of problems that leave a given person less able to compete for scarce social and economic resources and thus at elevated risk for homelessness in a structural context that makes homelessness inevitable.

—Paul Koegel

Further Reading

Baum, A. S., & Burnes, D. W. (1993). *A nation in denial: The truth about homelessness.* Boulder, CO: Westview.

Baumohl, J. (1993). A dissent from the Manichees. *Contemporary Drug Problems, 20,* 329–353.

Baumohl, J. (Ed.). (1996). *Homelessness in America.* Phoenix, AZ: Oryx Press.

Blau, J. (1992). *The visible poor: Homelessness in America.* New York: Oxford University Press.

Burt, M. R. (1992). *Over the edge: The growth of homelessness in the 1980s.* New York: Russell Sage Foundation.

Burt, M. R., Aron, L. Y., Douglas, T., Valente, J., Lee, E., &

Iwen, B. (1999). *Homelessness: Programs and the people they serve*. Washington, DC: U.S. Department of Housing and Urban Development.

Hopper, K. (2003). *Reckoning with homelessness: The anthropology of contemporary issues*. Ithaca, NY: Cornell University Press.

Hopper, K., & Baumohl, J. (1994). Held in abeyance: Rethinking homelessness and advocacy. *American Behavioral Scientist, 37*, 522–552.

Hopper, K., & Hamberg, J. (1986). The making of America's homeless: From skid row to new poor, 1945–1984. In R. G. Bratt, C. Hartman, & A. Meyerson (Eds.), *Critical perspectives on housing* (pp. 12–40). Philadelphia: Temple University Press.

Hopper, K., Susser, E., & Conover, S. (1985). Economies of makeshift: Deindustrialization and homelessness in New York City. *Urban Anthropology, 14*, 183–236.

Jencks, C. (1994). *The homeless*. Cambridge, MA: Harvard University Press.

Koegel, P., Burnam, M. A., & Baumohl, J. (1996). The causes of homelessness. In J. Baumohl (Ed.), *Homelessness in America* (pp. 24–33). New York: Oryx Press.

Koegel, P., Melamid, E., & Burnam, M. A. (1995). Childhood risk factors for homelessness among homeless adults. *American Journal of Public Health, 85*, 1642–1649.

Lehman, A. F., & Cordray, D. S. (1993). Prevalence of alcohol, drug, and mental disorders among the homeless: One more time. *Contemporary Drug Problems, 20*, 355–383.

O'Flaherty, B. (1996). *Making room: The economics of homelessness*. Cambridge, MA: Harvard University Press.

Rosenheck, R., & Fontana, A. (1994). A model of homelessness among male veterans of the Vietnam War generation. *American Journal of Psychiatry, 151*, 421–427.

Rossi, P. H. (1989). *Down and out in America: The origins of homelessness*. Chicago: University of Chicago Press.

Shinn, M., Weitzman, B. C., Stojanovic, D., Knickman, J. R., Jimenez, L., Duchon, L., James, S., & Krantz, D. H. (1998). Predictors of homelessness among families in New York City: From shelter request to housing stability. *American Journal of Public Health, 88*, 1651–1657.

Snow, D. A., & Anderson, L. (1993). *Down on their luck: A study of homeless street people*. Berkeley and Los Angeles: University of California Press.

Sommer, H. (2001). *Homelessness in urban America: A review of the literature*. Berkeley, CA: Institute of Governmental Studies Press.

Sosin, M. R. (1992). Homeless and vulnerable meal program users: A comparison study. *Social Problems, 39*, 170–188.

Sosin, M. R., Piliavin, I., & Westerfelt, H. (1990). Toward a longitudinal analysis of homelessness. *Journal of Social Issues, 46*, 157–174.

Sullivan, G., Burnam, A., & Koegel, P. (2000). Pathways to homelessness among the mentally ill. *Social Psychiatry and Psychiatric Epidemiology, 35*, 444–450.

Sullivan, G., Burnam, A., Koegel, P., & Hollenberg, J. (2000, September). Quality of life of homeless persons with mental illness: Results from the Course-of-Homelessness Study. *Psychiatric Services, 51*(9), 1135–1141.

Susser, E., Moore, R., & Link, B. (1993). Risk factors for homelessness. *American Journal of Epidemiology, 15*, 6546–6556.

Susser, E. S., Lin, S. P., Conover, S. A., & Struening, E. L. (1991). Childhood antecedents of homelessness in psychiatric patients. *American Journal of Psychiatry, 148*, 1026–1030.

Weitzman, B. C. (1989). Pregnancy and childbirth: Risk factors for homelessness? *Family Planning Perspectives, 21*, 175–178.

Wolch, J., & Dear, M. (1993). *Malign neglect: Homelessness in an American city*. San Francisco: Jossey-Bass.

Wright, J. D., Rubin, B. A., & Devine, J. A. (1998). *Beside the golden door: Policy, politics, and the homeless*. New York: Aldine de Gruyter.

◉ CHICAGO SKID ROW

When nineteenth-century Seattle lumberman Henry Yesler skidded logs to his waterfront sawmill, he rolled them down an inclined street lined with lodging houses, taverns, restaurants, brothels, pawnshops, and other stores. This original "Skid Road" later gave rise to the pejorative slang term "skid row," referring to any place in a U.S. city where drunkenness and social pathology were said to concentrate. One current dictionary definition: "a district of cheap saloons and flophouses frequented by vagrants and alcoholics."

This stereotype exaggerates one dimension of residential life among single working men while obscuring other important features that made these communities viable resources for the single working poor between 1870 and 1930. America's skid row lodging house districts emerged in the industrial cities that also served as railway hubs. New York, Philadelphia, Detroit, Minneapolis, Salt Lake City, San Francisco, and Seattle all harbored diverse lodging house districts. The largest and most prosperous developed in Chicago. There, at the peak of its rail activity, 2,840 miles of steam railway switched and sorted freight cars linking the city to 44,000 shipping points in forty-four states. Alice Solenberger estimated that as many as 50,000 men inhabited Chicago's lodging house district in 1911. The men lived in thousands of hotel dwellings arrayed along three streets: Madison to the west, Clark to the north, and State to the south.

THE TRANSIENT POOR

The urban homeless exhibited a social order that valued independence and personal freedom, tolerating a wide range of social behavior. Inhabiting the lodging house districts were three types of transient workers, commonly known as hoboes, tramps, and bums. Hoboes worked steadily at a variety of jobs that took them to destinations across the inner frontiers of an urbanizing

Residents of Chicago's skid row or "Main Stem" c. 1950.
Source: Hulton-Deutsch/Corbis; used with permission.

nation. They built infrastructure, mines, and factories. The hobo lexicon described "gandy dancers" who laid railroad ties, "muckers" who labored on construction sites, and "splinter bellies," or bridge workers. "You are as you work" was the hobo's motto. Their labor was frequently seasonal so they traveled to cities to bed down for the winter months. Few hoboes married, and cities offered the opportunity for sociability without the domesticity of family life.

Tramps were travelers who did not share the hobo work ethic, earning derogatory labels such as "jungle buzzard" (a beggar for food at hobo camps), "road egg" (a thief who stole from hoboes on the road), and "fuzzy tail" (a smart-aleck wise guy). Those transients who settled down and found occasional work in the local "slave markets" (labor exchanges) were known as bums. The bums worked as construction laborers, handbill distributors, or other unskilled temporary jobs.

THE "MAIN STEM"

In the early decades of the twentieth century, housing speculators, developers, and religious philan-

thropies such as the Salvation Army built residential hotels to shelter the burgeoning ranks of the working poor near the rail terminals of rapidly industrializing cities. Other rooming houses catered to skilled clerical and service workers, many of them female. Few of these were located near lodging houses on skid row; instead they clustered closer to the office and commercial activities at the city center. Skid row lodging houses welcomed migratory workers and local day laborers who needed cheap quarters. These lodgers settled for a single sleeping room—unlike today's renters who expect a place for sleeping, eating, food preparation, bathing, and other daily activities. The transients met their other needs through nearby shops and services that catered to the working poor.

Skid row housing offered a range of inexpensive shelter. The cheapest provided dormitory-style accommodations: makeshift quarters in obsolete warehouses, religious missions, or in some cases municipally run lodging houses. These commercial flophouses cost a nickel or less per night at the turn of the century. The best of these offered three tiers of bunk beds, their frames webbed with wide leather straps as a sleeping surface. The worst offered space on a floor. Philanthropic and municipal shelters might provide a free night's sleep, but there was a catch. Missions required attendance at a religious service, while municipal lodging houses imposed a work requirement such as splitting wood.

Cubicle hotels offered the next step up in housing quality. These multistory buildings might contain as many as 400 cubicles for residents. The interior walls did not extend floor to ceiling, but left space for air to circulate. Chicken wire nailed across the top of the units prevented tenants from climbing over. A single hanging bulb shed light on little more than bed, chair, and stand. Such cubicles provided the bulk of housing on skid row. Tenants paid just enough for personal privacy and security in the "cages," but not enough to escape the noise and stench of a shared atmosphere. As many as forty tenants might share the same toilet and bath.

At the top of the lodging house hierarchy were the working men's hotels, which provided rooms with a window and attached bath. The most luxurious included daily cleaning and linen service. In 1921, such a hotel might charge as much as seventy-five cents a night, while a flophouse might cost a dime.

The residents of skid row called their neighborhood the "main stem"—referring to the primary street leading from the rail depot to their clusters of lodging houses with storefronts sandwiched among them. Employment agencies, eateries, saloons, and many other enterprises provided plenty of commercial services for the thousands coming and going along the densely packed residential corridors. Nels Anderson's map of two blocks along Chicago's main stem in 1921 depicts the activity on Madison between Des Plaines and Jeffries. Seven hotels provided rooms for more than 2,000 residents, most in three huge cubicle-style buildings. This extremely high density channeled the small earnings of the poor tenants into a purchasing stream that supported eight restaurants, six saloons, five clothing shops, four barber colleges, two fortune-tellers, two gambling joints, a cigar store, and a drugstore. The entire district stretched for fifteen blocks from Canal Street to Ogden Avenue.

THE COMMUNITY OF HOBOHEMIA

Social life in the lodging house districts was part of a larger trend that saw increasing numbers of single people moving to the city from small towns and farms. Skid row offered a residential infrastructure for the diverse assortment of single men who congregated there to meet their basic needs and find companionship and support. The hobo's freedom and independence could flourish in part because he relied upon a fraternity of mutual give and take. The lone traveler was as likely to find work through the tip of a fellow traveler as he was through the "slave master" of a labor exchange. None ate "mulligan stew" who had not contributed ingredients. The warnings, gifts, and stories exchanged among comrades built the solidarity that each used to maintain a proud independence. The lodging house held a peculiar social appeal, as Nels Anderson described:

> To the homeless man it is home, for there, no matter how sorry his lot, he can find those who will understand. The veteran of the road finds other veterans; the old man finds the aged; the chronic grouch finds friends' fellowship; the radical, the optimist, the crook, the inebriate, all find others here to tune in with them. The wanderer finds friends here or enemies, but, and that is at once a characteristic and pathetic feature of Hobohemia, they are friends or enemies only for the day. They meet and pass on. (Anderson 1998, 33)

THE DEMISE OF SKID ROW

The economic hardships of the Great Depression expanded the demand for cheap shelter and increased housing pressures in many skid row districts. Edwin Sutherland and Harvey Locke studied the impact of the Depression in Chicago, where twenty municipal shelters built between 1931 and 1935 housed an additional 20,000 homeless each year. The federal government authorized and funded many of these shelters for the temporarily unemployed. But the new residents differed from the long-term hoboes, tramps, and bums for whom the district had served as an urban community. The professional staff treated the newly homeless as morally superior to the diminishing ranks of transient poor. When prosperity returned after World War II and the need for shelters collapsed, the skid row stigma remained. Land values in aging downtowns plummeted with the rapid suburbanization of U.S. cities, fueled by new modes of industrial production, improved wages, new highways, and federal home ownership policies.

The transient labor pool diminished drastically after 1930. The poor men inhabiting the skid rows of the 1950s and 1960s included elderly hoboes and tramps whose traveling days were finished, as well as an increasing share of people suffering from mental and physical disabilities and alcohol addiction. In Chicago, the skid row population had dwindled to less than 12,000 by 1958. New York City's Bowery housed fewer than 8,000 in 1964. Vacancy rates in the aging hotels soared. Owners deferred maintenance and repairs. Municipal officials scrimped on improvements to sidewalks and streets. Building inspectors enforced codes more vigorously. Police increased arrests for drunkenness and vagrancy. Newspapers ran lurid stories of skid row deviance and despair. Yet despite all these pressures, the lodging houses continued to make money. The poor tenants stayed because they had nowhere else to live.

When federal dollars for urban renewal became available, big-city mayors made plans to demolish obsolete buildings, hoping to attract new commercial and residential development. Many of them targeted dilapidated residential districts with low-income residents. Skid row districts proved especially attractive for renewal since they were centrally located and harbored populations with little political power. Studies documenting the disaffiliation and alcoholism of skid row tenants provided powerful rationales for demolition. As early as 1964, the commissioner of the Urban Renewal Administration of Housing and Home Finance could report the successful demolition of 129,000 buildings in more than 1,300 renewal projects nationwide. But the wave of demolition had yet to peak. Along Chicago's West Madison Street, more than 10,000 units were demolished between 1960 and 1980, wiping out more than 90 percent of the remaining hotel rooms. The juggernaut of renewal flattened hotels from San Francisco to New York City, eliminating skid rows across the entire United States.

THE LESSON FROM SKID ROW

Skid row neighborhoods harbored a diverse assortment of inexpensive, high-density, single-room hotels clustered near the center of the city. This concentration enabled the single poor to use the physical and social resources of the district to find a job, a place to sleep, food, clothing, and companionship without relying exclusively on public or private philanthropy. Homeless Americans in the twenty-first century are entitled to a much wider array of public services and shelters than were their skid row predecessors. But most enjoy less social flexibility and companionship. Today's homeless must learn to navigate their service providers' continuum of care to achieve independence—and they often do so without benefit of a diverse residential community. But nonprofit groups in some American cities have launched community-building initiatives to construct and rehabilitate buildings for single-room occupancy (SRO) and tie them to local networks of social and economic support. These organizations include the SRO Housing Corporation in Los Angeles, the Burnside Consortium in Portland, Oregon, and the Lakefront SRO in Chicago. Such groups are developing models for housing that will adapt the economic advantages of the old skid row to the social realities of the present. Their efforts are modest, but promising.

—*Charles Hoch*

Further Reading

Anderson, N. (1998). *On hobos and homelessness.* Chicago: University of Chicago Press.

Bahr, H., & Caplow, T. (1973). *Old men drunk and sober.* New York: New York University Press.

Blumberg, L., Shipley, T., & Barsky, S. (1978). *Liquor and poverty: Skid row as a human condition.* New Brunswick, NJ: Rutgers University Press.

Bogue, D. (1963). *Skid row in American cities.* Chicago: Community and Family Study Center, University of Chicago.

Groth, P. (1994). *Living downtown: The history of residential hotels in the United States.* Berkeley: University of California Press.

Hoch, C., & Slayton, R. (1989). *New homeless and old: Community and the skid row hotel.* Philadelphia: Temple University Press.

Kusmer, K. L. (2002). *Down and out, on the road: The homeless in American history.* New York: Oxford University Press.

Lee, B. (1980). The disappearance of skid row. *Urban Affairs Quarterly, 16,* 97.

Monkkonen, E. (Ed.). (1984). *Walking to work: Tramps in America, 1794–1935.* Lincoln: University of Nebraska Press.

Solenberger, A. W. (1911). *One thousand homeless men.* New York: Russell Sage Foundation.

Sutherland, E. H., & Locke, H. J. (1936). *Twenty thousand homeless men.* Chicago: University of Chicago Press.

Wallace, S. (1965). *Skid row as a way of life.* Totawa, NJ: Bedminster Press.

▣ CHILD CARE

Children and families make up the fastest growing segment of the homeless population in the United States. While many Americans tend to picture the homeless as armies of men and women pushing shopping carts through city streets and sleeping in subway tunnels, in cast-off boxes, and on heating grates, the new face of homelessness more accurately includes an increasing number of children and their families. Provision of child care and early education for these youngsters will be necessary to ensure that the homeless children of today do not become the homeless adult population of tomorrow.

THE SCOPE OF CHILDHOOD HOMELESSNESS

Homeless families are defined here as those with no permanent place to live; instead, they may live in shelters or other transitional programs, in motels or welfare hotels, in campgrounds or cars, or doubled up with relatives or friends. This definition is not limited to those dependent on government support. There are approximately one million children in the United States who are homeless each night (Helburn and Howes 1996, 5). In Massachusetts, according to Department of Transitional Assistance statistics, as of March 2003 there were 1,700 families homeless each night in congregate shelters, scattered site shelters, and motels—this represents 60 percent of all the homeless in the state. More than half of the children of these families were under school age. These families tend to lead nomadic lives that take them from one homeless venue to another. A 1997 study indi-

cated that homeless children have an average of 2.8 such temporary addresses each year, a rate sixteen times greater than the relocation rate of an average American family (Bartlett 1997, 122). Homelessness is often compounded by other family problems. Not only the lack of affordable housing, but other issues such as substance abuse, mental health problems, and domestic violence are often related to homelessness in the United States. These factors can be found in combination, doubling or tripling the potential for a slide into homelessness and increasing the negative effects on children.

THE IMPACT OF HOMELESSNESS ON CHILDREN

Compared with their housed counterparts, homeless children experience more developmental delays, emotional problems such as anxiety and depression, and behavioral problems, as well as a myriad of school-related troubles. All children require stability and consistency, individual attention, appropriate stimulation, protection from harm, and structure and routine in order to grow and develop normally. These conditions also allow a child to develop resiliency and gain appropriate skills for later success. All of these desirables are compromised by homelessness.

Living in automobiles, in welfare motels or hotels, or in shelters or transitional housing can create in children certain behaviors that are a response to their environment. Infants growing up in these circumstances can display slower motor development because they are not allowed the time or space to learn to grasp and crawl. Shelter rules may hinder a toddler's freedom to run, hop, and climb. Homeless infants cry more than their housed peers, and are less apt to receive the proper amount of stimulation and attention. Given the stressed nature of their parents' lives, these children often have scarce adult interaction, which in turn limits their sensory development. Lacking a consistent environment, homeless children may have difficulty focusing and paying attention. They also may be slower to develop language skills, and the inability to come up with words might result in negative behavior, such as biting instead of saying the word "mine." Lack of routine may make the primary caregiver seem unreliable, creating a mistrust that can lead to later emotional problems.

Homelessness Plus

Added to the negative impact of homelessness on children's growth and development are the other common factors of parental substance abuse, mental health issues, and domestic violence. For some youngsters, all three are a part of their childhood.

In a family where substance abuse occurs, young children may not receive the attention they require and therefore may be at risk for neglect and for attachment difficulties. Older children may become "parentified," taking on parental roles for younger siblings and thereby losing out on the benefits of play—which would help develop their own skills and readiness for school.

As for parental mental health issues, depression in particular can hinder a mother's ability to interact with her child in a positive manner. Often this depression can be linked to experiencing and/or witnessing violence and living in poverty. Whether in therapy or on medication, depressed mothers benefit from three interventions: programs that nurture the mother; guidance on how to enhance parent-child interaction; and help in strengthening the caregiving environment, including finding options for good child care (Gowen and Nebrig 2002, 239–244).

Each year, between 3 and 4 million children from ages three to seventeen are at risk of witnessing violence in their homes. Karen Miller (1996) writes of the impact violence can have on children; it can strip them of the feeling of safety they require in order to develop. The child in a household where there is domestic violence may feel that the world is a truly unsafe place. Psychologically the child may have to choose between remaining helpless and emulating the violent parent—a serious problem particularly for young boys. Domestic or even community violence can cause children to "tune out" their surroundings, which undermines their ability to learn.

Homelessness in itself is difficult for children. Adding any of the above to the mix—substance abuse, parental mental health issues, domestic vio-

lence—increases the likelihood of even more negative consequences. Compared to their housed peers, homeless children are both more likely to experience mental health problems and less likely to receive the attention they need to resolve them. A 1999 study by the National Center for Family Homelessness (formerly the Better Homes Fund) reports that more than 20 percent of homeless children three to six years of age have emotional problems that warrant professional care.

EARLY EDUCATION AND CHILD CARE: WHY AND HOW

"Children in high-quality early childhood education programs are more likely to be emotionally secure and self-confident, proficient in language use, able to regulate impulsive and aggressive inclinations, and advanced in cognitive development"(Helburn and Howes 1996, 62). Homeless children, like their housed counterparts, are increasingly likely to find themselves in child care programs—especially when their mothers join the work force or enter school or professional programs to acquire skills that will improve the family's prospects. Studies have documented the elements that make such programs successful for all children: small group size, trained and supervised staff in a high teacher-to-child ratio, and a curriculum that addresses the particular needs of the population it serves (Gomby et al. 1995, 16).

It remains the task of the parent to secure an optimal child care situation. Ideally, the parent locates and inspects the potential site, interviews the caregiver, and pays the provider directly from wages earned. Figures gathered by the Children's Defense Fund show that the cost of a year of center-based child care varies widely by region: from $3,900 in Conway/Springdale, Arkansas, to about $13,000 in Boston (Phillips and Adams 2001, 45). Unfortunately, all of the circumstances cited above—lack of permanent housing, parental substance abuse or mental health problems, domestic violence—can impair access to child care.

As for the programs themselves, the issue of homelessness must be considered and a curriculum developed that will benefit this population.

A Curriculum That Makes a Difference

An effective curriculum for homeless children addresses the particular nature of their difficulties, given their unstable living environment. The suggestions below have been developed in a child care setting specifically serving the needs of homeless children living in shelter. Such a curriculum might be organized by age group around four basic developmental areas: motor, sensory, language and cognitive, and social-emotional.

Infants (birth to 15 months)

Motor Development. Some infants have had little chance to practice motor activities, perhaps because of too much time spent in car seats or strollers. These babies benefit from a curriculum that makes the floor a clean, safe space and brings child care workers to floor level, encouraging the infant to roll over and sit, and later to crawl and walk. Parents, too, should be encouraged to do "floor time" with babies. Caregivers should provide crawling room and furniture so infants can practice pulling themselves upright. They should give infants objects to hold such as rattles, stuffed animals, bottles, or cups; provide containers and simple toys for "dump and fill" activities; introduce opportunities to pretend; play imitating games; and introduce board books, letting the infant hold them and turn the pages.

Sensory Development. Stressed parents may neglect to provide the sensory stimulation necessary for growth. Their infants, in turn, may find touch or sounds intrusive and may cry frequently or be "fussy." To address these needs, caregivers should hold and carry the infants frequently, pointing out objects and scenes and talking constantly about what they are seeing. They should make frequent eye contact with the infant when talking; sing to the child; provide colors and patterns for the infant to look at; and offer a wide range of toys and books for the infant to handle. Recognizing that infants also learn by putting things in the mouth, caregivers should make sure that the environment is safe and offer food of various tastes and textures.

Language and Cognitive Development. Infants in stressed homeless families may be slower to develop language than their housed peers and may progress more slowly from sounds to words to simple sentences. Because of the number of transitions homeless children often face, infants may have trouble focusing on and attending to new people or activities. A curriculum to address these issues would ensure that child care providers are "talking their way through the day," and, given the many transitions and strangers these children face, would establish a consistent and stable routine with one full-time caregiver rather than several part-timers. Caregivers should imitate the sounds the infant makes and urge the infant to imitate back the same sound; offer pop-up toys that can help teach cause and effect; read simple books frequently; teach songs and repeat favorite ones over and over again; create "go and find" games with toys; play peek-a-boo or simple hiding games; point out similarities in toys—color, shape, texture; count or sing the alphabet; and help the infant learn to anticipate activities by announcing them earlier in the day.

Social-Emotional Development. Parents who are stressed may not interact with their infants as they would otherwise. With their needs unmet, these infants may have learned to distrust their world. Homeless infants may become less interested in people, may smile less, make less eye contact, and generally be less responsive. A curriculum to address these issues would include plenty of reassuring words that soothe; a high caregiver-to-child ratio so that infants may be held often; conversation by caregivers about feelings; prompt response to infants' needs; and helping older infants develop autonomy—for example by encouraging use of cups or spoons at snack time.

Toddlers (15 months to 2.9 years)

Motor Development. Toddlers living in shelters and welfare hotels may suffer from cramped space and rules that prohibit them from running, climbing, and handling objects. Stressed parents may not fully engage, and may tend to view the normal activity of a toddler as too loud, too active, and too messy. Toddlers require a curriculum that provides for the development of both gross and fine motor skills. This includes space for climbing, running, and jumping; music and movement activities; use of objects such as balls, push toys, and baskets that require lifting and carrying; and "dump and fill" activities with all sorts of containers. Simple puzzles, stacking toys, blocks, finger paints, play dough, and big crayons and paper are also helpful.

Sensory Development. Toddlers' natural curiosity about sights, smells, and sounds around them may be harder to satisfy in a shelter setting that is characterized by multiple families living in close proximity. Or they may suffer from overstimulation, which can cause them to "tune out." In either case, caregivers can help compensate by responding to what toddlers are noticing. Toddlers need opportunities to use both an "outdoor voice" and an "indoor voice"; to echo sounds heard in the environment (trucks, fire engines, ambulances); they also enjoy rhyming games, especially those using their names. Caregivers should provide a sand or water table for experiencing various textures, and help toddlers explore flavors by varying snacks and talking about how food tastes, smells, and looks.

Language and Cognitive Development. Growing up in the stressful environment of a shelter, toddlers may experience delays both in acquiring language and extending their attention span. Child care providers should recognize that toddlers love to talk about what they are doing and should be encouraged to describe their actions, their feelings, and the objects they are handling. In addition, toddlers should be encouraged to speak in complete sentences; the caregiver can add adjectives so that sentence length gradually increases. Picture books are critical at this age; caregivers should allow time to look at pictures and comment on each one.

Social-Emotional Development. Homeless toddlers may be slow to trust people in their environment—for example, to know that hunger will be met with food and that individuals who leave them will eventually come back. This lack of trust will delay the toddler's growth toward independence and may hinder curiosity. Their language delays may cause behavioral problems; a toddler might substitute hitting or biting for expressing anger in words. The homeless toddler may appear sad and may have difficulty with toilet training and with learning to share.

Good child care providers can overcome these problems by creating independent activities for toddlers; celebrating accomplishments; modeling how to express feelings with words and offering books that do the same; making sure that toddlers are praised for sharing; and using a positive vocabulary ("walking feet" instead of "no running"; "inside voice" instead of "no shouting").

Preschoolers (2.9 to 6 years)

Motor Development. If a homeless preschooler has had limited access to large play spaces, motor skills may be underdeveloped. Some children may also show a disinclination to draw, paint, or work on puzzles. A good setting for these children would offer opportunities for active songs that include gross motor activity, and outdoor space where they can run, climb, swing, and slide. Fine motor skills can be developed with an ample supply of simple puzzles, play dough, finger paints, sidewalk chalk, and large crayons. A water play area equipped with food coloring and items such as droppers, cups, spoons, and ice cubes will encourage fine motor skills. So will building blocks, small cars and trucks, and activities that mimic daily life, such as shopping for groceries, setting the table, and cooking.

Sensory Development. Homeless preschoolers may have experienced many transitions in their short lives and be ultra-sensitive to stimulation. Some environments may have been unpredictable, noisy, or unresponsive to their needs. At the same time, lack of appropriate stimulation can lead to diminished interest in the environment just when this interest should be expanding. A preschool curriculum that addresses these needs would include games that focus on spotting slight differences between things, perhaps beginning with colors and then progressing to numbers and letters. Rhyming games, name games, and listening games can improve the preschooler's auditory awareness; use of a "mystery box" with a variety of objects can help children differentiate through touch; and a variety of foods increases awareness of smells, tastes, and textures.

Language and Cognitive Development. Homeless preschoolers may be delayed in both receptive language (understanding what is said) and expressive language (verbalizing thoughts and feelings). Attention spans may be short, and preschoolers may need help to organize their thoughts. Strategies that are particularly helpful with this population include role-playing and dramatic play opportunities; using literature as a basis for arts and crafts projects; using puppets to tell stories or share feelings. Photos can be used to demonstrate a process from start to finish, such as daily cleanup or cooking a meal. They can also be used for name games and for identifying classmates when attendance is taken.

Social-Emotional Development. Children without homes may feel self-conscious about being homeless. With the "magical thinking" characteristic of this age, preschoolers may believe that they are responsible for living in a shelter, or for the violence that might have landed the family there. Preschoolers—even at this very young age—may already be serving as parents to younger siblings and may not feel entitled to play themselves. Child care programs can enhance their social and emotional growth by including in their curriculum songs that model safe ways to express feelings like anger or sadness; establishing clear and stable routines; ensuring an adult-child ratio that allows plenty of individual attention; planning activities at which the preschooler can be successful; establishing clear and consistent limits for behavior; using books, puppets, or storytelling to talk about solving conflicts and airing feelings; providing dress-up clothes that allow the preschooler to take on other roles; and maintaining an awareness that some activities and some stories may affect homeless and housed children differently.

WHERE TO GO FROM HERE

Ideally, to lessen the problems that homeless children face, the answer is to end homelessness and all the additional challenges—substance abuse, mental health issues, domestic violence—that both increase the potential for homelessness and exacerbate its consequences. In the interim, it is important to identify the steps that will help ensure that homeless children receive an early childhood education that

specifically addresses the problems they face. Karen Miller writes,

> The child care program can be an enormous positive influence in the life of a family. The child may have his first opportunity to play, paint, dig, have friends and feel safe. The parent may feel supported for the first time and, consequently, feel optimistic about the future. (Miller 1996, 267)

Thoughtfully designed child care specifically created for homeless children can play a part in breaking the cycle of homelessness.

—Nancy Owens Hess

Further Reading

Bartlett, S. (1997). The significance of relocation for chronically poor families in the USA. *Environment and Urbanization, 9*(1), 121–131.

Better Homes Fund. (1999). *Homeless children: America's new outcasts.* Newton, MA: A Public Policy Report from National Center on Family Homelessness.

Choi, N., & Snyder, L. (1999). *Homeless families with children: A subjective experience of homelessness.* New York: Springer.

Friedman, D. H. (2000). *Parenting in public: Family shelter and public assistance.* New York: Columbia University Press.

Gomby, D. S., Larner, M. B., Stevenson, C. S., Lewit, E. M., & Behrman, R. E. (1995). Long-term outcomes of early childhood programs: Analysis and recommendations. *The Future of Children, 5*(3), 6–24.

Gowen, J. W., & Nebrig, J. B. (2002). *Enhancing early emotional development: Guiding parents of young children.* Baltimore: Brookes.

Harms, T., Ray, A. R., & Rolandelli, P. (Eds.). (1998). *Preserving childhood for children in shelters.* New York: Child Welfare League of America.

Helburn, S. W., & Howes, C. (1996). Child care cost and quality. *The Future of Children, 6*(2), 62–82.

Homes for the Homeless and The Institute for Children and Poverty. (1999). *Homeless in America: A children's story.* New York: Author.

Kozol, J. (1988). *Rachel and her children.* New York: Ballantine.

Miller, K. (1996). *The crisis manual for early childhood teachers: How to handle the really difficult problems.* Beltsville, MD: Gryphon House.

Molnar, J. M. (1988). *Home is where the heart is: The crisis of homeless children and families in New York City.* Bank Street College of Education. ERIC Document Reproduction Service, No. ED 304228.

Nunez, R. D. (1994). *Hopes, dreams and promise: The future of homeless children in America.* New York: Homes for the Homeless.

Phillips, D., & Adams, G. (2001). Child care and our youngest children. *The Future of Children, 11*(1), 35–51.

Purvin, D. (1996). Child witness to domestic violence: Common questions. Retrieved January 7, 2003, from http://www.janedoe.org/know/know_children_witnessfaq.htm

Walsh, M. E. (1992). *"Moving to nowhere": Children's stories of homelessness.* Westport, CT: Greenwood.

Wen, P. (2002, September 1). Stuck in a day care dilemma: Working-class families struggle with shortage. *Boston Globe.*

CHILD SUPPORT

In the United States, two types of child support are available to children. The first (the focus of this entry) is private child support, which is largely regulated by state law. The second is the public assistance or "welfare" system that provides cash support to children in poverty who live apart from a biological parent, usually their father. During the past thirty years, the federal government has taken several steps to strengthen the private child support system, particularly with respect to the treatment of children living in poverty. At the same time, the value of public assistance for children in poverty has dropped by nearly one-third. Overall, these changes have privatized the costs of supporting children and shifted some of the costs of raising children from mothers to fathers.

WHAT IS PRIVATE CHILD SUPPORT?

The vast majority of the nation's 23 million children who live with one parent live with their single, divorced, or never-married mothers. This is true even though state law is now gender neutral regarding custody arrangements. These mothers are eligible to apply for and receive child support on behalf of that child from the noncustodial biological parent. Even if the custodial parent (almost always the mother) has sufficient funds to support a child, the noncustodial biological parent still must provide financial support. If a child's parents were not married at the time the child was born, however, legal paternity must first be established before an application for child support can be made against the alleged father. If the father denies paternity, a court may order a DNA test to determine whether or not he is the biological father.

Once a child support order is issued by a court, a child is entitled to receive a set amount of money, paid bimonthly or once a month. For low-income mothers and their dependent children, child support is an important source of income. For women receiving child support, it adds an average of $2,000 a year to their family's budget, increasing their total income by 26 percent. In addition, child support reduces the total number of children in poverty by half a million and lessens income inequality among children who are eligible for it. For example, the poverty rate for families who receive all the child support they are owed is 15.2 percent, compared with the 35.7 percent poverty rate for families that do not receive any of the child support they are due.

CHILD SUPPORT AND THE LAW

In the United States, child support policy is a province of state law, so child support systems vary dramatically from state to state. Courts are the main decision makers in these systems. Although state law establishes the duty of noncustodial parents to financially support their children, judges have the authority to decide whether to grant a support order, and if so, for how much. Judges also often decide what sanctions will be taken if the father fails to meet his support obligation. In some jurisdictions, little is done about nonpaying fathers: The burden of collecting overdue support falls to the custodial mother, who must hire an attorney and take the father to court.

This case-by-case handling of child support orders results in a system that works very differently for poor/low-income families and children and their high-income counterparts. Low-income and poor fathers pay a higher percentage of their incomes than high-income fathers. Studies indicate that low-income fathers are likely to be ordered to pay amounts that exceed those set out in guidelines than middle- and high-income fathers. This happens in part because courts sometimes base child support orders on imputed income rather than actual income, assuming that any father could have earnings equal to full-time work at the minimum wage. If a father cannot attain this level of earnings, his child support order will be a very high percentage of his actual income. Fathers with very low incomes will thus have orders that amount to a very high percentage of their income. In addition to these high support orders, fathers of children receiving public assistance may be ordered to pay back all of the money the state has paid to their children in Medicaid and public assistance. The overall effect of these child support guidelines is regressive: Fathers in the lowest income group pay a much higher percentage of their income (when they pay at all) than fathers in the highest income category—28 percent versus 10 percent.

CHILD SUPPORT REFORMS

Some of these inequities have been addressed by Congress, which passed several major pieces of legislation, beginning in the 1970s, designed to (1) establish the legal obligation of noncustodial parents to pay child support, (2) increase the level of the child support orders, and (3) more effectively enforce support obligations.

Legal Obligation to Pay

In the 1970s, most divorced mothers already had a child support order, so the child support reforms undertaken beginning in the late 1970s were not aimed at divorced men. Instead, laws passed in this area focused on obtaining child support from men who have fathered children outside of traditional marriage. For these men, paternity must be established before a child support order can be issued by the court. Before the 1980s, paternity establishment in most states was a difficult and costly judicial procedure in which the rights of the accused were relatively well protected. Most courts admitted blood tests as evidence in paternity establishment cases only if they excluded the putative father. This changed with passage of the 1988 Family Support Act (FSA), which required all states to use blood tests and genetic tests without the need for a court order. The 1996 Personal Responsibility and Work Opportunity Reconciliation Act (PRAWORA) goes much further by requiring states to give administra-

tive agencies authority to order blood tests and genetic tests without a court order. The law also requires states to have available in hospitals and birth records agencies a paternity acknowledgment form. Signing it is voluntary, but when signed, it becomes a legal finding of paternity after sixty days. In 1980, paternity was established in only 22 percent of non-marital births. By 1996, the percentage had reached 57 percent. Not surprisingly, the proportion of never-married mothers with a support order has increased from 8 percent in 1979 to 23 percent in 1991. In view of PRAWORA, the percentage is almost certainly higher today.

Increasing Support Payments

Before the 1980s, child support orders were set on a case-by-case basis, and fathers in poverty were treated more harshly than their well-to-do counterparts. The old system also produced unacceptably low child support orders that failed to keep up with inflation. The 1984 Child Support Amendments requires states to adopt numerical guidelines for determining child support obligations that courts could use. The 1988 Family Support Act (FSA) requires states to make these guidelines the presumptive order. Judges who depart from the guidelines are required to provide a written justification.

Enforcing Payment Obligations

To help ensure that noncustodial parents pay what they owe, Congress passed the nation's first federal child support legislation in 1974—the addition of Part D to Title IV (IVD) of the Social Security Act. This act established the Child Support Enforcement (CSE) program, created the federal Office of Child Support Enforcement (OCSE), required all states to establish comparable state offices, and authorized federal funding for three-quarters of the states' expenditures on child support enforcement. Ten years later, Congress passed the 1984 Child Support Amendments, which require states to enact laws to require employers to withhold child support obligations of delinquent parents. The 1988 FSA goes further by requiring automatic withholding of child support obligations from the outset for all child support cases, beginning in 1994. Many states, however, failed to implement withholding for non-IVD cases because they neither had nor wanted to develop the bureaucratic capacity to administer universal withholding of payments. The 1996 PRAWORA requires all states to develop the bureaucratic capacity to monitor child support payments and to administer wage withholding of support payments from delinquent parents' wages.

EFFECTS OF CHILD SUPPORT REFORMS

What impact have these changes in child support policy had on women and children? While there has been an increase in child support orders among women in poverty receiving public assistance, from 8 percent in 1979 to 23 percent in 1991, the proportion of eligible families with a child support order remained at about 60 percent, which is where it was in the late 1970s. This is because divorce cases, which generate most child support orders, now make up a smaller share of the child support caseload, whereas cases due to non-marital births, which have a low, albeit growing, proportion of child support orders, make up a larger share of the caseload.

Data on child support receipts of single mothers from 1979 to 1999 indicate virtually no improvement in the receipt rate for all mothers: It rose from 30 percent to 31 percent. On the other hand, the increase in child support payments from the fathers of children in poverty and receiving public assistance doubled, from 8 percent to 16 percent. Likewise, the federal Office of Child Support Enforcement (OCSE) reported that the proportion of single mothers in poverty receiving public assistance and a child support payment nearly doubled between 1978 and 1998, from 13 percent to 25 percent. Thus, efforts to strengthen child support enforcement have not increased payment from all fathers but have increased support payments from fathers whose children live in poverty and are receiving public assistance.

Stronger enforcement of child support orders has increased the incomes of single mothers. One study found that the increases in child support payments between 1978 and 1998 increased the incomes of single mothers by 16 percent and the incomes of single

mothers with a high school degree or less by 21 percent. On the other hand, even perfect enforcement would leave one-third to one-half of single mothers poor and insecure. This is true for several reasons. First, support orders rarely keep pace with inflation or with increases in the living standards of noncustodial fathers. Custodial mothers and children receive too little financial support by almost any standard. Second, many fathers with support orders live in poverty: 30 percent of noncustodial fathers earn less than $14,000. Of all mothers who receive child support payments, mothers in poverty receiving public assistance obtain less support than others. Among mothers receiving public assistance who were supposed to receive child support payments, only 5 percent obtain their full award, while about 40 percent do not collect anything. Thus, the women who most need child support income are least likely to receive it.

Third, many women in poverty do not and will likely never have a child support order. This is true for several reasons. One is fear of violence. Some mothers, particularly those who experienced violence at the hands of their male partners or husbands during their marriage or relationship, will not apply for child support because they fear their ex-partners will be violent toward them if they do. A recent study found that 30 percent of all women stated that they were fearful during their negotiations for child support, with few race and class differences among them. These women's fears caused some of them to reduce their requests for child support. There is a statistically significant relationship between feeling fearful during negotiations for child support and receipt of child support. Only 6 percent of the women who reported being fearful received regular child support, in contrast to 34 percent of those who did not report fear during negotiations for child support.

Some mothers do not have support orders because they do not want to reveal the identity of their child's father. The 1996 PRAWORA stipulates that any mother applying for public assistance must reveal the identity of her child's father. Since the purpose of paternity establishment is to assign child support obligations to biological fathers, the second condition is that mothers who need public assistance must cooperate in establishing, modifying, and enforcing the support orders for their children. The PRA-WORA requires states to reduce a family's public assistance grant by at least 25 percent when a mother fails to comply with these rules; it also permits states to deny the family's grant altogether. Women may fear that revealing their child's father may result in abuse for themselves or their children. They may not want to seek child support because they have chosen to parent alone or with another man or woman. They may know their child's father is impoverished and may fear exposing him to harsh penalties when he cannot pay what a court stipulates.

Finally, women's vulnerability to poverty and homelessness is increasingly viewed as resulting from an unfair division of resources that leaves mothers and children with too little and absent fathers with more than their appropriate share. When parents separate, the average dollar income of the noncustodial parent, usually the father, is generally much higher than the income of the custodial parent. In this view, child support payments can help, but they rarely equalize the loss of income from the family's splitting. With no child support payments at all, the husband's living standard would rise to 2.33 times the poverty level, while the mother and children fall to 60 percent of the poverty line.

SUCCESSFUL REFORM?

Since the mid-1970s, homelessness has increased faster among single-mother families than among any other group. Their children now account for nearly 40 percent of the homeless population in the United States. One of the reasons for this is that noncustodial parents, mostly fathers, do not pay the child support they owe. If only 80 percent of the child support owed were collected, child poverty in the United States would be reduced by almost half. However, child support reforms of the past thirty years have focused on collecting support from unwed fathers whose children receive public assistance. It is likely that these children will continue to receive little or no child support because their fathers are, on average, more disadvantaged than the parents of children who already receive child support.

—*Susan L. Thomas*

Further Reading

Beller, A. H., & Graham, J. W. (1993). *Small change: The economics of child support.* New Haven, CT: Yale University Press.

Cancian, M., & Meyer, D. (1996). Changing policy, changing practice: Mothers' incomes and child support orders. *Journal of Marriage and the Family, 58*(3), 618–627.

Davis, M., & Kraham, S. J. (1995, Summer). Protecting women's welfare in the face of violence, *Journal of Marriage and the Family, 22,* 1141–1157.

Edin, K. (1995). Single mothers and child support: The possibilities and limits of child support policy. *Children and Youth Services Review, 17*(1–2), 203–230.

Garfinkel, I., McLanahan, S., Meyer, D., & Seltzer, J. (1998). *Fathers under fire: The revolution in child support enforcement.* New York: Russell Sage Foundation.

Mink, G. (1998). *Welfare's end.* Ithaca, NY: Cornell University Press.

Mink, G. (Ed.). (1999). *Whose welfare?* Ithaca, NY: Cornell University Press.

Raphael, J. (1996, Spring). Domestic violence and welfare receipt: Toward a new feminist theory of welfare dependency. *Harvard Women's Law Journal, 19,* 201–227.

Robins, P. (1992). Why did child support award levels decline from 1978 to 1985? *Journal of Human Resources, 27*(2), 362–379.

Sidel, R. (1998). *Keeping women and children last.* New York: Penguin Books.

Sorenson, E. (1997, November). A national profile of nonresident fathers and their ability to pay child support. *Journal of Marriage and the Family, 59,* 785–797.

U.S. Department of Health and Human Services (HHS), Office of Child Support Enforcement (1999). *Child support enforcement: Twenty-third annual report to Congress.* Washington, DC: Government Printing Office.

▣ CHILDREN

See Child Care; Child Support; Children, Education of; Children, Impact of Homelessness on; Families; Foster Care; Parenting; Youth, Homeless

▣ CHILDREN, EDUCATION OF

An estimated one million children in the United States experience homelessness in a given year.

Children who are homeless confront abject poverty and experience a constellation of risks that have a devastating impact on their well-being. Research studies have linked homelessness among children to hunger and poor nutrition, health problems, psychological problems, developmental delays, and academic underachievement. Such factors often converge in the educational problems confronting young people who are homeless. In addressing these issues, the federal Education for Homeless Children and Youth program was designed both to alleviate those obstacles and to enhance these students' ability to achieve academic success. However, ongoing challenges to service delivery remain.

EDUCATIONAL PROBLEMS CONFRONTING HOMELESS CHILDREN

School is especially important for homeless children because it is one of the few factors in their lives that provide stability, structure, and accomplishment during a time of great upheaval. When families lose their housing, they are often forced to move from one temporary placement to another. When children simultaneously lose both their home and school, they are doubly unanchored. They lose their neighborhood friends and have to make new ones. At the same time, they must get used to a new school, new teacher, and schoolwork that is often discontinuous with their previous curriculum. The instability associated with homelessness makes regular school attendance and success a daunting challenge for these children. Research studies investigating these impacts show that homeless children have poorer rates of school attendance, lower scores on standardized achievement tests, and higher rates of grade retention than their permanently housed peers.

THE EDUCATION FOR HOMELESS CHILDREN AND YOUTH PROGRAM

When the United States Congress passed the first comprehensive legislation to aid the homeless, it acknowledged the threat of homelessness to school success. The 1987 Stewart B. McKinney Homeless Assistance Act, and its subsequent amendments,

authorized a range of programs and benefits to provide urgently needed relief to the nation's unhoused and poor. It spoke to the educational needs of children and youth who are homeless by providing formula grants for states to carry out the Education for Homeless Children and Youth program, or EHCY (Subtitle VII-B). It also provided grants to local education agencies to help homeless young people enroll in, attend, and succeed in school. In 2001, the McKinney Act was reauthorized as part of the "No Child Left Behind" Act; it was also renamed the McKinney-Vento Homeless Assistance Act.

In reauthorizing the Act in 2001, Congress reaffirmed these intentions by substantially strengthening the EHCY program. Changes were based on proven practices contributed by educators from across the country, aimed at improving stability, access, and support. The program mandates that homeless children and youth have equal access to the same free and appropriate public education as their permanently housed peers, including preschool. It requires all state and local education agencies to review and revise any laws, regulations, practices, and policies that may act as a barrier to the enrollment, attendance, or academic success of homeless students. It requires states to ensure that local educational agencies do not create a separate education system for children and youth who are homeless. It mandates equal access to educational programs and services. It also specifies that homeless children and youth be provided with the opportunity to meet state and local academic achievement standards and be included in state- and district-wide assessments and accountability systems. One section of the "Statement of Policy" mandated by Congress calls for the removal of identified obstacles to school enrollment, attendance, and success, noting practical issues such as transportation, guardianship, and immunization requirements.

Obstacles to Enrollment and Regular School Attendance

The EHCY program addresses the need for policies and procedures to identify children and youth who are homeless. Each state education agency is required to have a State Coordinator of Education of Homeless Children and Youth to identify all such young people in their state, assess their educational needs, facilitate cooperation between state and local education agencies, and collaborate with other education, child development, and preschool programs, as well as other service providers, to ensure comprehensive services. Each school district must also designate a liaison to ensure that its homeless students are identified (by school personnel and through coordination with agencies and other agencies) and enrolled in school. The liaison must also ensure that they receive educational services for which they are eligible, including Head Start and other preschool programs, and family literacy programs such as Even Start. The liaison also ensures referrals to health, mental health, dental, and other appropriate services.

The EHCY program also mandates that parents of homeless children be informed of their children's rights under the McKinney-Vento Act. Posters must be displayed in places where homeless families might congregate, such as emergency shelters and soup kitchens. One key issue pertains to school selection. Children have the right to stay in their current schools to the extent feasible, unless they or their parents choose otherwise. They also have the right to attend any school that housed students in the same geographic area are eligible to attend. If there is a dispute, the district must enroll the child in the school of his or her choice, pending resolution.

For children transferring into local schools, the program mandates timely enrollment: Children have the right to enroll immediately, even if they lack required documents such as school records, medical records, or even proof of residency within the school district. For children who are staying in their school of origin, the EHCY program mandates districts to provide transportation, if required.

Obstacles to School Success

The state coordinator must provide technical assistance, in coordination with local liaisons, to all local education agencies to ensure compliance with a number of requirements: school choice, feasibility

determination, enrollment and disputes over enrollment, records, comparable services, coordination, local liaison duties, review and revision of policies, and the prohibition on segregation from students who are housed. States are also required to award competitive subgrants to local education agencies, based on need and application quality. Not surprisingly, research has found that school districts that had received McKinney-Vento subgrants provided a broader range of educational and recreational services than districts that were not awarded federal funds. Funding from Title I provisions and community organizations also enhanced services by school districts.

The Segregation Issue

The concept of separate schools for homeless students is one of the most controversial topics in the education of students who are homeless. States are prohibited from segregating homeless students in separate schools, or even in separate programs or settings within schools, except for short periods of time. Subtitle VII-B maintains, "Homelessness alone should not be sufficient reason to separate students from the mainstream school environment." However, states that were operating special schools for the homeless prior to the 2001 reauthorization—such as Arizona—were grandfathered under the new law and may continue to do so.

ONGOING CHALLENGES TO SERVICE DELIVERY

As a result of the McKinney-Vento Education for Homeless Children and Youth program, school access has significantly improved for these young people. Even so, obstacles continue to prevent them from achieving regular attendance and academic success. The U.S. Department of Education issued a report in 2002 on state and local efforts to serve the educational needs of homeless children and youth and overcome barriers that affect their enrollment, attendance, and school success. Titled *Reducing Barriers for Homeless Children and Youth for Access and Achievement,* the report noted that "transportation remains the most prominent enrollment barrier for homeless children and youth" (Vol. 1, p. 18). It also reported that "homeless students' frequent moves from school to school were their most significant barrier to academic success" (Executive Summary, p. 4). Other major barriers to school success included the lack of awareness and sensitivity among school administrators and teachers to the specific educational needs of homeless children, and children's lack of an appropriate study area in which to complete school assignments. Moreover, when state coordinators were asked to what extent eligible students had difficulty accessing educational services, more than half identified specific programs and services as particularly problematic for homeless children. The programs that were difficult for homeless students to access included special education, Head Start and other publicly funded preschool programs, "gifted and talented" programs, Even Start and other family literacy programs, and programs for English language learners. Finally, despite the 1994 McKinney requirement that states remove preschool enrollment barriers for homeless children, only 15 percent of homeless preschoolers were enrolled in such programs in 2002. According to the United States Department of Education, "preschool age homeless children are greatly underserved by homeless education programs" (Volume 2, p.1).

THE FUTURE

Schools and communities have a vital role to play in meeting the educational needs of unhoused children and in mitigating the potentially harmful effects of homelessness. Children and youth who are homeless require educational stability and the opportunity to maintain regular and consistent attendance in school,

---

The McKinney-Vento Homeless Assistance Act, Subtitle VII–B

Subtitle B: Education for Homeless Children and Youths

Sec. 721. Statement of Policy

The following is the policy of the Congress:

1. Each State educational agency shall ensure that each child of a homeless individual and each homeless youth has equal access to the same free, appropriate public education including a public preschool education, as provided to other children and youth.

2. In any State that has a compulsory residency requirement as a component of the State's compulsory school attendance laws or other laws, regulations, practices, or policies that may act as a barrier to the enrollment, attendance, or success in school of homeless children and homeless youth, the State will review and undertake steps to revise such laws, regulations, practices, or policies to ensure that homeless children and youths are afforded the same free, appropriate public education as provided to other children and youths.

3. Homelessness alone is not sufficient reason to separate students from the mainstream school environment.

4. Homeless children and youths should have access to the education and other services that such children and youths need to ensure that such children and youths have an opportunity to meet the same challenging State student academic achievement standards to which all students are held.

Source: Text of the McKinney-Vento Legislation. (2001). Retrieved November 18, 2003, from http://www.serve.org/nche/downloads/Reauthorizationtext.pdf

---

so that they acquire the skills necessary to escape poverty and lead productive, healthy lives as adults. Because their educational needs and problems are many and the solutions are complex, no agency or school can solve these problems alone. These needs can be best met through support, coordination, and collaboration among the various local agencies that work with homeless families, as well as communication with agencies at the state level. A coordinated model of service delivery would enhance the provision of programs and services to homeless children and their families.

At the very least, the mandates set forth in the McKinney-Vento Act should be enforced to promote continuity of educational services. School personnel must provide outreach services to locate and identify homeless children and thus minimize the disruption to their education. Parents should be informed of their children's rights, particularly with regard to remaining in their current schools. Homeless children should not have the additional instability of a mid-year school shift. Instead, the goal should be for them to remain in their original schools, with familiar teachers, curricula, and peers. For children who continue to attend their original schools, transportation problems should be expeditiously resolved, attendance should be monitored, and follow-up services should be provided if attendance is not satisfactory. For children who transfer to new schools, appropriate placement must be made quickly and every effort made to ensure that students receive services comparable to those given to permanently housed students. There must be effective procedures for transferring student records. Special attention must be paid to bilingual students and those who need special education services.

Ultimately, however, broader issues must be addressed. The United States must develop a coherent and comprehensive national family policy with a strong concern for the social problems confronting children in poverty. There must be a more serious and sustained investment in children by the federal government helping order to secure promising futures for them. The federal government must recognize that programs to reduce or eliminate poverty would, in the long term, cost society less than the persistence of current levels of poverty and its consequences.

Whatever vulnerabilities to homelessness may exist, an abundance of research continues to indicate that homelessness is associated with deficiencies in six areas: the availability of affordable permanent housing, the opportunity to earn an adequate income, education to prepare people to be productive, safe communities, a supportive and stable childhood environment, and accessible health and mental health services. Policies must be developed to meet the needs of families as a whole and, at the same time, the needs of children within them. In view of the continuing crisis in the nation's housing system, and the great suffering that vulnerable children who lack permanent housing continue to endure each night, there is an urgent need for action.

—*Yvonne Rafferty*

Further Reading

Children's Defense Fund. (2003). *The state of America's children: Yearbook 2002.* Washington, DC: Author.

Masten, A. S., Sesma, A., Jr., Si-Asar, R., Lawrence, C., Miliotis, D., & Dionne, J. A. (1997). Education risks for children experiencing homelessness. *Journal of School Psychology, 35,* 27–46.

Rafferty, Y. (2000). Educating homeless students: An overview of legal entitlements and federal protections. In R. Mickelson (Ed.), *Children on the streets of the Americas: Globalization, homelessness, and education in the United States, Brazil and Cuba* (pp. 107–117). New York: Routledge.

U. S. Department of Education (2002, October). *The education for homeless children and youth program: Learning to succeed.* Elementary and Secondary Education Division, Planning and Evaluation Services, Washington, DC. Retrieved January 21, 2003, from http://www.ed.gov/offices/OUS/PES/ed_for_disadvantaged.html

◉ CHILDREN, IMPACT OF HOMELESSNESS ON

In most American cities, homeless children are situated in a family shelter or transitional housing, although a minority can be found sleeping with other family members in such places as campgrounds or cars. According to a 1989 Government Accounting Office report, on any given night, upwards of 200,000 children are homeless—not counting unaccompanied homeless adolescents. In the course of a year, roughly one million U.S. children will experience an episode of homelessness.

A "first generation" of research on homeless children, mostly conducted during the 1980s, identified problems that children were experiencing while homeless and raised concerns over their unmet needs. A second generation of research, funded by the federal government during the 1990s, attempted to more accurately pinpoint the effects of homelessness, per se, on children.

While shelter life can be deeply troubling, it is but one of many stressors experienced by children living in poverty. In most cases, living in a shelter is only moderately stressful for youngsters compared to an event such as being exposed to violence, which can have a pronounced negative effect on children's mental health. Although homelessness is unlikely to have a long-term effect on children's cognitive or motor development (as found by Cynthia Garcia Coll and colleagues), it can certainly have an impact on their mental health. According to John Buckner and colleagues, living in a shelter appears to cause children psychological distress such as anxiety and depression, especially for those who are of school age. Children age six and older are usually more affected than younger children, due to greater awareness of their living circumstances and because of the possible shame they may feel about it. Homelessness is likely to affect children's academic performance to the extent that it impedes their school attendance, among other factors. This may vary from city to city, depending on the level of intervention in place to ensure that homeless children regularly attend school.

As Linda Weinreb and colleagues have found, the congregate nature of family shelters makes homeless children more likely to contract communicable illnesses such as colds, ear infections, and diarrhea. Chronic illnesses such as asthma are also more prevalent among them. According to Buckner and Bassuk (1997), their rate of severe mental illness is no higher than that of low-income housed children. However, low-income and homeless children as a group show elevated rates compared to children in the general population. Moreover, they are unlikely to be receiving the mental health treatment they need.

There is some evidence that a "dose-response" relationship exists between length of time in shelter and level of distress (Buckner et al., 1999). In other words, in children who remain homeless for some time, symptoms appear to gradually increase, then level off after a few months. It is unclear at this time what specific aspects of shelter experience are stressful for children. Shelters vary widely in their quality and size, factors that likely influence the degree of stress incurred.

The majority of homeless children are with a single parent, typically the mother, although two parent families are somewhat common in certain areas of the country, particularly the Southwest. The parents' mental health and stressors can also affect their children, especially younger ones. Parenting is made more stressful by shelter rules and the watchful eyes of others. A reciprocal interplay between the mental

A child in New York City in February 2002 waiting for a bus to take him and his family to a shelter.
Source: Mark Peterson/Corbis; used with permission.

health status of a mother and that of her children can often be observed among homeless families: A mother's psychological distress can affect her children's well-being and the behavior and distress of her children can, in turn, affect her own coping abilities.

GUIDANCE FOR FUTURE RESEARCH

Research conducted to date on homeless children has illuminated a fair amount of knowledge on current needs and the impact of shelter life. Future research should be guided by relevant policy and programmatic questions aimed at drawing clear conclusions on how to better help homeless children. The value of conducting more refined observational research without clear practical benefits is questionable. Researchers have not systematically examined what happens to children who are separated from their families as a result of a homeless episode (K. Cowal et al., 2002). Prior studies of such families have not included the separated youths, largely due to the complicated logistics that would be involved.

Future studies might also focus on better understanding which factors influence the experience of homelessness for children, including type of shelter, length of time homeless, parents' mental health, and so on. Such research could try to identify the most at-risk subgroups of homeless children, those who might be targeted for mental health interventions. Interventions that address the needs of homeless children are sorely needed, and should continue after children become re-housed, since these relationships take time to build. These interventions should be grounded in empirical research and undergo rigorous evaluation to ensure they have beneficial effects.

Further complicating the picture, homelessness can be a mixed or, in some ways, positive experience for families. While living in a shelter is often the result of a family life crisis, it is not always a negative event. In some instances, time in a shelter can help some families develop needed relationships with service providers, offer a respite from domestic violence and residential instability, and facilitate efforts to secure permanent housing and benefits. Shelters can provide a useful setting for intensive, time-limited services to families in crisis. But these potential benefits notwithstanding, shelter life is usually stressful and unpleasant for families. Societal efforts at reducing family homelessness would certainly include increasing the affordable housing supply. Other solutions might address broader issues faced by low-income families: increasing the wages of low-income workers, providing decent child care as well as transportation alternatives for parents who work, and reducing community and family violence.

—*John C. Buckner*

Further Reading

Bassuk, E. L., Weinreb, L. F., Dawson, R., Perloff, J. N., & Buckner, J. C. (1997). Determinants of behavior in homeless and low-income housed preschool children. *Pediatrics, 100,* 92–100.

Buckner, J. C., & Bassuk, E. L. (1997). Mental disorders and service utilization among youths from homeless and low-income housed families. *Journal of the American Academy of Child and Adolescent Psychiatry, 36,* 890–900.

Buckner, J. C., Bassuk, E. L., Weinreb, L., & Brooks, M. (1999). Homelessness and its relation to the mental health and behavior of low-income school aged children. *Developmental Psychology, 35,* 246–257.

Buckner, J. C., Bassuk, E. L., & Weinreb, L. F. (2001). Predictors of academic achievement among homeless and low-income housed children. *Journal of School Psychology, 39,* 45–69.

Cowal, K., Shinn, M., Weitzman, B. C., Stojanovic, D., & Labay, L. (2002). Mother-child separations among homeless and housed families receiving public assistance in New York City. *American Journal of Community Psychology, 30,* 711–730.

Garcia Coll, C., Buckner, J. C., Brooks, M. G., Weinreb, L. F., & Bassuk, E. L. (1998). The developmental status and adaptive behavior of homeless and low-income housed infants and toddlers. *American Journal of Public Health, 88,* 1371–1374.

General Accounting Office. (1989). *Children and youths: About 68,000 homeless and 186,000 in shared housing at any given time.* Washington, DC: Author.

Masten, A. S., Miliotis, D., Graham-Bermann, S. A., Ramirez, M., & Neemann, J. (1993). Children in homeless families: Risks to mental health and development. *Journal of Consulting and Clinical Psychology, 61,* 335–343.

National Center on Family Homelessness. (1999). *Homeless children: A public policy report from The Better Homes Fund.* Newton, MA: Author.

Rafferty, Y., & Shinn, M. (1991). The impact of homelessness on children. *American Psychologist, 46,* 1170–1179.

Weinreb, L., Goldberg, R., Bassuk, E., & Perloff, J. (1998). Determinants of health and service use patterns in homeless and low-income housed children. *Pediatrics, 102,* 554–562.

▣ CINEMA

See Appendix 2: Filmography of American Narrative and Documentary Films on Homelessness; Images of Homelessness in Contemporary Documentary Film; Images of Homelessness in Narrative Film, History of

▣ CONTINUUM OF CARE

The "continuum of care" concept came to national attention early in the Clinton administration, when the Department of Housing and Urban Development (HUD) published *Priority Home! The Federal Plan to Break the Cycle of Homelessness.* The concept encompasses two quite different meanings, one related to service availability, and the other related to pathways that homeless people may take through a service network.

With respect to service availability, a continuum of care (hereafter "CoC") is a system of services within a community that contains all the major elements for averting and ending homelessness. These elements include prevention, outreach and drop-in programs, emergency shelter, transitional housing, permanent supportive housing for people with disabilities, and affordable housing without supports. The CoC concept also calls for a system that is community-wide—that is, not just within one or two agencies—and brings all the elements together, working in a coordinated fashion to assure that people get the services and supports they need, either to avoid homelessness or to leave it permanently.

With respect to service pathways, a continuum of care is sometimes interpreted to mean that individual homeless people are expected to traverse *all* the components in a linear fashion, progressing from emergency to transitional shelter and then either to regular or supported housing situations. In the original formulation of the idea, everyone would begin with an assessment stage, but few systems ever did this. In reality, the service pathway is a fairly common meaning of the continuum concept if one counts systems that place almost all homeless people into emergency shelter first, before making opportunities available for transitional and permanent housing, with or without supports.

This entry focuses primarily on the "service availability" meaning of CoC, its components, and its recent changes, including those due to federal funding policies. As to the "service pathways" aspect, several new approaches are also addressed here—among them the "housing first," which offers the primary alternative model to an individual's stepwise progression through the components of a given CoC system.

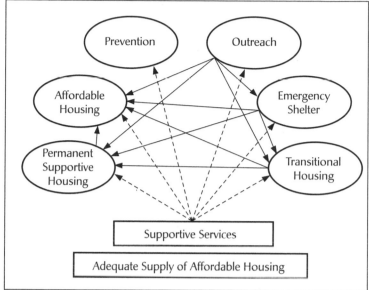

Figure 1. Model of a Continuum of Care

COMPONENTS OF A CONTINUUM OF CARE

What constitutes a service network in a given community? Figure 1 illustrates the typical components and the links between them. The solid arrows in Figure 1 indicate pathways along which people may move from one component to another. The dotted arrows from "supportive services" to each component indicate that all components may include supportive services of many varieties. The bar at the bottom, "adequate supply of affordable housing," is included to signify that the success of each CoC component in preventing or ending homelessness depends on being able to locate housing in the community that is affordable for people who are homeless or at risk for homelessness.

Prevention

Homelessness prevention for families and individuals at imminent risk should be an integral part of any CoC, but relatively few communities devote significant resources to prevention. Mainstream agencies dealing with alcohol, drug, and mental health problems and foster care, as well as prisons and jails—critical components in effective prevention of homelessness—vary in regard to discharge planning efforts and coordination. Without provision of housing resources and the supportive services to keep people in housing once they are discharged, these agencies often become feeders for homeless programs rather than serving as a line of defense against homelessness for their clients.

Outreach

Outreach and engagement strategies are critical for reaching the hardest-to-serve homeless people and bringing them into the homeless assistance system. Outreach focuses on finding homeless people who might not use services, due to lack of awareness or active avoidance, and who would otherwise be ignored or underserved. Outreach programs often serve persons with mental health and/or substance abuse issues who may be highly vulnerable and often cannot meet the requirements of traditional service providers—or bring themselves to trust them.

Outreach efforts focus on establishing rapport, developing trust, caring for immediate needs, providing linkages to services and resources, and helping people get connected to mainstream services and, ultimately, to the community. Some outreach programs are designed to find individuals and link them to other providers, while outreach workers in other programs serve as clients' case managers during their participation in various programs and services.

Emergency Shelter

For many people, emergency shelters are the point of entry into a homeless assistance system. Most are congregate buildings, but some may offer hotel or motel vouchers and short-stay apartments. Emergency shelters generally have an official length of stay ranging from one to ninety days; however, many chronically homeless people manage to live in them for years. Communities typically dedicate separate shelters to singles and families, or to single men and women with or without children, unless the community is very small. In addition, some communities have specialized shelters for veterans, victims of domestic abuse, teen parents, chronic substance abusers, or runaway youth.

Transitional Housing

A part of many communities' response to homelessness, transitional housing provides time-limited placement (usually for up to twenty-four months) for persons who are believed to need help resolving some issues before they will be able to maintain themselves in permanent housing. Transitional housing facilities differ from permanent supportive housing (the next CoC component) in their time-limited nature—people must move on to other housing within twenty-four months. They differ from regular affordable housing in the community because they offer supportive services connected to residence. Within these settings, residents have access to intensive services, often provided on-site or through community partners. These range from alcohol and drug abuse treatment to financial counseling and employment services. As residents become stabilized, providers are expected to help them find permanent housing.

The role of transitional housing in CoCs has evolved, with some communities having second thoughts about its importance as well as about which types of clients might profit from it. These communities are trying to reduce their reliance on transitional housing facilities for many homeless households, particularly families. Instead, programs place families in housing units where they will be able to stay indefinitely, and to which they hold the lease. The programs offer transitional supportive services as needed until families are stabilized and able to maintain housing on their own. Yet other communities continue to develop and provide transitional housing facilities and view them as a key component in their CoC.

Permanent Supportive Housing

Permanent supportive housing (PSH) combines housing assistance and supportive services for homeless persons with disabilities, primarily serving individuals (and increasingly their families) who have serious mental illnesses, chronic substance abuse problems, physical disabilities, AIDS and related diseases, and combinations thereof. Permanent supportive housing programs use many housing configurations, including scattered-site apartments, dedicated buildings (in which every unit is a PSH unit), and mixed-use buildings (in which as many as 75 to 80 percent of the units are not occupied by formerly homeless people). Supportive services are also provided on-site or through partnering agencies, depending on individual and community needs.

Affordable Housing

Housing without services (that is, "regular" housing) that is affordable to poor people is the key to ending homelessness for most of those who pass through homeless assistance networks. Until recently, very few communities tried to systematically increase the supply of affordable housing. But as more communities acknowledge a crisis in housing affordability, more are using rent subsidies, tax credits, housing trust funds, targeted tax levies, and other mechanisms to expand the supply.

EXPANSION OF HOMELESS ASSISTANCE NETWORKS

CoCs for homeless people in communities across the United States have developed substantially since the mid-1990s, thanks to expanded federal funding for homeless assistance programs and to HUD's requirement that to secure these funds, communities must organize themselves to provide coherent systems of care.

In 1987, Congress passed the first federal law specifically addressing homelessness, the Stewart B. McKinney Homeless Assistance Act of 1987, later named the McKinney-Vento Homeless Assistance Act. McKinney-Vento has been a major federal avenue for supporting the development of homeless assistance systems. Its funding levels since the mid-1990s have been slightly more than $1 billion a year.

Two McKinney-Vento programs focus on emergency services. The Emergency Shelter Grant Program's funding is one staple; these monies also sup-

port homelessness prevention activities, to some extent. Emergency Food and Shelter Program (EFSP) funds may also be used for these purposes, as well as for emergency feeding programs. The EFSP (which began in 1983 as a one-time emergency measure and was extended six times before the McKinney Act made it a permanent program) became the mainstay of homeless assistance through most of the 1980s.

By 1987, when the McKinney Act was passed, provider experience with homeless individuals and families had shown that for some homeless people, short-term emergency shelter was not enough to end their homelessness. Based on this experience, Congress included additional program types in the original McKinney Act, and McKinney-Vento added still more program types. The intention was to offer a federal incentive for local communities to develop comprehensive homeless assistance systems. Some of these new program types focused on people with disabilities, improving their access to both transitional and permanent supportive housing through the Supported Housing Program. To increase the permanent supportive housing supply for this population, Congress added the Shelter Plus Care funds program. In addition, several provisions were created for using Section 8 Moderate Rehabilitation grants to increase the supply of single-room occupancy units and give homeless individuals priority for them.

Also part of the initial premise was that once federally financed programs had proved their merit locally, local governments and other funding organizations would step up and assume responsibility for their survival. However, most programs begun with these federal funds continue to rely on them, thus creating tensions between the need to continue funding for existing programs and the desire to develop new programs and approaches.

For the first six or seven years of federal funding for homeless assistance programs, HUD did not impose any requirements for systematic planning and comprehensiveness at the local level. Funds for HUD's transitional and permanent supportive housing programs are distributed through national competitions. Initially, individual programs applied to these national competitions. Most communities could not be described as having "a system," and providers developed programs for which they saw a need and could find money, without regard to the larger pattern of services in the community.

Just as there was no comprehensive planning or intentional structure to the array of homeless assistance programs and services before the mid-1980s, initial uses of funds under McKinney and later McKinney-Vento increased capacity but were not structured to "complete" a service system. Nor were they structured to assure that homeless people received all the care they needed that the system had to offer.

In contrast, since 1996 HUD has used a competitive application process for the supportive housing programs authorized by McKinney-Vento to promote the development of CoCs. By requiring communities to come together to submit a single comprehensive application, HUD has stimulated many to move toward greater structure and a more strategic vision of their programs and services for homeless people. This increased system structure and rationality is expected to improve services for homeless people and to increase the chances that their needs will be met.

SERVICE PATHWAYS

Homeless people in most communities still enter the assistance system through emergency shelters. Then, if they cannot return to independent living in a short while, they may go on to transitional housing and perhaps ultimately to permanent supportive housing. But in recent years, some communities have developed several alternative pathways. Two of these are oriented toward families, two toward chronically homeless single adults.

Options for Families

The first alternative for families separates transitional *services* from transitional *facilities*. This approach is used for families who are capable of returning to independent living. Families needing more help after leaving emergency shelter are placed directly into housing units where they can continue to live after

services end. This is coupled with receipt of transitional services as long as necessary (up to two years) to help them stabilize their situation.

The second option, for parents with long histories of homelessness and failure to retain housing without supportive services, is permanent supportive housing for families. In both alternatives, the families bypass residence in a transitional housing facility.

Options for Singles

For chronically homeless single adults, the goal of the new alternatives is to avoid even emergency shelter. Again two alternatives exist, both of which make few or no demands on their residents for service participation or "improvement"—a principle known as "low/no demand." "Safe havens" are one example; these residences take people directly from the streets. Residents are not expected to remain in these safe havens indefinitely. Most safe havens have an official two-year time limit, but most will allow a resident to stay longer if necessary. "Housing first" approaches move people directly from the streets into permanent supportive housing units that are expected to be their permanent home. Tenants may, but do not have, to use a variety of supportive services. Recognizing the needs of these hard-to-serve homeless subgroups, some communities around the country are developing one or both, while other communities and provider groups remain skeptical.

"Low/No Demand" Options

Controversy surrounds shelter and housing programs that place few or no demands on their clients: to undertake certain activities, to change their behavior, or even to make "progress" at all. These programs do not lack supportive services—indeed, many are quite service-intensive—but they are merely offered, not required. Most often the need for such programs is discussed in terms of system entry. It is indeed an issue at that point, but in fact, such programs are evolving along the entire CoC, including the permanent supportive housing component.

The basic idea of a low/no demand facility is that offering a place for extremely vulnerable peo-

Integrating Group Homes into Neighborhoods

PORTLAND, Ore. (ANS)—Social service providers increasingly are recognizing the benefits of integrating homeless women and children, psychiatric patients and youthful offenders into residential communities.

Locating support networks close to or where the people who need them live makes sense, agencies say. Transportation is no longer an issue and help is close at hand in a crisis.

But established neighborhoods are often wary of low-income or challenging newcomers. So, looking for ways to ease the tensions and avert problems the arrival of these "group homes" often engender, a pilot program in Portland used mediators to get neighbors, developers and facility residents talking about their worries.

Because of client confidentiality considerations, agencies often cannot provide people with much information about a given facility. But when they can, the Siting Dispute Resolution Program appears to offer a chance for understanding.

The eight-month pilot project that ended in September brought neighbors, developers, social service workers and residents of proposed facilities together to hash out worries and ease fears. Often, non-binding "good neighbor agreements" were written up that outlined everyone's responsibilities and how the groups would work together.

"Siting is a huge issue," said Judith Mowry, who helped mediate the eight test cases. "We have a community struggling with complex issues, like How much citizen involvement do people have? How do we provide services to folks that need assistance? How do we deal with adjudicated youth and psychiatric facilities? How do we deal with serious felons who are living in residential neighborhoods?

"This is the first project we've seen in the country that tries to bring in collaborative processes to address these challenges," she said.

Mediators say the first step in resolving a dispute is giving participants the tools for dialogue. There is a longing and a need in many communities to talk about policy and how to share the load of these facilities but little understanding of how to begin, they say. "We're not skilled innately in dealing with the collaborative process," Mowry explained. Helping neighbors design and facilitate public meetings and making them work are some of the skills mediators say they can teach people facing difficult changes.

For example, Portland mediators worked hard to hammer out an agreement between developers of a proposed low-income housing project and residents of Portland's Boise neighborhood. Upset with how similar facilities nearby were being managed, neighbors in the low-income community were at odds with the idea of another one.

"During many hours and weeks of work, we identified the concerns and developed common areas of agreement," said Barbara Hunt, who coordinated the resolution program for the city. "We then came up with a workable neighborhood agreement that talks about how the facility would be managed, and how they would work together."

In the Concordia neighborhood, mediators brought developers planning to build a drug store together with neighbors who wanted a grocery store. By teaching the neighborhood association how to leverage the builder's interest in retail development with their own, the neighborhood got an agreement for a small grocery adjacent to the drug store.

Critical to this kind of success is getting people together before building plans are finalized and permits secured, Hart said. Often, neighbors are notified when the planning process has already begun. Change at that point is costly and difficult.

"Having a conversation early means the antagonism goes way down," Hart continued. "People's fears are addressed and reduced, and the stereotypes are able to be put aside because they're dealing with real people."

Of course, not every case has a picture perfect ending. Mediators were brought in at the late stages of a conflict between neighbors and a local convalescent care facility that wanted to expand. They worked with developers, the facility and the neighbors and came up with a revised plan that moved parking to the back of the building, modified the front of the facility and those units that offended neighbors.

Nevertheless, the groups could not agree on the size of the facility. The city ultimately gave the developers the okay for the size they wanted. Hart still sees the benefit of having gotten everyone together.

"They didn't get 100 percent but [they got] the opportunity for tinkering that wouldn't have happened otherwise," she pointed out. "And that's part of the goal. Maybe people won't always agree, but if they truly understand the point at which they agree—that's what we're looking for."

Affiliated with the city's Office of Neighborhood Involvement, the siting program has received permanent funding. The office has also been selected by the non-profit group Partners for Democratic Change to receive additional training and assistance in collaborative problem solving.

Source: "Mediation Can Ease Integration of Group Homes Into Neighborhoods," The American News Service, n.d.

ple to come in off the street is better for them, and better for the community, than leaving them on the street. In parallel with traditional shelters, this set of services works to assist chronically homeless persons with mental illness and/or substance abuse problems who might otherwise be excluded or hard to place.

For such programs, the problems of attracting and retaining chronically homeless people often vary with different subgroups. Substance abusers may be willing to enter facilities, but not if they have to be clean and sober, and not if the staff are going to try to make them do things they do not want to do. The challenge is to keep them in the program and reduce harm to self and others. Persons with major mental illnesses are much harder to attract into facilities, and considerable outreach contact may be required to win their trust. But once they accept services, they tend to retain their housing. These new low/no demand programs are often designed specifically to serve people with both problems, who are used to being rejected everywhere.

A key element of many low/no demand programs is their willingness to tolerate continued use of alcohol and drugs. Virtually all of these programs forbid substance use on the premises, and some also in the immediate vicinity of the facility, in the interest of community relations. Still, tenants are not required to be clean and sober.

Many communities and providers resist the general low/no demand approach on the grounds that people will do better if programs have expectations for their behavior, and that required participation in services is a means of helping homeless people "to help themselves." Others, following classic assumptions about substance abuse recovery, insist on requiring complete sobriety. Providers within the same community may also be split in their willingness to offer no-demand accommodations. But in the debate among providers of low/no demand shelter, those housing mentally ill people seem less involved than those working with substance abusers. The nature of mental illness, and the difficulties of attracting and winning the trust of people suffering from it, call for a different type of overture than is the case with substance abusers. The need is to make the

service attractive and nonthreatening, and to build trust gradually through very gentle approaches.

"Housing First"

"Housing first" approaches take the idea of low/no demand beyond the system entry level and place disabled chronically homeless people directly into permanent supportive housing units. Federal demonstration projects in the early 1990s showed that people with major mental illnesses could be moved directly from chronic street homelessness into permanent supportive housing, with excellent retention rates (upward of 85 percent at eighteen months). Among street homeless people, interest in moving into these units is usually very high, and once they are in, most stay. This approach bypasses the concepts of transition, preparation, and readiness. As with safe havens, "housing first" programs make many supportive services available, but do not require participation. Over the long run, most residents participate voluntarily in services—often motivated by issues that might threaten their housing stability.

Low/no demand programs play a key role in the provision of homeless services for some communities, and will probably play an even greater part in the future. These alternative approaches complement outreach and emergency shelter efforts, providing a haven for the hardest-to-serve, chronically homeless people whose needs may not be addressed by other CoC components.

IMPLICATIONS

Public policy decisions to promote a full range of homeless assistance approaches within communities have stimulated significant growth in CoCs. Linking federal funding with planning and coordination has boosted collaboration at the community level. Each component of a CoC is necessary for some homeless people. The challenges are to let people use the components they need without pushing them through components they resist, and to keep developing approaches that work for the hardest-to-serve homeless people as well as those who need only a short stay in emergency shelter to get back on their feet.

—Martha R. Burt

See also Case Management; Corporation for Supportive Housing; Housing, Transitional; "Housing First" Approach; Prevention of Homelessness: Overview; Service Integration

Further Reading

Burt, M. R., Pollack, D., Sosland, A., Mikelson, K. S., Drapa, E., Greenwalt, K, & Sharkey, P. (2001). *Evaluation of continuums of care for homeless people: Final report.* Washington, DC: Department of Housing and Urban Development. Retrieved April 16, 2003, from http://www.huduser.org/intercept.asp?loc=/Publications/pdf/continuums_of_care.pdf

Dennis, D. L., Cocozza, J. J., & Steadman, H. J. (1999). What do we know about systems integration and homelessness? In L. Fosburg & D. Dennis (Eds.), *Practical lessons: The 1998 National Symposium on Homelessness Research.* Washington, DC: U.S. Departments of Housing and Urban Development and Health and Human Services.

Erickson, S., & Page, J. (1999). To dance with grace: Outreach and engagement to persons on the street. In L. Fosburg & D. Dennis (Eds.), *Practical lessons: The 1998 National Symposium on Homelessness Research.* Washington, DC: U.S. Departments of Housing and Urban Development and Health and Human Services.

Interagency Council on the Homeless. (1994). *Priority home! The federal plan to break the cycle of homelessness.* Washington, DC: Department of Housing and Urban Development.

McMurray-Avila, M. (1997). *Organizing health services for homeless people: A practical guide.* Nashville, TN: National Health Care for the Homeless Council, Inc.

Shern, D. L., Felton, C. J., Hough, R. L., Lehman, A. F., Goldfinger, S., Valencia, E., Dennis, D. L., Straw, R., & Wood, P. A. (1997). Housing outcomes for homeless adults with mental illness: The results of the second-round McKinney programs. *Psychiatric Services, 48,* 239–241.

Shinn, M., & Baumohl, J. (1999). Rethinking the prevention of homelessness. In L. Fosburg & D. Dennis (Eds.), *Practical lessons: The 1998 National Symposium on Homelessness Research.* Washington, DC: U.S. Departments of Housing and Urban Development and Health and Human Services.

COPENHAGEN

Copenhagen Metropolitan Area is, with a population of approximately 1.2 million, the largest urban area in Denmark. The city of Copenhagen is also the capital. The metropolitan area consists of three large administrative units: The Municipality of Copenhagen, the Municipality of Frederiksberg, and the Regional County of Copenhagen. The homeless people are by and large concentrated in the Municipality of Copenhagen.

SHELTER-BASED COUNTS

Many estimates of Copenhagen's homeless population have been made, but none have been based on quantitative research methods. Rather, they have been based on social workers' general impressions or on rough calculations by researchers. Thus, no accurate count of the homeless in Copenhagen—nor in Denmark as a whole—exists. However, in the late 1990s, a national register of shelter users was developed; it has tracked such data since 2000. Still, there is no scientifically based information on, for example, the numbers of people "sleeping rough" (i.e., sleeping outside) or living doubled up.

It is known that women comprise 36 percent of shelter clients, but only 25 percent of the nationwide homeless population generally. As for the facilities themselves, almost all Copenhagen shelters provide single-occupancy rooms, spartanly furnished, with a lockable door—not the dormitory-style accommodations seen in many other countries. In a few shelters, one also might find double-occupancy rooms. Shelters are open to tenants twenty-four hours a day.

EXITS FROM HOMELESSNESS

Drawing upon information from various shelter registers, a follow-up study of people who had used Copenhagen shelters in 1988–1989 (Stax 1999) compared the shelter users' initial situations in regard to such factors as employment and income to their situations eight years later. The study found that women who had used shelters were twenty-four times more likely to have died in the eight-year period, adjusted for age, than women in Denmark as a whole. The rate for homeless males was fourteen times higher. Stax also showed that most of the deaths were linked to use of drugs. Eight years after having experienced homelessness, few people had returned to an ordinary life of employment and self-reliance. Only one in five of those alive were unemployed for less than half a year in 1996—that is,

Table 1. Shelter Space and Usage and Number of Beds in Special Housing in Copenhagen Metropolitan Area, 2001

	Total population	Shelter beds	Beds per 10,000 inhabitants	Total enrollments	Total clients enrolled	Clients per 10,000 inhabitants	Beds in special housing
Municipality of Copenhagen	499,148	589	12	2,217	1,725	35	217
Municipality of Frederiksberg	91,076	32	4	243	155	17	N.A.
Regional Council of Greater Copenhagen	615,115	79	1	691	329	5	N.A.

Source: Den Sociale Ankestyrelse, 2002; Lisberg, 2000.

about eight years after they stayed at a shelter—while 90 percent had received some kind of transfer payments during 1996. With regard to housing, between half and three-quarters were living in an ordinary flat eight years after they had stayed at a shelter. Finally, the study showed a high correlation between the use of drugs and duration of homelessness (see also Stax 2003).

Two primary measures are aimed at rehousing Copenhagen's homeless people—those with problems that make reintegration difficult, and those without such problems. For the former, "special housing for special people" offers housing arrangements targeted toward specific groups who might otherwise tend to stay continuously in shelters, such as heavy alcohol users with a psychiatric diagnosis. This strategy has been used relatively frequently in the Municipality of Copenhagen; Table 1 shows 217 places in such housing arrangements in Copenhagen. In Copenhagen, close to half the clients spend more than 120 days per year at these institutions, compared to one-third of clients nationwide. Special housing approaches are tailored for specific groups; for example, at one of the larger shelters for substance users in Copenhagen, one floor has been converted into special housing for those substance users not thought capable of skipping their drugs (primarily composed of heroine users). These tenants are not urged to look for alternative and permanent housing. Instead, it is acknowledged that they may live their entire lives here, outside the ordinary

housing market. And they can do so with no sanctions imposed due to their intake of illegal substances (Stax 2001). Another project, also located in a converted part of a shelter, targets heavy alcohol users.

The general aim of these arrangements is to allow certain groups of homeless people to live without being forced to continuously search for alternative housing. Indeed, special housing is more focused on providing room for people with their social deviance—mental health issues, heroin addiction, or a heavy alcohol use—than on reintegrating them, at least at first. Moreover, if eventual reintegration is to occur, it is seen as more likely to grow from a foundation of acceptance, rather than stigmatization.

For homeless people not considered deviant, many municipalities aim for reintegration into the ordinary housing stock. Although public authorities are not legally obligated to provide permanent housing, some municipalities have chosen to do so in practice. Very little information is available on this practice nationwide, but a recent study has focused on the practice in the Municipality of Copenhagen (Anker et al. 2002; Christensen and Stax 2002). To obtain a permanent dwelling through the Municipality of Copenhagen, an applicant must be incapable of solving his or her own housing difficulties, and must also have some problems in addition to lack of housing—mental health issues, drug problems, or trouble keeping a job. On the other hand, their problem must not be so severe that the client is seen as incapable of sustaining an independent life in ordinary housing. Furthermore, the applicant has to wait; in Copenhagen, the waiting period is about one year. It has been shown that 26 percent of the 1,171 assigned dwellings in the Municipality of Copenhagen in 2001 were assigned to people staying in shelters, and 5 percent to people temporarily accommodated by the municipality in hotels (Christensen and Stax 2002). In 2001, about 30 percent of the clients leaving shelters were moving into municipally assigned dwellings. The study also showed that the criteria for obtaining such dwellings had been tightened due to a decrease in the housing stock that the Municipality of Copenhagen can assign to.

—Tobias Børner Stax

Further Reading

Anker, J., Christensen, I., Romose, T. S., & Stax, T. B. (2002). *Kommunal boliganvisning til almene familieboliger: En analyse af praksis og politik i fire kommuner* [Municipal assignments of tenants to council housing. An analysis of practices and policies in four municipalities]. Copenhagen, Denmark: Socialforskningsinstituttet.

Christensen, I., & Stax, T. B. (2002). *Kommunal boliganvisning: En analyse af praksis og politik i Københavns Kommune* [Municipal housing assignment: An analysis of practice and policy in Copenhagen]. Copenhagen, Denmark: Socialforskningsinstituttet.

Den Social Ankestyrelse. (2002). *Brugere af botilbud efter servicelovens § 94: Personer, der er hjemløse eller som har problemer med at fungere i egen bolig* [Clients in housing arrangements established in accordance with §94 in Bill on Social Services: People homeless or unable to function in an independent dwelling]. Copenhagen, Denmark: Author.

Lisberg. (2000). *Statusbeskrivelse for hjemløseområdet i Københavns Kommune* [Status on measures for homeless in Copenhagen]. Copenhagen, Denmark: Municipality of Copenhagen.

Stax, T. B. (1999). *Én gang socialt marginaliseret, altid . . . ?* [Once socially marginalized, always . . . ?]. Copenhagen, Denmark: Socialforskningsinstituttet.

Stax, T. B. (2001). Understanding homelessness and social policy in Denmark. In V. Polakow & C. Guillean (Eds.), *International perspectives on homelessness* (65–84). Westport, CT: Greenwood.

Stax, T. B. (2003). Estimating the use of illegal drugs among homeless people using shelters in Denmark. *Substance Use & Misuse, 38*(3–6), 443–462.

▣ CORPORATION FOR SUPPORTIVE HOUSING

The mission of the Corporation for Supportive Housing (CSH), according to its own statement, is "to help communities create permanent housing with services to prevent and end homelessness." Since 1991, CSH has been working to prevent and end homelessness across the United States. Through technical assistance, grant-making and lending, advocacy, research, and other activities, CSH has been developing supportive housing and services to prevent and end homelessness for the several hundred thousand families and individuals who are at risk or become and remain homeless for long periods of time. As of the end of 2002, CSH's technical assistance, grant-making and lending, and direct community support had helped create almost 10,000 supportive housing units, with another 7,000 units in CSH's development pipeline.

THE SUPPORTIVE HOUSING CONCEPT

Supportive housing is a successful, cost-effective combination of affordable housing with support services that help people live more stable, independent, and productive lives. Supportive housing works well for people who face the most complex challenges—individuals and families who are not only homeless, but who also have very low incomes and serious, persistent issues that may include substance use, mental illness, and HIV/AIDS.

One of supportive housing's most important features is that it is *permanent* housing. People who live in supportive housing sign leases and pay rent, just like their neighbors. Unlike shelters, which work well for emergencies and short-term situations, supportive housing aims to provide long-term housing solutions.

By providing tenants with stable housing—along with accessible and voluntary mental health, substance addiction, employment and other support services—supportive housing helps people find strength, dignity, and community. Formerly homeless tenants have testified to the success of supportive housing. As one supportive housing tenant summed it up as she accepted the first CSH Julie Sandorf award, "I've never won anything in my life before. No, wait, I did. I won my life back."

Research sponsored by CSH and others has backed up these anecdotes. Studies have shown that supportive housing reduces tenants' use of expensive, emergency health services; helps tenants find employment and reduces their dependence on entitlements; and provides needed stability for the treatment of mental illness.

For example, an evaluation of California's Health, Housing and Integrated Services initiative (Proscio 2000) found that once participants had lived in supportive housing for a year, their use of the costliest health and mental health systems decreased significantly. In examining tenants' records one year prior to move-in and one year after, the study found a 57 percent reduction in emergency room visits; a 58 percent drop in the number of inpatient days; and a 100 percent decrease in the usage of public residential mental health program facilities.

CSH and its partner organizations have also proven that ending long-term homelessness is as fiscally responsible as it is humane. A University of Pennsylvania analysis of supportive housing for mentally ill homeless individuals in New York City (Culhane et al. 2002) that CSH helped to facilitate concluded that supportive and transitional housing created an average annual public savings of $16,282 by reducing the use of public services: 72 percent of savings resulted from a decline in the use of public health services; 23 percent from a decline in shelter use; and 5 percent from reduced incarceration of the homeless mentally ill. Researchers found that it costs essentially the same amount of money to house someone in stable, supportive housing as it does to keep that person homeless and stuck in the revolving door of high-cost crisis care and emergency housing.

CSH'S FIRST DECADE— AND THE WORK AHEAD

CSH was the first and remains the only national intermediary organization dedicated to building the supportive housing industry as the means of ending long-term homelessness in the United States. In 1991, CSH began building a network of nonprofit partners, governmental agencies, and private funders across the country. As of 2003, CSH program offices were located in California, Illinois, Michigan, Minnesota, New Jersey, New York, Ohio, and southern New England.

CSH's work is being guided by the *Compact to End Long-Term Homelessness,* a document unveiled in November 2002. The *Compact* was crafted by a coalition of supportive housing providers and advocates, and is being signed by organizations, individuals, and communities across the United States. It commits its endorsers to working to create and sustain at least 150,000 units of permanent supportive housing by 2012.

This campaign is part of a broader national movement to end homelessness. CSH specializes in supportive housing, which is one vital piece of the solution to homelessness in this country. But CSH and its partners emphasize that supportive housing should not be created at the expense of other necessary interventions; it can succeed only as part of a well-funded continuum of care that prevents homelessness, offers shelter and emergency care to everyone in need, and provides affordable housing to all.

For more on CSH, supportive housing, and the *Compact to End Long-Term Homelessness,* visit http://www.csh.org.

—*Carla Javits*

Further Reading

Culhane, D., Metraux, & S., Hadley, T. (2002). Public service reductions associated with placement of homeless persons with severe mental illness in supportive housing. *Housing Policy Debate, 13*(1): 107–163.

Proscio, T. (2000). *Supportive housing and its impact on the public health crisis of homelessness.* Oakland, CA: Corporation for Supportive Housing.

▣ COST-EFFECTIVENESS ANALYSIS

Most social program decision makers are interested in more than just whether homelessness programs work; they are also interested in whether such programs are cost-effective: Are they economical in terms of benefits produced by the money spent? Yet, few studies have addressed cost-effectiveness (C-E). Cost-effectiveness studies of homeless programs are difficult to conduct. Because interventions (efforts) to help the homeless generally involve more than one type of service, calculating the value of services offered is complicated and time-consuming. Moreover, compared to most medical and psychiatric conditions, homelessness—and efforts that reduce homelessness—can have a huge ripple effect on services outside the effort and costs to the community well beyond the immediate situation. The researcher must try to anticipate what secondary effects, such as reductions in police and jail costs and reductions in the need for foster care, will need to be measured.

STUDY DESIGN

In any study, researchers are faced with a choice between conducting a true experiment (e.g., assigning homeless people to intervention A or B at random) and studying by using a naturalistic design. For example, a recent study by social psychologist Dennis Culhane and his colleagues (2002) evaluated the New York/New York cooperative program for homeless people. Instead of considering a particular comparison group, these researchers identified matched cases from non-research (program) data sets showing service utilization. This is a creative way to develop cost data without a real (single) comparison group; the matched people were different for each administrative data set. Unfortunately, despite the matching procedure, one cannot be confident that the groups are similar with regard to such factors as readiness to change behavior.

PERSPECTIVE

Perspective is a central concept to the researcher conducting C-E studies. Whose costs (and whose benefits) need to be analyzed? Examples of perspectives that a study could employ include those of an agency, of the state, of the affected individual, of the family, and of society. Many economists believe that all C-E

studies should, at a minimum, specify which perspective is being used in the analysis, and unless there is a compelling reason not to do so, C-E analyses should present societal costs. Societal costs include use of any resource (i.e., anything of value), regardless of who pays for those resources. In a complete social cost analysis, the time value of a family member who has been burdened is as relevant as the time value of the case manager, who is paid with public funds. Because information about cost shifting (moving the burden of care from one party to another) is also useful for decision makers, the best C-E studies include analyses from multiple perspectives. Because of practical concerns, however, some studies are limited in the perspective taken and include only treatment costs (costs to treatment agencies affected).

Usually the bias created by limiting the perspective in homelessness C-E studies will favor Type II errors: failure to detect a difference in C-E, even though a difference does exist. For example, a C-E study by public health psychiatrist Anthony Lehman and colleagues (1999) compared treatment conducted by a community-based multidisciplinary team called assertive community treatment (ACT) for homeless persons to treatment as usual but limited the cost analysis to treatment costs. Although ACT, the experimental intervention, was more effective in reducing residential instability, the C-E results were not significant. From the standpoint of the treatment system, the ACT intervention was not significantly more cost-effective than treatment as usual. However, from the standpoint of society, the intervention well may be more cost-effective than treatment as usual. The comparison group experienced more homeless days, and in general, homelessness is associated with a variety of costs, such as shelter use, crime, and "social justice costs" (the general citizenry's sense that something is wrong). However, these costs—particularly the cost of social justice—are difficult to measure.

CALCULATING COSTS

To calculate costs, the researcher must measure units of utilization (e.g., of health services) or events (e.g., arrests) for each individual in the study and multiply these units by the cost per unit. Costs per unit are best estimated from actual expenditures rather than from budgets and from the costs of delivering the service rather than from fees. However, it is usually impractical to obtain actual costs for every type of service used in homelessness interventions because so many agencies are involved. Most C-E researchers therefore try to most carefully calculate unit costs of the services that will dominate the cost pie chart because they are frequently used and/or expensive. Common practice is to use fees for services that are infrequently used or inexpensive (such as emergency room fees).

Analyses also should be conducted during a period of time that accurately represents typical expenditures for similar programs. If a program usually operates with a staff-to-client ratio of 1:15, but during one six-month period a staff member was on extended leave, and the ratio changed, that period of time should not be used to calculate unit costs. Psychologist Barbara Dickey and colleagues (1997) conducted a C-E study of an intervention, called the "Evolving Consumer Household," in which formerly homeless persons sharing housing increasingly are responsible for their own care until they achieve independence. For this study, tracking of expenditures began before the program was mature and caused the unit costs to be unreasonably high. The authors point out that the C-E ratio is therefore not representative of the resource use that would normally face the agency.

In calculating the costs of a resource, such as homeless shelter services, the cost that will best capture the value of a resource is the opportunity cost— the value of the resource in the best alternative use. A homeless shelter that belongs to a charitable organization may be rented at a rate below market value and would thus not reflect the value of the shelter if it were to be used for other purposes. Also, the food offered at shelters is often donated, and staff resources may be supplemented by volunteer labor. When calculating the costs of shelters, it is appropriate to calculate the opportunity costs of these resources rather than the amounts paid.

To date, no homelessness C-E study has attempted to calculate the full social costs associated with homelessness. Many studies have documented the medical and social conditions connected with homelessness, and these studies provide evidence of the high costs associated with homelessness. Medical conditions that are associated with homelessness include hypothermia, vascular and skin disorders, and other problems of the legs and feet, as well as conditions that result from injuries. Homeless children exhibit low birth weight, infant mortality, malnutrition, under- or non-immunization, and elevated lead levels. All of these conditions imply future costs that have not been a part of homelessness C-E studies. (Indeed, studies have not considered the long-time horizons, i.e., period of collection of data on costs, that would be needed for such analyses.) Homelessness also causes emotional problems resulting from stigma and low self-esteem related to street and shelter living. Homeless people are more likely to be victims of crime and less likely to obtain employment. In children, homelessness is related to developmental delays, learning problems, and increased living apart from parents. Because of the future social and psychiatric problems of these children, the cost of homelessness of children and their parents is likely to be extremely high. In addition, citizens experience distress about the homelessness of their fellow citizens, which represents another social justice cost. These costs might be measured through studies of the population's willingness to pay for additional programs to reduce homelessness, but so far, researchers have not included this type of cost in C-E equations.

ANALYTIC APPROACH, SIGNIFICANCE TESTING, AND INTERPRETATION OF RESULTS

C-E studies also are difficult to conduct and to interpret because the analyses are problematic. In C-E studies, nontraditional analyses must be conducted because the distribution of costs is seldom shaped like a normal bell-shaped curve, and average costs do not reflect typical costs. Under these circumstances, the statistics most often used to test group differences can be misleading. Sometimes the researcher can use logarithms to make the cost distribution more normal distribution, and then parametric tests (tests of statistical significance based on the assumption of normal distribution) can be applied. Another approach is to use nonparametric tests. For example, the Mann-Whitney U test looks at differences between median costs, which have intuitive appeal because the value is more representative of the overall sample.

No matter which technique is used to analyze costs, because of the irregular shape of the cost distribution, the sample size needs to be large in order to detect significant differences (therefore lacking statistial "power"). Few of the C-E studies published have enough statistical power (the ability to find differences when they exist), so the most common finding of these studies is that there are no group differences in costs. However, actual costs should be inspected to make sure that the no-difference finding is not simply related to lack of power. For example, economist Nancy Wolff and her colleagues (1997) concluded that ACT, with better outcomes but not significantly different costs, was more cost-effective than brokered case management, where case managers link clients to treatment through referrals. However, upon inspection of the actual costs, groups did appear different, and the failure to reach statistical significance may have resulted from low power; when the distribution is not normal, it is more difficult to conclude that differences are unrelated to chance.

One approach to C-E analysis is to construct what are called "incremental C-E ratios" (ICERs) by dividing the difference in cost (treatment minus comparison) by the difference in effectiveness (treatment minus comparison). However, because of the variability in costs noted earlier, using a single value to represent the C-E ratio can be misleading since it fails to characterize the broad distribution of possible outcomes that are likely to occur across individuals. Thus, investigators often construct confidence intervals around the point estimates of the ICER. That is, they provide plus or minus values that show the

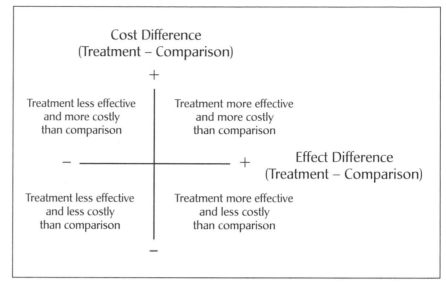

Figure 1. Cost-Effectiveness Plane.
Source: Black 1990, 212–214.

range of possible outcomes with a particular percentage level of confidence. This approach was applied by psychiatrist and researcher Robert Rosenheck and colleagues (2003) to examine the incremental cost-effectiveness of supportive housing for homeless veterans over case management and standard care from multiple perspectives. These investigators found that those veterans receiving supportive housing had significantly more nights housed but that they consumed about $45 more of societal resources per additional day of housing. However, the confidence interval around the point estimate of $45 ranged from -$19 to $108. Because the confidence interval includes the value of $0, these groups did not incur significantly different costs.

Another method of examining the ranges of costs is to create sampling distributions for costs and effectiveness measures to show the precision of estimates as well as their means. For example, a special technique called bootstrapping, which involves drawing multiple samples from the same group of numbers to create a larger hypothetical sample based on the actual data, uses every study participant's data to create an empirical sampling distribution of the test statistic and plot these estimates on a C-E plane. (See Figure 1.) For each estimate, the difference in effectiveness (treatment minus comparison) is plotted on the x-axis, and the corresponding difference in cost (treatment minus comparison) is plotted on the y-axis. The resulting cluster of points displays the sampling distribution of the ICER. The lower righthand quadrant contains ICERs where the treatment is less costly and more effective than the comparison, whereas the upper righthand quadrant contains estimates where the treatment is both more effective and costly. Both of the lefthand quadrants indicate that the treatment is less effective (with the upper lefthand quadrant indicating that the treatment is more costly and the lower lefthand quadrant indicating that the treatment is less costly).

In many homelessness C-E studies, more effective treatments were also more costly. However, payers may be willing to increase spending to improve the probability that a treatment improves outcome. One can construct vectors (lines specified by magnitude and direction, e.g., $y = mx$ or a line defined by a formula following $y = mx$) on the C-E plane that correspond to different ceiling ratios (the maximum amount someone is willing to pay for one unit of improvement) for a payer's willingness to pay. For example, if a payer is unwilling to spend anything, the vector of the ceiling ratio would follow the equation $y = 0x$. If a payer is willing to spend \$1,000 for each unit of improvement, the vector of the ceiling ratio would follow the equation $y = 1000x$ and so on. In this case, the probability that the treatment is more cost-effective is represented by the percentage of bootstrap replications falling below the constructed vector (which includes all of the points in the lower righthand quadrant plus the points in the upper righthand quadrant that fall below the vector).

The value of the ceiling ratios corresponding to what a payer is willing to pay will differ across payers. The information from the C-E plane can be used to create a C-E acceptability curve. The x-axis of the C-E curve represents the value of the ceiling ratios, which is equal to the ceiling ratios in the C-E plane. The y-axis represents the cumulative probability that the treatment is cost-effective and is calculated as the percentage of bootstrap replications that falls below the vector that corresponds to each value of the ceiling ratio on the x-axis. Given what a payer considers an appropriate incremental expenditure to achieve a given outcome, the C-E curve shows the likelihood

that the intervention will, on average, reach that threshold.

Another approach to C-E analysis is to calculate the statistical frontier in the willingness-to-pay/net-health-benefit (NHB) plane. With this approach, the treatment expected to provide the greater NHB for a given willingness to pay is established and plotted as the frontier. The health gain expected from a particular treatment is compared to the health gain that a decision maker stipulates to justify its cost. For both treatments, the NHB is plotted as a function of a decision maker's willingness to pay (x-axis)—the statistical frontier, the locus of points representing the maximum NHB between the alternative treatments. In this way, decision makers can see which treatment is preferable given their particular resources by locating the amount they are willing to pay on the x-axis and determining which treatment, at that value, yields the greatest net health benefit. One treatment may be preferable when a decision maker has fewer monetary resources for the intervention, whereas a different treatment may be preferable when more resources are available. This approach has been applied successfully by economist Kristine Jones and colleagues (2003) to study the effects of a critical time intervention (CTI) (brief case management to support homeless people in transition) to enhance continuity of care for persons shifting from shelter to community living. Specifically, these authors were able to demonstrate that CTI was more cost-effective than usual care when a payer's willingness to pay exceeded \$152 per night not homeless.

Based on the small number of C-E studies, it appears that most interventions are effective in reducing homelessness. Within the limited scope of costs studied and time frames considered, the costs of most interventions do not appear to be completely offset by savings. However, because decision makers may be willing to accept a modest amount of additional costs for assisting homeless people, they might consider these programs to be cost-effective. Furthermore, if it were possible to include more information about savings accrued through reducing homelessness—such as savings in conditions associated with homelessness, future savings related to the effects of homelessness, and the savings related to social justice—then the costs of many more interventions would be completely offset by savings.

—Linda Frisman, Nancy Covell, and Robin Hoburg

Further Reading

Cowal, K., Shinn, M., Weitzman, B. C., Stojanovic, D., & Labay, L. (2002). Mother-child separations among homeless and housed families receiving public assistance in New York City. *American Journal of Community Psychology, 30*(5), 711–720.

Culhane, D. P., Metraux, S., & Hadley, T. (2002). Public service reductions associated with placement of homeless persons with severe mental illness in supportive housing. *Housing Policy Debate, 13*(1), 107–163.

Dickey, B., Latimer, E., Powers, K., Gonzalez, O., & Goldfinger, S. M. (1997). Housing costs for adults who are mentally ill and formerly homeless. *Journal of Mental Health Administration, 24*(3), 291–305.

Hoch, J. S., Briggs, A. H., & Willan, A. R. (2002). Something old, something new, something borrowed, something blue: A framework for the marriage of health econometrics and cost-effectiveness analysis. *Health Economics, 11*(5), 415–430.

Jones, K., Colson, P. W., Holter, M. C., Lin, S., Valencia, E., Susser, E., & Wyatt, R. J. (2003). Cost-effectiveness of critical time intervention to reduce homelessness among persons with mental illness. *Psychiatric Services, 54*(6), 884–890.

Lehman, A. F., Dixon, L., Hoch, J. S., Deforge, B., Kernan, E., & Frank, R. (1999). Cost-effectiveness of assertive community treatment for homeless persons with severe mental illness. *British Journal of Psychiatry, 174*(4), 346–352.

Levstek, D. A., & Bond, G. R. (1993). Housing cost, quality, and satisfaction among formerly homeless persons with serious mental illness in two cities. *Innovations & Research in Clinical Services, Community Support, and Rehabilitation, 2*(3), 1–8.

Lewit, E. M., & Schuurmann Baker, L. (1996). Homeless families and children. *The Future of Children, 6*(2), 146–158.

Lindsey, E. W. (1998). The impact of homelessness and shelter life on family relationships. *Family Relations, 47*(3), 243–252.

McGeary, K. A., French, M. T., Sacks, S., McKendrick, K., & DeLeon, G. (1999). Service use and cost by mentally ill chemical abusers: Differences by retention in a therapeutic community. *Journal of Substance Abuse, 11*(3), 265–279.

Molnar, J. M., Rath, W. R., & Klein, T. P. (1991). Constantly compromised: The impact of homelessness on children. *Journal of Social Issues, 46*(4), 109–124.

Phelan, J., Link, B. G., Moore, R. E., & Stueve, A. (1997). The stigma of homelessness: The impact of the label "homeless" on attitudes toward poor persons. *Social Psychology Quarterly, 60*(4), 323–337.

Rafferty, T., & Shinn, M. (1991). The impact of homelessness on children. *American Psychologist, 46*(11), 1170–1179.

Rosenheck, R. (2000). Cost-effectiveness of services for mentally ill homeless people: The application of research to policy and practice. *American Journal of Psychiatry, 157*(10), 1563–1570.

Rosenheck, R., Kasprow, W., Frisman, L., & Mares, W.-L. (2003). Cost-effectiveness of supported housing for homeless persons with mental illness. *Archives of General Psychiatry, 60*(9), 940–951.

Salit, S. A., Kuhn, E. M., Hartz, A. J., Vu, J. M., & Mosso, A. L. (1998). Hospitalization costs associated with homelessness in New York City. *New England Journal of Medicine, 338*(24), 1734–1740.

Schumacher, J. E., Mennemeyer, S. T., Milby, J. B., Wallace, D., & Nolan, K. (2002). Costs and effectiveness of substance abuse treatments for homeless persons. *Journal of Mental Health Policy and Economics, 5*(1), 33–42.

Smollar, J. (1999). Homeless youth in the United States: Description and developmental issues. In M. Raffaelli & R. W. Larson (Eds.), *New Directions for Child and Adolescent Development, 85,* 47–58. San Francisco: Jossey-Bass.

Wolff, N., Helminiak, T. W., Morse, G. A., Calsyn, R. J., Klinkenberg, W. D., & Trusty, M. L. (1997). Cost-effectiveness evaluation of three approaches to case management for homeless mentally ill clients. *American Journal of Psychiatry, 154*(3), 341–348.

CRIMINAL ACTIVITY AND POLICING

Society historically has associated criminal activity with homelessness. As early as the late nineteenth and early twentieth centuries, observers such as Jack London and Nels Anderson provided vivid accounts of the lawlessness of hoboes, tramps, and bums. The numerous arrests of chronically alcoholic men living on American skid rows made criminal activity a major characteristic of homelessness until the decriminalization of public drunkenness. As substantial numbers of apparently mentally ill people began to spread throughout U.S. cities during the late 1970s, researchers' interest in criminal activity was displaced by investigations of deinstitutionalization as the primary cause of homelessness. During the past decade, researchers have become more interested in examining criminal activity among homeless populations as reports have emerged about substantial and possibly increasing proportions of jail inmates with histories of homelessness and mental illness. Criminalization of mental illness due to deinstitutionalization and criminalization of homelessness due to gentrification aroused interest in examining the implications of shifting the responsibility for these two overlapping populations from the mental health and social services systems to the criminal justice system.

SOURCES OF INFORMATION

Although criminal activity per se has not been the major focus of most contemporary research on homeless people, information can be gleaned from many of the encyclopedic surveys of the homeless population conducted since 1980. Information on numbers and characteristics of arrests and incarceration is elicited directly from interviews or review of records, and indirect indicators of criminal activities can be found in descriptions of other aspects of the homeless lifestyle. For example, measures of employment may include information on illegal income procurement such as panhandling, prostitution, drug dealing, and the like. However, differences in definitions of both *homelessness* and *criminal activity* impede comparing rates or generalizing findings from studies. For example, studies employing broad descriptors, such as "trouble with the law," fail to distinguish between arrest and conviction or between jailing and imprisonment, and the fact that such studies do not use standard offense categories makes it difficult for one to assess the character or magnitude of criminal activity in the homeless population.

Information about the nature of criminal activity engaged in by homeless people can reduce NIMBY (not in my back yard) barriers to services for homeless people by demonstrating to concerned people in the area that homeless people are not generally violent or dangerous. Researchers need information on arrest patterns correlated with personal and health characteristics to assess whether homelessness is being criminalized, particularly among specific subgroups of the homeless population, such as persons with mental illnesses. Examination of patterns of criminal activity and incarceration can identify gaps in service systems and determine the extent to which the responsibility for providing health, mental health, and other essential services is being shifted to the criminal justice system.

RATES OF ARRESTS AND INCARCERATION

Homeless persons are substantially more likely to be arrested and incarcerated than are persons in the general population, even when compared with low-income persons. One-fifth to two-thirds of the homeless persons questioned in studies conducted since 1980 reported having been arrested or incarcerated. Studies using comparison groups show striking differences. For example, nearly three-fifths of homeless men in Baltimore reported having been arrested, compared with about one-quarter of housed men. Recidivism is also high among homeless adults. For example, homeless shelter residents with arrest histories in Detroit averaged 5.3 prior arrests, and more than one-half of a Los Angeles homeless sample reported adult arrests, with nearly two-thirds having had multiple arrests.

Although rates of arrests and incarceration are frequently reported, we have little information on characteristics of criminal activity or its distribution in the homeless population. The ratio of jail incarceration to prison incarceration gives a good indicator of the seriousness of offenses committed. Homeless persons report being jailed more frequently than being imprisoned. For example, homeless people in Baltimore were about twice as likely to have been in jails as in prisons, suggesting that either they were not convicted of a crime or they were convicted of a misdemeanor or other offense punishable by a sentence of up to one year. The pattern of criminal activity of 125 residents of a temporary shelter in Detroit was described as primarily nonviolent crimes against property resulting in brief jail sentences. Although most offenses reported by homeless persons are relatively trivial offenses against property and the public order, evidence indicates that homeless people also commit serious crimes often associated with psychotic symptoms or intoxication.

RELATIONSHIP TO HOMELESSNESS

The chronology of homelessness relative to arrests is not clear. The majority of studies examining criminal activity are cross-sectional rather than longitudinal (involving the repeated observation of a set of subjects over time) and typically ask questions—such as whether a person has been arrested "as an adult," "during your lifetime," "recently," "in the past year," and so forth—that do not allow researchers to date arrests relative to homelessness. High rates of homeless people surveyed report having been arrested within a year prior to being interviewed. Furthermore, higher rates of arrests among the subgroup identified as chronically homeless provide evidence that the risk of arrest increases with the length of homelessness.

Criminal activity varies across homeless subgroups. Homeless men are more likely than homeless women to engage in criminal activity. However, when compared with their counterparts in the general population, women have a greater rate disparity by homelessness than do men. High rates of arrest and illegal activities are reported by both younger and older homeless persons but for different reasons. Largely ineligible for income support and other social services available to adults, homeless youth engage in numerous illegal activities to survive on the streets, reporting activities such as "survival sex" (prostitution) and drug dealing more frequently than do homeless adults. For example, in 1999, J. M. Greene and her colleagues reported that more than one-quarter of a national survey of street youth had engaged in survival sex. High rates of arrests of older people may reflect longer periods of homelessness that result in greater exposure to police attention. However, the arrests of some homeless people reflect a pattern established early in life, with substantial proportions reporting juvenile arrests and detention.

Both homeless men and homeless women with adverse early life experiences, mental illnesses, or addiction disorders are found in greater numbers among the subgroup of homeless persons with arrest histories. Adverse life experiences during childhood that are associated with adult criminal histories reported by homeless people include family dysfunction, such as parental death, parental mental illness, and parental substance abuse; foster care placement; physical and sexual abuse; and delinquent behavior, such as running away, being expelled from school, using alcohol and drugs, fighting, and being arrested and detained as a juvenile. In 2000, R. A. Desai and her colleagues reported findings from a study of a large sample of homeless people with serious mental illness demonstrating that early antisocial behavior predicted recent arrests.

MENTAL ILLNESS AND CRIMINAL ACTIVITY

Homeless persons with mental illness and addictive disorders have higher rates of contact with the justice system, as reflected in their being picked up by the police, arrested, and incarcerated, mainly in jails. "Like the old asylums, the jail increasingly functions as the one place in town where troubled persons can be deposited by law enforcement officers and not be turned away. As a result, the jail is, perhaps, our most enduring asylum" (Briar 1983, 388). Because of the overlap in populations, much of the debate concerning whether mentally ill persons are more violent than persons in the general population also applies to homeless persons. However, homeless people exhibiting symptoms of mental illness that appear frightening or threatening are considerably more likely to be reported to the police and to be arrested than are housed persons with mental illnesses who seldom attract public attention. In addition, antisocial behavior associated with personality disorders found at higher rates in homeless populations might contribute to greater incidents of arrests.

Despite widespread decriminalization of public drunkenness, alcohol abuse remains the greatest risk factor for arrest among the homeless population.

> Alcoholics and drug abusers . . . are probably the least likely of any group in the homeless population to elicit public sympathy . . . not only are some communities losing patience with the plight of the homeless in general, they are even more frustrated when it comes to tolerating the problem behaviors associated with homeless substance abuser. (Garrett 1992, 353)

Illicit drug use also increases risk of arrest and incarceration among homeless people. Few major drug dealers become homeless, but minor drug dealing is reported by homeless people. Criminal activity is associated with substance abuse in three ways. First, homeless substance abusers are less likely to be employed and must engage in illegal endeavors to obtain income to buy alcohol and drugs for consumption. Second, intoxicated persons have reduced inhibitions and may more easily engage in behavior that is illegal or that escalates into a crime, such as assaults. Third, certain aspects of consumption are illegal, such as using illicit drugs or drinking in public spaces.

CRIMINAL ACTIVITY
AS A COPING STRATEGY

Unemployment, low educational levels, and scant work histories are prevalent among the homeless population, and participation in entitlement programs is low relative to need, particularly after changes to welfare policies resulting from passage of the Personal Responsibility and Work Opportunity and Reconciliation Act in 1996. Thus, criminal activity may provide needed income. Panhandling may be the most common form of illegal income procurement, but other forms are also common, such as shoplifting and other petty theft and nonpayment of restaurant tabs and taxi fares. Other illegal activities present considerable risks to homeless people beyond potential arrest and incarceration. Arson can be an unintended consequence of basic life-sustaining activities when fires built for heating or cooking in vacant buildings consume property and cause injuries and deaths. Volitional activities such as engaging in survival sex and selling illicit drugs place participants at risk for sexually transmitted diseases (STDs) and exposure to violence. Evidence from a number of cities suggests that prostitution among homeless persons is most prevalent among youth and substance abusers, compounding the risk to these subgroups for STDs, particularly HIV.

CRIMINAL ACTIVITY AS A
HELP-SEEKING MECHANISM

Some homeless people appear to use arrest as a survival strategy, maneuvering the police into placing them in the relative safety of a jail. This behavior may be reinforced by pervasive police beliefs in the benefits of "three hots and a cot" (hot meals and a bed), especially for debilitated chronic street dwellers, or those in need of detoxification. For example, one homeless man in Baltimore reported that much of his extensive criminal history accrued from intentional arrests to gain temporary respite from the streets. He started by setting fires, then soon turned to setting off false alarms to ensure arrest without putting others at risk. Other homeless people report strategies such as throwing bricks through shop windows to catch the attention of the police.

When skid rows existed in most large American cities, jails were described as revolving doors for chronic inebriates who were regularly thrown into jail "drunk tanks" to be "dried out" or detoxified. Today, jails and prisons represent the only institutions where health care is mandated. For some homeless people, incarceration provides their only source of treatment for health, mental health, and substance abuse problems. In addition, incarceration offers relief from victimization that is a consequence of street life. However, despite some beneficial consequences, incarceration is a poor substitute for adequate services and housing for this population. The quality of assessment and treatment in jails and prisons is variable, and there is seldom continuity of care following incarceration. To address the lack of continuity of care, there is a growing interest in developing reentry programs to link homeless people with mental illnesses and substance abuse problems to community services. Ideally, persons in need of reentry services will be identified early with planning for linkages to appropriate services in the community made during their incarceration to prevent subsequent homelessness and exacerbation of problems.

CRIMINALIZATION OF HOMELESSNESS

Following the contention by advocates and researchers that mental illness has been criminalized, there is growing speculation among advocates that homelessness itself is also being criminalized. Researchers have used two criteria to determine whether homelessness per se is being criminalized.

The first criterion considers whether communities enact legislation prohibiting people from engaging in basic life-sustaining activities in public. For example, activities frequently prohibited in public include camping or sleeping, bathing, urinating, defecating, and the like. The second criterion relates to selective enforcement of generally applicable laws. For example, a well-dressed person waiting on a sidewalk is typically less likely to be charged with loitering than is a shabbily dressed or malodorous person engaging in the same behavior. Beginning in 1991, the National Law Center on Homelessness and Poverty and the National Coalition for the Homeless began documenting the trend toward criminalizing homelessness in a series of reports. For the report issued in 2003, information was gathered from a number of cities indicating the extent to which communities enact legislation limiting the use of public space. All of the cities surveyed reported some form of restriction on use of public space despite insufficient numbers of homeless shelters to accommodate the local needs. Banned activities included bathing in public waters, creating odor, sleeping or camping in public places, living in a vehicle, maintaining junk/storage of property, loitering, failing to disperse, begging, washing automobile windows for money, and performing on the street.

Enforcement of these laws has resulted in "sweeps" to remove homeless people from city centers, often in response to pressure from businesses or in anticipation of events expected to draw large crowds. During these sweeps, police check identities of persons suspected of being homeless, search for outstanding warrants, and either move the homeless people away or arrest them. Homeless people caught in these sweeps may be forced to abandon makeshift living quarters and encampments, losing personal property, including difficult-to-replace identification. Homeless people forced to disperse from city centers lose proximity to health and social services typically located there. Although communities justify such policies as necessary to protect the public health and safety, advocates for homeless people contend that such policies criminalize inherently noncriminal behavior and challenge these policies as violations of civil rights of homeless people.

POLICING

For a number of reasons, police officers probably have the highest rate of contact with homeless people of all public service providers. Citizens expect police to respond to all problems and not merely when crimes are being committed. Thus, in the absence of other solutions, police are frequently called upon by business proprietors as well as by ordinary citizens to deal with homeless persons who appear disheveled, intoxicated, confused, injured, or display symptoms of mental illness. In addition, police encounter homeless people on the street during their rounds as well as under directives from community officials to "clean up" specific areas of cities. Lastly, homeless people themselves frequently turn to police officers for assistance, asking to be taken to a shelter or hospital.

POLICE AS HELPERS

Although the law enforcement agencies (the police and jails) appear to be among the most important providers of services to the homeless population, provision of these services is not always seen by police as falling in their bailiwick. For example, the public inebriate formerly consumed a disproportionate amount of time from the law enforcement system, and currently police are frequently first responders to problems related to homeless people. Police routinely are asked by the public, as well as by homeless people themselves, to transport homeless people to shelters, hospitals, and other programs, and jails and precinct houses are routinely thrown open to homeless people in extreme weather conditions. Many individual police officers befriend the homeless people they encounter on their rounds, bestowing myriad small acts of kindness.

However, these encounters can be time-consuming and may be viewed by police as taking time from their "proper" duties. Police officers report that when they have attempted to have homeless mentally ill persons hospitalized (sometimes requiring both the officer and the homeless individual to wait hours in an emergency room for psychiatric evaluations), the persons fail to meet criteria for involuntary commitment and are released back to the street. Repeated too often, this discouraging experience makes police more likely to resort to arrest rather than less drastic and more appropriate dispositions that are viewed as wasting time and effort.

POLICE HARASSMENT

Advocates as well as homeless people themselves report incidents of police harassment of homeless people ranging from minor annoyances, like waking them up and moving them on, to more serious incidents, such as confiscation of belongings and destruction of camps. Police have been accused and sometimes charged with using excessive force during arrests and other encounters with homeless people, particularly those with mental illnesses. Among the incidents of violence perpetrated against homeless people and labeled as hate crimes by the National Coalition for the Homeless were two cases where police used excessive use of force, including one in Florida where a mentally ill homeless man brandishing a putty knife was shot despite pleas of acquaintances that he was mentally ill and harmless. Reports of police harassment ranged from 1 to 41 percent in studies conducted during the 1980s.

As a result of such experiences bolstered by street lore, many homeless people regard police as enemies rather than champions and avoid contact as much as possible. Homeless crime victims frequently do not report crimes to the police. Studies conducted during the 1980s determined that 16 to 60 percent of crimes against the homeless sought police intervention, with reporting more likely for serious or violent crimes. Nearly half of the homeless in a Los Angeles study said they went out of their way to avoid the police. Consequently, the homeless adopt "street smart" strategies for self-protection, including such things as avoidance of unsafe places, avoidance of people, the companionship of a trusted person or group, being secretive about sleeping spots, becoming hypervigilant to the approach of others, sleeping during the day, keeping a dog, and carrying a weapon. Women are particularly vulnerable to attack and frequently report developing adaptive strategies, including reclusiveness, wearing multiple layers of clothing, and being malodorous or otherwise offensive, to prevent being victimized.

TRAINING

The relationship between homeless people and the police becomes volatile as police are required to balance multiple and often conflicting demands from various interest groups within communities in addition to their law enforcement role. For example, businesses and homeowners exert pressure on police to maintain established social boundaries by moving homeless people away from shopping and residential areas. Police may be called upon to act as social workers or therapists to homeless persons needing services after hours or to fill gaps in the service system. In these non-crime situations, police must exercise a great amount of discretion without clear mandates or established protocols.

Although communities rely heavily upon police to respond to non-criminal problems and emergencies, police officers generally value these activities less than crime fighting. Despite devoting the majority of police time to peacekeeping and order maintenance, police in most communities do not receive specific training to discharge these types of responsibilities, particularly with problematic subpopulations such as homeless people and persons who have mental illnesses. In recognition of this lack, *The Police in America,* a textbook widely used in courses in law enforcement undergraduate programs, was expanded in the 2002 edition to include strategies for responding to special populations including homeless people, people with mental illnesses, and juveniles. In addition, there is a growing trend for communities to provide training in techniques of community policing and problem-oriented policing. Using these strategies, police become problem solvers, and individual officers are given latitude to devise community-specific or problem-specific solutions rather than relying solely on arrest and prosecutions.

MODEL PROGRAMS

Communities are recognizing the need to address the movement of homeless people, many of whom have mental illness and co-occurring substance abuse problems, through the criminal justice system, especially police and jails. Arrest records and other legal problems, such as outstanding warrants, present nearly insurmountable barriers to receipt of needed services, especially public housing, and exclude individuals from benefits and entitlements, such as Medicaid. Because of the overlap between the populations and similarity of problems, programs to alleviate legal problems among mentally ill persons may serve as effective models for the people who are homeless. Examples include programs to provide special training and support to police officers to promote more appropriate disposition of encounters, jail diversion and pretrial release programs, reentry programs, and special homeless courts.

A number of promising programs are being implemented. For example, Philadelphia has written a police protocol for interacting with homeless persons, developed as part of a larger community collaboration between community leaders and homeless advocates, including an outreach hotline and increases to the numbers of shelter beds. Fort Lauderdale has developed a Homeless Outreach Program, which includes a training program called "Homelessness 101" that instructs police officers on how to be more sensitive to the needs of homeless people and trains police to provide aid and referrals rather than rely on arrests. The proactive approach teams police with formerly homeless consumers. New Orleans has established a homeless assistance unit that pairs social workers with police to direct homeless people to appropriate services rather than arrest them. San Diego has established a Homeless Court Program, which operates a courtroom in shelters, and the city also offers services as part of the annual Stand Down for homeless veterans (a yearly intervention "event" that introduces service providers to this population). This program is organized according to rehabilitative rather than punitive principles and offers alternative sentencing to resolve offenses and clear up outstanding warrants.

Although these programs appear to offer great promise in resolving some of the issues related to criminalization of homelessness, it is not clear which programs or elements of programs will prove

to be the most successful. It appears that having community-wide coalitions facilitates addressing systemic issues and provides support for police to exercise a broader range of dispositions beyond arrests and incarcerations. In addition, a number of studies have shown that access to appropriate services, including supportive housing, reduces criminal activity among homeless persons as measured by arrests and incarcerations. However, advocates have pointed to pitfalls in implementing programs designed to be beneficial to homeless people. For example, sentencing homeless people to public service or fines in lieu of jail time in special homeless courts may be unduly burdensome, and sentencing persons with mental or addictive disorders to attend treatment programs can be viewed as coercive rather than humanitarian.

IMPLICATIONS

Reports of homeless people with histories of incarceration indicate that criminal activity is a prominent characteristic of homeless people. However, little is known about the nature of their criminal behavior. The role of criminal activity in homelessness can be interpreted in four ways. First, for a small proportion, homelessness may be a natural part of the life cycle of career criminals, reflecting alternately waxing and waning fortunes. Furthermore, for some individuals, particularly those with antisocial personality and drug disorders, histories of arrest and incarceration may be a function of chronic deviant behavior. Chronic criminal behavior of this type probably will be relatively unaffected by services aimed at ameliorating homelessness since homelessness per se is a by-product, not the root cause.

Second, for many homeless people, criminal activity may be one of the few means available to augment meager resources to meet subsistence needs. Homeless persons have difficulty in obtaining gainful employment, with those who report current employment commonly only able to obtain part-time, temporary work, casual labor, and "jobs" such as selling blood or participating as paid research subjects. Despite high rates of unemployment, substantial proportions are not enrolled in public support programs.

Thus, many resort to such criminal endeavors as petty theft, shoplifting, small-scale drug dealing, nonpayment of cab fares and restaurant tabs, and prostitution. Criminal activity of this kind reflects necessity and might be substantially reduced by improving the flow of eligible homeless people into mainstream health and social services including housing.

Third, behavior that is functionally adaptive in the homeless ecology may lead to arrest. Skills that enhance the survival prospects of homeless persons on the streets—such as breaking into an abandoned building or parked vehicle for shelter, trespassing, or sleeping on benches in violation of park laws—are often illegal or readily criminalized. The extreme case of functional criminal behavior occurs when homeless people manipulate police into arresting them in order to obtain temporary asylum in jail. It is mainly this pattern of behavior that advocates contend leads to the criminalization of homelessness itself.

Fourth, arrests may result from diminished mental capacity. Homeless people who exhibit poor judgment or bizarre behavior may be sent to correctional institutions rather than placed in appropriate social services and treatment. Psychotic behavior—sometimes violent—or the disorientation associated with intoxication, mental illness, and mental retardation may capture the attention of the police. Contentions that mental illness has been criminalized in the post-deinstitutionalization era apply to persons having mental illnesses who are homeless as well.

Consideration of these issues may lead to innovations in provision of services to homeless individuals and prevention of entrenchment into chronic homelessness. For example, homeless people frequently cite criminal behavior as a pathway into homelessness. Re-entry programs may prevent persons being released from correctional institutions directly to the streets with few resources to reassimilate into society. Prevention of criminal activity in this population is vital given that criminal records present barriers to gaining housing and needed benefits, perpetuating both the cycle of crime and the homeless condition. While it is critical to provide training to enable police to resolve problems between citizens and homeless people with resorting to unnecessary arrests and incarcerations, researchers and advocates agree that elimination of the bulk of criminal activity among homeless persons requires increasing access to safe and affordable housing with appropriate services.

—*Pamela J. Fischer*

See also Deinstitutionalization; Homeless Court Program; Homeless Organizing; Mental Illness and Health; National Coalition for the Homeless; Panhandling; Prostitution; Skid Row Culture and History; Street Youth and Violence; Survival Strategies; Vagrancy; Work on the Streets

Further Reading

Anderson, N. (1923). *The hobo.* Chicago: University of Chicago Press.

Baron, S. W. (2003). Self control, social consequences, and criminal behavior: Street youth and the general theory of crime. *Journal of Research in Crime and Delinquency, 40,* 403–425.

Barr, H. (2001). *How to help when a person with mental illness is arrested.* New York: Urban Justice Center Mental Health Project.

Bogue, D. J. (1963). *Skid row in American cities.* Chicago: University of Chicago Press.

Breakey, W. R. (1987, Spring). Treating the homeless. *Alcohol Health & Research World, 11,*42–47.

Briar, K. H. (1983, September). Jails: Neglected asylums. *Social Casework,* 387–393.

Burt, M. (1992). *Over the edge: The growth of homelessness in the 1980s.* New York: Russell Sage Foundation.

Desai, R. A., Lam, J., & Rosenheck, R. A. (2000). Childhood risk factors for criminal justice involvement in a sample of homeless people with serious mental illness. *Journal of Nervous and Mental Disease, 188*(6), 324–332.

Draine, J., Salzer, M. S., Culhane, D. P., & Hadley, T. R. (2002). Putting social problems among persons with mental illness in perspective: Crime, unemployment and homelessness. *Psychiatric Services, 53*(5), 565–572.

Fischer, P. J. (1988). Criminal activity among the homeless: A study of arrests in Baltimore. *Hospital and Community Psychiatry, 39*(1), 46–51.

Fischer, P. J. (1992). Criminal behavior and victimization of the homeless. In R. Jahiel (Ed.), *Homelessness: A prevention-oriented approach* (pp. 87–112). Baltimore: Johns Hopkins University Press.

Fischer, P. J. (1992). The criminalization of homelessness. In M. J. Robertson & M. Greenblatt (Eds.), *Homelessness: The national perspective* (pp. 57–64). New York: Plenum.

Fischer, P. J. (1992). Victimization and homelessness: Cause and effect. *New England Journal of Public Policy, 8*(1), 229–246.

Fischer, P. J., Ross, A., & Breakey, W. R. (1993). Correlates of arrest in a Baltimore homeless population. *Contemporary Drug Problems, 20*(3), 385–414.

Garrett, G. R. (1992). Homelessness, alcohol, and other drug abuse: Research traditions and policy responses. *New England Journal of Public Policy, 8*(1), 353–370.

Greene, J. M., Ennett, S. T., & Ringwalt, C. L. (1999). Prevalence and correlates of survival sex among runaway and homeless youth. *American Journal of Public Health, 89*(9), 1406–1409.

Husted, J. R., & Nehemkis, A. (1995). Civil commitment viewed from three perspectives: Professional, family, and police. *Bulletin of the American Academy of Psychiatry and the Law, 23*(4), 533–546.

London, J. (1907). *The road.* New York: Macmillan.

Massaro, J. (2003). *Successfully working with people with mental illness involved in the criminal justice system: What mental health service providers need to know.* Delmar, NY: Technical Analysis and Policy Analysis Center for Jail Diversion.

National Coalition for the Homeless. (2003). *Hate, violence, and death on Main Street USA: A report on hate crimes and violence against people experiencing homelessness from 1999–2002.* Washington, DC: Author.

National Coalition for the Homeless. (2003). *Illegal to be homeless: The criminalization of homelessness in the United States.* Washington, DC: Author.

National Law Center on Homelessness and Poverty. (2003). *Punishing poverty: The criminalization of homelessness, litigation, and recommendations for solutions.* Washington, DC: Author.

Robertson, M. J., Koegel, P., & Ferguson, L. (1989). Alcohol use and abuse among homeless adolescents in Hollywood. *Contemporary Drug Problems, 16*(3), 415–452.

Snow, D. A., Baker, S. G., & Anderson, L. (1989). Criminality among homeless men: An empirical assessment. *Social Problems, 36,* 532–549.

Susser, E., Struening, E. L., & Conover, S. (1987). Childhood experiences of homeless men. *American Journal of Psychiatry, 144,* 1599–1601.

Teplin, L. A. & Pruett, N. S. (1992). Police as street corner psychiatrist: Managing the mentally ill. *International Journal of Law and Psychiatry, 15,* 139–156.

Walker, S., & Katz, C. M. (2002). *The police in America.* New York: McGraw-Hill.

▣ CUBA

At beginning of the twenty-first century, Cuba is one of the few remaining communist-socialist societies in the world. Notably, it exhibits neither the extremes of destitution and poverty known in many developing countries, nor the street homelessness seen in some wealthy nations. Nevertheless, Cuba's housing problems are severe, though they may not be immediately obvious to the casual observer.

DEVELOPMENTS AFTER THE 1959 REVOLUTION

The Cuban revolution of 1959, led by Fidel Castro, ousted the previous U.S.-dominated regime, and was subsequently declared a socialist revolution, with Castro remaining as President up to the time of writing (2003). In the ensuing program of social change, housing received a relatively high priority. Early in the 1960s, legislation was passed to provide security of tenure, to reduce rents, and to transform many tenants into owners. These reforms were quickly followed by mass-scale building programs to relieve the worst of the prerevolutionary slum conditions. The state took the lead in policy and implementation. However, much of the construction was undertaken on a state-supported "self-help" basis through the "microbrigade" system, which relied on workers given leave from their usual occupations to contribute labor to the construction projects.

Cuban housing law, consolidated in 1984 and 1988, provided for the transfer of existing and newly built dwellings to their occupants, at a subsidized price through cheap state loans. Today, 85 percent of Cuba's dwellings are owner occupied. The general right of individuals to a dwelling is enshrined in law, and vacant dwellings are allocated according to factors of need and merit, not economic capacity. As a consequence of these policies, Cubans tend to have a high level of security in their housing—and they pay relatively little for it.

The Cuban revolution also sought to promote equal development geographically across the island. As of 1999, 2 million of the nation's 11 million people live in Havana, making the capital significantly larger than even the second city, Santiago de Cuba, with 440,000 inhabitants. But development has been promoted primarily in areas other than Havana; arguably, this policy has contributed to the long-term decline of the historic buildings of the capital.

HOUSING AND HOMELESSNESS IN CONTEMPORARY CUBA

Since 1990, Cuba has been in a "special period" of austerity measures in response to a severe and enduring economic crisis. This was precipitated by the loss of economic and political support from the former communist countries of Eastern Europe, and exacerbated by the tightening of America's economic blockade of the island.

While an overall national housing deficit is acknowledged, homelessness is not considered to be a significant problem. In 2001, the Cuban government estimated the island's total housing stock at 3 million dwellings with a nationwide average of 3.7 inhabitants per dwelling (Instituto Nacional de la Vivienda [INV] 2001). As in 1999, 55 percent of all dwellings across the island were considered to be in good condition, 28 percent in average condition, and only 17 percent were classified as poor (INV 2000, 2001). An estimated 95 percent had a piped water supply and an electricity supply (INV 2001). But population growth, combined with the added pressure of internal migration to Havana, means that the city faces an absolute shortage of housing and severe overcrowding. Newly forming households, or those moving for work-related reasons, tend to share quarters with immediate or more extended family, often for long periods of time. Cuba's apparently strong family culture, which tolerates a high level of sharing and crowding, appears to be an important factor in averting absolute homelessness. Nevertheless, these conditions place immense pressures on relationships and family life.

In the older parts of Havana, extreme structural deterioration adds to the city's contemporary housing problems. In the historic center of Old Havana, many old buildings have been repaired or restored. However, adjacent neighborhoods have severe housing problems, without the benefit of any of the resources that the historic district attracts. In the most extreme cases, buildings can collapse, resulting in the deaths of inhabitants. Still, occupants of life-threatening buildings are rarely referred to as homeless.

Debating Homelessness in Cuba

Policies pursued between 1960 and 1990 appear to have succeeded in providing basic, adequate housing for the majority of the population. But since 1990, housing has suffered the impact of severe economic austerity, as have other sectors of the economy and welfare provision. Older households appear to retain many of the early benefits of the revolution, while housing options for newly forming households seem to be extremely limited. Moreover, individual households have very limited economic resources with which to maintain their homes. State-led housing programs are currently small in scale and often dependent on funding from overseas nongovernmental organizations.

Although Cuba has avoided the extremes of destitution known in many of the world's developing countries—and the street homelessness of wealthier nations—its housing problems are severe. Quite possibly, its "people without homes" may simply remain hidden in overcrowded and/or structurally dangerous housing conditions.

Cuban authorities have reasonably sound information on the scale and nature of their housing problems. Indeed, most housing research and policy debate seems focused on properties, rather than people. There seems to be a relative lack of research and debate on the nature of home and homelessness for Cuban citizens, as compared to a wealth of technical information on the size and condition of the housing stock. More explicit consideration of what constitutes adequate housing—and homelessness—could help to more accurately reflect the reality of the lived experience of Cuban people.

—*Isobel Anderson*

Further Reading

Anderson, I. & Escobar, M. (2002, July). *Housing in Cuba: A culture of participation?* Paper presented to European Network for Housing Research, International Conference, Vienna.

Cole, K. (1998). *Cuba: From revolution to development.* London: Pinter.

Hamberg, J. (1990). Cuba. In K. Mathéy (Ed.), *Housing policies in the socialist third world* (pp. 35–70). London: Mansell.

Instituto Nacional de la Vivienda (INV). [Official Government Publication]. (2000). *Ley de reforma urbana 40 aniversario* [Law of urban reform: Cuba 40th Anniversary]. Havana, Cuba: Author.

Instituto Nacional de la Vivienda (INV). [Official Government Publication]. (2001). *Istanbul + 5: Cuba's national report.* Havana, Cuba: Author.

Mathéy, K. (1992). Self-help housing policies in Cuba. In Mathéy, K. (Ed.), *Beyond self-help housing* (pp. 181–216). London: Mansell.

Mickelson, R. A. (Ed.) (2000). *Children on the streets of the Americas: Homelessness, education and globalization in the United States, Brazil and Cuba.* New York: Routledge.

Segre, R., Coyula, M., & Scarpaci, J. (1997). *Havana: Two faces of the Antillean metropolis.* New York: Wiley.

D

◉ DALLAS

Homelessness is a serious and visible problem in the central city of Dallas. According to the 1999 Single Point Homeless Count, conducted by the City of Dallas, about 3,100 homeless persons reside on the city's streets. And because Dallas shelters report serving as many as 6,000 clients during a year, the actual number of homeless is probably much higher than the census tally.

Dallas's homeless population is concentrated in the southern half of the central business district (DCBD), mainly because most of the shelters and service providers are located in this part of town. It has been suggested that the visible presence of a large homeless population in the southern sector of the DCBD has been a factor in retarding commercial and residential redevelopment compared to the northern half of the DCBD.

HOW DALLAS DEALS WITH THE HOMELESS

The City of Dallas, along with a slew of voluntary, charitable and faith-based organizations, has been extraordinarily diligent in recognizing the needs of the city's homeless. More than forty-five agencies—in addition to various departments of the City of Dallas, Dallas County, and the state of Texas—are currently providing a wide range of housing, food, medical and employment services to these individuals. Dallas's delivery system can be best described as "fragmented" in that homeless persons must visit a number of different sites in order to avail themselves of the full range of services.

The "official" homeless programs administered by the City of Dallas are managed by the Department of Environmental and Health Services (DEHS). In fiscal 1999–2000, the department reportedly spent $4,329,913 on eight different programs funded primarily by HUD. Less than 7 percent of this total—$301,907—came from own source revenues. The vast majority of expenditures were allocated to shelters, health care, and day resources.

DEHS expenditures, however, represent only a portion of city outlays related to homeless individuals and families. Homeless persons also use a number of services provided by voluntary and faith-based institutions as well as by Dallas County. For example, most homeless persons and families receive medical care from Parkland Hospital, a county facility. They also impose "costs" on the city and county to the extent they use police time, stay in local jails, appear in court, or become patients in a detoxification center. The Central Citizens Association has estimated that the total public and private costs of providing services to Dallas' nearly 4,000 homeless persons is more than $20 million annually.

CENTRAL BUSINESS DISTRICT PROPERTY VALUATION COMPARISON: NORTH VERSUS SOUTH

Any visitor to downtown Dallas is struck by the disparities in development between the northern and southern halves of the central business district (DCBD). The northern half is dominated by relatively new high-rise office buildings while the southern half is characterized by older low-rise structures and vacant land. Though some redevelopment is occurring in the southern sector, the pace of growth has been extremely slow. The visible concentration of Dallas' homeless population may be one impediment to the commercial revival of the southern sector.

Comparative Property Valuations

In 2000, real property valuations in the northern half of the DCBD averaged $93.32 per square foot of building space while properties in the southern sector were valued at an average of $63.54. Furthermore, this gap in property valuations has been growing since 1995.

In addition, planning and urban renewal efforts have not been particularly successful in reversing a long-term trend of slower development in the southern half of downtown. Building space densities are much higher in the northern sector compared to the southern part of the DCBD. Development in the northern sector, as measured by land-to-building space ratios, is between three and four times as dense as the southern sector—even allowing for the preponderance of public buildings in the southern half, and accounting for low building-to-land-area uses such as the convention center. This suggests even greater disparities in taxable property valuations between the sectors.

Tax Revenue Losses from Lagging Development in the Southern DCBD

There are three major consequences for properties (and owners) in the southern sector not fully enjoying the resurgence in market demand being experienced by the northern half of the DCBD. First, there is less justification for encouraging new development in vacant land areas. Second, lower market performance of southern sector properties inhibits property owners' interest in investing in significant renovation of older properties. Perhaps most important at a time of increasing demands on public services, the southern sector's comparatively poor performance means lower revenues for local taxing entities.

Based on 2000 tax rates and total average real and business personal property valuations, the City of Dallas, Dallas County, and the Dallas Independent School District are losing at least $4.1 million per year due to valuation disparities from a lack of development in the southern sector. In other words, if existing southern sector properties were valued by the marketplace as highly as properties in the northern sector on a per-square-foot basis, the City of Dallas would add a little over $1 million per year to its revenues. Similarly, the Dallas Independent School District, struggling to afford major upgrades in facilities, equipment, and teaching personnel at its most distressed schools, would realize over $2.3 million in new revenues each year.

IMPLICATIONS

The northern and southern halves of the Dallas central business district present a stark contrast. Whereas the northern sector will soon be built out with commercial, residential, and entertainment venues, the southern sector is languishing with comparatively little development activity and depressed property values. Without question, the concentration of homeless persons is contributing to the slow pace of redevelopment in the southern sector. And despite more than $20 million spent annually on programs for the homeless, their numbers have not declined.

If these individuals and families could be served from a central location near the DCBD, commercial and residential development in the southern sector would likely accelerate dramatically, with attendant economic and fiscal benefits to local taxing jurisdictions. Indeed, the new economic activity and tax revenue resulting from revival of the southern sector would actually enable the City of Dallas to broaden its programs targeted to the homeless. At the same time, the experience of other cities suggests that providing services to the homeless at a centralized location helps to avoid duplication, hold down costs, and enhance the quality of life for these individuals and families.

—Bernard L. Weinstein and Terry L. Clower

Further Reading

City of Dallas. (1999). *Dallas homeless count, 1999.* Dallas, TX: Department of Environmental and Health Services.

Glomm, G., & John, A. (2002). Homelessness and labor markets. *Regional Science and Urban Economics, 32*(5), 591–606.

Kilgannon, C. (2002, February 26). A census that can't go door to door. *New York Times,* p. A23.

Morgan, P. (2002, November/December). A permanent solution. *Journal of Housing and Community Development, 59*(6), 19–22.

Quigley, J., Raphael, S., & Smolensky, E. (2001, February). Homeless in America, Homeless in California. *The Review of Economics and Statistics, 83*(1), 37–55.

Stein, J. (2002, January 20). The real face of homelessness. *Time Magazine, 161*(3), 52–57.

Urban Institute. (1999). *Homelessness: Programs and the people they serve.* Washington, DC: Author.

U.S. Department of Housing and Urban Development, Office of Policy Development and Research. (1995, January). *Review of Stewart B. McKinney homeless programs administered by HUD.* Washington, DC: Author.

U.S. Department of Housing and Urban Development, Office of Policy Development and Research. (1999, May). *Assessing property value impacts of dispersed housing subsidy programs.* Washington, DC: Author.

U.S. Department of Housing and Urban Development, Office of Policy Development and Research. (2002, October). *Evaluation of continuums of care for homeless people.* Washington, DC: Author.

▣ DEINDUSTRIALIZATION

Deindustrialization refers to the structural processes of industrial decline through disinvestment, relocation, or both. It results from corporate decisions to reduce costs and enhance profits by relocating manufacturing facilities to cheaper labor markets elsewhere or simply shutting down in the face of lower-priced goods from abroad. Increased worker productivity can also cause deindustrialization. Industrial decline may be followed by an increase in the service sector, which then provides jobs for some displaced industrial workers, but these are often lower-paying, impermanent, or dead-end jobs. Deindustrialization causes major problems, especially for industrial workers who lose relatively well-paid and secure jobs. It also impacts their families, their neighborhoods, and the small businesses and institutions that depend upon them and their communities. It can produce extreme poverty and homelessness. The term was first used by the Nazis during the World War II period to describe their policy of stripping conquered regions of industrial activities. In the 1970s, scholars in Great Britain adopted it to describe industrial decline there.

In the early 1980s, American economists Barry Bluestone and Bennett Harrison wrote a seminal study of deindustrialization in the United States, at a time when manufacturing's share of employment fell significantly. They date the process from the economic slowdown of the 1970s, when domestic industries appeared unable to compete in the international market; corporate leaders "systematically disinvested in the nation's basic productive capacity" (Bluestone and Harrison 1982, 6). Some corporations acquired other companies rather than reinvest in their own industry (for example, U.S. Steel acquired the Marathon Oil Company); others, like General Electric, shipped production overseas at the expense of domestic workers. During the 1970s, between 32 and 38 million jobs disappeared as a result of this disinvestment. Besides the loss of their well-paid industrial jobs, the newly unemployed experienced sustained and significant income loss and underemployment, loss of family wealth, and an increased likelihood of physical and mental health problems.

Blue- and white-collar workers alike suffered from deindustrialization. Those most likely to experience longer and more sustained unemployment were women and African-Americans and other minority workers. These patterns resulted from long-standing corporate and union discrimination and from a seniority system that caused workers with the shortest job tenure to be laid off first. Bluestone and Harrison, however, do not link deindustrialization to the period's growing homelessness.

PRE-1945 DEINDUSTRIALIZATION

While economists and sociologists have largely focused on deindustrialization as a post–World War II phenomenon, historians have demonstrated the concept's relevance for the decline of pre-machine handicraft industries. Recent studies have, for example, traced the deindustrialization of the woolen industries of late thirteenth- and fourteenth-century Flanders, seventeenth-century northern Italy, and the mid-nineteenth-century Languedoc region of France. Major parts of Italy and France were not industrialized or centers of woolen production; hence reference to specific region is important. These studies reveal that the industrial decline, as painful as it was for each region, was not complete; some parts of the industry remained competitive in the larger world markets. These findings hold relevance for the later U.S. experience where some segments of declining industries persisted. In all these dislocations, as historian Christopher Johnson concluded, "those who paid [the price for these changes] were the ordinary workers" (Johnson 2002, 27). Another classic case of deindustrialization is the decline in the cotton industry in Massachusetts after World War I, when the number of wage earners dropped by nearly 40 percent. Historians and others have also documented deindustrialization in the coal industry of the U.S. Appalachian region as well as in Belgium, France, India, Scotland, South Africa, and Wales; they also reported industrial decline in other industries in India and South Africa.

A BROADER THEORY OF DEINDUSTRIALIZATION

Since the work of Bluestone and Harrison, the deindustrialization thesis has been broadened and refined. Despite historians' work, some U.S. economists consider the process as old as capitalism, but most focus on recent manifestations in the United States in the post–World War II period. From 1967 to 2001, manufacturing jobs declined nationally by 9 percent; in the industrial Midwest and Northeast, job loss exceeded 40 percent while poorer-paying service employment grew rapidly. In contrast to Bluestone and Harrison, later studies found that males were more directly affected by deindustrialization than women, but minority men were more likely to experience more and longer periods of underemployment or unemployment than white men. This job and income instability produced additional problems; the unemployed confronted a range of social consequences including higher divorce rates, mental health problems, substance abuse, and criminality. These social problems clearly had repercussions for women and children as well. Their communities, which experienced a sharp decline in tax receipts, struggled to provide the necessary social services.

Deindustrialization in Detroit: 1945–1980

While all U. S. regions experienced some deindustrialization and its related consequences, the industrial Midwest experienced the greatest job losses, dislocations, and industrial decline. Thomas Sugrue's 1996 study, *The Origins of the Urban Crisis,* reveals the extent to which Detroit's industrial employment declined in the post–World War II period. While automation played a role in this decline, clearly disinvestment, plant closings, and relocations (to Detroit suburbs and elsewhere in the United States and abroad) played major roles in the growing unemployment. Total manufacturing employment plummeted by over half from 1947 to 1977. Joblessness for all Detroit adult males grew from 7.5 percent in 1950 to 11.7 percent in 1980; African-American men, however, experienced much greater unemployment—from 11.8 to 22.5 percent. Even more striking is the fact that while 45 percent of the total work-age male population was unemployed or not in the labor force in 1980, for African-American Detroiters it was 56 percent.

Black Detroiters faced growing unemployment at the same time that southern African-Americans continued to migrate there in search of work; both groups confronted a dramatically shrinking labor market. Although all unemployed workers experienced great difficulties, Sugrue concluded that the "combination of discrimination and deindustrialization weighed most heavily on . . . young African

American men" (Sugrue 1996, 147). As early as the end of the 1950s, black workers, unable to find work, grew increasingly demoralized and angry; these frustrations fed the city's brutal rebellion, the riot of 1967.

Midwest Deindustrialization: The 1980s

In the period after 1980, industrial decline remained more prominent in the Midwest than in the rest of the nation. Between 1979 and 1986, manufacturing jobs nationally declined 10 percent; in the Midwest they declined by over 17 percent. From 1972 to 1986, Illinois and Ohio lost 28 and 18 percent of their manufacturing employment, respectively, but ten states and the District of Columbia also suffered double-digit percentage losses. These included states in practically every region of the country: West Virginia (29 percent), Pennsylvania (27 percent), New York (22 percent), Indiana, Maryland, and New Jersey (15 percent each), Montana (14 percent), and Hawaii (11 percent). In their study of deindustrialization in the Midwest, Ann Markusen and Virginia Carlson concluded, "Some of this job loss has been the result of automation and outsourcing, but a good share was due to plant closings and disinvestment" (Markusen and Carlson 1989, 29).

CHALLENGES TO THE ECONOMIC THEORY OF DEINDUSTRIALIZATION

It is important to note that the deindustrialization thesis has been questioned by some scholars almost from its inception. Some economists, focusing on the recent U.S. experience, argued that deindustrialization was a cyclical recessionary period; recovery would bring industrial growth and reemployment. The recent econometric analysis of Robert Rowthorn and Ramana Ramaswamy found, however, that manufacturing's percentage of employment in the most advanced countries fell from 28 percent in 1970 to 18 percent in 1994. They saw deindustrialization as the product of "successful economic development" instead of the result of decline (Rowthorn and Ramaswamy 1997, 7). They concluded that it was increased worker productivity, which made it possi-

ble for fewer workers to produce the same amount of goods, that accounted for nearly two-thirds of the job loss rather than global competition. However, neither of these theories speaks to the problems of the long-term unemployed and the homelessness produced by the deindustrialization process.

Deindustrialization (Macro) and Homelessness (Micro) Studies

Whatever their discipline, scholars who focus primarily on macro-level structural changes seldom consider the micro-level enough to tease out how homelessness might result from deindustrialization. In contrast, studies of homelessness tend to focus on the micro-level of analysis, that is, on an individual's reasons for being homeless. They often ignore the structural conditions that cause poor people to become homeless. Increasingly, however, studies of homelessness have begun to link macro level economic restructuring to the growth of the homeless population since 1975.

The Limits of Individual Disability as a Cause of Homelessness

Traditionally, students of homelessness theorized that individual deficits or disabilities such as substance abuse or mental illness led to homelessness; *A Nation in Denial* by Alice Baum and Donald Burnes represents an application of this theory. However, even though these are important causes of homelessness, the theory does not convincingly account for the sudden increase in both the numbers and the kinds of homeless people that emerged in 1975. Although enumerations or estimates of homeless populations are fraught with methodological and other problems, as are definitions of homelessness, both anecdotal and statistical evidence confirm the fact that there has been a significant increase in the number of homeless people in American cities. The first federal census of homeless people in 1984 reported that from 250,000 to 350,000 people were homeless on a given night; by 2000, an Urban Institute study estimated the number at 460,000.

Questioning the individual deficits theory as an

explanation for the rapid growth in homelessness, sociologist Martha Burt concluded that the proportion of mentally ill and some substance abusers remained constant in the overall population. Other scholars, like psychiatrist H. Richard Lamb, linked the increased numbers of homeless people to the deinstitutionalization of mental hospitals, a process that began in the mid-1950s, with most patients discharged during the 1960s. The time gap between their release from mental institutions to their appearance in the homeless population beginning in the late 1970s indicated that they did not become homeless immediately. Ironically, homelessness could cause disabilities as well as the other way around. As sociologist Karin Ringheim suggested, "[For] a substantial proportion of homeless the trauma of homelessness itself precipitated mental illness" (Ringheim 1990, 25).

THE NEW HOMELESS POPULATION

Beginning in the 1970s, the demographics of homelessness began to change dramatically. The typical homeless people of the 1950s and 1960s were relatively homogeneous: elderly single white males who lived on an urban skid row. The new homeless people were strikingly heterogeneous: There were more women, families, and younger men (who were disproportionately minority). These demographics described those most affected by deindustrialization.

Deindustrialization as a Structural Cause of Homelessness

The confluence of the rise in the number of homeless people with the growing unemployment resulting from deindustrialization and of the similarities in the demographics of the new homeless and the industrially unemployed led some scholars to theorize that the new homelessness resulted from several structural changes. They saw deindustrialization as one of several causes of the post-1975 explosion of homelessness.

Studies that analyze structural causes are complex. Anthropologist Kim Hopper and urban planner Jill Hamberg argue that a "perfect storm" of dein-

dustrialization, economic downturn, sharp reductions in affordable housing, and steep cuts in public programs for the poor came together beginning in the late 1970s and accelerated rapidly in the 1980s, causing a rapid rise in the number of poor and homeless people. Between 1978 and 1983, the number of Americans living below the poverty line increased more than 40 percent; at the same time, the federal government reduced benefits for the poor, including welfare, energy assistance, and food stamps, by over 16 percent. Redevelopment, abandonment, displacement, and gentrification sharply reduced the number of affordable housing units; between 1970 and 1982, nearly one-half of single-room occupancy units (SROs) disappeared, while housing vacancy rates declined and rental prices increased significantly. These elements continued through the 1990s and accelerated from 2000 to mid-2003; they impacted on former residents of mental hospitals, substance abusers, and the newly unemployed and their families.

These structural studies tease out the various elements, personal and structural, that lead to homelessness. One study estimated that between 20 and 25 percent of homeless people "have at some time experienced severe . . . mental illness," and that half of all homeless people may have had substance abuse disorders (Koegel, Burnam, and Baumohl 1996, 31). Yet their analysis of Los Angeles's homeless people found that half of the interviewees had experienced a job loss or reduction of public benefits in the year before first becoming homeless, and that others had confronted significant increases in expenses or undergone divorce or separation traumas. Another study reported that most "homeless people . . . readily identify the lack of housing and . . . money . . . as the source of their troubles" (Wright, Rubin, and Devine 1998, 28).

In a study of New York City homelessness, researchers held that the homeless "represent the most marginalized persons from a community that is getting poorer" rather than being typical members of their respective communities (Hopper, Susser, and Conover 1985, 204). The young homeless men in their sample reported some erosion from their parents' generation, especially in education. For most of them, their last job was in service or sales, and few had had access to higher-paying industrial work. Most showed "no evidence of serious psychiatric disorder (or drug/alcohol) problems" (Hopper, Susser, and Conover 1985, 209). Finally, while earlier studies portrayed homeless people as deficient or impaired, this study found them trying to control their lives by utilizing several survival strategies, including the use of homeless shelters.

*Statistical Studies Supporting
Deindustrialization as a Cause*

Several quantitative studies have sought to determine what factors are most associated with increased homelessness; these tended to support broader multicausational models. Martha Burt's analyses of data for 182 cities "consistently point[ed] to the effects of local economic structure and the relationship between manufacturing and service jobs, homeless rates and increases in those rates over the decade of the 1980s" (Burt 1992, 222). She found that homelessness was associated with increased unemployment, single parenthood, reduced public benefits, and high housing and living costs.

GLOBAL DEINDUSTRIALIZATION AND PUBLIC POLICY

Deindustrialization's impact on the unemployed and the homeless varied significantly among advanced countries. Where governments played a major role in providing mitigating programs, as in Germany's industrial Ruhr Valley, most workers maintained employment and moved successfully to white-collar work. In contrast, the U.S. government reduced existing programs and failed to respond effectively, which resulted in significant harm to unemployed individuals, their families, and their larger communities.

Deindustrialization resulted from disinvestment, plant relocation, and improved worker productivity. It led to long-term unemployment, especially for young minority males, and to poverty for women and children. Since 1975, deindustrialization has combined with a decline in affordable housing and public benefits to produce a rapid increase in the number

of poor people. From this heterogeneous group, increasing numbers of the most marginal, including substance abusers and the mentally ill, have become homeless.

—*James Borchert*

Further Reading

Althena, B., & van der Linden, M. (Eds.). (2002). Deindustrialization: Social, cultural, and political aspects. *International Review of Social History, 47*(Supplement 10).

Baum, A., & Burnes, D. (1993). *A nation in denial: The truth about homelessness.* Boulder, CO: Westview Press.

Baumohl, J. (Ed.). (1996). *Homelessness in America.* Phoenix, AZ: Oryx Press.

Bluestone, B., & Harrison, B. (1982). *The deindustrialization of America: Plant closings, community abandonment, and the dismantling of basic industry.* New York: Basic Books.

Burt, M. (1992). *Over the edge: The growth of homelessness in the 1980s.* New York: Russell Sage Foundation.

Dear, M., & Wolch, J. R. (1987). *Landscapes of despair: From deinstitutionalization to homelessness.* Princeton, NJ: Princeton University Press.

Hopper, K., & Hamberg, J. (1986). The making of America's homeless: From Skid Row to new poor, 1945–1985. In R. G. Bratt, C. Hartman, & A. Meyerson (Eds.), *Critical perspectives on housing.* Philadelphia: Temple University Press.

Hopper, K., Susser, E., & Conover, S. (1985). Economies of makeshift: Deindustrialization and homelessness in New York City. *Urban Anthropology, 14*(1–3), 183–236.

Johnson, C. H. (2002). Introduction: Deindustrialization and globalization. *International Review of Social History, 47*(Supplement 10), 3–33.

Koegel, P., Burnam, M. A., & Baumohl, J. (1996). The causes of homelessness. In J. Baumohl (Ed.), *Homelessness in America.* Phoenix, AZ: Oryx Press.

Kusmer, K. L. (2000). *Down and out, on the road: The homeless in American history.* Oxford, UK: Oxford University Press.

Lamb, H. R. (1984, September). Deinstitutionalization and the homeless mentally ill. *Hospital and Community Psychiatry, 35*(9), 899–907.

Markusen, A. R., & Carlson, V. (1989). Deindustrialization in the American Midwest: Causes and responses. In L. Rodwin & H. Sazanami (Eds.), *Deindustrialization and regional economic transformation: The experience of the United States* (pp. 29–59). Boston: Unwin Hyman.

Quigley, J. M., Raphael, S., & Smolensky, E. (2001, February). Homeless in America, homeless in California. *Review of Economics and Statistics, 83*(1), 37–51.

Ringheim, K. (1990). *At risk of homelessness: The roles of income and rent.* New York: Praeger.

Rowthorn, R., & Ramaswamy, R. (1997, April). Deindustrialization: Causes and implications. Working Paper of the International Monetary Fund WP/97/42. Retrieved May 5, 2003, from http://www.eldis.org/static/doc3900.htm

Sommer, H. (2000). *Homelessness in urban America: A review of the literature.* Conference on Urban Homelessness and Public Policy Solutions. Berkeley, CA: Institute of Government Studies Press.

Sugrue, T. J. (1996). *The origins of the urban crisis: Race and inequality in postwar Detroit.* Princeton, NJ: Princeton University Press.

Wallace, M., & Rothschild, J. (Eds.). (1988). *Deindustrialization and the restructuring of American industry: A research annual.* Greenwich, CT: JAI Press.

Wright, J. D., Rubin, B. A., & Devine, J. A. (1998). *Beside the golden door: Policy, politics and the homeless.* New York: Aldine de Gruyter.

⊡ DEINSTITUTIONALIZATION

Deinstitutionalization is an awkward and often misunderstood term. Simply stated, it refers to a policy intended to reduce a society's reliance on large residential facilities that congregate people for care and control under sequestered conditions, frequently against their will and often in centralized public accommodations. Under deinstitutionalization, welfare and control aspects of social regulation are carried out on a smaller scale, largely under voluntary circumstances, in close (or closer) proximity to a person's home—and more often under the auspices of nongovernmental organizations. Although the process of deinstitutionalization has been most often associated with the management of persons with severe mental illness since the mid-1960s, in the United States the process descended from changes in the child welfare and criminal justice systems of many states beginning early in the twentieth century (for example, the shift from orphanages, often called "industrial homes," to family foster care or the use of probation and parole as an alternative to incarceration). Indeed, during the past few decades, deinstitutionalization has been seen to one degree or another in the management of lawbreakers, people with alcohol and other drug problems, and those with developmental disabilities and severe musculoskeletal impairments—that is, all groups historically subject to institutional concentration.

INSTITUTIONAL CARE AS HOUSING POLICY

Deinstitutionalization has been a long-evolving reaction to the dominant institutional solution for a variety of problems. Institutional care and control were appealing for a variety of reasons, but none was more important than the institution's ability to provide an alternative to a conventional home for those people who had no kin, were extremely burdensome to their families (often because of their disruptive behavior), or whose legal and social transgressions were deemed to warrant isolation in the service of social order. Many famous U.S. citizens were "institutionalized" in private or public facilities: As a boy, baseball great Babe Ruth spent several years before World War I in a Baltimore industrial home that was run by the Catholic church, because his parents couldn't afford to raise him; during the 1960s, saxophone masters Art Pepper and Frank Morgan, both heroin addicts, played in the same jazz band at San Quentin State Prison near San Francisco, and bebop genius (and polypharmacist) Charlie Parker wrote the famous song "Relaxin' at Camarillo" in reference to his sojourn of several months at a state mental hospital in southern California in 1947.

Most institutions were intended to be transitional settings. They were to subject their residents to a disciplined and beneficial regime of living that would prepare them to resume a place in the noninstitutional world. As it happened, however, a large percentage of institutional residents stayed for a long time or returned repeatedly when their lives outside unraveled. Young men and women grew up in orphanages because their families could never manage to support them or had brutalized them; adults with severe mental illness languished for years in mental hospitals for lack of another receptive home; alcoholics, addicts, and criminals returned repeatedly to hospitals and prisons when their "community adjustment" soured. Institutions of all sorts grew well beyond the population size for which they had been designed. Many, most notably mental hospitals and the "poorhouses" or "county farms" that evolved into public old-age homes, became internally differentiated to separate "chronic" from "acute" cases or, in less clinical language, those with some hope of getting out and those who would never leave. Inevitably, the "hopeful cases" got the most attention, and the others, the "custodial cases," were left to spin out their lives in sordid conditions of neglect. The term *back ward,* used to describe those institutional regions inhabited by the hopeless cases, derives from the location of these areas in the rear parts of buildings hidden from public view.

DISMANTLING THE INSTITUTIONAL SOLUTION

The institutional solution for impairment and waywardness often was degrading, ineffective, expensive—and impervious to meaningful reform. To be sure, mental hospitals, prisons (modern Western prisons, at least), and other institutions did not set out to brutalize and incapacitate at huge public and private cost. In the end, however, many of them did just this (and still do), and their scale, complexity, and resistance to outside interference created formidable barriers to generations of those who would change them. Deinstitutionalization was intended not merely to change but also to dismantle.

Regardless of the population concerned, deinstitutionalization originated from considerations of standards of human liberty and dignity and the creation of cost-effective mechanisms of care and control. However, the historical processes of deinstitutionalization have varied considerably depending on the population at issue. The extraordinary growth of the U.S. prison population since the late 1980s, due in large measure to the long-term incarceration of federal drug offenders under strict minimum sentencing provisions, reminds us that deinstitutionalization occurs under specific historical and political circumstances and that it may proceed quickly on one front while being stalled or reversed on another.

Conceptually, though, the dismantling of the institutional solution has some basic component processes. First, institutional residents must be transferred to other sites of care and control; second, routes into institutions must be changed so that those people who leave are not just replaced by new inmates; and third, the regulatory functions of the

institution must be reproduced in noninstitutional settings. As a practical matter, these processes should be undertaken in just the opposite order in which they are listed. It makes little sense to depopulate an institution by transferring residents and preventing the admission of new ones if sufficient and appropriate noninstitutional settings are not in place beforehand.

However, policymaking is not always logical or sufficiently forward-looking. Thus, the controversy about deinstitutionalization mainly concerns this last component of the process. Indeed, some analysts distinguish between institutional depopulation and "community care" rather than invoke the term *deinstitutionalization* to cover both. Such a distinction emphasizes that although community care might have a logical connection to institutional depopulation, its achievement is neither a political nor a technical given. A government can depopulate institutions quite successfully without providing the resources required if alternative settings are to provide adequate care and control for the same populations. (Early critiques of deinstitutionalization in the mental health field stressed that the new "community-based" programs were serving a relatively healthy population that was categorically distinct from its institutional counterpart.) Further, programs may not be able technically to translate all of the institution's regulatory functions (notably, secure detention) or its substitute livelihoods to other settings. The state mental hospital census in the United States has declined from its zenith of 559,000 in 1955 to less than 75,000 today, but few would argue that community care is without significant problems.

In theory, the widespread development of "supportive" and "substitutive" services facilitates the dismantling of the institutional solution. Supportive services are intended to maintain people in their own homes with restrictions on their activities only as necessary for their safety or the safety of others. In mental health policy and mental health law parlance, this is known as the principle of "housing in the least restrictive environment." Substitutive services involve the provision of alternative, supervised environments, with limitations consistent with safety but designed to help someone live the most independent life of which he or she is capable. In their most complete expressions, substitutive services comprise alternative homes that may be permanent or transitional.

A number of factors have contributed to the erosion of political support for deinstitutionalization in the United States. The most important of these factors have been the necessary scale and thus the cost of community care in an era when the huge baby boom generation (those people born between 1946 and 1964) has reached maturity; the persisting shortage of low-income housing that could provide sites of supportive services; and the general reduction in social welfare benefits and services, particularly by state and local governments. One result has been what is sometimes called "transinstitutionalization," or the transfer of institutionalized persons from one large, congregate institution to another of only somewhat lesser scale and restriction. The most frequently cited example of transinstitutionalization is the transfer of elderly state hospital patients to large nursing homes that began during the 1960s and 1970s. However, during the 1980s and 1990s, the reappearance of mammoth homeless shelters not seen since the Great Depression (1929–1941) raised a similar issue.

HOMELESSNESS AND DEINSTITUTIONALIZATION

The high prevalence of serious mental disorders among homeless shelter residents often is used as evidence that homelessness is a direct outcome of deinstitutionalization, that homelessness results from the dismantling of institutional solutions in the absence of effective community care. During earlier eras, so the reasoning goes, today's sheltered mentally ill, including many of those people with concurrent substance use disorders, would have been in state hospitals. In fact, although more permissive civil commitment laws and a much greater institutional capacity significantly prevented homelessness in the past, they did not eliminate it. The grasp of the asylum was never sure, and—the gradual accumulation of "chronic" cases notwithstanding—most institutional sojourns were short. The term *revolving door*, which has been in use for about fifty years to describe the rapid cycling of people in and out of

institutions, is the successor metaphor to *rounder*, a late nineteenth-century term applied to those people who moved frequently in and out of jails, hospitals, and other similar facilities, making what is sometimes called the "institutional circuit."

Viewed this way, the relationship between homelessness and deinstitutionalization alerts us to the fact that homelessness is a failure of "abeyance mechanisms" more generally. (Abeyance mechanisms are social arrangements that provide niches for surplus people.) As well, it makes clear that homelessness represents failures in interrelated policy domains, especially those of income maintenance and housing policies, from which deinstitutionalization and the problems of community care cannot be separated.

The presence in shelters of substantial numbers of persons with mental illness provides a good illustration of this interrelatedness. The vast majority of persons with mental illness do not become homeless. However, the intersection of mental illness and abject poverty often results in homelessness. Although landlords sometimes shun prospective tenants because their symptoms are obvious and difficult to cope with, homeless people with mental illness end up in shelters mainly for the same reason as their healthy peers: In the absence of work or a significant work history, no income maintenance program provides a cash benefit large enough to allow them to purchase housing in a seller's market. This problem has become more acute since the early 1970s and has been worsened by the stagnant inflation-adjusted value of welfare benefits especially and by the destruction or "conversion to higher use" of the single-room occupancy hotels and other forms of cheap group quarters that once housed the denizens of U.S. skid rows. Indeed, due to the availability of cheap flophouses, the members of that population (no strangers to crime, substance use, and psychiatric problems) rarely were homeless as we most commonly use the term today.

THE FUTURE CONNECTION

As noted, deinstitutionalization has proceeded unevenly across the various domains of social care and social control, and we have no reason to think that this will change. To the extent that their members are not perceived to be dangerous, groups with a claim on public sympathy—for example, abused and neglected children, the ill or poor elderly, and the mentally ill or physically impaired—almost certainly will continue to be shielded from a policy of systematic (re)institutionalization. With resentment of minimum sentencing laws growing rapidly among federal judges and with community treatment and criminal justice diversion measures gaining favor in many states, a high percentage of nonviolent drug offenders soon may be steered away from institutionalization. At the same time, though, a large population of long-term inmates of the baby boom generation soon will begin to emerge from U.S. prisons without much in the way of "human capital"—the skills and formal and informal knowledge required for economic survival. Under current circumstances, they are likely candidates for shelter residence.

Whether the supportive and substitutive functions of community care can adequately settle the members of this and other groups depends at least as much on the future of economic and housing policy as it does on innovations in therapy and social rehabilitation. The latter are important, particularly in connection with managing persistent and severe mental illness and substance use without the secure detention afforded by institutional regimes—but without income and housing for those affected, deinstitutionalization will contribute to growing shelter populations.

—*Jim Baumohl*

See also Abeyance Theory; Mental Health System; Mental Illness and Health; Social Welfare Policy and Income Maintenance

Further Reading

Bachrach, L. L. (1978). A conceptual approach to deinstitutionalization. *Hospital and Community Psychiatry, 29,* 573–578.

Baumohl, J., & Huebner, R. (1991). Alcohol and other drug problems among the homeless. *Housing Policy Debate, 2,* 837–865.

Currie, E. (1993). *Reckoning: Drugs, the cities, and the American future.* New York: Hill and Wang.

Hopper, K., Jost, J., Hay, T., Welber, S., & Haugland, G. (1997). Homelessness, severe mental illness, and the institutional circuit. *Psychiatric Services, 48,* 659–665.

Oakley, D., & Dennis, D. L. (1996). Responding to the needs of homeless people with alcohol, drug, and/or mental disorders. In J. Baumohl (Ed.), *Homelessness in America* (pp. 179–186). Phoenix, AZ: Oryx Press.

Rothman, D. J. (1980). *Conscience and convenience: The asylum and its alternatives in progressive America.* Boston: Little, Brown.

White, W. L. (1998). *Slaying the dragon: The history of addiction treatment and recovery in America.* Bloomington, IL: Chestnut Health Systems.

◉ DENMARK

In the early 1980s, if asked about homelessness in Denmark, most Danes would probably have shaken their heads, looked a little amazed, and told the questioner to head abroad to find such social problems. Today, the question calls for a different response: Homelessness has become a social problem that is discussed and acted upon by the nation's politicians, journalists, researchers, students, and social workers.

WHO ARE THE HOMELESS?

It has been argued that the Scandinavian welfare model (see, for example, Esping-Andersen, 1990) prevents widespread poverty relatively well, especially when compared to the models of the United States or the United Kingdom, for example. Denmark provides a wide span of social measures—such as rent subsidies, welfare payments, old age and early retirement pensions—at a comparatively high standard. It offers these benefits to all citizens, regardless of where they reside or their degree of contact with the labor market, and it administers them not by the principles of the insurance industry but simply on the basis of legal residency in Denmark. With this model, the state has been able to limit the problems of poverty and homelessness; indeed, homelessness caused by inability to pay rent is almost nonexistent.

However, still some people are considered homeless. But it is a situation understood to be correlated more with social deviation than with housing policy, market forces, or poverty: The homeless population is understood to consist of people with a variety of personal problems in addition to having no permanent dwelling—such as excessive use of illegal drugs (see Stax, 2003) or alcohol, mental illness (see Brandt, 1992), or a combination of these and other problems (Järvinen, 1993; Koch-Nielsen & Stax, 1999; Stax, 1999). It is these personal troubles, perhaps compounded by housing issues, that are found to cause homelessness.

ORGANIZING AND COUNTING THE HOMELESS

But while the housing situation has not been found to be of central importance in understanding the causes of homelessness in Danish research, it has played a significant role in categorizing the people considered homeless. Stax (2001) presented a typology of homelessness based on where they sleep, which, he argued, underlies the current Danish understanding of the phenomenon. He distinguished between people living on the streets, in shelters for those without a permanent place to stay, doubled up with friends or family, and in "special housing" arrangements—that is, those targeted toward people considered in need of permanent housing but not able to live in an ordinary, independent dwelling.

Notably, shelter standards in Denmark are high. Almost all shelters provide a single-occupancy room, spartanly furnished, with a lockable door, rather than the large-scale dormitories known in other countries. (In a few shelters, almost all located in Copenhagen, one might still find some double-occupancy rooms.) Moreover, shelters are open to tenants twenty-four hours a day.

Estimates of the homeless population have thus far been based on counts of shelter clients, since no scientifically based information on other groups is available—for example, people "sleeping rough" (i.e., sleeping outside) or living doubled up with others. Within the shelter population, however, some data have been gleaned since the late 1990s, when a national register with information on users of shelters was established.

The number of clients using the facilities that year was equivalent to 15 per 10,000 Danes. Drawing information from the register, one finds that one-

Table 1. Homeless Facility Use in Denmark, 2001

Number of institutions	67
Number of beds	2,854
Number of registered clients	8,341
Number of enrollments	20,514
Average days per enrollment	49
Average length of stay per client, in days	121
Number of clients staying one whole year	1,111

Source: Den Sociale Ankestyrelse, 2002b.

third of the clients spent over four months at a facility that year. During the same period, these one-third of the clients accounted for 70 percent of the overnight stays. Furthermore, out of the 20,514 enrollments, 75 percent were clients who had already used a similar institution that same calendar year (Den Sociale Ankestyrelse, 2002b).

SERVICE MEASURES FOR THE HOMELESS

This high number of long-term and repeat users has spurred a new initiative known as "special housing for special people." It offers housing arrangements tailored to specific types of people, particularly those continually moving in and out of shelters or staying for long periods. These facilities provide alternative and more permanent accommodation for the "highest-demand" third of the shelter population—those who draw most heavily on the shelters' resources. The aim is to enable the shelters to focus more upon the clients in acute and time-sensitive need of shelter. Such "special housing" varies widely; it might be, for example, ten freestanding dwellings in an urban setting with no restrictions on intake of alcohol or loudness in effect. It might be living units modified from the staircase of a housing complex, perhaps with a common area for watching television and dining, targeted to people preferring not to live alone in ordinary flats. Or it might be a shared flat or villa where tenants have private rooms but share kitchen, bath, and living room with four or five other people. Special housing measures are so recently initiated that no precise counts or in-depth evaluations of them are available.

There also exists a possibility for providing ordinary housing to homeless people who are considered capable of sustaining a life—perhaps with social support—in an ordinary neighborhood without burdening other people too much. Providing ordinary flats is a possibility that the municipalities can choose to include in their social policy. Municipalities are not obliged to provide permanent housing, but they have the right to assign tenants to up to every fourth vacant apartment in low-cost permanent housing, in these cases overruling the ordinary waiting lists for these dwellings. Seventy percent of Danish municipalities, including those of all larger cities, exercise this right to provide permanent housing (Anker et al., 2002). Very little is known about the actual practice of assigning tenants and how it influences homelessness nationwide, but Denmark's 2001 facility registers show that in 905 cases, a person left a homeless institution for an assigned dwelling. Assuming that a client would seldom obtain more than one assigned dwelling in a given year, this amounts to about 10 percent of those enrolled at shelters that year.

—*Tobias Børner Stax*

Further Reading

Anker, J., Christensen, I., Romose, T. S., & Stax, T. B. (2002). *Kommunal boliganvisning til almene familieboliger: En analyse af praksis og politik i fire kommuner* [Municipal assignments of tenants to council housing: An analysis of practices and policies in four municipalities]. Copenhagen, Denmark: Socialforskningsinstituttet.

Brandt, P. (1992). *Yngre hjemløse i København* [Younger homeless in Copenhagen]. Copenhagen, Denmark: FADL's forlag.

Den Social Ankestyrelse. (2002a). *Brugere af botilbud efter servicelovens § 94: Personer, der er hjemløse eller som har problemer med at fungere i egen bolig* [Clients in housing arrangements established in accordance with 94 in Bill on social services: People being homeless or unable to function in an independent dwelling]. Copenhagen, Denmark: Author.

Den Social Ankestyrelse. (2002b). *Det sociale Danmarkskort 2002* [The social map of Denmark 2002]. Copenhagen, Denmark: Author.

Esping-Andersen, G. (1990). *The three worlds of welfare capitalism.* Cambridge, UK: Polity Press.

Järvinen, M. (1993). *De nye hjemløse: Kvinder, fattigdom og vold* [The new homeless: Women, poverty and violence]. Holte, Denmark: Forlaget Socpol.

Kautto, M., Fritzell, J., Hvinden, B., Kvist, J., & Uusitalo, H. (Eds.). (2001). *Nordic welfare states in the European context.* London: Routledge.

Koch-Nielsen, I., & Stax, T. B. (1999). The heterogeneity of homelessness and the consequences for service provision. In D. Avramov (Ed.), *Coping with homelessness: Issues to be tackled and best practices in Europe* (pp. 429–453). Ashgate, UK: Aldershot.

Stax, T. B. (1999). *Én gang socialt marginaliseret—altid . . . ?* [Once socially marginalized—always . . . ?]. Copenhagen, Denmark: Socialforskningsinstituttet.

Stax, T. B. (2001). Understanding homelessness and social policy in Denmark. In V. Polakow & C. Guillean (Eds.), *International perspectives on homelessness* (pp. 65–84). Westport, CT: Greenwood.

Stax, T. B. (2003). Estimating the use of illegal drugs among homeless people using shelters in Denmark. *Substance Use & Misuse, 38*(3–6), 443–462.

▣ DISORDERS AND HEALTH PROBLEMS: OVERVIEW

The relationship of social disparities and health is a long-standing area of concern in public health policy and practice. Early interest in social disparities in health occurred in the late 1960s, when the war on poverty and the civil rights movement heightened public awareness of broad disparities. Poor populations were reported to suffer disproportionately from higher mortality rates, a higher incidence of major diseases, and a lower availability and utilization of medical services. More than three decades later, major disparities persist in "the burden of death and illness experienced by low-income groups as compared with the nation as a whole" (National Center for Health Statistics 1998, 23).

The individual risk of illness cannot be considered in isolation from the disease risk of the population to which a person belongs. It has long been recognized that social and environmental forces and a strong governmental health infrastructure capable of influencing these forces are critical in ensuring a community's health. Lower socioeconomic (SES) groups have lagged in health largely because the gains in social and environmental conditions enjoyed by higher SES groups have not been widely distributed. Areas populated by low-income groups tend to be fraught with air, water, and soil pollutants, poor access to supermarkets and healthy food choices, poor working conditions, crowded and substandard housing, unsafe settings that do not support physical activity, and other similar deficits. Indeed, lower SES groups are at "risk of risks" (Link and Phelan 1995, 80–94). The greatest impacts in improving population health and reducing health disparities will not be made by modifying one or a few risk factors, but will be the consequences of gradual developmental changes in areas populated by lower SES groups.

Homeless persons, as a group, are exposed to the highest levels of virtually all social and environmental risk factors for health, and as a result pose serious public health concern. Even relatively short bouts of homelessness expose individuals to severe deprivations (for example, hunger and a lack of adequate hygiene) and victimization (for example, physical assault, robbery, or rape). Homeless children, growing up in shelters and without a stable home, often have unmet emotional, social, and educational needs. Many health problems, such as the high rates of infection that result from overcrowded living arrangements in shelters, hypothermia from exposure to cold, and poor nutrition due to limited access to food and cooking facilities, are a direct result of the homeless experience.

Further, in the context of the pressing demands for day-to-day survival, the use of health care may become a lower priority, which commonly exacerbates even minor illnesses and makes treatment more difficult. While there are many commonalities among subgroups of the homeless population in terms of their health, mental health, and use of services, there are unique features that characterize homeless adult individuals, adult family members, children, and youth. The following provides an overview of the health issues that face each homeless subgroup.

HOMELESS ADULT INDIVIDUALS

Homeless adults are subject to the same risk factors for physical illness as the general population, but they may be exposed to excessive *levels* of such risk, and they also experience some risk factors that are unique to the homeless condition. Risk factors include the excessive use of alcohol, illegal drugs, and cigarettes; sleeping in an upright position (resulting in venous disease); extensive walking in poorly fitting shoes; and inadequate nutrition.

Health Status

About 37 percent of homeless adults report having poor health compared to 21 percent of lower SES adults and 4 percent of higher SES adults. The most common self-reported medical conditions among homeless adults include joint problems, respiratory infections, high blood pressure, and problems walking. Contagious diseases, such as tuberculosis and HIV, are also more common among the homeless than the general population. The prevalence of tuberculosis infection among homeless adults ranges from 32 to 43 percent. These TB prevalence rates are three to six times greater than among the general population. The high rate of tuberculosis has been found to be related to the duration of homelessness, living in crowded shelters or single-room occupancy hotels, injection drug use, and increasing age. Tuberculosis may be more difficult to treat among the homeless because of the difficulty of screening and maintaining tuberculosis treatment for this population, and because many have multidrug-resistant organisms.

The prevalence of HIV infection among the homeless is also higher than in the housed population. Studies reveal an HIV infection rate of 9 percent among San Francisco's homeless adults. Among 649 women in the same study, HIV sero-prevalence was 6.3 percent. Risk factors for HIV infection included being black, injection drug use, and chronic homelessness. Rates of HIV infection nationally are estimated to be between 0.3 percent and 0.4 percent.

Mortality

A growing number of studies have documented the powerful and persistent association between a person's socioeconomic status and mortality. Lower SES persons live six to nine years less than higher SES persons. The mortality rate among homeless adults is even greater. Among homeless adults, the age-adjusted number of years of potential life lost before the age of seventy-five years is twenty-eight. Mortality rates for homeless adults are highest among white men (8.9 deaths per 1,000 person-years of observation), followed by nonwhite men (7.1), then nonwhite women (6.7) and white women (5.4). The three leading age-adjusted causes of death for homeless persons are injury (for instance, homicide, suicide, or unintentional poisonings), heart disease, and liver disease.

While the prevalence of infectious diseases among homeless people is commonly emphasized in reports, the excess in mortality observed among homeless adults results primarily from noninfectious causes. Injuries, poisoning, and liver disease—each of which may be associated with substance abuse—play a large part in causing death among the homeless. While substance abuse increases the risk of death, homeless people who do not use substances also experience much higher mortality rates than the general population. Finally, chronic homelessness is also associated with higher rates of mortality. Factors that increase mortality among the homeless—for instance, injury and long-term homelessness—support an emerging population health perspective that confirms the importance of context. The cumulative effect of homelessness points to unequal exposure to social, psychological, and ecological conditions that affect both mortality and health.

Lifestyle Practices

Smoking is the leading cause of preventable deaths and disease in the United States. Smoking leads to an increased risk of heart disease, lung disease, emphysema, and other respiratory diseases. Current smoking among homeless adults (between 69 and 78 percent) is more than double that of lower SES groups and more than three times the rate observed in the general population, placing homeless adults at the highest risk of the serious health implications of smoking.

Despite variations in estimates, most studies of homeless adults describe high rates of alcohol and drug use. Heavy alcohol and drug use may result in numerous health problems such as liver disease, poor pregnancy outcomes, and physical injury. The prevalence of heavy alcohol use among homeless adults is more than twice (42 percent) that of lower SES men and about seven times (29 percent) that of lower SES women. Rates of illicit drug use are also high among homeless adults (they are estimated to be between 25 percent to 50 percent). Reflecting gender-associated findings in the general population, the prevalence rates for both alcohol and drug problems are higher among homeless men than homeless women.

The prevalence of obesity, which places adults at increased risk for hypertension, heart disease, diabetes, and some cancers, is 39 percent for homeless adults, almost three times the rate of the general population. Low rates of physical activity are significantly more common among homeless adults, with 47 percent reporting limited physical activity compared to only 15 percent of the general population. The risk of heart disease, diabetes, hypertension, and colon cancer is higher among those with sedentary lifestyles.

Mental Health

Rates of serious mental disorders are disproportionately high among the homeless, with almost 60 percent of homeless adults experiencing a lifetime disorder, a rate that is four times that observed in the general population. Rates of a recent psychiatric problem are also very high: 39 percent of homeless adults report having had mental health problems in the past month. Lifetime major depression (20 percent) and recent major depression (15 percent) are the most prevalent problems. More than half of homeless adults who suffer from a chronic mental health disorder experience comorbid substance abuse dependence problems as well. Rates of mental disorders are not higher for women than they are for men, with the exception of lifetime depression and serious mental disorder without co-occurring substance dependence.

Women's Health

Homeless women have serious gynecological and obstetrical health concerns, but they lack women's health services. Almost half (48 percent) report a history of sexually transmitted diseases or pelvic inflammatory disease. Non-use of contraception is high. About half of homeless women forty years old or older had not received a clinical breast exam in the past year, and 53 percent of homeless women forty years old or older had not received a mammogram in the past year. In addition, 46 percent of homeless women had not received a Pap smear in the past year, compared to fewer than 23 percent of women in the general population. This is alarming given that 23 percent of homeless family-planning-clinic users had an abnormal Pap smear.

Pregnancy and recent births are risk factors for becoming homeless. Homeless women have a lifetime average of 3.4 pregnancies. Among the 28 percent who reported being pregnant in the past year, 73 percent said that the pregnancy was unintended. In addition, homeless women are more likely to receive inadequate prenatal care than poor but housed women (39 percent versus 15 percent). It follows that homeless women are more likely than the general population of women to have poor birth outcomes; 16.8 percent of women report low-birthweight babies (less than 2,500g) (national average: 7.4 percent); 18.5 percent report giving birth pre-term (before thirty-seven weeks) (national average: 11 percent). However, homeless women's rates of infant mortality are the same as those of housed women.

Trauma and Victimization

Physical traumatic disorders, including injuries such as burns and lacerations, and violent victimization occur at high rates among homeless adults. Rates of sexual assault among homeless persons are considerably higher than those observed in the general population. As many as one-third to two-thirds of homeless adults have been a victim of crime. The reasons for homeless adults' higher risk of traumatic life events include the lack of a safe and protective home, increased vulnerability from mental health or drug-related problems or medical illness, and living in unfamiliar environments.

Health Care Access and Utilization

Seventy-five percent of homeless adults reported receiving some form of health care in the past year. However, 25 percent of homeless adults reported that they needed to see a doctor in the past year but were unable to do so. In addition, the majority of homeless persons seek care at places that do not provide the continuous quality care that can address their multifaceted and complex health problems. Of those homeless persons who sought care in the past year, 32 percent reported receiving medical care at a hospital emergency room, 27 percent at a hospital outpatient clinic, 21 percent at a community health clinic, 20 percent at hospitals as inpatients, and 19 percent at private doctors' offices. High rates of emergency room use among homeless adults represented the substitution of emergency room care for outpatient primary care. More than half lacked a regular source of care, and having such a source is strongly associated with access to health services and the use of preventive health services.

One in four homeless adults is hospitalized during the course of a typical year. About 75 percent of hospitalized homeless adults are hospitalized for conditions that are often preventable (for instance, substance abuse, mental illness, trauma, respiratory disorders, skin disorders, and infectious diseases), a rate that is fifteen times that observed in the general population. Following hospital discharge, almost half (40 percent) of homeless adults are readmitted to a hospital within fourteen months, usually with the same diagnosis as on the initial hospitalization. The finding that most of homeless inpatients could have been treated less expensively in an outpatient setting highlights the difficulty in sustaining treatment intensity for homeless persons outside of a hospital.

Despite higher rates of medical hospitalization and higher rates of disease, homeless adults are in fact less likely than other sectors of the population to use medical ambulatory services. It is not uncommon for homeless adults to delay seeking medical attention at a time when more severe stages of illness could be prevented. Homeless adults, given their increased need for care, may benefit from improvements to and increased availability of primary and preventive care.

Gradients of Health

An accumulating body of research has shown that unsheltered homeless adults and homeless adults with longer lengths of homelessness have poorer physical health than their sheltered or recently homeless counterparts. Compared to those in shelters, unsheltered homeless adults are more likely to use illegal drugs or alcohol, to have been victimized, and to have experienced an accident or injury. An emerging literature on homeless women has shown similar results, with those who are unsheltered more likely to report fair or poor health, to be engaged in risky sex, and to have higher rates of victimization, poor mental health, and alcohol and non-injection drug use than sheltered women. Finally, the fact that adults experiencing extended homelessness are twice as likely to die as those with shorter episodes highlights the cumulative impact of the homeless condition—the unequal exposure to adverse conditions and the unequal access to health care.

HOMELESS ADULT FAMILY MEMBERS

The majority of homeless families are headed by females in their late twenties with an average of two to three children. The health and mental health profile of homeless adult family members, while overlapping with that of adult individuals, also differs. Unlike solitary adults, homeless families are more likely to have opportunities for shelter and are less likely to be living on the streets with little protection from the elements.

Health

One in four homeless mothers report their health to be fair or poor. Just under half suffer from a chronic illness, with rates of asthma, anemia, and ulcers more than four times higher than the rates in a general population sample of comparably aged women. Similar to adult individuals, common acute illnesses include upper respiratory infections, skin problems, and dental and trauma-related problems. When compared to a general population, homeless mothers experience lower levels of physical and social functioning, limitations in completing role responsibilities due to physical or mental health, and higher rates of bodily pain. Health limitations may be explained by the high levels of acute and chronic ill-

ness, environmental stressors, and high rates of childhood and adulthood victimization reported by homeless mothers.

Lifestyle Practices

Three-quarters of homeless mothers report either smoking, using intravenous drugs, a lifetime prevalence of alcohol or drug abuse or dependency, or obesity. More than half of homeless mothers smoke cigarettes, a rate that is considerably higher than that observed in a general population of women.

Homeless mothers, like homeless individual women, are at high risk for contracting sexually transmitted diseases, including HIV. Homeless mothers are twice as likely as low-income housed mothers to have had multiple sexual partners during the past six months; they report twice as many lifetime sexual partners and are more likely to report a younger age of first sexual contact. Homeless mothers who have experienced victimization in childhood or adulthood are at substantially higher risk for HIV.

Trauma, Mental Health, and Substance Abuse

Ninety percent of homeless mothers report severe physical or sexual abuse during childhood or adulthood. Two out of three homeless mothers report childhood physical abuse and almost half report that they had been sexually molested as a child. For most homeless mothers, violence continued into adulthood with just under two-thirds of homeless mothers reporting severe violence by an adult partner. Victimization experiences may significantly compromise a woman's physical and mental health and are associated with many short- and long-term health and mental health consequences.

Experiences of childhood or adult abuse may also result in long-lasting mental health problems, fear and lack of trust, difficulty forming and sustaining supportive relationships, parenting challenges, and substance abuse. Lifetime rates of psychiatric disorders are disproportionately represented among homeless mothers compared to the general population and are a likely consequence of the high rates of victimization. Seventy percent of homeless mothers have at least one lifetime psychiatric disorder, with depression, posttraumatic stress disorder, and substance abuse most common. One in three homeless mothers has lifetime posttraumatic stress disorder, a rate that is three times higher than the rates found in general population studies. Forty percent of homeless mothers have a lifetime prevalence of substance abuse or dependence.

HOMELESS CHILDREN

When compared to mothers of low-income children who are housed, mothers of homeless children are more than two times as likely to report their children as being in fair or poor health; they also report more acute and chronic illness.

Health

High rates of asthma, recurrent ear infections, and gastrointestinal disturbances are reported more commonly among homeless children than among low-income children who are housed. Homeless children are also twice as likely to have been hospitalized during the prior year, a fact that may reflect higher levels of illness or barriers to accessing services.

Factors that may contribute to the adverse impact that homelessness has on children's health include the instability and frequent moves that often precede the homeless episode, environmental and maternal factors, and specific conditions of shelter life. Sheltered mothers may have fewer resources to cope with a child's illness. A mother's emotional distress or diminished availability during the acute homeless period may lead to physical symptoms in a child who needs emotional attention. Also, shelters are often crowded and provide shared food preparation facilities, increasing the likelihood of transmitting infection. Sometimes the exigencies of shelter life and competing demands for survival make a timely use of health care difficult, leading to increased illness severity.

Nutrition and Hunger

Homeless children are at risk for poor nutrition and hunger. Some studies have reported homeless chil-

dren to be at high risk for iron-deficiency anemia, delayed growth, and obesity. Homeless families may not have access to supermarkets and healthy foods. Some shelters may not be able to provide a diet that is balanced and appropriate for children at different developmental stages. Poor nutrition and hunger can compromise a child's growth, contribute to higher rates of illness, and are associated with poorer academic achievement. Children who are hungry are also more likely to experience mental health problems such as anxiety or depression.

Development, Behavior and Emotional Health, and Learning

Many homeless children have experienced a range of stressful life events in addition to homelessness and frequently come to a shelter demonstrating developmental, emotional, and behavioral problems. Stressors include residential instability, with homeless children having moved an average of three times in the year prior to their homelessness. Other stressors include being witness to violence, frequent school moves, and high levels of maternal distress. One in five homeless children have been placed in foster care in the past.

Coping with the homeless episode is often difficult for children. Shelters may be crowded and lack privacy. Children commonly share a room with parents and siblings and are subject to many rules. For some children, the homeless episode may lead to depression or withdrawn behavior, while for others it may lead to acting out and aggressive behavior. It is not uncommon for homeless toddlers and preschoolers to regress in developmental milestones, for example, to lose recently acquired language. Some of these behaviors may be an attempt to express their stress or to gain attention from parents who may be preoccupied with daily demands and distressed themselves.

Homeless children experience delays in development and demonstrate emotional and behavioral health problems. While homeless infants appear to be on track with developmental milestones, research demonstrates that their development slows as they get older. This delay in achieving critical cognitive, social, and language milestones, which begins to appear at approximately eighteen months of age, probably results from the accumulation of multiple stressors over time. Among homeless older children, one in five preschoolers and at least one in three school-aged children manifest emotional or behavioral problems severe enough to warrant professional care. One-third of homeless school-aged children have a current mental health disorder that impairs their functioning. These rates are twice that found in a general population of children. Common disorders include depression, anxiety, and disruptive or aggressive behavior. Despite these high rates of mental health problems, fewer than a third of children with a disorder receive mental health treatment.

Homeless children are also at risk for poor academic achievement, repeated grades, and absenteeism. According to some reports, three out of four homeless children perform below grade level in reading and one in two homeless children perform below grade level in math. As many as 20 percent of homeless children do not attend school at all. Many homeless children have moved frequently before the homeless episode, resulting in numerous school changes, disruption of learning and teacher and peer supports, and potential delays in transfer of school records. Once in school, homeless children often have unmet learning needs, with as many as three-quarters of those meeting the criteria for special education evaluation failing to receive these essential and legally required services and appropriate class placements.

Health Care Access and Utilization

Both homeless mothers and children have higher rates of emergency department use when compared to their housed counterparts. Rates of hospitalization are four times greater among homeless mothers than in the general population of comparably aged women, suggesting gaps in the receipt of primary care services.

Homeless mothers frequently have delays in receiving essential preventive services, including screening for tuberculosis, cervical cancer, and sexually transmitted diseases, and dental care. Homeless children commonly fail to receive essential preventive care including immunizations, periodic health examinations, screening for lead poisoning or ane-

mia, and dental care. A significant subgroup of homeless children do not have a regular health care provider or source of medical care. In the context of daily demands, preventive health care needs may go unmet. Delays in receiving critical preventive services may lead to more illness among homeless children and result in exacerbations of common medical problems that may be easily treated if recognized early. Delays in immunizations may interfere with timely school enrollment. While ending the homeless episode may be the most important preventive health measure to accomplish, health promotion and preventive screening measures can significantly improve the health and well-being of homeless mothers and their children.

HOMELESS YOUTH

National estimates of the number of homeless and runaway youths are close to one million. Reasons vary as to the cause of homelessness and include running away from dysfunctional families, being pushed out of these families, or exiting from involvement in the social service network (for instance, "aging out," foster home failure, or an unsatisfactory institutional placement by the welfare system). Estimates report that one-third of runaway youths have been physically and sexually abused as children. Whatever the reasons, these youths infrequently utilize the shelter system; instead, they attempt to survive on the street. This puts them at risk for victimization and trauma, and introduces numerous physical and mental health challenges.

Homeless youths are on the streets with minimal social and economic resources during a critical developmental stage. Adolescence is characterized as a time for establishing a stable identity, refining a self-image, and developing sexually and socially. When homeless, accomplishing these tasks is made far more difficult given the exigencies of street life and a paucity of supports.

Vulnerabilities and Risk Behavior

Homeless youths generally rely on themselves or peers for survival. In order to support themselves, homeless youths must often participate in illicit activities and risky behaviors, such as panhandling, theft, drug dealing, and exchanging sex for food, shelter, or money. They are frequently victims of violent crime including assault, robbery, and rape. Survival sex is itself a form of repetitive victimization. These activities may cascade into numerous physical and mental health problems.

Experiences of trauma and the lack of a safe environment during adolescence contribute to the mental health, substance abuse, and risk behavior profile manifested by homeless youths. Mental health problems, particularly depression, suicidal symptoms, and anxiety are commonly reported among homeless youths. As many as one-third of youths report a previous suicide attempt. Homeless boys are more likely to engage in antisocial behavior than homeless girls. Some antisocial behaviors, such as stealing money or food to avoid hunger, are, in many instances, required for survival.

High rates of substance abuse are also common among homeless youths, as high as 84 percent according to some reports. Commonly used substances include alcohol, marijuana, crack cocaine, and intravenous drugs. Drug use may be a method of self-medicating a depression as well as of dulling the fear of the dangers on the street. Trading in drugs may also be a means of survival for some street youths. Whether receiving free drugs for sex or exchanging sex for drugs because of an addiction, the resulting risky behaviors expose adolescents to sexually transmitted diseases, including HIV, and to unplanned pregnancies.

Health

The medical needs of homeless youths commonly include exposure-related problems and malnutrition. Poor hygiene, scabies, skin infections, hepatitis, and acute fractures and other traumatic injuries are frequently reported. As discussed above, the rates of sexually transmitted diseases are considerably higher than rates observed among comparably aged housed youths. Lifetime pregnancy rates for homeless youths range from 33 percent to 50 percent in sheltered and non-sheltered youths, respectively, compared to less than 10 percent for non-homeless youths. The pregnant homeless adolescent is at high risk for complications during pregnancy. Poor nutrition, risk exposure, and limited access to or utilization of prenatal care services increase the potential for adverse birth outcomes among homeless pregnant youths.

Health Care Access and Utilization

Numerous barriers lead to a limited use of traditional health care and mental health services by homeless youths. Homeless youths tend to distrust adults and institutions and have concerns regarding confidentiality of personal information. This distrust may be rooted in the history of abuse and neglect in their families of origin or in their unsatisfactory placements in foster care or institutions by the social service network. Lack of insurance poses another significant barrier to their use of health care services. Many youths believe that without money or insurance they cannot receive care, which results in delays in seeking needed medical attention. Limited knowledge of available services may also result in emergency department use, and as with homeless adults, may limit a homeless youth's access to continuous health care that meets preventive as well as urgent health needs.

Successful approaches to the provision of health care to homeless youths combine outreach and drop-in type services with nonjudgmental and confidential caregiving practices.

OUTLOOK FOR THE FUTURE

Homeless populations must struggle not only with the health consequences of being poor, but also with the added burden of residential instability and life on the streets. Structural changes that eliminate homelessness by developing increased affordable housing and opportunities to earn a living wage will ultimately be necessary to improve the health and well-being of the homeless. Reducing persistent health disparities among the poor and the homeless requires a broad strategy that can address the social and environmental conditions that result in adverse health outcomes.

—Linda Weinreb, Lillian Gelberg,
Lisa Arangua, and Mary Sullivan

See also Alcohol and Drugs; Continuum of Care; Health Care; HIV and AIDS; Mental Health System; Mental Illness and Health

Further Reading

Adler, N. E., Boyce, T., Chesney, M. A., Cohen, S., Folkman, S., Kahn, R. L., et al. (1994). Socioeconomic status and health: The challenge of the gradient. *American Psychologist, 49*(1), 15–24.

Andersen, R. M., Rice, T. H., & Kominski, G. F. (Eds.). (2001). *Changing the U.S. health care system.* San Francisco: Jossey-Bass.

Barrow, S. M., Herman, D. B., Cordova, P., & Struening, E. L. (1999). Mortality among homeless shelter residents in New York City. *American Journal of Public Health, 89*(4), 529–534.

Bassuk, E., Weinreb, L., Buckner, J., Browne, A., Salomon, A., & Bassuk, S. (1996). The characteristics and needs of sheltered homeless and low-income housed mothers. *JAMA, 276*(8), 640–646.

Brickner, P. W., Scharer, L. K., Conanan, B. A., Savarese, M., & Scanlan, B. C. (Eds.). (1990). *Under the safety net.* New York: W. W. Norton.

Centers for Disease Control and Prevention. (1999). Ten great public health achievements: United States 1900–1999. *MMWR, 48*(12), 241–243.

Council of Scientific Affairs. (1989, September 8). Health care needs of homeless and runaway youths. *Journal of the American Medical Association, 262,* 1358–1361.

Hibbs, J. R., Benner, L., Klugman, L., Spencer, R., Maccia, I., Mellinger, A. K., et al. (1994). Mortality in a cohort of homeless adults in Philadelphia. *New England Journal of Medicine, 331,* 304–309.

Institute of Medicine. (1988). *Homelessness, health and human needs.* Washington, DC: National Academy Press.

Klein, J. D., Woods, A. H., Wilson, K. M., et al. (2000). Homeless and runaway youths' access to health care. *Journal of Adolescent Health, 27,* 331–339.

Koegel, P., Sullivan, G., Burnam, A., Morton, S., & Wenzel, S. (1999). Utilization of mental health and substance abuse services among homeless adults in Los Angeles. *Medical Care, 37*(3), 306–317.

Kushel, M. B., Vittinghoff, E., & Hass, J. S. (2001). Factors associated with the health care utilization of homeless persons. *JAMA, 285*(2), 200–206.

Link, B., & Phelan, J. (1995). Social conditions as a fundamental cause of disease. *Journal of Health and Social Behavior, Special Issue,* 80–94.

Lynch, J. W. (1997). Cumulative impact of sustained economic hardship on physical, cognitive, psychological and social functioning. *New England Journal of Medicine, 337,* 1989–1995.

McGinnis, M. J., Williams-Russo, P., & Knickman, J. R. (2000). *IOM: Promoting health: intervening strategies from social and behavioral research.* Washington, DC: National Academy Press.

National Center for Health Statistics. (1998). *Health United States, 1998 with socioeconomic status and health chartbook.* Hyattsville, MD: Author.

Robertson, M. J., & Greenblatt, M. (Eds.). (1992). *Homeless, a national perspective.* New York: Plenum Press.

Weinreb, L. F., Goldberg, R., & Perloff, J. (1998). Determinants of health and service use patterns in homeless and low-income housed children. *Pediatrics, 102,* 554–562.

Weinreb, L. F., Goldberg, R., & Perloff, J. N. (1998). The health characteristics and service use patterns of sheltered homeless and low-income housed mothers. *Journal of General Internal Medicine, 13,* 389–397.

Wood, D. (Ed.). (1992). *Delivering heath care to homeless persons.* New York: Springer.

E

EGYPT

Homelessness is less visible in Egypt than it is in many countries. However, indicators are readily apparent throughout Egyptian society, as serious housing shortages, overcrowded urban areas, and poverty have resulted in the creation of squatter settlements. In addition, Egypt has witnessed an increasing number of children who work or live on the streets.

As in other developing countries, poverty is a pervasive problem in Egypt. In recent years, it has increased in prevalence and intensity, as the gap between the rich and the poor has widened. Unemployment and inflation have also increased. Estimates indicate that between 32 and 40 percent of the country's population live at or below the poverty line; indeed, it is often hard to distinguish homelessness from extreme poverty.

STREET CHILDREN

Although homelessness is not viewed as a major public concern in Egypt, street children are now recognized as a social problem requiring urgent governmental attention. The phenomenon of large numbers of children who live or work on the nation's urban streets, often in groups, is considered a relatively new problem. Studies have attributed its rising prevalence to rapid urbanization, deteriorating economic conditions, declining social programs, and weakening family ties (see Bibars 1998; Human Rights Watch 2003).

It is unclear how many street children there really are. Surveys have found that they range between nine and eighteen years, with the majority around thirteen. Most are members of the local urban poor. However, some are older children who have migrated from rural areas in the hope of finding employment, often having left families facing extreme poverty.

Many street children do not attend school, do not receive health care, and are unprotected by adults. The trajectory that leads children from poor families to resort to the streets typically involves poverty, dysfunctional families, child abandonment, and physical and sexual abuse. Some of these children live on the streets to escape violence at home. Others are abandoned by their families who cannot afford to support them or are unable to do so because of death, imprisonment, or illness. Some resort to begging and pickpocketing because these are the only sources of income for their destitute families. To survive, many of these children eventually engage in other petty crime, which often leads them to jail or juvenile correctional facilities.

In 2001, there were more than 11,000 arrests of street children. Under current Egyptian law, they are

Homeless people in Cairo's City of the Dead.
Source: Johannes Armineh/Corbis Sygma; used with permission.

considered "children at high risk" and therefore can be arrested and placed in correctional institutions. While in police custody, street children are given the same treatment as juvenile delinquents and children who have committed more serious crimes. They are often physically abused by supervisors and older children, do not receive adequate services, and sometimes end up being trained to become professional criminals by other children. Human rights groups have documented widespread abuse and exploitation of these children once they are detained or placed under institutionalized care.

Traditionally, care for street children has been provided by religious institutions in the form of charity. These children are often viewed by average citizens as "troublemakers" and criminals. Although Egyptian law makes a distinction between street children (who are considered vagrants) and juvenile delinquents, the distinction breaks down once they enter the legal system. There are few governmental programs designed to deal with street children, and those staffing such programs often lack the necessary skills to address these children's social and psychological needs.

In part as a result of publicity generated in recent years by nongovernmental organizations and human rights groups, Egypt's municipal governments have begun to improve their treatment of street children and to develop programs to help them. Governmental as well as nongovernmental organizations are beginning to seek ways to return these children to their families or find them alternative housing until they reach adulthood.

URBAN HOUSING SHORTAGES

In 2000, the population of Egypt reached 68 million, with an annual growth rate of 1.72 percent. The majority of Egypt's population lives on 5 percent of the country's land, and fully one-quarter live in the capital city of Cairo (Cairo is the most populated city in the Middle East and Africa). Large-scale migrations from rural areas in recent decades have transformed all of Egypt's cities, resulting in massive housing shortages in Cairo and other urban centers.

The Egyptian government has attempted to respond to these shortages with government-subsidized housing. However, such programs have not been adequate to meet the population's needs. Not only has the demand for housing far outstripped what the government programs have been able to supply, but even this limited housing has been slow to appear and is often located in remote towns, where there is little work.

PRECARIOUS HOUSING SITUATIONS

As public, private, and cooperative housing efforts have proven insufficient, the number of slums and squatter settlements has increased dramatically. Squatter settlements, which involve the illegal occupation of mainly publicly owned land, have grown in both inner-city and rural areas. Such settlements now represent 20 percent of the total population in Cairo, 11 percent in Alexandria, 18 percent in Ismailia, 25 percent in Suez, and 12 percent in Port Said. Construction in these settlements is typically of poor quality and is unregulated by building enforcement agencies. Inhabitants receive minimal or no services, including water, electricity, and basic sanitation, and they are especially vulnerable when natural disasters such as earthquakes or flooding occur. Such conditions are not just a concern for settlement residents—they serve as a reservoir for disease and other health dangers whose effects could be widespread.

—*Sawssan R. Ahmed, Mona Amer,*
and Paul A. Toro

Further Reading

Bayat, A. (1997). Cairo's poor: Dilemmas of survival and solidarity. *Middle East Report, 27*(1), 2–6.

Bibars, I. (1998). Street children in Egypt: From the home to the street to inappropriate corrective institutions. *Environment and Urbanization, 10*(1), 201–216.

Denis, E., (1997). Urban planning and growth in Cairo. *Middle East Report, 27*(1), 7–12.

Degg, M. (1993). The 1992 "Cairo earthquake": Cause, effect and response. *Disasters, 17*(3), 226–238.

Evin, A. (1985). *The expanding metropolis: Coping with the urban growth of Cairo.* Singapore: Concept Media/The Aga Khan Award for Architecture.

Human Rights Watch. (2003). *Charged with being children: Egyptian police abuse of children in need of protection, 15*(1).

Nagi, S. Z. (2001). *Poverty in Egypt: Human needs and institutional capacities.* Lanham, MD: Lexington Books.

Soliman, A. (1988). Housing the urban poor in Egypt: A critique of present policies. *International Journal of Urban and Regional Research, 12*(1), 65–86.

ENCAMPMENTS, URBAN

The past fifteen years have seen a rapid growth in the number of homeless men, women, and children living in street camps. Although shelters and emergency services are available, most are filled early in the day or have restrictions, both formal and informal, that limit access to their programs. As a result, shelters and other homeless services programs are unable to meet the complex needs of the broader homeless population. For example, many restrict services to adults, or to men or women, and others do not accept people with health problems such as HIV, mental illness, or drug or alcohol addiction. Thus, semipermanent encampments of homeless people have emerged in many urban settings. These encampments are generally collections of makeshift dwellings constructed of cardboard boxes, scrap wood, plastic sheeting, and other discarded materials. While some encampments are assembled in public places such as on sidewalks or in vacant lots, others are more concealed from public view, springing up along riverbanks and train tracks, under freeway overpasses or bridges, and in alleys or in shrubbery along open highways, freeway on-ramps, and access roads. This entry focuses on encampments in Los Angeles (Cousineau 1997, 2001), the location of the most recent and comprehensive research on the topic.

Researchers studied the physical conditions in the camps and the health status of encampment residents, including substance use and abuse and substance abuse treatment and their access to and use of health care services, including tuberculosis and HIV screening services. The study area was limited to the central Los Angeles area, which includes the financial district, skid row, and the areas surrounding the immediate downtown area: Chinatown, South Park, MacArthur Park, and the industrial areas on the east, among them. Residents of these encampments were interviewed by one of fourteen formerly homeless people who are currently employed as peer counselors in organizations serving the homeless.

Although more than 100 sites were mapped, 54 sites were selected in the target area for site visits and resident interviews. Interviews were conducted with 134 residents of 42 camps, with only two people refusing to be interviewed. The camps ranged in size from one to twenty people and had an average of five occupants. The majority were men; children were seen in only one camp. Two-thirds of the respondents were men. Two people described themselves as transgendered. More than 94 percent of respondents were under the age of 65, with 42 percent between the ages of 30 and 39. More than 50 percent of the respondents were African-American, 34 percent were Hispanic, and 7 percent were Caucasian. Two of the respondents were Asians. Fewer than 20 percent of the men (and none of the women) were veterans, and more than 65 percent were born in the United States; 20 percent, in Los Angeles.

Encampment residents may differ somewhat from

homeless people living in the heart of downtown skid row. For example, 21 percent of the respondents in earlier studies in skid row were Latino, compared with about 33 percent of encampment respondents. Downtown and shelter residents overall tend to be slightly younger compared with encampment residents, and nearly two-thirds were single compared with a little more than half of the encampment residents.

Approximately 65 percent of the respondents had been homeless for at least one year, and 20 percent had been homeless for over five years. The majority of respondents had spent at least one night in an average of three places within the previous year (range of one to ten places). Almost half reported having lived in another camp, but many had spent at least one night in an abandoned building, a mission or shelter, a cold-weather or wet-weather shelter, a hospital, a drug or alcohol program, a room either rented by the respondent or paid for with a government voucher, or with friends or relatives. Thirty-three percent of the respondents reported having lived in the camp for at least one year and 5 percent more than five years.

WHY WON'T ENCAMPMENT RESIDENTS GO TO A SHELTER OR MISSION?

Only 41 percent of the respondents reported having ever lived in a shelter or mission, and 34 percent had spent time in a shelter or mission within the previous year. When asked why they weren't staying in a shelter at present, the majority indicated that they did not like the rules, including religious requirements (34 percent), that they could not afford it (22 percent), that they feared crime or violence in the shelters (15 percent), that the shelters were too crowded (14 percent), or that they were turned away from a shelter (10 percent). Investigators assessed the conditions of the encampment and their potential as threats to health because of such factors as poor sanitation, proximity to on-ramps, and exposure to toxic substances.

Living conditions in the camps are health threatening. Researchers visiting the camps observed the ways people lived and conditions in the camp, including those that might be health threatening. In several encampments, couches, barbecue grills, beds, chairs, and other furniture were observed. Also present were dogs and cats; in one case, chickens, presumably used for food, were kept. In six camps, residents were seen sleeping or sitting amidst piles of garbage and trash. Residents in these and other camps reported that rodents and insects were a problem, and some had obtained rat poison, which they spread on the ground near where they slept at night. Clean water was seldom available. These conditions made it difficult to maintain cleanliness and personal hygiene. Residents in eight camps retrieved water from nearby businesses, while others extracted water that is not potable from the Los Angeles River, which collects the water from street drains. For toileting, people reported that they used portable toilets found at construction sites (7 percent) or missions (7 percent), although most respondents reported exclusively or sometimes using the river, bushes and shrubbery, the street or sidewalk, or some other outdoor location.

Health status and access to health and screening services. Nearly 38 percent of the respondents reported their health as being either poor or fair. More than 30 percent reported having health problems that required ongoing medical attention, including life-threatening, chronic health conditions, without receiving the appropriate medical care. These conditions include heart disease, diabetes, and hypertension. In spite of the low health status of the respondents, encampment residents experienced several formidable barriers to obtaining health care services. Seventy-five percent of the respondents had no health coverage; only one person was covered by Medi-Cal. Although nearly 50 percent had visited a doctor or clinic sometime in the previous six months, 41 percent reported that there was a time when they felt they needed to go to the doctor but did not go. Financial access barriers—no money or insurance—were cited by half as reasons for not going, but other access barriers were reported, including lack of transportation, concern about long waits, and not knowing where to go for health care. Access to dental care was even more limited, with about 12 percent having visited a dentist in the previous six months and 61 percent reporting that they felt like they needed to see a dentist right away. However, access to screening services for HIV and tuberculosis was better than expected. Nearly a third of the respondents said they had received a TB test and a third an HIV test within the previous twelve months. Los Angeles and several other urban areas have seen an increase in the number of funded outreach programs specifically supporting HIV and tuberculosis screening, which may account for this finding. Still, 35 percent had never had an HIV test, and 16 percent had never had a TB test.

Table 1. Length of Time Respondents Have Been Homeless and Have Been Living in the Present Encampment (N = 134)

| | Homeless | | Encampment | |
	Number	Percent	Number	Percent
Less than 1 month	1	1%	3	2%
1 to 6 months	19	14%	61	46%
7 to 12 months	9	8%	23	17%
1 to 2 years	30	22%	20	15%
2 to 5 years	31	23%	12	9%
More than 5 years	27	20%	7	5%
Didn't know	7	5%	NA	NA
No answer	10	8%	8	6%

** Defined as where the person had their own place where they paid rent and could receive mail.

THE OUTLOOK

The health of residents is jeopardized by the living conditions found in downtown encampments. Residents cook and eat in places where food cannot be stored properly and where dishes cannot be washed with hot water. The proximity of garbage, animals, vermin, and human excrement to cooking areas expose residents to infectious diseases, particularly hepatitis, shigella, and salmonella. Lack of proper hygiene can also lead to dental decay and skin problems such as lice, scabies, and impetigo. Many encampments are adjacent to freeways, and residents constantly breath toxic exhaust fumes and risk being hit by moving vehicles as they move in and out of encampments.

Plans to dismantle and outlaw encampments and force people to go to shelters or government camps will at best have only a short-term effect in reducing the number of urban encampments. Many encampment residents will not go to shelters or downtown missions because they fear violence or dislike the rules and regulations. If forced to go there, many would eventually return to an urban encampment.

There have been several financial crises that have threatened the health care safety net in Los Angeles. These crises have led to proposals and in some cases decisions to reduce support for public health and hospital programs and will eliminate or seriously cut back on the major source of care on which many homeless people depend. More protected, however, are federally funded programs such as the Ryan White CARE Act programs for HIV prevention and treatment, the federally sponsored Health Care for the Homeless Program, and CDC-sponsored tuberculosis programs that have supported health-related outreach to homeless people, including many living in encampments. Many encampment residents had contact with these programs, and many had obtained services as a result.

Activities designed to reduce the number of encampments must include efforts to address substance abuse in this population. Homeless people require programs with more tolerant and flexible approaches to treatment that emphasize social support and housing and case management and minimize requirements to achieve and maintain sobriety within time frames designed for more stable populations. Although encampment conditions are health threatening, the conditions are not unlike those found in many low-rent, slumlord-owned apartments and hotels in large cities. Programs that engage residents of homeless encampment through creative outreach and effective case management should be supported. These efforts will encourage camp residents to choose alternatives to encampments while providing them with services that promote and protect their health and welfare and put them on a road to self-sufficiency, employment, and stable housing.

—*Michael R. Cousineau*

Further Reading

Cousineau, M. R. (1997, February). Health status and use of health services of encampment dwellers. *Journal of Health Care for the Poor and Underserved, 8*(1).

Cousineau, M. R. (2001, November). Comparing adults in Los Angeles County who have and have not been homeless. *Journal of Community Psychology, 29*(6).

▣ EPIDEMIOLOGY

Over the years, Americans have expressed considerable interest in and concern about the extent of alcohol, drug, and mental health problems among homeless persons. In recent decades, the nature of these problems has changed, as a function of both demographic and social policy changes, especially in the realms of mental health and housing. During the mid-twentieth century, the homeless population was more homogenous than it is today and was typified by men living in inner cities, many of them alcohol abusers. But beginning in the late 1960s and early 1970s, the homeless population became more diverse. A number of factors contributed to this trend, including the broad-scale release of patients from state mental hospitals, a demographic shift toward younger homeless individuals, the destruction of cheap housing in the inner cities, increased use of illicit drugs, and reduced federal spending for new housing construction, restoration, and rental assistance.

Today, in the United States and elsewhere, it is useful to distinguish three important subgroups among homeless persons: single adults, families (that is, one or more parents with children in tow), and unaccompanied adolescents. Different types of shelters have been created in most U. S. cities to house these subgroups, provide them with better protection and care, and more effectively respond to their somewhat different needs.

While rates of mental illness and substance abuse are higher in all three of these homeless subpopulations than for their domiciled peers, there are salient differences among these subgroups in terms of the type, severity, and origins of their psychiatric conditions. By understanding these differences in homeless subgroups, it is possible to tailor service programs to best respond to their needs.

PSYCHIATRIC EPIDEMIOLOGY

Epidemiological research typically begins with a descriptive phase in which the incidence and/or prevalence of one or more diagnosable conditions is ascertained in a defined population. The term *prevalence* refers to the proportion of a population possessing a certain characteristic or condition over a specified period of time. *Incidence* refers to the proportion of people who *develop* the condition in a defined time interval. Expressed as a formula, incidence times duration equals prevalence, generally speaking. For instance, a condition that has both a high rate of incidence and a long duration leads to a highly prevalent condition in the population. Reducing either factor will lower the prevalence.

The vast majority of psychiatric epidemiological research on homeless populations has been descriptive in nature, documenting the prevalence of various mental illnesses and substance abuse disorders. To the extent that these studies have enrolled representative samples of homeless persons in a particular area, they shed light on the types of problems homeless persons experience. Such research helps us better understand the characteristics of a population and how to best meet their treatment needs.

Mental Illness Variables

The term *mental illness* covers a number of specific conditions, which can be diagnosed by trained clinicians. While the full spectrum of mental disorders is quite varied, some disorders principally affect one's thought processes, as in the case of schizophrenia. Others reflect disorders of mood or affect, such as major depression. Mental illnesses can vary in their severity as well as degree of impairment or disruption they cause to a person's daily life. They can also differ in terms of chronicity. For example, schizophrenia is both a very disabling and chronic condition, whereas depression can vary in the extent of psychosocial impairment it can cause and tends to be more episodic. The term *severe mental illness* refers to both disorders of thought and mood that typically cause extensive impairment in level of functioning for those who experience them.

SINGLE ADULTS

A number of studies in various regions of the United States and in other countries have documented that the prevalence of severe mental illnesses, as well as alcohol and other drug abuse, is much higher among the homeless than among the general population. In the United States, the most sophisticated and largest-scale epidemiological research on this issue took place in the mid-1980s. One such study was conducted by Paul Koegel and colleagues (1988), who interviewed single homeless adults in Los Angeles to learn about their past mental health and substance use difficulties. They found that, over the prior six months, 16 percent had experienced an episode of major depression, 12 percent were diagnosed with schizophrenia, 27 percent had an alcohol abuse or dependence disorder, and 10 percent had abused an illicit drug, some addictively. The researchers then compared their results to those of another study—one sampling the *general* adult Los Angeles population using an identical interview. They found the homeless were thirty-eight times more likely to have schizophrenia, five times more liable to have a major depression, and three times more prone to have abused alcohol. The researchers found similar rate gaps in terms of the lifetime prevalence of these three conditions. (As a point of comparison, less than 1 percent of the general population would currently be diagnosed with schizophrenia, 2 to 3 percent with major depression.)

Another comprehensive psychiatric epidemiological survey of homeless single adults was conducted by William Breakey, Pamela Fischer, and colleagues (1989) in Baltimore. They too found elevated rates of various psychiatric conditions among their homeless sample. For instance, the then-current prevalence rate of schizophrenia was 14 percent, major depression 13 percent, alcohol abuse or dependence 54 percent, and illicit drug abuse 20 percent. Many such adults suffer from both a severe mental illness and a substance abuse disorder. In the Baltimore study,

such comorbid conditions were found in about 31 percent of the total sample; the Los Angeles homeless group's rate of comorbidity was 12 percent.

Outside the United States, researchers have also found high rates of alcohol, drug, and mental disorders among homeless single adults. For example, Helen Herrman and her colleagues conducted a descriptive investigation of homeless persons in Melbourne, Australia and found that 12 percent were suffering from schizophrenia, 7 percent from major depression, 22 percent from alcohol dependence, and 10 percent from illicit drug dependence. A study in Madrid by Claudia Vazquez and colleagues determined that half the sample had a substance-related disorder at some point in their lives and 35 percent a mental disorder. The findings of these two investigations, and those from such other cities as Paris, Belfast, and Juiz de Fora, Brazil, have many more similarities to studies conducted in the United States than differences.

In general, homeless single adult populations are noteworthy for their relatively high rates of psychotic disorders such as schizophrenia—particularly among women—as well as high rates of alcohol and drug dependence, particularly among men.

FAMILIES

The vast majority of homeless families in the United States are headed by single mothers. Although two-parent families and families headed by single fathers can be found, the epidemiological research on adults in these households has focused exclusively on mothers. The most comprehensive study to date was conducted by Ellen Bassuk and colleagues (1998) in Worcester, Massachusetts. The researchers interviewed mothers living in shelters with their children. They then compared them to two other groups: low-income single mothers who had never been homeless and women of similar age in the general population who participated in the National Comorbidity Survey—a large-scale epidemiological study. Compared to domiciled low-income mothers, the homeless mothers looked remarkably similar in terms of lifetime and one-month prevalence rates of mental health and substance abuse disorders. Approximately two-thirds of both the homeless and poor housed women had had a psychiatric condition in their lifetimes. All the women were especially likely to have experienced major depression, posttraumatic stress disorder (PTSD), or an addiction to alcohol or other drugs. When compared to women in the general population, homeless mothers (and low-income women more broadly) had much higher rates of all three conditions. For instance, 45 percent had experienced major depression at some point in their lives, versus 20 percent of women in the general population. About 10 percent (versus 6 percent) had been depressed in the past month. Thirty-six percent had suffered from PTSD, 17 percent in the past month alone; these rates are about triple the rates of their domiciled peers. Lastly, 41 percent (versus 20 percent) had experienced at least one form of alcohol or drug dependence in their lifetimes.

Homeless mothers are noteworthy for their high prevalence of mood and anxiety disorders (such as depression and PTSD), but also for very *low* rates of psychotic disorders (such as schizophrenia) when compared with their homeless *solitary* counterparts. In the Worcester study, only 3 percent of mothers had experienced a psychotic condition in her lifetime (usually not schizophrenia), a rate much more comparable to the general population's rate than to that of homeless solitary women. (It should be noted that some in the latter group are, in fact, mothers but have had their children taken away from them and placed with relatives or in foster care due to their psychiatric condition.)

For homeless mothers, it is quite likely that these elevated rates of mood, anxiety, and substance use disorders are primarily due to past experiences of violent victimization, both in childhood and adulthood. In the Worcester study, Bassuk and her colleagues found that 67 percent had been physically abused in childhood; 43 percent had been sexually abused. Twenty percent had been placed in foster care as children. As adults, 63 percent had experienced severe physical violence at the hands of an intimate male partner. Cumulatively, 92 percent of homeless mothers had been physically or sexually assaulted at some point in their lives. The psychological sequelae of violent victimization often includes the very conditions that are common among homeless mothers: PTSD and other anxiety disorders, major depression, and substance abuse.

Homeless and low-income housed children in the Worcester study showed nearly identical rates of mental disorders. Approximately 32 percent of both groups were diagnosed as having either a conduct, mood, or anxiety disorder in the previous six months. This rate is two-thirds higher than the prevalence rate of 19 percent among their domiciled peers.

UNACCOMPANIED ADOLESCENTS

While some homeless adolescents live with relatives in family shelters, a growing number of them now live on the streets or in shelters designated for runaway youths. This problem is especially acute in many Latin American countries and in several European and Asian ones, although it is also significant in the United States. Some youth leave their homes because of abuse or extreme domestic turmoil. In the United States, some homeless youths, especially those in their late teens and early twenties, have "graduated" from the foster care system with no relatives or family they can rely on for assistance and with limited skills that would enable them to work and live independently. Life on the streets is especially hard for this subgroup, and they are at high risk of being sexually exploited. Numerous descriptive studies involving relatively small sample sizes have reported high rates of suicide attempts, alcohol and other drug abuse and dependence, major depression, and PTSD. However, schizophrenia has not been found to be especially elevated in this group, possibly because its onset is typically a bit later: in the early twenties for men and late twenties for women.

THE ROLE OF MENTAL HEALTH AND SUBSTANCE USE DISORDERS IN THE ETIOLOGY OF HOMELESSNESS

The findings of psychiatric epidemiological research involving homeless populations have at times been met with skepticism. They have also been misconstrued in terms of their implications for addressing the systemic causes of homelessness. Indeed, the question is controversial: How do we appropriately view the complex relationship between homelessness and mental illness?

When homelessness first emerged as a major social problem in the United States during the late 1970s and early 1980s, the finding of high prevalence rates of psychiatric disturbance, especially among single adults, seemed unsurprising to many, but was nonetheless controversial. Advocates for the homeless were primarily concerned with solving the homelessness crisis. Appropriately, they saw its chief causes as the affordable housing shortage brought on by cuts in government funding, as well as the destruction of single-room occupancy (SRO) hotels in inner cities. To them, raising the issue of severe mental illness and substance abuse in homeless persons only detracted from public sympathy for their plight. Alternatively, clinicians and researchers who were concerned that the acute needs of homeless persons be met believed it morally necessary to point out the extent and severity of these psychiatric conditions. The issue stirred disagreement and debate, especially when some politicians and social commentators—to account for the increasing visibility of homeless persons on the streets and in shelters—inaccurately portrayed the findings of psychiatric epidemiological research. Over time, these differing points of view have begun to converge, as people have grown more sophisticated in perceiving the links between homelessness, mental illness, and substance abuse.

While these issues are indeed related, the relation is not causal. Homelessness is not a cause of severe mental illness, nor can mental health and substance abuse disorders be accurately viewed as fundamental causes of homelessness. To better understand the nuances, it is useful to separate the question of *who* is most at risk to experience homelessness from the issue of *why* homelessness exists as a major social problem in the first place. Various writers have referred to the game of musical chairs as an analogy to clarify this "who versus why" distinction.

The game of musical chairs is premised on the creation of a structural problem, namely a shortage of chairs given the number of people competing for them. Similarly, members of a population experience homelessness when the housing supply (particularly housing affordable to persons with low to moderate incomes) is not sufficient to meet demand. While many factors affect both housing supply and demand, in a nutshell, the extent of homelessness is a direct function of this structural imbalance. Why is there homelessness? For the same reason people are left standing in the game of musical chairs after the music stops: There is a structural imbalance between supply and demand.

Of course, in the game, the suspense lies not in *whether* someone will be left standing when the music stops, but specifically *who* will fail to find a seat. Similarly, homelessness is no surprise when there is an inadequate supply of housing. What is less apparent is *who* is most vulnerable to losing in this competitive struggle. What constitutes this vulnerability? Factors such as a severe mental health or substance abuse disorder, or even having sole responsibility for the care of dependent children, can render some individuals less able to effectively compete for housing. The same factors, of course, can interfere with finding or maintaining employment—usually a prerequisite for housing. In sum, given a structural imbalance between housing supply and demand, it is not a question of whether some people will be rendered homeless, but rather who they will be. Homelessness occurs not on account of personal characteristics, but rather because there is not enough housing. Epidemiological research helps to answer the question of who is likely to be homeless, but does not address why homelessness is occurring in the first place.

METHODOLOGICAL CONSIDERATIONS

Estimates of the prevalence of mental health and substance abuse disorders can vary widely from study to study. One reason for this variation is straightforward: namely, that there are real differences in the populations being investigated. But sometimes disparities emerge because of dissimilar methodologies. Several variables commonly lead to these problems.

What definitions are used for alcohol, drug, and mental disorders? Descriptive epidemiological research is usually premised on clear-cut definitions of the conditions under investigation. Typically, these characteristics are measured in a categorical manner, rather than on a continuous scale. People either meet the criteria for a condition or they do not. These "case definitions" are usually derived from classification systems that establish such criteria, such as the American Psychiatric Association's *Diagnostic and Statistical Manual of Mental Disorders*. But different systems have been created, and studies that do not use the same one can produce discrepant findings reflecting different operational definitions. Likewise, since classification systems evolve over time, studies that use different versions of the same system may employ slightly different definitions of particular conditions.

What retrospective time period is employed? Use of dissimilar time frames for tracking a psychiatric disorder will also produce inconsistencies. For example, a study that assesses whether a condition has been experienced during the past year will likely find a higher prevalence rate than one whose time frame refers to the past month.

What type of psychiatric assessment tool is used, and what kind of interviewer conducts the assessment? These choices can also influence a study's findings. Some instruments are highly structured and allow for no alternative questioning. Others are only semi-structured and permit the interviewer—usually a trained clinician—to probe for clarity by asking follow-up questions to determine whether the criteria have been met for a particular diagnostic element. A trained clinician using a semi-structured format can draw upon clinical experience and judgment, and will usually generate a more valid assessment than a lay interviewer using a structured instrument. Yet hiring trained clinicians can be expensive, especially in larger investigations. Moreover, such professionals may be in short supply.

How do investigators sample or enroll homeless persons for an epidemiological investigation? An important methodological goal is to select participants who truly represent the broader population under study. Representative sampling of homeless persons in a delineated area can be very challenging, as such individuals often move from place to place, can be difficult to find, may be mistrustful of investigators when answering questions, or may decline to participate entirely. Many sampling variables can shape findings; for example, a bias can result if individuals are sampled from shelters without consideration for how long they have resided there. Although longer-term residents have a better chance of participating, they may be systematically different—for example, more psychopathological—than their shorter-term peers.

Finally, how "homelessness" is itself defined will influence who is enrolled in a study and the findings that emerge. For example, one study might include only those living in shelter or on the streets, whereas another might broaden the definition to include persons who are in jail or doubled up with family or friends.

THE FUTURE

In summary, the extent and nature of alcohol, drug, and mental health issues among homeless persons have been and are likely to remain important topics of research. Such information furthers our understanding of how to best meet the needs of those single adults, families, and adolescents who find themselves without homes. However, psychiatric epidemiological research on homeless populations does not cast light on the structural causes of homelessness. In the long term, the incidence of homelessness in a population can only be reduced by increasing the supply of affordable housing. Nonetheless, in the short run, it is important to understand the characteristics and needs of persons who are homeless so that effective programs can be developed to increase their residential stability and improve their quality of life. Psychiatric epidemiological research has an important place in this endeavor.

—*John C. Buckner*

Further Reading

Bassuk, E. L., Buckner, J. C., Perloff, J. N., & Bassuk, S. S. (1998). Prevalence of mental health and substance use disorders among homeless and low-income housed mothers. *American Journal of Psychiatry, 155*(11), 1561–1564.

Breakey, W. R., Fischer, P. J., Kramer, M., et al. (1989). Health and mental health problems of homeless men and women in Baltimore. *Journal of the American Medical Association, 262,* 1352–1357.

Buckner, J. C., & Bassuk, E. L. (1997). Mental disorders and service utilization among youths from homeless and low-income housed families. *Journal of the American Academy of Child and Adolescent Psychiatry, 36,* 890–900.

Fischer, P. J., & Breakey, W. R. (1991). The epidemiology of alcohol, drug, and mental disorders among homeless persons. *American Psychologist, 46,* 1115–1128.

Herrman, H., McGorry, P., Bennett, P., et al. (1989). Prevalence of severe mental disorders in disaffiliated and homeless people in inner Melbourne. *American Journal of Psychiatry, 146,* 1179–1184.

Koegel, P., Burnam, M. A., & Farr, R. K. (1988). The prevalence of specific psychiatric disorders among homeless individuals in the inner city of Los Angeles. *Archives of General Psychiatry, 45,* 1085–1092.

Vazquez, C., Munoz, M., & Sanz, J. (1997). Lifetime and 12-month prevalence of DSM III mental disorders among the homeless in Madrid. *Acta Psychiatrica Scandinavica, 95,* 523–530.

◙ ETHNOGRAPHY

Private Lives/Public Spaces, the groundbreaking study that was published in 1981 and heralded the emergence of contemporary homelessness, was not one of the many quantitative surveys of homeless populations that began appearing in rapid succession during the mid-1980s. Rather, it was an ethnographic account—a rich, compelling, qualitative record of what two investigators, Ellen Baxter and Kim Hopper, had learned about homelessness and homeless people by spending three years observing and talking with them as they eked out their precarious existences. Baxter and Hopper's work was compelling because of the real, immediate sense it provided of who homeless people were, where they had come from, the very difficult circumstances they faced, and how they felt about and dealt with those circumstances. This was not a distilled set of percentages and numbers that somehow lost sight of the individuals behind them. This was the human drama itself, portrayed in a way that allowed one to grasp the world from a homeless person's perspective.

In turning to ethnography as a way of documenting the phenomenon of contemporary homelessness, Baxter and Hopper were actually drawing upon a long tradition of using intensive qualitative methods to understand homelessness. As far back as the early 1920s, for example, sociologists such as Nels Anderson were closely examining the world of the hobo as part of a newly emerging school of urban ethnographic research emanating out of the University of Chicago. Similarly, as part of the broad scholarly interest in skid rows and public inebriates that occurred toward the middle of the twentieth century, scholars such as Jacqueline Wiseman, a sociologist, and James Spradley, an anthropologist, used ethnographic methods to shed light on the subtle relationships between homeless alcoholics and the institutions meant to control and/or provide services to them.

This tradition continues today. Although a spate of largely quantitative studies followed Baxter and Hopper's qualitative wake-up call, additional ethnographic efforts soon began surfacing in at least a dozen cities across the United States. Some of these efforts—such as David Snow and Leon Anderson's work in Austin, Texas, Rob Rosenthal's work in Santa Barbara, California, Jackson Underwood's work in Los Angeles, and Gwendolyn Dordick's work in New York—zeroed in on the lives of homeless people in street and shelter settings, painting detailed portraits of how they meet their material and social needs. Other efforts, such as Elliot Liebow's sensitive portrayal of homeless women, focused on identifiable subpopulations among the broader homeless population. Still other efforts, exemplified by the work of researchers such as Michael Rowe and Rae Bridgman, explored the intersection between homeless people and the programs and service providers attempting to meet their needs. Together, these efforts have played a pivotal role in expanding our understanding of contemporary homelessness and contemporary homeless people.

WHAT IS ETHNOGRAPHY?

Ethnography emerged as an approach to understanding human behavior as anthropologists sought to understand faraway cultures about which they knew virtually nothing. Anthropologists such as W. H. R. Rivers and Bronislaw Malinowski increasingly realized that making sense of very different people in foreign settings required *going* to them and *staying* with them. Almost independently, early twentieth-century U.S. sociologists interested in obtaining detailed, qualitative understandings of people living in their midst—but often outside the mainstream—were reaching a similar conclusion. Both groups of researchers learned the value of living among the people they were studying for extended periods of time, asking questions, observing and participating in their daily lives, documenting all of this on an ongoing basis, and ultimately analyzing this rich set of textual data to understand how the pieces fit together.

For anthropologists and sociologists alike, this set of activities culminates in an ethnography—a rich, holistic, description of a different way of life. As such, ethnography is both process and product. As a process, it involves encountering alien worlds and trying to make sense of them, as anthropologist Michael Agar has said. In this sense, ethnography is something that one does. As a product, it is the written account that artfully weaves together the cultural understandings that the ethnographic process has yielded—it is something that one produces.

In practice, ethnography is an end to which many methods might be applied. Depending on his or her specific interests, an ethnographer might engage in archival/historical research, map the layout of a particular physical space, conduct a census, chart genealogical and other network relationships, measure economic productivity, administer psychological tests, conduct formal observations, take life histories—the list is endless. However, two features distinguish ethnography from alternative strategies for understanding people and are essential to any ethnographic effort. These features can be used, in a sense, as yardsticks against which to measure the extent to which studies claiming to be ethnographic are actually justified in doing so.

The first of these features is a reliance on participant observation, a method so intimately associated with ethnography that the two terms are often used interchangeably. The use of participant observation as a backdrop against which all other methods are applied is fundamental to ethnography and is virtually a precondition to producing the kind of "thick description" that is ethnography's signature

characteristic. Participant observation involves immersing oneself in the lives of a particular people over long periods of time through a process referred to as "fieldwork." This means living among the people or spending long periods of time with them; learning their language; participating in their daily routine and extraordinary activities; observing their behavior; asking them questions; using everyday conversation as an interview technique; watching them behave across the many contexts in which they live their day-to-day lives; listening to what they say during natural interactions; recording and interpreting their behavior; and ultimately formulating an understanding of their culture. Participant observers become involved because involvement is necessary to achieve an understanding of the psychological realities of culture and because involvement translates into levels of rapport and trust that reduce reactivity and open the door to information that might otherwise be withheld. However, participant observers also remain detached, in part because they want to retain their objectivity but also because one can never be an absolute part of a culture that isn't one's own. In essence, they walk the line between being insider and outsider, struggling all the while to arrive at holistic cultural understandings. In the end, these understandings are deeper, more valid, and more nuanced because the data supporting them have been carefully contextualized, emerge over long periods of time, come from multiple perspectives, and consist not only of what people say but also observations of what they do.

A second feature that is relatively unique to ethnography is its concern with what anthropologists refer to as an "emic" perspective, or an "insider's" point of view. The ethnographic approach relies on far more than an outside observer's descriptions and observations. At its core, ethnography is an attempt to understand the *meaning* that behavior and social life hold for the people in question—how *they* see the world and make sense of it. In this sense, ethnography is the godchild of the German sociologist Max Weber and others who recognized that people are unique as objects of study because they *think* and *feel* and because what they think and feel affects how and why they behave as they do. In keeping with this, anthropologist Clifford Geertz has pointed out that because "man is an animal suspended in webs of significance which he himself has spun" (Geertz 1973, 5), science must at least in part be an interpretive one in search of meaning. Chasing after "meaning" by watching and listening to people over long periods of time and searching for evidence of how they construct their worlds are an essential part of the ethnographic domain.

Ethnography, then, is the documentation of a way of life that emerges from long-term participant observation (and other methods, but always participant observation) and that highlights the meaning that social life holds for the individuals in question—that is, that seeks to understand their values, beliefs, and the implicit assumptions that make up their worldview. One-hour qualitative interviews conducted with a group of individuals on a single occasion may reveal important insights that could not have been obtained by quantitative surveys, but it would be wrong to call such research "ethnographic." How much participant observation is necessary in order to say a piece of work is ethnographic? What level of the actor's perspective must one penetrate before one can say "meaning" has been obtained? These are really unanswerable questions. However, the degree to which participant observation has been engaged in and the extent to which an emic perspective has been pursued provide us with a relevant yardstick against which the use of the term *ethnographic* can be measured. One should take more seriously a study that logged one thousand hours in the field over the course of a year than one that logged twenty hours during a six-week period, although important insights can emerge even from the latter. One should take more seriously a study that reveals how the social and psychological realities of a group of people affect the group's choices and behaviors in complex ways than a study that states the obvious or doesn't really attend to the issue at all. In the end, it is difficult to imagine that someone who has pursued knowledge over long periods of time, focusing on beliefs and values as well as behaviors and context, won't produce a richer, more detailed, more explanatory account.

Ultimately, that is the final arbiter of what a successful ethnography is.

APPLYING AN ETHNOGRAPHIC PERSPECTIVE TO THE STUDY OF HOMELESSNESS

As mentioned earlier, the 1980s were dominated by cross-sectional surveys of homeless populations in virtually every major city across the United States. These studies collectively provided a quantitative snapshot of contemporary homelessness that guided important insights into relevant demographic and diagnostic characteristics of the homeless population and that began pointing to salient aspects of the problem and how to solve it. However, they did not tell the full story. Indeed, they often unintentionally distorted the story. Interestingly, the gaps they left were, in many cases, precisely the issues that an ethnographic approach is best able to address.

Ethnographic work, for instance, has been instrumental in enhancing our understanding of homelessness and homeless people by providing rich, qualitative descriptions of how homeless people live day to day. Ethnographic accounts provide vibrant portraits of how those experiencing homelessness juggle the scarce resources available to them to meet their subsistence needs, how they take advantage of formal and informal economies to generate income, how they interact with both homeless and non-homeless social network members, how they experience the service providers and settings that are often at the heart of their survival, how they interpret the events that have led to their current circumstances, and how they sustain a positive identity in the face of constant assaults to their sense of self-worth.

These accounts, at a minimum, document the experiences behind the percentages that emerge from quantitative surveys of the homeless—the *what, how,* and *why* that explain the numbers. Surveys, for instance, inevitably report low rates of stable wage employment and underutilization of public benefits for which homeless people may be eligible. A book such as *Down on Their Luck,* David Snow and Leon Anderson's ethnography of homeless street people in Austin, Texas, provides the story behind those numbers. Snow and Anderson explored the work histories of the homeless people they came to know over time, compared them to the available employment opportunities in Austin, described the way in which a homeless lifestyle impeded the ability of people to pursue the few available jobs for which they could compete, documented the bureaucratic nightmare that the process of applying for benefits tended to be, and provided detailed descriptions of the "shadow work" to which homeless people turned because these more conventional pathways were closed to them. Their account highlighted the fact that numbers suggesting low participation in formal wage labor notwithstanding, homeless people—even the homeless people they typed as "outsiders" (i.e., people who had been on the street for a long time and had accommodated themselves to street life)—displayed a strong orientation toward work and in fact worked hard on a daily basis. By necessity, however, their work was typically part of an informal economy that surveys did not always sufficiently acknowledge, explore, or understand.

Ethnographic description has also expanded our understandings of the social lives of homeless people. Countless surveys, for instance, have documented quantitatively the fact that homeless people are often unable to count on family members for support, an observation that has led to the conclusion that homeless people lack the social ties that serve as a buffer against the experience of homelessness. An ethnographic account such as Elliot Liebow's *Tell Them Who I Am,* an intimate look into the lives of homeless women in Washington, DC, puts flesh on these quantitative bones. Liebow's rich depictions of the family relationships of homeless women certainly included those who were without family and reconciled to that fact, providing insight into the experience of being "familyless." However, Liebow also described many women who had regular and intense contact with their families. His sensitive portrayal of these relationships showed how easily they were strained by a myriad of factors—a lack of resources, imbalances of power, bad circumstances, and many others. As such, his work contributed to a richer understanding of how people in touch with family members could still find themselves on the

street. His poignant descriptions of the extent to which these women were emotionally tied to their children—even children who were no longer in their care—made it clear that homeless people often experience a sense of emotional connectedness to others that is impossible to glean from quantitative accounts.

A real contrast emerges between the depictions in the survey literature of a homeless population with few viable ties to friends and the ethnographic accounts of the ways in which homeless people create and rely on a complex, intricate set of relationships that helps them sustain and enjoy themselves. Jackson Underwood's depiction of the interdependent lives of a group of individuals living under a freeway bridge in Los Angeles is a striking portrait of sociability, as are Gwen Dordick's renditions of homeless life across a variety of settings—a large, bustling urban transportation station, an improvised shantytown, an enormous public shelter, and a smaller private shelter. Indeed, Dordick concluded that the homeless people with whom she spent time would be lost without their companions and that the complexity of those relationships notwithstanding, homelessness "transforms personal relationships into the principal currency of survival" (Dordick 1997, 194). Other ethnographic accounts, particularly in New York, make it clear that for many homeless individuals, such personal relationships include ties to non-homeless family and friends and that these relationships are activated and deactivated in complicated and strategic ways.

These examples show how vivid descriptions and documentation of the lives of homeless people have allowed an important ethnographic corrective, replacing quantitative depictions that catalog pathology and dysfunction with a more balanced rendering that includes compelling examples of strength, innovation, integration, and resiliency. However, the ethnographic corrective arises not only from the process of documenting and describing. It also arises from "contextualizing."

One of the primary strengths of the ethnographic approach stems from its insistence on examining a phenomenon in context, the assumption being that only by looking at a phenomenon in relationship to its surroundings can it be truly understood. "Context," on the one hand, refers to the big picture—what Kim Hopper refers to as "framework." Thus, his ethnographic *Reckoning with Homelessness* includes a historical account of how New York City has dealt with its marginal poor; a depiction of the neighborhoods in which homeless populations of the past resided; a discussion of relevant developments in labor markets, housing stock, and policies affecting the care and containment of those people on the margins; and an examination of relatively recent changes in the configuration of the African-American family. Hopper reminds us that these factors have shaped how and why homelessness exists and that together they form a critical backdrop against which the behavior of homeless people must be considered if it is to be understood and interpreted correctly.

Context is also "setting"—the immediate physical and social environments in which homeless people live their lives. These environments exert a similarly profound influence on the behavior of homeless people. The ethnographic descriptions of shelters offered by Dordick and by Hopper, for instance—descriptions that are filled with images of violence, degradation, and abuse of power   allow a very different interpretation of the decision that many homeless people make to forsake a guaranteed shelter bed for what would otherwise seem like a harsher life on the street. The carefully contextualized interactions between shelter staff and homeless women that Elliot Liebow so skillfully documented similarly make it clear that what might otherwise be dismissed as an inclination toward violence on the part of homeless women was actually a product of a complex interactive dance between "the servers and the served." In this dance, palpable fear on the part of shelter providers that their charges will be violent induced an arbitrary display of power that often provoked the very reaction it was meant to forestall.

Attention to context/setting can sometimes provide an alternative explanation of the results of the psychological and functioning scales relied on in surveys. For instance, anthropologists who have incorporated ethnographic work into evaluations of homeless people and programs have pointed out how poor performance by homeless people on scales meant to capture their ability regarding everyday tasks—evidence interpreted as suggesting inadequate money management skills—could take on a different light when these people were observed making decisions in the everyday contexts of their lives. Ongoing fieldwork among homeless people has suggested a functional approach to money management in which spending down large sums is a necessary response to the requirements of entitlement programs, celebrations are a way of encouraging reciprocal debts that hedge against future risk, and cash or other surplus is quickly consumed to mitigate vulnerability to having it stolen. Again, attention to context allows a more nuanced understanding.

Ethnographic accounts have contributed to our understanding of homelessness in a myriad of additional ways. For instance, the methods used by ethnographers, in contrast to those researchers conducting surveys, have made it possible to gain insights into homeless subpopulations that quantitative surveys tend to exclude. Many of the seriously mentally ill homeless adults included in Paul Koegel's ethnographic work, to take one example, were either far too leery of strangers or too unable to communicate to be included in surveys. A combination of time, patience, observation, and relationship building, however, made it possible to learn a lot about these people, ultimately yielding important understandings of how they manage that often included real surprises. Likewise, ethnographers have been able to study homeless individuals in unique settings in which survey methodologists would have had trouble either gaining access, such as transit tunnels, or identifying their targets without the requisite degree of ethnographic investment, such as municipal airports or transportation depots. In many instances, ethnographers have paved the way for those researchers trying to count or survey, providing the lay of the land and the understandings of the targeted populations that are a necessary foundation to such efforts. The ethnographic work coordinated by Matt Salo to support the inclusion of as many homeless people as possible in the 1990 U.S. census—and to evaluate the efforts to enumerate homeless people—is a case in point. Ethnographers have also successfully studied issues that might otherwise have been overlooked. Rob Rosenthal's emphasis on resistance and collective political activity on the part of homeless people, documented in his ethnography of homelessness in Santa Barbara, California (*Homeless in Paradise*), is one such example.

Yet another way in which ethnography has made substantial contributions has less to do with describing homelessness itself and more to do with shedding light on efforts to address the needs of homeless people. Ethnographers have played a key role in evaluations of innovative programs by helping to "open up the black box"—by documenting, in other words, what actually occurs in these programs and how they are experienced by those who participate in them. Several large evaluations of service demonstrations funded by the U.S. National Institute of Mental Health and the National Institute of Alcohol Abuse and Alcoholism, for instance, included ethnographic components that explored such diverse issues as the implicit principles embedded in treatment, discrepant ways in which recipients and providers define success, factors that promote or inhibit the ability of people to achieve desired outcomes, issues related to the provision of meaningful choices during street outreach, and the dynamics of an empowerment ethic in consumer-run households of seriously mentally ill homeless adults.

Along these lines, researchers Darin Weinberg and Paul Koegel used an ethnographic approach to document how a social model treatment program for adults with dual diagnoses of serious mental illness and substance abuse was playing out "on the ground." Their analysis identified key elements that would not have appeared in a manual characterizing the program's approach but that explained how therapeutic practice actually occurred. As part of this analysis, these researchers also described several impediments to recovery that homeless people taking part in this program faced. These impediments included the challenge of trying to reconcile attitudes, skills, and behaviors that had served them well in the homeless environments from which they had come with what was expected of them as program participants; the tension between pursuing a program of recovery and simultaneously meeting basic survival needs; and the devastating disap-

pointment that often followed recognition that treatment would not necessarily eradicate all of the long-standing problems that had complicated their lives. These findings became the basis for a targeted set of recommendations on how the intervention could be modified to mitigate the impact of these impediments.

NEXT STEPS

Ethnographers, then, have contributed extensively to our understanding of contemporary homelessness by documenting the experiences of homeless people across multiple settings—including both community and program settings—and by helping us piece together a more valid and complete sense of this population. Although ethnographers can take pride in the value of these contributions, it would be a mistake to conclude that the job is complete. Kim Hopper, a constant and careful observer of homelessness over the last three decades, observes "that ethnographic work is essentially unfinished if it pulls up short at description and commentary" (Hopper 2003, 205). Not everyone will subscribe to Hopper's notion that witnessing must be the prelude to engagement and action, although his argument is both passionate and persuasive. However, it is difficult to ignore his admonishment that ethnographers must move upward and outward from a familiar and comfortable focus on the traditional habitats of the homeless—that they must take on the more pressing, difficult challenge of linking "framework" and "fieldwork" by applying ethnographic tools to the conditions that produce, sustain, and combat homelessness. This means turning their attention from a focus on street people to such issues as the pressures impinging on precariously poised households, the nature and impact of changing urban landscapes, the contours of neighborhood opposition to ameliorative programs, the processes that move proven intervention strategies to broadly implemented policies, and so forth. Broadening the scope of their inquiry in these ways will allow ethnographers to continue expanding our understandings of homelessness and will enhance their role in shaping effective solutions.

—*Paul Koegel*

Further Reading

Anderson, N. (1923). *The hobo*. Chicago: University of Chicago Press.

Baxter, E., & Hopper, K. (1981). *Private lives/public spaces*. New York: Community Service Society.

Bridgman, R. (2003). *Safe haven: The story of a shelter for homeless women*. Toronto, Ontario, Canada: University of Toronto Press.

Desjarlais, R. (1995). *Shelter blues*. Philadelphia: University of Pennsylvania Press.

Dordick, G. A. (1997). *Something left to lose: Personal relations and survival among New York's homeless*. Philadelphia: Temple University Press.

Geertz, C. (1973). *The interpretation of cultures*. New York: Basic Books.

Glasser, I. (1988). *More than bread: Ethnography of a soup kitchen*. Tuscaloosa: University of Alabama Press.

Golden, S. (1992). *The woman outside*. Berkeley and Los Angeles: University of California Press.

Harper, D. A. (1982). *Good company*. Chicago: University of Chicago Press.

Hopper, K. (2003). *Reckoning with homelessness*. Ithaca, NY: Cornell University Press.

Koegel, P. (1992). Through a different lens: An anthropological perspective on the homeless mentally ill. *Culture, Medicine and Psychiatry, 16*(1), 1–22.

Liebow, E. (1993). *Tell them who I am: The lives of homeless women*. New York: Free Press.

Lovell, A. M., & Cohn, S. (1998). The elaboration of "choice" in a program for homeless persons labeled psychiatrically disabled. *Human Organization, 57*(1), 8–20.

Quimby, E. (1995). Homeless clients' perspectives on recovery in the Washington, DC, dual diagnosis project. *Contemporary Drug Problems, 22*(2), 265–289.

Rosenthal, R. (1994). *Homeless in paradise: A map of the terrain*. Philadelphia: Temple University Press.

Rowe, M. (1999). *Crossing the border: Encounters between homeless people and outreach workers*. Berkeley and Los Angeles: University of California Press.

Salo, M. T., & Campanelli, P. C. (1991). Ethnographic methods in the development of census procedures for enumerating the homeless. *Urban Anthropology, 20*(2), 127–140.

Snow, D. A., & Anderson, L. (1993). *Down on their luck: A study of homeless street people*. Berkeley and Los Angeles: University of California Press.

Spradley, J. P. (1970). *You owe yourself a drunk*. Boston: Little, Brown.

Underwood, J. (1993). *The bridge people: Daily life in a camp of the homeless*. Lanham, MD: University Press of America.

Wagner, D. (1993). *Checkerboard Square: Culture and resistance in a homeless community*. Boulder, CO: Westview Press.

Ware, N. C., Desjarlais, R. R., AvRuskin, T. L., Breslau, J., Good, B. J., & Goldfinger, S. M. (1992). Empowerment and the transition to housing for homeless mentally ill people: An anthropological perspective. *New England Journal of Public Policy, 8,* 297–314.

Weinberg, D., & Koegel, P. (1995). Impediments to recovery in treatment programs for dually diagnosed homeless adults: An ethnographic analysis. *Contemporary Drug Problems, 22*(2), 193–236.

Weinberg, D., & Koegel, P. (1996). Social model treatment and individuals with dual diagnoses: An ethnographic analysis of therapeutic practice. *Journal of Mental Health Administration, 23*(3), 272–288.

Wiseman, J. (1970). *Stations of the lost: The treatment of Skid Row alcoholics*. Englewood Cliffs, NJ: Prentice Hall.

▣ EUROPEAN NETWORK FOR HOUSING RESEARCH

The European Network for Housing Research (ENHR) is an organization comprising social science professionals who work together to target and research issues of housing and urban development in Europe. The ENHR's quarterly newsletter and secretariat are based out of the Institute for Housing and Urban Research in Gävle, Sweden. Established in 1988, the ENHR has a membership of some 1,000 individuals and almost 100 institutions representing every country in Europe. A democratically elected board known as the Coordination Committee runs the organization, and this committee is responsible for arranging and organizing the ENHR's biyearly conferences. The main goal of the ENHR is to support research on housing and urban issues and to promote contacts and communication between researchers and professionals in the housing field.

In congruence with these main goals, the ENHR is responsible for sponsoring a General Assembly every two years, publishing a newsletter four times a year, providing a framework and guidelines for approximately twenty working groups, encouraging smaller conferences and seminars every year, and maintaining a group of PhD students as housing researchers.

WORKING GROUPS AND CONFERENCES

Working groups exist to perform extensive research on specific topics related to housing issues, such as homelessness, rural housing, housing finance, or housing for elderly adults. Members of working groups generally come from a variety of locations throughout Europe and represent a wide range of disciplines. Working groups either schedule meetings on a regular basis or simply meet at conferences. The ENHR sponsors periodic conferences, each with a specific theme such as "Methodologies in Housing Research" or "Housing: Regeneration and Growth."

ENHR MEMBERSHIP AND MEMBER BENEFITS

ENHR offers two types of membership: individual and institutional. An individual membership allows one to work closely with other researchers in a working group, be directly involved in the ENHR's international conferences where researchers present the latest information on housing and urban issues, receive the ENHR newsletter four times a year, participate in the election of members to the Coordination Committee, and place a vote in the General Assembly held every two years.

An institutional membership allows a member organization to publish news about its activities in the ENHR newsletter, come in contact with research institutions and other organizations in Europe, start and facilitate cooperative projects, and have access to the addresses of the every organization with an ENHR membership to make publicizing conferences and other research events easier and more efficient.

Applications for both individual and institutional memberships, along with contact information, are available for download on the ENHR website at www.enhr.ibf.uu.se.

—*Emily A. Colangelo*

FAIR HOUSING LAWS

Since the 1980s in the United States, as a continuum of care has developed to respond to the day-to-day needs of individuals and families who are homeless, very little attention has been paid to the civil rights issues involving shelter, housing, and service providers and the rights of homeless people themselves. Often, the law has the effect of protecting entrenched interests, thereby magnifying the advantage of those who have accumulated wealth or power. But civil rights laws, which are designed to provide equal opportunity and to prohibit discrimination by public and private entities, have had a great leveling effect. More vigorous enforcement of fair housing laws could both expand the supply of housing for homeless people and dramatically reshape the way such housing is operated.

POVERTY AND DISABILITY CONTRIBUTE TO HOMELESSNESS

While many social problems may be entangled in the issue of homelessness, one of the most critical problems is the nation's general scarcity of affordable housing. Whether a person's homelessness is described as situational or chronic, poverty has likely been a major ingredient in losing one's permanent housing. Rental housing in many cities is entirely out

of reach for individuals and families who rely on welfare, disability, or veterans' benefits to survive. Starting in the 1970s, as the federal government reduced its financial support for subsidized housing and as redevelopment claimed previously affordable housing in the private sector, more and more people with mental and physical disabilities and addiction disorders fell into homelessness. By 1992, a federal task force on homelessness estimated that at least one-third of homeless people had severe disabilities.

WHAT KIND OF HOUSING AND SERVICES DO HOMELESS INDIVIDUALS AND FAMILIES NEED?

Because of the failure (or inability) of the mainstream rental housing market to accommodate homeless individuals and families, many social service agencies have entered the housing business, becoming landlords. Their choice of housing models has profound implications for providers and homeless people under the Fair Housing Act. To the extent that a larger institutional model is chosen, it is more difficult to argue that such housing belongs in residential neighborhoods. To the extent that shelter, transitional, and supportive housing congregate people on the basis of homelessness or disability status, the housing becomes identifiable as a place for people with social problems. On the other hand, approaches that emphasize smaller programs and scattered-site housing that mixes homeless and disabled people with mainstream residents are less likely to engender community opposition and more likely to help clients achieve reintegration into the community.

When homelessness came to public consciousness in the 1980s, it was thought to be a state of temporary dislocation, and the public policy response clearly accepted that premise. By the early 1990s, it was clear that, for many people, homelessness was not just structural or situational, but might continue for months or years. The "continuum of care" approach promoted the development of a wide array of housing models and services to help people who had hit bottom to reconnect with housing and employment. Often this approach has required people to move from one place of residence to another, eventually graduating back to independent housing if they can convince their caseworkers that they are responsible enough to do so.

Since the 1980s, in an effort to respond to growing homelessness, federal, state, and local governments have spent billions of dollars annually to provide shelter, transitional housing, and supportive services. In a collective hurry to respond to the crisis, the private and public sectors devised and established shelter and housing programs that bore little resemblance to mainstream housing. Out of a conviction that homelessness was caused by factors other than the mere lack of affordable housing, these programs were meant to get at the roots of homelessness. These models tended to identify social and moral deficits among shelter residents and program participants—such as lack of parenting or budgeting skills, poor decision making, addiction, and disability—and define new paths for them to reclaim their lives.

By the end of the twentieth century another model had emerged, organized under the banner of supportive housing. This model assumes that homeless people need and want supportive services, and so provides permanent housing with non-mandatory services. As practiced by the Corporation for Supportive Housing, this model requires that homeless people be treated as tenants, with their own individual leases and keys to their units. Some providers have gone even further in an attempt to reach the hardest-to-serve homeless people. Employing a "housing first" philosophy, Pathways to Housing and others seek to cure the problem of homelessness immediately by providing permanent housing with no requirements whatsoever to participate in treatment or services.

THE SCOPE OF FAIR HOUSING LAWS

Originally passed in 1968, the federal Fair Housing Act (FHA) is the nation's primary law ensuring equal housing opportunity. On its face, it protects against housing discrimination on the basis of race, color, religion, national origin, gender, disability, and familial status (the presence of one or more children under the age of eighteen in the household). While the law does not mention homelessness or poverty, it has become clear that many homeless people will benefit from their membership in one of the seven protected classes enumerated by the law: race, color, religion, sex, familial status, national origin, or disability. Some cities and states prohibit discrimination based on source of income, meaning that people whose income derives from welfare, disability, veterans' or other benefits cannot be denied housing.

The federal Americans with Disabilities Act of 1990 (ADA) requires that people with disabilities be served "in the most integrated setting appropriate" to [their] needs. The Supreme Court of the United States has recognized that the ADA imposes an affirmative obligation on city and state disability and homelessness agencies to provide housing and services in a setting in which people with disabilities have the maximum opportunity to interact with people who do not have disabilities. Because large numbers of homeless people qualify for disability status under federal law, the FHA and the ADA have become powerful tools for ensuring greater housing and community-based service opportunities.

For purposes of this discussion, the FHA contains two important provisions. The first prohibits discrimination on the basis of membership in any protected class. The second requires landlords, realtors, city officials, and anyone affecting the housing market to make reasonable accommodations—or changes in rules, policies, practices, and services when such accommodations are necessary—to ensure that people with disabilities have an equal opportunity to use and enjoy housing. Combined, these provisions of the FHA offer strong protection for shelter and housing providers who face opposition from community members and elected officials. They also suggest that housing and service providers serving homeless individuals and families are required to respect their residents' civil rights and to provide a higher degree of flexibility in the application of program rules and policies.

The right of disabled persons that is protected under the FHA is the right to live in the residence of their choice in the community, according to *Marbrunak, Inc. v. City of Stow, Ohio.* It is not the province of zoning officials or neighbors to choose the neighborhoods in which people with disabilities, including homeless people, will live. In 1988, Congress made clear its intention that the prohibition against discrimination against those with handicaps should also apply to zoning decisions and practices. The Act is intended to prohibit the application of special requirements through land-use regulations, restrictive covenants, and conditional or special use permits that have the effect of limiting the ability of such individuals to live in the residence of their choice in the community (House Report No. 100–711, n. 18, at 24).

USING FAIR HOUSING LAWS TO OVERCOME ZONING AND LAND-USE BARRIERS

While there is still significant resistance in many communities to the presence of shelters and transitional and supportive housing, the FHA has given homeless people and their service providers powerful tools to overcome such resistance. Beyond granting specific protections from discrimination, the FHA (and lawsuits brought pursuant to it) has also fostered a broad national debate about the inclusion of people who are homeless. Despite its "two steps forward, one step backward" quality, this debate has demonstrated that federal laws can have an important impact on public attitudes. In many ways, the FHA embodies a level of tolerance and inclusion that is not yet embraced by the general public.

Prior to 1988, when the FHA was amended to include disability as a protected class, many communities developed zoning and land-use policies with the explicit purpose of excluding or limiting shelters, transitional housing, and other congregate living arrangements for homeless people. The unsurprising result has been that such housing, when it was permitted, was disproportionately located in commercial and industrial areas, which were not conducive to reintegration into the community. The persistent problem of NIMBYism ("Not In My Back Yard") has further reduced the number of units of housing available to homeless people, particularly when they have disabilities.

Despite the recent public commitment by coalitions of government and nonprofit agencies to end chronic homelessness by 2010, many major cities still employ zoning restrictions that make placement of shelter, transitional, and supportive housing very difficult. In attempts to regulate the makeup of their neighborhoods, many localities have enacted spacing ordinances requirements that transitional or supportive housing units not be located within a specified distance of one another. These requirements impose significant restrictions on providers because they place absolute limits on the number of units in the whole community.

The FHA can serve as a valuable weapon to combat these spacing restrictions because it requires communities to make reasonable accommodations to allow people with disabilities access to housing similar to the access enjoyed by people without disabilities. This requires that communities change, waive, or make exceptions to their zoning rules (*United States v. City of Philadelphia*). Under this test, if the waiver of a spacing requirement would not impose an undue financial or administrative burden on the defendant, and would not undermine the basic purpose that the requirement seeks to achieve, then the waiver is reasonable and is therefore mandated by the FHA.

OTHER LAND-USE RESTRICTIONS WITH DISCRIMINATORY IMPACTS

Many localities have enacted occupancy rules that prohibit certain unrelated people from living together in the same dwelling. On their face, such rules may appear neutral. But if they have the effect of limiting the housing opportunities of people with disabilities, such rules are unlawful. Such rules might be valid when applied to college students, for example, but not when they have the effect of excluding people with disabilities.

Local governments must not require such special or conditional use permits unless they are also required of other dwellings of similar size, such as those occupied by families. The general rule of nondiscrimination applies: If a family of six may occupy a particular dwelling without a special use permit, then a shelter, or transitional or supportive housing, for six people with disabilities must not be required to obtain one either. On the other hand, if a special use permit is required for apartment construction in a particular zone, the fact that people who would live in the apartment have disabilities would not exempt them (or the builder) from the requirement.

The enforcement of restrictive covenants that preclude occupancy of a dwelling by people with disabilities is specifically identified in the regulations as a discriminatory housing practice; indeed, even representing a covenant in such a way is regarded as discriminatory. Courts have uniformly invalidated such covenants, whether they seek to exclude people with disabilities directly, or to exclude them by characterizing group homes as business enterprises.

FAIR HOUSING LAWS HAVE EXPANDED HOUSING OPPORTUNITIES

Housing and service providers serving homeless people have made profitable use of the courts to overcome discriminatory zoning and land-use barriers. In a 1990 case in Providence, Rhode Island, a nonprofit advocacy group challenged the city's decision to move a homeless shelter—a move the group considered racially motivated. Refusing to dismiss the lawsuit, a federal trial court found there was sufficient evidence of a potentially racially discriminatory impact to allow the case to proceed.

In the early 1990s, Project HOME faced intense political and community opposition to its single-room occupancy (SRO) project on Fairmount Avenue

in Philadelphia. Its proposed residents would be formerly homeless people with mental illnesses and addiction histories. To block the project, the city refused to issue a permit, claiming that the rear-yard setback was insufficient and refusing to consider a very large side yard as fulfilling the requirement. The U.S. Department of Justice sued on behalf of Project HOME and required the city to issue the permit.

Two years later, another legal challenge was filed against the city of Caldwell, Idaho, which had restricted occupancy of a shelter to fifteen residents and required an annual review of a special use permit. Because three-quarters of its residents had mental and physical disabilities, and because stability in residence was determined critical to their well-being, the shelter operator challenged the city's restrictions in federal court. Finding that the city had failed to make accommodations that were necessary to ensure equal housing opportunity for shelter residents with disabilities, the federal court of appeals found the city in violation of the Fair Housing Act, increased the shelter's occupancy to twenty-five residents, and eliminated the annual review provision in the conditional special use permit.

Finally, in 2003, a federal trial court in Washington, D.C., upheld a claim that the city government had discriminated against the nonprofit Community Housing Trust and five formerly homeless men with mental illnesses who resided in a small group home known as Zeke's House. Although the local zoning ordinance permitted Zeke's House as a matter of right, the city's Department of Consumer and Regulatory Affairs (DCRA) declared the home an illegal boarding house and imposed fines of $100 per day. Noting that DCRA's action was motivated in part by the strong opposition of a vocal minority of neighbors, the court found DCRA liable for disability discrimination. Zeke's House remained open during the litigation, despite the deleterious effect of DCRA's actions on its ability to secure charitable contributions.

FAIR HOUSING LAWS GUARANTEE FAIR TREATMENT FOR RESIDENTS

Just as the fair housing laws protect shelter and service providers from discrimination by city officials and neighbors, they also require providers to respect the civil rights of their clients and residents. That the FHA covers temporary abodes was established in the mid-1970s in an influential case in Virginia. There, the court had to determine whether the U.S. Department of Justice could, under the FHA, sue a home for abused and neglected children for its racially exclusive policies. The court reasoned that the FHA's definition of "dwelling" covered any building or portion thereof designed for occupancy, and that where residents had no other place to live, even temporary quarters would qualify under the FHA. In 1995, then, it was a short step for a federal court in Chicago to declare explicitly that the FHA covered homeless shelters as well.

Building on that decision, courts in New York (*Metalsky v. Mercy Haven, Inc.* 1992), Massachusetts (*Carr v. Friends of the Homeless* 1990; *Serreze v. Y.W.C.A. of Western Mass.,* 1991), and several other states have held that transitional housing providers may not simply eject tenants at will, but must adhere to a fair eviction process governed by an impartial decision maker. Subsequently, the federal government has required these same safeguards in a number of programs serving homeless people (Code of Federal Regulations: 24: Sections 582.320, 583.300(i), 574.310[e][2]), including Shelter + Care, the Emergency Shelter Grant Program, and Housing Opportunities for Persons with HIV/AIDS (HOPWA).

EXEMPLARY MODELS COMBINE FORWARD THINKING WITH ADHERENCE TO FAIR HOUSING LAWS

Research indicates that residents of supportive housing experience stability in housing, greater satisfaction, and dramatic reductions in hospital days (Culhane et al. 2002). Greater respect for residents' rights and choice in housing are also positively correlated with happiness and life satisfaction ratings and, ultimately, with community success (Schutt and Goldfinger 1996). Some research even suggests that of all criteria considered, client preference may best predict success in different housing options. Reliance on congregate models has led to poor-quality housing in many states (Tsemberis and Eisenberg 2000).

Research also shows that housing programs serving homeless people with very severe psychiatric disabilities (and, in many instances, co-occurring substance abuse problems) can be successfully placed in independent housing that complies with the FHA and ADA, and whose outcomes are significantly better than those of the older models focusing on treatment compliance. Pathways to Housing has demonstrated that such outcomes are possible, even for people coming in directly off the street, and even in a hyperinflated market like New York City. The key has been the provision of comprehensive but entirely voluntary mental health, addiction, and other services. Pathways allows clients to determine the type and intensity of services, or to refuse them entirely.

A study published in 2000 reveals that after five years, Pathways' clients are between two and four times more likely to have been continuously housed than clients in New York's traditional linear residential treatment programs. Most importantly, for the homeless clients in these programs, living in apartments of their own with assistance from a supportive and available clinical staff teaches them the skills and provides them with the necessary support to continue to live successfully in the community (Tsemberis and Eisenberg 2000, 492). A number of other communities have developed similar outreach services and housing programs that have proven effective with treatment-resistant or hard-to-serve clients, and have implemented them with virtually no coercion. In 2000, the Connecticut legislature authorized and funded the Pilot Peer Engagement Specialist Program, which employs people with psychiatric disabilities to conduct outreach to consumers who have not been engaged with the community mental health system. Similarly, since 2000, under the rubric of "AB 34" programs, the California Department of Mental Health has funded innovative outreach and engagement practices that have shown significant promise.

LAW AND SOCIAL CHANGE

In many instances, only when the full force and effect of the law have been brought to bear have homeless people actually been able to enjoy the rights granted to them by the FHA. But lawsuits are expensive and time-consuming; sometimes the mere prospect of having to litigate the legality of a zoning ordinance is enough to scare away a housing or service provider. As important as court decisions are to the development and protection of fair housing rights for people who are homeless, the FHA cannot become a more progressive force for social change if it is confined to the courtrooms. The creation of statutory rights is a necessary, but not a sufficient, condition for the realization of greater housing choice. To be effective, the principles of the FHA must infuse the entire housing community.

The barriers to more universal respect for the fair housing rights of homeless people are familiar: lack of knowledge about the existing protections of the law, a perception that the law is too complicated, the dearth of lawyers fully conversant with the intersection of housing and civil rights laws, and resistance by landlords and municipal officials.

The passage of the FHA and related civil rights laws has clearly changed the advocacy focus from supplication to legal entitlement. The litigation, community education, and consciousness raising that have taken place in the years since the FHA was enacted have built a sturdy foundation of housing rights for homeless people. But the progressive aims of the law can only fully be realized when all parties affected by it integrate it into their operations and expectations. The next challenge for all stakeholders is to preserve the vitality of the law, and to ensure that its protections do not become empty promises.

—*Michael Allen*

Further Reading

Allen, M. A. (1996, November). Separate and unequal: The struggle of tenants with mental illness to maintain housing. *Clearinghouse Review 720.* Retrieved December 3, 2003, from http://www.povertylaw.org/fulltext/pdfarticles/1996/nov/housing.pdf

Allen, M. A. (2002, Winter). Why not in our back yard? *Planning Commissioners Journal.* Retrieved December 3, 2003, from http://www.bazelon.org/issues/housing/articles/Why-Not-In-Our-Back-Yard.pdf

Bazelon Center for Mental Health Law. (2003). *Digest of cases and other resources on fair housing for people with disabilities.* Washington, DC: Author.

Building Better Communities Network and National Low Income Housing Coalition. (n.d.). *The NIMBY report.* Retrieved July 22, 2003, from http://www.bettercommunities.org/index.cfm?method=nimby

Code of Federal Regulations: 24: Sections 100.50(b) (1995) 24 C.F.R. 100.50(b), 100.70(b). (1996). Consortium for Citizens with Disabilities Housing Task Force and Technical Assistance Collaborative: Opening Doors: Recommendations for a Federal Policy to Address the Needs of People with Disabilities.

Cook, T. M. (1991). The Americans with Disabilities Act: The move to integration. *Temple Law Journal 64,* 393–425.

Corporation for Supportive Housing (2001). *Between the lines: A question and answer guide on legal issues in supportive housing.* Retrieved December 3, 2003, from http://www.csh.org/index.cfm?fuseaction=Page.viewPage&pageID=602

Culhane, D., Metraux, S., & Hadley, T. (2002). Public service reductions associated with placement of homeless persons with severe mental illness in supportive housing. *Housing Policy Debate, 107*(13). Retrieved December 3, 2003, from http://www.fanniemaefoundation.org/programs/hpd/pdf/hpd_1301_culhane.pdf

Dear, M., & von Mahs, J. (1996). *Case studies of successful and unsuccessful siting strategies.* Washington, DC: Building Better Communities Network.

Fair Housing Amendments Act. (1988). United States Code: 42: Sections 3601–3617, Fair Housing Amendments Act.

Outcasts on Main Street: A report of the federal task force on homelessness and severe mental illness. (1992). Washington, DC: GPO.

HomeBase. (1996). *Building inclusive community: Tools to create support for affordable housing.* San Francisco. Author.

Iglesias, T. (2002). Managing local opposition to affordable housing: A new approach to NIMBY. *Journal of Affordable Housing, 78*(12). Retrieved July 22, 2003, from http://www.bettercommunities.org/IglesiasMLOinprint.pdf

National Alliance to End Homelessness. (n.d.) *The ten-year plan to end homelessness.* Retrieved July 22, 2003, from http://www.endhomelessness.org/pub/tenyear

National Law Center on Homelessness and Poverty. (1995). *No room for the inn: A report on local opposition to housing and social services facilities for homeless people in 36 United States cities.* Washington, DC: Author.

National Law Center on Homelessness and Poverty. (1997). *Access delayed, access denied: Local opposition to housing and services for homeless people across the United States.* Washington, DC: Author.

National Low Income Housing Coalition (2002). *Rental housing for America's poor families: Farther out of reach than ever.* Retrieved July 22, 2003, from http://www.nlihc.org/oor2002/index.htm

Newman, S. J., Reschovsky, J. D., Kaneda, K., & Hendrick, A. M. (1994). The effects of independent living on people with severe mental illness. *Housing Center Bulletin, 2,* 8–12.

Newton, P. (n.d.). *Community relations handbook for providers of community-based housing and services.* Washington, DC: Building Better Communities Network.

Proscio, T. (2000). *Supportive housing and its impact on the public health crisis of homelessness.* Washington, DC: Corporation for Supportive Housing. Retrieved December 3, 2003, from http://www.csh.org/html/supportiveimpact-final.pdf

Schutt, R. K., & Goldfinger, S. M. (1996). Housing preferences and perceptions of health and functioning among homeless mentally ill persons. *Psychiatric Services, 47,* 381–386.

Technical Assistance Collaborative, Inc. (2003). *Priced out in 2002.* Retrieved July 22, 2003, from http://www.tacinc.org/cms/admin/cms/_uploads/docs/PO2002.pdf

Tsemberis, S., & Eisenberg, R. (2000). Supported housing for street-dwelling homeless individuals with psychiatric disabilities. *Psychiatric Services, 51,* 487–493.

Turner, L., & O'Hara, A. (1995). Supported housing and services: A view from the field. *Housing Center Bulletin, 3*(3), 6–7.

U.S. House of Representatives. (1988). House report no. 100–711 at p.18. Reprinted in U.S. Code Congressional and Administrative News (pp. 2173, 2179).

Court Cases

Carr v. Friends of the Homeless, No. 89-LE-3492-S, Trial Court, Commonwealth of Massachusetts, Hampden Div., Housing Court Dept. (1990).

Community Housing Trust v. Department of Consumer and Regulatory Affairs, 257 F.Supp.2d 208 (D.D.C. 2003).

Marbrunak, Inc. v. City of Stow, 974 F.2d 43 (6th Cir. 1992).

Mctalsky v. Mercy Haven, Inc., 594 N.Y.S.2d 129 (N.Y. Sup. Ct. Nassau Co., 1993).

Olmstead v. L.C., 527 U.S. 581 (1999).

Project B.A.S.I.C. v. City of Providence, 1990 WL 429846 (D.R.I. April 25, 1990).

Serreze v. Y.W.C.A. of Western Mass., 572 N.E.2d 581 (Mass.App. 1991).

United States v. Hughes Memorial Home, 396 F.Supp. 544 (W.D.Va. 1975).

United States v. City of Philadelphia, 838 F.Supp. 223, 228 (E.D. Pa. 1993).

Woods v. Foster, 884 F.Supp. 1169 (N.D.Ill. 1995).

FAMILIES

Families, usually defined as one or more adults accompanied by one or more children under eighteen, constitute an important subset of homeless people. The reasons for homelessness and the resources available to prevent or end it are different for families than for single adults or unaccompanied adolescents. On the other hand, distinctions between homeless families and homeless individuals also reflect the passage of time and the actions of service systems. Thus, in understanding homeless families, it is important to understand their characteristics as well as the systems that shape them.

EXTENT OF FAMILY HOMELESSNESS

One way to estimate the extent of family homelessness is to determine the percentage of homeless people who are members of homeless families. The 2002 U.S. Conference of Mayors report on homelessness in twenty-five large cities concluded that 41 percent of those who were homeless on any given night were members of homeless families. But because the report relied largely on counting people in shelters and because families are more likely than single individuals to seek shelter, this proportion was probably an overestimate. The Urban Institute's National Survey of Homeless Assistance Providers and Clients (NSHAPC), which included a broader and more representative sample of clients of sixteen types of homeless assistance programs in seventy-six geographical areas, provides better data. It found that 34 percent of homeless service users in 1996 were members of homeless families: 23 percent were children and 11 percent were their parents. This survey also noted that families remained homeless for shorter periods and were less likely to have several episodes of homelessness than single adults. Because the turnover of families was more rapid than the turnover of single adults, it was therefore only logical that the proportion of families who were homeless over the course of the year would be larger than the proportion of people who were homeless on any given night. The sample did not include families or individuals who did not access services and were more likely to be chronically homeless.

Another way of measuring the extent of family homelessness is to determine the proportion of poor families who become homeless. Psychologist Dennis Culhane and his colleagues investigated this in

Philadelphia and New York in the late 1980s and early 1990s by examining shelter records. They found that 10.5 percent of poor families and 13.6 percent of poor children had stayed in shelters during a three-year period in Philadelphia; in New York the percentages were 15.5 percent of poor families and 15.9 percent of poor children over five years. Sociologist Bruce Link and his colleagues, using data from a national telephone survey, found that 7.4 percent of adults in households with phones had been homeless (sleeping in places such as shelters, abandoned buildings, and bus and train stations) over their lifetimes. The comparable figure for those who had ever received public assistance was 19.8 percent. If the definition of homelessness was expanded to include doubling up, 31.2 percent of people who received public assistance had been homeless. Thus it is clear that homelessness is a common experience for poor families.

FAMILY SEPARATION

Numbers based on people who are sheltered along with their families underestimate the extent to which individual family members experience homelessness. The NSHAPC reported that 60 percent of all homeless women in 1996 had children below age eighteen, but only 65 percent of those women lived with at least one child; 41 percent of all homeless men had minor children, but only 7 percent lived with a child. These numbers are consistent with other studies. The extent to which separations are caused by service systems is unknown. According to the 2002 U.S. Conference of Mayors report, in 40 percent of cities in 2002, families sometimes had to break up to be sheltered, primarily because many family shelters excluded fathers and teenage boys.

Several studies have also found that mothers in family shelters have children living elsewhere. Psychologist Kirsten Cowal and her colleagues in New York found that five years after entering a shelter, 44 percent of a representative sample of mothers had become separated from one or more of their children (compared to 8 percent of poor mothers in housed families). A majority of the separated children lived with relatives, although a substantial minority were in foster care. Among both homeless families and the housed comparison group, three factors predicted separations: maternal drug dependence, domestic violence, and institutionalization, most often for substance abuse treatment. But at any level of risk, homeless families were far more likely to become separated from children than housed families, so that a homeless mother with no risk factors was as likely as a housed family with both drug dependence and domestic violence to become separated from a child. Because of family separations, what we know about homeless families pertains only to families who manage to maintain themselves as family units.

CHARACTERISTICS OF HOMELESS FAMILIES

Homeless families are very poor. Families with more resources might become homeless briefly, as a result of a fire or other disaster, but are likely to be quickly rehoused. Thus it makes sense to compare families who are homeless to single homeless individuals and to poor families who remain housed. For the first comparison, the NSHAPC is the best source. There are a number of studies that compare homeless families to families receiving public assistance or living in poor neighborhoods. In many respects, homeless families are more similar to other poor families than to homeless single adults.

Demographic Characteristics

Compared to homeless single adults, adults in homeless families are more likely to be female (23 percent versus 84 percent, according to the NSHAPC). They are also substantially younger, typically averaging between twenty-five and thirty, than homeless single adults and adults in other poor families. Adults in homeless families, which have an average of two children, are more likely than homeless single adults to be married (23 percent vs. 7 percent, according to the NSHAPC). Poor families generally are likely to be headed by women, but the relative number of homeless and poor families that are headed by married couples depends greatly on whether the homeless families are recruited from shelters that exclude men.

Homeless families are more likely than poor families generally, and substantially more likely than the general population, to be members of minority groups, especially African-American. This is also true of homeless single adults. For example, according to the NSHAPC, 62 percent of families and 59 percent of single adults, compared with 24 percent of the general population, were members of a minority group.

Adults in homeless families and other poor families have low levels of educational attainment and minimal work histories, but typically do not differ from each other. High school graduation rates for mothers in homeless families range from 35 percent to 58 percent. The graduation rates for these women are lower than for homeless single adults (47 percent versus 63 percent according to the NSHAPC). Incomes are slightly higher in homeless families than for homeless single adults, because families have greater access to means-tested benefit programs such as welfare and more help from relatives and friends. Nonetheless, the median income for a homeless family in 1996, according to the NSHAPC, was only $418 per month, or 41 percent of the poverty line for a family of three.

Stresses in the Lives of Homeless Parents

Homeless parents are severely stressed. Psychiatrist Ellen Bassuk and her colleagues in the Worcester Family Research Project (WFRP) found that homeless mothers faced multiple stressful events in three main areas: interpersonal, child-related, and medical and emotional. In the WFRP, a case-control longitudinal study conducted from 1992 to 1996, more than two-thirds of both homeless and housed mothers described severe interpersonal conflicts with significant others, including abusive relationships (see next section). As parents living in extreme poverty, their ability to take care of their children while working was frequently compromised by the lack of child-care vouchers, child support, jobs that paid livable wages, and flexible job hours. As described above, many parents were also coping with the out-of-home placement of a child. Pregnancy or the recent birth of a child placed poor women at higher risk for becoming homeless. Further complicating their situation was that many homeless children had high rates of medical hospitalization as well as significant emotional and medical problems.

Trauma, Mental Health, and Substance Abuse Problems

One of the major stresses in the lives of homeless mothers and mothers in other poor families is interpersonal and random violence. Many suffer from traumatic childhood experiences, such as physical and sexual abuse, and therefore may not be able to establish secure relationships during critical developmental years. This may explain why some of these women have difficulty forming and maintaining supportive relationships as adults. In the Worcester study, only 8.4 percent of homeless mothers and 18.2 percent of housed mothers had *not* experienced at least one form of severe violence during their lifetime. A majority of both groups had been severely physically assaulted as children and more than 40 percent had been sexually molested at least one time before adulthood. As adults, nearly two-thirds of the entire sample had been severely assaulted by an intimate partner. Although largely unrecognized, many of the mental health and medical needs of poor women are directly associated with violence and trauma.

In the Worcester study (but not in the New York study described below), interpersonal violence, especially during childhood, was closely associated with a woman's ability to remain rehoused after an episode of homelessness. Mothers who had been homeless more than once had had higher rates of childhood sexual abuse and random violence than those who had been homeless only once. First-time homeless mothers who were in violent domestic relationships when they were rehoused were more likely to become homeless again.

Not surprisingly, given their experience of extreme poverty, multiple stresses, and severe violence, poor women, including homeless women, suffer from an array of emotional problems. The lifetime rates of mental health problems among homeless mothers, such as major depression, anxiety disorders, and posttraumatic stress disorder (PTSD), are similar to the rates of other poor mothers, but considerably higher than rates in the general female population, as reported in the National Comorbidity Survey. Compared to the general population, very poor homeless and housed mothers had twice the rate of depression, twice the rate of PTSD, and twice the rate of substance abuse. Psychotic disorders, such as schizophrenia, were *not* more common among homeless mothers than among the general population. Compared to poor housed mothers, significantly more homeless mothers had been hospitalized for emotional or substance use problems.

The proportion of adults in homeless families who suffer from mental health, alcohol, or drug problems depends on how these problems are defined and the period over which problems are assessed. For example, the NSHAPC counted people who attend Alcoholics Anonymous (or met a variety of other criteria) as having a current alcohol problem, whether or not they had had a drink recently. Thus, 18 percent of adults in homeless families were classified as having an alcohol problem in the past month whereas only 11 percent reported having drunk alcohol three times within any week in the past month. Using careful diagnostic interviews, Bassuk and her colleagues found that 2.7 percent of homeless mothers met diagnostic criteria for alcohol abuse or dependence in the past month. These rates may be underestimated given that shelters excluded active substance users. Figures for the current drug problems of poor and homeless women (20 percent of adults in families based on an expansive definition in the NSHAPC; 3.6 percent based on diagnostic interviews in the Worcester study) are equally disparate. Lifetime rates of substance use problems in both groups were far higher in both studies—with 41 percent of homeless mothers and 34.7 percent of poor housed mothers in Worcester reporting alcohol- or drug dependence. Whatever the definition or period used, studies consistently find that mothers in homeless families have fewer substance problems than single homeless adults (who are mostly male), but more than mothers in poor families and more than women in the general population.

The NSHAPC found comparable levels of mental health problems among homeless families and homeless single adults, although the single adults were more likely to have been hospitalized. However, this study did not distinguish among different types of mental health problems, or between problems that are more prevalent for women and for men. Homeless single men and women are more likely than mothers in homeless families to have schizophrenia.

Taking alcohol, drug, and mental health problems together, the National Survey found that 49 percent of adults in homeless families had had some problem in the current month compared to 69 percent of homeless single adults. In the Worcester study, using tighter definitions, 35 percent of homeless mothers, compared to 33 percent of housed low-income mothers, had had current problems. Again, although the specific numbers depend on definitions, the finding that mothers in homeless families are more like other poor mothers than like homeless single adults is consistent with other studies.

Medical Problems

Homeless mothers have many acute and chronic medical problems—far more than the general population of women aged twenty-five to thirty-four. In the Worcester study, homeless mothers had significantly higher rates of asthma, anemia, chronic bronchitis, and ulcers.

Characteristics of Children in Homeless Families

Children in homeless families are very different from unaccompanied homeless adolescents. Their parents are young and so are they, with 42 percent in the National Survey below school age. The most lasting legacy of homelessness for many children may be separation from their families, as described above. In the New York study, less than a quarter of separated children had been returned to their families five years after the family first entered a shelter. Children who remain in homeless families may have fewer problems than those who leave.

Psychologist Ann Masten has described a "continuum of risk" in which homeless children are worse off than other poor children (although often not significantly so), and poor children are worse off than middle-class children, along a variety of dimensions. Compared to other poor children, children in shelters may experience more health problems. They report somewhat more psychological distress (although typically not higher rates of diagnosable mental disorders). Despite federal legislation (the McKinney Act) that entitles homeless children to remain in their previous schools, many change schools frequently as their families move around and in and out of shelters. They are frequently absent and often need to repeat a grade.

CAUSES OF FAMILY HOMELESSNESS

Experts generally agree that the structural causes of homelessness are poverty and a lack of affordable housing, with individual vulnerabilities playing an important role in determining which poor people are unable to secure or maintain access to housing. Families compete in the same housing market as single individuals, although they typically require at least a two-bedroom unit. The Department of Housing and Urban Development (HUD) has traditionally maintained that housing is affordable if it costs no more than 30 percent of income. The National Low Income Housing Coalition found that, by this standard, a minimum-wage worker would have needed to work from 66 hours per week (in Puerto Rico) to 146 hours per week (in New Jersey) to afford the fair-market rent (as calculated by HUD) for a two-bedroom apartment in 2002. HUD reported that 33 percent of families with incomes below half of the median income in their area had worse-case housing needs in 1997—that is, they were renters without subsidies who paid more than half their income for housing and utilities or lived in severely substandard housing.

The importance of housing in understanding which families become homeless is demonstrated in a New York City study by Psychologist Marybeth Shinn and her colleagues in which families requesting shelter were compared to families from the public assistance caseload. None of the families had been homeless previously, so characteristics that

A group of homeless children who live in a slum in the Milpillas dump in Miacatlan, Morelos, Mexico. During the day, the children are taken to an orphanage to attend school, shower, and eat, and are then returned to the dump in the evening to be with their parents.
Source: Lynsey Addario/Corbis; used with permission.

might be the consequences of shelter stays could not be confused with characteristics that might cause them. Mothers in the families requesting shelter were younger than those in housed families, more likely to be African-American, and much more likely to be pregnant or have a newborn, factors that may have affected both housing needs and the ability to generate income. They were also far more likely to be doubled up, to have moved recently, and to live in overcrowded dwellings, and far less likely to have housing subsidies. Together, these housing and demographic factors accurately predicted 65 percent of families who would become homeless (but the same factors wrongly predicted that 10 percent of housed families would be homeless). Other factors that together improved prediction to 66 percent were marriage (heads of homeless families were *more* likely to be married), growing up in a family on welfare, experiencing domestic violence, and early childhood abuse or separation from the family of origin. Factors that did not add any predictive power included education, work history, prior teen pregnancy, mental illness, substance abuse, health problems, history of incarceration, and social networks.

Five years later, only one factor made an important contribution to understanding which formerly homeless families would be stably housed in their own apartments for at least a year without a move.

This was whether or not the family had received some form of subsidized housing. Among families that did, 80 percent met this definition of stability, the identical proportion as for public assistance recipients generally. Among those who did not, only 18 percent were stable. Unlike the findings in Worcester, neither early childhood experiences of abuse or out-of-home placement, adult experiences of domestic violence, nor any other factors that influenced seeking shelter affected later stability. Of all other factors measured, only age additionally contributed to stability, and the effect was quite small. Families in this study received no special services.

Psychologist Debra Rog and her colleagues, in a six-city study conducted in the early 1990s, found that 86 percent of families with multiple problems who had been provided with both Section 8 certificates (which subsidize housing) and services were still in the same Section 8 housing after eighteen months. No differences were found across cities or service models. These studies suggest the centrality of housing resources to ending family homelessness.

Some observers, such as sociologist Christopher Jencks, have argued that declines in marriage rates are a central cause of family homelessness. Single parenthood may well contribute to poverty, and hence to making housing less affordable. But once families are poor, marriage or cohabitation does not seem to protect them against homelessness. Studies that find higher rates of single parenthood among homeless families than among other poor families tend to have been conducted in shelter systems that sometimes exclude men.

SOLUTIONS TO FAMILY HOMELESSNESS

Solutions to family homelessness can be divided into efforts at preventing and ending homelessness, making homelessness less disruptive to children and families, and improving the quality of life for families who become homeless. With respect to preventing and ending homelessness, research suggests that creating more affordable housing is critical. This can be done with direct housing subsidies and subsidies or tax breaks for the development of affordable

housing, or with efforts to raise wage rates and benefits from government transfer programs at the bottom of the income distribution. Both strategies are important. Because in some cities homeless families come disproportionately from specific neighborhoods (not simply poor neighborhoods), and because homelessness is associated with life stage (youth, having a new child), it may be worth targeting prevention efforts to young families in high-risk neighborhoods. Greater efforts to eliminate persistent discrimination in housing might lower rates of homelessness for African-American families.

To make homelessness less disruptive to families, temporary shelter should be a right. The U.S. Conference of Mayors reported in 2002 that 60 percent of cities in their survey sometimes turned families away for lack of space. Families, especially families with young children or members who are sick, should not be required to leave shelters during the day, as they were in 32 percent of cities. Providers should try to house entire families together and to avoid arbitrary limits on the length of stay. To avoid disruptions in schooling and social networks, temporary shelters should be located near the neighborhood of origin, the neighborhood in which families will be rehoused, or both.

Shelters are difficult places in which to rear children. Shelter rules frequently usurp parental authority, and establishing routines for meals or homework can be difficult in crowded and shared facilities. To minimize the disruptions associated with shelters, families should be moved to permanent housing as quickly as possible. Social service personnel should consider the long-term interests of children as well as their immediate circumstances in determining whether they need to be removed from a family, and they should make provisions for reuniting families. For example, separated mothers should be given priority access to apartments large enough to accommodate all their children if reunification is desired.

Many services may be important to a family's quality of life, including health services, help with employment, quality child care and after-school programs, and counseling for mental health problems. Substance abuse programs should accommodate children, so that mothers do not have to choose between getting treatment and keeping their children. An important question is whether services should be based in shelters and transitional housing programs, or whether they should be sited in poor communities, where they would be more widely available. Shelters and housing programs might then link homeless families with community-based services that offer more continuity. Some evidence suggesting the value of community-based services comes from a study in New York, which has excellent health services in shelters. Nevertheless, five years after entering shelters, formerly homeless families in New York were less likely than other poor families to have a regular source of medical care. A small number of families may need ongoing supportive housing where services are more intensive and coordinated.

Many of these services have the primary purpose of undoing the damage caused by homelessness. If homelessness can be prevented, by raising the incomes of poor families and providing more affordable housing, other specialized services will be less necessary. Thus, prevention should be the primary goal.

—*Marybeth Shinn and Ellen Bassuk*

Further Reading

Bassuk, E. L., Buckner, J. C., Perloff, J. N., & Bassuk, S. S. (1998). Prevalence of mental health and substance use disorders among homeless and low-income housed mothers. *American Journal of Psychiatry, 155,* 1561–1564.

Bassuk, E. L., Perloff J. N., & Dawson, R. (2001). Multiply homeless families: The insidious impact of violence. *Housing Policy Debate, 12,* 299–320.

Bassuk, E. L., Weinreb, L., Buckner J., Browne, A., Salomon A., & Bassuk, S. (1996). The characteristics and needs of sheltered homeless and low-income housed mothers. *JAMA, 276,* 640–647.

Baumohl, J. (Ed.). *Homelessness in America.* Phoenix, AZ: Oryx Press.

Buckner, J. C., Bassuk, E. L., & Weinreb, L. F. (2001). Predictors of academic achievement among homeless and low-income housed children. *Journal of School Psychology, 39,* 45–69.

Buckner, J. C., Bassuk, E., L., Weinreb, L., & Brooks, M. (1999). Homelessness and its relation to the mental health and behavior of low-income school aged children. *Developmental Psychology, 35,* 246–257.

Burt, M., Aron, L. Y., Douglas, T., Valente, J., Lee, E., & Iwen, B. (1999). *Homelessness: Programs and the people they serve: Findings of the National Survey of Homeless Assistance Providers and Clients.* Technical report prepared for Interagency Council on the Homeless. Washington, DC: The Urban Institute.

Cowal, K., Shinn, M., Weitzman, B. C., Stojanovic, D., & Labay, L. (2002). Mother-child separations among homeless and housed families receiving public assistance in New York City. *American Journal of Community Psychology, 30,* 711–730.

Culhane, D. P., Dejowski, E. F., Ibanez, J., Needham, E., & Macchia, I. (1994). Public shelter admission rates in Philadelphia and New York City: The implications of turnover for sheltered population counts. *Housing Policy Debate, 5,* 107–140.

Culhane, D. P., Lee, C.-M., & Wachter, S. M. (1996). Where the homeless come from: A study of the prior address distribution of families admitted to public shelters in New York City and Philadelphia. *Housing Policy Debate, 7*(2), 327–365.

Duchon, L., Weitzman, B. C., & Shinn, M. (1999). The relationship of residential instability to medical care utilization among poor mothers in New York City. *Medical Care, 37,* 1282–1293.

Jencks, C. (1994). *The homeless.* Cambridge, MA: Harvard University Press.

Kessler R. C., McGonagle K. A., Zhaos S., et al. (1994). Lifetime and 12-month prevalence of DSM-III-R psychiatric disorders in the United States: results from the National Comorbidity Survey. *Archives of General Psychiatry, 51,* 8–19.

Link, B. G., Susser, E., Stueve, A., Phelan, J., Moore, R. E., & Struening, E. (1994). Lifetime and five-year prevalence of homelessness in the United States. *American Journal of Public Health, 84,* 1907–1912.

Masten, A. S., Miliotis, D., Graham-Bermann, S. A., Ramirez, M., & Neemann, J. (1993). Children in homeless families: Risks to mental health and development. *Journal of Consulting and Clinical Psychology, 61,* 335–343.

National Low Income Housing Coalition. (2002). *Rental housing for America's poor families in 2002: Farther out of reach than ever.* Retrieved April 6, 2003, from http://www.nlihc.org/oor2002/index.htm

Rafferty, Y., & Rollins, N. (1989). *Learning in limbo: The educational deprivation of homeless children.* New York: Advocates for Children. (ERIC Document Reproduction No. Ed 312363).

Rafferty, Y., & Shinn, M. (1991). The impact of homelessness on children. *American Psychologist, 46,* 1170–1179.

Rog, D. J., Holupka, C. S., & McCombs-Thornton, K. L. (1995). Implementation of the homeless families program: 1. Service models and preliminary outcomes. *American Journal of Orthopsychiatry, 65,* 502–513.

Shinn, M., & Weitzman, B. C. (1996). Homeless families are different. In J. Baumohl (Ed.), *Homelessness in America* (pp. 109–122). Phoenix: Oryx Press.

Shinn, M., Weitzman, B. C., Stojanovic, D., Knickman, J. R.,

Jiménez, L., Duchon, L., James, S., & Krantz, D. H. (1998). Predictors of homelessness from shelter request to housing stability among families in New York City. *American Journal of Public Health, 88,* 1651–1657.

United States Conference of Mayors. (2002). *A status report on hunger and homelessness in America's Cities.* Retrieved April 6, 2003, from http://www.usmayors.org/uscm/hunger survey/2002/onlinereport/HungerAndHomelessReport 2002.pdf

U.S. Department of Housing and Urban Development (2000). *Rental housing assistance: A report to Congress on worst case housing needs.* Retrieved April 6, 2003, from http://www.huduser.org/Publications/AFFHSG/WORST CASE00/worstcase00.pdf

Weinreb, L., Goldberg, R., Bassuk, E., & Perloff, J. (1998). Determinants of health and service use patterns in homeless and low-income housed children. *Pediatrics, 102,* 554–562.

Wood, D. L., Valdez, R. B., Hayashi, T., & Shen, A. (1990). Health of homeless children and housed poor children. *Pediatrics, 86,* 858–866.

▣ FAMILY SEPARATIONS AND REUNIFICATIONS

Wars and natural disasters that uproot and displace whole communities produce both homelessness and family dispersal. But in twentieth-century urban America, losses of home and family usually occur under the more insidiously destructive conditions of poverty, discrimination, and disability. Understanding the varied processes linking homelessness to the rupture of family ties in these contexts must be part of any effort to avert both kinds of losses and the suffering they entail.

Homelessness in the United States changed markedly in the last half of the twentieth century. In the decades after 1950, urban skid rows were populated by men whose lack of family and other intimate ties, limited participation in the labor market, and residence in nonconventional "flophouse" or single-room occupancy dwellings, bespoke a disaffiliation from mainstream life and institutions. Indeed, contemporaneous notions of homelessness assumed such a disengagement. Though skid row residents were poor, their poverty was usually described as a by-product of the disaffiliation that infused their personalities and lifestyles. By the

1980s, however, the global deployment of capital to low-wage regions of the world, and its effects on the industrial economies of U.S. cities, had pushed many more persons into poverty. With both affordable housing and entitlement benefit dollars shrinking rapidly, urban poverty generated a growing population of homeless or marginally sheltered individuals. Meanwhile, related changes increased that population's diversity: shifts in the gender and race structure of the labor force, immigration patterns, and family organization. Those on the streets or seeking shelter included rising numbers of women and people of color, as well as individuals with psychiatric problems and drug addiction. The most striking change was the growth of family homelessness, as exemplified in New York City, where the number of sheltered families—usually single mothers and their children—increased by a factor of 160: from 30 in 1969 to 5,000 in 1985. These new demographics challenged prior understandings of homelessness as an outgrowth of disaffiliation, even as they reflected the new hardships faced by poor families.

TYPES OF FAMILY SEPARATION

Family disruptions are implicated in several recent and current manifestations of homelessness: homeless youth, homeless adults who themselves were in out-of-home care as children, and homeless parents whose children live with others. Disrupted families and residential instability often precede homelessness for both youth and adults. Researchers estimate that in any given year, more than a million twelve- to seventeen-year-olds experience homelessness on their own. Family conflict is the primary reason, though neglect and abuse are also common precipitants. By most accounts, these young people come from less impoverished backgrounds than do homeless adults. Over half—57 percent in one study of federally funded youth shelters—return home eventually, though this is not an option for significant subgroups such as those who "age out" of foster care or state youth care institutions. Youth homelessness increases the risk for mental disorders, and for both divorce and arrest later in life, though only those with a long history of residential instability and foster care are at special risk of becoming homeless as adults.

Childhood family disruptions, particularly foster care placements, are also precursors of homelessness for up to a quarter of homeless adults. It is unclear what factors this reflects: damaged family networks that otherwise buffer hard times, foster children's increased vulnerability to emotional or behavioral problems that interfere with social functioning, foster settings that provide inadequate preparation for independent living, or other factors.

For homeless adults, high rates of family separation during childhood are paralleled by high rates of separation from their own children. Surveys of homeless populations routinely find that more than half are parents, though most are homeless alone. Homeless women are especially likely to be parents: More than 70 percent were mothers in studies in Chicago, Baltimore, New York, St. Louis, and Alameda County, California, and most research on homeless parents has focused on women. Mothers are more likely than fathers to be accompanied by some or all of their children, but separations are nonetheless frequent. In local surveys of homeless women, between 20 and 58 percent of mothers were separated from all of their children. If the mother had mental illness, the rate was higher: 73 percent, according to one national study. And in studies of homeless mothers accompanied by children, between 18 and 44 percent report that some of their children live elsewhere.

REASONS FOR PARENT-CHILD SEPARATION

Some of the processes leading to separations of homeless parents and children have been well documented: certain social service policies, shelter admission rules, child welfare agency practices, stresses of shelter life, surveillance of homeless families, and parental efforts to spare their children the experience of homelessness. Other factors, such as mental illness, substance abuse problems, and domestic violence, have been inferred from their high prevalence among separated mothers. But the mechanisms that link these processes to separations, in varying ways under varying conditions, are not well understood. And since few studies have compared homeless mothers' separation experiences with those of other poor mothers, it has been hard to determine what role homelessness itself plays in dismantling families.

On the agency level, several social and child welfare policies encourage family dispersal: Eligibility criteria for entitlement benefits favor single-parent families, and shelters themselves often exclude larger families, older children, adult and adolescent males, or families that cannot prove biological or marriage relationships. Although child welfare systems rarely remove children from families solely because of homelessness, many features of shelter life increase the risk of child placement elsewhere. Crowded and inadequate facilities increase stress, shelter rules and practices can undermine parental authority and parenting practices, and staff surveillance and the stigma of homelessness influence how mothers' parenting behaviors are assessed by the agencies that serve and observe them.

Some mothers who become homeless choose to place children with relatives or friends to avoid school disruption or exposure to negative shelter environments. While African-American and Latino families have historically used extended-kin networks to share resources, provide for children, and reaffirm family ties, many homeless families have already strained these resources through doubled-up living arrangements and other support needs before "officially" becoming homeless, and many homeless families lack access to such support. Moreover, regardless of who initiates such placements, their voluntary nature must be understood against a background of options constrained by poverty and homelessness.

Personal problems may also contribute to separations. Unaccompanied homeless mothers have higher rates of mental illness and substance abuse than mothers accompanied by children, and researchers have inferred that these problems may account for the children's absence. There is evidence that drug abuse increases the risk of separation, though in one study institutional drug treatment increased the risk of separation even more than drug dependence itself. The role of mental illness is less

Homeless families waiting to board a bus at the Emergency Assistance Unit in the Bronx, New York, to take them to an overnight shelter in January 2002.
Source: Mark Peterson/Corbis; used with permission.

ents and children, research comparing homeless with other poor families found that homelessness had almost twice the impact of other risk factors for separation. It is not clear whether the same factors affect separations for unaccompanied homeless mothers, since no studies have compared this group to similar mothers who are housed. Moreover, no controlled studies of homeless family separations have included both accompanied and unaccompanied parents. In fact, research on the timing and circumstances of separations raises the possibility that the terms *accompanied* and *unaccompanied* denote overlapping rather than distinct groups that include some of the same mothers at different points in a process of family dispersal that ultimately leaves some homeless alone.

clear. Major depression has been associated with parenting deficits in non-homeless populations and is highly prevalent among mothers in homeless families. But research has not confirmed its link to homeless mothers' separations from their children. Moreover, research on homeless mothers with serious mental illness indicates that psychotic behavior, specifically, is a feature of those separated from their children, suggesting that "serious mental illness" may be too broad a category to be useful in identifying parents at risk for separation.

Homeless women experience high rates of domestic violence. Across several studies, between one-third and two-thirds reported violence on the part of a male partner. Domestic violence has also been shown to increase the risk of family separation, though there are contradictory findings on its frequency among homeless mothers versus other poor mothers. Inconsistent measures of domestic violence create further problems in clarifying both the mechanisms that might link it to family separation and the nature of its risk for children. Additional research is needed on this subject.

While studies have found it hard to determine what role homelessness itself plays in separating par-

TIMING AND CIRCUMSTANCES OF SEPARATION

Over the course of their homelessness, mothers' decisions about their children may be increasingly preempted by others. In one study, mothers themselves chose whether and how to separate the family before, or, as it became homeless, often sending children to live with relatives. But during shelter stays, separations were more likely to be imposed by the child welfare system or family court, which more often sent children to foster care. Fathers, children, and other relatives played a greater role in later separations, when children often went to live with the relative most involved in the decision. For some mothers, a diminished role in decisions about their children culminates in eventual separation from all of them. A significant minority of unaccompanied homeless mothers—proportions range from 20 to 31 percent—were previously homeless *with* children.

One study found that such separated mothers were more likely to have recurrent homelessness, suggesting that once underway, losses of home and family are mutually reinforcing.

While separations from children do not bode well for homeless mothers, little is known about the characteristics or experiences of separated children. Most stay with relatives in either informal placements or kinship foster care, though as many as one-quarter may be in non-kin foster arrangements. Studies show that homelessness negatively affects children's short-term school achievement and some mental health measures, but once housed, they recoup these losses over time. There is virtually no information, however, on how separated children fare over time, as compared to children who remain in homeless families.

ONGOING PARENTAL INVOLVEMENT AND PROSPECTS FOR REUNIFICATION

Many homeless mothers stay in regular contact with absent children and actively work toward reunification. An early New York City study reported that almost two-thirds of unaccompanied mothers had cared for their children in the past two years, were maintaining contact with them, and planned to rejoin them. However, homelessness can make these complex and exhausting endeavors, especially for parents with substance abuse and mental health problems. When homeless parents are separated from children, they often lose the financial entitlements and housing eligibility that would be needed to restore their families. Moreover, contact is complicated by distance, shelter rules—about phone calls, visits, curfews, and required activities, for example—and the demands of treatment programs. When children stay with faraway relatives, mothers may be unable to pay for long-distance calls or visits. Even local visits may require expensive travel, and contact may be inhibited by poor relationships with caregivers, court-mandated schedules or supervision of visits, or foster care policies that reward agencies for arranging adoptions but not for reuniting families. And when visiting schedules or family court appearances conflict with other appointments arranged by shelter staff, mothers must choose which demands to satisfy.

Visits themselves can also be emotionally challenging, as mothers and children readjust to each other; children may have clinging, withdrawn, or "acting-out" responses to separation. Mothers with several children must juggle visits around the schedules of multiple caregivers and schools while also complying with treatment programs or required housing searches. Failures to make planned visits not only damage fragile mother-child relationships but can become part of the "case" for termination of parental rights.

In the case of court-ordered separations, reunification plans specify what homeless parents must do to regain custody. In addition to visiting children, parents are routinely required to find appropriate housing, attend parenting classes, and successfully complete job training and treatment programs. For accompanied mothers in shelters, arranging child care while pursuing these tasks is difficult. In treatment programs or shelters for single adults, staff may be unaware or unwilling to accommodate mothers' parenting needs and goals, and may limit their help with housing to semi-independent or single-room settings that preclude children either as residents or visitors. Moreover, treatment program timetables are increasingly at odds with federal time limits for parents to complete reunification plans or lose their parental rights.

Given these hurdles, it is not surprising that reunification is rare. In a study of family shelter users and other poor mothers in New York City, only 23 percent of separated children were living with their mothers five years later. In research on unaccompanied homeless mothers with mental illness, only 17 percent were reunited with children after one year. Improvements in housing status, reduced psychotic symptoms and drug use, and improved relationships with service providers predicted reunification for this group, but it is unclear how these findings might apply to other separated homeless families.

UNANSWERED QUESTIONS AND FUTURE CHALLENGES

Evidence to date shows that children with out-of-home placements are at risk of becoming homeless adults, while homelessness itself further undermines the integrity of poor families and increases the likelihood of parent-child separations. Among homeless adults, various personal circumstances—substance dependence, domestic violence, institutional treatment—are implicated in separations, and homeless mothers with severe mental illness may also be at higher risk. Moreover, once separated, homeless mothers have increased risk of recurring homelessness, so that losses of home and children reinforce each other.

Many questions remain. Mothers report their own anger, sadness, and guilt about separations, but we know little about how separated children fare, although their "best interests" are regularly invoked. We also know little about how separation affects the extended-kin networks that often take children in, though homelessness and separation have widespread ramifications within extended families and need to be understood from multiple perspectives.

Another omission from the literature is the issue of race. Studies have repeatedly documented that African-Americans are overrepresented in both homeless and foster care populations, but the processes involved remain inadequately investigated. There is persuasive evidence that racial disparities emerge from decision making about assessment, placement, and service at every stage of the foster care process, but this understanding has yet to be incorporated into research into the links between foster care, homelessness, family separation, and service system responses.

Preventing homelessness would go a long way toward preventing the devastation of families that occurs in its wake. But resolving families' homelessness does not by itself repair families once they are dismantled. Many homeless mothers go to great lengths to maintain contact and actively seek reunification, but even when re-housed, only a minority rejoin separated children. Apart from research showing that reunifications for homeless mothers with mental illness occur when housing, symptoms, and treatment stabilize, we know little about what promotes reunification for other homeless families, or how reunified families fare over time.

Finally, efforts to end homelessness and reunite families must contend with growing poverty in the early twenty-first century, time limits on welfare benefits, and short federally imposed timetables for terminating rights of separated parents. These policies and processes will affect not only parents' ability to exit from homelessness but also the extended-family networks that often care for separated children, perhaps impelling further displacement. Future research must address the individual characteristics and experiences implicated in separations of homeless families; document the policies and processes, both local and large-scale, that foster dispersal of homeless families; and consider interventions that will change systems as well as people.

—Susan M. Barrow

Further Reading

Bahr, H. M. (Ed.). (1970). *Disaffiliated man: Essays and bibliography on skid row.* Toronto, Ontario, Canada: University of Toronto Press.

Bassuk, E. L., Buckner, J. C., Weinreb, L. R., Browne, A., Bassuk, S. S., Dawson, R., & Perloff, J. N. (1997). Homelessness in female headed families: Childhood and adult risk and protective factors. *American Journal of Public Health, 87*(2), 241–248.

Bernstein, N. (2001). *The lost children of Wilder: The epic struggle to change foster care.* New York: Pantheon.

Browne, A., & Bassuk, S. S. (1997). Intimate violence in the lives of homeless and housed women: Prevalence and patterns in an ethnically diverse sample. *Journal of Orthopsychiatry, 67*(2), 261–278.

Burt, M. R., & Cohen, B. E. (1989). Differences among homeless single women, women with children, and single men. *Social Problems, 36*(5), 508–524.

Connolly, D. R. (2000). *Homeless mothers: Face to face with women and poverty.* Minneapolis: University of Minnesota Press.

Cowal, K., Shinn, M., Weitzman, B. C., Stojanovic, D., & Labay, L. (2002). Mother-child separations among homeless and housed families receiving public assistance in New York City. *American Journal of Community Psychology, 30*(5), 711–730.

Crystal, S. (1984). Homeless men and homeless women: The gender gap. *Urban and Social Change Review, 17,* 2–6.

Curtis, P. A., Dale, G., Jr., & Kendall, J. C. (1999). *The foster care crisis: Translating research into policy and practice.* Lincoln: University of Nebraska Press.

D'Ercole, A., & Struening, E. (1990). Victimization among homeless women: Implications for service delivery. *Journal of Community Psychology, 18,* 141–151.

DiBlasio, F. A., & Belcher, J. R. (1992). Keeping homeless families together: Examining their needs. *Children and Youth Services Review, 14,* 427–438.

Hoffman, D., & Rosenheck, R. (2001). Homeless mothers with severe mental illness and their children: Predictors of family reunification. *Psychiatric Rehabilitation Journal, 25*(2), 163–69.

Johnson, A. K., & Kreuger, W. (1989). Toward a better understanding of homeless women. *Social Work, 34,* 537–540.

Metraux, S., & Culhane, D. P. (1999). Family dynamics, housing and recurring homelessness among women in New York City homeless shelters. *Journal of Family Issues, 20*(3), 371–396.

Roberts, D. (2002). *Shattered bonds: The color of child welfare.* New York: Basic Civitas.

Robertson, M. J., & Toro, P. (1999). Homeless youth: Research, intervention, and policy. In L. B. Fosburg & D. L. Dennis (Eds.), *Practical lessons: The 1998 National Symposium on Homelessness Research* (pp. 3.1–3.32). Washington, DC: U.S. Department of Housing and Urban Development and U.S. Department of Health and Human Services.

Robertson, M. J., & Winkleby, M. A. (1996). Mental health problems of homeless women and differences across subgroups. *Annual Review of Public Health, 17,* 311–336.

Rossi, P. H. (1989). *Down and out in America: The origins of homelessness.* Chicago: University of Chicago Press.

Shinn, M., & Weitzman, B. C. (1996). Homeless families are different. In J. Baumohl (Ed.), *Homeless in America* (pp. 109–122). Phoenix, AZ: Oryx.

Smith, E. M., & North, C. S. (1994). Not all homeless women are alike: Effects of motherhood and the presence of children. *Community Mental Health Journal, 30*(6), 601–610.

Susser, I. (1996). The construction of poverty and homelessness in U.S. cities. *Annual Review of Anthropology, 25,* 411–435.

Susser, I. (1999). Creating family forms: The exclusion of men and teenage boys from families in the New York City shelter system 1987–1991. In S. M. Low (Ed.), *Theorizing the city: The new urban anthropology reader* (pp. 67–82). New Brunswick, NJ: Rutgers University Press.

Stein, T. J. (2000). The Adoption and Safe Families Act: Creating a false dichotomy between parents' rights and children's rights. *Families in Society: The Journal of Contemporary Human Services, 81*(6), 586–592.

▣ FEANTSA

FEANTSA (www.feantsa.org), the European Federation of National Organisations Working with the Homeless, was established in 1989 as a European nongovernmental organization (in French, FEANTSA stands for la Fédération Européenne d'Associations Nationales Travaillant avec les Sans-Abri).

The more than ninety member organizations of FEANTSA come from twenty-three European countries, including all fifteen member states of the European Union (EU). FEANTSA members represent a substantial part of the organized homeless sector in the fifteen EU countries, with membership expanding to additional organizations in countries seeking accession to the EU. Members are nongovernmental organizations (NGOs) that provide a wide range of services to homeless people including accommodation and social support. Most of the members of FEANTSA are national or regional umbrella organizations of service providers. They often work in close cooperation with public authorities, social housing providers, and other relevant actors.

FEANTSA is the only major European network that focuses exclusively on homelessness at the European level. FEANTSA receives financial support from the European Commission for the implementation of its activities. FEANTSA works closely with the EU institutions, and has consultative status at the Council of Europe and at the United Nations.

STRUCTURE

FEANTSA is democratically structured to involve member organizations in as many aspects of its work as possible. The guiding bodies of FEANTSA are the general assembly (which involves all member organizations), an administrative council (consisting of one representative for each EU member state), and an executive committee (comprising up to 7 members drawn from the administrative council). FEANTSA also has a small office based in Brussels that is responsible for the day-to-day operations of the network.

INFLUENCING POLICY

FEANSTA engages in constant dialogue with the European institutions and national and regional governments to promote the development and implementation of effective measures to fight homelessness. It also works to make European, national, and regional decision makers aware of the urgent need to develop proactive policies aimed at effectively preventing homelessness. FEANTSA raises public awareness about the complexity of homelessness and the multidimensional nature of the problems faced by homeless people.

TRANSNATIONAL EXCHANGES

FEANTSA promotes and facilitates the exchange of information, experience, and best practice among its member organizations. This exchange gives members access to effective and innovative approaches to the problem of homelessness. To this end, FEANTSA organizes regular European seminars and conferences that bring together service providers, researchers, and decision makers. In addition, FEANTSA has four working groups, where members discuss relevant issues and themes surrounding housing, employment, health and social protection, and data collection (statistics and indicators). The working groups are composed of experts in their field and, in addition to sharing information and experience, are responsible for following developments at the EU level (in terms of policy, programs, initiatives, etc.) in their respective areas.

FEANTSA prepares regular policy documents on relevant issues based on the results of transnational exchange. Both these reports and the resulting policy statements are available on the website and through the FEANTSA office in Brussels.

RESEARCH

FEANTSA is dedicated to facilitating research to promote better understanding of the complexity and the changing nature of homelessness. Research findings are circulated to other academics, as well as to the service providers for homeless people and policymakers. This research provides insights into the theoretical nature of homelessness, as well as trends, and provides a strong scientific base for service providers and policymakers to construct policy and programs.

FEANTSA established the European Observatory on Homelessness in 1991. This network is composed of fifteen national research correspondents from the fifteen EU countries who have built up extensive experience in the field of homelessness and housing exclusion.

By 2002, the Observatory produced a series of national reports on specific research themes related to homelessness. These reports formed the basis of a European publication that examines and analyzes transnational trends. These national and transnational reports are available for sale through the FEANTSA office in Brussels.

In 2002, FEANTSA changed its research strategy. Now, the fifteen national correspondents draft a national statistics update, research review, and policy update. The coordinators of the Observatory use these key national reports to write three European synthesis reports on statistics, research, and policy. The Observatory also operates three thematic working groups with five researchers per group. In 2003, these groups drafted papers on (1) Intervention Strategies and the Changing Role of the State, (2) Profiles of Homelessness, and (3) Services for Homeless People.

More information on the Observatory's publications can be found at www.feantsa.org/research.htm.

NETWORKING

An important goal of FEANTSA is to strengthen cooperation with other international organizations. Based on established trans-sectoral cooperation at the national level, FEANTSA develops similar partnerships at the European level. These partnerships enhance FEANTSA's ability to influence policymaking. For example, FEANTSA works closely with CECODHAS (European Liaison Committee for Social Housing) and EUROCITIES (a European network of large cities). FEANTSA is a founding member of the European Housing Forum (a forum of European organizations active in the field of housing), the Platform of European Social NGOs, and EAPN (European Anti-Poverty Network).

COMMUNICATIONS

To inform FEANTSA members, as well as a wider audience involved in fighting homelessness, the organization's website provides all visitors, be they member organizations, policymakers, researchers, service providers, or members of the general public, with important information, analysis, and links on homelessness and housing exclusion issues. The website is a central resource center for information and expertise on homelessness in Europe.

Three times each year, FEANTSA publishes *Homeless in Europe,* an online electronic magazine. The magazine has a thematic approach, and each issue focuses on a different aspect of homelessness in Europe. Each month, "FEANTSA Flash," an e-mail update, provides readers with information and analysis on European issues, as well as contributions from its member organizations and news items from across Europe.

—*Donal MacManus and Freek Spinnewijn*

FOOD PROGRAMS

Nongovernmental food programs in the United States include food banks, food pantries, and shelters operated by nonprofit organizations and faith-based agencies. This emergency food assistance network provides food to people who lack the resources to obtain adequate amounts of food through conventional means. Food banks solicit donations of surplus or salvage food which they then distribute to food pantries (which provide emergency grocery packages), soup kitchens and shelters (which provide on-site meals), and other feeding programs. Soup kitchens and shelters typically serve one meal a day on-site, although some shelters permit their residents to prepare and cook their own meals. Although religious organizations and nonprofit agencies have historically distributed food and meals to people in need, such requests sharply increased beginning in the 1980s. This increase was associated with high unemployment, cuts in the social safety net, a decline in the value of public assistance benefits, and increases in housing and other costs, and it led to a proliferation of food banks, food pantries, soup kitchens, and government

programs that defined hunger and homelessness as temporary "emergency" problems.

HUNGER, POOR NUTRITION, AND HOMELESSNESS

Homeless people in the United States are particularly vulnerable to poor nutrition and hunger. Although their food deprivation is not as extreme as it is in many other countries, many of them are often chronically undernourished. Compared to other groups at risk for hunger, the homeless are at greatest risk, being ten times more likely to go without food for a day than other poor people. One contributing factor is their extremely low participation rate in the federal Food Stamp Program. Homeless advocates argue that barriers such as documentation of identity prevent many from participating. The difficulty of making effective use of food stamp benefits without adequate cooking and storage facilities is also a barrier.

Few homeless persons are able to obtain three meals a day, and many go at least one day a month without any food. Some research indicates that many have caloric intakes far below recommended levels and may have inadequate intakes of calcium, folacin, iron, magnesium, or zinc. Such low-calorie diets are often high in fat, cholesterol, and sodium and inadequate in essential nutrients. The lack of a stable home environment and cooking and storage facilities contributes to an inability to obtain an adequate, varied, and healthy diet. Many homeless persons depend on food banks, food pantries, soup kitchens, and shelters for daily nourishment.

Food Banks

Food banks in the United States are centralized warehouses that collect, sort, and store food and distribute it to member agencies. Member agencies include food pantries, soup kitchens, shelters, child care agencies, senior centers, and residential programs. Food banking began in Phoenix, Arizona, as an outgrowth of a church-sponsored soup kitchen. In 1967, a group of local volunteers from St. Mary's Catholic Church expanded the feeding program's functions to include the solicitation and storage of large amounts of edible but unmarketable food. The resulting operation became a clearinghouse that redistributed food to other charitable programs in the area. It was as much a conservation program aimed at eliminating food waste as a charitable effort to feed hungry people, and the originators envisioned the creation of a national network of food banks linked by a central solicitation and coordination agent. In 1979, Second Harvest was incorporated as the organizational link between the three food banks that had developed in addition to the Phoenix prototype. Second Harvest was originally funded through federal grants from the now-defunct Community Services Administration and later through the Department of Health and Human Services. By 1984, the Second Harvest budget was funded totally through food bank fees and private-sector support. Second Harvest solicits food from large national firms and distributes it among certified food banks. Because of the Tax Reform Act of 1976, corporate donors can take advantage of tax deductions for their contributions—for 100 percent of production costs and 50 percent of the difference between the product cost and the normal sale price. The Good Samaritan Act, passed by Congress in 1981, serves as the model for similar state legislation and absolves donors from liability for a product's safety, as long as they make an effort to determine that the food is edible and fit for human consumption when donated. The Tax Reform Act of 1986 expanded inventory-costing rules, which provided additional tax deductions. There are numerous administrative requirements associated with tracking and receipting national and local food donations.

U.S. food banks are subject to numerous Second Harvest and food industry inspections as well as to those required by state and local governments. In addition, to retain Second Harvest certification, food banks must regularly monitor their member agencies. The funding for food banks comes from private contributions, foundations, government agencies, shared maintenance fees, and handling/processing fees (assessed per pound) from their member agencies.

Food banks multiplied from a few dozen in the 1980s to more than 250 in 2002. Today, approximately 80 percent of all food banks in the United States are members of America's Second Harvest and collectively distribute nearly a billion pounds of food annually, feeding more than 23 million needy Americans, including 8 million children and 4 million senior citizens. These needy Americans include 21.3 million food pantry users, 1.3 million soup kitchen users, and 0.7 million shelter users. Overall, about two-fifths (39 percent) of the needy households include at least one employed adult, two-thirds (64 percent) have incomes at or below the federal poverty level, and 10 percent are homeless.

Food Pantries

In 2001, America's Second Harvest provider network included approximately 26,300 food pantries in the United States, three-quarters of which were run by faith-based agencies affiliated with churches, mosques, synagogues, and other religious organizations. The number of pantry programs operated by faith-based agencies between 1997 and 2001 increased by approximately four percentage points. These food pantries received more than half (59 percent) of the food they distributed from food banks, and religious organizations, direct purchases, and federal government commodity programs supplied the remainder. More than 90 percent of these food pantries use volunteer staff and many rely entirely on volunteers. Only one-third of the pantry programs have any paid staff.

Food pantries, also known as food closets, food shelves, or grocery programs, distribute nonprepared foods and other grocery items to needy clients, who then prepare and use these items where they live. Some food pantries distribute special grocery packages for the homeless that do not require extensive preparation. In the United States, food pantries operate primarily through referral systems, in which trained staff at nonprofit organizations screen clients and refer them to pantries operated by volunteers. The majority of food pantries prebag the food distributed to clients, while others allow clients to select their own food "grocery-store style." To the extent possible, pantries use several different factors, including household size, household composition (the number of children, adults, and elderly people), and the health status of household members, to determine the contents of a food order. Some follow nutritional guidelines in selecting pre-bagged items. On average, food pantries distribute food items to provide three meals per day per household member for three to five days. A sample list of items distributed to a single adult by a Pittsburgh, Pennsylvania, food pantry includes cereal, canned vegetables, Jell-O, juice, bread, canned beef stew, ground turkey, canned fruit, pasta, spaghetti sauce, and paper products.

Some food pantries provide additional services. In 2001, 18 percent of the food pantries in America's Second Harvest food provider network also provided nutrition counseling, 15 percent provided eligibility counseling for food stamps, 20 percent provided utility bill assistance, and 43 percent provided clothing assistance.

Many food pantries require recipients to run out of food before they request assistance and categorize this condition as a food emergency. Their focus is on serving clients compatible with their service mission, and they have much less need for documentation and much more trust in recipients' testimonies than government agencies. Only recently have U.S. food pantries begun to enforce explicit eligibility standards, such as income or residency, and to require documentation of eligibility.

Emergency Shelters

In 2001, America's Second Harvest provider network included 4,100 shelters in the United States, 43 percent of which were run by faith-based agencies affiliated with churches, mosques, and other religious organizations. This is a 15-percentage-point increase since 1993, when only 28 percent of shelters were run by faith-based agencies. Shelters in 2001 received more than one-third (36 percent) of the food they distributed from food banks, and direct purchases, religious organizations, and federal government commodity programs supplied the remainder. Three-quarters (76 percent) of these shelters use volunteer staff, and some rely entirely on volunteers.

Shelters provide shelter services and serve one or more meals a day on a short-term basis to low-income clients. Shelter may be either the primary or the secondary purpose of the service. Examples include homeless shelters, shelters with substance abuse programs, and transitional shelters such as those for battered women. In 2001, nearly three-quarters (72 percent) of the shelters in the America's Second Harvest food provider network also provided clothing assistance, more than one-third (36 percent) provided nutrition counseling, 33 percent provided employment training, and 32 percent provided eligibility counseling for food stamps.

CAPACITY OF THE EMERGENCY FOOD ASSISTANCE NETWORK

Surveys of the twenty largest American cities made in the late twentieth century by the U.S. Conference of Mayors Task Force on Hunger and Homelessness revealed steady increases in the demand for emergency food assistance. A rising proportion of those requesting food assistance were families with children. There were more requests from working families and individuals; there was an unmet demand for emergency food assistance; and in numerous cities, food assistance facilities had to turn people away. In 2001, nearly two-thirds (60 percent) of the food pantries and more than half (56 percent) of the shelters in America's Second Harvest food provider network served more clients than they had in 1998. They also faced problems that threatened their continued operation. More than two-thirds (68 percent) of the pantries and 87 percent of the shelters experienced problems related to funding, and about two-fifths (39 percent) of the pantries and 16 percent of the shelters had problems related to food supplies. More than one-third (35 percent) of the shelters also experienced problems related to paid staff or personnel, while about one-third (32 percent) of the pantries had problems related to volunteers. About one-third (32 percent) of the pantries and more than half (60 percent) of the shelters had turned away clients in the year 2000.

IMPACT OF SOCIAL POLICY CHANGES

When widespread hunger emerged as a national issue in the 1960s, an array of federal programs was designed to ameliorate it. In the 1980s, hunger returned to the United States in association with economic and tax policies that redistributed income from poor and middle-income groups to the wealthy, and with a corresponding failure of the federal government to protect high-risk groups from undernutrition. In the early 1990s, the poor were less well fed than in the previous two decades because of reduced purchasing power (due to increased food costs relative to wages and public benefit levels) and restricted access to affordable food sources, and also because fewer of them received government food assistance, and those who did, received less of it.

A convergence of social, economic, and political developments—rising caseload trends, increasing welfare costs, and judgments about the relationship between welfare and poverty—produced a major change in the American welfare system in 1996. The Personal Responsibility and Work Opportunity Reconciliation Act of 1996 (PRWORA) was the most substantial welfare reform legislation since the establishment of the Supplemental Security Income program and the revision and expansion of the Food Stamp Program in the 1970s. The most significant change was the termination of the 61-year-old entitlement of cash assistance to families provided under Title IV-A of the Social Security Act. The 1996 Act converted AFDC, emergency assistance, and work programs to a block grant, the Temporary Assistance for Needy Families program, with essentially fixed funding, and it instituted work requirements and a five-year-maximum lifetime limit on assistance. PRWORA also included $27.7 billion in Food Stamp reductions.

One of the harshest changes limits individuals between the ages of 18 and 50 who are not raising children to three months of food stamp receipt while unemployed in any three-year period. Some advocates argue that this provision disproportionately affects the homeless. PRWORA also denies food stamp assistance to legal immigrants. As of July 2000, participation in the Food Stamp Program had declined by nearly 40 percent from its peak in March 1994. In 2000, the Food Stamp Program reached about 60 percent of individuals who were eligible for program benefits, a significant decline since 1994,

when over 74 percent of eligible households were participating in the program. During fiscal year 2001, the program served over 17 million people in an average month at a total annual cost of nearly $16 billion in benefits. The average monthly food stamp benefit was about $170 per household.

The Food Stamp Reauthorization Act of 2002 (Title IV of the Farm Security and Rural Investment Act of 2002) restored eligibility for many legal immigrants and increased benefit levels for larger households. The act also benefits other groups, such as disabled persons, homeless persons, and responsible noncustodial parents. It gives states new flexibility to administer the program in ways that improve access and benefits. The flexibility allows states to remove barriers that discourage many needy households from applying for, or remaining on, the program. The act includes an improved homeless shelter deduction which gives states the option of providing a standard homeless shelter deduction to homeless households that incur any shelter expenses.

OUTLOOK IN THE TWENTY-FIRST CENTURY

Government data indicate that at least 9.2 million households in the United States were food insecure (defined as running out of food, reducing the quality of meals, feeding their children unbalanced diets, or skipping meals) in 1999 and that approximately 3 million households had experienced hunger at some point in that year. The food-insecure households contained an estimated 27 million people, of whom 11 million were children. The existence of large numbers of people without secure access to adequate amounts of nutritious food represents a serious national concern. An important response to this problem has been the growth of the private-sector institutions that were created to provide food for the needy.

Throughout the United States, food pantries, soup kitchens, and homeless shelters play a critical role in meeting the nutritional needs of America's low-income population. These organizations help meet the needs of people and households that otherwise would lack sufficient food. However, emergency feeding organizations are ultimately limited by the depth of the hunger problem, their reliance on volunteers, the availability of government and food industry surpluses, the lack of legally enforceable rights for food recipients, and discrepancies between where food providers are located and where those who need food live. Seeing these organizations as the primary solution to the problem of hunger diverts attention from the societal relationships that produce hunger, including economic restructuring, the erosion of public assistance benefits, major cuts in social welfare programs, and high housing, medical, and other costs.

—*Karen A. Curtis*

Further Reading

Andrews, M., Nord, M., Bickel, G., & Carlsen, S. (2000). *Household food security in the United States, 1999.* Washington, DC: U.S. Department of Agriculture, Food and Nutrition Service.

Burt, M. R., et al. (1999). *Homelessness: Programs and the people they serve.* Washington, DC: U.S. Department of Housing and Urban Development, Office of Policy Development and Research.

Carillo, T., Gilbride, J., & Chan, M. (1990). Soup kitchen meals: An observation and nutrient analysis. *Journal of the American Dietetic Association, 90*(7), 989–992.

Cohen, B., & Burt, M. (1989). *Eliminating hunger: Food security for the 1990s.* Washington, DC: The Urban Institute.

Cotterill, R., & Franklin, A. (1995). *The urban grocery store gap: An issue paper.* Storrs, CT: Food Marketing Policy Center, Department of Agricultural and Resource Economics, University of Connecticut.

Curtis, K. A. (1997). Urban poverty and the social consequences of privatized food assistance. *Journal of Urban Affairs, 19*(2), 207–226.

Daponte, B. O., Lewis, G., Sanders, S., & Taylor, L. (1994). *Food pantries and food pantry use in Allegheny County.* Pittsburgh, PA: H. John Heinz III School of Public Policy and Management, Carnegie Mellon University.

Dean, S., & Rosenbaum, D. (2002). *Implementing new changes to the food stamp program: A provision by provision analysis of the Farm Bill.* Washington, DC: Center on Budget and Policy Priorities.

Fitchen, J. (1988). Hunger, malnutrition, and poverty in the contemporary United States: Some observations on their social and cultural context. *Food and Foodways, 2,* 309–333.

Food Research and Action Center. (2002). *Good choices in hard times: Fifteen ideas for states to reduce hunger and stimulate the economy.* Washington, DC: Food Research and Action Center.

Food Research and Action Center / America's Second Harvest. (2000). *State government responses to the food assistance gap 2000.* Washington, DC and Chicago: Authors.

Kim, M., Ohls, J., & Cohen, R. (2001). *Hunger in America 2001: National report.* Princeton, NJ: Mathematica Policy Research.

Lindsey, A. T. (1998). *Food and nutrition resource guide for homeless shelters, soup kitchens and food banks.* Washington, DC: U. S. Department of Agriculture.

O'Brien, D., Pendergast, K., Thompson, E., Fruchter, M., & Aldeen, H.T. (2001). *The red tape divide: State-by-state review of food stamp applications.* Chicago: America's Second Harvest.

Poppendieck, J. (1998). *Sweet charity?: Emergency food and the end of entitlement.* New York: Viking.

Riches, G. (1997). *First world hunger: Food security and welfare politics.* New York: St. Martin's Press.

Second Harvest. (1989). *The story of Second Harvest: 1979–1989: A decade of feeding America's hungry.* Chicago: Author.

Second Harvest. (1998) *Hunger: The faces and facts.* Chicago: Author.

U.S. Conference of Mayors. (2001). *A status report on hunger and homelessness in America's cities: 2001.* Washington, DC: Author.

▣ FOSTER CARE

In most Western countries, homeless populations include many people who have spent time in foster care as children. Such placements in foster homes or families, or in institutional settings, generally result from decisions made by children's social service agencies or by the legal system. Foster children can live in such places as the following:

foster care family homes, either non-kin family (the most frequent in the United States) or kinship family (i.e., with relatives);

institutions, that is, child care facilities providing 24-hour care and/or treatment for children who need to leave their own homes and require a group living experience (such as the Burke Foundation, Texas, which offers therapeutic camp for neglected, abused, or disturbed boys);

group homes, which provide 24-hour care for children in a small group setting, generally seven to twelve children (e.g., the SOS Children's Village in Europe and the United States, which offers permanent foster care in "village" of about ten homes,

Table 1. Homeless People with Foster Care History:
Selected Western Nations (North America, Western Europe)

Study (and year published)	Year of data collection	Survey site	Age range sampled	Sample size	Percentage with a history of foster care placement
Burt et al. (2001)	1996	United States	18 and older	2,938	26%
			20–24	217	34%
Anderson (1997)	1993	England	18 and older (single persons)	1,769	15%
Lussier et al. (2000)	1998	Montreal, Quebec (Canada)	18–35	60	33%
Marpsat et al. (2000)	1998	Paris, France, including inner suburbs	18–24	461	31%
Brousse et al. (2002)	2001	France (cities over 20,000 inhabitants)	18 and older	4,066	23%
			16–24	807	35%

each one sheltering ten to twelve children, enabling sibling to remain together).

These two last categories can include short-term emergency shelters (generally fifteen days), specifically for runaway youths. Possible scenarios for children at the end of a placement are multiple: return to the natural family, adoption, imprisonment, admission to a mental health or other care facility, or transfer to another foster institution or to a foster family. Others simply leave statutory care upon coming of age.

The proportion of homeless adults who have been "fostered" reaches one-fourth to one-third in some nations, as noted below. In contrast, only a small fraction of the general population in the West (typically less than 5 percent) has experienced foster care.

CHALLENGES TO DATA COLLECTION AND ANALYSIS

When studying the effects of childhood foster care on housing and economic status in adulthood, it is extremely hard to determine which problems are attributable to placement per se, and which to the circumstances that have preceded, caused, or followed it. Accurate data on these effects are therefore difficult to quantify. In fact, some young people experience placement as a haven of stability in which to rebuild their lives after a distressing period in a dysfunctional family: a period possibly including physical or sexual abuse, alcohol or drug misuse, or various types of deprivations. For others, placement represents a painful separation from their parents, a traumatic event possibly precipitated by a death in the family, serious illness, imprisonment, or loss of home. Further disruption may result from poor living conditions during placement or unsuccessful attempts to live in group homes or foster families. The problems of those who become homeless may be traceable to such factors, both before and during a placement.

DOCUMENTING THE LINK

The high proportion of homeless people with a foster care background is observed in most Western countries (see Table 1), apparently indicating the greater social vulnerability of people who lack the support of their families during childhood and youth.

In some Western nations, however, this phenomenon is not observed. In Spain, where the institutionalized system of child protection is less developed than in northern Europe, placements are mainly with relatives and seldom in institutions (except in the case of orphans). The reality of placement is therefore experienced differently, and the number of people involved is very small. In Spain, therefore, "being in care" is not considered a relevant factor when estimating the extent of childhood disadvantage.

Notably, however, 11 percent of homeless people in Madrid have lived in orphanages as children; this factor is examined in surveys of homeless people.

A COMPLEX PROCESS

Among homeless young people, the likelihood of foster care history is greater than in older homeless people. Young people who have been "fostered" thus appear to have a high vulnerability at the beginning of adulthood. After this especially unstable period, homelessness becomes less frequent. This interpretation is valid primarily for countries where the resort to foster care has not increased in recent decades (as in France and the Netherlands but unlike in the United States where the annual numbers of young people placed in care rose by 60 percent between 1980 and 1995).

In France, 31 percent of homeless young people aged 16 to 24 have spent time in some form of foster care, a very high proportion compared with 1 percent for young people in the general housed population and 2 percent for children of manual workers. It is also higher than the 23 percent rate for homeless adults in general.

In the United States, the figure is similar for homeless young people aged 20 to 24 (34 percent). But for 18- and 19-year-olds, fully 61 percent have a history of foster care placement, compared with 26 percent for homeless adults generally and 3 percent for the general housed population.

A young person's "risk" of being placed in foster care is also related to the socioeconomic status of the family of origin. A family's financial well-being certainly affects its children's educational attainment, health status, and so on; it may also affect their eventual risk of homelessness. In some cases, foster placement is made for primarily economic reasons: It is believed that removing a child from the family will offer protection from potential dangers such as domestic accidents or deprivations associated with poor housing, and that the foster family or institution will offer better living conditions in terms of food, clothing, and educational support, for example. But such a placement may be traumatic for the child who is *not* escaping from an abusing family. Moreover, the family may feel unjustly punished.

SPECIAL VULNERABILITIES

The hypotheses put forward to explain this increased risk of homelessness tend to be formulated in terms of vulnerability rather than of direct causality.

A family history of violence or conflict can result in a lack of strong attachment during youth, with negative consequences for the young person's development and future social behavior: relational instability and mistrust of adults, for example. Abusive or violent relationships prevent young people from acquiring the practical skills necessary to construct and manage harmonious social relations. Settings that lack such models often also lack emotional warmth and supportive, consistent discipline for children. These environments, whether in a natural family or a foster family, tend to produce lower levels of self-esteem among adolescents.

Young people who have contact with persons with criminal behavior, perhaps as runaways or in group homes, are at risk of adopting delinquent or predelinquent behavior through emulation or peer group pressure. This increases the likelihood of later troubles such as conflictual relationships, heavy drinking, or substance abuse, all obstacles to successful social integration. Life in a congregate care home (i.e., group home or institution) can also expose young people to negative effects such as institutionalized dependence and emotional deprivation, which may leave them poorly equipped for independent living.

Some observers make a causal linkage: Young people in foster care are at greater risk of becoming runaways, and thus of living "on the street." In this view, foster care acts as a trigger for running away, given an often negative combination of placement circumstances. Indeed, runaway rates for homeless youths are much higher than for older homeless population (and than for housed population): 43 percent among young homeless people aged 18 to 24 in the United States as a whole (50 percent among young homeless people aged 16 to 24 in Paris). Among the homeless youths, if we look at those with an out-of-home placement history, we find that they have even higher runaway rates than the other young homeless persons (in Paris: 60 percent versus 41 percent for the males, 69 percent versus 49 percent for the females). (Notably, some may have been runaways *before* being placed in care.) Running away, even for short periods, could represent a form of initiation that facilitates a subsequent decision to leave home. It is thus interpreted as a risk factor, even though for some young people the choice may be reasonable. Running away or "sleeping rough" may be an appropriate response to certain traumatic or pathogenic situations, either in a family or institutional setting.

LEAVING CARE AND ENTERING ADULTHOOD: A CRITICAL TRANSITION

Many who try to interpret the connection between foster care and homelessness note the difficulties young people face when they leave care upon coming of age. Often their families give them little or no help; indeed, they may be estranged from their families or suffer from past conflict and abuse. These young people's disrupted lives and the experience of foster care living may have compromised their development of personal friendships. This lack of support—financial, practical, and relational—at the entry into adulthood is a serious obstacle in making the transition to independent living. Moreover, young people who leave the care system when they come of age are rarely entitled to social benefits. In France, for example, although a benefit is available for young people leaving institutional care (the *jeune majeur* allowance), it is not awarded automatically; the young person must first submit a substantive "project" plan. In the United States, the federal government provides no direct financial support for young people leaving the foster care system. However, help is available through the Independent Living Program aimed at encouraging life skills, coping with the psychosocial problems associated with leaving care, and so on. Initiatives also exist at the local level, such as the Bridges to Independence program in Los Angeles County, operating since 1996.

THE CHALLENGES AHEAD

Foster care for young people spans a wide variety of situations. Placement may occur early or late in childhood and may last for weeks, months, years. The sequence of events might range from a single foster placement with a family or an institution, to a series of such placements, to repeated alternations between placement and family of origin. Reasons for the placement might include physical or sexual abuse, an economically deprived household, or many other factors.

Difficulties experienced within families—or troubles that arise from having no family—are central to the phenomenon of youth homelessness. But this factor of vulnerability alone cannot explain why people become homeless. Unfavorable social and economic contexts are also a powerful influence. Being placed in foster care constitutes a rupture in young people's lives, and when added to the psychosocial problems associated with separation, residential instability, institutional living, and unhappy memories of family life, it can adversely influence their personal development by depriving them of individual and family resources. When foster placement ends, the young person is frequently left unsupported during the transition to independent living. This is a clear failing of a foster care system that makes inadequate provisions for the time when the young person ceases to be its responsibility.

—*Jean-Marie Firdion*

Further Reading

Anderson, I. (1997). Homelessness and social exclusion: The situation of single homeless people in Great Britain. In M. J. Huth & T. Wright (Eds.), *International critical perspectives on homelessness* (pp. 107–137). Westport, CT: Praeger.

Brousse, C., de la Rochère, B., & Massé, E. (2002). Hébergement et distribution de repas chauds. Qui sont les sans-domicile usagers de ces services? [Shelter and hot meals. Which homeless people use these services?]. *INSEE Première, 824.*

Burt, M., Aron, L. Y., & Lee, E. (2001). *Helping America's homeless: Emergency shelter or affordable housing?* Washington, DC: Urban Institute.

Curtis, P. A., Dale, Jr., G., & Kendall, J. (1999). *The foster care crisis.* Lincoln: University of Nebraska Press.

de Feijter, H., & Blok, H. (1997). *Youth homelessness in the Netherlands: Nature, policy, good practices.* Brussels, Belgium: FEANTSA.

Herman, D. B., Susser, E. S., & Struening, E. L. (1994). Childhood out-of-home care and current depressive symptoms among homeless adults. *American Journal of Public Health, 84*(11), 1849–1851.

Koegel, P., Melamid, E., & Burnam, A. (1995). Childhood risk factors for homelessness among homeless adults. *American*

Journal of Public Health, 85(12), 1642–1649.

Little Hoover Commission. (2003). *Still in our hands: A review of efforts to reform foster care in California.* Los Angeles: State of California.

Lussier, V., & Poirier, M. (2000). Parcours de rupture ou quête de reconnaissance et d'identité? L'impact des représentations parentales sur l'itinéraire de jeunes itinérants et itinérantes de Montréal [A history of rupture or a quest for recognition and identity? The impact of parental representations on the itineraries of young runaways in Montréal]. In D. Laberge (Ed.), *L'errance urbaine* (pp. 161–178). Sainte-Foy, Quebec, Canada: Editions MultiMondes.

Mangine, S. J., Royse, D., Wiehe, V. R., & Nietzel, M. T. (1990). Homelessness among adults raised as foster children: A survey of drop-in center users. *Psychological Reports, 67,* 739–745.

Marpsat, M., Firdion, J.-M., & Meron, M. (2000). The difficult past of homeless young people. *Population et Sociétés* (English version), *363,* 1–4.

Muñoz, M., Vazquez, C., Bermejo, M., & Vazquez, J. J. (1999). Stressful life events among homeless people: Quantity, types, timing and perceived causality. *Journal of Community Psychology, 27*(1), 73–87.

Whitbeck, L. B., Hoyt, D. R. (1999). *Nowhere to grow: Homeless and runaway adolescents and their families.* New York: Aldine de Gruyter.

◉ FRANCE

In France as in other countries, the term *homeless* (usually rendered in French as *sans-domicile*) can connote a range of meanings, the broadest of which extend beyond housing circumstances to include one's level of social integration and various other characteristics. But even when judged solely by the criterion of housing, the number and characteristics of homeless persons will vary depending on which housing situations are equated with homelessness. Another variable is the temporal framework of observation: Does one include only people who are homeless on a given date—or also those who drift in and out of homelessness over a period of time?

A VARIABLE DEFINITION

In the narrowest sense of the term, the homeless are the persons who regularly "sleep rough," either in the street or in other places not intended for human habitation, such as parking lots, stairwells, cellars, or public parks. They are the target population for a number of French agencies which, for example, send teams around towns and cities at night to provide assistance for rough sleepers. A slightly broader definition would include users of the various accommodation facilities for the homeless, such as night shelters, extended-stay hostels known as CHRS, or *Centres d'Hébergement et de Réadaptation Sociale* (Accommodation and Social Rehabilitation Centers), or hotel rooms and flats provided through voluntary agencies. This broader definition was used for statistical surveys conducted in 1995 and 1998 by the National Institute of Population Research (INED, or *Institut National d'Etudes Démographiques*) in Paris and its suburbs, and in 2001 by the National Institute of Statistics and Economic Research (INSEE, or *Institut National de la Statistique et des Etudes Economiques*) in a representative sample of French towns and cities of 20,000 inhabitants or more. This is also the target population for a wide range of services, free or low-cost meals, day centers, and so on.

Even more broadly, the term *homeless* can also refer to anyone identified as inadequately housed on the basis of several criteria. These criteria might include their dwelling's physical characteristics (a wooden hut, for example, might be deemed inadequate), other living conditions and amenities (perhaps overcrowded or unsanitary), the person's occupancy status (squatting, for example, or reluctantly "doubling up" with friends or relatives), and their personal stability over time (perhaps they are under threat of eviction). The voluntary agencies working on behalf of the poorly housed usually employ definitions that encompass all or some of these situations.

Moreover, the time variable plays a role in any attempt to survey homeless people. People without a permanent home of their own typically move between different situations. For example, a few days in a hotel may be followed by a stay in a hostel, perhaps interspersed by periods of doubling up with friends.

ATTITUDES AND APPROACHES

Vagrants, tramps (*clochards*), "roofless," and homeless people have been a central social concern in

France for hundreds of years. But often the compassion inspired by their miserable condition has been outweighed by the unease about their rootless, unattached state—as people with "neither house nor home" *("sans feux ni lieux")*. The housing shortage and harsh economic conditions that followed World War II exacerbated the difficulty of obtaining adequate housing. The "excluded" and "poorly housed" received renewed attention after May 1968, and they were the subject of several official reports. It was during the 1980s, however, in a context of severe economic downturn, that these "marginal" and "most deprived" members of society became a priority issue for organizations such as activist groups, charities, and trade unions; for academics; and for a number of regulatory bodies and government departments, including the National Statistical Council (CNS), and the Social Services Directorate.

In 1989, a working group of the National Council of Statistical Information (CNIS), which succeeded the CNS in 1984, called for a "specific study of the homeless." A national law on the implementation of the right to housing (*Loi visant la mise en oeuvre du droit au logement*), was introduced in 1990 by Louis Besson, the Minister of Housing at the time. This law established a right to housing and obliged local authorities in each *département* to provide housing for "people and families without housing or threatened by eviction without re-housing, or living in slums or insalubrious, insecure or improvised dwellings." Activist organizations such as "Right to Housing" (*Droit au logement*) and the "Committee of the Unhoused" (*Comité des sans-logis*) joined forces with other voluntary nonprofit agencies to campaign for action on behalf of those living on the margins of society.

In October 1993, the CNIS set up a homelessness working group with the aim of conducting a methodological investigation to improve understanding of these populations. As part of this work, INED developed a methodology for selecting representative samples of this population. In addition, a series of ethnographic monographs was commissioned by the Ministry of Housing, and many local studies of the homeless were made.

SOCIAL POLICY: REPRESSION AND ASSISTANCE

Social policy directed at the poorest populations has often combined elements of repression with efforts at assistance. By the time the offense of vagrancy was removed from the French Penal Code in 1994, prosecutions for vagrancy and begging had already declined sharply since the end of the 1960s. The state's role in helping the homeless expanded during the 1970s, evidenced by the growth of public funding for shelters and hostels, among other indicators. Agencies working with the homeless expanded their interventions into several areas: social rehabilitation, health care, and links with social workers and administrative bodies—particularly for reestablishing social security entitlements.

Since the 1990s, however, the balance has been shifting again. In parallel with the development of support services for the homeless—accommodation, meal distribution, day centers, mobile night services—a return to a more repressive approach can be discerned in the "anti-begging" laws, and the law on domestic security (2002) made begging an offense again.

CHARACTERISTICS OF THE HOMELESS TODAY

An INSEE survey conducted in January 2001 focused on people using a shelter or hot meal distribution center at least once in the course of a single week. The scope was a representative sample of French cities and towns of over 20,000 inhabitants. A large proportion of these service users—two-thirds in Paris and its suburbs, three-quarters in the rest of France—had no permanent home of their own. The full questionnaire was administered only to French-speaking adults aged eighteen or over. The survey estimated that 63,500 adults and 16,000 children under eighteen visited hot-meal distribution centers or shelters, including the long-term facilities (for up to several years) known as *centres maternels,* where mothers can stay with their children until the youngest reaches the age of three. The decision to include these facilities in the French sample resulted in the percentage of women being higher than it would be if the shelters visited had been similar to those chosen in, for example, the U.S. Census 1996 survey, and in the number of children being more significant in the survey (there are few children in homeless shelters in France). The survey did not cover homeless people who slept in the street and who did not use meal distributions. However, complementary studies established that the great majority of homeless people were covered by the survey.

The characteristics of the homeless identified in the INSEE survey are consistent with the findings obtained by INED in Paris and the suburbs. Women are in a minority, though this pattern is less marked at the youngest ages. There are fewer old people than in the rest of the population. A very large majority come from working-class backgrounds and manual labor service occupations. Non-nationals are more numerous among the homeless, as they are among the poor in general. Resources are particularly scarce for those who have only recently entered France and do not have the right to work legally.

Three-quarters of the homeless have had a place of their own at some stage, while the remainder have lived primarily in the parental home or an institution—former foster children, for example. Roughly one-third are currently employed, and most have worked in the past. Six in ten receive a welfare payment of some sort, including unemployment benefits or social safety net payments such as the Disabled Adult Allowance (AAH) or the Minimum Guaranteed Allowance Income (RMI). One in ten has no source of income at all. It is relevant to note that since January 2000, access to primary health care has become easier, thanks to the Universal Sickness Coverage (CMU), obtained by 60 percent of the homeless people INSEE surveyed.

Future research and action on behalf of the poorest members of society must focus on the role of the socioeconomic context in which homelessness has developed, and in particular on the changes affecting the housing stock that can be accessed by the poorest. More consideration is due to those in intermediate housing situations, perhaps doubling up with friends or relatives; these at-risk people number more than 80,000 in France. More attention should also be paid to the factors that increase the likelihood of exiting homelessness, in order to effectively help those in greatest need.

—Maryse Marpsat and Jean-Marie Firdion

Further Reading

Brousse, C., de la Rochère, B., & Massé, E. (2002a, January). Le cas des sans-domicile [The case of the homeless. Minimum guaranteed allowance.]. *INSEE-Première, 823*, 1–4.

Brousse, C., de la Rochère, B., & Massé, E. (2002b, January). Hébergement et distribution de repas chauds. Qui sont les sans-domicile usagers de ces services? [Shelter and hot meals: Which homeless people use these services?]. *INSEE-Première, 824*, 1–4.

Brousse, C., de la Rochère, B., & Massé, E. (2002, December). L'enquête de l'INSEE auprès des usagers des services d'hébergement et de distribution de repas chauds: une méthodologie inédite pour étudier la population des sans-domicile [The INSEE survey of homeless users of shelters and hot meals: A new methodology to study the homeless population], *INSEE-Courrier des Statistiques, 104*, 33–39.

Conseil National de l'Information Statistique. (1996, March). *Pour une meilleure connaissance des sans-abri et de l'exclusion du logement* [Improving understanding of the homeless and housing exclusion]. Final Report. Paris: Author.

Damon, J. (2002). *La question SDF: Critique d'une action publique.* [The homelessness issue: A critique of public policy]. Paris: Presses Universitaires de France, collection Le Lien Social.

Marpsat, M., & Firdion, J.-M. (1996). Becoming homeless: Who is at risk. *Population et Sociétés* (English version), *313*, 1–4.

Marpsat, M., & Firdion, J. M. (1998). The homeless in Paris: A representative sample survey of users of services for the homeless. In D. Avramov (Ed.), *Coping with homelessness: Issues to be tackled and best practices in Europe* (pp. 221–251). Aldershot, UK: Ashgate.

Marpsat, M., & Firdion, J. M. (Eds.). (2000). *La rue et le foyer: Une recherche sur les sans-domicile et les mal-logés dans les années 90* [The street and the shelter: Research on the homeless and housing exclusion in the 1990s]. Travaux et Documents de l'INED, 144. Paris: INED.

Marpsat, M. (2000). An advantage with limits: the lower risk for women of becoming homeless. *Population: An English selection, 12*, 247–292.

Marpsat, M., Firdion, J.-M., & Meron, M. (2000). The difficult past of homeless young people. *Population et Sociétés, 363*, 1–4. Retrieved July 8, 2003, from www.ined.fr

G

◉ GENTRIFICATION

Gentrification refers to residential change that brings new residents who are disproportionately young, well educated, salaried, and professional into urban neighborhoods where poor people live. Gentrification has been occurring in cities throughout the world since the 1970s. The change in an urban population can be dramatic. For example, in Ottawa, Canada, in 1971, 10 percent of downtown residents held university degrees and 42 percent worked in white-collar jobs.

New York, San Francisco, Cincinnati, Toronto, London, Berlin, Sydney, and Washington, D.C., are some of the cities where gentrification has been dramatic and controversial. Some cities welcome gentrification as a revitalization of neighborhoods mired in poverty. They argue that it boosts the urban tax base while reducing blight and density. For example, between 1971 and 1996, Canada's four major cities experienced a loss in population density of 25 percent because only some people were welcome. Hotels and businesses in San Francisco have actively supported gentrification and promoted policies to push homeless people out of downtown areas in order to make tourists and businesspeople feel more welcome and safe. In many cities, however, community activists argue that gentrification disrupts traditional neighborhood life, displaces vulnerable residents, and causes homelessness.

Urban scholars debate the causes of gentrification. Some stress the cultural or individual inclinations of the newer residents to experience the excitement and diversity of urban life. Some scholars liken the new residents to pioneers braving a challenging, changing urban frontier. Others explain gentrification by a rent gap between the potential and current value of the land, which grows when older urban housing deteriorates and becomes devalued and thereby a good investment. By purchasing properties cheaply, investors can renovate them and take advantage of a changing real estate market to sell them for a handsome profit. These scholars link gentrification to the cycling of capital investment in and out of cities and to recurrent processes of decline and regrowth in urban neighborhoods. Gentrification also reflects larger processes of changing employment structures and opportunities and public policies for redesigning cities.

The simplest way to visualize gentrification is in its residential form. Older houses are rehabilitated and resold; inexpensive apartment buildings are converted to condominiums; old warehouses are transformed into lofts. Affordable multifamily rental dwellings are converted and "restored" into upscale single-family homes. Single-room occupancy hotels (SROs), which often house poor, homeless men, are torn down or remodeled. Toronto lost 300 SROs since 1986, and in Sydney, Australia, between 1992 and 2000, 340 boarding houses were demolished, renovated into expensive apartments, or turned into backpackers' hostels. Commercial life also changes, because shops that serve the poor, such as thrift stores or carry-outs, give way to boutiques and antique stores.

Sometimes homeless shelters themselves are removed from gentrifying neighborhoods. In Cincinnati, for example, the Drop Inn Center Shelterhouse in the Over the Rhine community was removed to make way for a Fine Arts and Education Center linked to Cincinnati's historic Music Hall. The shelter was considered a danger to the children using the new facility, although it housed 16,000 people, some of them children. In downtown Cincinnati, the Salvation Army Hostel building was sold to the Senator Steakhouse chain, where a retail/restaurant/loft complex is planned.

DISPLACEMENT

Displacement through gentrification occurs when inflated rents and prices in a changing neighborhood push out low-paid or unpaid older residents. Residents are displaced in several different ways. Sometimes homeowners find that as the value of their homes rises, they cannot afford to pay their property taxes. For renters, rents can become unmanageably high, or buildings may become unlivable as they are readied for conversion into luxury apartments or condominiums. Older, poorer residents may simply feel a strong pressure to sell their homes because they cannot afford not to take advantage of the new market. Families who try to stay may feel such financial stress that they triage relatives whom they could once afford to support. Finally, a kind of exclusionary displacement occurs because poorer people who could once have afforded to live in the neighborhood no longer can, or the social networks that once helped support them thin out. Displacement also affects more people than those who are directly displaced. There is an effect on other residents who see their area changing, businesses closing to make way for more expensive services, and friendship and kinship networks being abandoned as people move away. People may leave simply because their relatives, friends, and neighbors have left and they no longer feel comfortable in the neighborhood.

Gentrification-induced displacement is hard to measure, and estimates range from 6,000 households a year in one small section of Philadelphia, to 10,000 to 40,000 households a year in New York City, and as many as 2,000,000 households a year in the United States. In Britain, Leckie (1995) estimates that 144,000 people are evicted each year and that many go unregistered.

WHERE DO THEY GO?

The destination and new living circumstances of those displaced after gentrification vary. Many of them have to pay more for poorer accommodations. Many remain near their prior residences in an effort to keep social networks intact. Some move in with friends or relatives, which leads to overcrowding. Some return to rural homes; others move to less expensive suburbs. Often cities don't keep any record of what happens to those who are displaced by gentrification. Authorities in South Sydney, Australia, for instance, declare themselves baffled about where the older traditional boarding house residents have gone, and speculate that they have moved into shelters or onto the streets. Overcrowded shelters are especially dangerous in cold climates and during the winter. In Toronto, during the winter months of 2003, 3,200 beds were needed each night and the number of available beds fell at least 500 short. Many families refuse to use shelters.

IDEOLOGIES

Frequently, the language that accompanies gentrification celebrates it as revitalization or rebirth and links the traditional neighborhood to images of dirt, disease, pathology, and decay. In part, such language reflects fears that poor and homeless people will hurt business and tourism.

Activists believe that stereotypes of traditional neighborhoods, which include squeegee kids, beggars, crack houses, sex workers, substance abusers, and mentally ill wanderers, harm institutions that serve the poor. They point out that such representations are often used to control or exclude undesirable people from public space, urban parks, and public transportation.

AVOIDING THE DISPLACEMENT THAT LEADS TO HOMELESSNESS

Many cities have experimented with ways to protect vulnerable residents from gentrification-induced displacement. These include rent control, offering tenants the right of first refusal, and passing laws that prevent landlords from harassing tenants or denying them proper living conditions through disinvestment in their buildings. City governments can closely monitor and regulate evictions, grant lifetime tenancy to elderly tenants, offer emergency assistance to poorer renters, fix assessments or institute tax circuit breakers so that residents on fixed or limited incomes do not get forced out of their homes because they cannot pay their taxes, provide long-term tenants and owners the tools to maintain or rehabilitate their homes themselves, and institute commercial rent control to preserve public space and the stores that poor people need. Governments can also offer tax credits for poorer homeowners to do repairs and maintenance on homes in gentrifying or abandoned neighborhoods, and they can raise or lower assessments to discourage or encourage gentrification.

Cities can protect single-room occupancy housing by bringing it under public control or insisting that developers replace it on a one-to-one basis. Governments can require developers to build affordable housing whenever they are granted rights to build luxury or commercial facilities; use zoning provisions to preserve mixed-use districts; pour public resources into areas of potential abandonment; and develop discouragement and encouragement zones for development, protecting some areas from rapid change.

More drastic measures might include capping the mortgage interest deduction for affluent homeowners, placing a surcharge on luxury housing; or instituting an anti-speculation tax to control resale prices. Lenders' regulations might encourage low down payment policies for poorer prospective buyers and

enforce the Community Reinvestment Act and nondiscrimination in mortgage and home equity laws. Landlords could be regulated to prevent tax delinquencies, illegal conversion of rooming houses into condominiums or backpackers' hostels, limitation of properties to adults-only buildings that exclude families, illegal evictions, and discrimination against minorities and people who depend on Section 8 vouchers. At the heart of the problem worldwide is that housing is treated as a commodity; as long as that remains the case, the use values that people find in their homes and the exchange values that properties sustain in cities will be in conflict. Unless some properties are removed from the market through community land trusts or cooperatives, or governments support use values over exchange values in some instances, gentrification will inevitably create displacement and homelessness.

—*Brett Williams*

Further Reading

Andersen, H. S. (1988). Gentrification or social renewal? Effects of public supported housing renewal in Denmark. *Scandinavian Housing and Planning Research*, *15*(3), 111–128.

Atkinson, R. (2000a). The hidden costs of gentrification: Displacement in central London. *Journal of Housing and the Built Environment*, *15*(4), 307–326.

Atkinson, R. (2000b). Measuring gentrification and displacement in Greater London. *Urban Studies*, *37*(1), 149–165.

Bratt, R., Hartman, C., & Meyerson, A. (Eds.). (1986). *Critical perspectives on housing*. Philadelphia: Temple University Press.

Brodie, M. (1980). *Social and economic change in the inner city. The gentrification process: A review of the literature*. London: Greater London Council.

Carr, L. G. (1994). The can't move-must move contradiction: A case study of displacement of the poor and social stress. *Journal of Social Distress and the Homeless, 3*(2), 185–201.

Chernoff, M. (1980). Social displacement in a renovating neighborhood's commercial district: Atlanta. In S. Laska & D. Spain (Eds.), *Back to the city: Issues in neighbourhood renovation* (pp. 204–219). Oxford, UK: Pergamon Press.

Dangschat, J. (1991) Gentrification in Hamburg. In J. van Weesep & S. Musterd (Eds.), *Urban housing for the better-off: Gentrification in Europe*. Utrecht, Netherlands: Stedelijke Netwerken.

Dehavenon, A. L. (Ed.). (1996). *There's no place like home: Anthropological perspectives on housing and homelessness in the United States*. Westport, CT: Bergin & Garvey.

Ellin, N. (1997). *The architecture of fear*. Princeton, NJ: Princeton Architectural Press.

Garside, J. (1993). Inner city gentrification in South Africa: The case of Woodstock, Cape Town. *Geojournal, 30*(1), 29.

Gelb, J., & Lyons, M. (1993). A tale of two cities: Housing policy and gentrification in London and New York. *Journal of Urban Affairs, 15*(4), 345–366.

Goldfield, D. (1980). Private neighbourhood redevelopment and displacement: The case of Washington. *Urban Affairs Quarterly, 15*(4), 435–468.

Grier, G., & Grier, E. (1980). Urban displacement: A reconnaissance. In S. Laska and D. Spain (Eds.), *Back to the city: Issues in neighbourhood renovation* (pp. 252–268). Oxford, UK: Pergamon Press.

Griffith, J. M. (1996). Gentrification: Perspectives on the return to the central city. *Journal of Planning Literature, 11*(2), 241–255.

Hamnett, C., & Williams, P. (1980). Social change in London: A study of gentrification. *Urban Affairs Quarterly, 15*(4), 469–487.

Hartman, C. (1979). Comment on 'Neighborhood revitalization and displacement: A review of the evidence.' *Journal of the American Planning Association, 45*(4), 488–491.

Henig, J. (1980). Gentrification and displacement within cities: A comparative analysis. *Social Science Quarterly, 61*(3), 638–652.

Kasinitz, P. (1984). Gentrification and homelessness: The single room occupant and the inner city revival. *Urban and Social Change Review, 17*(1), 9–14.

Klinenberg, E. (2002). *Heat wave*. University of Chicago Press.

Larkham. P. J. (1991). *Gentrification, renewal and the urban landscape*. University of Birmingham, UK: School of Geography.

Leckie, S. (1995). *When push comes to shove: Forced evictions and human rights*. Utrecht, Netherlands: Habitat International Coalition.

Lee, B., & Hodge, D. (1984). Social differentials in metropolitan residential displacement. In J. Palen & B. London (Eds.), *Gentrification, displacement and neighbourhood revitalization*. Albany: State University of New York Press.

Lees, L. (1994). Gentrification in London and New York: An Atlantic gap? *Housing Studies, 9*(2), 199–217.

Logan, J., & Molotch, H. (1987). *Urban fortunes*. Berkeley: University of California Press.

Lyons, M. (1996). Gentrification, socioeconomic change, and the geography of displacement. *Journal of Urban Affairs, 18*(1), 39–62.

Marcuse, P. (1984, May). Measuring gentrification's impact: The city tells just part of the West Side's story. *City Limits,* May, p. 26.

Marcuse, P. (1987, April 4). Why are they homeless. *The Nation, 244*(13).

Marcuse, P. (1989). Gentrification, homelessness, and the work process: Housing markets and labour markets in the quartered city. *Housing Studies, 4*(3), 211–220. Reprinted as "Housing markets and labour markets in the quartered city" in J. Allen and C. Hamnett (Eds.) (1991), *Housing and labour markets: Building the connections* (pp. 118–135). London: Unwin Hyman.

Marcuse, P. (1993). Degentrification and advanced homelessness: New patterns, old processes. *Netherlands Journal of Housing and the Built Environment, 8*(2), 177–192.

Mele, C. (1995). Private redevelopment and the changing forms of displacement in the East Village of New York. In M. P. Smith (Ed.), *Marginal Spaces* (pp 69–93). New Brunswick, NJ: Transaction.

Muniz, V. (1998). *Resisting gentrification and displacement. Voices of Puerto Rican women of the barrio*. New York: Garland.

Nelson, K. P. (1988). *Gentrification and distressed cities—an assessment of trends in intrametropolitan migration*. Madison: University of Wisconsin Press.

Palen, J., & London, B. (Eds.). (1987). *Gentrification, displacement and neighbourhood revitalization*. Albany: State University of New York Press.

Robinson, T. (1995). Gentrification and grassroots resistance in San Francisco's Tenderloin. *Urban Affairs Review, 30*(4), 483–513.

Rofe, M. W. (2000). Gentrification within Australia's 'problem city': Inner Newcastle as a zone of residential transition. *Australian Geographical Studies, 38*(1), 54–70.

Ruddick, S. (1996). Constructing difference in public spaces: Race, class, and gender as interlocking systems. *Urban Geography, 2*(S), 132–151.

Schaffer, R. & Smith, N. (1996). The gentrification of Harlem? *Annals of the Association of American Geographers, 76,* 347–365.

Smith, A. (1989). Gentrification and the spatial constitution of the state: The restructuring of London's Docklands. *Antipode, 21*(3), 232–260.

Smith, N., & Williams, P. (Eds.). (1986). *Gentrification of the city*. London: Unwin & Hyman.

Smith, N. (1996). *The new urban frontier. Gentrification and the revanchist city*. London: Routledge.

Sumka, H. J. (1979). Neighborhood revitalization and displacement. A review of the evidence. *Journal of the American Planning Association, 45*(4), 480–487.

Taylor, M. M. (1994). Gentrification in Harlem: Community, culture and the urban redevelopment of the black ghetto. *Research in Race and Ethnic Relations, 7,* 147–188.

Urban Habitat Program. (1999). *There goes the neighborhood: A regional analysis of gentrification and community stability in the San Francisco Bay Area*. San Francisco: Urban Habitat.

Wagner, G. R. (1995). Gentrification, reinvestment, and displacement in Baltimore. *Journal of Urban Affairs, 17*(1), 81–96.

White, P., & Winchester, H. P. M. (1991). The poor in the inner city: Stability and change in two Parisian neighbourhoods. *Urban Geography, 12*, 35–54.

Williams, B. (1988). Upscaling downtown: Stalled gentrification in Washington, DC. New York: Cornell University Press.

Wilson, F. H. (1992). Gentrification and neighborhood dislocation in Washington, DC: The case of black residents in central area neighborhoods. *Research in Urban Sociology, 2*, 113–143.

Wittberg, P. (1992). Perspectives on gentrification: A comparative review of the literature. *Research in Urban Sociology, 2*, 17–46.

Wolch, J. & Dear, M. (1993). *Malign neglect—Homelessness in an American city.* San Francisco: Jossey Bass.

Wright, T. (1997). *Out of place: Homeless mobilizations, subcities, and contested landscapes.* New York: State University of New York Press.

Widespread homelessness is often a consequence of war. Here, a homeless man sleeps in public in post-World War II Berlin in October 1945.
Source: Hulton-Deutsch/Corbis; used with permission.

▣ GERMANY

Generally speaking, the term *homeless (wohnungslos)* is used in Germany to refer to those people who do not have their own self-contained dwelling with a regular, unlimited tenancy (either as owner or under the German Tenancy Act) and who are unable to obtain such housing without support from the government or charitable organizations. This usage includes those temporarily housed in shelters or similar facilities by municipalities or nonprofit groups, those "sleeping rough" (i.e., sleeping outside) or in accommodations unfit for human habitation, and those who have lost or given up their own residences and are sharing temporarily with friends or relatives.

LEGAL PROVISIONS

German law plays a central role in defining the nature of homelessness in the country. Although there is no legal right to permanent housing in Germany, "rooflessness"*(Obdachlosigkeit)* has traditionally been considered a danger to the public order. Thus, it has fallen upon municipalities to enforce the laws of the regional states *(Bundesländer)* that grant temporary accommodations to persons in danger of becoming roofless. However, since the minimum standards for such accommodations are very low, there are great differences in local practices across the country.

A second important legal provision that grants support to homeless people is in Section 72 of the Federal Act on Social Assistance (*Bundessozialhilfegesetz*). It states, in translation here, that "Persons who live in exceptional living circumstances which are connected with social difficulties are to be granted support in overcoming these difficulties, if they are not able to overcome them on their own." Specifically, the law stipulates measures for acquiring and maintaining a dwelling, getting help with advocacy and personal needs, job training, and finding and maintaining a job.

Under Section 11 of the Federal Act on Social Assistance, homeless people without sufficient income, like other people in need, also have a right to social assistance covering subsistence costs and "reasonable" costs of accommodation.

SERVICES FOR THE HOMELESS

Homeless services in Germany are characterized by a division of responsibilities and service between municipalities and the voluntary sector. This division is deeply rooted in German history and reflected in its system of law.

Municipalities are responsible for activities designed to avert homelessness. For example, they may

Table 1. Estimated Number of Homeless in Germany, 1994–2000*

		1994	1995	1996	1997	1998	1999	2000
Homeless persons excluding repatriates	Living in multi-person households	370,000	390,000	380,000	370,000	330,000	260,000	220,000
	Single	180,000	190,000	210,000	220,000	200,000	180,000	170,000
	Total	**550,000**	**580,000**	**590,000**	**590,000**	**530,000**	**440,000**	**390,000**
Homeless repatriates		330,000	340,000	340,000	270,000	150,000	110,000	110,000
Total Homeless*		**880,000**	**920,000**	**930,000**	**860,000**	**680,000**	**550,000**	**500,000**

Source: Bundesarbeitsgemeinschaft Wohnungslosenhilfe (BAWG) (2002). 39–40.

*Actual numbers of homeless are estimated to fall within a range of +/- 10% of these figures; rounded to ten thousands.

assume a tenant's rent arrears to forestall eviction. In many towns, the local government concentrates on providing temporary accommodation for evicted families and, in some cases, for single persons who have been evicted from their former dwellings. A variety of temporary accommodations are provided, including shelters, hostels, cheap hotels, substandard housing settlements created primarily for homeless families, and ordinary dwellings. However, even when the accommodations provided are in normal dwellings, those being helped have no legal rights as tenants and are still treated as homeless persons. They can be transferred to other shelters at any time and remain obliged to look for permanent housing.

Those who are homeless for other reasons, in particular single people who become homeless outside the borders of their municipal district, are referred to charitable institutions in the voluntary sector. Most of these institutions belong to organizations associated with the two largest churches in Germany, the Protestant church and the Catholic church. These institutions for "non-local" single homeless persons have a tradition of more than a hundred years, formerly being institutions for the itinerant poor. While today they are mainly financed by local (or regional) authorities under Section 72 of the Federal Social Assistance Act, they continue to focus on housing single homeless people from other areas, but with an increasing number of local single homeless as well.

Increasingly, modern homeless policy has emphasized both prevention and providing individuals and families with normal housing. Services are now aimed at enabling a homeless person to lead as normal a life as possible, including reintegration into society. Recently a number of pilot projects and longitudinal evaluations (Bundesamt für Bauwesen und Raumordnung 1998 and 2003) have shown that if certain basic requirements are met, it is possible to rehouse larger numbers of long-term homeless people than previously, even those having substantial social difficulties. Most important are provisions giving the homeless preferential access to normal housing and to social support in such housing suitable to their needs (see Busch-Geertsema 2001 and 2002).

NUMBERS AND KEY FEATURES

There are no nationwide official data on the extent of homelessness in Germany. Although studies by the Federal Institute of Statistics have shown that data on the most important subgroups of the homeless could be collected relatively easily (König 1998), no steps have been taken to introduce such data collection.

In the absence of official counts, the best estimate of the scale of homelessness in Germany (with its 83 million inhabitants) has been produced annually by the national coalition of service providers for the homeless (*Bundesarbeitsgemeinschaft Wohnungslosenhilfe,* or BAGW). For the year 2000, it estimated the overall number of homeless people at about 500,000, including 110,000 repatriates from former Eastern Bloc countries living in special temporary accommodations (asylum seekers were not included). Not including the repatriates, about 55 percent were men, 23 percent women, and 22 percent children and teens under eighteen. About 24,000 were estimated to have slept outdoors during the year 2000.

Table 1 shows that the total number of homeless people has been declining since 1996. One reason for the drop was a relaxation of the German housing market in the latter half of the decade; this was due to demographic developments—such as a declining birth rate and a massive decrease in immigration and repatriation—on top of the substantial increase in the construction of new housing during the first half of the decade. However, long-term analysis since World War II shows that the housing market is cyclical, with repeated waves of shortage and oversupply over time (see Ulbrich 1991). Housing policy tends to reflect this cyclical movement, and it is likely that homelessness will increase again in the future.

—Volker Busch-Geertsema

Further Reading

Bundesarbeitsgemeinschaft Wohnungslosenhilfe (BAGW) (2002). Zahl der Wohnungslosen in Deutschland [Number of homeless people in Germany]. Pressemitteilung. In *Wohnungslos*, 4(1), 39–40.

Bundesamt für Bauwesen und Raumordnung (BBR). (1998). *Dauerhafte Wohnungsversorgung von Obdachlosen* [Permanent housing for the homeless; evaluation report]. Werkstatt: Praxis Nr. 3/1998, Bonn: BBR Selbstverlag.

Bundesamt für Bauwesen und Raumordnung (BBR). (2003). *Dauerhafte Wohnungsversorgung von Obdachlosen* [Permanent housing for the homeless; follow-up study]. Werkstatt: Praxis Nr. 3/2003, Bonn: BBR Selbstverlag.

Busch-Geertsema, V. (2001). Homelessness in Germany: Housing poverty in a wealthy country. In T. Pollakow & C. Guillean (Eds.), *International perspectives on homelessness* (pp. 85–117). Westport, CT: Greenwood.

Busch-Geertsema, V. (2001). *Access to housing for disadvantaged and vulnerable groups in Germany.* National Report 2000/2001 for the European Observatory on Homelessness. Bremen/Brussels: FEANTSA.

Busch-Geertsema, V. (2002). When homeless people are allowed to decide by themselves: Rehousing homeless people in Germany. *European Journal of Social Work,* 5(1), 5–19.

Busch-Geertsema, V., & Ruhstrat, E. U. (1994). *Wohnungsnotfälle. Sicherung der Wohnungsversorgung für wirtschaftlich oder sozial benachteiligte Haushalte* [Cases in urgent need of housing. Procuring housing for economically and socially disadvantaged households]. (Bundesministerium für Raumordnung, Bauwesen und Städtebau and Bundesministerium für Familie und Senioren, Eds.). Bonn, Germany: Eigenverlag.

Enders-Dragässer, U., Sellach, B., Feig, A.., Jung, M.-L., Roscher, S. (1999). *Frauen ohne Wohnung. Handbuch für die ambulante Wohnungslosenhilfe für Frauen* [Homeless women. Handbook for ambulant services for homeless women]. Bundesministerium für Familie, Senioren, Frauen und Jugend (BMFSFJ). Stuttgart, Germany: Kohlhammer.

König, C. (1998). *Machbarkeitsstudie zur statistischen Erfassung von Wohnungslosigkeit* [Feasibility study for the implementation of statistics on homelessness]. Wiesbaden, Germany: Statistisches Bundesamt.

Kunstmann, W. (1999). Germany. In C. O. Helvie & W. Kunstmann (Eds.), *Homelessness in the United States, Europe and Russia: A comparative perspective* (pp. 33–61). Westport, CT: Greenwood Press.

Ruhstrat, E.-U., et al. (1991). *'Ohne Arbeit keine Wohnung, ohne Wohnung keine Arbeit!' Entstehung und Verlauf von Wohnungslosigkeit* ['No home without work, no work without home!' Origin and development of homelessness]. (Evangelischer Fachverband Wohnung und Existenzsicherung. (Eds.). Bielelfeld, Germany: Verlag Soziale Hilfe.

Ulbrich, R. (1991). Wohnungsmarktsituation in den westlichen Bundesländern [Situation on the housing market in West German regional states]. *Wohnungswirtschaft und Mietrecht, Heft 5,* 234–247.

☐ GOODWILL INDUSTRIES INTERNATIONAL

Goodwill Industries International is a network of 207 community-based, autonomous member organizations in the United States, Canada, and twenty-two other countries. Each organization serves people with disabilities and disadvantages—such as homelessness, welfare dependency, and lack of education or work experience—by providing job training and employment services, as well as job placement opportunities and post-employment support.

Founded in Boston in 1902 by Methodist minister Edgar J. Helms, Goodwill Industries first put people to work by hiring them to repair and sell donated goods. Today, Goodwill Industries not only provides employment, it also trains people for careers in a variety of fields, including financial services, computer programming, and health care. To pay for its programs, Goodwill sells donated clothes and other household items in more than 2,000 retail stores and online at www.shopgoodwill.com. The organization also builds revenues and creates jobs by contracting with businesses and government to provide a wide range of commercial services, including janitorial work, packaging and assembly, food service preparation, and document shredding. Since 1902, Goodwill Industries has helped more than 6 million people enter the workforce and support their families.

In 2002, of the more than 583,000 people who benefited from Goodwill's career services, 10,568 were homeless. More than sixty Goodwill agencies have specialized services to reach this population, many of them offered through partnerships with other nonprofit and private organizations and government agencies. Goodwill's goal is to help people move into stable employment by providing them with a wide range of support programs, including transitional housing, clothing vouchers, skills assessment, job search assistance, job retention skills, and help with transportation.

PROGRAM SUCCESSES

In West Palm Beach, Florida, Gulfstream Goodwill Industries provides transitional housing for up to two years for people who are homeless. Its thirty-bed program is funded through the U.S. Department of Housing and Urban Development (HUD) and Palm Beach County Division of Human Services, and offers job placement services, work adjustment training, vocational evaluation, life skills training, and case management. It started in 1996 and serves about 100 people in residential services annually. Participants have obtained jobs as hairdressers, telemarketers, landscapers, sales representatives, and truck drivers. In 2001 and 2003, Goodwill added two new HUD programs to provide permanent supported housing services for adults with disabilities who had been homeless. These programs serve twenty-four persons in their own apartments in scattered sites in their communities.

Since 2002, Wall Street Mission Goodwill Industries in Sioux Falls, South Dakota, has provided people who are homeless with social and employment-related skills and assistance, as well as referrals for housing. In the first eight months of operation, 103 people benefited from this program, 40 percent of them obtaining jobs in fields such as clerical, warehouse, production, and retail.

Goodwill Industries of Kentucky (Louisville), through Goodwill Temporary Services (GTS) staffing, operates a job program to help people who are homeless obtain housing through their employment. The program requires participants to attend two job search groups per week, be available for vocational assessment to evaluate employment aptitudes and skills, and maintain monthly contact with a job coach after employment. An important goal of the program is to match participants' work skills with the right jobs. Goodwill also helps with the cost of suitable interview clothes and provides transportation for one month after the client has been hired. In 2002, GTS staffing through the Kentucky Goodwill served 505 homeless people, compared with 116 in 2001.

In Indiana, the Goodwill Family Center of Evansville Goodwill Industries provides quality transitional housing and supportive services to meet the identified needs of homeless families, including services not found in other homeless shelters in the community, such as on-site child care and comprehensive vocational services. At any one time, the Center can handle between eight and ten families, who may reside there for up to two years as long as the adults are working or in school at least thirty hours per week.

In 1999, Goodwill Industries of Greater Detroit (Michigan) began a partnership with Mariners Inn, a residential facility for homeless men with a history of substance abuse, and the Michigan Department of Career Development/Rehabilitation Services. Transitional work experience is available through Goodwill's Industrial Work Center, which does contract work for Daimler Chrysler, Ford Motor Company, and General Motors.

The job center of The Helping Hand of Goodwill Industries in Kansas City, Missouri, is a job-hunting staging room for homeless job seekers where they use phones, access a personal voice mailbox, find and share job leads, participate in workshops, write resumes, and receive bus ride cards. The Goodwill agency also provides vouchers for haircuts and local

Goodwill retail stores, as well as referrals for housing, counseling, health care, and legal services.

Since 1998, Youngstown Area Goodwill Industries (Ohio) has provided vocational evaluation, work adjustment, job placement, instruction, and follow-up. About twenty-five homeless people enroll each year, of whom three-fourths are placed in jobs such as sales, janitorial, and food service.

Goodwill Industries of Northern Michigan (Traverse City) has owned and operated a homeless shelter called the Goodwill Inn since 1979. It provides emergency shelter, access to donated food, housing placement services, job placement services, vocational services, veterans' services, and children's services. The Inn also offers temporary work for participants until they obtain a job in the community. The children's program, New Beginnings, involves organized play, limited day care, mentoring, and tutoring. Residents also receive direct financial assistance for emergency expenses such as car repair, prescriptions, clothing, and even the first month's rent. In 2002, 397 benefited from services at the Goodwill Inn. One-fourth of adults come to the shelter with full- or part-time work, and 52 percent maintain employment upon leaving. Classes on independent living skills, as well as health care on a limited basis are also being provided.

Goodwill Industries of South Texas (Corpus Christi) has been providing services to the homeless population since October 1999. Goodwill provides two weeks of classroom instruction, including twenty-five hours of social and life skills training, and one week of job search training. In the program's first year, it served 209 homeless people. In 2000–2001, 325 participants were served, with 120 placed in jobs and 89 in housing.

—*Goodwill Industries International*

GREAT DEPRESSION

No experience defined the predicament of the Great Depression in the United States more forcefully than homelessness. As unemployment, rural collapse, and business failure mounted after 1930, millions of Americans lost their housing through evictions and

bank foreclosures. More than the mere loss of shelter, homelessness symbolized the larger breakdown of the American economic system. Ubiquitous images of snaking breadlines, urban shantytowns, migrant camps, and railroad boxcars overflowing with vagrant passengers captured the broader sense of dislocation and disillusionment that had swept across the country during the Depression. In response to this crisis, President Franklin Delano Roosevelt (1882–1945), first elected in 1932, launched his sweeping New Deal program of reforms. Roosevelt's New Deal ended neither the Great Depression nor homelessness, but it did transform the political economy of employment, housing, and welfare in such ways as to change permanently the nature and experience of homelessness.

THE EARLY CRISIS, 1927–1934

During the prosperity of the 1920s, most Americans believed rail-riding hoboes to be a thing of the past. In 1927, however, a slump in the auto, steel, and construction industries coincided with a sharp increase in the number of homeless men seeking overnight shelter in municipal lodging houses. As the Depression set in across the economy over the next three years, old skid row districts swelled steadily with the unemployed, while freight trains brimmed with illegal passengers. By 1930, homelessness had reached crisis proportions.

The crisis touched every corner of America, but industrial cities were especially hard hit. Between 1930 and 1931, the number of those resorting to public shelters increased over sevenfold in Detroit and Cleveland. By 1932, Chicago sheltered more men in *one day* (20,000) than it had during any given year of the 1920s. Shortly after Roosevelt took office in January 1933, sociologist Nels Anderson gave a Senate subcommittee his conservative estimate that there were 1.5 million people in America without any shelter of their own.

The "New Homeless" of the Great Depression

Depression-era homelessness increased dramatically not only in number, but also in variety. For the

"Hardluck Town," located at Ninth Street and the East River in New York City, on 3 August, 1932. The town's residents were 200 men willing and ready to go to work at any time. Those not willing to work were not allowed in.
Source: Bettmann/Corbis; used with permission.

increased dramatically during the Great Depression. Until World War I, when 500,000 African-Americans migrated to the urban industrial North, black homelessness was relatively rare. Racial discrimination in the North made black workers more vulnerable to economic downturns both because African-Americans made less money to tide them over during periods of unemployment, and also because employers tended to lay off black workers first. As a result, African-Americans in the North suffered higher rates of homelessness than the general population, making up between 15 and 27 percent of urban shelter residents in 1931.

Far more alarming to politicians, social workers, and relief officials than the increases in black and female homelessness, however, was the highly publicized plight of the "respectable" white-collar homeless. While homelessness rates among the middle class were far lower than among working people, the mere presence of businessmen, managers, and professionals in public shelters, miniscule though it was, sparked fear among the propertied classes. Along with lurid tales of "lady hoboes" and "wild boys and girls of the road," which became staples of popular journalism during 1930–1933, stories of the "worthy," genteel, down-on-their-luck poor helped to generate public sympathy for federal action on behalf of the homeless. Such action finally came in 1933 as part of the "first hundred days" of Franklin Roosevelt's New Deal.

first time, women, families, African-Americans, and middle-class persons became vulnerable to mass homelessness.

While single men gathered in hobo "jungles" and along skid rows, families built shantytowns on abandoned lands. These shantytowns were called "Hoovervilles" in cutting reference to Roosevelt's predecessor President Herbert Hoover (1874–1964). They also took to the road in search of work and relief, but unlike hoboes of old, they traveled mainly by automobile rather than by railroad.

Single women also composed a larger share of the homeless than in earlier eras, in part because of their increased participation in urban labor markets after World War I. Single wage-earning women suffered higher rates of unemployment than men in the early 1930s. Rarely, however, did single women resort to the road where, as one relief official put it, they were "likely to encounter both suspicion and prejudice from citizen and police alike," not to mention assault, rape, and sexual harassment by the men they encountered (DePastino 2003, 202).

Homelessness among African-Americans also

Local Responses

No matter what their background, destitute persons confronted with the loss of housing sought relief first and foremost in the informal networks of kin and community that have sustained the poor from time in memoriam. "In most cities," one commentator noted in 1932, "the poor are taking care of the poor" (Kusmer 2002, 201). When family, friends, churches, unions, ethnic and benevolent societies, and other forms of neighborhood-based support proved inadequate, as they did very early during the Great Depression, the next recourse was to larger private charity organizations and municipal relief services.

By 1930, rescue missions and wayfarers lodges, the primary charitable institutions of skid row, turned away far more applicants than they could serve. Municipal authorities faced similar dilemmas and strains on their resources. With hordes of men and women seeking aid, municipalities scrambled for shelter space and also for new policies to accommodate the emergency. Vacant buildings of all sorts were pressed into service, and most large cities provided casework and other services for the homeless in addition to food and shelter. The rigid and often punitive policies that had characterized both charity and municipal shelter regimens earlier in the century persisted in some places. In New York City, for example, authorities continued its practice of limiting stays at the shelter to five days a month until a thousand homeless and unemployed people marched in protest against the policy. Conditions in shelters also varied. Some were clean and modern, while others resembled medieval dungeons. One investigator in 1933 found the New York Shelter for Homeless Men at South Ferry to be a "horror . . . crowded, dank, undoubtedly rat-ridden" and in desperate need of reform (Wickenden 1987, 82).

With cities and charities so woefully ill-equipped to handle the crisis (many communities in the South had no homeless shelters whatsoever), the homeless quickly took matters into their own hands, reviving the old hobo jungles near railroad yards and erecting shantytowns that sometimes housed hundreds or thousands of men, women, and children. Building shacks out of scrap lumber, corrugated tin, and tar paper or digging hovels out of the ground, the homeless congregated in vacant lots and unused land in virtually every major city. In St. Louis, a Hooverville with a thousand residents appeared next to a dump along the banks of the Mississippi. "Hoovervilles are a separate nation," remarked one investigator, "with separate codes" (Kusmer 2002, 202).

Such social cleavage rose to the level of national spectacle in the summer of 1932 when 25,000 protesting World War I veterans, demanding early payment of a "bonus" that had been awarded to them for their overseas service, descended upon Washington, D.C., and formed a massive shantytown in the heart of the nation's capital. When General Douglas MacArthur (1880–1964) evicted the marchers at the point of bayonets on 28 July, outraged public opinion linked the draconian treatment of the marchers to President Hoover's meager relief policies. Franklin Roosevelt, the Democratic candidate running against Hoover that summer, took advantage of the national mood by promising large-scale federal relief for America's impoverished masses. Shortly after taking office, President Roosevelt and the newly elected Democratic Congress created the Federal Emergency Relief Administration (FERA), which included the first federal program specifically for the homeless: the Federal Transient Program (FTP).

The Federal Transient Program

During the 1930s, most states still adhered to archaic settlement laws that entitled only legal residents of the state to receive any form of public relief. With millions of persons crossing state lines during the Depression, homeless "transients," as they were called, were ideal candidates for federally funded relief.

Originally budgeted at $15 million, the FTP was established as a part of FERA in May 1933. State relief administrators ran the program with the federal government paying for 100 percent of state expenses toward transients, which the FTP defined as anyone who had lived within the state for less than one year. The so-called local homeless were then served under the state's general relief funds, which FERA financed on a matching basis.

Directed for most of its existence by twenty-four-year-old Elizabeth Wickenden, the FTP was a highly decentralized program that took on different forms in different communities across the nation. In larger cities, the FTP financed state-run and municipal shelters that served hundreds or even thousands of persons a day. In smaller communities, the federal government contracted with private charities, hotels, and restaurants to feed, house, and clothe transients. Over 300 rural camps, resembling the famous camps of the Civilian Conservation Corps (CCC), were also built and equipped with Army surplus materials in order to employ transients on public works projects. By the summer of 1934, the FTP had almost 500,000 Americans under its care. By the time the program was terminated in the fall of 1935, it had run over 600 facilities and had registered an estimated 1 million persons.

Unattached non-family men made up the bulk of transients housed in urban centers and rural camps. Like rail-riding hoboes of previous eras, Depression-era transients were overwhelmingly young, white, native-born members of the industrial working class. Two-thirds were under thirty-five years of age, and 20 percent were nineteen years old or younger. Scattered among this young white male cohort were significant numbers of women, African-Americans, and older Americans, which distinguished the transient army from the hobo armies of old.

Although conditions varied from place to place, the FTP promoted a high standard of care for transients. Shelters were expected to offer not only clean, comfortable, and nonrestrictive accommodations, but also opportunities for recreation, education, medical care, and work relief. Some places managed to employ their clients at the required thirty hours a week, but most had little work to offer. Rural camps paid up to three dollars a week, plus room and board, for outdoor labor. Camps also departed from the prevailing practices of racial segregation, whereas urban FTP centers tended to assign African-American and white clients to separate dining and sleeping quarters.

Unlike unattached men, single women and families, who made up about 40 percent of transients, received individualized case treatment, which included private housing in apartments and hotels. Such gender discrimination conformed to the general opinion that mass shelters had a deleterious effect on family life. Concerns with protecting women, bolstering nuclear family life, and promoting masculine breadwinning proved an important motive in the New Deal's termination of the FTP a little more than two years after its creation.

THE HOMELESS AND THE LATER NEW DEAL, 1935–1942

In September 1935, the Roosevelt administration began phasing out the FTP and other direct relief programs under FERA in favor of a "Second New Deal" that shifted policy toward public works, unemployment compensation, old-age pensions, and welfare benefits for children and the disabled.

The FTP was a victim of its own success in several ways. First, the program proved so effective in pulling men and women off the road that public concern about the homeless diminished significantly by 1935. Without active and widespread public support, the FTP, in the words of one historian, "was in a weaker position than most federal programs" because most transients could not vote (Kusmer 2002, 220). Furthermore, direct relief programs like the FTP raised concerns about the federal government creating a class of demoralized and dependent citizens. "I don't think anybody can go year after year, month after month, accepting relief without affecting his character in some way unfavorably," wrote Harry Hopkins (1890–1946) in 1933 before he became the director of FERA (quoted in Schlesinger 1958, 267). After liquidating the FTP, Hopkins elaborated on the harmful effects of transient camps, arguing that the camps separated men from the "normal" world of masculine breadwinning and nuclear family life. "It was the men who became so well adjusted to the secure, if limited, life of the transient camp who hoped, like certain soldiers, that the war would never end" (Crouse 1986, 169). In replacing FERA with the Works Progress Administration (WPA) and Social Security, the Roosevelt administration shifted its focus from alleviating immediate suffering to helping struggling households remain intact, with men as breadwinners and women as caregivers.

The result of this gender-based policy shift was an almost instantaneous revival of the transient crisis that had plagued the nation during the early 1930s. Breadlines, shantytowns, and hobo jungles sprang up like mushrooms, while lines of overloaded jalopies and freight trains filled to capacity with human cargo crisscrossed the continent. Cities and states resumed their practice of "passing on" those with no legal residence and launched harsh new anti-vagrancy measures that included clearing public spaces of squatters and the unemployed. In 1936, the Los Angeles Police Department launched its "Bums Blockade," closing off California's borders to migrants for six weeks. When the so-called Roosevelt Recession struck in 1937–1938, millions more workers lost their jobs and joined the throngs already on the streets and roads. After five years of the New Deal, conditions were almost as bad as they had been during the dark years of 1932–1933.

In addition to transients, a half-million migrants from Oklahoma, Texas, Arkansas, and Missouri, the so-called Okies, driven to the road by drought, eviction, farm foreclosure, and agricultural unemployment added a new dimension to the homelessness crisis of 1935–1940. Although the vast majority of Southwest migrants flocked to urban areas in the Southwest, many sought work in the fields of California, where they shared the appalling living and working conditions of Mexican, Filipino, Japanese, and other agricultural laborers. Unlike their non-white counterparts, native-born Okies won widespread public attention to their plight through such works as Dorothea Lange and Paul S. Taylor's *An American Exodus* (1940) and John Steinbeck's *The Grapes of Wrath* (1939), as well as through a Congressional investigative committee headed by California Congressman John Tolan. By the time the Tolan Committee completed its work in 1941, California's burgeoning defense industries had begun to absorb Okie migrants. Economic mobilization for World War II, not the New Deal, finally brought the Great Depression and the homelessness crisis that accompanied it to an end.

LEGACIES

The FTP established an important precedent in directing the power and resources of the federal government to relieve the suffering of the homeless. But it would take over fifty years before the United States Congress would again approve any large-scale federal relief for the homeless (the McKinney Homeless Assistance Act of 1987).

The New Deal's most lasting legacy would be in laying the foundation of the modern welfare state through Social Security and what later became Aid to Families with Dependent Children, programs that have prevented generations of unemployed, underage, elderly, and disabled persons from becoming homeless. Moreover, in placing the federal government in the role of brokering the competition among interest groups, the New Deal strengthened the hand of many groups, especially industrial workers, vulnerable to poverty and destitution. Finally, New Deal housing policies, especially those administered under the Federal Housing Authority, vigorously promoted single-family housing, which eventually resettled millions of wage earners in the suburbs while systematically inhibiting the construction of low-cost housing in cities. This last trend played a key role in creating the conditions that encouraged the revival of homelessness among the urban poor during the last quarter of the twentieth century.

—*Todd DePastino*

Further Reading

Anderson, N. (1940). *Men on the move*. Chicago: University of Chicago Press.

Crouse, J. M. (1986). *The homeless transient in the Great Depression: New York State, 1929–1941*. Albany: State University of New York.

Daniels, R. (1971). *The bonus march: An episode of the Great Depression*. Westport, CT: Greenwood.

DePastino, T. (2003). *Citizen hobo: How a century of homelessness shaped America*. Chicago: University of Chicago Press.

Golden, S. (1992). *The women outside: Meanings and myths of homelessness*. Berkeley: University of California Press.

Gordon, L. (1994). *Pitied but not entitled: Single mothers and the history of welfare, 1890–1935*. New York: Free Press.

Gregory, J. N. (1989). *American exodus: The dust bowl migration and Okie culture in California*. New York: Oxford University Press.

Groth, P. (1994). *Living downtown: The history of residential hotels in the United States*. Berkeley: University of California Press.

Kromer, T. (1968). *Waiting for nothing*. New York: Hill and Wang. (Originally published 1935)

Kusmer, K. L. (2002). *Down and out, on the road: The homeless in American history*. New York: Oxford University Press.

Lange, D., & Taylor, P. S. (1969). *An American exodus: A record of human erosion in the thirties*. New Haven: Yale University Press. (Originally published 1940)

Minchan, T. (1934). *Boy and girl tramps of America*. New York: Farrar and Rinehart.

Schlesinger, A. M., Jr. (1958). *The coming of the New Deal.* Boston: Houghton Mifflin.

Steinbeck, J. (1999). *The grapes of wrath.* New York: Penguin Books. (Originally published 1939)

Sutherland, E. H., & Locke, H. J. (1971). *Twenty thousand homeless men: A study of unemployed men in the Chicago shelters.* New York: Arno Press. (Originally published 1936)

Uys, E. L. (1999). *Riding the rails: Teenagers on the move during the Great Depression.* New York: TV Books.

Webb, J. N. (1935). *The transient unemployed: A description and analysis of the transient relief population.* Washington, DC: Works Progress Administration.

Webb, J. N., & Brown, M. (1938). *Migrant families.* Washington, DC: Works Progress Administration.

Wickenden, E. (1987). *Reminiscences of the program for transients and homeless in the thirties.* In R. Beard (Ed.), *On being homeless: Historical perspectives* (pp. 80–87). New York: Museum of the City of New York.

H

⊡ HARM REDUCTION

While the lack of affordable housing and poverty remain the primary causes of homelessness among Americans, diagnoses of severe mental illness and substance abuse or addiction can act as double locks on an already closed door. For a substantial number of the homeless, these conditions create an almost impenetrable barrier to housing and strand these individuals in the most remote margins of society. To gain access to housing for the dual-diagnosed homeless, "consumers" are almost invariably required to abstain completely from using alcohol or street drugs and participate in psychiatric treatment. In addition, because most housing programs insist on the twelve-step abstinence mode or other sobriety-contingent models as a condition for remaining in housing, formerly homeless people with histories of substance abuse are at great risk of repeated housing loss and long periods of homelessness. Pervasive sobriety and treatment requirements, despite well-researched evidence of the barriers they pose to the dual diagnosed (Coalition for the Homeless, 1999; Rowe et al., 1996; Interagency Council on the Homeless, 1992), prevent the most persistently homeless individuals from obtaining housing; moreover, such requirement often hinder them from retaining housing when they relapse.

One of the major dilemmas surrounding abstinence/treatment-contingent housing, also known as "linear residential continuum of care" programs, is that while concurrent mental illness and substance abuse increase one's risk of becoming homeless (Goldfinger et al., 1999), homelessness and residential instability exacerbate addiction (Coalition for the Homeless, 1999; Interagency Council on the Homeless, 1992). Such a situation often confronts the dual-diagnosed homeless person who lives in treatment-contingent housing. Treatment for substance abuse and mental health is typically provided by different providers and, in many cases, by different agencies. A client making an earnest effort to comply with his or her twelve-step treatment programs is told to abstain completely from all alcohol and conscious-altering drugs. However, the same individual may also have a comorbid mental illness and need to comply when a treating psychiatrist prescribes consciousness-altering medications for psychiatric symptoms. And if such persons are living in treatment-contingent housing and, as often happens, begin to relapse, they cannot discuss drug problems or emerging psychoses with a housing counselor, for fear of eviction. Residential instability is also a risk factor for a number of other conditions that inhibit recovery, including physical illness, social dysfunction and isolation, joblessness, poverty, criminal involvement, and criminal punishment (McQuistion et al., 2003, Rossi et al., 1987). Thus, people with dual diagnoses remain "system misfits" because of the frustrating and con-

189

tradictory expectations and requirements that could be easily remedied by using an integrated approach to treatment and services (Mueser, Noordsy, Drake, & Fox, 2003; George & Krystal, 2000) that incorporates a harm reduction approach (Tsemberis & Asmussen, 1999).

Harm reduction provides a pragmatic, effective, and compassionate approach that can be used to address the problem of treatment and housing for individuals who are homeless, substance abusing, and mentally ill. Harm reduction is a public health alternative to the moral, criminal, and disease models of drug use and addiction (Marlatt, 1998). It seeks to engage and stabilize the addict and then work to address the factors that contribute to the addiction. In fact, the harm reduction strategy is already being effectively employed in a number of similar contexts. Two recent examples are needle exchange and jail diversion programs, which have successfully mitigated needle-related infectious disease transmission (Langendam, van Brussel, Coutinho, & van Ameijden, 2001) and reduced the psychological, economic, and socially hazardous conditions experienced during incarceration (Klein, 1997).

The Pathways to Housing program in New York City uses a harm reduction approach in providing services to the homeless who live with concurrent mental illness and addiction, by offering immediate access to permanent, independent housing without requiring treatment or sobriety. Housing first stipulates unequivocally that housing is a right: No one should be denied housing for any period of time because of failure in treatment, or for failure to choose treatment. Seriously mentally ill adults, even those who are abusing substances, can and should live in a home of their choice while retaining the right to choose or refuse. Using this "housing first" approach significantly reduces the risks and trauma endured by people who remain homeless, and it is consistent with the harm reduction philosophy of creating a low threshold access to services—in this case, housing.

Once housed, the program staff offer services and support that include an acceptance and tolerance of symptoms, use, and relapse while the individual is housed (Marlatt, 1998). Psychotic or addictive behaviors are not a cause for alarm, but rather are events that staff anticipate. Clients typically move from stage to stage at their own pace, but when they stop moving or move backward, they are still accepted and supported. Relapse is an expected and natural step in the long course of recovery, and clients are able—indeed encouraged—to discuss their psychoses and addictions with staff in an open and accepting manner. Staff are able to gain the confidence of clients by reassuring them that the use of addictive substances, relapse, or recurrent symptoms will not result in eviction from the program (Tsemberis, 1999). Although abstinence is considered an ideal outcome of harm reduction, this model allows alternative paths to complete sobriety as long as they serve to contain or reduce the many harms—for example, drug overdose, incarceration, impoverishment, malnourishment, unending homelessness, and ill health—that might otherwise befall a person who is homeless and striving to achieve abstinence.

HARM REDUCTION: THEORETICAL FOUNDATIONS

Harm reduction is rooted in Prochaska and DiClemente's transtheoretical model of change (Prochaska & DiClefmente, 1992). A distillation of the most widely used approaches to psychotherapy, the transtheoretical model focuses on practices common to all models that have proven to motivate patients to change their behavior. Often referred to as the "stages of change," the transtheoretical model guides substance-addicted clients and their clinicians through a rewarding process of tracking milestones— the stages of change—along a path of decreasing personal risk and toward the ideal of sobriety (DiClemente, 2003; Marlatt, 1998). The stages of change—precontemplation, contemplation, preparation, action, and maintenance—can be effectively employed in helping clients avoid the self-esteem deflating Abstinence Violation Effect (AVE; Marlatt & Gordon, 1985), thought to be a primary contributor to addicts' failure to achieve and maintain sobriety through abstinence. Based on the theory of cognitive dissonance, the AVE approach counters the most prominent weakness of the abstinence-only model:

that each of the addict's failures to abstain leads to an adjustment of his self-opinion in tune with the failure just experienced. This negative readjustment of self-opinion feeds on itself, lowering self-esteem and diminishing the belief—and hope—in the possibility of making changes on one's own.

Harm reduction avoids the downward spiral of AVE, by focusing on helping clients take small steps forward and maintain a positive attitude and direction, while rewarding each small step along the way. "Even though some people can stop just like that," opined one recovering addict, snapping his fingers. "I couldn't stop like that. I thought it was good when I went from a 40-ouncer to a 12-ouncer." Indeed, this kind of improvement, which is not recognized by the abstinence model, is rewarded by the harm reduction approach as a sign of developing self-esteem and momentum necessary to progress through the stages of change.

In addition to being noticed and rewarded for victories small and large, clients are assisted in identifying factors that will motivate their recovery. In the harm reduction approach, motivation for treatment is considered to be multidimensional and includes how clients perceive internal pressures, external pressures, readiness for treatment, and the suitability of the treatment program. The aim of harm reduction is to find methods that work for the client in terms of his or her goals, and not to blame clients for failure to change by labeling them "treatment resistant," "unmotivated," or "not housing ready." The therapist's or peer's judgment of failure is replaced with a compassionate acceptance of errors as opportunities for learning and thoughtful analysis of the circumstances that led to relapse.

Once a client is engaged in a therapeutic relationship and there is a candid discussion concerning the symptoms of mental illness or drug and alcohol use, the stressors leading to these conditions are addressed. Harm reduction places engagement of the individual in a potentially healing, self-affirming relationship at the forefront. Just as in effective models of psychotherapy (Denning, 2000), the clinician who works with a harm reduction philosophy believes the choice of goals is client driven and the role of the therapist is to support that goal. This approach stands in stark contrast to the sobriety and traditional medical models that treat the client as incapable of making the right decisions, instead capable only of "stinking thinking" that must replaced with the tenets of the group, sponsor, and a higher power—or medication. In a harm reduction approach, clients are invited to examine the options of becoming active or remaining abstinent, and to discuss the relative pros and cons of each choice. Harm reduction treats clients as rational beings who are capable of directing their own lives.

PATHWAYS TO HOUSING: PROGRAM AND EFFECTIVENESS

"What's good about this program is that I can deal with my problems honestly," noted a Pathways to Housing client named Armando. "I can tell you I'm on drugs or that I stopped taking my medication because the greatest fear—being homeless again—is gone. I won't be evicted because I started getting sick again."

Pathways to Housing, a program designed to end homelessness and improve overall well-being for the hardest-to-serve street-dwellers of New York City, has found that harm reduction is especially effective in ending homelessness for people with dual diagnoses (Gulcur, Stefancic, Shinn, Tsemberis, & Fischer, 2003). Housing is considered a basic right; housing and treatment are seen as separate domains. Clients are housed because they are homeless. Treatment is provided for their illness. They are not expected to cure their illness in order to end their homelessness. Individuals who are homeless face inordinate stress simply tending to the demands of daily survival in an inhospitable world. In this state, seeking treatment is not among their priorities (Maslow, 1987). In fact, as Pathways' clients attest, homelessness often serves to reduce the motivation for treatment, as they use drugs and alcohol to escape from the daily exhaustion and humiliation associated with being homeless.

Providing a person with an apartment of their own, without requiring sobriety or participation in psychiatric treatment in return, immediately transforms individuals who are chronically homeless into the new neighbor on the block. Because their most urgent and compelling need was met first, without compromise or coercion, clients are much more likely to enter into a trusting relationship with support staff. Individuals are more willing and able to discuss, understand, and accept the clear and reasonable terms of a program—two visits a month and 30 percent of income toward the rent paid through money management—that offers them housing on their own terms. The majority of clients served have never previously experienced a program that accepts them first as people and regards their needs and priorities as more legitimate that any program rules or requirements.

The belief that people should be allowed to make choices is one of the fundamental principles of Pathways' "housing first" program, and it is also the foundation of the harm reduction approach (Inciardi & Harrison, 2000). Clients are able to define their needs and goals at every step of the way, and they can set the pace and sequence of their journey toward recovery. Placing the clients at the center of their own "treatment plans" ensures their participation and cooperation and opens the way for support staff to facilitate, witness, or be guests in the lives of their clients.

The Pathways "housing first" program provides the client with access to accepting an interdisciplinary team (an Assertive Community Treatment team) of skilled clinicians who offer assistance on the person's own terms. Clients who continue to use addictive substances or remain symptomatic are gently invited to examine their behaviors and consider alternatives. Cognitive behavioral strategies are well suited to a harm reduction approach, as are group treatment and support (Marlatt, 1998). While clients strive to achieve abstinence, harm reduction is employed to provide practical, individualized solutions to the risky behaviors that accompany chronic drug use: harmful and self-destructive behaviors resulting from addiction or relapse (including accidental overdose), infection with AIDS or hepatitis C, prostitution, violence, imprisonment on theft and drug charges, or selling all the apartment furniture. Some newly housed clients are spontaneously motivated to reduce substance abuse or seek psychiatric treatment to avoid jeopardizing

their housing. Others seek treatment for their depression or other psychiatric symptoms once their survival is no longer in jeopardy. Their security assured, they become ready to address higher-order needs such as treatment, employment, or family reunification (Maslow, 1987).

Contrary to the expectations of those who insist on sobriety-contingent and medication-contingent models of housing, people who are provided housing first without pretreatment requirements, consistent with the harm reduction approach, are able to end their homelessness and remain stably housed without risking more frequent psychiatric symptoms or substance use. In a longitudinal study comparing the "housing first" approach to residential continuum of care, after 24 months only 3 percent of the housing first clients remained literally homeless, compared to 24 percent for the continuum group. Similarly, approximately 78 percent of the "housing first" clients were stably housed, as compared to 27 percent of the continuum group. Another finding thus far is that the "housing first" group did not use any more drugs or alcohol than the continuum group. Finally, clients not requiring initial psychiatric treatment experience no differences in subsequent symptoms between the groups (Tsemberis, Gulcur & Nakae, in press). Given that the most important outcomes for dual-diagnosed homeless clients are either neutral or improved when harm reduction is employed, it is clear that a more humane approach to helping the "hardcore" homeless can be successful.

Harm reduction lowers two enormous barriers to housing: access and retention. It also reduces the risks faced by both the individual and society, while improving the chances that clients who have resisted treatment will accept help willingly, and thereby significantly improve the chances of becoming and remaining sober. Although for decades the abstinence-contingent model was the only one available to homeless individuals with concurrent substance use and mental illness, current research does not support the idea that providers who employ abstinence-contingent models will be able to attain their own goals of ending homelessness for 100 percent of their clients. Such programs will not succeed until they are able to overcome the obstacle of clients' risk aversion by accepting the greater leniency of a harm reduction program. Providers must overcome their fears of out-of-control, dangerous behavior and be willing to take more risks on behalf of their clients' well-being. Otherwise, people who are homeless and dually diagnosed will simply continue to be locked out of care, without shelter and without hope.

—Sam Tsemberis and Seana O'Callaghan

Further Reading

Coalition for the Homeless (1999). *Addiction disorders and homelessness,* NCH Fact Sheet #6. Retrieved June 25, 2003, from http://www.nationalhomeless.org/addict.html

Denning, P. (2000). *Practicing harm reduction psychotherapy: An alternative approach to addictions.* New York: Guilford Press.

DiClemente, C. C. (2003). *Addiction and change: How addictions develop and addicted people recover.* New York: Guilford Press.

Drake, R. E., McHugo, G. J., Clark, R. E., Teague, G. B., Xie, H., Miles, K., & Ackerson, T. H. (1998). Assertive community treatment for patients with co-occurring severe mental illness and substance use disorder: A clinical trial. *Journal of Orthopsychiatry, 68*(2), 201–215.

Felton, B. (2003). Innovation and implementation in mental health service for homeless adults: A case study. *Community Mental Health Journal, 39*(4).

George, T. P., & Krystal, J. H. (2000). Comorbidity of psychiatric and substance abuse disorders. *Current Opinion in Psychiatry, 13*(3), 327–331.

Goldfinger, S. M., Schutt, R. K.,Tolomiczenko, G. S., Seidman, L., Renk, W., Eturner, W., & Caplan, B. (1999). Housing placement and subsequent days homeless among formerly homeless adults with mental illness. *Psychiatric Services, 50,* 674–679.

Gulcur, L., Stefancic, A., Shinn, B., Tsemberis, S., & Fischer, S. (2003). Housing, hospitalization, and cost outcomes for individuals with psychiatric disabilities participating in housing first and continuum of care programs. *Journal of Community & Applied Social Psychology, 13*(2), 171–186.

Inciardi, J. A., & Harrison, L. D. (2000). Introduction: The concept of harm reduction. In J. A. Inciardi & L. D. Harrison (Eds.), *Harm reduction: National and international perspectives.* Thousand Oaks, CA: Sage.

Interagency Council on the Homeless (ICH). (1992). *Outcasts on Main Street: Report to the Federal Task Force on Homelessness and Severe Mental Illness.*

Klein, A. R. (1997). *Alternative sentencing, intermediate sanctions and probation* (2nd ed.). Cincinnati, OH: Anderson.

Langendam, M. W., van Brussel, G. H. A., Coutinho, R. A., & van Ameijden, E. J. C. (2001). The impact of harm-reduction-based methadone treatment on mortality among heroin users. *American Journal of Public Health, 91,* 774–780.

Marlatt, G. A. (1998). Basic principles and strategies of harm reduction. In G. A. Marlatt (Ed.), *Harm reduction: Pragmatic strategies for managing high-risk behaviors.* New York: Guilford Press.

Marlatt, G. A., & Gordon, J. R. (Ed.s). (1985). *Relapse prevention: Maintenance strategies in the treatment of addictive behaviors.* New York: Guilford Press.

Maslow, A. (1987). *Motivation and personality* (3d ed.). Reading, MA: Addison-Wesley.

McQuistion, H. L, Finnerty, M., Hirschowitz, J., & Susser, E. S. (2003). Challenges in psychiatry in serving homeless people with psychiatric disorders. *Psychiatric Services, 54,* 669–667.

Morse, G., Calsyn, R., Klinkenberg, W. D., et al. (1997). An experimental comparison of three types of case management for homeless mentally ill persons. *Psychiatric Services, 48*(4), 497–503.

Mueser, K. T., Noordsy, D. L., Drake, R. E., & Fox, L. (2003). *Integrated treatment for dual disorders: A guide to effective practice.* New York: Guilford Press.

Prochaska, J. O., & DiClemente, C. C. (1992). In search of how people change: Applications to addictive behaviors. *American Psychologist, 47,* 1102.

Rossi, P. H., Wright, J. D., Fisher, G. A., & Willis, G. (1987). The urban homeless: Estimating composition and size. *Science, 235,* 1336–1341.

Rowe, M., Hogue, M. A., & Fisk, D. (1996). Critical issues in serving people who are homeless and mentally ill. *Administration and Policy in Mental Health, 23,* 555–565.

Substance Abuse and Mental Health Service Administration (SAMHSA). (2003). *Best practices: An overview of mental health and substance abuse services and systems coordination strategies.* Section 1: evidence-based and promising practices. Retrieved June 25, 2003, from http://www.samhsa.gov/grants/content/2003/sm03006_homeless.htm#reference

Tsemberis, S. (1999). From streets to homes: An innovative approach to supported housing for homeless individuals with psychiatric disabilities. *Journal of Community Psychology, 27,* 225–241.

Tsemberis, S., & Asmussen, S. (1999). From streets to homes: The pathways to housing consumer advocacy supported housing model. *Alcoholism Treatment Quarterly, 17*(1), 113–131.

Tsemberis, S., Gulcur, L., & Nakae, M. (in press). Housing first, consumer choice, and harm reduction for individuals who are homeless with dual diagnosis: A 24-month follow-up. *American Journal of Public Health.*

▣ HEALTH CARE

We know little of the health status of urban homeless populations, although frustrated clinicians in the emergency rooms and clinics of our inner-city hospitals and health centers have long lamented the seeming impossibility of providing primary and continuous care for this itinerant and vulnerable population.

"Homelessness" is an elusive descriptor for a population seeking health care and is perhaps best viewed as an indicator of extreme and persistent poverty within an eclectic group of individuals and families of diverse backgrounds. Poverty is a social determinant of poor health, and the population of impoverished persons who lack stable housing experiences extraordinary health risks and daunting obstacles to quality health care services.

BACKGROUND

Western history and literature are replete with the ills and misfortunes that have plagued the homeless poor. The sanctuary of medieval churches and cathedrals, the Victorian almshouses, the lodging houses of the British writer George Orwell's London and Paris, and the burgeoning shelters of the U.S. urban landscape during the past several decades of economic largesse have witnessed the burden of illness carried by those wandering homeless on the fringes of society. Malnutrition, poor sanitation, overcrowding in poorly ventilated warehouse shelters, repeated exposures to the extremes of weather and temperature, the habitual use of alcohol and drugs, the relentless torment of intrusive voices and hallucinations, and inadequate access to primary and preventive health care only begin the litany of hazards faced by those people struggling to survive on the streets and in shelters.

Defining a Diverse Population with an Elusive Denominator

Despite an emerging and impressive body of literature on homelessness, a striking lack of data exists on the health and health status of this vulnerable population. Several reasons can be surmised, including the exasperating difficulty in defining "the homeless." The often romanticized hoboes and skid row denizens of American lore have yielded to a cross-

section of our society, including families with children, runaway and throwaway adolescents, young men of color, middle-aged workers, and the fragile elderly.

Homelessness has proven a complex social phenomenon that thwarts simple definition, a murky chasm beneath the safety net known to a heterogeneous cross-section of society's most vulnerable persons. Darwinian rules apply; housing is a scarce and valued commodity in our market economy. Those people least able to compete—impoverished individuals and families beset with problems—fail in this intense competition for housing. Opportunity and choice are limited not only by abject and persistent poverty, but also by the challenges of chronic mental illness, substance abuse, physical and sexual violence, illiteracy, complex acute and chronic medical problems, the nightmares of recent and remote wars, and advancing years with meager financial reserves and atrophied gray matter. Extreme poverty and a lack of housing are perhaps the only shared characteristics of this eclectic population, and the complexity of need and rich diversity of the homeless have confounded and bewildered researchers.

The corollary to an imprecise definition of "homelessness" has been an elusive denominator. No research methodology has been able to accurately enumerate the homeless. Estimating the size of this population in the United States and in any particular city has been contentious, hampered by the geographic and temporal transience of homeless persons as well as daunting logistical difficulties with sampling techniques. Estimates have ranged from 250,000 to 3 million on any specific night; some researchers estimate that 13.5 million U.S. citizens have experienced "literal" homelessness in their lifetimes.

Medical Problems of Homeless Persons

Researchers have written much about the problems of substance abuse and mental illness among homeless individuals and families. In contrast, studies of the medical problems and patterns of disease among homeless persons have been largely descriptive. Nonetheless, a composite emerges of a population suffering disproportionately from a plethora of medical problems.

The medical problems of homeless persons are rarely exotic but are rather common illnesses magnified by prolonged neglect during the daily struggle for survival on the streets. The medical problems facing homeless populations cross the boundaries of both medicine, which refers to individual care, and public health, which refers to the care of an entire population. One person sleeping in a crowded shelter who suffers from a communicable disease such as influenza or meningococcal meningitis creates an urgent public health crisis. Many cities, including Boston, have shelters in former tuberculosis sanatoriums. These buildings had been emptied as the spread of this ancient disease was controlled by aggressive public health interventions. The several outbreaks of tuberculosis among homeless populations sheltered in facilities once used to treat this disease in many of our cities are a glaring irony. Shelters harbor perhaps the poorest of U.S. citizens, and the conditions of poverty, overcrowding, malnutrition, and exposure to the elements create a cascade of medical and public health maladies: tuberculosis, infestations with lice and scabies, trauma, the ravages of chronic use of alcohol and other drugs, sexually transmitted diseases and HIV infection, exposure to the extremes of weather and temperature, influenza, upper respiratory infections, pneumonia, and peripheral vascular disease.

Clinicians treating homeless people frequently see common primary care problems, including hypertension, diabetes, peripheral vascular disease, respiratory problems, and chronic liver and renal disease. Tuberculosis and HIV/AIDS are endemic in this population and have been well documented. The HIV epidemic has exposed many shortcomings in the health care system and has illustrated the critical need for flexibility in caring for vulnerable populations. In 1985, only one person was known to have AIDS in Boston's shelter system. An alarming rise in the numbers of homeless persons diagnosed with AIDS began in 1986, particularly among women and persons of color whose primary risk behavior was the use of injection drugs. At that time, homeless persons had little access to specialty clinics and were

Orwell's *Down and Out in London and Paris*

Almost two decades before he wrote his classic novels Animal Farm *(1945) and* 1984 *(published in 1949), George Orwell lived in poverty and later wrote about those years. Here he describes the indignity of undergoing a medical examination.*

Naked and shivering, we lined up in the passage. You cannot conceive what ruinous, degenerate curs we looked, standing there in the merciless morning light. A tramp's clothes are bad, but they conceal far worse things; to see him as he really is, unmitigated, you must see him naked. Flat feet, pot bellies, hollow chests, sagging muscles-every kind of physical rottenness was there. Nearly everyone was under-nourished, and some clearly diseased…

The inspection was designed merely to detect smallpox, and took no notice of our general condition. A young medical student, smoking a cigarette, walking rapidly along the line glancing us up and down, and not inquiring whether any man was well or ill. When my cell companion stripped I saw that his chest was covered with a red rash, and, having spent the night a few inches way from him, I fell into a panic about smallpox. The doctor, however, examined the rash and said that it was due merely to under-nourishment.

Source: Orwell, George. (1933). *Down and out in London and Paris.* San Diego, CA: Harcourt Brace, pp. 147–148.

usually found ineligible for experimental medications because of the lack of a permanent address and the high likelihood of non-adherence. That year, Boston Health Care for the Homeless Program (BHCHP) physicians began to conduct regular sessions in the newly formed AIDS Clinic at Boston City Hospital in order to work closely with specialists and keep abreast of a rapidly changing epidemic. Most importantly, homeless persons engaged in the shelters by BHCHP clinicians would then receive up-to-date specialty care and access to appropriate protocols. With the advent of highly active antiretroviral therapy (ART) (a combination of medications that target various aspects of HIV infection) in the mid-1990s, AIDS has become a chronic illness, and access to these medications is life preserving. Many experts doubted that persons without homes would be able to adhere to the strict ART regimen, but the experience in Boston and many other cities across the country has been that homeless persons have excellent outcomes when provided with appropriate support. BHCHP continues to provide primary and specialty care for more than 500 homeless persons with HIV infection.

Other infectious and communicable diseases have been described, many of which hearken to earlier times and are seldom seen by today's clinicians, such as diphtheria, infestations that result in endocarditis and bacteremia (the usually transient presence of bacteria in the blood) from *Bartonella quintana* (the organism carried by lice that is the cause of trench fever), and Haemophilus influenza bacteremia and septic arthritis among adults.

Skin diseases are extraordinarily common and can lead to costly hospital admissions for cellulitis (lumpy fats found in the thighs, hips, and buttocks of some women). Foot care is a critical component of the health care of homeless persons; timely podiatry services can avoid limb-threatening and life-threatening infections. Hypothermia and frostbite are dreaded hazards of life on the streets and are risk factors for early death. Trauma and violence are more common among homeless poor than among the housed poor. Poor nutrition among homeless populations causes anemia as well as growth and development problems in children and worsens medical problems in adults.

Homeless persons have been shown to have high mortality rates in studies from Atlanta (1987) and San Francisco (1991). In Philadelphia, the mortality rate in a population of homeless adults was 3.5 times that of the general population. Stephen W. Hwang and his colleagues in Boston found that homeless men aged eighteen to twenty-four years were 5.9 times more likely to die than housed counterparts and that men aged twenty-five to forty-four years were 3.0 times more likely to die.

These studies highlight the medical and public health problems associated with homelessness. Homelessness worsens chronic illnesses, causes an array of illnesses and injuries, facilitates the spread of communicable and infectious diseases, places individuals at risk for trauma and exposure to the elements, and all too often leads to premature mortality.

Utilization of Health Care Services by Homeless Populations

Homeless persons live in abject poverty without the security of stable homes and constitute a population with higher health care costs. The lack of accessible primary care and the severity and comorbidity of medical, psychiatric, and substance abuse problems in this population result in increased utilization of emergency departments and more frequent acute care hospital admissions.

EMERGENCY ROOM VISITS AND RATES OF HOSPITALIZATIONS

In a study by Martell and Seitz (1992), homeless people in Hawaii had higher rates of admissions to acute care medical and psychiatric hospitals than the general population. The study's researchers performed a retrospective chart review to determine hospitalization rates among a group of homeless persons from 1988 to 1990. Of a total of 1,751 persons, 564 hospitalizations were identified (92 psychiatric admissions to Hawaii State Hospital and 472 to seven acute care hospitals in Honolulu). The age- and sex-adjusted hospitalization rate for the psychiatric hospital was 106 per 1,000 person-years, more than one hundred times the state rate of 0.8 per 1,000 person-years. Homeless persons accounted for 3,837 days in the psychiatric hospital, compared with a predicted 139 days. The primary diagnoses were schizophrenia (39 percent), bipolar disorder (22 percent), and schizo-affective disorder (12 percent). The hospitalization rate to acute care hospitals was 542 per 1,000 person-years, more than five times the state rate of 96 per 1,000 person-years. These admissions accounted for 4,766 hospital days, compared with a predicted 640 hospital days. The primary causes of admission were psychiatric illness (23 percent), trauma (11 percent), cellulitis (subcutaneous inflammation of connective tissue) (9 percent), and illness related to substance abuse (8 percent). The average length of stay for acute care hospitalization was 10.1 days, compared to the statewide average of 7.9 days at that time.

Christina Victor and James Connelly found that homeless families in one health authority in London accounted for 9 percent of the inpatient beds in the local hospital. This inner-city district had a large concentration of homeless families because 200 of London's approximately 600 bed-and-breakfast hotels that accommodated homeless families were situated within this district. The population of the district totaled 124,000 persons; authorities identified 1,569 homeless families and 5,595 individuals, of whom 2,787 were children aged zero to fourteen. St. Mary's Hospital had 1,105 total admissions during May 1988, of which 71 were from homeless families living in the hotels. This admission rate was four times that of the resident population: 12.8 admissions per 1,000 person-months, compared with 2.8 per 1,000. Homeless children were more than twice as likely to be admitted to the hospital (6.4 per 1,000, compared to 2.9 per 1,000). Victor also examined use of the emergency services and found that homeless persons were 2.6 times more likely to use the emergency department than were the local residents.

Hospitalization rates and emergency department utilization were higher among homeless persons than among housed persons at San Francisco General Hospital (SFGH). A cross-sectional analysis by Braun and colleagues (1995) found 400 adults who used SFGH's Emergency Department during a one-year period (December 1992 through November 1993) and who also slept in shelters or ate in free-lunch programs. All patients were interviewed, and the medical charts were reviewed. The hospitalization rate for homeless persons was 2.7 times greater than that of the general population: 368 days per 1,000 person-years, compared to 136 days per 1,000 person-years.

The Boston Health Care for the Homeless Program followed homeless people who utilized the BHCHP Primary Care Clinic at Boston Medical Center during two successive years (July 1995 through June 1996 and July 1996 through June 1997). All admissions to this former municipal hospital were tracked. The hospitalization rates were strikingly similar for each year of the two-year study period: 2,815 hospital days per 1,000 person-years. These utilization rates are from a single inner-city hospital and are likely to underestimate the true use of acute care hospitals because admissions of this homeless population to other hospitals in Boston and elsewhere in the state were not captured in this study.

A 1995 national survey of Veterans Affairs medical centers and domiciliary programs found that homeless veterans were seven times more likely to be hospitalized than were other low-income veterans.

The Boston Health Care for the Homeless Program collaborated with the Massachusetts Rate Setting Commission in an effort to understand the population-based statewide hospitalization rate for a large population of homeless people who received primary and episodic care within BHCHP's citywide network. Beginning in 1994, the Rate Setting Commission maintained a database of all Massachusetts hospitalizations, including both the insured and uninsured. During 1994, BHCHP provided medical services for 5,926 homeless adults aged eighteen and older in the program's two hospital-based primary care clinics and the seventy shelter and outreach clinics in the greater Boston area. From those records, 3,962 unique Social Security numbers were available. Of the 3,962 identifiable homeless persons seen by BHCHP, 1,498 had been admitted to acute care medical or psychiatric hospitals, for a total of 4,055 admissions from 30 January 1994 through 30 September 1995. The sobering reality is that clinics caring for homeless persons must be prepared for an average of one acute care hospitalization per enrolled adult homeless patient per year. Such data have potentially profound implications for the ability of managed care plans to provide care for homeless persons without data and strategies for identification of enrolled homeless persons as a high-risk group that requires accurate risk adjustment.

PREVALENCE OF HOMELESSNESS AMONG HOSPITALIZED PERSONS

Several studies have examined populations of hospitalized patients to determine the prevalence of homelessness. In these selected populations, from 5 to 46 percent of the inpatients have been homeless or without permanent addresses.

Homeless persons accounted for 8 percent of acute admissions in two district health authorities in inner-city London in 1990. In the study noted earlier, Victor and colleagues found that homeless families living in hostels in London were responsible for 9 percent of admissions to the local district hospital.

Using unpublished data, James O'Connell and Joan Lebow reviewed admissions to one of the four medical teams at Boston City Hospital during September and November of 1993. Homeless persons living on the streets, in shelters, or in transitional programs comprised 24 percent of the admissions in September and 28 percent of the admissions in November. A comparison month at Massachusetts General Hospital during December 1993 found that homeless persons accounted for 12 percent of the admissions to the ward medical service.

Herman and Galanter found that 46 percent of patients with dual diagnosis admitted to a large New York psychiatric hospital were homeless at the time of admission. No significant differences in diagnoses were noted between the housed and homeless patients.

Marcos and Cohen (1990) evaluated a New York City program to serve homeless persons with severe mental illness and found that almost all participants had been previously hospitalized for psychiatric care. Schizophrenia, generally seen in 2 to 17 percent of homeless populations, was diagnosed in 80 percent of this population. Interestingly, 73 percent of these people also had significant medical problems. Two years after initiation of this program, 55 percent of these people were living either in an institution or a community setting.

LENGTHS OF STAY AND COSTS OF HOSPITALIZATION

In the study of homeless persons in Hawaii conducted by Martell and Seitz (1992), the total costs for the admissions for homeless persons were almost $4 million: Acute care hospitalizations cost $3.3 million, whereas the Hawaii State Hospital admissions cost $690,000. These figures are based on average daily costs of $695 and $179, respectively. The authors estimate that the expenditure for "excess" hospitalization of this homeless population was $3.5 million. The average length of stay in the psychiatric hospital was considerably shorter for homeless individuals: 41.7 days, compared to 103 days for housed residents. The average length of stay for acute care hospitalization was 10.1 days, compared to the statewide average of 7.9 days at that time.

Salit and colleagues (1998) attempted to untangle the hospital costs associated with homelessness that are not explained by the severity and complexity of illnesses alone. In this retrospective study, discharge data from the Department of Health and Hospitals of the City of New York were used to compare 18,864 homeless adults with 383,986 other low-income adults admitted to all general hospitals in New York City during 1992 and 1993. Maternity admissions were excluded from this study. Mental illness and substance abuse accounted for more than one-half (51.5 percent) of the homeless admissions and less than one-fourth (22.8 percent) of the admissions for low-income housed individuals. Mental illness and substance abuse, when included as either a primary or secondary diagnosis, were involved in 80 percent of the homeless admissions, about twice the rate for the nonhomeless admissions. The primary diagnoses of another 20 percent of the homeless admissions were for potentially preventable conditions: trauma, infectious diseases (excluding HIV/AIDS), and respiratory and skin disorders.

After adjustments were made for the differences in mental illness and substance abuse, as well as demographic characteristics and other clinical issues, the authors determined that the lengths of stay for homeless people averaged an additional 4.1 days (36 percent) per admission. These days are thus attributable to homelessness, and the costs of the additional days per discharge averaged $4,094 for psychiatric patients, $3,370 for patients with AIDS, and $2,414 for all patients. The authors conclude that homelessness causes considerable excess cost per hospitalization in New York City and argue for the funding of housing and supportive services as a

Foreign-Trained MDs Give Vital Service to Poor

CHAPEL HILL, N.C. (ANS)—While major medical institutions worry that an influx of foreign-trained physicians is contributing to an oversupply of doctors and have called for a cutback in their numbers, community health centers in poorer and rural areas rely on them, a recent study found.

Community clinics that serve poor, migrant and homeless patients could suffer if the number of doctors trained overseas and allowed to practice in this country is curtailed, study co-author Leonard Baer said.

One-quarter of the nation's 2,500 public health centers rely on doctors who were educated abroad, completed their residency training in this country and agreed to practice in an underserved area in order to remain here, said Baer.

Of the 100 health centers surveyed by researchers at the University of North Carolina, one-quarter said they were highly dependent on international medical graduates. Administrators at the facilities said if the physicians were no longer available, more than 50 percent of those positions would go unfilled.

Curtailing the number of international medical school graduates in residency programs was recommended in a 1997 report by six of the nation's leading medical associations. The "Consensus Statement on Physician Workforce" said the nation was on the verge of an oversupply of doctors and should limit the number of foreign-trained students entering residency programs.

Many positions at public health centers are filled by international doctors who agree to serve in these relatively low paid positions in return for permission to remain in this country. Since 1990, the study found, more than half of the surveyed health centers in rural areas and inner cities employed one or more foreign-trained doctors.

The overwhelming majority of community clinic patients are minorities, including 3.5 million Latinos, said Dan Hawkins, policy director of the National Association of Community Health Centers. As competent medically as their U.S. counterparts, foreign doctors "more than fit the bill" culturally, linguistically and attitudinally, he said.

In recent years, the number of foreign medical school graduates in residency programs in this country has doubled, approaching 40 percent of U.S. graduates, whose numbers have remained stable. According to Baer, in 1990 there were only 70 requests from international students

for visa waivers that would allow them to stay and practice. In 1995, there were 1,374.

"There appears to be a policy consensus that the U.S. has too many doctors and there are concerns about unnecessary expenditures," said Baer, who is a doctoral candidate in geography at UNC. "But while there are concerns about a national oversupply, there are local shortages. It's a distributional problem. How do you correct that?"

According to the medical associations, one way to address regional shortages is by expanding the National Health Services Corps. Doctors in this program agree to work in underserved areas for several years in exchange for scholarships or loan repayments.

Funding for the health corps was cut dramatically during the Reagan Administration, and it has suffered from "benign neglect" ever since, Hawkins said. The corps has only 2,000 clinicians in the field, who meet just 10 percent of the need, he said. Up for reauthorization by Congress next year, the corps would need a massive infusion of cash if it were to plug spots now filled by physicians trained abroad.

Medical schools should also expand the opportunities students have to intern in rural and inner-city communities, the associations said. Because minority physicians are more likely than their white counterparts to establish practices in minority communities, medical schools should also work harder to diversify their student bodies.

Nevertheless, many public health centers would have difficulty keeping their doors open without international medical graduates, said Baer. More than 10 million people are served by the centers annually. "It raises questions about medical care," he said.

Hawkins said while there was growing discussion in health policy circles about cutting the number of foreign physicians who practice here, no steps have been taken to do so. Without a greatly enlarged Health Services Corps, he said his association would fight any such effort "tooth and nail."

Results of the study, entitled "The Need of Community Health Clinics for International Medical Graduates," were published in the October issue of the *American Journal of Public Health*. It was funded in part by the federal Office of Rural Health Policy.

Source: "Foreign-Trained MDs Give Vital Service to Poor," American News Service, n.d.

means of reducing the high costs of hospitalization in this population.

Paul Starr (1998) notes in an accompanying editorial in the *New England Journal of Medicine* that the costs of failures in other public sectors, such as housing and education, have been shifted onto health care. Health maintenance organizations (HMOs) and safety net providers (health care providers, clinics, health centers, and hospitals who care for the poor and uninsured) who must operate in the health care marketplace are unlikely to be able to absorb these excess costs without public subsidies or risk-adjusted capitation rates (the amount of money an insurance company or health plan pays for the care of each enrolled person per month).

Homeless persons caused excess costs in mental health hospitalizations and accounted for 26 percent of all Veterans Affairs inpatient costs in 1995. S. A. Shalit and colleagues found that homeless persons accounted for 26 percent of public hospital expenditures for inpatient mental health and substance abuse treatment, even though this group represented only 10 percent of discharges.

EMERGENCY DEPARTMENT UTILIZATION

Padgett and Struening (1995) analyzed a survey of 1,260 homeless adults in New York City in 1987 and found that one-third of the women and one-fourth of the men had visited an emergency department during the previous six months. Trauma and victimization, with resulting limb fractures, concussions, burns, and skull fractures, occurred 30 times more frequently in this population than in the general population. This study tested a multivariate conceptual model—a common type of analysis that looks at many different variables that may influence a particular outcome—for predicting emergency department use. The high-risk profile for men was African-Americans or Hispanics of higher education, poorer health, injuries or victimization as risk factors, and less alcohol dependence; men in this group were 58 times more likely to use the emerging department than were homeless men in the low-risk profile. The high-risk women were 146 times more likely to use the emergency department and were characterized as being currently or previously married with higher levels of alienation, physical disability, poor physical health and injuries, and less alcohol dependence. The rather startling finding was the failure of mental health and substance abuse to predict high use of the emergency department.

This study has interesting implications. Mental illness and substance abuse are common problems faced by homeless persons, but in this study they appear to play only a minor role in utilization of the emergency department. Rather, treating physical health problems and reducing vulnerability to injuries and victimization are paramount. The authors argue that more aggressive enrollment in medical entitlement programs such as Medicaid should be vigorously pursued if we are to reduce utilization of costly emergency department services.

In the San Francisco study performed by Braun, homeless persons averaged 2.5 visits to the emergency department each year, compared to 1.6 visits for the general SFGH emergency department population. The most frequent reasons for visits to the emergency department and for admissions to the hospital were trauma (18 percent), skin disorders (cellulitis, abscess) (16 percent), cardio-pulmonary (16 percent), and psychiatric/substance abuse (13 percent). Only 7 percent had a diagnosis of HIV. High rates of self-reported current or past substance abuse were found. The authors conclude that the homeless represent a vulnerable population that relies on the emergency room for urgent/emergent and primary health care.

In the two-year unpublished study conducted in Boston by Robert Taube, Ph.D., 1,084 persons followed in the BHCHP's primary care clinic also visited the public hospital's emergency department an average of 1.6 times each year. This population also visited the hospital's urgent care center an average of 1.1 times per year. The total rate of 2.7 emergency or urgent care visits per patient per year is similar to the data reported by Braun in San Francisco.

Barriers to Health and Health Care

The U.S. urban landscape offers a dramatic background to the problem of health care and homelessness. The finest academic medical centers in the world tower over many of our cities, serving as beacons of learning and science while providing state-of-the-art care to people from all over the world. Yet, the homeless of these cities wander literally in the shadows of these buildings, unable to access even basic health care services.

Homelessness is a struggle for daily survival that mandates responses to immediate needs. Meals, clothing, refuge from the elements, and a safe place to sleep are of utmost concern, and health care needs are rendered a distant priority. Encounters with the health care system are episodic and often come after wounds have festered or illnesses have grown severe. The emotional scars from long waits in hectic and impersonal emergency rooms and ambulatory clinics are often indelible. The immediacy of life on the streets means that appointments made next week or next month are long forgotten and rarely kept, further alienating both patient and clinician.

The lives of homeless persons are fragmented and full of losses; the health care system for those without insurance and without primary care doctors and clinicians often mirrors this fragmentation. Trust, consistency, and continuity of care are essential components of any delivery system designed to overcome these barriers and engage homeless persons in primary and preventive care.

The financial barriers can be daunting for homeless persons. More than 40 million U.S. citizens are without health insurance, and the richest nation in the history of civilization does not regard health care as a right and fails to provide universal health care insurance. Although necessary for the care of poor and disenfranchised populations, universal health care insurance is still not sufficient to ensure quality health care for homeless populations. A study conducted by the Massachusetts Housing and Shelter Alliance found that 70 percent of persons living in shelters across the state had health care insurance. Yet, many reported that the system remained unable to address their needs and that too few physicians were available or willing to care for them. The Street Team of Boston's Health Care for the Homeless Program has followed a population of high-risk street dwellers for more than four years. More than 80 percent of this population have insurance, yet the health care system continues to struggle to overcome the special needs of this group of "rough sleepers."

The nursing profession has been the health system's vanguard in understanding the unique health care needs of homeless persons. Boston offers an instructive example. During the early 1970s, nurses in the emergency department at Boston City Hospital became exasperated by the growing number of homeless persons seeking care for preventable illnesses and injuries. An intrepid group of these nurses began to volunteer at Boston's Pine Street Inn, the oldest and largest adult shelter in New England. Understanding that health care needs to be brought directly to places familiar to homeless persons, these nurses maintained a consistent presence in the shelter. The cornerstone of the shelter clinic was the foot soak, a practical and symbolic gesture of service and respect by the clinic staff to weary sojourners. After the shelter guests had secured a bed ticket and eaten the evening meal, the nurses would invite the guests into the clinic to rest and soak their feet after the day's weary journey. All persons were called by name, often the only time these persons would hear their names for many weeks in the anonymity of the streets and shelters. The nurses were patient, never judged or prodded, and allowed trust to build slowly. This practice was in marked contrast to fifteen-minute visits with doctors at hospitals and clinics, where chief complaints needed to be elicited within minutes and treatment plans conceived and implemented immediately after an often invasive physical examination.

Service Delivery Models: Blurring the Boundaries

Caring for homeless persons requires a deliberate blurring of the traditional boundaries among institutions and among health care disciplines and professions. Although physicians, nurse practitioners, and physician assistants can diagnose and treat according to *Harrison's Principles of Internal Medicine,* a homeless person with a leg ulcer and cellulitis needs access to antibiotics and a place to keep the leg elevated, an impossibility while living in shelters or on the streets. Thus, the clinician's treatment plan is only as effective as the social worker who obtains the medications, the nurses who perform the twice-daily dressing changes, and the shelter supervisor who permits the person to remain in the lobby during the day.

The remarkable degree of comorbidity of acute and chronic medical problems, severe and persistent mental health illness, and active substance abuse within homeless populations requires an integrated approach to health care.

In 1985, the Health Care for the Homeless Program of the Robert Wood Johnson Foundation and the Pew Charitable Trust funded four-year projects in nineteen cities across the country. Modeled after an innovative program under the direction of Dr. Philip Brickner at St. Vincent's Hospital in New York City, these projects were envisioned to bridge the gulf between hospitals and shelters and serve as a catalyst for change within the mainstream health care system. The success of these projects resulted in the creation of the Health Care for the Homeless Program of the Bureau of Primary Health Care (BPHC) of the U.S. Public Health Service. Projects are now funded in 155 sites, spanning every state as well as Puerto Rico. More than half a million homeless persons receive medical, behavioral, and oral health care each year. Outreach and direct clinical services on the streets and in the shelters, assistance with benefits and entitlements, and wrap-around services—the supportive services that are often needed for people trying to get health care—such as transportation are core components of the service delivery models of these projects.

Multidisciplinary teams are essential for homeless health care; medical, nursing, public health, psychosocial, and holistic approaches to health care must blend into a single workable model. To illustrate, an elderly man with a high fever and a raging cellulitis of his right lower extremity was in a shelter clinic one night in 1985 and was admitted directly to the hospital for intravenous antibiotics. Despite the wonderful care of the intern, the man absconded from the hospital the following morning after removing his intravenous lines. He was found soon afterward in a downtown soup kitchen, but he politely declined pleas to return to the hospital for treatment of his life-threatening illness. Given that he was competent to make his own decisions, the only alternative was a two-week course of a powerful antibiotic that could be given by intramuscular injections four times each day. He agreed to have injections each morning and evening at the shelter clinic and each noon at the soup kitchen where he ate lunch and BHCHP conducts a daily clinic. The fourth injection involved more cre-

ativity: The bartender at the man's favorite bar agreed to keep the medication in his refrigerator, and he called a nurse each afternoon when this man came for a cocktail. The man recovered fully from his cellulitis and probable bacteremia but on his own terms and without relinquishing his dignity or his resolve to continue drinking.

Clinicians involved in the care of homeless persons must use modern technology and clinical skills in a model that harkens to the early days of U.S. medicine. The paradoxical concept of a country doctor in the inner city is a tantalizing metaphor. To meet the needs of persons without homes, clinicians must venture out from traditional hospital and clinic settings to visit and care for homeless persons in their "homes," whether in a shelter, under a bridge, down a back alley, or in an abandoned car. Homeless people migrate throughout our cities, crossing the boundaries that separate hospitals and neighborhood health centers. Quality health care ideally requires a consistent primary care clinician who is not only willing to hold "office hours" at dependable times in accessible and familiar shelters and soup kitchens, but also able to be involved in the all-too-frequent hospitalizations of a population with such a complex burden of medical, psychiatric, and substance abuse problems.

The U.S. health care delivery system has increasingly turned to home care and home-based services as lengths of hospital stays have been dramatically foreshortened during the past two decades. Persons recovering from coronary artery bypass surgery stayed in the hospital an average of twelve days in 1985 but now return home after about four days. The majority of surgery is now done on an outpatient basis. Chemotherapy, once delivered during a several-day hospitalization, is now done at home or in a specialty clinic. When persons have no home and no family supports, our current system has no viable alternative. In 1985, respite care programs for homeless persons were created by health care for the homeless programs in Boston and Washington, D.C. These freestanding medical facilities provide acute, subacute, perioperative (pre- and post-surgical), recuperative, rehabilitative, palliative, and end-of-life care for homeless persons who would otherwise require costly hospital admissions. The Bureau of Primary Health Care has funded a three-year pilot program to replicate this critical service in ten cities across the country.

All persons deserve a voice in shaping their health care, and many projects throughout the country have aggressively recruited homeless persons to serve on governing and advisory boards. This involvement of consumers in the design and scope of service delivery models has assured that the special needs of homeless persons are recognized and addressed.

Homeless persons live on the margins of our society and expose the failures in human services, including our health care system. Caring for the poorest of U.S. citizens requires that traditional concepts of health care must be seen as part of an intricate community mosaic of housing, income, education, jobs, crime, violence, race, and politics. The creation of affordable housing is necessary for any solution to the vexing problem of homelessness in the United States but may not be sufficient. The causes of persistent poverty must be addressed, including poor schools, blighted neighborhoods, troubled foster care systems, disappearing jobs and the escalating gap between the minimum and the living wage, and an ominous growth in the income chasm between the rich and the poor.

—James J. O'Connell

See also Alcohol and Drugs; Continuum of Care; Disorders and Health Problems: Overview; HIV and AIDS; Mental Health System; Mental Illness and Health

Further Reading

Allen, D. M., & Lehman, J. S. (1994). HIV infection among homeless adults and runaway youth, United States, 1989–1992. *AIDS, 8,* 1593–1598.

Bassuk, E. L., & Buckner, J. C. (1997). Homelessness in female-headed families: Childhood and adult risk and protective factors. *American Journal of Public Health, 87*(2), 241–248.

Black, M. E., & Scheuer, M. A. (1991). Utilisation by homeless people of acute hospital services in London. *British Medical Journal, 303,* 958–961.

Braun, R., Hahn, J. A., Gottlieb, S. L., Moss, A. R., & Zolopa, A. R. (1995). Utilization of emergency medical services by homeless adults in San Francisco: Effects of social demographic factors. *AHSR & FHRS Annual Meeting Abstract Book;* 12:114.

Breakey, W., & Fischer, P. (1989). Health and mental health problems of homeless men and women in Baltimore. *Journal of the American Medical Association, 262*(6), 1352–1357.

Brickner, P. W., & Scharer, L. K. (1990). *Under the safety net: The health and social welfare of homeless in the United States.* New York: W. W. Norton.

Brudney, K., & Dobkin, J. (1991). Resurgent tuberculosis in New York City: Human immunodeficiency virus, homelessness and the decline of tuberculosis control programs. *American Review of Respiratory Diseases, 144,* 745–749.

Burt, M. R., & Cohen, B. E. (1989). *America's homeless: Numbers, characteristics, and programs that serve them.* Washington, DC: Urban Institute Press.

Drancourt, M., & Mainardi, J. L. (1995). *Bartonella (Rochalimaea) quintana* endocarditis in three homeless men. *New England Journal of Medicine, 332*(7), 419–423.

Ferenchick, G. S. (1991). Medical problems of homeless and non-homeless persons attending an inner city health clinic: A comparative study. *American Journal of Medical Science, 301,* 379–382.

Harnisch, J. P., & Tronca, E. (1989). Diphtheria among alcoholic urban adults: A decade of experience in Seattle. *Annals of Internal Medicine, 111,* 71–82.

Herman, M., & Galanter, M. (1991). Combined substance abuse and psychiatric disorders in homeless and domiciled patients. *American Journal of Drug & Alcohol Abuse, 17,* 415–422.

Hibbs, J. R., & Benner, L. (1994). Mortality in a cohort of homeless adults in Philadelphia. *New England Journal of Medicine, 331*(5), 304–309.

Hoombs, M. E., & Snyder, M. (1982). *Homelessness in America: A forced march to nowhere.* Washington, DC: Community for Creative Non-Violence.

Hwang, S. W., & Lebow, J. M. (1998). Risk factors for death in homeless adults in Boston. *Archives of Internal Medicine, 158*(13), 1454–1460.

Hwang, S. W., & Orav, E. J. (1997). Causes of death in homeless adults in Boston. *Annals of Internal Medicine, 126*(8), 625–628.

Institute of Medicine. (1988). *Homelessness, health, and human needs.* Washington, DC: National Academy Press.

Lebow, J. M., & O'Connell, J. J. (1995). AIDS among the homeless of Boston: A cohort study. *Journal of Acquired Immune Deficiency Syndromes and Human Retrovirology, 8,* 292–296.

Link, B., & Susser, E. (1994). Lifetime and five-year prevalence of homelessness in the United States. *American Journal of Public Health, 84,* 1907–1912.

Marcos, L., & Cohen, N. (1990). Psychiatry takes to the streets: The New York City initiative for the homeless mentally ill. *American Journal of Psychiatry, 147,* 1557–1561.

Martell, J. V., & Seitz, R. S. (1992). Hospitalization in an urban homeless population: The Honolulu Urban Homeless Project. *Annals of Internal Medicine, 116*(4), 299–303.

O'Connell, J. J. (1991). Non-tuberculous respiratory infections among the homeless. *Seminars in Respiratory Infections, 6*(4), 247–253.

Orwell, G. (1933). *Down and out in Paris and London.* San Diego, CA: Harcourt Brace Jovanovich.

Padgett, D., & Struening, E. L. (1995). Predictors of emergency room use by homeless adults in New York City: The influence of predisposing, enabling, and need factors. *Social Science & Medicine, 41,* 547–556.

Robbins, J. M., & Roth, L. S. (1996). Stand down for the homeless podiatric screening of a homeless population in Cleveland. *Journal of the American Podiatric Medical Association, 86,* 275–279.

Rosenheck, R., & Kizer, K. (1998). Hospitalizations and the homeless. *New England Journal of Medicine, 339,* 1166.

Rosenheck, R., & Leda, C. (1996). *Fiscal year 1995 end of year survey of homeless veterans in VA inpatient and domiciliary care programs.* West Haven, CT: Northeast Program Evaluation Center.

Salit, S. A., Kuhn, E. M., Hartz, A. J., Vu, J. M., & Mosso, A. L. (1998). Hospitalization costs associated with homelessness in New York City. *New England Journal of Medicine, 338,* 1734–1740.

Smith, E., & North, C. (1992). A systematic study of mental illness and treatment in 600 homeless men. *Annals of Clinical Psychiatry, 4,* 111–120.

Spach, D. H., & Kanter, A. S. (1995). *Bartonella (Rochalimaea) quintana bacteremia* in inner-city patients with chronic alcoholism. *New England Journal of Medicine, 332*(7), 424–428.

Starr, P. (1998). The homeless and the public household. *New England Journal of Medicine, 338,* 1761–1763.

Stratigos, A. J., & Stern, R. (1998). Prevalence of skin disease in a cohort of shelter-based homeless males. *Journal of the American Academy of Dermatology, 41*(2), 197–202.

Torres, R. A., & Mani, S. (1990). Human immunodeficiency virus infection among homeless men in a New York City shelter. *Archives of Internal Medicine, 150,* 2030–2035.

Victor, C., & Connelly, J. (1989). Use of hospital services by homeless families in an inner London health district. *British Medical Journal, 299,* 725–727.

Wiecha, J. L., & Dwyer, J. T. (1991). Nutrition and health services needs among the homeless. *Public Health Reports, 106*(4), 364–374.

Wlodarczyk, D., & Prentice, R. (1988). Health issues of homeless persons. *Western Journal of Medicine, 148,* 717–719.

▣ HIDDEN HOMELESSNESS

Concerns for the visible and invisible homeless and the causes of their estrangement from society have been actively with us from biblical times to the present day. We have come to know that our understanding of "hidden" homelessness, and its personal and social pain and suffering, is anchored in our ways of "seeing" each other. Our cultural perspectives, religious and ethical norms, and the support community's philosophy of life need to be acknowledged because these become *the light* we turn on in the process of interpreting what we see. How we see shapes how we talk about and then how we act on social problems.

An interdisciplinary partnership illuminates how our many perspectives impact both (1) informal observations, such as those made by family members and that are reported in the social network, and (2) formal observations, such as scientific qualitative and quantitative data made by trained observers and reported in official government population reports, the news media, and research studies. Sociologist Serge Paugam writes, "The living conditions and experiences of 'the poor' must be analysed in this light of interdependence, which varies throughout history and in different sociocultural contexts" (Paugam 1999, 44).

INVISIBILITY

The people whose homelessness is not seen are called the "hidden homeless." First among the reasons for the persistent undercount of the hidden homeless is that some hidden homeless are not on the streets and are by historical and contemporary definitions not roofless. The poor that we have with us always are often intergenerationally cohabiting or doubled and tripled up with friends and other families. Social geographers and environmental planners Paul Cloke, Paul Milbourne, and Rebekah Widdowfield argue that the hidden homeless are further undocumented by their reluctance to believe that they are homeless and that they are at risk of becoming shelterless and so fail to register with formal social service agencies as homeless. Also undercounted are unseen rural people sleeping in "the woods, country paths, open fields, isolated hedges, ditches, and barns" (Cloke, Milbourne, and Widdowfield 2001b, 64). Medical anthropologist Hans

Baer provides us with a widely accepted definition of homelessness as the condition in which people literally do not have "a permanent home and address" (Baer et al. 1997, 66).

PAIN AND SUFFERING

As is often the case in the social sciences, a look at the simplest case often provides the best clues for the most difficult situation. A good way to gain insight into our aversion to social pain is to leave the complicated nature of urban life and to look at rural homelessness. In rural areas, where there are fewer social relief agencies and low-income housing alternatives, and where one is exposed to the criticism of local gossips, there would be few reasons for a homeless person to come forward and request services.

However, when people do know that local resources exist and that they are likely to get them and not be humiliated, they do come forward. Rural resources remain inadequate largely due to widespread understandings of the country as an *ideal* setting not beset by personal and social failures. Also at fault is a lack of ethnographic studies that help officers in their "struggle to present informed discourses of the scale and scope of rural homelessness, let alone generate innovative policy responses" (Cloke, Milbourne, and Widdowfield 2001b, 105).

SEEING THE UNSEEN

The mythology of the rural area as "purified space" and as "anti-urban utopia" prevents local authorities and people from making the connections between housing, homelessness, and rural policy problems (Cloke, Milbourne, and Widdowfield 2001a, 2000b). Doubling and tripling up is attributed to being a good family member or a good friend; rarely do people name the situation as one of homelessness. To admit to a lack of housing is to admit to a lack of rural goodness and wholesomeness where needs are met.

In order not to expose a contradiction in a widely held philosophy of care in a romantic, mutually supportive rural network, the needy person is as likely to cover up homelessness and an inability to secure long-term, affordable shelter, as is the local authority.

Failing to name the reasons for a lack of housing, such as the loss of rooms for rent in exchange for the higher incomes of bed-and-breakfast tourism, and the inability of commuters to move to affordable housing in the city, maintains the mythic façade.

SPEAKING THE UNSPOKEN

Rural geographer Mark Lawrence argues that we insist "on primarily viewing homelessness as an occupation of particular spaces rather than as a sign of overall processes" (Lawrence 1995, 305). Examining the mythology of rural homelessness challenges us to name the process by which rural invisibility becomes visible and to speak what is not said about other hidden homeless life issues. Speaking the truth challenges us to respond to real human suffering with real solutions.

Immigrants are often not seen as homeless or are thought to be voluntarily homeless. Reexamining the reasons immigrants leave or even flee their homelands gives us a more complex picture of poverty, natural disasters, and political oppressions. One reason we "do not see" the economic reasons immigrants have for living in overcrowded dormitories and doubled and tripled up in single-family apartments is our mythology of the United States as a land of milk and honey, where everyone's dreams come true. In fact, we overlook immigrants' hidden homelessness in their real-life spaces because our economy depends on their marginality. Writes sociologist Roger Waldinger: "Had there been no immigration, New York would have suffered an even more severe decline. As in Los Angeles, the arrival of the new immigrants provided a direct stimulus to the local economy. With a growing immigrant labor force, wage pressure eased up" (Waldinger 1989, 223).

Women, unmarried mothers, and divorcees are another misread population that is continuously on the verge of homelessness. Against the stereotype of mother–daughter relations, "one may expect mothers to take in their homeless daughters and children, they rarely do" (Goldberg 1997, 96). Relatives have their limits even when they may know that women head the majority of homeless families. Working against mothers are popular concepts of, and official govern-

A "squatter," a person who lives in abandoned buildings, in a squat in Philadelphia, c. 1989.
Source: David H. Wells/Corbis; used with permission.

mental polices determining, what it means to be self-sufficient. The widespread encouragement of marriage as a solution to poverty largely disregards marriage disruptions that almost always leave the mother unable to take on expanded labor market responsibilities. Divorce is a worldwide poverty indicator. Sithembiso Nyoni, Zimbabwe's Deputy Minister for Public Construction and National Housing reports: "When there is a divorce, you find that the woman is thrown out of the home together with the children, unless of course, the woman is educated and well-off and contests this through the courts" (Nyoni 2003, 11–13). She found that for reasons of pride, not only do women hide their poverty, they hide their homelessness also.

Children make up a growing population of hidden homeless. Adolescence is a stressful time of life, especially for homosexual youth, whose sexual identities may put them at risk in their family and friendship networks, causing hidden homelessness. The public expectation of seeing youth on street corners and in public places like parking lots and train stations further shields their problems. Runaway youth are often escaping abusive parents who have rejected them for a host of reasons. Youth also escape from many kinds of substitute parental care and are per-

haps the most hidden of all, as social welfare agencies race to keep track of their wards. Too often they are further victimized and hidden from view in detention centers, houses of prostitution, and drug dens.

COMMUNITY MEDICINE– NOT JUST MEDICINE

Ronald Paul Hill, professor of business administration and social responsibility, details the movement of the hidden homeless to homeless status—from being cared for by family and friends to receiving care from a "shadow community" (Hill 2001, 9). Alternative communities spring up in situations requiring human responses to the disruption of normative systems, thereby attesting to the profound sense of responsibility humans have to care for one another. Shadow communities may range from a loose collection of unsheltered individuals on the street to large and complicated social networks, such as food, electric, and banking cooperatives.

Still largely unidentified in the literature is the shadowing role of the medical community that has attempted to fill the gaps that exist between a strict sense of medical care and the healing of the whole individual. As the idea and practice of community medicine takes hold in the United States, we are seeing the medical community apply its knowledge of the human body to social problems, therein advancing our thinking about the causes of homelessness and treatment of homeless people as members of a social body.

AMENDING SOCIAL NORMS

The suffering body of homeless people requires society to amend social norms, just as the suffering physical body requires the sufferer to amend its activities. Anthropologist and nurse Janice Morse writes that in order to maintain integrity of self, one "endures" (Morse 2000, 2). The sufferer calls forth a comforting response from the other. The housed hidden homeless are frequently not available for comforting and intervention by local help agencies such as the Health Visitors (Britain) or Visiting Nurse Services (United States). Professional caregivers often find that social and personal boundaries, such as historic myths and prejudices that create unresponsiveness, pride, and denial, acerbating uneducated definitions of the situation, are difficult to negotiate.

However, when helping professionals and academic researchers cross boundaries, they are able to hear the stories of patients and social sufferers and see the structural, social, and personal violence hidden in the context of everyday life. This awareness often brings a moral obligation to end violence of all types. Nurse Kathy Carlson encourages her peers to question and change social norms that produce cruel life situations. She believes that medical workers are agents in "reframing the paradigm" of authority structures that keep some people in abusive systems. "The social attitude of violence is no longer acceptable. We've had enough. Partnership was once a social norm—it could be again" (Carlson 1992, 225).

NAMING THE VALUES THAT CONSTRUCT THE SOCIAL BODY

Like the human body, society has a body, made up of many bodies. When the social body is sick, it goes through healing, and sometimes the mourning processes of member loss. For example, even the most understanding of families goes through a normal sense of loss and mourning when a family member who was assumed to be heterosexual discloses homosexuality (Harrison, 203). The loss is a social one that responds to expected roles and norms.

Unlike non-understanding families that push the individual into hidden forms of homelessness, understanding families choose love relations instead of violent acts of exclusion as they negotiate cultural and social constructs, creating out of their loss a new found identity and normality. In doing so, their loved ones do not need to be hidden in a shadowy world of unsatisfactory care but are able to thrive in the light that illuminates their humanity.

RETHINKING AND REMAKING THE SOCIAL BODY

Zimbabwe's Sithembiso Nyoni credits Habitat for Humanity and NGOs, nongovernmental organizations associated with the United Nations, with bringing the many plights of the hidden homeless, especially women and children, to worldwide attention. Zimbabwe's consulting of specialists in empowering housing strategies produced a simple yet varied housing plan that allowed each cottage to be adapted to both family needs and a woman-run business.

Put into interdisciplinary dialogue, recent medical contributions to the philosophy of care shed light on our understanding of the sheltered but hidden homeless and their descent to the street and public shelters. Janet Younger, professor of nursing, argues that the "suffering that accompanies adversity is compounded by a suffering of a second type: the loss of community and the sense of connectedness it entails" (1995, 3). Healing requires a transformation of the situation through "finding a voice for suffering" (Younger 1995, 57). Acting as moral beings, nurses and doctors, professors and students, journalists and foreign aid officials, you and I are capable of addressing the social suffering that affects the suffering body. As we saw in Zimbabwe, when officials and the global society take the suffering of the hidden homeless seriously and talk about their pain, seeking ways to end it, creative solutions materialize.

—*Victoria Lee Erickson*

Further Reading

Baer, H. A., Singer, M., & Susser, I. (1997). *Medical anthropology and the world system: A critical perspective.* Westport, CT: Bergin & Garvey.

Biehal, N., & Wade, J. (1999). Taking a chance? The risks associated with going missing from substitute care. *Child Abuse Review, 8,* 366–376.

Boyer, J. (1986). Homelessness from a health visitor's viewpoint. *Health Visitor, 59,* 332–337.

Carlson, K. (1992). Violence: Amending a social norm. *Journal of Post Anesthesia Nursing, 7*(3), 225–226.

Cloke, P., Milbourne, P., & Widdowfield, R. (2001a). Interconnecting housing, homelessness and rurality: Evidence from local authority homelessness officers in England and Wales. *Journal of Rural Studies, 17*(1), 99–111.

Cloke, P., Milbourne, P., & Widdowfield, R. (2001b). *Rural homelessness: Issues, experiences and policy responses.* Bristol, U.K.: The Policy Press.

Goldberg, J. E. (1997). Mutuality in the relationship of homeless women and their mothers. *Affilia, 12*(1), 96–105.

Harrison, T. W. (2003). Adolescent homosexuality and concerns regarding disclosure. *Journal of School Health, 73*(3), 107–112.

Hill, R. P. (2001). *Surviving in a material world: The lived experience of people in poverty.* South Bend, IN: University of Notre Dame Press.

Lawrence, M. (1995). Rural homelessness: A geography without a geography. *Journal of Rural Studies, 11*(3), 297–307.

Morse, J. M. (2000). Responding to the cues of suffering. *Health Care for Women International, 21,* 1–9.

Nyoni, S. (2003). Interview with Mrs. Sithembiso Nyoni, Zimbabwe's deputy minister for public construction and national housing. *WomanPlus, 1*(3), 11–13.

Paugam, S. (1999). Weakening and breaking of social ties: Analysis of explanatory factors. In D. Avramov (Ed.), *Coping with homelessness: Issues to be tackled and best practices in Europe* (pp. 29–45). Aldershot, UK: Ashgate.

Waldinger, R. (1989). Immigration and urban change. *Annual Review of Sociology, 15,* 211–232.

Younger, J. B. (1995). The alienation of the sufferer. *Advances in Nursing Science, 17*(4), 53–72.

▣ HISTORY OF HOMELESSNESS

See Appendix 4: Documentary History of Homelessness; Bowery, The; Chicago Skid Row; Deindustrialization; Great Depression; Hobo and Tramp Culture and History; Literature, Hobo and Tramp; Missions; Poorhouses; Skid Row Culture and History; Workhouses

▣ HIV AND AIDS

People who are living with human immunodeficiency virus infection (HIV) or acquired immunodeficiency syndrome (AIDS) are often at risk of becoming homeless, and people who are homeless are often at increased risk for HIV and AIDS. As a result, the homeless population has been estimated to have a median rate of HIV prevalence at least three times higher—3.4 percent versus 1 percent—than the general population, while surveys of people living with HIV/AIDS have found that more than a third report having been homeless at some point.

TRANSMISSION OF HIV

During the course of HIV infection, crucial immune cells called CD4+ T cells are disabled and killed, and their numbers progressively decline. Because people infected with HIV may not feel or look sick, they are usually not diagnosed with AIDS until they develop certain opportunistic infections or take blood tests related to the immune system. The virus is spread through sexual contact with an infected person, through sharing needles (usually for drug injection) with someone who is infected, or through transfusions of infected blood or blood products, although this last source of infection is now very rare in countries like the United States where blood is screened for HIV antibodies. Women living with HIV can transmit the virus to their babies before or during birth or through breast-feeding after birth, but treatments are available in the United States that reduce the risk of transmission. As of 2002, the Centers for Disease Control and Prevention (CDC) had estimated that between 850,000 and 950,000 Americans were living with HIV/AIDS.

THE LINKS BETWEEN HIV/AIDS AND HOMELESSNESS

Substance use, higher-risk sexual activities while using substances, a lack of prevention education designed for people with serious substance use issues and/or mental illness, and trading sex for money, drugs, or protection have all been identified as factors in the prevalence of HIV/AIDS among people who are homeless. A 1995 survey of homeless adults found that 69 percent were at risk for HIV infection from unprotected sex with multiple partners, injection drug use (IDU), or sex with IDU partners. Homeless women and adolescents are particularly at risk due to the prevalence of domestic violence, sexual abuse, exploitation (sexual as well as other), and substance use among the homeless. HIV infection rates as great as 62 percent have been measured in certain segments of the homeless population.

Conversely, people with HIV/AIDS are more likely to become homeless, due in part to the impoverishing effects of chronic disease. For example, although a person disabled by HIV/AIDS may qualify for Supplemental Security Income (SSI), this was only $545 per month in 2003. Because it is nearly impossible to pay for housing as well as food and other living expenses anywhere in the United States on $545 per month, people living on this income are often forced to sell or spend their assets, as the national average rent for a modest one-bedroom rental unit was 105 percent of the SSI income. Of 13,475 people living with HIV/AIDS surveyed by AIDS Housing of Washington, 41 percent reported having been homeless. People who are living with HIV/AIDS may be forced to choose between health care and housing; a 1999 UCLA/Rand Corporation study found that a third of people living with HIV in the United States went without medical care or postponed it at least once in a six-month period in order to pay for food, clothing, or housing.

THE IMPACT OF HOMELESSNESS ON PEOPLE LIVING WITH HIV/AIDS

Whether homelessness follows HIV infection or vice versa, people who are homeless and living with HIV/AIDS are likely to have poorer health, less access to health care, and more challenges in adhering to medical treatments than those who are housed.

People who are homeless have higher rates of chronic disease than people who are housed—regardless of HIV—due to the effects of lifestyle factors such as drugs and alcohol, exposure to extreme weather, chronic nutritional deficiencies, and the experience of violence. These factors have an even greater impact on people with weakened immune systems. While homeless shelters offer some protection and stability, they may also be hazardous to people living with HIV/AIDS because they expose them to infectious diseases, including skin infestations, pneumonia, hepatitis A, and tuberculosis.

People who are homeless have trouble accessing appropriate health care because they often lack medical benefits, adequate transportation, and an awareness of services and resources. They also may have concerns about confidentiality and face providers that lack comprehensive and/or culturally appropriate services. A 1999 U.S. Department of Housing and Urban Development study found that more than two-thirds of those who are homeless suffer from chronic or infectious diseases, yet more than half lack health insurance and almost a quarter said they needed to see a doctor in the last year but were unable to do so; homeless mothers frequently subordinated their own health care needs to the needs of their children. Barriers to health care have significant implications for people living with HIV/AIDS because of the importance of early intervention and care.

Homelessness also poses challenges in adhering to HIV medications. Medical advances in treating HIV have greatly reduced mortality rates but have added new challenges of their own. A person living with HIV/AIDS may have fifteen or more different medications to take every day, each with a specific dosing schedule and set of requirements (for example, to be taken with or without food). Adhering to a particular regimen is critical in preventing the virus from becoming resistant to the medications, and studies have shown that a much higher rate of adherence is required for HIV medications than for other types.

People with a regular place to sleep, regular access to food and clean water, and a refrigerator find adherence challenging; adherence is far more complicated for people who are homeless. For example, meal programs for people who are homeless often offer meals at specific times of the day, which may or may not coincide with times for taking a medication with food. The medications themselves also have side effects, such as nausea, diarrhea, fatigue, and nerve problems. A person who is homeless may not have a place to lie down or a regular bathroom to use during the day, when many shelters close, and therefore may have few resources for managing side effects.

The difficulties in adhering to HIV medications make some physicians reluctant to prescribe them to people who are homeless. A San Francisco study found that only 7 percent of the HIV-positive homeless people studied had had previous access to protease inhibitors, a type of drug commonly used in current recommended therapies, compared to 50 to 70 percent reported in standard clinical settings. Despite the challenges of adherence while homeless, however, several studies have found that people who are homeless can have excellent adherence rates in programs that are designed for them and provide adequate and accessible information and offer flexible services. These studies show that homelessness itself is not a sufficient reason to deny access to medications.

Engaging support services and accessing stable housing can significantly improve access to health care and adherence to prescribed regimens. A study in New York found that formerly homeless people with HIV were four times more likely to enter medical care when living in supportive housing than homeless people with case management services. Although supportive housing was the most effective intervention, homeless people with case management services were still 10 times more likely to enter medical treatment than those without any services.

—*Amy Davidson*

Further Reading

Adams, M. (n.d.). *HIV and homeless shelters: Policy and practice.* American Civil Liberties Union AIDS Project. Retrieved April 14, 2003, from http://archive.aclu.org/issues/gay/hiv_homeless.html

Aidala, A. A., Jackson, T., Fuentes-Mayorga, N., & Burman, R. (2000). *Housing, health and wellness study.* Columbia University School of Public Health and Bailey House Inc. Retrieved April 14, 2003, from http://www.aidshousing.org/ahw_library2275/ahw_library_show.htm?doc_id=76999

Bangsberg, M. P. H., Tulsky, J. P., Hecht, F. M., & Moss, A. R. (1997, July 2). Commentary: Protease inhibitors in the homeless. *Journal of the American Medical Association, 278*(1), 63–65.

Burt, M. R., Aron, L. Y., Douglas, T., Valente, J., Lee, E., & Iwen, B. (1999). *Homelessness: Programs and the people they serve.* Interagency Council on the Homeless. Retrieved April 14, 2003, from http://www.huduser.org/publications/homeless/homeless_tech.html

Centers for Disease Control and Prevention, National Center for HIV, STD and TB Prevention, Divisions of HIV/AIDS Prevention. (n.d.). *U.S. HIV and AIDS cases reported through December 2001,* Year-end edition, *13*(2). Retrieved April 14, 2003, from http://www.cdc.gov/hiv/dhap.htm

Culhane, D. P., & Gollub, E. L. (2001). Connections between AIDS and homelessness. *LDI Issue Brief, 6*(9). Leonard Davis Institute of Health Economics, University of Pennsylvania. Retrieved April 14, 2003, from http://www.upenn.edu/ldi/issuebrief6_9.pdf

Cunningham, W. E., Andersen, R. M., Katz, M. H., Stein, M. D., Turner, B. J., Crystal, S., Zierler, S., Kuromiya, K., Morton, S. C., St. Clair, P., Bozzette, S. A., & Shapiro, M. F. (1999). The impact of competing subsistence needs and barriers on access to medical care for persons with HIV receiving care in the United States. *Medical Care, 37*(12), 1270–1281.

Curry, J. (2000). Homelessness and HIV/AIDS. *CRIA Update, 9*(3). Community Research Initiative on AIDS. Retrieved April 14, 2003, from http://www.thebody.com/cria/summer00/homeless.html

DeCarlo, P., Susser, E., & Tulsky, J. P. (1996). *What are homeless people's HIV prevention needs?* UCSF, AIDS Research Institute, Center for AIDS Prevention Studies. Retrieved April 14, 2003, from http://www.caps.ucsf.edu/capsweb/homelesstext.html

Moss, A. (1997, December 1). *Adherence to TB and HIV therapy among the homeless and marginally-housed in San Francisco.* UCSF AIDS Research Institute Inaugural Event. Retrieved April 14, 2003, from http://hivinsite.ucsf.edu/InSite.jsp?page=kbr-03–02–09&doc=2098.36de

National Alliance to End Homelessness. (n.d.). *Homelessness and HIV/AIDS.* Retrieved April 14, 2003, from http://www.endhomelessness.org/back/AIDS.htm

National Coalition for the Homeless. (1999). *Fact sheet #9: HIV/AIDS and homelessness.* Retrieved April 14, 2003, from http://www.nationalhomeless.org/hivaids.html

National Resource Center of Homelessness and Mental Illness. (2002). *Annotated bibliography: HIV/AIDS, homelessness, and serious mental illness.* Retrieved April 14, 2003, from http://www.nrchmi.com/text/bibliographies/HIV_AIDS.htm

O'Hara, A., & Miller, E. (2001). *Priced out in 2000: The crisis continues.* Technical Assistance Collaborative Inc. (TAC) and the Consortium for Citizens with Disabilities Housing Task Force. Retrieved April 14, 2003, from http://www.tacinc.org/resourcesframe.html

Song, J. (1999). *HIV/AIDS & homelessness: Recommendations for clinical practice and public policy.* National Health Care for the Homeless Council, Health Care for the Homeless Clinician's Network. Retrieved April 14, 2003, from http://www.nhchc.org/Publications/HIV.pdf

United States General Accounting Office. (2000). *Homelessness: Barriers to using mainstream programs.* GAO/RCED-00–184.

Zerger, S. (2002). A preliminary review of literature: Chronic medical illness and homeless individuals. *Healthcare for the Homeless.* Retrieved April 14, 2003, from http://www.nhchc.org/Publications/literaturereview_chronicillness.pdf

⊡ HOMELESS ASSISTANCE SERVICES AND NETWORKS

By 2003, homeless people in most communities across the United States had access to a much broader array of programs and services than existed even as recently as a decade ago. The availability of federal resources has stimulated much of this expansion, and federal program requirements have also stimulated service coordination. Community experience over the years of developing service networks for currently homeless people has also had an important effect. Many communities with good service networks have realized that they will never end homelessness as long as all they do is help currently homeless people. The result is an effort to expand prevention activities, develop affordable housing, and devise networks to address the factors that push people into homelessness. To discover what differentiates true systems from loose associations of providers, this entry examines the variety and structure of homeless programs and services, including intake procedures, service linkages, and other "system" aspects of homeless assistance networks, as well as funding fragmentation and other challenges.

THE VARIETY OF PROGRAMS AND SERVICES

In 1994, the U.S. Department of Housing and Urban Development (HUD) began promoting homeless assistance networks called Continuums of Care (CoCs). The core elements of these networks are outreach/drop-in (making first contacts with the hardest-to-serve homeless people who do not use shelters), emergency shelters, transitional housing, and permanent supportive housing. Because people who become homeless may have myriad issues and needs in addition to their basic need for housing, a homeless assistance network will have to provide an extensive array of services in order to meet its users' needs. These typically include the following: care for physical health, mental health, and substance abuse problems; housing-related issues (finding housing, linking to subsidies, household skills, landlord negotiations,

move-in money, and deposits); daily living skills (budgeting and time management); employment-related issues (GED, job readiness, training, development, and coaching); social skills development and reconnection with family; child-related issues for custodial parents (child care and parenting skills development); and the basics of food and clothing.

Because client needs are often complex, assembling the appropriate array of services is virtually impossible without the help of a case manager who knows where to find services and how to access them, and who will invest the time needed to work out the best program for each client. Case management can differ in intensity between individual clients and for the same client over time, from as little as a twice-yearly check-in to a daily contact. The services the case manager assembles and coordinates may actually be provided by the staff of homeless-specific residential programs, the staff of agencies that specialize in serving homeless people but do not offer shelter or housing, and/or the staff of agencies whose missions extend well beyond serving homeless people.

THE STRUCTURE OF PROGRAMS AND SERVICES

Two of the most important structural dimensions of programs and services are openness and completeness. An open agency relies on other agencies—public, nonprofit, or for-profit—to supply most or all services. A closed agency uses its own staff and resources to supply virtually everything that clients receive. "Completeness" refers to the extent to which an agency or a network has all the types of services that even the hardest-to-serve client may need. How open and complete the homeless assistance agencies in a community are depends in large part on the degree to which the community's mainstream public agencies—especially its health, mental health, substance abuse, income maintenance, and housing agencies—accept responsibility for homeless people and offer them appropriate services.

In communities characterized by open and complete homeless assistance agencies, these agencies typically supply services through their own staff to meet more common, less specialized client needs such as assessment and general case management. Open agencies may offer an entire spectrum of contact and housing opportunities, from outreach and drop-in to permanent supportive housing, or they may specialize in one or two of these program types. They are able to offer their clients a full spectrum of residential and supportive services because the mainstream public agencies in their community supply the rest. Mainstream agency services may be delivered on-site at these open agencies through co-location or regularly scheduled visits, or clients may get services at the mainstream agency. Cooperation among the staffs of residential programs and mainstream agencies assures that clients are able to get what they need.

In communities without mainstream public agency involvement in homeless-related service delivery, homeless assistance agencies are most likely to be closed; they may be either complete or incomplete, depending on their ability to raise resources. In some communities with resistant public agencies, homeless assistance agencies have developed into self-contained mini-continuums that are closed and complete. A single agency operates programs that range from outreach to permanent supportive housing, and it maintains specialists on its staff who can provide health, mental health, substance abuse, life skills, and other specialty services. Communities may have several of these agencies, which know each other and work together on advocacy and other external issues, but do not usually refer clients back and forth.

Only a few homeless assistance networks can be called complete. Likewise, most homeless assistance agencies fall in between these two extremes—they are partially open and incomplete. When clients need something an agency cannot supply internally, agency staff refer them to other agencies. Completeness then depends on what else is available in that community. If public agencies are not cooperative, referrals will usually occur within the homeless assistance network. For instance, agencies offering only outreach and emergency shelter will refer appropriate clients to transitional housing programs. If some public agencies are willing to provide sup-

portive services, then the referral network can extend beyond homeless-specific agencies to include whatever specialized services are available from the cooperative public agencies.

Other important dimensions of homeless assistance agencies and networks are sufficiency, quality, and inclusiveness. Very few communities have enough services to meet the needs of their homeless populations, so even if all types of service are available and they are all excellent, some people will not get what they need. Service quality may also vary considerably. Homeless assistance networks in some communities have established quality standards that the agencies agree to maintain. They may hold themselves responsible to each other to meet the standards, or community funding may be made conditional on meeting the standards.

An inclusive homeless assistance network will accommodate homeless people regardless of their conditions, illnesses, or other difficulties. Networks in many communities have gaps in the types of people they can accommodate. In the early 1980s, homeless assistance networks did not have facilities for women with children; that gap has largely been filled. A long-standing gap in most communities has been providing facilities willing and able to address the needs of people with co-occurring mental illness and substance abuse disorders. Public agencies providing services for one of these disabilities are only now beginning to recognize the need to work together to address the needs of people with both. Among homeless assistance providers and mainstream agencies, the idea that their staff members should be dual-qualified to address both needs simultaneously has only recently begun to spread. A few communities have merged their public mental health and substance abuse agencies because they recognize that co-occurrence is an issue for far more of their clientele than just those who experience a spell of homelessness. Changes in Medicaid administration—in particular, the creation of "managed behavioral health" agencies that address the needs of Medicaid beneficiaries with mental health or substance abuse problems, or both—have also moved mainstream public agencies in this direction. However, dual-certified staff and agencies are still the exception in homeless assistance networks, and homeless people with co-occurring disorders are often excluded from care.

"SYSTEM" ASPECTS OF HOMELESS ASSISTANCE NETWORKS

Homeless assistance networks have developed mechanisms to increase the likelihood that people will get the services they need and that available programs and services will be fully used. Formal mechanisms include bed-tracking systems, common intake and assessment forms, centralized intake, multi service centers, access to public agency management information systems, and homeless management information systems. Only a few communities will have all of these mechanisms, but many communities will have at least one of them.

Bed-Tracking Systems

Having empty beds in shelters, transitional housing, and permanent housing is expensive and inefficient; program expenses do not shrink when occupancy is low, and homeless people who could have received services do not get them. Some communities have developed either telephone- or Internet-based systems through which programs can notify a central location of bed availability. Agencies can check availability and refer a person to a program where they know that space is available. Some systems even allow the referring agency to book the bed, so the program can prepare for the person being referred. A few cities that themselves pay for most homeless-related beds manage bed availability centrally, and have succeeded in cutting vacancies to no more than 1 percent.

Common Intake and Assessment Forms

Communities that are trying to understand the scope and characteristics of homelessness often have difficulty doing so because every agency keeps different information on its clients, or the same information in different formats. Some communities, and at least one whole state, have developed intake and assessment protocols that several agencies have agreed to

use. Emergency shelters are the most common type of agency involved in these arrangements, but the arrangements may extend to other types of housing within a homeless assistance network. Common forms are sometimes, but not always, found in combination with centralized intake mechanisms and/or full-fledged homeless management information systems (HMISs).

Centralized Intake

Entry into homeless assistance networks may be described in one of three ways: fragmented, "no wrong door," and centralized. Most communities in the United States probably still fall into the fragmented category, which means that the homeless people who live there must approach any provider directly, may or may not gain entry, and may or may not get connected to other programs and services. Some communities with good cross-program communications operate with a "no wrong door" approach. In these communities, a homeless person may approach any program, after which the program staff will augment this first contact by sharing their knowledge of what is available and providing systemic linkages to help this person get to the right programs and services. Multiservice centers often facilitate access to services in these communities, but they are not essential to this approach.

A centralized intake system through which every homeless person desiring emergency shelter or other accommodation has to pass can increase system efficiency. According to proponents, centralized entry minimizes prolonged and misdirected searches for emergency shelter and services. It also allows for uniform intake and assessment, which helps ensure equity of access to services. Some centralized intake agencies also have resources to prevent entry into literal homelessness if a person or family has not already lost housing but is facing eviction or will not be able to stay in temporary lodging for more than another day or two. To prevent homelessness, these agencies can pay back rent or utilities bills, assist with moving expenses, negotiate with landlords, work out budgets and payment plans, enroll the person or family into a rent-subsidy program, handle credit issues, and pursue whatever it takes to assure that literal homelessness does not occur.

Some communities have centralized intake only for families, others have separate centralized intake systems for families and singles, and a few have combined centralized intake functions. Centralized intake structures are often linked to bed-tracking systems, so referral to a program with availability can immediately follow the intake process. At a minimum, the accepting program usually receives some information from the intake agency so the homeless person does not have to repeat the information. In networks with fully computerized systems, the intake and assessment information will be available to the accepting program electronically, and records will be periodically updated as a resident receives services or passes various milestones.

Multiservice Centers

Some communities without fully centralized intake nevertheless have established multiservice centers where homeless people can access a wide variety of services. They may still apply directly to emergency shelters, because although many multiservice centers handle intake, assessment, and referral to shelters, some serve only a case management and service linkage function. The most commonly used public and private agencies offering supportive services to homeless people usually place at least one staff member at a multiservice center for at least some hours during a day or week. Some multiservice centers have as many as fifteen or twenty agencies represented, from public mental health, physical health, substance abuse, and income-maintenance agencies to veterans programs, Travelers' Aid, child care, immigrant and undocumented worker organizations, translators/interpreters, employment training and referral agencies, and education agencies. Usually a core case manager interviews a new client and assesses the needs. The manager may then arrange referrals or may simply take the client around to the different offices, introduce him or her to the representatives of relevant agencies, and then leave the client to work with the representatives to establish eligibility and arrange for needed services.

Access to Public Agency Records

In some communities, transitional and permanent supportive housing programs serving specialized populations may link with the mainstream public agency responsible for that population to assure appropriate services and treatment. This is particularly important for people with severe mental illness, and the crucial link will be with the mental health agency. Public mental health agencies in many communities maintain a spectrum of residential settings for their clients. It is fairly common for the agencies that develop and run these types of housing for non-homeless people with severe mental illness to begin developing and running permanent supportive housing programs within homeless assistance networks, so they can better serve people whose mental illness has contributed to a sometimes long history of homelessness. The parent housing developer was probably already tied into the mental health agency's computer system because its residents were system clients. It was a small step in some communities for that agency to extend that system to programs within the homeless assistance network.

Linking permanent supportive housing programs into the computerized records of public mental health agencies helps both the housing programs and the public agency keep track of what their shared clients are getting and how well they are doing. A less complete version of system linkage occurs in some communities where outreach teams can check to see whether new people they contact on the streets are already being served through the public mental health agency. If they are, then the outreach teams can refer them to the agency that has served them before, or have their case transferred to an agency that will be more able to meet their needs.

Homeless Management Information Systems

An HMIS pushes the advantages of a centralized intake and assessment system several steps further. In its ideal form, it links all homeless assistance programs in a community and integrates each person's multiple service records into one complete record. It has distinct advantages for serving individual clients, keeping track of service delivery communitywide, and conducting analyses that can provide feedback on the success of current policies and projections of what will be needed in the future. At present, few communities have an HMIS approaching this ideal, but many communities are developing HMISs both for their intrinsic advantages and because they are under pressure from Congress and HUD to do so. Communities whose information systems come the closest to a full HMIS have benefited from their access to good data that have helped them shape policy and even make dramatic policy changes.

CHALLENGES: GAPS AND EXCLUSIONS

Some communities have been willing and able to extend the full array of programs and services defining a CoC to most homeless people. However, different parts of the homeless population inspire different degrees of sympathy from funding institutions, the general public, and even homeless assistance providers. As a consequence, many communities have partial homeless assistance networks that omit either certain types of programs or certain types of people. Most communities have emergency shelters or the capacity to respond to housing emergencies. Transitional housing programs have become more common during the past ten to fifteen years, and permanent supportive housing programs have recently been developed. Inclusion of permanent housing alternatives with supportive services for chronically disabled homeless people stems from a recognition that some people's physical health and/or mental health render them unable to sustain housing without help and an acceptance of the fact that the community has a responsibility to provide both housing and help.

Communities appear most willing to establish homeless assistance networks for homeless families. For single homeless people, more programs have been developed to serve those with severe mental illness than have been created to aid chronic substance abusers; the fewest programs of all are for homeless people with both mental illness and substance abuse problems. Oddly, given the emphasis over many years on developing programs for homeless families, homeless parents with chronic mental health and substance abuse problems have only recently been the focus of a new type of program—family permanent supportive housing. Sympathy for homeless families has tended to downplay the very real disabilities and disadvantages of some homeless parents, so programs with full cognizance of their particular issues have taken a long time to develop.

CHALLENGES: FUNDING FRAGMENTATION

It is hard for agencies that provide homeless assistance programs and services to attract the funding to support an approach that deals with the whole person or the whole family. Funding sources are usually structured around single problems—for example, severe mental illness or substance abuse but not both, or a history of violence and abuse or substance abuse but not both. They are often further restricted by eligibility criteria relating to family structure, income, residence, and even gender or age. Trying to make the money come together to serve a particular person is never easy; in this respect, homeless assistance funding sources do not differ from funding programs that address other social problems.

Some communities have developed mechanisms to streamline provider access to funding and reduce the frustration of trying to put all the pieces together. One mechanism, a funding funnel agency, facilitates provider access to multiple funding sources through a single application. The funnel agency may be permanent—serving this function year after year—or may be created anew through an interagency memorandum of understanding for each integrated request for proposals. A single agency, either public or nonprofit, assembles funding from many sources. Sometimes these sources are all public, but in some communities even foundation funding and United Way funding flow through the funnel agency. The funnel agency then issues a request for proposals, providers respond, and the funnel agency has the task of figuring out how to match available funds with provider requests. The providers need to deal with only one proposal, get one grant or contract, and respond to one set of reporting requirements. The funnel agency assembles reports from all providers and reports as necessary to the different funding agencies.

TRENDS

Homeless assistance began in the early 1980s with bare-bones emergency shelters. Over the past two decades, programs offered by both providers and whole communities have become increasingly complex and differentiated, in a process that still continues. Two important trends are apparent at this writing—the increasing involvement of mainstream agencies and the growing number of options for responding to the needs of people whose substance abuse complicates programmatic responses to their other problems.

No community will end homelessness, or even chronic homelessness, without the involvement of mainstream public agencies, as communities across the country are recognizing. Only these public agencies have the resources to address the ongoing physical and mental health care and housing subsidies that will be necessary to end chronic homelessness. Only mainstream mental health and corrections agencies, through improved discharge policies and recognition that housing is part of their responsibility, can prevent having their discharged clients become new additions to the homeless population. Only mainstream housing and redevelopment agencies, including private and nonprofit housing developers, have the resources to create enough affordable housing for people already homeless and those at risk of homelessness. Mainstream public agencies in many communities have begun to accept these responsibilities, but few communities today have the active involvement of all the necessary public agencies. Substance abuse is pervasive among homeless people, especially among those who have been homeless the longest. An important development in the last few years has been the creation of programs that work with substance abusers, many of whom also have other issues that keep them homeless. One such program type could be called "pre-recovery." These programs help substance abusers leave the streets and enter residential programs that do not require them to be clean and sober, although they do require them to refrain from using a prohibited substance on program premises. Services, including those aimed at reducing and ultimately ending substance use, are available but not required. Many of these pre-recovery programs, also referred to as "low/no demand" or "safe haven" programs, serve populations with co-occurring mental illness and substance abuse problems. In this way, they represent the second trend noted above—the willingness to provide staff qualified to work with people who have both mental illness and substance abuse problems. Even more promising is the movement in some communities for public mental health and substance abuse agencies to develop effective working relationships with each other and even, in some instances, to merge. These changes will make homeless assistance networks more effective in ending homelessness for those with the most complex and long-standing problems.

—*Martha R. Burt*

Further Reading

Burt, M. R., Pollack, D., Sosland, A., Mikelson, K. S., Drapa, E., Greenwalt, K., et al. (2001). *Evaluation of continuums of care for homeless people: Final report.* Washington, DC: Department of Housing and Urban Development. Retrieved May 29, 2003, from http://www.urban.org/url.cfm?ID= 310553

Burt, M. R., Zweig, J. M., Hedderson, J., & Aron, L. Y. (2003, forthcoming). *Best practices for ending chronic street homelessness.* Washington, DC: U.S. Department of Housing and Urban Development and Urban Institute.

Dennis, D. L., Cocozza, J. J., & Steadman, H. J. (1999). What do we know about systems integration and homelessness? In L. Fosburg & D. Dennis (Eds.), *Practical lessons: The 1998 National Symposium on Homelessness Research.* Washington, DC: U. S. Departments of Housing and Urban Development and Health and Human Services.

Goldman, H. H., Morrisey, J. P., Ridgeley, M. S., Frank, R. G., Newman, S. J., & Kennedy, C. (1992). Lessons learned from the program on chronic mental illness. *Health Affairs, 11*(3), 51–68.

Interagency Council on the Homeless. (1994). *Priority home!: The federal plan to break the cycle of homelessness.* Washington, DC: U.S. Department of Housing and Urban Development.

Kahn, A., & Kamerman, S. (1992). *Integrating services integration: An overview of initiatives, issues, and possibilities.*

New York: National Center for Children in Poverty.

McMurray-Avila, M. (1997). *Organizing health services for homeless people: A practical guide.* Nashville, TN: National Health Care for the Homeless Council, Inc.

Ridgeley, M.S., Lambert, D., Goodman, A., Chichester, C., & Ralph, R. (1998). Interagency collaboration in services for people with co-occurring mental illness and substance use disorder. *Psychiatric Services, 49*(2), 236–238.

Rosenheck, R., Morrissey, J. M., Lam, J., Calloway, M., Johnsen, M., Goldman, G., et al. (1998). Service system integration, access to services and housing outcomes in a program for homeless people with mental illness. *American Journal of Public Health, 88*(11), 1610–1615.

Shern, D. L., Felton, C. J., Hough, R. L., Lehman, A. F., Goldfinger, S., Valencia, E., et al. (1997). Housing outcomes for homeless adults with mental illness: The results of the second-round McKinney programs. *Psychiatric Services, 48,* 239–241.

Shinn, M., & Baumohl, J. (1999). Rethinking the prevention of homelessness. In L. Fosburg & D. Dennis (Eds.), *Practical lessons: The 1998 National Symposium on Homelessness Research.* Washington, DC: U.S. Departments of Housing and Urban Development and Health and Human Services.

Shinn, M., Baumohl, J., & Hopper, K. (2001). The prevention of homelessness revisited. *Analyses of Social Issues and Public Policy,* 95–127.

▣ HOMELESS COURT PROGRAM

The Homeless Court Program (HCP) is a special session of the Superior Court of San Diego held in local homeless shelters. Homeless misdemeanants satisfy court orders with participation in rehabilitation programs. The HCP provides homeless defendants access to justice through four basic principles: a progressive plea agreement, alternative sentencing structure, assurance of "no custody," and proof of the homeless participants' accomplishments in program activities. The HCP addresses a full range of misdemeanor offenses.

THE PROBLEM

Resolution of outstanding misdemeanor criminal cases is a real and fundamental need for homeless people. Most homeless defendants fail to appear in court, not because of a disregard for the court system, but due to their status and condition. For many

homeless people, the day is consumed with a search for food, clothing, and shelter. Most homeless persons are not in a position to fight the procedural or substantive issues a case presents.

The homeless are aware that the court also requires a decent appearance. Not wanting to make a bad first impression, a homeless person with poor hygiene or without a place to store belongings may choose not to appear in court at all. Many homeless people are reluctant to attend court given the uncertainty of court proceedings and the threat of custody.

The homeless have requested assistance with outstanding criminal cases. In 1988, at the conclusion of the first Stand Down (an annual three-day tent community providing comprehensive services for 700 homeless veterans), 116 of 500 homeless veterans stated their greatest need was to resolve outstanding bench warrants.

HISTORY

In 1989, San Diego started the first Homeless Court Program in the nation, a special superior court session held on handball courts. Three gray concrete walls at San Diego High School's athletic field surrounded foldout tables and chairs. Desert camouflage netting sheltered the court from the sun. The flag of the United States anchored one corner; that of the State of California, the other. The defendants appearing before this outdoor Homeless Court were veterans who live outdoors on the streets of San Diego, but for three days they were sheltered in tents and received employment counseling, housing referrals, medical care, and mental health and other social services.

Following this first Homeless Court, 130 defendants had 451 cases adjudicated through Stand Down in 1989. Between 1989 and 1992, the court resolved 4,895 cases for 942 homeless veterans.

The continued large numbers of homeless people participating in the HCP, coupled with their efforts to overcome the obstacles their condition represents, fostered the program's expansion from an annual, to a quarterly, then a monthly schedule. Over the years the HCP expanded to serve battered and homeless women (1990), residents at the city-sponsored cold weather shelter (1994), and the general homeless population served at local shelters (1995). In 1999, the HCP started holding monthly sessions, alternating between two shelters (St. Vincent de Paul Village and Vietnam Veterans of San Diego).

PURPOSE

The HCP plea agreement addresses the cases/offenses involving homeless participants due to their condition—living on the streets—and a full range of misdemeanor offenses. Additionally, the plea agreement acknowledges the effort participants undertake before their appearance in court, satisfying the requirements of the court order before the court imposes a sentence.

Alternative sentencing substitutes participation in agency programs for fines and custody. This structure is not coercive or punitive but designed to assist homeless participants' move from the streets, through the shelter program, to self-sufficiency. The HCP gives "credit for time served" for a participant's activities that include, but are not limited to, life skills, chemical dependency, or AA/NA meetings; computer or literacy classes; training or searching for employment; counseling; or volunteer work.

The court agreement of "no custody" acknowledges that the participant's efforts in their program activities satisfy court requirements. This agreement respects the relationship and trust the homeless service agencies have with the participants who appear before the HCP, and it acknowledges that the time spent working with these agencies is equivalent to, and more constructive than, time spent in custody.

Local homeless shelters and agencies are the gateway for participants. Homeless persons who want to appear before this court must sign up through a local shelter. The shelter representatives write advocacy letters for each client. The advocacy letter includes a description of the service provider and its program, the client's start date and accomplishments, programs completed or in progress, the client's efforts and demeanor, and long-term goals. While more information usually is better, the participant's privacy is respected. With the advocacy letter in hand, the court has verification of a participant's activities and the framework to pronounce a sentence and terms and

conditions of probation, with "credit for time served." Under the HCP 90 percent of the cases are dismissed.

PROCESS

The HCP coordinates interagency linkages with key players from the criminal justice system and homeless service agencies in a series of synchronized steps for a one-month calendar.

These steps include the following:

Week One: The defense attorney receives the list of participants interested in resolving their cases through Homeless Court. The attorney meets with case managers and potential homeless participants to explain the court's purpose, procedures, and schedule. The attorney delivers the participant list to the court and prosecution.

Week Two: The prosecution prepares a list of cases, relevant discovery, and the proposed plea bargain for each participant. The defense attorney receives and reviews the prosecution packet. The defense attorney contacts the participant and program representative to review difficult cases.

Week Three: The defense attorney counsels each defendant, reviews his/her cases and participation in program activities at the host shelter, and prepares for the court hearing.

Week Four: At the host shelter, the attorney approaches the court with each defendant. They stand before the judge with proof of progress in the participant's chosen program activities and resolve cases.

Unprocessed cases not only clog courts' calendars, they also are obstacles to individuals' reintegration into society because they deter use of social services and impede access to employment. The courts are open five days a week from 8:00 a.m. to 5:00 p.m., poised to fulfill their role in the administration and execution of justice.

RESULTS

Before 1989, the criminal justice system relied on the courthouse and jails to administer justice and order. In the wake of Stand Down, justice and order are found with programs that include rehabilitation, counseling, recovery, and life skills and employment training. Handball courts and shelter meeting rooms house courts that work for the criminal justice system, the homeless participants, and society. In short, the Homeless Court Program brings law to the streets, the court to the shelters, and the homeless back into society.

—Steve Binder

Further Reading

American Bar Association Policy Positions on Homelessness and Poverty. (2001/2002). Retrieved August 6, 2003, from http://www.abanet.org/homeless/recommend.html

Binder, S. (2002). *The Homeless Court Program: Taking the court to the streets.* Washington, DC: ABA Commission on Homelessness and Poverty.

▣ HOMELESS INTERNATIONAL

Homeless International (HI) is a charitable organization based in the United Kingdom that works alongside partners in Asia, Africa, and Latin America to support community-led housing and development. Initially formed as a trust, HI was established in 1989 and since then it has advocated housing initiatives and other potential solutions to poverty issues by providing information and technical assistance to partners and other housing organizations, providing people in poverty with methods of establishing credit through loans and guarantees, influencing policies, and conducting research focused on long-term solutions to housing issues and poverty issues in general. As stated on their website, Homeless International bases its efforts on the following beliefs:

(1) All people have an equal right to adequate, safe, and secure shelter and people who are unable to exercise this right are considered homeless; (2) Shelter is more than a house—it is a space for privacy, economic activity, social care, and personal fulfillment; (3) Shelter development is more than the building of houses—it is the development of neighborhoods and communities that provide opportunities for social and cultural expression; (4) Homelessness is a characteristic feature of poverty and the eradication of poverty requires investment in the development of shelter that is economically, socially, and environmentally sustainable;

(5) Sustainable solutions to homelessness can be created only if people have access to appropriate land, finance, information, organization, and technology and also have an opportunity to play a lead role in designing solutions that work for them; and (6) Sharing information about creating solutions to homelessness allows people to learn from and support each other.

PROGRAMS AND INITIATIVES

Homeless International takes part in numerous programs and initiatives in partnership with their colleague organizations in Asia, Africa, and Latin America, and they have helped provide many of those in need with shelter and support. Among these programs are the following:

Rehabilitation and Resettlement in India. Homeless International, along with its Indian partners Society for the Promotion of Area Resource Centres (SPARC), Mahila Milan, and the National Slum Dwellers Federation, worked on a slum resettlement project in Mumbai, India. World Bank and HI grants funded the voluntary relocation of more than 60,000 slum dwellers to safe and secure housing with basic services in order to make room for World Bank's proposed improvements to the railway, which is the "lifeline of the city." Currently half of Mumbai's population of 12 million is living in slums, and this project was the first effort to tackle this massive housing problem.

Successes and Prospects in Southern Africa. Homeless International is providing support and grant funding to partners in Namibia (The Namibia Housing Action Group and the Shack Dwellers' Federation of Namibia), South Africa (People's Dialogue and the South African Homeless People's Federation), and Zimbabwe (Dialogue on Shelter and the Zimbabwe Homeless People's Federation) to aid them in Federation processes and their fight against urban poverty. The methods of support that HI has offered include negotiating with local authorities for land access, collecting data and information about informal settlements, encouraging community-to-community correspondence, and creating and strengthening new savings groups (support groups that allow people to share about the problems of living in informal or inadequate housing).

Chartered Institute of Housing and Presidential Appeal. Focused on supporting Cambodian partner Solidarity for the Urban Poor Federation (SUPF), this proved to be one of the most successful fund-raising appeals in 2003, raising almost $40,000. After fires burned Basaac and Chbar Ampoe settlements to the ground, families from those settlements were moved to a temporary settlement just outside Phnom Penh. With money raised by this appeal, 1,857 such families were given plots of land to build and live on. SUPF continues to provide these temporary communities with emergency shelter and food and is negotiating with the Phnom Penh government for the acquisition of permanent, secure land close enough to the city to allow people to work.

Pragmatic Advocacy. Homeless International raises international support for organizations of urban poor through fund-raising and policy advocacy on both local and international levels. HI also contributes financial and other support to grassroots initiatives and builds communication with other agencies to facilitate discussion and understanding of these initiatives.

Community-Led Infrastructure Finance Facility (CLIFF). A new project managed by Homeless International and piloted in partnership with SPARC, the National Slum Dwellers Federation, and Mahila Milan, CLIFF provides funding to the Indian Alliance of these three organizations to provide loans for communities undertaking major construction projects. It also provides grants for assistance in project development and specified "knowledge grants," which ensure that outside organizations and those who are not directly involved learn about the project. The ultimate goal of the project is to increase deposits in the Guarantee Fund by $1 million in order to increase the Indian Alliance's ability to involve local commercial banks in urban regeneration.

COORDINATION WITH OTHER AGENCIES

Homeless International works with many international organizations such as the Asian Coalition on Housing Rights, the Department for International Development-UK, Dialogue on Shelter for the Home-

less in Zimbabwe, Fundacion Pro-Habitat-Bolivia, Groundswell-UK, the Namibia Homeless Action Group, People's Dialogue-South Africa, Slum/Shack Dwellers International, Urbanet, Women Advancement Trust, and YCO-India. More information concerning opportunities for support and fund-raising ideas are available on the Homelessness International website at www.homeless-international.org.

—*Emily A. Colangelo*

▣ HOMELESS ORGANIZING

The United States has a long history of organizing by and for those dispossessed by the nation's economic and political structures. In the decades between the Civil War and World War II, periodic recessions and depressions led to sporadic public demonstrations by those thrown out of work. In 1894, masses of men known as "Coxey's Army," many homeless as well as jobless, traveled by foot, train, and boat from all over the country to converge on Washington, demanding the establishment of a public works program to employ them. In the early years of the twentieth century, the Industrial Workers of the World (IWW) more systematically organized those on the fringes of society. The IWW was particularly successful in winning more decent conditions for the transient workers of the logging industry, known as "timber beasts" because they carried all their worldly goods on their backs from one job to the next. The Great Depression saw a good deal of organizing concerned with issues of housing—anti-eviction actions, for example—as well as unemployment.

But it wasn't until the late 1970s that organizers first began attacking the issue of homelessness per se. Their efforts were precipitated by the explosive growth in the homeless population and galvanized by two watershed events. The first was the November 1978 occupation of the National Visitors' Center in Washington, D.C., by members of the Community for Creative Non-Violence (CCNV). This activist group, with origins in the anti–Vietnam War movement, had been operating a soup kitchen for the previous decade, and demanding the creation of an emergency homeless shelter. The second landmark was a class action lawsuit filed by attorney Robert Hayes against the City and State of New York, arguing that a constitutional right to shelter existed in New York State—a suit that ultimately succeeded in establishing a local right to shelter. Legal challenges and direct action aimed at governmental officials have remained the basic weapons of anti-homelessness activists, although they have also adopted other strategies, including lobbying elites, appealing to public opinion, and advocating research by both academic and popular writers.

NATIONAL ADVOCACY GROUPS

The actions of the CCNV in Washington, and the Coalition for the Homeless, a New York group co-founded by Hayes, made them national models for groups elsewhere. The CCNV's highly innovative and confrontational tactics raised the issue's profile, stressing the moral question of homelessness in a land of plenty. Moreover, its location in the nation's capital led to media coverage that would not have been forthcoming otherwise. In November 1984, Mitch Snyder, their most charismatic leader, fasted for fifty-one days, gaining a great deal of media attention and winning a commitment from the White House to create a homeless shelter in an unused federal building.

The CCNV and the Coalition for the Homeless served as informal national leaders of the anti-homelessness movement in the early years (and episodically in later years), but the need for a truly national organization was quickly apparent. In 1984, a meeting attended by homeless and housed activists from across the country formed the National Coalition for the Homeless, headed initially by Hayes and attorney Maria Foscarinis. In 1989, Foscarinis left to form the National Law Center on Homelessness and Poverty and concentrate on legal strategies. Other national groups of major importance include the National Low Income Housing Coalition, the National Housing Law Project, the Legal Services Homelessness Task Force, the U.S. Conference of Mayors, and the National Alliance to End Homelessness. In the late 1980s, campus activists formed the National Student Campaign against Hunger and Homelessness.

The national groups have been largely directed and staffed by housed advocates, often professionals, although some have made substantial efforts to include homeless and previously homeless people as well. Much like institutionalized activist groups in other areas—such as race relations or environmental issues—these groups concentrate on public education, government lobbying, and in some cases legal advocacy. They raise the bulk of their funding from appeals to "conscience constituencies" rather than from homeless people themselves. To the extent that they actually organize people, it is largely (though not exclusively) housed supporters who are being mobilized.

These groups were extremely successful in the 1980s in changing the terms of the national debate about homelessness. When mass homelessness first surfaced as a public issue in the early years of that decade, most housed people were likely to see the problem in individual terms, strictly attributable to personal moral failure (irresponsibility, substance abuse, etc.) or incompetence (mental illness, drug dependency as a medical problem) But backed by a growing literature produced by activist, advocate, academic, and government researchers, the national organizations were able to raise an alternative vision of homeless people as the casualties of systemic failures far larger than individual actions. Public opinion became much more sympathetic to the plight of unhoused people; government spending at all levels, but particularly federal spending, skyrocketed from the mid-1980s to the mid-1990s (though remaining far below what was required).

This "politics of compassion" required convincing housed people that homeless people were neither slackers nor villains but victims caught in massive social processes such as deindustrialization and the collapse of affordable housing. Some organizations tried to present the view that unhoused people were "just like you and me," except for an unlucky break that took them away from a mainstream life. But even this perception of the homeless as victims—as well as the image presented by some of the most visible homeless people—tended to connote incompetence, an inability to adequately provide for themselves. Aid was thus seen by many as a form of charity that a civilized nation benevolently provided to its unfortunates.

LOCAL ORGANIZATIONS

Local groups arose and developed simultaneously with the national organizations. While some of these too were dominated by housed advocates, homeless activists were far more likely to play a significant role at the local level, including founding the groups and assuming leadership roles in many cases. One group, the Union of the Homeless, begun locally in Philadelphia in 1985, had chapters in fourteen cities by 1988.

While such groups were encouraged and shaped in part by events at the national level, local flash points typically led to their creation. As in other social movements, these flash points tended to be of two kinds: first, sudden new deprivations, such as police sweeps of areas traditionally sanctioned for homeless encampments; and second, new information about rights previously denied. Hayes's suit in New York, for instance, galvanized local homeless organizing efforts much as the U.S. Supreme Court decision in *Brown v. Topeka Board of Education* had galvanized civil rights activity in the 1950s.

Many localities have a variety of organizations representing various homeless subpopulations, from formerly middle-class single parents to long-term "street people." Though such groups typically develop out of preexisting networks of friends and acquaintances, most see outreach to others in similar situations as a basic survival strategy. That is, despite the need for support from housed people (and in contrast to the national groups), local groups led by homeless activists have typically placed a premium on organizing homeless people themselves.

In general, local groups have depicted homeless people as competent but wronged citizens—veterans, workers, and parents—rather than as pitiable victims. But the heterogeneity of the population also results in a wide array of images invoked and tactics used. Local groups dominated by street people, for example, are more likely to make immediate demands, threaten disruption, and in general engage in the politics of confrontation. Those representing

single parents are more likely to negotiate for aid, invoke moral authority, and engage in the politics of compromise. On the local level, legal strategies, appeals to public opinion, and lobbying are important, as they are on the national level. But often these local groups are effective only to the degree that they can produce not only housed advocates but also homeless activists as an ongoing visible presence—either as a form of moral suasion or, in contrast, to raise the threat of disruption and chaos.

Dilemmas of Local Groups

Establishing a visible presence is one of the dilemmas facing local groups. Being publicly identified as homeless can lead to significant legal, social, and financial problems, so most such people are extremely reluctant to be highly visible. Those most successfully hiding their homelessness from relatives, employers, child protection case workers, and so on, are the least likely to be willing to establish a public presence, though their very success in staying connected to mainstream life might present the most sympathetic image of homelessness to housed people.

Collecting and mobilizing the resources necessary for political work presents a second challenge. Mounting a demonstration, for example, is extremely difficult without a permanent staff or office, telephone, copy machine to make leaflets, and so forth. Since homeless people themselves have so few resources to pool, outside support is almost always necessary for the long-term survival and efficacy of local groups.

This leads to a third dilemma, however: the relations between housed advocates and homeless activists. Advocates typically enjoy advantages of class, including finances, connections to elites, and "respectability," which can easily translate into assuming leadership positions. But since these advocates lack the actual experience of homelessness, activists generally resent their speaking for and making decisions in the name of homeless people. Activists often feel that advocates spend too much time appealing to other housed people for charity and not enough time helping organize homeless people for further empowerment. In addition, they may tend to depict homeless people in different terms, with advocates highlighting "unfortunates" while activists stress "wronged citizens."

Other divisions and disagreements also may weaken anti-homelessness groups. Some homeless people, for instance, oppose all activism, merely wishing to be left alone by activists as well as police. Others feel they are connected only to certain subsets of the greater homeless population, sometimes reproducing the basic "deserving versus undeserving poor" distinction that elites have long maintained.

Finally, groups of all compositions struggle with the question of goals: What is it they hope to achieve? Some argue that simple freedom from arrest and harassment is enough; others believe a right to emergency shelter is essential. At the other pole, some activists and advocates have argued for a basic right to housing, similar to the right to education, to which all residents of the country are entitled, as well as support services to cope with employment, education, and issues of physical and mental health.

VICTORIES AND CHALLENGES

Despite the many dilemmas involved in organizing homeless people and their housed supporters, the overwhelming lack of resources, and the challenge of simply establishing homelessness as a social issue rather than an individual problem, anti-homelessness groups have won many impressive victories in various localities over the last quarter century. Homeless people have gained the right to vote, the right to emergency shelter, the repeal of laws prohibiting "illegal" sleeping or camping, and greater access to medical, welfare, and social services. But these have largely been temporary victories, and their very local nature means they must be won and then protected over and over in each town, city, and state.

Still, organizing efforts have benefits aside from whatever collective concessions are gained. Participants often report increased feelings of efficacy and decreased feelings of self-doubt and isolation, as they experience the solidarity of political work. Thus activists may spark their own individual escape from homelessness by engaging in collective struggle.

Public and governmental support for anti-homelessness measures waxes and wanes; the pendulum moves back and forth from individual—often punitive—approaches to those that stress collective and systemic strategies. While many factors are involved in policymaking, the level of organizing by and for homeless people is clearly of central importance, as homelessness is ultimately a political issue. Lacking most of the necessities of mainstream political power—money, political connections, pure numbers—the strength of anti-homelessness organizations in the future depends in large part on the alliances they can make: alliances with other housing groups and with the larger universe of groups advocating for greater social justice.

—*Rob Rosenthal*

See also International Union of Tenants; National Alliance to End Homelessness; National Coalition for the Homeless; Washington, D.C.

Further Reading
Barak, G. (1991). *Gimme shelter.* New York: Praeger.
Blau, J. (1992). *The visible poor: Homelessness in the United States.* New York: Oxford University Press.
Baumohl, J. (1996). *Homelessness in America.* Phoenix, AZ: Oryx Press.
Cress, D., & Snow, D. (1996). Mobilization at the margins. *American Sociological Review, 61,* 1089–1109.
Dubofsky, M. (2000). *We shall be all: A history of the Industrial Workers of the World.* Urbana: University of Illinois Press.
Foscarinis, M. (1991). The politics of homelessness. *American Psychologist, 46,* 1232–1238.
Hombs, M. (1992, Summer). Reversals of fortune. *New Formations,* 109–125.
Hombs, M. E., & Snyder, M. (1983). *Homelessness in America.* Washington, DC: Community for Creative Non-Violence.
Katz, M. (1989). *The undeserving poor: From the war on poverty to the war on welfare.* New York: Pantheon.
Miller, H. (1991). *On the fringe.* Lexington, MA: D.C. Heath.
Piven, F. F., & Cloward, R. A. (1977). *Poor people's movements: Why they succeed, how they fail.* New York: Pantheon.
Rosenthal, R. (1994). *Homeless in paradise: A map of the terrain.* Philadelphia: Temple University Press.
Rosenthal, R. (1996). Dilemmas of local antihomelessness movements. In J. Baumohl (Ed.), *Homelessness in America.* Phoenix, AZ: Oryx Press.
Wagner, D. (1993). *Checkerboard square: Culture and resistance in a homeless community.* Boulder, CO: Westview Press.
Wagner, D., & Cohen, M. B. (1991). The power of the people. *Social Problems, 38,* 543–561.

Wright, T. (1997). *Out of place.* Albany: State University of New York Press.

Yeich, S. (1994). *The politics of ending homelessness.* Lanham, MD: University Press of America.

▣ HOMELESS POPULATIONS

See African-Americans; Children; Epidemiology; Families; Homelessness, Definitions and Estimates of; Homelessness, Patterns of; Homelessness, Rural; Homelessness, Suburban; Latino(a)s; Older Homeless Persons; Street Youth; Veterans; Women; Youth, Homeless

▣ HOMELESSNESS, COURSE OF

Many of the early "first-generation" studies on homelessness—cross-sectional studies seeking a better descriptive sense of who the contemporary homeless are, what their needs are, and whether those needs are being met—collected data on history of homelessness but did so only with regard to current episodes of homelessness. Homeless respondents, in other words, were simply asked how long they had been homeless. The implicit assumption seemed to be that homelessness is something into which individuals fall and remain.

As researchers learned to ask more pointed questions about homelessness history, however, they realized that homelessness is not a chronic condition for the majority of those referred to as "homeless." Rather, it is a dynamic state that individuals enter, exit, and then often reenter repeatedly over time. This finding prompted the realization that in addition to understanding why people become homeless in the first place, we must understand what is now commonly referred to as the "course" of homelessness—the process by which homeless people exit and reenter homelessness over time.

In response, a "second-generation" set of prospective, or longitudinal, studies took on the considerable challenge of tracking samples of homeless individuals in order to better understand movement out of, and back into, homelessness. Some of these studies focused on community-based probability samples of homeless adults. Others relied on comprehensive administrative databases that documented stays in municipal shelter systems. Still others addressed this issue in the process of evaluating interventions designed to end homelessness.

As a result, a growing literature exists on the extent to which people move into and out of homelessness, the factors that determine who eventually exits from homelessness, and the factors that distinguish successful from unsuccessful exits.

CROSS-SECTIONAL STUDIES: THE EARLY EVIDENCE

Most of the studies of homelessness that began emerging in the mid-1980s were cross-sectional in nature. These studies drew samples of homeless individuals at one point in time and interviewed them to determine their demographic and diagnostic characteristics and their life circumstances. With regard to homelessness itself, questions tended to focus on the amount of time individuals reported being homeless, usually in simplistic ways that obscured as much as they revealed. In some cases, questions were posed only in terms of an individual's current episode of homelessness, ignoring the possibility that there may have been past episodes. In other cases, the question of duration was posed without reference to time frame, leaving it unclear whether the answer pertained to lifetime homelessness or current homelessness. More often than not, the question of how long the individual had been homeless was asked without precisely defining for the individual what an entry into homelessness, or an exit from homelessness, actually was. Given this confusion, people often had difficulty interpreting the results.

With time, more precisely worded questions—and more precise data—emerged. These data suggested that recurrent homelessness is in fact a common experience among cross-sectional samples of homeless individuals. For example, in the Los Angeles Skid Row Study, conducted by Paul Koegel, Audrey Burnam, and Rodger Farr between 1984 and 1986 (reported in Burnam and Koegel

1988) an extensive set of questions on homelessness history was asked. It yielded information not only on the current episode of homelessness but also on the extent to which people had moved into and out of homelessness since their first entry into homelessness. In this study, respondents were asked when they first became homeless, "homelessness" being defined as not regularly sleeping in a room, apartment, or house of their own but instead sleeping in shelters, the streets, or other places not meant for sleeping. They were then asked whether, since that time, they had ever lived in their own room, apartment, or house for a month or more and whether, since their first episode of homelessness, they had ever lived with family or friends for a month or more. Those individuals who responded affirmatively were then asked when they had last done so.

The answers to these questions made it possible to determine not only the precisely defined length of a respondent's current episode of homelessness but also how many times a respondent had experienced homelessness since first becoming homeless. The results were surprising. The vast majority—two-thirds—had experienced multiple episodes of homelessness during the course of their adult lives. Indeed, slightly more than one-quarter (26 percent) had experienced six or more such episodes. Clearly, homelessness was not a one-time phenomenon for most of these people.

By crossing the number of times respondents had been homeless by the length of respondents' current episode, it was also possible to use these data to begin understanding patterns of homelessness. Doing so made it clear that "newly" homeless individuals—people who were experiencing a relatively short-lived first episode of homelessness—were a distinct minority: Only 13 percent of the sample were in a first episode of homelessness lasting less than six months, a figure that rose to only 18 percent if the definition was stretched to include those in a first episode lasting less than a year. By the same token, those who had fallen into homelessness once and remained there for long periods of time were a small minority as well: Only 10 percent were experiencing first episodes of homelessness lasting more

than two years, a figure that climbed to 15 percent if the definition was stretched to first episode of homelessness lasting more than one year. Again, multiple episodes were the rule. Homelessness, it was becoming clear, is not so much an event as a process.

The Los Angeles Skid Row Study, of course, focused on a restricted geographic area in which almost the entire local homeless population consisted of unattached homeless men, raising questions about generalizability. The patterns revealed by this study, however, were confirmed by findings from other locales as well, although their intensity proved to be more closely associated with the single adults who dominated the Los Angeles Skid Row sample than with adults who had children in their care. The 1996 National Survey of Homeless Assistance Providers and Clients (NSHAPC), conducted by Martha Burt and colleagues of the Urban Institute, provides the clearest evidence of this. The NSHAPC study drew a nationally representative sample of homeless people from a broad range of homeless assistance programs, including not only shelters, vouchers, and housing programs, but also meal, mental health, substance abuse, medical, outreach, and drop-in programs. In this sample, single men were still the modal (largest) group (61 percent), but single women (15 percent), women with their own children in their care (12 percent), men with children in their care (2 percent), and a remaining group of men and women attached to others in a myriad of ways (10 percent) were also represented.

In findings that were remarkably similar to those for Los Angeles, only 13 percent of the single men and 15 percent of the single women in this national sample were in a first episode of homelessness that had lasted six months or less. The experience of people who were homeless with their children was quite different, however. Fully 50 percent of the adult men in homeless families and 30 percent of the women in homeless families were in a first episode of homelessness lasting six months or less, providing a vivid reminder of the fact that the experience of homeless families is often different. Even so, approximately half of the singles and adults in homeless families alike had experienced multiple homeless episodes during the course of their lives, suggesting again that homelessness is a dynamic phenomenon and that understanding transitions between being homeless and being housed is critically important.

Because the studies from which these understandings were emerging relied on point-in-time samples, they likely overrepresented people with long-term and multiple episodes of homelessness relative to those who experience brief episodes of homelessness and never become homeless again. We know that those who are homeless at one point in time are only a fraction of those who experience homelessness during longer periods of time. Bruce Link and colleagues, for instance, determined that 3.1 percent of a random sample of households across the nation with telephones—a total of 5.7 million people—had experienced homelessness (living in a shelter or in public spaces) during the previous five years, a number that is significantly higher than the (one-week) national estimate of 508,300 reported by Martha Burt and Barbara Cohen in 1987. Similarly, Dennis Culhane and colleagues found that although the estimated size of the homeless populations in New York and Philadelphia on a given night was between 0.2 and 0.3 percent of each city's population, the number of different shelter users during a single year was approximately 1 percent of each city's population, whereas the three-to-five-year rates increased to 2.8–3.2 percent. This high turnover in the homeless population over time suggested that a significant number of people exit homelessness and do not return. Even so, the recurrent nature of homelessness among a significant segment of the homeless population remained a startling fact that warranted further attention.

Cross-sectional studies, then, pointed to an issue that needed exploring. They were also the basis for the first attempts to systematically address the factors that were affecting course of homelessness. These attempts involved comparing currently homeless individuals with similar groups who were not currently homeless on relevant characteristics. For instance, Michael Sosin and his colleagues utilized a cross-sectional design to identify predictors of homeless transitions by retrospectively examining the experience of 535 randomly sampled persons in

Chicago who were using free meal services. Approximately one-third (34 percent) had never been homeless, 34 percent were currently homeless, and 32 percent had previously been homeless but were currently housed. Domiciled, never-homeless individuals were compared to the first-time homeless to consider determinants of first entry into homelessness, and domiciled, previously homeless individuals were compared to repeatedly homeless individuals to understand factors associated with returns to homelessness. Comparisons between these groups suggested that variables related to social institutional factors—that is, the "safety-net" resources that potentially protect people from homelessness, such as living with others or receiving public assistance—were more closely associated with homeless transitions than were disabilities or occupational deficiencies.

Although illuminating, studies of this nature were limited in their explanatory power because cross-sectional studies, by definition, can establish only associations between variables; they cannot disentangle predictors from consequences or cause from effect. To achieve these kinds of understandings, longitudinal designs were necessary. Longitudinal studies, needless to say, are far more challenging than cross-sectional studies. The challenges faced by homelessness researchers interested in exploring homelessness over time were even greater than is usually the case given the unique circumstances in which homeless people lead their lives.

THE CHALLENGES OF CONDUCTING LONGITUDINAL RESEARCH

Of the many challenges confronted by those researchers interested in course of homelessness, three stand out as particularly noteworthy: (1) arriving at the optimal design; (2) appropriately defining the phenomena at hand; and (3) successfully tracking homeless people over time.

The optimal design for a study of course of homelessness would begin with a sample of individuals who are "at risk" for but have never experienced homelessness and would follow the individuals for a long time to determine who becomes homeless and what happens to them after they do. The idea would be to follow people long enough for the universe of patterns of homelessness to emerge. Such a design would make it possible to establish rates of and predictors of first entry into homelessness, suggesting critical points of early intervention. Even further, assuming the baseline sample was large enough and people were followed long enough, it would ultimately produce unbiased rates and predictors of the different ways in which homelessness unfolds over time.

Unfortunately, such a design was not a viable option for researchers who, in the late 1980s, were contemplating how to study course of homelessness longitudinally—and probably this design isn't an option today. To begin with, too little was known about the prehomeless backgrounds and communities of homeless individuals to design an efficient yet representative sample of those "at risk" for homelessness. Moreover, even if such information were available, homelessness is probably a rare enough event that baseline samples would have to be extremely large and follow-up periods extremely long for researchers to have enough first entries into homelessness to support an analysis of determinants. The sample would have to be even larger and followed for even longer periods of time to analyze transitions out of and back into homelessness. As a result, studies that began with a baseline sample of at-risk individuals—even if it were possible to conduct them—would be both prohibitively expensive and slow to produce findings capable of addressing what was an immediate policy need.

Recognizing these problems, researchers interested in course of homelessness instead chose as their starting point samples of individuals who were already experiencing homelessness. They knew that such a design would not allow examination of first entry into homelessness but reasoned that following samples of homeless individuals prospectively would at least allow researchers to identify predictors of exits from and reentries into homelessness and to understand what distinguishes successful from unsuccessful exits. In some cases (for example, in studies of homelessness transitions in Minneapolis, Minnesota, and Alameda County, California), researchers

attempted to focus exclusively on samples of newly homeless individuals in order to eliminate the bias introduced by what is referred to as "lefthand censoring." This refers to the fact that when you draw a sample of homeless adults, you capture the adults while they are in the midst of homeless episodes of varying durations, so that they are not all beginning at an equivalent "starting gate." Such studies ultimately discovered that identifying newly homeless individuals within a short enough time period was difficult, and researchers ended up supplementing their "recent arrivals" with a cross-section of homeless adults. Other studies, such as the Course of Homelessness Study in Los Angeles, intentionally focused not only on newly homeless individuals but also on individuals at later stages of their homeless careers in an attempt to estimate what might be found if newly homeless individuals were followed for longer periods of time.

Ultimately, then, community-based studies that were explicitly designed to examine course of homelessness relied on designs that involved following baseline samples of currently homeless adults over time. Admittedly, this alternative sacrificed information on first entry into homelessness and introduced biases associated with using cross-sectional comparisons of "slices" of the homeless population (e.g., the new versus the experienced homeless) to inform individual changes over time. Nevertheless, the longitudinal nature of these "second-generation" designs represented an important advance over the "first-generation" cross-sectional studies that were the norm during the first half of the 1980s. This was equally true of the longitudinal designs, typically associated with Dennis Culhane, that relied exclusively on the analysis of large municipal shelter system administrative databases to understand the movement of homeless people into and out of shelter and of the service demonstrations and evaluations that followed homeless people over time to understand the impact of innovative interventions.

A second challenge faced by researchers interested in course of homelessness prospectively in community-based samples was how to define exits from homelessness. Defining homelessness itself was a straightforward matter. Virtually all researchers agreed that a person is homeless if he or she spends at least one night in a temporary dwelling designated for homeless individuals or in any number of places not meant for sleeping (although there was often disagreement on how to handle doubling up with family and friends and long-term but temporary stays in housing programs). Defining exits was more complicated. For instance, should an individual be counted as exiting homelessness if he or she spends a week in a hotel? Does it matter whether the person pays for the hotel or whether it is paid for with a voucher received by a community-based organization? What about stays in board-and-care facilities? What about jails or hospitals? What about a long stay in the home of family or friends? Does it matter whether the individual is contributing to the rent?

With time it became clear that researchers had to consider two dimensions in defining homelessness exits. The first of these dimensions pertains to the *type* of place to which a person is exiting. Some places unequivocally connote an exit from homelessness, such as when someone who is homeless obtains a room, apartment, or house that he or she owns or pays rent for. These exits have been referred to as "independent" exits. Other exits clearly involve changes in homelessness status that are less closely associated with what we think of as a "home," such as doubling up with family or friends, living in voucher-paid housing, living permanently in lodging facilities for which pay is not expected, or staying in institutions such as hospitals or jails. These exits have been referred to as "dependent" exits.

The second relevant dimension is *duration*—the length of time someone has to *remain* in an exit category before researchers can say that an exit has taken place. The first longitudinal study of homelessness, conducted in Minneapolis by Michael Sosin, Irving Piliavin, and Herb Westerfelt, set a minimum threshold of fourteen consecutive days. This was rejected by most researchers as too lenient, especially given that during a given month, many homeless people—especially those who receive some kind of public assistance—find housing for as long as two or three weeks at a time but regularly find themselves homeless when their monthly income runs out before the months does.

Researchers eventually arrived at thirty consecutive days in housing as the most common threshold, although at least one study, seeking to be sensitive to the idea that even thirty-day exits may be too shallow to be real, also looked at a ninety-day threshold.

Crossing these two dimensions—type and duration—yields a wide variety of homelessness exit definitions. For instance, one can define an exit from homelessness as thirty consecutive days in independent exit settings, or thirty consecutive days in dependent exit settings, or thirty consecutive days in either of the preceding. Similarly, one can look at the same categories but defined on the basis of sixty or ninety, rather than thirty, consecutive days. Each of these definitions is defensible depending on what the researcher is trying to explain. In practice, most community-based studies of course of homelessness have selected thirty-day independent exits as their definition of exit from homelessness, although substantial variation exists and must be attended to in interpreting results. Similarly, longitudinal studies relying on municipal shelter system databases have used departure from the system for thirty days as their primary exit criterion. Alternatively, evaluations of innovative services aimed at ending homelessness have often relied on a continuous measure of days homeless after the intervention as a measure of program success.

Researchers who follow people over time traditionally rely on the anchors that tie people to a particular place—their addresses, phone numbers, and workplaces—and, even so, struggle mightily to track people successfully. Homeless people, almost by definition, lack these anchors and thus present a challenge that goes well beyond the traditional one. Indeed, the extent of this challenge was reflected in the substantial rates of attrition that characterized early attempts to follow homeless people. More than 40 percent of the baseline sample was lost to follow-up in the Minneapolis study during a six-month period, for instance. Similar proportions were lost to follow-up in early longitudinal studies of homeless people in St. Louis and Baltimore as well. Such levels of attrition are generally viewed as unacceptable because of the potential bias they introduce. This bias stems from the possibility that those lost to follow-up may differ from those who have been retained in ways that haven't been measured and accounted for.

More recent longitudinal studies of homeless samples have achieved significantly higher retention rates. For instance, in the Alameda County and Course of Homelessness studies, 85 percent and 87 percent of those interviewed at baseline were successfully recontacted at least once. Likewise, in a longitudinal study of homeless persons with alcohol and other drug problems conducted in New Orleans, at least one follow-up interview was completed with 93 percent of the sample during a twelve-month period.

These improvements are the outcome of a series of innovative techniques and strategies that was developed simultaneously and independently by a number of research teams. Basically, researchers learned that to successfully recontact homeless individuals, researchers had to (1) collect the right information from respondents at baseline, (2) make sure that respondents are given meaningful incentives to remain in contact and that doing so is as easy for them as possible, and (3) be ready to use a myriad of tracking strategies to find people if they fail to keep in touch. Each of these issues is worth talking about in greater detail.

The first steps toward achieving successful follow-up occur at the end of the baseline interview. Successful researchers have learned to collect detailed recontact information. This means learning as much as possible about the daily, weekly, and monthly cycles of individuals in their samples so that researchers can determine the people, places, and institutions with which respondents periodically interact that might know about their whereabouts. This also means recording as much contact information on these collaterals as possible—and confirming that this information is accurate. This also means learning about aliases and nicknames, the multiple Social Security numbers under which individuals might be known, and their distinguishing physical characteristics. Successful researchers have taken photographs of subjects (with their permission) and have made sure that subjects sign consent-to-be-tracked forms that can be used later to reassure collaterals who are asked for help in finding the subjects.

Researchers also learned that they must make it as easy as possible for subjects in longitudinal samples themselves to initiate contact at the appropriate time so that tracking resources can be channeled toward those not able or willing to take on this responsibility. Along these lines, recontact or calendar cards are provided to research subjects to remind them when they are supposed to be back in touch. Cash and other incentives, which are generally available at each follow-up interview, are increased for those subjects who initiate contact at the appropriate time so that subject initiative is rewarded. Incentives are similarly available for those who touch base between interviews to update contact information. Researchers set up field offices and/or toll-free, twenty-four-hour phone lines so that subjects can do this as easily as possible. Research participants are recontacted immediately after baseline to solidify the relationship and to enhance the rapport between interviewer and participants. Indeed, rapport is often nurtured as another incentive that motivates participants to continue staying in touch with researchers.

Despite these efforts, a substantial number of participants will not make contact at the time of their follow-up interview and will have to be more aggressively tracked. Successful studies have used a combination of phone tracking, mail follow-up, agency and systems-level tracking, and field-level tracking, usually pursuing each of these strategies simultaneously. Systems-level tracking, for instance, may involve searching shelter records, calling jail and prison information numbers, obtaining state-level Criminal Information and Investigation Reports, having the Social Security Administration forward mail, checking Department of Motor Vehicles Records, linking into the Veterans' Administration record system, and using other agency-related strategies. Field-level tracking may mean making frequent visits to local places where a missing person is known to hang out, sitting in the local welfare or assistance office and listening to names being announced, staking out local check-cashing businesses at the beginning of the month, or, as reported by Wright and his colleagues, posting flyers "which are printed on obnoxiously colorful paper so as to be impossible to miss" (Wright, Allen, and Devine 1995, 273). Effective organization of interview staff can be critical as well. As part of the Course of Homelessness Study, for instance, interviewers were regularly given time to peruse a "lost list" and the study's "Family Album," which included photographs of all participants. Interviewers were organized into teams who were given collective responsibility for missing individuals. A "Most Wanted" incentive program was initiated to provide rewards to interviewers who were successful in finding hard-to-reach people. Those interviewers who exhibited a flair for successful sleuthing were designated "Re-Contact Experts" and assigned to follow-up tracking full-time.

Studies that have followed homeless people over time tend to endorse what Wright and colleagues refer to as the "90–10 rule": It takes 10 percent of the time to accomplish 90 percent of the work, and the remaining 90 percent of the time to accomplish the remaining 10 percent of the work. Although that rule may often be more of an 80–20 rule, or even a 70–30 rule, the point is an important one. Easily implemented strategies will account for the vast majority of recontact success. However, the difference between marginally acceptable retention rates and exemplary retention rates will likely be related to a study's willingness to engage in any number of additional labor-intensive efforts. Each of these may yield only a smattering of successful recontacts. Experience has proven, however, that collectively they make a critical difference.

WHAT WE KNOW ABOUT COURSE OF HOMELESSNESS FROM LONGITUDINAL STUDIES

As indicated earlier, three types of longitudinal studies inform issues related to course of homelessness. These are (1) community-based panel studies that have followed and reinterviewed baseline samples of homeless people over time, (2) studies that rely entirely on large municipal shelter system administrative databases to trace the movement of people into and out of shelters, and (3) experimen-

tal evaluations of innovative service programs for homeless adults.

Community-based panel studies are probably our best source of information on course of homelessness because their reliance upon probability samples of community-based homeless adults ensures broad representation and because they have focused explicitly on collecting data that can inform homeless/domicile transitions. These panel studies generally tell a similar story—a story that carries both good and bad news. The good news is that among samples of homeless adults followed over time, the vast majority of them get out of homelessness. The actual percentage of those who exit, of course, is in part a function of how *exit* is defined. For instance, in the Course of Homelessness Study, 72 percent exited homelessness during a fourteen-month period using the least conservative definition of *exit*—a thirty-day exit in either a place the person paid for (independent exit) or other arrangements, including doubling up, staying in institutions, and so forth (dependent exit). That figure falls to 52 percent if the definition is thirty days in an independent exit setting only, to 51 percent if the definition is ninety consecutive days in either independent or dependent exit settings, and 30 percent if the definition is ninety days in an independent exit setting only. Exit rates also differ by subpopulations. For instance, in the Alameda County study, 94 percent of women with children exited within a year (defined as at least thirty days, excluding institutional stays), whereas 82 percent of women without children in their care and 65 percent of men exited. Still, the general pattern is the same: Substantial numbers of homeless people exit from homelessness within relatively short periods of time.

The bad news is that most of these individuals fall back into homelessness within those same time periods. For example, in the Course of Homelessness sample, more than three-quarters of the 72 percent who experienced a thirty-day exit to either independent or dependent exit settings experienced homelessness again; two-thirds of the 30 percent who experienced at least ninety consecutive days of housing for which they paid fell back into homelessness again. (Clearly, type of exit affects likelihood of return, a fact that emerges from the Alameda County study as well.) Moreover, multiple cycles of exiting and reentering were not unusual: More than half of those persons with thirty-day exits and approximately one-quarter of those with ninety-day exits experienced two or more exits during the fourteen-month follow-up period. Again, differences were quite apparent with regard to subgroups. More than half of the women without children in their care and more than two-thirds of the men who exited homelessness in the Alameda County study transitioned back into homelessness during the time they were followed, although only one-third of the women with children in their care did so. Still, the general trend is the same. Particularly among single homeless adults, exits are shallow for most people, making the typical pattern of homelessness, as Sosin and colleagues have pointed out, "one of *residential instability, rather than constant homelessness over a long period*" (Sosin, Piliavin, and Westerfelt 1990, 171). Moreover, what appears to drive that residential instability, based on multivariate (considering multiple variables simultaneously) analyses of predictors of exit and reentry, is not the individual deficits that people may have (such as psychiatric disorders or substance abuse problems) but rather the institutional and economic resources available to them (such as formal or informal income support or subsidized housing).

The Alameda County data show that homeless families appear to differ significantly from single people in their movement into and out of homelessness. This fact is even more apparent in a study of homeless families in New York City that was conducted by Beth Shinn, Beth Weitzman, and colleagues. This study interviewed a sample of families as they were requesting shelter for the first time and then reinterviewed them approximately five years later. Among the 256 families who actually entered a shelter, 79 percent were housed in their own apartments five years later, and another 17 percent were living with family or friends. Only 4 percent were in a shelter. Receipt of subsidized housing proved to be the best—and virtually only—predictor of who was in their own housing. Controlling for all other factors, those who received subsidized housing at some

point between time 1 and time 2 were twenty-one times more likely to be housed in their own places than were those who hadn't. (Receiving subsidized housing was not confounded with individual characteristics, eliminating the hypothesis that factors affecting selection into subsidized housing are responsible for this finding.) Closer analysis of these data suggested that 96 percent of families who left a shelter with subsidized housing were housed in their own apartments at time 2; only 15 percent had returned to a shelter at any point, usually because of serious building problems or safety issues related to their housing. Alternatively, 71 percent of the families who went into unsubsidized housing situations were in their own place at time 2; 43 percent had returned to a shelter at some point during the interim between time 1 and time 2. These findings point to the critical contribution of subsidized housing, foreshadowing the findings from service demonstrations, discussed later.

Several studies have taken advantage of the comprehensive administrative databases that document stays in New York's and Philadelphia's large, centralized municipal shelter systems to try to understand residential transitions among homeless adults. Dennis Culhane and Randall Kuhn, for instance, used these databases to examine shelter utilization first among homeless single adults over time and then, along with Yin-Ling Irene Wong, among family shelter users. Tracking people through administrative data confers many advantages. These advantages include the large numbers of people captured, the ability to focus on new entries and to deal with both left (see above) and right (ending data collection before an episode has played itself out) censoring, the actual documentation of stays (thus avoiding the need to rely retrospectively on self-report and all the bias associated with this), and the ability to avoid underrepresenting short-term stays. The disadvantages, of course, are that information on periods of homelessness outside of the public shelter system are not captured and that specific information on potential predictors of interest may not be available. Overall, such studies are best suited to understanding the dynamics of shelter utilization per se, rather than homelessness more generally, and speak more specifically to policy issues related to shelter administration.

In general, the findings of these studies parallel those of panel studies. All of the index cases (those tracked over time) in each of these studies exited the shelter system within a two-year period, but substantial numbers returned. Again, recidivism (relapse) was much higher among single males (50 percent) and single females (33 percent) and lowest among adults with children in their care (22 percent). Interestingly, among the single adults, short-term use of the shelter system was the rule. The majority of single men (55 percent) and single women (65 percent) had only one episode of shelter use during a two-year period. Moreover, even when all shelter stays were combined, half of these adults spent fewer than forty-five days in a shelter. For many, then, shelter stays represented a short-term transition. On the other hand, a smaller group of adults made significant use of the shelter system—18 percent of users accounted for 53 percent of the shelter usage during that two-year period—suggesting a critical target group for intervention. A host of demographic and personal deficit variables were associated with probability of exit, but no resource utilization variables were available for inclusion in the multivariate analyses of predictors. Findings from the family shelter study were somewhat more complex but paralleled the findings from panel studies in that exiting to subsidized housing was clearly linked with a lower rate of readmission to the family shelter system.

Panel and shelter studies provide a window into what happens to homeless people in naturally occurring situations—people who are receiving what might be referred to as "usual care." A growing literature has also documented the extremely positive impact of subsidized and supportive housing interventions on subsequent course of homelessness. Debra Rog and Scott Holupka recently reviewed this literature, focusing not only on single-site studies but also on large-scale, multisite supportive housing initiatives such as the Robert Wood Johnson (RWJ)/HUD Homeless Families Program and the McKinney-supported studies of housing and services for seriously mentally ill homeless adults. Several lessons emerge from these studies. First, the vast majority of homeless people placed in housing stay housed. In the McKinney demonstration projects, for instance, 78 percent of those people placed in housing were stably housed in the community twelve to eighteen months later. In the RWJ/HUD program, more than 85 percent of the homeless families who received Section 8 housing certificates (subsidies that make apartments affordable) were still in permanent housing eighteen months later. Housing by itself, however, may not always be enough. Subsidizing the cost of housing increases stability, especially where subsidies allow people to live in safer, more decent housing. Supportive services may be needed to help establish, maintain, and enhance stability. However, providing secure housing *first* is the most effective way of stabilizing homeless adults and families.

WHERE WE GO FROM HERE

Clearly, we need to learn more about who becomes homeless, patterns of homelessness over time, and the factors that predict movement into and out of homelessness. We do understand, however, that a large number of people experience homelessness and then never experience homelessness again, that homelessness is a chronic condition for a much smaller number of people, and that in between, a substantial number of people experience ongoing residential instability, moving into and out of homelessness repeatedly over time. Similarly, we understand that access to institutional resources, including the safety net meant to support economically marginal households, plays a critical role in determining which group people find themselves in. Finally, we know that proven models for successfully intervening with the full range of homeless subpopulations exist. What remains is the will to translate these understandings into broad policy initiatives that are capable of both preventing homelessness and ameliorating it when it occurs.

—*Paul Koegel*

Further Reading

Burnam, M.A., & Koegel, P. (1988). Methodology for obtaining a representative sample of homeless persons: The Los Angeles Skid Row Study. *Evaluation Review; 12*(2):117-152.

Burt, M. R. (2001). Homeless families, singles, and others: Findings from the 1996 National Survey of Homeless Assistance Providers and Clients. *Housing Policy Debate, 12*(4), 737–780.

Culhane, D. P., Dejowski, E. F., Ibanez, J., Needham, E., & Macchia, I. (1994). Public shelter admission rates in Philadelphia and New York City: The implications of turnover for sheltered population counts. *Housing Policy Debate, 5*(2), 107–140.

Culhane, D. P., & Kuhn, R. (1998). Patterns and determinants of public shelter utilization among homeless adults in New York City and Philadelphia. *Journal of Policy Analysis and Management, 17*(1), 23–43.

Dworsky, A. L., & Piliavin, I. (2000). Homeless spell exits and returns: Substantive and methodological elaborations on recent studies. *Social Service Review, 74*(2), 19–213.

Hough, R. L., Tarke, H., Renker, V., Shields, P., & Glatstein, J. (1996). Recruitment and retention of homeless mentally ill participants in research. *Journal of Consulting and Clinical Psychology, 64*(5), 881–891.

Hurlburt, M. S., Wood, P. A., & Hough, R. L. (1996). Providing independent housing for the homeless mentally ill: A novel approach to evaluating long-term longitudinal housing patterns. *Journal of Community Psychology, 24*(3), 291–310.

Link, B. G., Susser, E., Stueve, A., Phelan, J., Moore, R. E., & Struening, E. (1994). Lifetime and five-year prevalence of homelessness in the United States. *American Journal of Public Health, 84*(12), 1907–1912.

Marshall, G. N., Burnam, M. A., Koegel, P., Sullivan, G., & Benjamin, B. (1996). Objective life circumstances and life satisfaction: Results from the Course of Homelessness Study. *Journal of Health and Social Behavior, 37*(1), 44–58.

Piliavin, I., Entner, B. R., Mare, R. D., & Westerfelt, A. H. (1996). Exits from and returns to homelessness. *Social Service Review, 70*(1), 33–57.

Rog, D. J., & Holupka, C. S. (1999). Reconnecting homeless individuals and families to the community. In L. B. Fosburg & D. L. Dennis (Eds.), *Practical lessons: The 1998 National Symposium on Homelessness Research* (pp. 11.1–11.38). Washington, DC: U.S. Department of Housing and Urban Development and U.S. Department of Health and Human Services.

Rog, D. J., Holupka, C. S., & McCombs-Thornton, K. L. (1995). Implementation of the homeless families program: 1. Service models and preliminary outcomes. *American Journal of Orthopsychiatry, 65*, 502–513.

Shinn, M., Weitzman, B. C., Stojanovic, D., Knickman, J. R., Jimenez, L., Duchon, L., James, S., & Krantz, D. H. (1998). Predictors of homelessness among families in New York City: From shelter request to housing stability. *American Journal of Public Health, 88*(11), 1651–1657.

Sosin, M. R. (1992). Homeless and vulnerable meal program users: A comparison study. *Social Problems, 39*(2), 170–188.

Sosin, M., Piliavin, I., & Westerfelt, H. (1990). Toward a longitudinal analysis of homelessness. *Journal of Social Issues, 46*(4), 157–174.

Stojanovic, D., Weitzman, B. C., Shinn, M., Labay, L. E., & Williams, N. P. (1999). Tracing the path out of homelessness: The housing patterns of families after exiting shelter. *Journal of Community Psychology, 27*(2), 199–208.

Stretch, J. J., & Kruegerk, L. W. (1992). Five year cohort study of homeless families: A joint policy research venture. *Journal of Sociology and Social Welfare, 19*(4), 73–88.

Susser, E., Valencia, E., Conover, S., Felix, A., Tsai, W-Y., & Wyatt, R. J. (1997). Preventing recurrent homelessness among mentally ill men: A "critical time" intervention after discharge from a shelter. *American Journal of Public Health, 87*(2), 256–262.

Toro, P. A., Goldstein, M. S., Rowland, L. L., Bellavia, C. W., Wolfe, S. M., Thomas, D. M., & Acosta, O. (1999). Severe mental illness among homeless adults and its association with longitudinal outcomes. *Behavior Therapy, 30*, 431–452.

Weitzman, B. C., Knickman, J. R., & Shinn, M. (1990). Pathways to homeless among New York City families. *Journal of Social Issues, 46*(4), 125–140.

Wong, Y. I. (1997). Patterns of homelessness: A review of longitudinal studies. In D. P. Culhane & S. P. Hornburg (Eds.), *Understanding homelessness: New policy and research perspectives* (pp. 135–164). Washington, DC: Fannie Mae Foundation.

Wong, Y. I., Culhane, D. P., & Kuhn, R. (1997). Predictors of exit and reentry among family shelter users in New York City. *Social Service Review, 71*(3), 441–462

Wong, Y. I., & Piliavin, I. (1997). A dynamic analysis of homeless-domicile transitions. *Social Problems, 44*(3), 408–423.

Wright, J. D., Allen, T. L., & Devine, J. A. (1995). Tracking nontraditional populations in longitudinal studies. *Evaluation and Program Planning, 18*(3), 267–277.

Zlotnick, C., & Robertson, M. J. (1999). Getting off the streets: Economic resources and residential exits from homelessness. *Journal of Community Psychology, 27*(2), 209–224.

◉ HOMELESSNESS, DEFINITIONS AND ESTIMATES OF

Definitions and counts or estimates of a phenomenon are inextricably intertwined. One cannot count something—widgets, for instance—if one cannot tell whether an object is or is not a widget. In other words, the first problem that arises when trying to count "homeless people" is that defining the term is extremely difficult, both in the abstract and in the practical methods of social research. Further, definitions of a phenomenon such as homelessness usually embody one or more social purposes. They are not neutral, but rather are constructed to influence public concern and action. Thus they are "programmatic." They may be trying to make a phenomenon visible, to get it defined as a problem and therefore worthy of intervention and amelioration, or to do the opposite. They may be trying to limit, or to expand, the scope of action expected or demanded. Or they may be trying to influence the value placed on one way of life in comparison to others.

Yet definitions are essential. From the perspective of immediate action, definitions identify who is eligible to receive whatever assistance is available specifically for homeless people. From a research perspective, definitions are necessary to identify who should be counted and described. And from a policy perspective, definitions are necessary to identify who should be planned for and what types of assistance they will need. The problem is, each of these purposes may require that homelessness be defined and measured in a different way. For this reason, the most useful research methods do not rely on a single definition of homelessness, but collect enough information about housing situations to allow analysts to construct samples based on different definitions for different purposes.

This entry looks first at the rather simple definition of homelessness used to allocate federal funding and at national estimates of the size of the homeless population based on that definition. It then discusses several issues surrounding definitions of homelessness and examines the issues involved in selecting various methods for obtaining estimates of population size.

THE FEDERAL DEFINITION OF HOMELESSNESS

At present in the United States, government policy and access to particular kinds of government-supported assistance are driven by a clear but narrow definition of "literal" homelessness, which is based upon a person's sleeping arrangements. Literal homelessness is defined on a day-by-day basis and refers to sleeping either in places not meant for human habitation, in an emergency shelter or transitional housing program serving homeless people, or in emergency accommodations paid for by a voucher from a program serving homeless people. This federal definition narrows the group of people identified as homeless to a fairly small proportion of the precariously housed or unhoused population. It is meant to help providers determine whom to serve, and to help planners calculate the levels of service to provide.

1996 ESTIMATES OF THE NUMBER OF HOMELESS PERSONS

The most recent reliable source of national estimates of homelessness is the 1996 National Survey of Homeless Assistance Providers and Clients (NSHAPC). NSHAPC did not use a single definition of homelessness, but collected information that allows researchers to construct samples based on a variety of definitions.

Point-in-Time Estimates

Burt and her colleagues used NSHAPC data to develop point-in-time estimates for February and October of 1996 using the federal definition of homelessness. Their results indicated that between 444,000 (October) and 842,000 (February) people were homeless at those particular points in time and using homeless assistance services. These estimates include the children in homeless families as well as all service-using homeless adults.

Point-in-time estimates like these were the only type produced for more than a decade after homelessness was acknowledged to be a national problem in the early 1980s. However, during that period, awareness increased of the complexities of homelessness. One aspect of that complexity is the amount of movement into and out of homelessness over time, including the exit and reentry of the same people and the first entry of new households into homelessness. Making reliable estimates of period prevalence—the number of people who have experienced homelessness during a specified period of time such as one year—is much harder than taking a point-in-time count, because one needs a way to be sure that each person is counted only once.

Annual Prevalence

The first good estimates of annual prevalence were not national. Dennis Culhane and his colleagues (1994), analyzing data from the Philadelphia and New York homeless management information systems (HMISs), found that four to six times the number of people homeless on a given day passed through the shelter systems of these cities in the course of a year. Calculations for Philadelphia and New York showed that during a single year's time, these people included about 1 percent of the entire city population, and came close to or exceeded 10 percent of its poor people.

No HMIS exists on the national level that could produce annual prevalence estimates for the country as a whole. Nevertheless, as appreciation grew for the very great differences between point-in-time and annual numbers, the issue of annual estimates was important enough for Burt and her colleagues to develop a way to make projections using the February and October 1996 NSHAPC point-in-time estimates based on the federal definition of homelessness. The results: From 2,325,000 (based on October estimates) to 3,494,000 (based on February estimates) people experienced homelessness in a year's time. As large as these projections seem, they are completely in line with the documented shelter use rates in New York, Philadelphia, and a few other cities—0.9 to 1.3 percent of the entire population, and 6.3 to 9.6 percent of poor people in the United States.

ISSUES IN DEFINING HOMELESSNESS

Definitions of a phenomenon such as homelessness frequently require balancing between the two horns of a dilemma. If definitions are too inclusive, they become useless because too many people are ultimately covered and the phenomenon becomes too diffuse. With homelessness, this tendency is manifested by definitions that threaten to include the entire population of people in poverty, or everyone who is poorly housed. But if definitions are too specific, they focus too exclusively on the homelessness of the moment. They lead to policies and practices that are ameliorative but not preventive, because they do not address the larger question of desperate poverty and the pool of people at high risk for periodic bouts of literal homelessness.

During the past two decades, we have become increasingly sophisticated in our policy approaches to homelessness. We no longer can sustain the belief of the early 1980s that homelessness is an emergency situation that will go away as a national issue, and we increasingly look for ways to prevent homelessness as well as to end it for those to whom it occurs. As policy needs change, so too must we reconsider the value of definitions that were created to serve a particular policy purpose.

For instance, the federal definition of literal homelessness that served throughout the 1990s, with its emphasis on being without a bed tonight or last night, is conveniently precise from some perspectives (it is relatively easy to ascertain where a person slept on the previous night and therefore easy to use in determining whom to help). However, it is overly precise and therefore misleading from other perspectives. If people can afford to pay for a motel room three nights a week but sleep in the park for the other four, week after week, because they cannot afford a room, it seems relatively meaningless to say that they are homeless only on the nights they sleep in the park. Truly helping them would mean helping them achieve stable housing. Similarly, if someone has no stable place to stay but a relative is willing to provide housing for two or three days until space is available in a homeless shelter, it seems relatively meaningless to say that the person is housed (because he or she is sleeping in conventional housing) and therefore not eligible for the homeless service. The ultimate failure of this narrow definition is that it does not help us address the larger issues of how to end homelessness for the long term, not just for a night. It only helps people decide who should receive services at any particular time.

ISSUES IN COUNTING AND ESTIMATING HOMELESS POPULATIONS

Every number claiming to represent the size of "the homeless population" is an *estimate,* regardless of the method used to obtain it. Even when the basis of the number is a street count and enumerators know they have actually seen every person in the count, the final number is still an estimate. Enumerators will always have missed some unknown number of people and will try to compensate for those not counted in various ways. It is a rare count that, when published, does not include a statement that "there are *at least* this many homeless people" or "we doubled the number we actually interviewed to account for those we missed" (note that the decision to increase the reported count by any percentage is pure guesswork). As most counts are done at night, the odds of missing people who do not want to be found are quite high. The only numbers that are not estimates are those that claim merely to be reporting the number of people contacted—either through a survey, a street count, or a shelter-tracking database—and *not* "the size of the homeless population."

Focusing on estimates of population size, we can try to understand the various factors that make an estimate more or less likely to reflect the population adequately. These include (1) where one looks, (2) how much information one gathers to help distinguish among different housing situations, (3) when and how long one looks, and (4) whether one uses a sample or tries to make contact with everyone.

Where One Looks

If one does not go to certain places where one might expect to find homeless people, the people staying in those places will not be included in one's estimate. This is the definitional bottom line—whatever the theory, the reality of who is included in an estimate depends on where the enumerators go. Therefore the first thing that should be checked when reading reports of homeless counts is what locations the enumerators did and did not include.

For example, studies that go only to shelters miss homeless people who do not use shelters. Many local efforts to count homeless people do only shelter counts. Studies that only search downtown streets miss anyone who stays outdoors in residential areas. Very few street counts cover an entire jurisdiction, yet in some communities homeless people with specific disabilities—mental illness in particular—avoid downtown areas because they feel too vulnerable there to harassment and victimization. Along with gaining agreement on which housing circumstances should be called homelessness, the biggest challenge to obtaining good estimates is finding people who do not use shelter arrangements.

It is relatively easy to count and interview people who sleep in a residential program. The challenge is choosing which programs to include in one's study. Emergency shelters are pretty obvious. But lines are increasingly blurred around programs that offer various degrees of permanence for people coming directly from the streets. For instance, some no/low demand residences such as safe havens allow residents to stay "as long as needed" although the housing is not intended to be permanent—are the people staying in them homeless or are they in permanent housing? Some transitional housing programs put households directly into housing they can retain even after supportive services end—are these tenants homeless or in permanent housing? Every study needs to make these decisions, but different studies may decide differently, making their estimates difficult or impossible to compare.

Finding people who do not use the homeless assistance network's shelter and housing resources is even more of a challenge. Various techniques have been used, including street searches, following outreach teams, and going to feeding programs (for example, soup kitchens and mobile food vans), health care programs, and drop-in or warming centers. All these approaches require a method for assuring that a particular person is not counted more than once, since the same person may use more than one service, either on a given day or during the days the enumeration is taking place. In general, no matter how thorough, street counts will miss many homeless people because they do not want to be found or because finding them might be dangerous to the searchers. For most communities, techniques involving sampling from relevant services (including outreach) will capture higher proportions of non-shelter-using homeless people than straight street counts, especially if the counts are done at night.

Finding people who are not presently homeless but are at imminent risk is the hardest task of all, and one that cannot be done within the same study framework as most studies of homeless populations. The places one would look for the imminent risk population include institutions (psychiatric hospitals or wards, jails, and prisons) and conventional housing units. As prevention becomes an increasingly important part of systematic efforts to end homelessness, we will need better techniques for estimating the population at imminent risk, which will indicate the demand for interventions to prevent homelessness.

Clarifying Information

The more places one includes as locations to search for homeless people, the greater the odds that some of the people in those places will not be homeless now and may never have been homeless. For instance, feeding programs such as soup kitchens are excellent locations for finding non-shelter-using homeless people, but on average about half of soup kitchen users are not currently homeless. If one includes soup kitchens in one's enumeration to increase the coverage of street homeless people, one will need to collect enough information to separate the homeless users from the non-homeless users. Therefore one cannot merely count heads; one needs to obtain specific information about housing situations, at present and in the past. The more details one has about current, recent, and even long-ago housing situations, the more flexible the data will be for accommodating a variety of definitions of current or former homelessness and housing instability.

Another consequence of searching in many types of places for homeless people is that the same people are likely to have used more than one of the places. Early homeless counts attempted to deal with the problem of duplicate counting by limiting their time frame to a few hours at night, and some still do so today. The problems and inaccuracies of night count-

ing quickly became apparent, however, and led to the search for alternative approaches for assuring that people are not double and triple counted in the final estimate. Two approaches emerged—developing unique identifiers, and getting service use information from each respondent. Unique identifiers, which are most likely to be used in studies that try to capture all homeless people, allow analysts to compare identifying information from interviews or contacts with homeless people done at many locations to detect and eliminate duplication in population counts, while still retaining the information about how many people use each different service location. Service use information from respondents allows analysts to use statistical techniques to unduplicate, and it is most common in studies that use sampling rather than trying to make contact with every homeless person.

When and How Long One Looks

"Point prevalence" refers to the number of people who are homeless at a single point in time—usually one day or one night. "Period prevalence" refers to the number of people who have been homeless during some longer time period such as a month or a year.

Most efforts to enumerate homeless people cover a very short time period and produce estimates of point prevalence. They give a count and provide descriptions based on the people who are homeless on a single day or single night. There have also been some attempts to use interview data from point-in-time samples to estimate the number of people who might be homeless during the course of a year. To come close to the results of shelter-tracking databases when doing this type of projection, one needs a large, statistically valid sample that is very inclusive of sampling sites and information from respondents about the length and pattern of their homelessness. The annual estimates derived from NSHAPC, presented above, used this technique.

Two alternatives to the one-night approach provide important techniques for getting accurate estimates of population size. The first is the computerized shelter-tracking database that covers all (or most) "homeless beds" in a jurisdiction. Because each person in these databases has a unique identifier, all service episodes (for instance, nights in shelter) used by one person can be linked to that person. These databases, now known most frequently as homeless management information systems, give a jurisdiction knowledge of how many distinct individuals have used the system during any time period of interest, from one day to one year to however long the system has been operating. The Philadelphia and New York data cited earlier come from systems of this sort. It is important to remember, when using population counts from an HMIS, that the counts cover only the types of people the HMIS covers—usually emergency shelter users. In most communities, this is not the entire homeless population.

The second alternative to a one-night count is an enumeration over an extended period of time—say six to eight weeks—conducted in mainstream agencies such as welfare offices, food pantries, food stamp offices, and community action agencies as well as in programs targeted specifically to homeless people. The Kentucky Housing Corporation has used this technique twice in statewide studies to estimate population size. The mainstream agencies use two brief screening questions to identify people among their clients who may be homeless, and a brief follow-up questionnaire gathers information to construct unique identifiers as well as answer some basic questions about the homeless condition. This technique is particularly appropriate for jurisdictions with relatively sparse populations and/or relatively few homeless-specific services. Kentucky developed the approach because all but 7 of its 120 counties are rural.

Sampling or Counting

Counting seems like a straightforward process. But in fact, producing an accurate estimate of the size of the homeless population at a particular point in time from simple counting techniques is extremely difficult. Understanding the flows of people into and out of homelessness cannot be accomplished with a simple count. HMISs can provide both literal counts and descriptions of flows (assuming they contain the right data fields), but an HMIS is a very difficult thing for a community to develop, and it will rarely cover the entire homeless population.

Studies based on sampling techniques require more methodological knowledge but also give more flexibility. One need interview fewer people for the same results and can go into greater depth with them about their circumstances and conditions. One can use screening questions to make it feasible to check for homeless people in places where they may be a small minority of service users, which is useful for finding homeless people in jurisdictions without many homeless-specific programs. The Kentucky Housing Corporation survey provides an example of a simple two-question screener: (1) In what type of place are you now staying? (2) Is that your permanent place to stay? If the answer to the second question is "no" or "unsure," the interview continues on the assumption that the person is homeless. Finally, if one wants to find people at imminent risk of becoming homeless (to estimate, for instance, the likely level of need for services), sampling techniques are essential for examining overcrowded households, particular neighborhoods, and institutionalized populations that are major senders of people into literal homelessness. However, when it comes to estimating the annual prevalence of homelessness, sample-based studies are limited to projections based on what currently homeless people say about their homeless experiences.

POLICY IMPLICATIONS

No one has done a perfect enumeration of homeless people, and no one is likely to do so. Resource constraints, the slipperiness of homeless definitions, and multiple policy purposes for homeless studies make this prediction almost certain. Also contributing to the difficulty are the different sources of data for estimating the size of the homeless population and the different legitimate uses to which such numbers can be put. There is no one right number. Different types of estimates serve different purposes, and all are useful. Someone interested in service planning needs to know about the expected level of service contacts on a given day and will not care so much whether the contacts are made repeatedly by a relatively small group of people or only once each day by a very large number of different people. Someone who wants to create permanent housing for the longest-term homeless people with disabilities will need to know the actual number of such persons, not just at one point in time. And someone who wants to stop family homelessness through prevention efforts needs to know how many families might be at risk of homelessness during a particular time period and whether they need temporary crisis assistance or long-term supports to remain in their housing.

The 1980s began with only the crudest ways to estimate the level of homelessness. Throughout the decade and into the 1990s, the assessment of homelessness has become more sophisticated, both in the use of numbers for different purposes and in the ability to determine these numbers. It is critically important for those who wish to make policy or to influence it to have a very clear understanding of what they are trying to do and for whom they want to do it. It will then be much easier to identify the right number for that specific purpose. It is also important to realize that bad policy will result from using the wrong numbers or from using numbers that confuse rather than clarify the nature of the policy task.

—*Martha R. Burt*

Further Reading

Burt, M. R. (1994). Comment. *Housing Policy Debate, 5*(2), 141–152. Retrieved April 14, 2003, from http://www.fannie maefoundation.org/programs/hpd/pdf/hpd_0502_burt.pdf

Burt, M. R. (1996). Homelessness: Definitions and counts. In J. Baumohl (Ed.), *Homelessness in America.* Phoenix, AZ: Oryx Press.

Burt, M. R. (1996). *Practical methods for counting the homeless: A manual for state and local jurisdictions.* Washington, DC: Urban Institute Press.

Burt, M. R. (1999). Demographics and geography: Estimating needs. In L. Fosburg & D. Dennis (Eds.), *Practical lessons: The 1998 National Symposium on Homelessness Research.* Washington, DC: U.S. Departments of Housing and Urban Development and Health and Human Services.

Burt, M. R., Aron, L. Y., & Lee, E. (2001). *Helping America's homeless: Emergency shelter or affordable housing?* Washington, DC: Urban Institute Press.

Bylund, R. A., Rudy, D. R., & Parkansky, S. (2001). *2001 Kentucky homeless survey.* Frankfurt, KY: Institute for Regional Analysis and Public Policy, Morehead State University, and Kentucky Housing Corporation. Retrieved April 14, 2003, from http://www.kyhousing.org/Publications/resources/2001HomelessReport.pdf

Culhane, D. P., Dejowski, E., Ibañez, J., Needham, E., & Macchia, I. (1994). Public shelter admission rates in Philadelphia and New York City: Implications for sheltered population counts. *Housing Policy Debate, 5*(2), 107–140. Retrieved April 14, 2003, from http://www.fanniemaefoundation.org/programs/hpd/pdf/hpd_0502_culhane.pdf

Culhane, D. P., & Hornburg, S. P. (1997). Section I: Defining, counting and tracking the homeless. *Understanding homelessness: New policy and research perspectives.* Washington, DC: Fannie Mae Foundation.

Kentucky Housing Corporation. (1993). *Kentucky homeless survey preliminary findings.* Frankfurt, KY: Author. Retrieved April 14, 2003, from http://www.kyhousing.org/publications/resources/1993HomelessSurvey.pdf

HOMELESSNESS, INTERNATIONAL PERSPECTIVES ON

Understanding homelessness in international perspective poses a general challenge: to approach each culture from an emic point of view—that of an insider—since what one culture regards as homelessness, another may not. For example, the communal apartments of Russia may be termed *precarious* or *marginal* housing by U.S. standards, but are not considered such in Russia. Or a shelter made from found material on land to which the builder has no legal claim could be seen as part of a *squatter settlement* or a part of an emerging community.

How widely does one cast the "homeless net"? What are the numbers and characteristics of the people included in the definition of homelessness? Worldwide, the answers vary. Studies comparing homelessness in two or more nations offer a step toward an international understanding of the issue (Daly 1990; Glasser 1994; Glasser, Fournier, and Costopoulos 1999; Helvie and Kunstmann 1999). These comparisons expose factors that might not be obvious in a one-site study—factors affecting both levels of homelessness and the society's response to it.

THE TERMINOLOGY OF HOMELESSNESS

Words used to describe homeless persons offer some insight into the varying conceptualizations of the

Table 1. Cross-Cultural Conceptualizations of Homelessness

Concept	Notes	Region
Lack of shelter		
roofless		India
sin techo	"without roof"	Latin America
sans-abri	"without shade"	France; Quebec, Canada
sleeping rough		United Kingdom
without permanent address, *sans adresse fixe*	generic term	United Nations
Person who is cut off from a household or other people		
clochard	tramp	France
Pennebruder	"prison brother"	Germany
desamparado	without protection or comfort from other people	Latin America
furosha	"floating people"	Japan
puliukko	elderly male alcoholic	Finland
bomzi (acronym for *bez opredilyonogo mesta zhitelstva*)	of no fixed abode	Russia
Homeless street child		
gamino, gamina	gamin, gamine; street urchin	Colombia
pivete or *pixote*	street child involved in crime; *pixote* is from the film of that title	Brazil
khate	"ragpicker"	Kathmandu, Nepal
Squatter settlement, spontaneous settlement		
bidonville	"tin city"	Francophone Africa
pueblo jóvene	"young town"	Lima, Peru
favela	squatter settlement	Brazil
kampung	village	Indonesia

Source: Adapted from I. Glasser (1994, 6).

term, as illustrated in Table 1 above. In countries such as India, the term for people living outside without shelter is *roofless,* a term that does not imply the social pathology so often associated with the word *homeless.* Developing countries tend to discuss the issue of lack of adequate housing from the point of view of rural-to-urban migration, or as the result of natural disaster or war. For Western nations, homelessness historically has been linked to alcoholism (as seen on the skid rows of major cities, for example). In the latter part of the twentieth century, homelessness was tied to widespread substance abuse and the deinstitutionalization of the mentally ill, coupled with the gentrification of the cities and a decrease in governmental support for social housing.

In Montreal, Quebec, *les itinérants* is the term used by the religious and advocacy communities; the newspaper sold on the streets of Montreal is *L'Itinéraire.* But the word *sans-abri* (without shelter, or literally "without shade") is used in professional and academic circles. Some people have suggested that *sans-abri* came into vogue in Montreal *after* the widespread media attention to the United Nations 1987 International Year of Shelter for the Homeless (Glasser, Fournier, and Costopoulos 1999).

Elsewhere, too, terminology reflects local conditions. Street children are often referred to by the job they do for survival, such as the "parking boys" of Kenya. It is interesting to note that originally the South American Spanish term *gamino* may have implied a petite and appealing child on the street, whereas now the word has taken on negative connotations, hinting at lawlessness. The Finnish term *puliukko* indicates the close historical relationship of alcoholism and homelessness. Finally, a *bidonville* ("tin city") may become a new community (that is, a *pueblo jóven*) with infrastructure support such as clean water, waste removal, and electricity.

Another way to understand homelessness internationally is to think of homelessness as the opposite of being adequately housed. In 1987, representatives from forty countries met in Limuru, Kenya, in order to address poverty and homelessness. The conference developed a definition of adequate housing that became known as the Limuru Declaration (as cited in Turner 1988, 187):

Adequate, affordable shelter with basic services is a fundamental right of all people. Governments should respect the right of all people to shelter, free from the fear of forced eviction or removal, or the threat of their home being demolished. . . .

Adequate shelter includes not only protection from the elements, but also sources of potable water in or close to the house, provision for the removal of household and human liquid and solid wastes, site drainage, emergency life-saving services, and easy access to health care. In urban centers, a house site within easy reach of social and economic opportunities is also an integral part of an adequate shelter.

Another interesting challenge in the effort to define homelessness is raised by this question: When is "no access to a conventional dwelling" *not* homelessness? The answer appears to be: When movement from place to place is a part of the *culture* of the group. For example, pastoralists who move with their herds and have no permanent settlement, such as the Kurds of Iraq, and hunters and gatherers such as the !Kung of the Kalahari desert, would fit this description. And, some would argue, so do the year-round recreational vehicle dwellers who do not maintain permanent dwellings anywhere else (Glasser and Bridgman 1999).

To further make the point, what would prevent a group of people from *naming* their lack of a permanent home a part of their culture? For example, Susan Hutson, an anthropologist who has widely studied homelessness in Wales, documents the appearance in Wales of self-styled nomadic groups known as the New Age Travellers, young people who travel around the United Kingdom in caravans or move into abandoned buildings. Is this an appropriation of the name "Travellers," (known as gypsies in other parts of the world) or is it an accurate description of their culture? Must a group have other markers of culture, such as language and common ancestry, in order to warrant membership in a culture, or is a loosely affiliated group, such as men living on the streets, enough?

Finally, consider the populations of refugees and immigrants—forced and voluntary transnational migrants—who have long been the subject of anthropological research. Should they be included under the rubric of "homeless"? At first glance, those who lack a "homeland," as in the case of

An older homeless man squats to rest outside a café in Athens, Greece, in July 2003.

Source: Karen Christensen; used with permission.

refugees, may appear to comprise a different category than those who live in shelters and on the streets of their own country. But there is some evidence of overlap. For example, there appears to be a high proportion of refugees in the squatter camps of the Sudan. One also finds a high proportion of African immigrants squatting in the vacant HLMs in and around Paris; these *Habitations de Loyer Modérés,* or "moderate rent housing," are similar to public housing in the United States. Indeed, in some cases, being a refugee or immigrant may increase one's vulnerability to various forms of homelessness. However, one should also be aware that government officials may often claim that the homeless are "not from here" as a way to turn a blind eye even to a community's indigenous people who have become homeless.

RESPONSES TO HOMELESSNESS

The industry and inventiveness of people in various parts of the world to create their own housing out of found materials have been well documented. For example, in *The Young Towns of Lima* (1980) the British anthropologist Peter Lloyd argued that rather than being squatter settlements of despair, the self-made houses of the *sin techo* ("roofless") poor on the periphery of Lima, Peru, were in fact the beginning

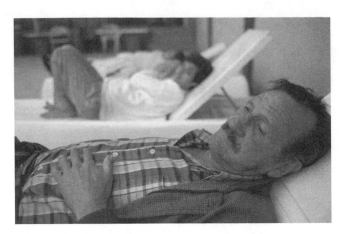

Men rest at a shelter for the homeless and mentally ill in Mexico City in 2000.
Source: David H. Wells/Corbis; used with permission.

of stable housing with the potential for vital communities, and were being called *pueblos jóvenes* ("young towns") in order to reflect that reality. Janice Perlman (1976) concluded from her research on urban poverty in the *favelas* of Rio de Janeiro that poor people, through their self-build redevelopment efforts, gave much more to the city than they took in return.

One of the greatest barriers to such self-build efforts is that residents in informal settlements do not actually own the land they build on, and therefore do not enjoy security of tenure. Many countries have instituted micro-credit financing programs—such as revolving loan programs—to assist people with gaining security of tenure, title to their lands, or economic self-sufficiency. Examples include the Self-Employed Women's Association Bank, started in 1972 in Ahmedabad, India; the Payatas Scavengers' Association Savings and Loan, begun in 1997 in Quezon City, Philippines, and the uTshani Fund, started in 1995 for members of the Homeless People's Federation, South Africa (Sheehan 2003).

The idea of self-made housing or mutual help efforts to challenge homelessness have also been tried in many North American cities, and at times, anthropologists have been involved in these efforts.

On the street, an intermediate level of service between outreach efforts and permanent shelter facilities can sometimes be found: the "daytime respite," or a place of rest and refuge for the home-

less person. In Montreal, Chez Doris is one such daytime shelter for women, where French, English, and increasingly, Inuktitut—the language of the Inuit—are all spoken. Chez Doris is a multilingual gathering spot for over sixty women a day; they come for food, clothing, baths, laundry facilities, and most of all, the companionship of the other women and the staff. The center is funded by both government and private donations, and the women who utilize Chez Doris also provide much of the labor needed to run the place. It is a low-demand, "no-questions-asked" service that accepts women who are poor, on the street, and may have psychiatric and/or substance abuse problems (Glasser and Bridgman 1999).

Another example of a "no-questions-asked" daytime respite is El Patio, a community program for street children including play, laundry services, and food in Bogotá, Colombia (Goode 1987). This program represents a first step in a series of programs that emphasize education for occupations (including the children's own current "street" livelihoods) and self-government. Such programs are often known as "street schools" in the developing world. But unlike many, El Patio does *not* emphasize reuniting children with their families, who are seen as having had to give up their children to the streets due to severe poverty. The former street children who become staff appear to be very effective and have a long-term commitment to the work.

The general rubric of "self-help housing" has been applied to many strategies that capitalize on the leadership and labor of the future residents. For example, StreetCity in Toronto was a nonprofit pilot housing project developed by the Homes First Society in direct consultation with the chronically homeless (Bridgman 1998; Canada Mortgage and Housing Corporation 1999). StreetCity occupied a vacant warehouse, and funding came from many levels of provincial, metropolitan, and municipal governments. The project grew from an idea generated by a group of homeless and formerly homeless men and hostel workers. The facility first opened in December 1988 while still under construction, and operated as a hostel dormitory with forty homeless men sleeping on the second floor. Some of the men

A Green Statement on Homelessness

Homelessness is a great issue for Greens, one on which we can clearly distinguish ourselves.

Ds and Rs are in thrall to "the market" and "economic growth" as the way to provide jobs, housing, and increased tax revenues for the government programs. Note the quotes: "the market" and "the economy" are abstractions based on statistical assumptions. Clearly, however, "the market" is dominated by individuals and corporations seeking to maximize profits; "the market" will not provide housing for people who cannot afford to pay for it. And "economic growth" is measured by GDP, which we all know is an absurd statistic that counts war, waste, crime, and disease as positive line items.

Most of what Ds and Rs propose to do about homelessness actually involves subsidies to homebuilders, real estate developers, and other corporations. Greens have to challenge them to be concrete and specific.

A lot of Greens talk about a living wage, and that's an important step. But we have to understand the problems a living wage creates for small business people, [who] fear higher payroll costs.

The one sure way to end homelessness—and an idea that is central to the economic platforms of most Green Parties in Europe—is to provide everyone with a guaranteed basic income at a subsistence level.

Basic income gives the same amount to everyone, rich and poor, employed and unemployed, as a baseline of economic justice and equality. (A progressive income tax would recover the money from those who don't really need it. That's much simpler and more efficient than any type of means-testing.)

With basic income, everyone will have enough money for food and shelter, which can be purchased through the market. It will no longer be necessary for government to create jobs or provide food or housing; such programs can be cut, the money used to pay for the basic income. Everyone will receive the same amount, so there would not be any loss of dignity in accepting it, in contrast with welfare payments that are need-based, means-tested, or otherwise conditional. And the distribution would be extremely efficient, with no welfare bureaucracy.

Basic income is not socialism. It would preserve markets and private property. And everyone will still be free to earn as much money as one can. So we can at the same time end homelessness and eliminate the rationale for a vast range of corporate welfare subsidies.

In other words, this is a great way to show that we are Greens, neither left nor right but above and beyond both sets of conventional policies. For a more thorough presentation, visit www.citizenpolicies.org/endinghunder.html.

Source: Steven Shafarman, Citizen Policies Institute, Washington, D.C. (2003).

worked as laborers on the construction crew. This kind of incremental building, in which housing may be partially occupied while still under construction, required a relaxation of municipal and provincial building standards. Over time, StreetCity residents developed an elaborate community structure including a biweekly residents' meeting known as Town Council, with an elected mayor.

The fact that StreetCity had no curfews, that it was a coed residence, and that drugs and alcohol were not banned in the building signaled its laissez-faire approach, in direct contrast to the conventional mores of hostel provision in Canada and the United States. A second, more permanent facility was modeled after StreetCity and named Strachan House, opened in 1997.

In Montreal, mentally ill residents benefit from supportive housing through the FOHM (Fédération

des organismes sans but lucratif d'Habitation de Montréal), which is a federation of nonprofit agencies that has developed housing for vulnerable populations, including the formerly homeless. The tenants receive ongoing help in the form of time with social workers, referrals to health and social service agencies, tenant organizations, and recreational activities. These help ensure that high-risk tenants (for example, the chronically mentally ill) will succeed in *keeping* their housing. The housing is affordable—defined in Canada as costing no more than 30 percent of a person's income. A key component of supportive housing is the role of the on-site concierge, whose services are integral to the stability of the tenants' lives. Research conducted by a team from the University of Quebec in Montreal, who closely interviewed a sample of thirty-three FOHM tenants, concluded that there were significant improvements in the tenants' overall quality of life, and that the tenants expressed a high degree of satisfaction with their housing (FOHM 1997).

International responses to homelessness vary from country to country, from city to city. It is clear, however, that those initiatives that involve homeless people themselves directly in their design and implementation show the most promise for challenging the great divide that separates those who lack safe shelter from those safely housed.

—Irene Glasser and Rae Bridgman

Further Reading

Bridgman, R. (1998). A "city" within the city: A Canadian housing model for the homeless. *Open House International, 23*(1), 12–21.

Canada Mortgage and Housing Corporation. (1999). Documentation of best practices addressing homelessness. (Research report). Ottawa, Ontario, Canada: Author.

Daly, G. (1990). "Health implications of homelessness: Reports from three countries." *Journal of Sociology and Social Welfare, 27*(1), 111–125.

FOHM (La Fédération des OSBL [Organismes Sans But Lucratif] d'Habitation de Montréal). (1997). *Evaluation of social housing with community support.* Roundup paper, preliminary research results. LAREPPS-UQAM, FOHM, CLSC du Plateau Mont-Royal, HQ.

Glasser, I. (1994). *Homelessness in global perspective.* New York: G.K. Hall Reference.

Glasser, I. and Bridgman, R. (1999). *Braving the street: Anthropological perspectives on homelessness.* New York and Oxford, UK: Berghahn Books.

Glasser, I., Fournier, L., & Costopoulos, A. (1999). Homelessness in Quebec City, Quebec and Hartford, Connecticut: A cross-national and cross-cultural analysis. *Urban Anthropology and Studies of Cultural Systems and World Economic Development, 28*(2), 141–164.

Goode, J. (1987). Gaminismo: The changing nature of the street child phenomenon in Colombia. (No. 28.). Indianapolis, IN: Universities Field Staff International.

Helvie, C., & Kunstmann, W. (1999). *Homelessness in the United States, Europe, and Russia.* Westport, CT: Bergin & Garvey.

Perlman, J. (1976). *The myth of marginality: Urban poverty and politics in Rio de Janeiro.* Berkeley: University of California Press.

Sheehan, M. O. (2003). Uniting divided cities. In G. Gardner et al. [Eds.], *State of the world 2003: A Worldwatch Institute report on progress toward a sustainable society* (130–151). New York: Norton.

Turner, B., (Ed.). (1988). Building Community: A Third World Case Book. *A Summary of the Habitat International Coalition Non-Governmental Organization's Project for the International Year of Shelter for the Homeless, 1987, in association with Habitat Forum Berlin.* (Monograph.)

Turner, J. (1976). *Housing by the people: Towards autonomy in building environments.* London: Marion Boyars.

▣ HOMELESSNESS, PATTERNS OF

The homeless population in the United States and other developed nations shows a diverse range of characteristics. Although certain groups are clearly at greater risk for homelessness, all types of people can be found among the homeless population. This entry reviews the broad characteristics of homeless people in the United States, where most of the recent relevant research has been done. It considers the different pathways that lead to homelessness and reviews the life course someone follows after becoming homeless.

DEFINING HOMELESSNESS

To the casual observer, it would appear that defining homelessness would be an easy task. However, this is not the case. Different definitions are used by advocates for the homeless, policymakers, and researchers. Complicating the definition are the duration of homelessness required (should a person homeless for one night be included?), the specific quality of housing (should a person living in grossly substandard housing be included?), and crowding (should someone temporarily doubled up with family or friends be included?). Most researchers have settled these issues by studying the "literally homeless," that is, people staying in shelters for the homeless, on the streets, or in other similar settings (e.g., in abandoned buildings, in makeshift structures, or in parks). There are many other persons who are precariously housed or at imminent risk for becoming homeless. Researchers may include such persons, but will define them as a group separate from the literally homeless. Many researchers and advocates now talk about homelessness in the context of a continuum of housing that runs from the stably housed to the literally homeless, with many persons falling between these two extremes.

THE THREE MAJOR HOMELESS GROUPS

Before proceeding with any research-oriented description of the homeless, it is important to distinguish three key subgroups in the overall homeless population: *homeless families, homeless adolescents,* and *homeless single adults.* These three subgroups are generally distinct on many dimensions, including their patterns of homelessness. In most cities in the United States (as well as in other developed nations), homeless families rarely include children of age ten or over and children under age twelve are very rarely found homeless on their own. Largely distinct service systems and research literatures have developed for each of these three subgroups, and recent research has documented many of the ways they differ from each other.

Homeless families typically include a single young mother with young children (often under age five). These families end up homeless for a variety of reasons, including extreme poverty, loss of benefits, eviction, domestic violence, or their own personal problems (e.g., substance abuse). Homeless families often include multiple siblings. Unlike single homeless adults and, to some extent, homeless adolescents, homeless families are rarely found on the streets. Rather, they tend to be found in homeless shelters, often ones specially designed for families. Many can also be found temporarily doubled up with friends or family or in domestic violence shelters (these families are sometimes referred to as the "precariously housed"). Few traditional families made up of couples with their children are found among the homeless. African-Americans and some other ethnic minorities (e.g., Native Americans) are found disproportionately.

Homeless adolescents differ from homeless adults by definition because they are under age eighteen, and from homeless children in families because they are homeless on their own. Although studies on homeless youth often include young people as old as twenty-four, the legal, policy, and intervention issues are quite different for adoles-

cents under age eighteen who are homeless on their own than for those eighteen or older. A variety of terms have been used to describe homeless adolescents, including *runaways,* who have left home without parental permission, *throwaways,* who have been forced to leave home by their parents, and *street youth,* who are found on the streets. These are not mutually exclusive groups. The definition of homelessness for adolescents is necessarily different from that for homeless adults and families because minors away from home without parental permission are typically breaking the law and so must be returned to their parents except under special circumstances (e.g., when there is clear evidence that they are being abused at home). Once adolescents turn eighteen, their legal status changes dramatically. Though most homeless adolescents have spent little or no time on the streets, much of the existing research has focused on "street youth" who can be found in certain large cities (especially on the East and West Coasts). Most research has found roughly equal numbers of girls and boys among homeless adolescents, though boys are much more common among studies of street youth.

Homeless single adults are mostly male (70–80 percent), and most have a history of alcohol and/or drug abuse and/or dependence (60–80 percent). Though the mentally ill are clearly overrepresented, only about 20 to 40 percent of the overall population of homeless single adults are severely mentally ill. Severe depression is probably the most common diagnosis (20–25 percent of the overall population), with schizophrenia less common (5–15 percent) but very noticeable to the casual observer. Most homeless single adults are between eighteen and fifty (usually over 80 percent), with people over sixty quite rare (less than 5 percent). As with homeless families, African-Americans and some other ethnic groups are found in disproportionate numbers among the population of homeless single adults. In American cities with large general populations of African-Americans, this ethnic group often constitutes a majority of the homeless population (including families, adolescents, and single adults). Most of the existing research on homelessness has been done on single adults.

SOME OTHER CHARACTERISTICS OF HOMELESS PEOPLE

While many women and adolescents from middle-class backgrounds who are fleeing difficult environments become homeless, in all subgroups homeless people usually come from poor backgrounds and thus share many characteristics with the larger population of poor people. Violence in the homes and communities of origin of homeless people has been well documented. This is perhaps especially true for homeless women (whether single or with their children) and homeless adolescents. Despite stereotypes to the contrary, most homeless people (including single adults) are in regular contact with members of their families (though this contact obviously may not always be positive). Substance abuse (of alcohol and/or drugs) is common in both the families of origin and among the homeless people themselves. While it is easy to see how a history of substance abuse would put someone at risk for becoming homeless, it has also been suggested that, once homeless, some persons may self-medicate to temporarily escape the hardships of being in a homeless state. This appears to be true for single homeless men, but many studies have found lower rates of substance abuse among homeless mothers and homeless adolescents. For homeless mothers, these lower rates could be either a result of the time and effort they need to care for their children or the consequence of underreporting due to the fears of having children removed by authorities (substance abuse and child abuse or neglect are often associated in the eyes of child protection workers). For homeless teens, the lower rates could be due either to having less access to alcohol and drugs or to being young and not having yet developed entrenched patterns of substance abuse. Many believe criminal behavior to be very common among the homeless. However, even among homeless young adults, only about one-quarter to one-third have a serious criminal history (felony conviction). It is also important to note that many homeless people get arrested for victimless crimes due to their homeless lifestyle (e.g., through panhandling, public drunkenness, or squatting in abandoned buildings).

CHANGES IN HOMELESSNESS OVER TIME

If we look solely at media coverage of homelessness over the past several decades in the United States, it might appear that homelessness was nearly nonexistent before the 1980s, showed a sharp rise during the 1980s, and then dropped or leveled off in the 1990s. However, it is not clear whether there was a significant rise in homelessness during the 1980s or just a rise in media coverage of the problem (and the associated interest of politicians). Some data suggest that with the booming economy of the 1990s, there may have been a small decline in the rate of homelessness (a five-year prevalence of 3.9 percent in a national sample in 1993–1994 vs. 1.9 percent in 2001). However, even if it has declined, the rate remains very high. With the poorer economic times of the early 2000s, it is possible that homelessness may soon rise again.

Martha Burt and her colleagues (2001) examined changes in the rates of homelessness from 1987 to 1996 and concluded that there is no simple answer to whether these rates have changed. They believe that the number of people homeless and using assistance services (e.g., soup kitchens and shelters) at any one time is highly variable and greatly affected by the season, with greater service use during the winter months. Although the increased number of homeless assistance programs affects her estimates, Burt points out that the availability of assistance programs does not cause need but illuminates a level of need that already exists.

Peter Rossi, one of the early pioneers in modern research on homelessness, has often noted that today's homeless people, who began to appear in the 1980s, differ greatly from the homeless of the 1950s and 1960s (1989). Homeless people in earlier decades were often middle-aged, white male alcoholics living in the skid-row areas of American cities. The new homeless population is more diverse; it has more ethnic minorities (especially African-Americans), more women (including those homeless with their children), and more younger people (including adolescents and young adults). It is less certain whether there have been changes in the characteristics of the homeless population over the past few decades, during which time research on the topic has become common. To assess whether there were, indeed, any such changes, Ouellette and Toro conducted a needs assessment that used the same methods in the early 1990s and early 2000s to obtain representative samples of homeless adults (including those with children) in Wayne County, Michigan (which includes the city of Detroit). Compared to the sample of 249 obtained between 1992 and 1994, the 220 adults in the sample obtained between 2000 and 2002 were older, had more physical health symptoms, reported less social support and fewer significant family and friends, and were more likely to receive a diagnosis of schizophrenia (see Ouellette and Toro 2002). Perhaps during the generally good economic times that existed between the collection of these two homeless samples, those most capable of escaping homelessness did so, leaving behind those who were older and who had fewer resources to obtain employment. The erosion of access to health care services and special services for the mentally ill in the past few decades could help explain the findings on physical health and schizophrenia.

PATHWAYS INTO HOMELESSNESS

To understand the paths people take into homelessness, it is necessary to consider the broader question of what causes homelessness. Although there has been a great deal of speculation on the causes of homelessness by the media, politicians, and researchers, firm scientific data are hard to come by. However, several research methods can shed some light on the causes, even though none can provide definitive proof. The simplest method is to carefully describe large representative samples of the homeless population. This approach fails to support the notion that severe mental illness and the closing of mental hospitals over the last several decades are the main causes of the rise in homelessness that has been observed over the past few decades. With most studies finding that fewer than 40 percent of the overall homeless adult population (and even fewer homeless adolescents and adolescents in homeless families) are severely mentally ill, it is not plausible that mental illness is the major cause, though it could be a

partial cause. On the other hand, substance abuse (observed in a clear majority of homeless single adults) could be a major cause. Another method that can help understand the causes of homelessness is to compare samples of homeless people to samples of similar poor, but not homeless, people. Such studies, especially those on homeless single adults and adolescents, often find that substance abuse does, indeed, distinguish homeless people from other comparable groups. Other factors often found to distinguish the homeless population from the poor include higher levels of stress and psychological distress, more experience of domestic and community violence, and disordered backgrounds (e.g., abusive families or foster care).

Yet another way to attempt to understand the causes of homelessness is to compare the prevalence and other features of homelessness around the world. An ongoing study of several of the world's most developed nations has found some important differences, both in the prevalence of homelessness and in the public's views of homeless people. In 2,000 telephone surveys of representative samples of citizens in seven different nations, researchers found the highest lifetime rates of (prior self-reported) homelessness in the United States and the United Kingdom, the lowest rate in Germany, and intermediate rates in Belgium, France, Italy, and Canada. The amount of compassion toward the homeless expressed by citizens matched the rates, with people in Germany and some of the other nations in Europe showing the greatest compassion and people in the United States and the United Kingdom showing the least. As researchers in this study collect more data on homelessness, they hope to identify national factors, such as family structures and welfare, housing, and health care systems, that might explain the varying rates of homelessness. One cause commonly mentioned by advocates for the homeless and researchers alike is the lack of low-cost (affordable) housing. While it may well be true that certain persons are more likely to end up homeless (e.g., those with substance abuse problems), it is also true that if there is not enough affordable housing, many poor people will be forced into homelessness. As in a game of musical chairs, because there are not enough housing units ("chairs") for all the poor people ("players") at any point in time ("when the music stops"), some people will have to go without. It is often the same people who lose the game (e.g., those with substance abuse problems or mental illness).

PATHWAYS OUT OF HOMELESSNESS

The patterns of housing and homelessness among the full range of homeless people are enormously diverse. Many homeless people are homeless only for very short periods of time. Large national telephone surveys that question people on their lifetime experiences with homelessness suggest that most homeless episodes are brief. Such surveys, though they tend to exclude the currently homeless and those so poor that they cannot afford a telephone, include the full range of people who have had experience with homelessness (whereas studies of the currently homeless may include only the neediest of cases, those who show up in homeless shelters or on the streets.). Studies by Bruce Link and his group (1994) and Paul Toro and his colleagues (1997; 1999) found lifetime rates of "literal homelessness" of 6 to 8 percent among adults in the United States. Among those who have been homeless, about 40 percent report a total lifetime history of homelessness of less than a month, with about 50 percent reporting between a month and a year and only about 10 percent reporting that they had been homeless for over a year. Studies of currently homeless families and adolescents also tend to find relatively short episodes of homelessness, with many studies finding half or more of their samples homeless for a month or less (in their current episode). Of the three subgroups, homeless single adults tend to show the most extensive histories of prior homelessness and the longest episodes of homelessness. For example, in our recent studies involving large representative samples of homeless adults in Detroit and Buffalo (937 people across three separate samples), we found lifetime histories (since age sixteen) of homelessness of over a year among about 40 percent of the sample (about 80 percent had been homeless for over a month).

A number of recent longitudinal studies followed large representative samples of homeless people over time. This allowed a determination not only of how long people were homeless in the past, but also of how much homelessness they were likely to experience in the future. Whether these longitudinal studies involve single adults, adolescents, or families, one common finding is that homeless people improve in many ways over time, including the time they were homeless. For example, in two different longitudinal studies of homeless adults who were followed for eighteen months or more, our research group found that about a third of the sample appeared to have escaped homelessness, showing no more homelessness once their current episode ended. At the other end of the continuum was about another third who were "chronically homeless," that is, they were homeless for a majority of the follow-up period. The final third typically showed an episodic pattern, and often experienced one or more additional episodes of homelessness during the follow-up period (although they were not homeless a majority of the time). These same longitudinal studies of homeless adults also found improvements in reported stress levels and symptoms of psychological and physical illness.

Longitudinal studies of homeless families, such as that by Beth Shinn and her colleagues (1998), typically show that most families obtain permanent housing relatively quickly and remain in the housing for at least five years. Longitudinal studies of homeless adolescents, such as that of Toro and Goldstein (2000), typically find that most adolescents return fairly quickly to their family of origin. Nearly all (93 percent) of the initially homeless adolescents in our sample from metropolitan Detroit were no longer homeless at a 4.5-year follow-up, with many living with their parents (33 percent), others living on their own (34 percent), and still others living with friends or relatives (21 percent). At the follow-up, the initially homeless adolescents also reported significantly less conflict with their family and fewer stressful events.

The general improvements observed among homeless samples could be a result of the fact that when they were initially found, they were in a particularly difficult period of their lives and were therefore observed rebounding to a previously better level of functioning. This is, perhaps, good news, given that very large numbers of people can expect to be homeless at some point in their lives (6–8 percent of all American adults, or between 16 and 22 million people, based on the large national telephone surveys reviewed above). A variety of intervention programs have been attempted with the various subgroups of currently homeless people. One increasingly common approach, called "intensive case management," has been used effectively with the homeless mentally ill by Gary Morse and his colleagues in St. Louis (1992), with homeless street youth by Ana Mari Cauce and her colleagues in Seattle (1994), and with the full range of homeless adults (including those with their children) by Toro and his research group (1997). A related approach, called "supportive housing," makes a full range of services readily available to homeless people at the same time that housing is provided. While such intensive programs may be necessary for many multiproblem homeless people, simpler interventions can be effective for others. For example, Beth Shinn and her colleagues (1998) found that one of the best predictors of prolonged stays in permanent housing among formerly homeless families in New York City was the provision of housing subsidies to these families. Many advocates for the homeless have called for increases in the very small numbers of federal and other housing subsidies available in the United States.

A variety of approaches for preventing homelessness from occurring in the first place have recently been proposed. Crisis intervention to avert eviction among low-income people could be effective. Given that violence and family conflict are common among the families of homeless adolescents, ready access to family-oriented services, including dispute resolution, could work for this subgroup. And, obviously, strategies that create more low-income housing or reduce the cost of existing housing (e.g., through housing subsidies), especially in large urban areas, could reduce the rate of homelessness.

—Paul A. Toro and Heather C. Janisse

Note: The authors thank Carolyn J. Tompsett for comments on an earlier draft of this article.

Further Reading

Baumohl, J. (Ed.). (2003). *Homelessness in America.* Phoenix, AZ: Oryx Press.

Burt, M., Aron, L. Y., Lee, E., & Valente, J. (2001). *Helping America's homeless: Emergency shelter or affordable housing?* Washington, DC: Urban Institute Press.

Cauce, A. M., Morgan, C. J., Wagner, V., Moore, E., Sy, J., Wurzbacher, K., Weeden, K., Tomlin, S., & Blanchard, T. (1994). Effectiveness of intensive case management for homeless adolescents: Results of a 3-month follow-up. *Journal of Emotional and Behavioral Disorders, 2,* 219–227.

Fosburg, L. B., & Dennis, D. L. (Eds.). (1999). *Practical lessons: The 1998 National Symposium on Homelessness Research* (pp. 3–32). Washington DC: U.S. Department of Housing and Urban Development and U.S. Department of Health and Human Services.

Jones, J. M., Levine, I. S., & Rosenberg, A. (Eds.). (1991). Special issue on homelessness. *American Psychologist, 46,* 1109–1111.

Link, B. G., Susser, E., Stueve, A., Phelan, J., Moore, R., Struening, E., & Colten, M. E. (1994). Lifetime and five-year prevalence of homelessness in the United States. *American Journal of Public Health, 84,* 1907–1912.

Morse, G., Calsyn, R. J., Allen, G., Tempelhoff, B., & Smith, R. (1992). Experimental comparison of the effects of three treatment programs for homeless mentally ill people. *Hospital and Community Psychiatry, 43,* 1005–1010.

Ouellette, N., & Toro, P. A. (2002, November). *Have the needs of the homeless changed over the past decade? An empirical assessment.* Retrieved July 9, 2003, from http://sun.science.wayne.edu/~ptoro/

Ringwalt, C. L., Greene, J. M., Robertson, M., & McPheeters, M. (1998). The prevalence of homelessness among adolescents in the United States. *American Journal of Public Health, 88,* 1325–1329.

Rossi, P. H. (1989). *Down and out in America: The origins of homelessness.* Chicago: University of Chicago Press.

Shinn, M. (1992). Homelessness: What is a psychologist to do? *American Journal of Community Psychology, 20,* 1–24.

Shinn, M., & Weitzman, B. C. (Eds.). (1990). Urban homelessness. *Journal of Social Issues, 46*(4).

Shinn, M., Weitzman, B. C., Stojanovic, D., Knickman, J. R., Jimenez, L., Duchon, L., James, S., & Krantz, D. H. (1998). Predictors of homelessness among families in New York City: From shelter request to housing stability. *American Journal of Public Health, 88,* 1651–1657.

Tompsett, C. J., Toro, P. A., Guzicki, M., Schlienz, N., Blume, M., & Lombardo, S. (2003). Homelessness in the United States and Germany: A cross-cultural analysis. *Journal of Community and Applied Social Psychology, 13,* 240–257.

Toro, P. A. (1998). Homelessness. In A. S. Bellack & M. Hersen (Eds.), *Comprehensive clinical psychology* (Vol. 9; pp. 119–135). New York: Pergamon.

Toro, P.A. (Ed.). (1999). Special issue on homelessness. *Journal of Community Psychology, 27,* 157–178.

Toro, P. A., Goldstein, M. S., Rowland, L. L., Bellavia, C. W.,

Wolfe, S. M., Thomas, D. M., & Acosta, O. (1999). Severe mental illness among homeless adults and its association with longitudinal outcomes. *Behavior Therapy, 30,* 431–452.

Toro, P. A., & Goldstein, M. S. (2000, August). *Outcomes among homeless and matched housed adolescents: A longitudinal comparison.* Retrieved July 9, 2003 from http://sun.science.wayne.edu/~ptoro/

Toro, P. A., Passero Rabideau, J. M., Bellavia, C. W., Daeschler, C. V., Wall, D. D., Thomas, D. M., & Smith, S. J. (1997). Evaluating an intervention for homeless persons: Results of a field experiment. *Journal of Consulting and Clinical Psychology, 65,* 476–484.

▣ HOMELESSNESS, RURAL

The two fundamental causes of homelessness in the United States—lack of affordable housing and inability to pay for adequate housing—are not limited to urban communities, and yet "poverty in rural America is often unseen, unacknowledged, and unattended" (National Catholic Rural Life Conference 2000; www.ncrlc.com). The same can be said of homelessness in rural America. Differences between urban and rural communities extend far beyond simple measures such as size, density, and distance; even definitions of the word *rural* can vary from agency to agency. Still, recent research has helped reveal the extent of homelessness in rural areas and the characteristics of the rural homeless. It has also called into question whether current approaches to defining and studying homelessness—approaches that have generally been developed in urban settings—are appropriate for rural areas. Perhaps these lessons can inform future efforts to end homelessness in rural America.

DEFINING "RURAL"

One challenge in studying homelessness in rural areas is that there is no single definition of "rural" for statistical and other purposes. Rural communities are generally thought to be places with small, low-density populations, often remote from larger cities and towns. In reality, these geographic characteristics exist on a continuum and there is no obvious dividing line between "urban" and "rural." Two of the most common definitions are based on stan-

dards developed by the Office of Management and Budget (OMB) and the Bureau of the Census. Both define rural areas as those that fall *outside* certain areas: "metropolitan statistical areas" (or MSAs) in the OMB standard, or "urbanized areas and urban clusters" in the Census definition. MSAs are composed of one or more counties, and are defined based on population size and density, and the extent to which fringe counties are economically tied to core metropolitan counties. Because county-level data are quite plentiful, MSAs are often used as a basis for comparing urban and rural America statistically. On the other hand, the Census defines "urbanized areas and urban clusters" by settlement size and density, ignoring county boundaries. The Census approach offers a somewhat purer measure of "rural" but is more difficult to use (Hewitt 1989). Data from the 2000 census show that 21 percent of the nation's population (or 59.1 million people) live in rural areas according to the Census definition, while a slightly lower share, 17.4 percent (or 49.2 million people), live in non-metropolitan areas as defined by OMB (U.S. Department of Agriculture 2003). But the two groups are not identical: About half (50.8 percent) of all Census-defined rural residents actually live in counties classified as falling within an MSA. Moreover, among residents of counties not included in MSAs, 41.1 percent live in urban areas.

WHY PLACE MATTERS

Whatever standard one uses to distinguish rural from urban areas, it is clear that the differences between them extend far beyond size, density, and distance. Living in a rural community has important economic, social, and cultural implications, and these in turn affect how people experience poverty and homelessness, and also how communities can best address these problems.

Housing costs are often lower in rural areas, but so too are incomes, with the result that rent burdens in rural communities are often as high or higher than those in urban places. Furthermore, opportunities for raising one's income are much more limited in rural areas. Lower levels of education, less competition for workers, and fewer high-skilled jobs in the occupational mix result in lower wages and higher levels of unemployment, underemployment, and seasonal employment in rural communities. In addition, low population density discourages the development of workplace supports and infrastructure such as education and training, child care, and public transportation.

Many of these factors also explain why homelessness is not evenly distributed across rural areas. Higher-than-average levels of homelessness are found in communities that are primarily agricultural, in regions with economies based on declining extractive industries (such as mining, forestry, or fishing), in areas with persistent poverty, and in places experiencing economic growth (Aron and Fitchen 1996; Burt 1996). Those with growing economies include, for example, communities with new or expanding industrial plants that attract more job-seekers than can be absorbed, and areas on the urban fringe that attract new businesses and higher-income residents; these trends can drive up taxes and other living expenses to the detriment of longtime residents. Such places include ski resorts, upscale retirement communities, and counties experiencing a boom in vacation home sales. In communities with persistent poverty, such as Appalachia, young able-bodied workers often relocate to urban areas in search of employment, but if unsuccessful, they return to their home communities and find themselves homeless. Other people in impoverished or primarily agricultural areas may become homeless because of changing economic conditions, including lower labor demand as a result of mechanized and corporate farming, and a shrinking service sector because of declining population. Finally, communities located along major transportation routes often receive homeless people literally "off the interstate"—people on the road looking for work, or transients who run out of resources.

The most recent statistics on poverty across the country reveal that not only is poverty disproportionately rural, it is a persistent problem. Data from the 2000 census indicate that 13.4 percent of rural Americans were living in poverty, compared to 10.8 percent of more urban Americans. Among the nation's 500 poorest counties, non-metropolitan (rural) counties outnumbered metro counties by 11 to 1. Among the 500 counties with the lowest per-capita income,

non-metropolitan (rural) counties outnumbered metro counties by 25 to 1 (Miller and Rowley 2002). The poorest counties—those with poverty rates of 20 percent or more—are found in Appalachia, the Mississippi Delta, the lower Rio Grande, and the Northern Plains. In many of these counties, such poverty rates have been documented in every decennial census since 1960.

Findings from the Rural Sociological Society's Task Force on Persistent Rural Poverty, as well as other sources, dispel many common myths about America's poor. The vast majority (73 percent) of poor rural Americans are white, another 24 percent are African-American, and the remainder are Native Americans (Hispanics of any ethnicity account for 5 percent of all poor Americans). The majority of poor rural families are among the "working poor." In almost two-thirds (64.6 percent) of the families, at least one person has a job; in about one-quarter of them, two or more members have a job. Poor people in rural areas are much less likely than their urban counterparts to live in female-headed families. Only 17 percent of them live in female-headed families with children at home—about the same share who live in married-couple families with children at home: 18 percent (Summers and Sherman 1997).

The majority (55 percent) of poor rural Americans live in the South, another quarter (25 percent) are in the North Central region, and the remaining are in the Mountain (8 percent), Pacific (5 percent), Middle Atlantic (5 percent), and New England (2 percent) regions of the country. These patterns also vary by race/ethnicity: Poor rural African-Americans are concentrated in the south (97 percent), while poor rural Hispanics or Latinos/as are concentrated in the Southwest and on the West Coast. Poor rural Native Americans are concentrated in the Southwest (particularly in the area where Arizona, Colorado, New Mexico, and Utah meet), the Upper Great Plains (especially North Dakota and South Dakota), and eastern Oklahoma (Summers and Sherman 1997).

CHARACTERISTICS OF RURAL HOMELESS

During the 1990s, a general picture of the characteristics of rural homeless people emerged from a variety of state and local studies. Compared to their urban counterparts, rural homeless people are more likely to be white, female, married, currently working, younger, homeless for the first time, and homeless for a shorter period of time than their urban counterparts (Burt 1996; National Coalition for the Homeless 1999). Other research has also suggested higher rates of domestic violence and lower rates of alcohol and substance abuse among the rural homeless, but these findings have not been not consistent across studies (National Coalition for the Homeless 1999; Burt, Aron, and Lee 2001). Finally, some rural communities have large shares of Native Americans and migrant workers among their homeless populations (Burt 1996).

Some of the most recent data on people homeless in the United States come from the 1996 National Survey of Homeless Assistance Providers and Clients (NSHAPC). As the name suggests, the data are national in scope and include communities outside MSAs in addition to central cities and those in the "balance of MSA" (see Burt, Aron, and Lee 2001 for a detailed description of this study and its findings). NSHAPC used a service-based sampling strategy, identifying and counting only those homeless people who had contact with some type of homeless assistance program; these included outreach programs, drop-in centers, and mobile food programs that serve homeless people who do not use shelters. NSHAPC documented an estimated 444,000 homeless adults and children using such services during an average week between October and November 1996 (Burt, Aron, and Lee 2001). Of this total, 69 percent were in central city areas, another 21 percent were in suburban or urban fringe areas of MSAs, and 9 percent (or about 41,000 people) were in rural areas (defined as outside an MSA). In terms of *rates* of homelessness, the NSHAPC data indicate that anywhere between about 7 and 14 people per 10,000 in rural areas were homeless. Projections to the entire rural homeless population (not just those using services) increase this range to about 9 to 17 people per 10,000. In all cases, these rates were about one-fifth those of central city locations, but were slightly higher than those of suburban–urban fringe locations.

The data also suggest that compared to poor peo-

ple generally (about 23 percent of whom live in rural areas), service-using homeless people are more concentrated in urban areas. Other NSHAPC findings point to the possibility that some urban homeless people may have originated in rural areas. Almost half (44 percent) of the homeless people interviewed had left the community where their current homeless spell began, and only 28 percent of these "movers" began their current homeless episode in a central city. The NSHAPC data also show that these people tended to move from smaller communities to larger ones and that the smaller the originating community, the more likely they were to move to a larger one. Interestingly, the lack of shelters or other social services was *not* a major reason for leaving their home communities—losing housing and needing work were more important—but central cities were their primary destination, and most of these movers *did* identify the availability of shelters and other homeless assistance services as a major draw.

NSHAPC also confirms many of the distinctive characteristics of people homeless in rural areas. Compared to other homeless people, they are less likely to be black or Hispanic, and have completed high school. They are also much more likely than others to be married, divorced, separated, or widowed. Those in rural areas are also heavily concentrated in the age range from 35 to 44 years, are more likely to be working, and less likely to be receiving any means-tested government benefits such as food stamps, welfare, supplemental security income, and so on. Rural homeless people are as likely as other homeless people to have problems with alcohol, drugs, or mental illness—about two-thirds do—but the types of problems differ by community. The rural homeless identified in NSHAPC are much *more* likely than their urban counterparts to have had recent problems with alcohol, and they are much *less* likely to have had recent problems with drugs or mental illness. They are also much more likely to have been incarcerated as juveniles and as adults. Other NSHAPC results indicate that people homeless in rural communities are much more likely to be homeless for the first time and for a shorter episode, to have no public or private health insurance, and to have needed—but not been able to see—a doctor or nurse in the past year. With the exception of the much higher rates of problems with alcohol, most of these findings are consistent with those of earlier smaller-scale studies of rural homelessness (National Coalition for the Homeless 1999).

In addition to homeless people, NSHAPC documented the nationwide presence of almost 40,000 homeless assistance programs of various types; a third of these were located in rural areas. There were some interesting urban-rural variations within the four broad types of programs. The majority (56 percent) of all programs distributing vouchers for emergency shelter in 1996, for example, were located in rural areas, but only 15 percent of transitional housing programs were. Conversely, soup kitchens were much more likely to be found in central cities than in rural areas (65 versus 15 percent). These findings reflect fundamental differences in the social service structures of urban versus rural communities. Permanent housing structures and soup kitchens designed to serve walk-ins are not efficient systems for helping homeless people in rural areas who are not concentrated in any one place geographically. The greater use of mainstream agencies programs by rural people, including public health programs and financial and housing assistance, is also confirmed by these NSHAPC findings.

The high rates of incarceration among rural homeless people documented by NSHAPC is of particular interest, given the large numbers of rural communities that have turned to new prisons and other correctional facilities as a way of supporting their local economies (Kilborn 2001; Beale 1996). Without effective discharge planning, one unintentional consequence of these large and growing prison populations may be higher levels of homelessness. Such plans typically include an estimated discharge date, programs that prisoners complete while in prison, medical records, and arrangements for post-release housing, medical and mental health care, and other community-based services. In some states, this planning is the formal responsibility of corrections administrations, while in other states it is done more informally by correctional health providers, community-based social service providers, or other prison-based social services staff (Community Shelter Board 2002). In the absence of effective policies and practices for discharge planning, many prisons simply release ex-offenders directly into local homeless shelters. There are similar concerns about people being released from hospitals, treatment facilities, and psychiatric institutions.

ADDRESSING HOMELESSNESS IN RURAL AREAS

While additional research is clearly needed on homelessness in rural communities, much has been learned since the first systematic, mostly local, studies of rural homeless people were conducted in the late 1980s and early 1990s. One ongoing challenge, which has not necessarily been resolved, has to do with definitions. Many perceive a fundamental disconnect between definitions of homelessness that have been developed with urban settings in mind—including, most importantly, the main federal definition as embodied in the Stewart B. McKinney Act—and the realities of homelessness in rural areas, where there are few or no shelters, and where settlement patterns are so dispersed that even "living on the street" may not be possible. Many homeless people in rural areas double up with relatives or other families, or live in abandoned homes or substandard or severely overcrowded housing, often without plumbing or heat. Also, while few people sleep on the streets of rural towns, many live in their vehicles at campgrounds or in woods or remote hills and valleys (Burt 1996).

It is debatable whether definitions of rural homelessness should be expanded to include people who are precariously housed, especially since there are many such people in urban areas too. But rural homeless advocates and service providers have argued against restrictive definitions that limit people's eligibility for critical homeless assistance services. Even those who find the McKinney Act definition adequate want more flexibility in how it is applied:

> In the final analysis, the total number of homeless persons, when homelessness has [such] a broad definition, is really less important than the segmentation of the homeless population into meaningful components, so that policy makers can design appropriate programs for specific groups. (Kondratas 1991, p. 646)

Many of the lessons of the 1990s have to do with how rural homeless people can be studied and effectively served. Like NSHAPC, most studies of rural homelessness rely on identifying homeless people through various service agencies (Kentucky Housing Corporation 2001; Koebel, Murphy, and Brown 2001). The absence of homeless-specific agencies in rural areas makes it essential that these studies include broad-spectrum mainstream ones such as welfare and social services agencies, public and mental health departments, community action agencies, public housing agencies, Salvation Army centers, Legal Aid offices, and faith-based and other nonprofit organizations that serve poor people. Even for the NSHAPC study, an interesting deviation from the original sampling design had to be made in rural areas because there were so few homeless-specific service programs: The standard for inclusion in the study was expanded to include programs serving homeless even if this group was not their intended population focus, and about one-fourth of all rural programs in NSHAPC were recorded as a result of this expansion. Interestingly, the duration of the data collection in rural areas has also expanded in recent years. Studies relying on one-night counts or "sweeps" of the shelter and street population have been replaced by one- or two-month-long periods during which service agencies collect information on all people they serve who may be homeless. (They also collect unique but anonymous identifiers that allow one to "unduplicate" counts over time and across agencies so that the same homeless person is not counted more than once.) This longer time period is especially helpful in rural areas where homeless people are not as visible or as easy to locate.

Mainstream social service agencies are important to include in studies of rural homelessness because it is these agencies that actually serve homeless people. This has led many to argue that rural homeless services should be improved by enhancing the capacities of existing mainstream agencies, rather than by building a highly specialized homeless-specific service structure similar to those in urban centers. Understanding differences in the social service systems of urban and rural communities also has important implications for how federal programs and funding streams are structured. For example, applications from rural agencies to the federal government should not be downgraded simply because they do not target specific subgroups of homeless people; such targeting simply may not make sense in many rural parts of the country. Moreover, services that are sometimes considered "nice extras" in urban areas can be critical to the success of rural service agencies. In rural communities, for example, outreach may literally be the "front door" of an agency; without it, many people would not be served. Other activities, such as improving communications through more or better technology, and improving transportation for agency staff and clients, are also very important in rural communities (Burt 1996). The Department of Housing and Urban Development recently sponsored a study profiling four different "model" approaches to developing homeless service systems in rural areas. The four partnerships included a county system in New York state, a multi-county/regional system in Alabama, a rural statewide system in Arizona, and a statewide system in Ohio (Housing Assistance Council 2002).

LOOKING AHEAD

Some observers believe that the United States has done an adequate job of building up an emergency response system for homeless people and must now go beyond this by focusing on prevention and longer-lasting housing and support services. Key support services include child care, substance abuse treatment, and in rural areas, transportation (National Alliance to End Homelessness 2000; Burt 2001). It is not clear from existing studies whether rural communities have adequate emergency response systems, but few would argue that they do need longer-lasting homeless prevention, housing, and support services. Indeed, in both national and local studies, rural homeless people and service providers consistently place transitional and permanent housing among the top needs of homeless people (Burt, Aron, and Lee 2001; Kentucky Housing Corporation 2001; Koebel, Murphy, and Brown 2001).

As in urban areas, effectively ending homelessness in rural communities will require comprehensive policies on affordable housing, economic development, employment and training, and on poverty more generally. It is also important to recognize that that because place really does matter when it comes to being homeless and poor, these policies may not resemble those that have been successful in urban areas. Rural and non-metropolitan communities have been largely neglected in public policy, and recent research on rural homelessness may help change this. Developing what has been called "a national rural public policy" (Castle 2001), and committing adequate resources to implementing these policies, can go a long way toward solving rural America's most persistent problems, including poverty and homelessness.

—*Laudan Y. Aron*

Further Reading

Andrews, D. (n.d.). Rural poverty, another world. Retrieved January 7, 2003 from http://www.ncrlc.com/rural_poverty.html

Aron, L., & Fitchen, J. (1996). Rural homelessness: A synopsis. In J. Baumohl (Ed.), *Homelessness in America*. Phoenix, AZ: Oryx.

Beale, C. L. (1996). Rural prisons: An update. *Rural Development Perspectives, 11*(2), 25–27.

Burt, M. R. (2001). *What will it take to end homelessness?* Urban Institute Brief. Washington, DC: Urban Institute.

Burt, M., Aron, L., & Lee, E. (2001). *Helping America's homeless: Emergency shelter or affordable housing?* Washington, DC: Urban Institute Press.

Burt, M., Aron, L., Douglas, T., Valente, J., Lee, E., & Iwen, B. (1999). *Homelessness: Programs and the people they serve, findings of the National Survey of Homeless Assistance Providers and Clients, technical report*. Washington, DC: Interagency Council on the Homeless.

Burt, M. (1996). *Rural homelessness: A report on the findings and implications of RECD's Rural Homelessness Conferences*. Washington, DC: U.S. Department of Agriculture, Rural Economic and Community Development.

Castle, E. N. (2001, Winter.). Wanted: A rural public policy. *Choices, The Magazine of Food, Farm and Resource Issues*.

Community Shelter Board (2002). *Preventing homelessness: Discharge planning from corrections facilities*. Columbus, OH: Author.

Hewitt, M. (1989). *Defining "rural" areas: Impact on health care policy and research*. Washington, DC: Office of Technology Assessment, Congress of the United States.

Housing Assistance Council. (2002). *Continua of care best practices: Comprehensive homeless planning in rural America*. Washington, DC: Housing Assistance Council.

Kentucky Housing Corporation. (2001). 2001 Kentucky homeless survey report. Retrieved January 7, 2003, from http://www.kyhousing.org/Publications/resources/2001HomelessReport.pdf

Kilborn, P. T. (2001, August 1). Rural towns turn to prisons to reignite their economies. *The New York Times* (p. A-1).

Koebel, C. T., Murphy, M., & Brown, A. (2001, September). *The 2001 Virginia rural homeless survey*. Retrieved January 7, 2003, from http://www.arch.vt.edu/caus/research/vchr/pdfreports/VaRuralHomeless_sum.pdf

Kondratas, A. (1991). Estimates and public policy: The politics of numbers. *Housing Policy Debate, 2,* 631–647.

Miller, K., & Rowley, T. (2002). *Rural poverty and rural-urban income gaps: A troubling snapshot of the "prosperous" 1990s,* RUPRI Data Report, P2002–5. Columbia, MO: Rural Policy Research Institute.

National Alliance to End Homelessness (2000). The ten year plan to end homelessness. Retrieved January 7, 2003, from http://www.endhomelessness.org/pub/tenyear/index.htm

National Coalition for the Homeless. (1999). *Rural Homelessness,* NCH Fact Sheet #13. Washington, DC: National Coalition for the Homeless.

Rural Welfare Policy Panel (1999). *Rural America and welfare reform: An overview and assessment*. Columbia, MO: Rural Policy Research Institute.

Summers, G. F., & Sherman, J. (1997). *Who's poor in rural America? Working together for a change*. Madison, WI: Rural Sociological Society.

U. S. Department of Agriculture. (2000). *Measuring rurality: What is rural?* Washington, DC: Economic Research Service. Retrieved January 7, 2003, from http://www.ers.usda.gov/briefing/rurality/WhatisRural/

▣ HOMELESSNESS, SUBURBAN

During the mid-1980s, homelessness and other problems associated with severe poverty began to emerge in many U.S. suburban communities. Although describing homeless persons has presented methodological challenges to social scientists, the characteristics and tendencies of the suburban homeless do not appear to be substantially different from those of their urban counterparts.

A 1996 report by the Urban Institute on findings of the National Survey of Homeless Assistance Providers and Clients (NSHAPC) estimated that one in five homeless individuals was living in suburban areas. Demographically, suburban homeless are similar in age distribution to their urban counterparts.

However, the suburban homeless are more likely to be female (45 percent) and white non-Hispanic (54 percent), compared to the female (29 percent) and white non-Hispanic (37 percent) homeless in the central city. The suburban homeless were found to experience homelessness and incidence of alcohol, drug, and mental health problems on a par with their central city counterparts. The suburban homeless report having been physically or sexually abused before the age of eighteen (33 percent) more than the homeless of the central city (24 percent). Furthermore, the suburban homeless use services geared toward them less than their urban counterparts, with only 50 percent reporting that they had used a soup kitchen and only 18 percent a drop-in center, compared to 68 percent and 30 percent for the urban homeless, respectively. This suggests a lack of availability of these programs outside the central city.

Like their urban counterparts, the suburban homeless utilize overnight shelters for many reasons. In an unpublished 1997 study of one Chicago suburb, Lewis and Nelson found that many of the homeless they interviewed working during the day but could not afford permanent housing. Others came to the overnight shelter only to eat a meal, and then they would work overnight shifts, sleep in their car, or stay with family and friends. Some were looking for work and divided their time between the shelter and the daytime drop-in program. Family problems were common. Mentally ill individuals, unable to afford housing on fixed incomes, were regular shelter users. Others were alcohol or drug addicted. The majority of homeless individuals interviewed had suburban roots. They had grown up, attended school, and had extended family in the immediate community or adjacent suburbs.

KEY FEATURES AND IMPLICATIONS

Since the 1980s, suburban areas have outpaced most cities in population growth and the creation of new jobs, notably in technology, light industry, and service sectors. As the suburban population has grown, so, too, have retail shopping malls, restaurants, and hotels, which depend upon a low-wage workforce. Employment opportunities are a relatively new phe-

nomenon in suburbia. The qualities that have traditionally attracted white middle-class families, such as safety, good schools, and quality of life, also appeal to the homeless. As the suburban population has become more heterogeneous, these communities have been confronted with social, economic, and ethnic class tensions that were previously unknown. Homelessness is one problem that has arisen as a result of social and economic changes.

Most suburbs have no history of dealing proactively (relating to acting in anticipation of a problem) with these problems. During the past several decades, gentrification (a process of renewal and rebuilding) has significantly reduced the stock of affordable urban housing, which has contributed to increasing homelessness. Affordable housing for the poor has largely been nonexistent as suburbs developed. Where social service networks exist, they have focused on the needs of the suburban middle class who can pay their own way. Many services are church based and not well positioned to respond to the increasing scope and scale of demand for basic needs such as food and shelter presented by the homeless.

The suburban growth phenomenon of the past fifty years has been seen by many as "white flight" from the perceived ills of the urban environment. The suburbs held the promise of an insulated, bucolic world, often at a geographical and social distance from low-income and minority groups. As political scientist Michael N. Danielson observed in his book *The Politics of Exclusion,*

> most of those moving outward have been seeking social separation from the lower classes as well as better housing and more spacious surroundings. Middle-class families commonly equate personal security, good schools, maintenance of property values, and general desirability of a residential area with the absence of lower-income groups. (Danielson 1976, 6)

The issue of homelessness challenges deep-seated beliefs about what suburban residents believe their community is and should be. Danielson noted, "Most suburban jurisdictions are small and relatively homogeneous populations, which makes it easier to secure consensus on exclusionary policies than is commonly the case in larger and more heterogeneous cities" (Danielson 1976, 4).

As more homeless, lower-income, and minority groups seek employment and housing in the suburbs, suburban residents, who once almost uniformly favored exclusion, have split into two camps: those who believe the community has a social responsibility to respond to residents in need and those who believe the community should be insulated from such people and their problems.

HISTORICAL ASSUMPTIONS OF URBANISM

The growth of cities during the nineteenth century brought the plight of the homeless and desperately poor into focus. The demand for temporary and seasonal unskilled labor attracted the transient homeless to the cities. Local communities struggled with the choice between providing a monetary stipend to the homeless and maintaining them in poorhouses. Instead, they created shantytowns on the cities' peripheries.

As cities became more populated and annexed new areas, they incorporated these shantytowns and their homeless inhabitants. Bricks and mortar replaced the makeshift dwellings that characterized the shantytowns, and skid row districts were born. During much of the nineteenth century, skid row and its denizens became an accepted part of the urban environment, seen as a necessary, although unpleasant, reality of the geographic and social structure of U.S. cities.

Several researchers have studied the inhabitants and conditions of postwar skid row areas across the United States. Sociologist Peter Rossi analyzed these studies and concluded that

> all presented the same picture of three dire conditions: extreme poverty, arising out of low earnings and low benefit levels; disability through advanced age, alcoholism, and physical or mental illness; and disaffiliation—absent or tenuous ties to family and kin and few or no friends. (Rossi 1989, 31).

Since the late 1960s, a steady process of urban renewal and gentrification has all but eliminated skid row districts in most cities. This process has dis-

placed the former and would-be residents of skid row into less hospitable surroundings. No longer contained in a geographically and socially segregated district of the city, they have had an unwelcome reception as they have been assimilated into the mainstream of urban life. Sociologists David Snow and Leon Anderson observed:

> The differences between the homelessness of the skid-row era and that of the 1980s extended beyond demographics. Most significantly, it included a shift in the public perception of the problem of homelessness. Urban renewal and the gentrification of skid rows around the country had destroyed the urban niche in which many of the homeless of the previous period had existed. As a result, the homeless of the 1980s were more visible and faced more frequent contact with domiciled citizens than had their earlier counterparts. (Snow and Anderson 1993, 17)

In his book *The Homeless*, sociologist Christopher Jencks asserted that political restrictions on the creation of flophouses have contributed to the spread of homelessness among single adults. Jencks wrote,

> Had cities been able to mothball skid rows during the affluent 1960s and 1970s the way that the Navy mothballed old battleships, entrepreneurs could perhaps have created new cubicle hotels when the demand revived in the 1980s. But once skid row was gone, it was hard to find any other area that viewed the very poor as a commercial asset rather than a liability. (Jencks 1994, 74).

This urban history provides the foundation for our current theories of homelessness, but it does not help us understand homelessness as it is manifested in most suburban areas. Suburban areas do not possess a history of planned geographic containment, political control, and social intervention with the poor and deviant, as do older urban areas. Suburbia has had from its beginning vast tracts of prime space that attracted affluent migrants from the city center. The destruction of skid row and gentrification of other marginal areas have reduced the supply of cheap urban housing. This change is viewed as a major reason for the recent emergence of homelessness as a problem in older cities. The suburbs by design never allowed the creation of these marginal

Homeless teenagers, nicknamed "Post Office Kids," often hang out at the Street Scene Teen Center located under the post office in Chapel Hill, North Carolina, in January 2002.
Source: Jeffrey Allan Salter/Corbis; used with permission.

areas of cheap housing to begin with, and thus we must look to other factors to understand suburban homelessness.

THE CHANGING CONTEXT OF SUBURBANIZATION

During the 1990s, a body of literature described the phenomenon of postsuburban development, which rendered obsolete the concepts of urban hub and suburban rim. Books such as journalist Joel Garreau's 1991 *Edge City: Life on the New Frontier* and historian Jon C. Teaford's *Post-Suburbia: Government and Politics in the Edge City* chronicled the evolution of suburbia into what are now considered urban villages, technoburbs, or edge cities, a grouping of suburban municipalities unified and coordinated through the expanding role of county government and commercial expansion. Teaford writes,

> The metropolitan world had been transformed, and formally suburban areas were now centers of commerce and industry, as well as residence and recreation. In fact, the edge had an economic life of its own, which challenged that of the older cities and in some cases seemed to supersede it. (Teaford 1997, 2)

With big government viewed as the antithesis of the suburban ideal, suburbanites lean toward volunteerism to address civic needs, governmental inti-

macy in the delivery of city services, and a sense of parochialism in their interests, opinions, and views. Teaford writes,

> Traditional American city government had evolved in the nineteenth century to foster urbanization and to provide public services and facilities necessary to enhance the development of a great metropolis. Post-suburban government, in contrast, evolved as a mechanism to maintain a suburban way of life and the creation of a big tax base. (Teaford 1997, 8)

Many new information-age industries are based in the suburbs. Most major cities have experienced the development of these "high-tech corridors" beyond their municipal boundaries. Increasing numbers of long-established corporations have abandoned their older city addresses and relocated to the suburbs seeking the promise of greener pastures, lower taxes, and a better workforce. The majority of the corporate workforce now lives in these suburban locations. This transformation has resulted in suburbs that are no longer simply bedroom communities.

SUBURBAN RESPONSES TO HOMELESSNESS

Societal responses to homelessness have mirrored, in many ways, the effects of the last thirty years of deinstitutionalization. As political sociologist Dan A. Lewis and his coauthors (1991) noted in *Worlds of the Mentally Ill: How Deinstitutionalization Works in the City,* society has moved away from large institutions and bureaucracies toward more inclusionary, streamlined, community-based measures for taking care of needy citizens. The price paid for this policy of deinstitutionalization is a growing public presence for groups who were previously hidden from society's view.

To some people, the emergence of homelessness in suburban communities represents a decline in social organization and control. Many community residents attribute the presence of the homeless to a weakening of the moral and political order in their communities. They feel threatened by the "incivility" they observe in the behavior of some of the homeless, which threatens their notion of community integrity and social control. Therefore, in examining the problem of suburban homelessness, it is helpful to view it from a social control perspective, in which a negative perception of the homeless is more than a response to a particular interaction or observed event. Rather, it is a consequence of the erosion of middle-class values, as suburban residents perceive them. Thus, the problem of suburban homelessness can be viewed in much the same terms as criminologist James Q. Wilson explains the perception of urban decline in general, namely, as the erosion of civility within the local community.

> The concern for "community" refers to one's desire for the observance of standards of right and seemly conduct in the public places in which one lives and moves, those standards to be consistent with, and supportive of, the values and lifestyles of the particular individual. Around one's home, the places one shops, and the corridors through which one walks there is for each of us a public space wherein our sense of security, self-esteem, and propriety is either reassured or jeopardized by people and events we encounter. (Wilson 1975, 24)

In their book *Fear of Crime: Incivility and the Production of a Social Problem*, Dan A. Lewis and political scientist Greta Salem find that communities with a high degree of social control have assurance that (1) residents adhere to a shared set of expectations about appropriate behavior; (2) private property is kept up in accordance with commonly held standards; (3) public areas are adequately maintained; and (4) access is regulated so as to control the incursion of population groups, private enterprises, and public institutions that are perceived to threaten the integrity of the neighborhood.

> The first two items reflect the moral order of the community. In neighborhoods where the majority of residents share common backgrounds, where there is minimal population movement, and where there is a high level of informal social interaction, commonly held norms are more likely to be held and enforced. The last two items reflect the political order of the community. To secure city services and control access to the community, local residents must have the capacity to influence municipal service bureaucracies and both the

> public and private decision-making agencies that play a role in determining the direction of neighborhood change. (Lewis and Salem 1986, 79)

Suburban residents confronted by emerging social problems such as homelessness are forced to take sides. One side views the suburban community as a fortress of middle-class affluence, in which it was inconceivable that the homeless could be residents. Members of that side argue that the homeless are outsiders for whom the community bears no responsibility and that providing assistance only encourages the homeless to remain in the community and attracts others from the outside seeking help. The opposing side contends that where the homeless came from does not matter. This side argues that, for whatever reason, the homeless are in their midst and thereby deserve the community's charity and assistance. Helping is the moral and responsible thing to do.

ADDRESSING THE PROBLEM

As a result of the rapid social and economic changes that have occurred in recent years, many suburbs are now faced with the problem of how best to assimilate the growing class of working poor and marginalized who are now in their midst.

Whereas the poor were concentrated and segregated in distinct neighborhoods in the older city, enabling them and their caretakers to influence electoral politics, the suburban poor have lacked a similar base of political representation. Poverty in the older city has long been the venue of patronage systems, city councils, and city planners. However, poverty has largely been irrelevant to suburban politics. In the suburbs, the historic low incidence of poverty and other related social problems has understandably warranted little attention from government in the past. Whereas the older cities accepted responsibility for the problem of homelessness, suburban governments continue to rely on the efforts of the private sector, opting for control by overseeing the problem rather than delivering direct services.

As a result, typical political dialogue in the suburbs occurs among community elites, who consist of officials, community residents, religious leaders, and service providers, through a politically appointed coalition or task force. Appointees to coalitions who judge the homeless problem often have strongly differing philosophical views of the problem, which can frustrate local initiative.

A central issue may be the perception of people that providing services for the homeless in their community unfairly burdens them because they take on the homeless problems of neighboring suburban municipalities. Because of the amorphous (shapeless) geographic and political nature of the suburbs, problems such as homelessness cross many boundaries. Suburban municipalities typically share no history of working collaboratively on such issues. County governments that serve these affluent suburban areas have not developed the leadership, expertise, or capacity to provide the type of services needed by the homeless. Suburban communities may lack the political will to appropriate funds and counter community opposition.

In the absence of government initiative, the challenge of ministering to the homeless in suburban communities is likely to be met by faith-based organizations, which have little experience in providing social services on a substantially different scale than what has been given to the suburban middle class. The needs of the homeless will be met by the volunteer efforts of local churches, who view this type of work as being consistent with their Judeo-Christian social mission philosophy. Churches enter this new territory of service with the expectation that they will develop expertise in the operation of overnight shelters, feeding programs, and provisions for the homeless.

Professional human service providers, lacking additional funds with which to provide these homeless services, take on roles of coordination and consultation that support church efforts and new agencies created to help the homeless. Seeking to establish some degree of social control over the homeless, local government may provide limited funds for professional human service providers to monitor the guests of church-based shelter operations, provide referral resources, intervene when behavior is inappropriate, and resolve personal crises. Establishing professional human service providers as benevolent agents of social control can create a tension with the philosophy of unconditional love and acceptance that is the foundation of the churches' mission of service to the homeless.

Suburban residents often perceive the presence of services for the homeless as the reason for increasing numbers and problems associated with the homeless in their community. Professional human service providers in this role run the risk of displacement, given that they can be held unrealistically accountable for the problems created by the homeless. Displacement occurs when the social problem that needs to be solved—in this case, homelessness—is replaced in the minds of the problem solvers and community members with the services that were developed as a partial response to the original problem. When this occurs, community pressure can develop to curtail services or severely restrict the scope and scale of services offered and which homeless individuals are eligible to receive them.

The fear of the homeless is a real issue among some residents of suburbia. For the most part, that fear is not based on personal experience but rather on what the homeless represent: the poor, the unclean, the deviant. The homeless are a constant reminder of what each of us might become, of a hometown that is rapidly changing, and of the potential for decline and social disorder.

IMPLICATIONS

Current urban theories of homelessness are not useful in understanding homelessness as it is manifested in most suburban areas. Suburban areas do not possess a history of planned geographic containment, political control, or social intervention with the poor and deviant, as do our older urban areas. Suburbia had from its beginning vast tracts of prime space that attracted affluent migrants from the city center. Poverty, where it existed, was scattered, occurring within a rural context very different from that of the inner city.

The destruction of skid row and the gentrification of other marginal areas resulted in the loss of cheap housing in cities. This is seen as a major reason for the emergence of homelessness as a problem in the older city. The suburbs by design never allowed the creation of these marginal areas of cheap housing.

Deinstitutionalization of the mentally ill has affected homelessness equally in the city and the suburb. This policy shift from inpatient to outpatient care has resulted in the release of thousands of patients from long-term hospitalization but also has resulted in people who once would have been sent to a mental hospital now being treated in the community. Indeed, as Christopher Jencks has noted, "The history of deinstitutionalization is the story of America's collective search for other places to send these disturbed and disturbing people" (Jencks 1994, 25).

As a result of the rapid social and economic changes that have occurred in recent years, suburbs are now faced with the problem of assimilating this growing class of working poor and marginalized. This problem will require creative thinking on the part of suburban leaders as they attempt to guide their communities from a past of exclusivity toward a future of diversity and inclusivity.

—*Dan Lewis and Bruce Nelson*

Note: The authors wish to acknowledge the contributions of Matthew A. Lewis as research assistant on this article.

Further Reading

Bogard, C. J. (2001). Advocacy and enumeration: Counting homeless people in a suburban community. *American Behavioral Scientist, 45*(1), 105–120.

Brickner, P. (Ed.). (1990). *Under the safety net: The health and social welfare of the homeless in the United States.* New York: W. W. Norton.

Burt, M. R. (1992). *Over the edge.* New York: Russell Sage.

Burt, M. R. (1999). *Homelessness: Programs and the people that they serve: Findings of the National Survey of Homeless Assistance Providers and Clients.* Washington, DC: Urban Institute.

Cohen, S. (1985). *Visions of social control.* Cambridge, MA: Polity Press.

Danielson, M. N. (1976). *The politics of exclusion.* New York: Columbia University Press.

Dehavenon, A. L. (1996). *There's no place like home: Anthropological perspectives on housing and homelessness in the United States.* Westport, CT: Bergin & Garvey.

Fahs, I. (Ed.). (1996). *From soup and sermon to mega-mission.* Milwaukee, WI: Christian Stewardship Association.

Fishman, R. (1987). *Bourgeois utopias: The rise and fall of suburbia.* New York: Basic Books.

Garreau, J. (1991). *Edge city: Life on the new frontier.* New York: Doubleday.

Jencks, C. (1994). *The homeless.* Cambridge, MA: Harvard University Press.

Lewis, D. A., & Nelson, B. A. (1997). *A study of homelessness in Wheaton, Illinois: A report to the mayor's task force on homelessness.* Unpublished report, Northwestern University, Institute for Policy Research.

Lewis, D. A., Riger, S., Rosenberg, H., & Wagenaar, H. (1991). *Worlds of the mentally ill: How deinstitutionalization works in the city.* Carbondale: Southern Illinois University Press.

Lewis, D. A., & Salem, G. (1986). *Fear of crime: Incivility and the production of a social problem.* New Brunswick, NJ: Transaction.

Rossi, P. H. (1989). *Down and out in America.* Chicago: University of Chicago Press.

Snow, D. A., & Anderson, L. (1993). *Down on their luck.* Berkeley and Los Angeles: University of California Press.

Teaford, J. C. (1997). *Post-suburbia: Government and politics in the edge cities.* Baltimore: Johns Hopkins University Press.

Wilson, J. Q. (1975). *Thinking about crime.* New York: Basic Books.

▣ HOMELESSNESS, URBAN

See Appendix 4: Documentary History of Homelessness; Bowery, The; Calcutta; Chicago Skid Row; Copenhagen; Dallas; Houston; London; Los Angeles; Minneapolis and St. Paul; Montreal; Mumbai (Bombay); Nairobi; New York City; Paris; Philadelphia; St. Louis; Sydney; Tokyo; Toronto; Washington, D.C.

▣ HOUSING

See Appendix 4: Documentary History of Homelessness; Corporation for Supportive Housing; European Network for Housing Research; Fair Housing Laws; Foster Care; Hidden Homelessness; Housing and Homelessness in Developing Nations; Housing, Affordable; Housing, Transitional; "Housing First" Approach; International Union of Tenants; Interventions, Housing; Low-Income Housing Development; Missions; Municipal Lodging Houses; National Alliance of State Housing Agencies; Self-Help Housing;

Shelters; Single-Room Occupancy Hotels; Survival Strategies; Workhouses

◨ HOUSING, AFFORDABLE

Without affordable housing, the problems of homelessness will never be solved. High housing costs often put individuals and families at risk of homelessness when their incomes are too low to pay for housing plus other basic necessities. People fleeing domestic violence frequently find themselves back in violent situations because they can't find affordable housing. People on fixed incomes find that rising housing costs outstrip their meager incomes. A high demand and a shortage of affordable housing make it even more difficult for people with disabilities, people with a history of substance abuse, and people with poor credit records to obtain housing. For people needing temporary or seasonal housing, affordable units are in short supply.

MEASURING HOUSING AFFORDABILITY

People measure housing affordability by the ratio of household income to the cost of available housing. For more than a century, the recommended standard for housing affordability was that households should spend no more than one-fourth of their income for shelter expenses. This ratio dates back to the writings of economist Ernest Engel. Using analysis of a survey of Belgian working-class families conducted in 1857, Engle proposed an economic law stating that the ratio of a household's income spent for housing is constant regardless of the household's income. Engel's law focused on food as the most essential expenditure within a household. Of necessity, food costs would vary depending on the number and age of people in a household and the ability to self-provision through foraging, hunting, gardening, or raising of livestock while the housing cost could remain constant even when household composition changed. The rule of thumb that emerged from this perspective was "one week's wage for one month's rent." This ratio could be readily applied in decision making for minimiz-

ing risk in renting an apartment or granting a mortgage to a given household. This ratio remained the norm until the mid-1970s.

Critics of Engel's economic law have proposed other measures of affordable housing. As early as 1868, other economists critiqued Engel's work. Herman Schwabe, for example, published detailed research on housing expenditures within the household budget. His research on wages and rent indicated that as income rose, the percentage of income spent on rent fell. Schwabe proposed an alternative economic law stating that the poorer the household, the greater the proportion of income must be spent on housing.

More recent critics of Engel's economic law note that over time, consumers' shifting expectations regarding their housing have also affected household consumption patterns. They propose that the proportion of income spent on housing would have increased over time as other costs have decreased and as housing expectations have increased.

Focusing on income as the primary factor in determining housing cost burdens fails to account for variability in households. Housing costs affect households with equal incomes differently depending upon the size of the households. A household with seven members has different needs than a single individual for food, clothing, transportation, medical care, and other basic necessities. In 2001, the average annual expenditures from the Consumer Expenditure Survey found that one-person households spent on average $1,477 for food at home, while five or more person households spent $5,111. One alternative means of measuring housing affordability would take household size and composition into account and base a recommended budget guideline for housing affordability on actually household expenditures. The U.S. Bureau of Labor Statistics (BLS), for example, has established typical household budgets based on their annual Consumer Expenditure Survey. In 2001, the typical family spent about 33 percent of their gross income on housing, 11.2 percent for food, and 3.5 percent for clothing. The use of a housing affordability standard based on BLS budgets is in contrast to measures based on the Census Bureau's Federal Poverty

Threshold levels. Social Security Administration economist Mollie Orshansky developed the poverty threshold levels in 1963 and 1964 using the Department of Agriculture's Economy Food Plan adjusting for family size. The limitation to affordability standards based on poverty levels is that these were not established as inclusive standard budgets of goods and services meeting minimum annual needs for a family of a particular size and composition. With the exception of food, acceptable standards for major consumption items were not available at the time the poverty threshold levels were established.

Another recommended measure of housing affordability not only recognizes the household composition but also incorporates Schwabe's economic law regarding income level. With the concept of "shelter poverty" as a basis, Michael Stone, a professor at the center for Community Planning and Public Policy at the University of Massachusetts in Boston, emphasizes the amount of money that a household needs to meet basic necessities and uses the residual of income less that amount as the affordable housing measure. Using this measure, some households may have a negative housing affordability; the cost of basic needs excluding housing may exceed their income. Under this measure, housing is unaffordable at any cost.

Although Stone's shelter poverty measure does account for income level and variations in cost of other needs, it fails to address concerns regarding the cost of housing as the cause of the difficulty in meeting basic necessities. Another alternative, "burden of housing cost," begins with housing costs to determine if the residual income following shelter expenditures is sufficient to meet other minimum household needs. It considers the impact of a proportional expenditure/income norm, such as an allocation of 25 percent of income for housing, and identifies households for which allocating the recommended percent of income find themselves unable to cover costs of other necessities. The burden of housing cost would then incorporate not only guidelines for household budgets based on size and characteristics of the household, but also the actual level of income.

Although alternative measures of housing affordability such as shelter poverty and burden of housing costs are more accurate than a set ratio of expenditures to income, the practicality of implementing them is limited. For example, determining an adjusted housing affordability threshold level would require considerably more information and effort in identifying eligible families for housing assistance, increasing the cost of providing housing assistance. Thus, people commonly employ a standard fixed housing affordability ratio when making policies and implementing programs.

The U.S. Department of Housing and Urban Development (HUD) has established a threshold level for housing cost burden based on a household paying 30 percent or more of its gross monthly income on monthly housing costs (rent or mortgage payments plus basic utilities including heat and electricity). The 30 percent cut-off point for housing affordability provides a straightforward measure of affordability and is an efficient measure for use in implementing federal housing programs. Using the housing cost burden level of shelter expenditures at 30 percent of household income or higher, the Joint Center for Housing Studies at Harvard University estimates, three out of every ten U.S. households struggle with housing affordability. In 2003, more than 14.3 million households were severely cost burdened, spending more than 50 percent of their incomes on housing.

The increase in the standard from 25 percent to 30 percent of household income as a reasonably affordable shelter cost occurred during the mid-1970s. Prior to that time, public housing residents were required to contribute 25 percent of their income toward rent, observing the rule of thumb for housing affordability. Federal budget deficits and political will at that time created pressure to reduce government costs. This pressure resulted in a policy change that shifted a greater proportion of housing assistance program costs from the taxpayer to the recipients, requiring program beneficiaries to contribute more of their incomes to rent. The decision to require households to contribute 30 percent of their income to housing was based more on an attempt to lower government costs of providing housing assistance than it was on actual household expenditures or recommended household management practices. The

30 percent housing cost burden measure has, however, become the standard for affordability and is used for both renters and home owners.

MEASURES OF HOUSING AFFORDABILITY AND HOME OWNERSHIP

The measures of housing affordability discussed previously are directed primarily at estimating rent levels appropriate for low-income households and their eligibility for housing assistance. Current policy priorities are directed at making the dream of home ownership a reality for more and more households. Providing home-ownership opportunities to lower-income households by adjusting the underwriting practices for residential mortgages is another way that the standard measure for housing affordability has changed over time.

Conventional mortgage underwriting practices typically considered a 20 percent down payment for borrowers. In addition, borrowers were required to meet qualifying ratios that kept the mortgage principle and interest payment under 28 percent of income and total payments for long-term debts under 36 percent of income. Lenders today consider much higher ratios for underwriting mortgages using a system of credit scoring that includes employment stability and credit payment histories along with loan characteristics.

Increasing the qualifying ratio for the mortgage principle and interest payment to as high as 40 percent of income increases the pool of potential borrowers substantially. One of the justifications for this increase is that many households manage to pay monthly rents costing more than 50 percent of their income, and they should have the opportunity to achieve the dream of home ownership.

The push to allow more people to own a home, deregulation of the banking industry, and the emergence of mortgage companies have led to an increase in unscrupulous lending. With the higher qualifying ratios, interest rates and loan terms are often adjusted to minimize the lenders' risk of financial loss in case of loan default. Many questionable lending practices are predatory, targeting loans with higher interest rates and less attractive terms to low-income neighborhoods and minority households. With a slowdown in the economy, the consequence of this shift in underwriting is beginning to be apparent.

Foreclosure rates are increasing, placing low-income households in precarious housing situations. They often lose the wealth built up in home equity, have poor credit ratings, and can be forced to relocate, increasing the risk of homelessness as they seek alternative housing in a market with rapidly escalating housing costs. Thus, the determination of a standard measure of housing affordability is linked to changing risk of homelessness for home owners as well as low-income renters.

TRENDS IN HOUSING COSTS

Refining the measure of housing affordability may contribute to more effective distribution of government housing assistance and a larger pool of potential home buyers, but it does not address the difficulty that households face in obtaining affordable housing presented by a rapid increase in housing costs. Although the Consumer Price Index (CPI) has limitations for direct application, it is often used to measure relative changes in consumer costs over time. For example, using the CPI, overall consumer costs were estimated to have increased by 3.8 percent between 1999 and 2000. This was the highest increase in a decade. A year later, the CPI was at the lowest rate in fifteen years at 1.6 percent. This fluctuation in consumer costs reflects economic shifts over time, but it fails to adequately reflect the way in which various costs changes affect household budgets. As indicated previously, housing is a major component of household budget requirements, and dramatic changes in the cost of housing have a direct effect on income available for other expenditures. For example, rent of primary residences increased 36.1 percent between 1990 and 2000. With the cost of renting increasing faster than incomes, a greater number of households are at risk of homelessness.

Costs of purchasing an existing home have also increased. The U.S. Census reported that in 2000 the average home sold for $177,000. The cost of home ownership simply prices many people out of the market. At the same time, increased rent levels limit their options.

The costs of operating and maintaining a home affect housing affordability. Utility costs have risen as well. Between 1990 and 2002, the cost of natural gas—the heating fuel for more than half of all metropolitan homes in the United States—increased 42.5 percent. Electricity costs increased 16.6 percent during the same twelve years. The rising costs of maintaining a home affect housing affordability for all households, regardless of whether they are renters, home buyers, or even people who own their home mortgage free.

Housing costs are not, however, constant. Variation in housing markets by location dramatically affects housing affordability. Regional variation in house price, utility costs, and rent levels for available units is significant. According to the National Association of Homebuilders, the average sales price of an existing home in the Elkart-Goshen, Indiana, metropolitan statistical area was $111,000 in 2002. At this price, 94.9 percent of homes for sale were affordable to prospective buyers with earnings at the median area household income. In comparison, the average sales price of an existing home in Salinas, California, was $319,000. At this price, only 7.7 percent of homes for sale were affordable to prospective buyers with earnings at the median household income of $53,800 (with the area median household income for Elkhart-Goshen at $59,300). Even within a local housing market, submarket variation exists across neighborhoods and among various housing units based on the type, size, condition, and amenities.

CONSTRUCTION TRENDS

Rising costs of residential construction are one reason for the increased cost of home ownership. In 2000, the U.S. Census reported that the average cost of a new single-family home was $207,000. In 1990, the average cost of a new single-family home was $149,800, whereas an average new home cost less than $80,000 in 1980. One explanation for the increase is that the cost of construction reflects market demand. The square footage of new single-family houses continues to increase, and the trend is toward

Participants in a national protest of the lack of affordable housing block off Constitution Avenue in Washington, D.C., on 7 November 1988.
Source: Bettmann/Corbis; used with permission.

including more amenities, ranging from three-car garages to a second kitchen for entertaining. Increasing market expectations have extended beyond quality construction and energy efficiency, contributing to the rapidly escalating cost of housing.

Standardizing construction costs to square-foot costs reveals the increased expense of land, materials, and labor that also affect housing affordability. Regulatory barriers, reviews, and construction code requirements also increase costs. Policies that require excessive lot sizes increase not only the cost of land per house but also costs for provision of utilities, streets, and services. Manufactured homes are often considered a more affordable housing alternative. The square-foot cost of manufactured homes is less than that of conventional homes; however, the cost of obtaining a suitable site and setting up a manufactured home can make the overall cost less affordable.

TRENDS IN HOUSEHOLD INCOME

Because housing affordability is determined not only by the cost of housing, but also by household income, income trends have a direct effect on housing affordability. The typical household in the United States today finds that its income has not kept pace with the cost of housing. Those people working at low-wage, insecure jobs are particularly vulnerable to becoming homeless. The Low Income Housing Coalition (LIHC) calculates a "housing wage" as the income that a full-time worker needs to be able to afford a basic two-bedroom apartment. Using the 30 percent housing cost burden measure and fair market rent levels used by the U.S. Department of Housing and Urban Development when establishing housing assistance payments, the wage level for affordable two-bedroom apartments in every state in the nation far exceeds the minimum wage.

The U.S. Census in 2000 reported the disparity in income distribution across the country. Income distribution is such that the 20 percent of households with the highest income in 2000 obtained 49.7 percent of all earnings while those households in the bottom 20 percent had a 3.6 percent share of earnings. Not only is there a disparity in distribution of income, but also the Economic Policy Institute reports that wages for workers with earnings at the bottom 10 percent of households found that their income fell by 9.3 percent between 1979 and 1999. Furthermore, between 2000 and 2001, the number of unemployed workers in the United States increased by 2.2 million.

AVAILABILITY OF AFFORDABLE HOUSING

The availability of affordable housing is affected by trends in construction, demand for existing housing units, and the demolition of substandard dwellings. In general, construction of multifamily rental units

has declined since the 1980s, when tax policies shifted away from benefiting individuals investing in affordable housing development. Low-income housing tax credits were created as a source of capital for constructing multifamily units. Low-income housing tax credits have been used to finance mixed-income developments, resulting in a limited increase of affordable housing units.

Renovation of housing and demolition of deteriorated units have reduced the U.S. housing stock that was considered substandard to less than 1 percent. At the same time, the number of homeless households has increased. Because less costly housing is often older and of lower quality, the trade-off for improved housing stock has been more expensive housing. In the process of upgrading housing quality, basic shelter options such as rooming houses, residential hotels, and other single-room occupancy alternatives were eliminated. Supply-and-demand economics results in the cost of housing exceeding reasonable affordability for low-income households. Preservation of affordable housing stock is essential. The real spending by owners of rental units fell at a 2.7 percent average annual rate between 1992 and 1999. Deferred maintenance has a deteriorating impact on the long-term availability of affordable housing. Long-term lack of maintenance results in deteriorating buildings and eventually in the need to demolish substandard units.

Beyond the shift in housing stock toward more costly housing, federally subsidized housing is being lost. In order to capitalize on higher prevailing rents, private owners have opted out of rental assistance programs or prepaid mortgages that required a unit to be available for low-income tenants. This shift has resulted in a loss of more than 90,000 affordable housing units. According to the Joint Center for Housing Studies at Harvard University (2000), 10 to 15 percent of the remaining project-based, assisted units with contracts expiring in the future may become market rate units.

Recent federal policies to deconcentrate racial minorities and persons in poverty by demolishing large-scale public housing projects further limit available affordable housing. Federal policy no longer requires a one-for-one replacement of demolished units, and under a policy priority to subsidize mixed-income development, fewer than one-third of the replacement housing units are for low-income households. A number of federal policies have created a net loss of affordable housing units, especially for low-income households.

LOCATION AS A FACTOR

In making the link between the lack of affordable housing and homelessness, one must consider the location of affordable housing and the impact of location on individuals and families. Housing markets are commonly based on locational factors. Housing units located near community amenities such as good schools, parks, and transportation access are priced higher, whereas those located in environmentally unsatisfactory areas or remote areas without employment opportunities or transportation access are frequently priced lower. Yet, the cost of getting to work, the availability of a job that pays a livable wage, and the need for a safe place to raise one's family or retire well are all linked to location.

The failure to provide affordable housing to keep pace with rapid economic development often results in an affordable housing shortage. In areas with natural amenities, tourism and second-home development often result in increased jobs but can have the unintended consequence of increasing pressure on housing affordability. Construction of high-end homes raises the value of existing homes, and the shortage of lower-cost housing affects the housing affordability across an entire area. Workers are forced to commute longer distances from affordable housing. Employers are forced to deal with a less-reliable labor force as workers commute longer distances. Families doubling up to afford the limited available housing live in overcrowded and/or substandard housing and face a greater risk of domestic violence and increased likelihood of homelessness.

HOUSING DISCRIMINATION AND HOUSING AFFORDABILITY

Further worsening the problems that people have in finding affordable housing is not having access to housing. Discrimination differentially impacts households of families of color, those with more children, and those with disabilities in terms of housing affordability. Not only are these households more likely to have lower incomes, but also they confront barriers to the affordable housing that is available.

Racial and ethnic minorities are a growing proportion of U.S. households. The Joint Center for Housing Studies estimates that by 2010 nearly three out of ten households will be headed by minorities. These households affect home ownership demand; they are also the households targeted for questionable lending practices and therefore are at a greater risk of foreclosure, affecting their continued housing stability.

IMPACTS OF HOUSING AFFORDABILITY

Lack of affordable housing is directly linked to homelessness. As the availability of affordable housing declines, the rate of homelessness increases. We cannot address the problem of homelessness without addressing the problem of lack of affordable housing.

Trends in household incomes, housing costs, construction, and demolition of housing indicate that concerns about housing affordability will continue to escalate. Strong public policies, private sector commitments, and public support are essential to lessen the affordable housing shortage.

At the same time, people are using a number of creative alternatives to address the lack of affordable housing. Communities are becoming aware of income factors that affect housing affordability and are promoting new job growth at more livable wages. People are reviewing regulatory barriers to construction of affordable housing across the country and establishing alternative policies. Builders are exploring the use of more affordable and sustainable building materials and techniques. People are scrutinizing policies regarding the demolition of public housing without replacement. People are implementing state-level policies that target housing development funding to areas of economic growth. People are studying mortgage lending practices and policy recommendations. We can hope that affordable housing will soon become a measure of community well-being.

—*Ann C. Ziebarth*

Further Reading

American Institute for Economic Research. (2001, January 8). The AIER cost-of-living guide. *Research Reports, 68*(1), 1–4.

American Institute for Economic Research. (2001, November 26). Employment outlook: The party's over. *Research Reports, 68*(22), 125–126.

American Institute for Economic Research. (2003, January 13). The AIER cost-of-living guide. *Research Reports, 70*(1), 1–4.

Fisher, G. M. (1997). *The development of the Orshansky Poverty Thresholds and their subsequent history as the official U.S. poverty measure.* Poverty Measurement Working Papers. Washington, DC: U.S. Census Bureau. Retrieved December 2, 2003, from http://www.census.gov/hhes/poverty/povmeas/papers/orshansky.html.

Hulchianski, J. D. (1995). The concept of housing affordability: Six contemporary uses of the housing expenditure-to-income ratio. *Housing Studies, 10*(4), 471–491.

Joint Center for Housing Studies of Harvard University. (2003). *The state of the nation's housing.* Cambridge, MA: President and Fellows of Harvard College.

Low Income Housing Coalition. (2003). *Out of reach.* Washington, DC: Author.

Stone, M. E. (1993). *Shelter poverty: New ideas on housing affordability.* Philadelphia: Temple University Press.

U.S. Department of Commerce, U.S. Census Bureau. (2001, September). Money income in the United States: 2000. *Current Population Reports P60–213.* Washington, DC: U.S. Government Printing Office.

Wills, D. S. (2002). Rural housing prices grew rapidly in the 1990s. *Rural America, 17*(3), 47–56.

▣ HOUSING, TRANSITIONAL

Transitional housing has come to play a major but controversial role as a public response to homelessness in the United States. Proponents assert that it offers the combination of housing and services that homeless families and individuals with multiple problems need to achieve residential stability. To critics, transitional housing disempowers its residents with intrusive rules and requirements, saddles them with the stigma of living in a "program" rather than normal housing, and diverts resources that might otherwise expand the supply of affordable permanent housing. Assessing these claims requires considering what transitional housing consists of, how and why such programs for homeless families and individuals developed, and what is known about their effectiveness in reducing homelessness.

WHAT IS TRANSITIONAL HOUSING?

For the U.S. Department of Housing and Urban Development (HUD), "transitional housing" refers to programs intended to facilitate the movement to permanent housing of homeless individuals with mental or physical disabilities and homeless families with children, usually within twenty-four months. Compared to emergency shelters, transitional housing programs tend to be smaller, offer more privacy, provide more intense goal-oriented services, and place more limits on the length of stay. For people with mental health or substance abuse problems, transitional housing often doubles as residential treatment, with both structure and services organized to address clinical and addiction issues. Compared to permanent housing, transitional programs are distinguished by time limits on stays, a focus on changing residents' behavior, the use of behavioral criteria for admissions and discharges, and the absence of leases or other protections of tenancy rights.

Transitional housing programs vary in the populations they serve (for instance, people with disabilities or families rather than individuals), the amount of privacy their physical structure allows (for example, congregate settings rather than scattered apartments), the services they provide, their requirement for participation in services, and their admission, tenure, and disposition policies for moving people through the program.

THE ROLE OF TRANSITIONAL HOUSING IN HOMELESS POLICY

The context for the development of transitional housing was the crisis of affordable permanent housing that was revealed when homelessness mushroomed in the 1980s. As the homeless population shifted to include more families and disabled adults, nonprofit agencies emerged to address housing and service needs not met by public services.

A major impetus for developing transitional housing for homeless families was to improve on inadequate shelters. In New York City, for example, a lack of affordable housing led to increasing lengths of stay in overburdened family shelters that had never been intended for long-term residence. Transitional housing programs with more private accommodations offered a more humane alternative. They also developed an array of services (assistance with budgeting, money management, housing search, vocational services, and parenting skills training) that were expected to enhance residential stability. For individual homeless adults with psychiatric and substance abuse problems, nonprofit agencies developed "low demand" transitional housing to attract those who were unwilling to enter shelters, and more service-intensive transitional housing that offered "housing readiness" services (including assistance with medication management, enforced sobriety, and money management) to help those with disabilities compete for the limited permanent housing slots.

When HUD took over the coordination of federally funded homelessness programs, it required localities seeking funds to establish a system of services called "continuum of care," codified transitional housing as an essential element of the continuum, and strongly encouraged the development of services. In effect, this approach shifted the policy focus away from the systemic problems of lack of housing to the more tractable issues of how best to address individual families and single adults through services.

IS TRANSITIONAL HOUSING EFFECTIVE?

Descriptive evaluations have found transitional housing programs viable and helpful to their graduates. A 1995 study of HUD-funded transitional housing reported that 70 percent of families graduating from these programs moved on to stable housing, though it noted that a lack of employment opportunities and of affordable housing remained barriers. Outcome studies of service-intensive transitional housing programs report improvements in residential stability, income, and clinical status, but dropout rates are invariably high. Controlled studies, which are rare, have found transitional housing to be more effective than shelter or drop-in programs at moving homeless individuals into permanent housing.

The question of whether transitional housing is a necessary step to permanent housing is only beginning to be asked. Sociologist Martha Burt suggests rethinking the utility of transitional housing for families and proposes that moving homeless families "from emergency shelter directly into a permanent unit and then providing the same type of supportive services commonly available in transitional housing residential programs may produce less disruption and help families more than the usual type of transitional program" (Burt 2001, 776). Models using this approach—"Transitioning in Place" in Seattle, Washington, and "Family Critical Time Intervention" in Westchester County, New York—are being tested as alternatives to lengthy stays in transitional facilities for families.

For homeless individuals with mental illness, the effectiveness of "housing first" approaches that bypass transitional "housing readiness" programs has been demonstrated in New York City. In the only controlled trial of "housing first" versus "continuum of care" approaches, those who were immediately offered apartments without treatment and sobriety prerequisites spent less time homeless and in hospitals and incurred fewer costs over the two-year follow-up than those in continuum-of-care programs.

UNKNOWNS AND NEXT STEPS

These recent developments in research and program development have challenged conventional wisdom about transitional housing. At the same time, new HUD funding formulas are shifting monies allocated for homeless programs away from services and toward permanent housing, which may further reduce the role of transitional housing programs.

The implications of these changes are unclear, and several issues warrant attention. First, emerging alternatives to transitional housing rely heavily on providing access and subsidies to units in the "normal" housing market, so expanding the supply of affordable permanent housing remains a prerequisite for their success. HUD's reallocation of homeless program monies will be grossly inadequate without significantly expanding mainstream programs for developing affordable housing. Second, both "housing first" and "transitioning in place" approaches require supportive services. Redirecting HUD monies will necessitate finding new funding sources for services. Finally, research is needed to assess the limits of "housing first" approaches, what array of permanent housing options it requires, which individuals and families will still require extra transitional structure and support, and how to tailor transitional programs to meet their needs most effectively.

—*Susan M. Barrow*

Further Reading

Barnard-Columbia Center for Urban Policy. (1996). *The continuum of care: A report on the new federal policy to address homelessness.* Washington, DC: U.S. Department of Housing and Urban Development.

Barrow, S. M., & Soto, G. (1996). *Closer to home: An evaluation of interim housing for homeless adults.* New York: Corporation for Supportive Housing.

Barrow, S. M., & Zimmer, R. (1999). Transitional housing and services: A synthesis. In L. B. Fosburg & D. L. Dennis (Eds.), *Practical lessons: The 1998 National Symposium on Homelessness Research* (pp. 10-1–10-31). Washington, DC: U.S. Department of Housing and Urban Development and U. S. Department of Health and Human Services.

Bogard, C. J., McConnell, J. J., Gerstel, N., & Schwartz, M. (1999). Homeless mothers and depression: Misdirected policy. *Journal of Health and Social Behavior, 40,* 46–62.

Burt, M. R. (2001). Homeless families, singles and others: Findings from the 1996 National Survey of Homeless Assistance Providers and Clients. *Housing Policy Debate, 12*(4), 737–780.

Gulcur, L., Stefancic, A., Shinn, M., Tsemberis, S., & Fischer, S. N. (2003). Housing, hospitalization and cost outcomes for homeless individuals with psychiatric disabilities participating in Continuum of Care and Housing First programmes. *Journal of Community and Applied Psychology, 13,* 171–186.

Interagency Council on the Homeless. (1994). *Priority: Home! The federal plan to break the cycle of homelessness.* Washington, DC: U.S. Department of Housing and Urban Development.

Matulef, M. L., Crosse, S. B., Dietz, S. K., Van Ryszin, G., Kiser, M. L., Puhl, L. M., & Ficke, R.C. (1995). *National evaluation of supportive housing demonstration program: Final report.* Washington, DC: U.S. Department of Housing and Urban Development and the Office of Policy Development and Research.

Murray, R., Baier, M., North, C., Lato, M., & Eskew, C. (1997). One-year status of homeless mentally ill clients who completed a transitional residential program. *Community Mental Health Journal, 33*(1), 43–50.

Nathan, R. P., Pulice, R., Nakamura, R. T., & Schwartz, M. (1995). *The New York State McKinney Transitional Housing Demonstration Project. Final report.* Prepared for the New York State Department of Social Services.

National Resource Center on Homelessness and Mental Illness Policy Research Associates. (1997). *Developing and operating safe havens programs.* Washington, DC: The Center for Mental Health Services, Substance Abuse and Mental Health Services Administration, U.S. Department of Health and Human Services, Office of Special Needs Assistance Programs, Office of Community Planning and Development, and U.S. Department of Housing and Urban Development.

Rahav, M., Rivera, J., Nuttbrock, L., Ng-Mak, D., Sturz, E. L., Link, B. G., Struening, E. L., Pepper, B., & Gross, B. (1997). Homeless, mentally ill, chemical abusing men in different, community-based treatment programs. In F. M. Tims, J. A. Inciardi, B. W. Fletcher, & A. M. Horton Jr. (Eds.), *The effectiveness of innovative approaches in the treatment of drug abuse* (pp. 84–97). Westport, CT: Greenwood Press.

Roman, A. M., & Zhu, X. D. (1996). *An evaluation of Massachusetts AFDC transitional housing demonstration project.* Prepared for the Massachusetts Department of Public Welfare and the U.S. Department of Health and Human Services.

▣ HOUSING AND HOMELESSNESS IN DEVELOPING NATIONS

At the turn of the twenty-first century, the number of homeless people worldwide was estimated as between 100 million and 1 billion—an estimate whose wide range reflects varying definitions of homelessness. Indeed, the current definitions and categories that are applied in industrialized countries often do not adequately capture the situations of chronically homeless people or squatters in developing countries. Moreover, the causes of homelessness differ in developed and developing countries, requiring different intervention strategies.

Nine developing nations—Peru, South Africa, Zimbabwe, Ghana, Egypt, India, Bangladesh, Indonesia, and China—were the subject of a study carried out in 2001 by the Centre for Architectural Research and Development Overseas (CARDO) at the University of Newcastle upon Tyne in England. The aims of the study were to explore the different definitions and causes of homelessness in developing countries and to highlight innovative campaigns underway to eradicate homelessness and support homeless people. While CARDO's research also focused on street children, the emphasis here is on homeless adults and households.

COMPARING HOMELESSNESS IN DEVELOPED AND DEVELOPING COUNTRIES

In developed countries, homelessness is generally more attributable to personal or household circumstances than to a failure of the housing supply system. Even when affordable housing exists, homeless people in the West frequently need a range of social support and welfare systems to help them gain access to it, and to the services that might lift them out of homelessness. In developing countries, however, formal housing supply systems simply fail to provide enough shelter to fill the demand, particularly among low-income groups. This leads to massive informal development and squatting which, in turn, places hundreds of millions of people in living conditions that would merit the term *homelessness* in developed nations.

Indeed, most of the world's population would be homeless if judged by the standards of the developed nations. For example, in its 1999 study of the issue in Europe, the European Federation of National Organizations Working with the Homeless (FEANTSA) defined four levels of homelessness based on housing adequacy. It described an adequate home as one that is secure and where available space and amenities provide a good environment for the satisfaction of physical, social, psychological, and cultural needs. Low quality, by these European standards, is manifested by overcrowding, high levels of noise, and pollution or infestation—conditions that many, if not most, people in developing countries endure.

Cooper (1995) also offers four categories, or degrees, of homelessness. At one end of this scale are those who are housed but without security, safety, and adequate standards for health or child develop-

ment; at the other end are people without a roof, living on the streets. In Cooper's model, the category of people without an acceptable roof over their heads could describe the countless millions in poor-quality squatter settlements around the world, as well as street dwellers.

DEFINING HOMELESSNESS IN DEVELOPING COUNTRIES

Official definitions of homelessness range from nonexistent, as in Peru, China, and Ghana, to so broad as to be virtually all-encompassing, as in Zimbabwe. However, for census purposes, most nations have working definitions that fall into four broad categories.

Tenure-Based Definitions

Some governments define homelessness primarily in terms of home ownership or secure land tenure. Two examples show the extremes of such definitions based on security of tenure. The National Housing Taskforce of Zimbabwe assumes that anyone who does not own a home in an officially approved residential area is homeless. Any adult not possessing a publicly provided dwelling is entitled to register for one on the Official Housing Waiting List. So embedded is this linkage of homelessness with the concept of ownership that government housing policy earmarks 90 percent of all new housing for ownership, and only 10 percent for rental. Furthermore, all urban local authorities are required to sell their housing stock to tenants, as a way of passing the maintenance burden on to the occupants.

Peru is at the opposite end of the tenure scale. Policymakers distinguish two very different—though only semi-official—categories of homeless people. The first consists of those who live in squatter settlements without legal title to land. One Peruvian program grants formal land title to squatters below the poverty level who do not own a registered plot or property. Existing squatter settlements are divided up, and plots are allocated to the residents for formal ownership. As a result, many thousands of people are squatting on poor-quality desert land, in makeshift dwellings of straw or plastic sheeting, and applying for legal tenure before they invest in building more substantial homes. In many cases, the process takes years.

The second group in Peru consists of those living on the street. These people are often branded variously as alcoholics, addicts, vagrants, criminals, and mentally ill. Being so far outside any formal community, people in this group are not granted land title.

Shelter-Based Definitions

For land allocation purposes, India's census agency defines homeless people as those not living in a "census house," that is, a structure with a roof. Planners charged with providing house sites to deserving cases classify a person as eligible if they do not have a structure with a roof or land. Thus, residents of squatter areas are entitled to a plot in a regularized area if authorities have driven them from their squatter homes. No household that holds a plot in a regularized area is regarded as homeless, even if its home consists only of a shack. By a quirk of policy, pavement dwellers are usually not counted among the homeless because they are rarely on the list of voters and do not possess ration cards, with which to claim food and fuel at controlled priced.

In shelter-based definitions, what constitutes an adequate roof is open to question. The Ghanaian Statistical Service includes sales kiosks, abandoned warehouses, offices, and shops in its definition of "house"; no other issues of quality or suitability are considered. Therefore, in Ghana, only the most destitute, without any form of roof, and without any family nearby to take responsibility for them, are officially defined as homeless.

Definitions Based on Suitability and Quality

Other countries—for example, Egypt and Bangladesh—class such shelter solutions as inadequate. In Egypt, people are considered homeless who live in *marginal* housing (*iskan gawazi* in Arabic), including shacks, kiosks, staircases, rooftops, public institutional buildings, and cemeteries. Similarly, the Bangladesh Bureau of Statistics' official definition of homelessness is used for census purposes:

> Floating population are the mobile and vagrant category of rootless people who have no permanent dwelling units whatever . . . and they are found on the census night . . . in the rail station, launch *ghat* [terminal], bus station, *hat-bazaar* [market], *mazar* [shrine], staircase of public/government buildings, open space, etc.

In South Africa, officials of the Provincial Housing Department and the Greater Johannesburg Metropolitan Council base their definition on quality. They accept as homeless those people without adequate shelter or secure tenure, including those living in squatter settlements, rooms built in the back yards of dwellings in official townships, or in slum conditions.

Definitions Based on Permanence and Stability

The Indonesian census of 2000 divided the population into two main categories, those with a permanent place to stay and those without. The latter included ship crewmen, nomadic people, and those living in houseboats or floating houses, as well as the more obvious *tunawisma*—houseless.

DIFFERENTIATING BETWEEN HOMELESSNESS AND SQUATTING

Squatters need not be excluded from a definition of homelessness, but a distinction is helpful. Without it, the sheer numbers of squatters might divert attention from those in more desperate circumstances. The more chronically homeless, such as street dwellers, generally have no protection from the elements; at most, they might improvise shelters of plastic sheeting, cloth, or cardboard, sometimes clustering together on the pavement or empty private or public space close by. Squatters tend to build somewhat more permanent, roofed structures. This gives them not only more physical security but also a de facto address that helps them develop a social network with people living in similar circumstances. Both of these factors facilitate help from both governmental and nongovernmental organizations (NGOs)—for example, providing water, sanitation, and opportunities for education and financial credit, especially where these rely on traceable networks to provide valuable social contacts in the absence of monetary assets.

Generally, but not always, squatters' shelters are of higher quality than street homeless people's, and tend to be improved over time. Squatters tend to settle in peripheral sites, while homeless people gravitate to city centers where their opportunistic lifestyle is possible.

In many countries, including India, China, Bangladesh, Indonesia, South Africa, and Zimbabwe, the legal position of squatters is no better than that of their counterparts on the street. All of them—but especially the street homeless

Once an upper-class area, the Cartucho district in Bogatá, Colombia, has become a ghetto in the heart of the city. Some 10,000 people live in poverty and violence in this district, shown here in January 2001.
Source: Jerome Sessini/Corbis; used with permission.

—suffer raids during which officials scatter or relocate the people. However, when this happens, squatters may be the more insecure as they have more to lose. When street homeless people are raided, it is generally because they are perceived as a nuisance or a blot on the attractiveness of the city. But squatter settlements are usually raided to clear land for more profitable uses, often favoring upper-income groups.

In Peru, however, squatters have much higher legal standing than other homeless people. A peculiarity in Peruvian law provides that people who occupy state-owned land and remain there for twenty-four hours, with no formal complaint being lodged, cannot be evicted immediately. Rather, they can apply for legal title to the land, and the case will be decided in court. The same provision applies to occupiers of private land. If such land has been undeveloped for ten years or more, the court is likely to give title to the invaders. Unlike street homeless people, squatters in Peru may consider themselves on an upwardly mobile housing trajectory.

In many countries, the street homeless population has higher occupational mobility, less secure jobs, and smaller income range than residents of squatter

settlements. Street homeless populations tend to be predominantly single and male, whereas squatter settlements have more mixed populations.

Interestingly, Ghana has virtually no squatters, as local chiefs control most land. Even the lowest-quality urban housing properties tend to be held legally under a traditional tenure system administered by the chiefs.

CAUSES

A fundamental cause of homelessness in developing countries is poverty, especially in rural areas. However, poverty alone does not necessarily lead to homelessness. There is also a failure of the housing supply system to provide at even the most basic level. These two problems are exacerbated, in some cases, by social and political changes and the breakdown of traditional family support systems, factors that can gradually push some people into homelessness.

From Rural Home to Urban Homelessness

In many of the developing countries studied, particularly Peru, India, Bangladesh, and Egypt, rural poverty has driven many to seek employment in cities. Most often, a single man moves to the city to work and sends money back to the family, often preferring homelessness to paying for accommodations. In bad weather, he might pay to stay in a hostel, if such places are available, but primarily he "sleeps rough." In some cases, other family members follow him to the city. In India, for example, entire families move to the city to work on construction sites and live on or near the site in rudimentary shelters.

Seasonal economic migration in Peru sees many indigenous people from the Alto Plano sleeping on the street and in parks at particular times of the year. A similar pattern occurs in Bolivia. These people have adequate homes back in their villages but are without any shelter for the time they spend trading in the cities.

Social Causes

Many people endure poverty without being tipped into homelessness—until the poverty is coupled with a breakdown in traditional family support or loss of a spouse through separation, divorce, or death. Rapid changes and disruptions in social relations can compound the stress of housing insecurity, while supportive family life and effective parenting can alleviate it. Homeless women and children are frequently casualties of family dissolution or escapees from family violence. This is especially true in a number of South American nations, such as Peru and Bolivia. Street children often also tell of fleeing an abusive stepparent. Indeed, social interventions such as family support and mediation, child protection, and the prevention of domestic violence can be effective in addressing homelessness.

Many developing countries have adopted legislation to protect women's rights. Nevertheless, cultural attitudes often result in a woman, and her children, being thrown out of their home by relatives if her husband dies or abandons them. Such women may be forced onto the streets (see "Rita: A Case Study," p. 276, this volume) and sometimes into prostitution to provide for their children.

In China, those who might elsewhere be deemed homeless are included within the "floating popula-

tion." This "floating" segment also includes some people who are trying to escape local enforcement of the Chinese government's "one family, one child" population policy. Some families who want more children choose to leave their household registration place. But women in these "over-procreated" families cannot obtain the official temporary living permit without the family planning certificate granted by their native neighborhood. Without official identification, children born to these couples will have difficulty obtaining education and employment.

Evictions

In developing countries, governments quite commonly use their powers to evict people to allow commercial development of the spaces they illegally occupied. Those affected have neither the money nor the power to defend themselves. The Delhi Development Authority (DDA), for example, has a land protection branch to detect and remove all squatter settlements. The inhabitants are first rendered homeless and are moved on to the pavement, then are chased off one pavement only to settle on another or on open ground, even at the coldest and wettest times of the year.

Such evictions generally involve the transfer of land from the poor and vulnerable to middle- or upper-income people, and the development of projects that particularly benefit wealthier groups. Such cases can be found in the developed as well as developing countries. In a Malaysian case, the evictions made room for a golf course to promote international tourism. Forced evictions are particularly disturbing for those in precarious housing. Often violent and discriminatory, they are officially sanctioned acts with many harmful consequences for those displaced.

CHARACTERISTICS OF HOMELESS PEOPLE

The characteristics of homeless people in developing countries are quite different from those in the developed countries and from common Western perception of homeless people as lone, unemployed vagrants and drunks.

While the majority of homeless people in developing countries are single and male, there is also a very high percentage of homeless families with children. This is especially true of countries such as Peru if squatters are included in the definition. In India and Bangladesh, households with children also feature highly among those who live on the streets.

Homeless people in developing countries fall predominantly into the twenty to fifty-nine age range. However, there are certain anomalies. For example, in Kumasi, Ghana, 70 percent are under twenty years of age. The figure also varies among some Indian cities. In Delhi, for example, only 14 percent of people living on the streets are under twenty; but in Calcutta the figure is 31 percent.

Homeless people sleep in the street in Bombay in December 1964.
Source: Hulton/Deutsch Collection/Corbis; used with permission.

Homeless people in developing countries live and sleep in a broad range of locations: on the street, in abandoned buildings, in stairwells, in and around rail and public transit stations, and in rudimentary shelters in squatter settlements. In India and Bangladesh, many hundreds of thousands of people live on the streets. In some cases, they live without shelter of any kind, carrying their belongings and simply sleeping where they can. In other cases, they construct dwellings of plastic sheeting, cloth, and cardboard—dwellings which have no security or services, but which may survive for years.

In Mumbai, for example, some makeshift shelters extend across the pavements up to the slow lane of the highway, which becomes the front porch for domestic activities. The dangers from passing traffic and pollution are extreme. In other countries, such as China, one rarely finds homeless people living on the street; anyone making the attempt would very quickly be removed by authorities.

In Egypt and Peru, many if not most homeless people live in poor, temporary dwellings in squatter settlements around the urban peripheries. Some of these colonies, particularly those on low-quality state-owned land of no commercial value, have survived for many years and may eventually be allocated to the residents for formal ownership.

While begging is common among homeless people in developing countries, the assumption that all homeless people are reduced to begging, or that all beggars are homeless, is clearly incorrect. Most homeless people in developing countries do work; this is particularly true if squatters are included in the proportion. For example, the Villa el Salvador squatter settlement in Lima, Peru, is home to 370,000 people, most employed in the informal sector as traders, taxi drivers, or laborers, although some are professionals such as teachers or nurses. However, in general, homeless people tend to have lower-paid and more insecure employment than adequately housed people.

Homeless people in developing countries are frequently victims of crime, abuse, and harassment, but there is little evidence to suggest they are any more likely to be criminals than housed people. It has been noted, particularly in South Africa and Bangladesh, that members of criminal gangs, while not homeless themselves, sometimes use the cover and anonymity of squatter settlements to hide stolen goods.

Rita: A Case Study

Rita (age 30) is a lone parent of two children aged six and one and half years. She was orphaned when she was only 12 years old. She was taken to a relative's house which was later lost due to river erosion. Rita has been living in Dhaka (Bangladesh) with her relatives for about twenty years. She had a steady job at a garment factory with a salary of Tk. 700. At one stage, her relatives became keen to arrange her marriage with the intention of using her marriage as an excuse to oust her from their home. She married, against her will, to a rickshaw puller. Shortly before their first child was born, Rita left her job, needing more time for household work and child caring. Soon afterwards her husband developed an extra-marital affair with one of her coworkers. While she was pregnant the second time, her husband deserted her and took with him many valuables not bought with his income. Following his desertion without a divorce, she fell into a deep crisis. A few weeks later, she became homeless due to failure to pay the rent.

Her present home is a cover of polyethylene over a small chunk of footpath alongside many other street dwellers in the Katobon area. She now begs as well as collects waste papers from which her daily income is Tk. 15. Even this income is irregular. This amount is insufficient to feed her two children and herself. At least Tk. 100 (US$1.76) are required daily for bare subsistence. One problem is that she could not take a steady job at garment factory again as there is no one to take care of her children while she is away from home.

—Suzanne Speak and Graham Tipple

INTERVENTIONS

In developing countries, official efforts to address homelessness are limited and indeed often negative or unhelpful. They may take the form of harassment, violence, eviction or displacement of settlers, and imprisonment. One intervention in India, the Bombay Prevention of Begging Act, is invoked to clear the streets of homeless people when important public events are to take place. Many other countries report similar "cosmetic" clearing of the streets.

Assisting the Street Homeless

For the street homeless, appropriate interventions might resemble those needed in developed countries.

Such people often need a range of advocacy and individual support to gain access to services, as well as needing immediate protection from the elements—preferably free of charge. The lack of such shelter was sadly illustrated by the deaths of several hundred people in Delhi in January 2003, when the temperature made a rare drop below freezing at night.

Very few countries provide overnight shelters, although they can be found in India and in South Africa. They are often of poor quality, dirty, unsafe, and lacking in necessities for some users. For example, the Municipal Corporation of Delhi's night shelters offer no safe parking for rickshaws, so cycle rickshaw drivers must look elsewhere.

But the provision of shelter need not entail building overnight shelters. Many municipal buildings are empty at night and could be used by homeless people as safe places to sleep. The simple measure of legitimizing this use of some public buildings, and providing additional services and support through them, might provide vital help to many thousands of street homeless people.

Nevertheless, some organizations do provide valuable interventions. Delhi's Aashray Adhikar Abhiyan, a shelter rights campaigning organization, works directly with street homeless people. It provides legal advice as well as one-on-one support for gaining access to a range of services, including medical help. Another Indian NGO, the Society for the Promotion of Area Resource Centres (SPARC), formed an alliance with the National Slum Dwellers Federation and a women's NGO called *Mahila Milan*. Together, they supported 60,000 low-income people in voluntarily moving from their settlements beside the railway tracks of Mumbai to make way for improvements to the infrastructure. With the support of these organizations, the people helped plan their new settlement and then moved there—without forced eviction and without the further impoverishment that usually accompanies such moves.

Addressing Mass Homelessness

To address mass homelessness and low-income squatter settlements, intervention approaches in developing countries differ greatly from those in developed countries. At this scale, people need some of the rights that security of tenure bestows. Especially important is the right not to be evicted. They also need more basic housing that can be occupied at virtually no cost, and then improved and enlarged over time. Land allocation policies, which aim to provide homeless people with legal tenure to land on which they can build their own homes, often fall short in several ways. They generally allocate only land of very poor quality, or of low or no value, and leave people on their own to construct habitable residences.

The latter is expensive and tends to result in higher-income groups buying out the original allocates for a fraction of the real value of their assets. The allocated land is usually some distance from the city and thus from employment opportunities. Moreover, land grants without any form of support to help people to build adequate shelter on it has resulted in many thousands of people living for many years in inadequate shelters without services.

Although policy reforms in this direction have been advocated since the Year of Shelter for the Homeless in 1987, few governments find such action attractive. As they are usually invisible to national statistics and policymaking, homeless people are not included in lists of development priorities. It is important to pay more attention to the presence of homeless people so that their needs are considered and, where possible, met.

—*Suzanne Speak and Graham Tipple*

Further Reading

Agbola, T., & Jinadu, A. M. (1997). Forced eviction and forced relocation in Nigeria: The experience of those evicted from Maroko in 1990. *Environment and Urbanisation, 9*(2), 271–288.

Aptekar, L. (1988). *Street children of Cali.* Durham, NC, and London: Duke University Press.

Chawla, L. (2002). *Growing up in an urbanising world.* London: Earthscan.

Cooper, B. (1995). *Shadow people: The reality of homelessness in the 90s.* Retrieved June 14, 1999, from gopher://csf.colorado.edu:70/00/hac/homeless/Geographical-Archive/reality-australia

Labeodan, O. A. (1998). The homeless in Ibadan. *Habitat International, 13*(1), 75–85.

McLeod, R. (2001). *SPARC: A case study.* Coventry, UK: Homelessness International.

Murphey, D., & Anana, T. (1994). Evictions and fear of evictions in the Philippines. *Environment and Urbanisation, 6*(1), 40–49.

Neale, J. (1997). Homelessness and theory reconsidered. *Housing Studies, 12*(1), 47–61.

Olufemi, O. (1998). Street homelessness in Johannesburg inner city: A preliminary survey. *Environment and Urbanisation, 10*(2), 223–234.

Patel, S., d'Cruz, C., & Barra, S. (2002). Beyond evictions in a global city: People-managed resettlement in Mumbai. *Environment and Urbanisation, 14*(1), 159–172.

Rahman, T. (1993). *The rural homeless in Bangladesh.* Dhaka, Bangladesh: UNICEF.

Springer, S. (2000). Homelessness: A proposal for a global definition and classification. *Habitat International, 24*(4), 475–484.

Taschner, S. P., & Rabinovich, E. P. (1997). The homeless in Sao Paulo: Spatial arrangements. In M. J. Huth & T. Wright (Eds.), *International critical perspectives on homelessness.* Westport, CT: Praeger.

United Nations Centre for Human Settlements (UNCHS). (2000). *Strategies to combat homelessness.* Nairobi, Kenya: Author.

◉ "HOUSING FIRST" APPROACH

This entry describes the "housing first" approach in the context of homeless individuals with psychiatric and substance use disorders; however, the philosophy of housing first is applicable to every person and every family that is homeless.

The problem of homelessness entered the purview of the American public in the 1980s with the alarmingly rapid growth in major urban centers of a highly visible population of homeless individuals with drastically elevated rates of mental illness and substance abuse disorders. This growth coincided with and coalesced from several economic changes, such as the removal of federal support for subsidized housing, the increasing scarcity of low-income housing, and a growing disparity of wealth, as well as with social changes such as deinstitutionalization and the crack epidemic. This new mass homelessness revealed what Kim Hopper described in 2003 as "[the formerly] hidden face of poverty ripped from its customary habitat" (Hopper 2003, 176).

Homeless individuals who were most difficult to assist—those afflicted with mental illness and substance use disorders—confounded the psychiatric and social service communities in short order. Even when assisted by social service organizations, these homeless individuals found it much more difficult to gain access to stable housing and to retain it than their less troubled counterparts. The social service organizations seeking to help them came to believe that it was the co-occurring disorders that hindered their progress toward stable housing. Assuming that persons who were diagnosed with mental illness and addictions would be too much of a risk to themselves and the community if they were housed before they overcame these conditions, the overwhelming majority of these organizations attempted to funnel clients into treatment programs to make them "housing ready." In most of these programs, rigid regulations control consumers' behavior, mandating that in order to become "housing ready" they *first* become clean and sober, take their psychiatric medications, and obey curfews.

These treatment-first programs seek to resurrect their consumers, releasing each of them like a phoenix into a blue sky of reason, sobriety, and social inclusion. To this illusory end, most housing programs for people who are homeless with psychiatric disabilities and substance use disorders continue to use housing as leverage to induce their compliance with treatment. It is widely believed that only by participating in treatment can a consumer truly become "housing ready." Thus, housing readiness gained primacy in the lexicon of homeless services and to this day is presented as the sole path of deliverance from homelessness. Yet, as a 2003 survey by the Coalition for the Homeless shows, chronic homelessness among the mentally ill persists. Hard-to-serve consumers are burned out by their efforts to end their homelessness via the mandatory treatment route, which is marred by our collective failure to respond adequately to their needs. For these consumers, the story of the phoenix is a myth. However, there is an effective solution to the problems of this seemingly intransigent population—the Pathways to Housing "housing first" model.

PHILOSOPHY AND VALUES

The Pathways to Housing program, founded in 1992, seeks out the hard-to-serve—that is, people with psychiatric disabilities, co-occurring substance use disorders, a history of incarceration or violence, and other serious difficulties—and offers them immediate access to an independent apartment of their own, without requiring sobriety or participation in treatment as a condition for housing.

The ethos that guides Pathways to Housing rests on two important beliefs. The first one is that housing is a basic right for all people. The Pathways to Housing program regards housing and treatment as two distinct domains with separate criteria for operation and evaluation. Thus, housing is not connected to a consumer's assent to treatment; consumers who are active substance users are not excluded from housing; and consumers who relapse while housed are given treatment, not evicted or moved to a more supervised setting. The second belief is that the choice to change must be the consumer's. As Michael Rowe wrote in 1999, "If we cannot trust others to know themselves and their needs, we will end by oppressing them." (Rowe 1999, 85). In this program, choice is a continuous process, not an isolated incident. When the program's Assertive Community Treatment (ACT) teams conduct outreach to engage people living on the streets, the service street-dwellers say they need most is housing. Hence, the program provides housing first because it is the consumer's first choice.

Pathways to Housing's application of these two fundamental beliefs—that housing should be separated from treatment and that consumers should make their own choices—incorporates the following ideas, which were contributed by both service providers and consumers:

- psychiatric rehabilitation and motivational interviewing, which easily lend themselves to the dictates of consumer choice;

- harm reduction practice for substance abuse and psychiatric disorders to reduce the deleterious consequences of a consumer's lifestyle without dictating a goal like sobriety or remission from symptoms;

- community integration, which is based on the conviction that scatter-site housing is ideal because it minimizes stigma and its psychological impact;

- consumer advocacy, which emphasizes self-direction, self-help, and self-advocacy; and

- recovery, which rests on the knowledge that people with mental illness can and do recover their lives completely.

PROGRAM STRUCTURE AND FORMAT

The philosophy of providing housing first and allowing consumers to make their own choices has been realized in the model called "supported housing": scatter-site independent apartments that are affordable, safe, secure, and permanent, and have services offered by off-site teams. While in other programs consumers are rejected for housing and removed from housing for violating rules, consumers in the housing first model lose their housing only in the ways that any tenant loses housing: by not paying their rent, by creating disturbances intolerable to neighbors, or by committing other ordinary violations of a standard lease. The rules of the standard lease apply to tenants in the program the same way that they do to everyone else. In its ten-year history, serving more than 450 consumers, the program has had only one eviction.

All clinical and support services, including outreach and housing-related services, are provided by ACT teams. As pioneered by Leonard Stein and Mary Ann Test in 1980 and defined by the current national standards for evidence-based practice, the ACT teams implemented by Pathways to Housing meet the current fidelity standards: They are community-based, multidisciplinary teams of service professionals who provide intensive, individualized programs; team members seek out consumers and address their emotional, psychiatric, medical, and human needs. ACT teams operate twenty-four hours, seven days a week, and their relationships with consumers extend indefinitely into the future; consumers leave the program only when they choose to leave. Seventy percent of consumers have an acute or chronic health problem, and in order to meet these needs, ACT teams have been expanded to include a nurse practitioner and a nutritionist. Using these basic program features, Pathways to Housing dedicates itself to working with those people whom others reject.

MEASURES OF SUCCESS

At its inception in 1992, Pathways to Housing employed five staff members and served fifty tenants. Ten years later, there were 73 full-time staff and 450 tenants housed in their own apartments and served by six ACT Teams. The program's housing retention rate has remained consistently high, at roughly 88 percent for periods up to five years long (compared to 47 percent of the homeless people from whom this population was excluded on the basis that they were not "housing ready").

In a 2003 federally funded Substance Abuse and Mental Health Services Administration (SAMHSA) clinical control study, 225 participants were randomly assigned to either the housing first condition or the continuum of care (treatment before housing) condition. Experimental participants were given a referral to Pathways to Housing. Most control participants were already working with an outreach worker at the first stage of the continuum; those who were not were referred to outreach workers or drop-in centers. Both experimental and control participants spent approximately half their time literally homeless and a third of their time in institutions (primarily psychiatric hospitals) in the six months prior to the start of the study; there were no differences between groups. The goal of the experimental program was to move respondents directly into stable housing (their own apartments), and experimental participants spent 61 percent of their time in the first half of the year and 80 percent of their time in the second half of the year in stable housing. By the second half of the year, participants assigned to the experimental program spent only 3 percent of their time literally homeless and only 4 percent in transitional facilities. The goal of the continuum of care programs was to move individuals off the streets into facilities deemed appropriate for their needs, not necessarily to move them into stable housing. Consistent with that goal, control group respondents spent far less time in stable housing (15 percent in the first half of the year and 23 percent in the second half of the year). Their time in the second half of the year was almost evenly divided among stable, transitional, institutional, and literally homeless states. Differences between the groups were highly significant at both the six- and twelve-month assessments (Shinn et al., 2001).

Remarkably, the program has proved not only successful but also cost-effective. In 2003, the average cost of rent plus ACT team services is approximately $22,500 per person per year. This is less than the annual cost of a municipal shelter cot, which ranges between $25,000 and $30,000 per person per year and approximately half the cost of providing supportive housing in congregate settings, where services are on-site and costs range between $40,000 and $65,000 per person per year. It is also much cheaper than allowing people to remain homeless, which costs approximately $40,000 per year (Culhane et al., 1999).

Most importantly, supportive housing with ACT works to improve substance abuse and mental health outcomes for consumers. It works so well, in fact, that it has been adopted as a "best practice" by SAMHSA.

CONCLUSION

Housing first is a clinically effective, cost-effective, proven method for stably housing people who are homeless and have psychiatric disabilities along with co-occurring substance abuse disorders. The offer of housing without treatment conditions is a practical manifestation of Pathways to Housing's ethos of respect for the ability of consumers to know their own needs and choose their own treatment; the offer dramatically illustrates the agency's confidence, based on experience and evidence, in a consumer's potential for recovery, ability to live independently, and right to decent housing. In addition, sequencing housing before treatment acts as a powerful tool of engagement; moreover, it cures homelessness.

—*Sam Tsemberis*

Further Reading

Allen, M. (2003). Waking Rip van Winkle: Why developments in the last twenty years should teach the mental health system not to use housing as a tool of coercion. *Behavioral Sciences and the Law, 21,* 503–521.

Anthony, W., Cohen, M., & Farkas, M. (1990). *Psychiatric rehabilitation.* Boston: Boston University Center for Psychiatric Rehabilitation.

Carling, P. J. (1993). Housing and supports for persons with mental illness: Emerging approaches to research and practice, *Hospital & Community Psychiatry, 44,* 439, 442.

Chamberlin, J. (1978). *On our own: Patient-controlled alternatives to the mental health system.* New York: McGraw-Hill.

Coalition for the Homeless. (2003, February 19). *State of the homeless 2003.* Retrieved May 6, 2003, from http://www.coalitionforthehomeless.org:8080/top/CFTH/downloads/stateofthehomeless2003.pdf

Culhane, D. P. (1997, March 5). Testimony to U.S. House of Representatives Committee on Banking and Financial Services Subcommittee on Housing and Community Opportunity H.R. 217, Homeless Housing Programs Consolidation and Flexibility Act. Retrieved May 6, 2003, from http://financialservices.house.gov/banking/3597culh.htm

Culhane, D. P., Metraux, S., & Hadley, T. (1999). The impact of supportive housing on services use for homeless mentally ill individuals. *Housing Policy Debate, 12*(1). [page nos. not available: summary available at http://www.csh.org/html/NYNYSummary.pdf.]

Deegan, P. E. (1988). Recovery: The lived experience of rehabilitation. *Psychosocial Rehabilitation Journal, 11*(4), 11–19.

Drake, R. E., Mueser, K. T., Torrey, W. C., et al. (2000). Evidence-based treatment of schizophrenia. *Current Psychiatry Reports, 2,* 393–397.

Frese, F. J., & Davis, W. W. (1997). The consumer-survivor movement, recovery, and consumer professionals. *Professional Psychological Research and Practice, 3,* 243–245.

Harding, C. M., Brooks, G. W., Ashikaga, T., Strauss, J. S., et al. (1987). The Vermont longitudinal study of persons with severe mental illness: I. Methodology, study sample, and overall status 32 years later. *American Journal of Psychiatry, 144*(6), 718–726.

Hopper, K., Jost, J., Hay, T., Welber, S., et al. (1997). Homelessness, severe mental illness, and the institutional circuit. *Psychiatric Services, 48*(5), 659–665.

Hopper, K. (2003). *Reckoning with homelessness.* Ithaca, NY: Cornell University Press.

Howie the Harp. (1990). Independent living with support services: The goals and future for mental health consumers. *Psychosocial Rehabilitation Journal, 13,* 85–89.

Jencks, C. (1994). *The homeless.* Cambridge, MA: Harvard University Press.

Korman, H., Engster, D., & Milstein, B. (1996). Housing as a tool of coercion. In D. Dennis & J. Monahan (Eds.), *Coercion and aggressive community treatment.* New York: Plenum Press.

Miller, W. R., & Rollnick, S. (1991). *Motivational interviewing.* New York: Guilford Press.

New York State Office of Mental Health. *Evidence-based practices: a primer.* Retrieved May 6, 2003, from http://www.omh.state.ny.us/omhweb/omhq/q0901/Primer.html.

New York City Department of Homeless Services (DHS).

(2003, February 24). *Homeless outreach population survey.* New York: Author.

Rossi, P. H., Wright, J. D., Fisher, G. A., & Willis, G. (1987). The urban homeless: Estimating composition and size. *Science, 235,* 1336–1341.

Rowe, M. (1999). *Crossing the border: Encounters between homeless people and outreach workers.* Berkeley: University of California Press.

SAMHSA. (2003). *Best practices: An overview of mental health and substance abuse services and systems coordination strategies.* Retrieved May 6, 2003, from http://www.samhsa.gov/grants/content/2003/Resource%20material.pdf

Shinn, M. B., Tsemberis, S., Assmusen, S., Toohey, S., & Moran, L. (2001, November). *Effects of housing first and continuum of care programs for homeless individuals with psychiatric diagnose.* Paper presented at the annual meeting of the American Public Health Association, Boston, MA.

Stein, L. I., & Test, M. A. (1980). Alternative to mental hospital treatment: I. Conceptual model, treatment program, and clinical evaluation. *Archives of General Psychiatry, 37*(4), 392–397.

Susser, E., Streuning, E. L., & Conover, S. (1989). Psychiatric problems in homeless men. *Archives of General Psychiatry, 46,* 784–859.

Teague, G. B., Bond, G. R., & Drake, R. E. (1998). Program fidelity in assertive community treatment: Development and use of a measure. *American Journal of Orthopsychiatry, 68*(2), 216–232.

Tsemberis, S., & Eisenberg, R. F. (2000). Pathways to housing: Supported housing for street-dwelling homeless individuals with psychiatric disabilities. *Psychiatric Services, 51,* 487–493.

Whitaker, R. (2002). *Mad in America.* Cambridge, MA: Perseus.

◉ HOUSTON

Like most large U.S. cities, Houston during the early 1980s began experiencing a degree and type of homelessness that stood in marked contrast to the more contained homelessness it had experienced until then. This time coincided with a deep national recession that, combined with a dramatic decline in oil prices, brought an abrupt end to the boom economy that Houston had enjoyed—an economy fueled by oil development and international trade. The city began recovering from its slump in the late 1980s after several years of high unemployment and stagnant economic growth, but the recovery seemed to leave the homeless population behind. Large numbers of homeless individuals, including increasing numbers of primarily African-American women with children in their care, remained visible throughout the 1990s and into the new century, continuing to present a challenge to a city not known for its largesse in meeting the needs of its less fortunate citizens.

CAUSES

Homelessness in Houston has been the product of the same complex set of factors that accounts for rapid increases in homelessness elsewhere during the last two decades: rising rental costs (especially at the lowest rungs of the housing ladder), multiple pressures on the income-generating ability of those living in poverty, and new policies such as deinstitutionalization and the decriminalization of public drunkenness that swelled the pool of vulnerable individuals competing for scarce low-income housing. After analyzing data from the U.S. Bureau of the Census Annual Housing Survey for 1976 and 1983, Karin Ringheim suggested that Houston was perhaps a classic example of how structural factors (such as factors affecting the housing and job markets) produce a context in which pervasive homelessness is inevitable.

During that seven-year period, for instance, poor African-Americans in Houston experienced rent increases of 41 percent while experiencing a drop in median per capita income of 20 percent. Over time, the gap between the affordable housing that was available and what was needed widened considerably. By 1983, approximately 10,000 households in Houston needed units renting for less than $50 per month (using federal standards suggesting that no more than 30 percent of one's income should go to rent). No such units existed. A similar number of households needed units renting for between $50 and $99 per month. Only 1,000 such units existed, many of which were occupied by people with much higher incomes. As a result, the most vulnerable of the poor found themselves devoting unprecedented portions of their income to rent, creating the instability that contributes to high risk for homelessness.

Ways of mitigating the problems of unaffordable rents and inadequate income exist, of course. Government can decrease the cost of rental housing for poor people by providing housing subsidies or can increase the income of the poor through cash assistance and other kinds of transfers. Both were scarce in Houston, however, because of a prevailing ideology, apparent both locally and statewide, that placed high value on self-reliance and the free enterprise system. Rates of income assistance in Houston were among the lowest of all large metropolitan areas in the United States during that period. Moreover, those people who managed to get public assistance actually received little relative to people in other parts of the country. A 1989 McKinsey and Company report on homelessness in Houston, for instance, noted that Texas ranked forty-eighth out of the fifty states and the District of Columbia in the maximum amount of Aid to Families with Dependent Children (AFDC) benefits a family could receive. Housing subsidies were equally rare. Although it was the nation's fourth-largest city, Houston at that time ranked fifteenth of sixteen large cities in its number of public housing units and thirteenth in Section 8 housing certificates—federal subsidies that Houston chose not to aggressively pursue. Similarly, only meager funding was available to support services for subpopulations at extremely high risk for homelessness, such as the seriously mentally ill. Texas ranked forty-eighth in per capita state funding for mental health care at this time and was one of only seven states that did not supplement federal income entitlements for the seriously mentally ill. The safety net, then, was a tattered one, creating a climate ripe for pervasive homelessness.

THE SIZE AND FACE OF THE HOMELESS POPULATION IN HOUSTON

Houston's homeless population, which has historically been concentrated in the central city, is estimated to be approximately 10,000 people on a given night, according to two local—and somewhat dated—counts of the homeless population. The first count, conducted in 1989 by McKinsey and Company, indicated that approximately 20 percent of the population were in shelters, 20 percent were on the

streets, and 60 percent were in abandoned buildings. The second count, a sophisticated one-night count conducted by the Center for Public Policy at the University of Houston in the spring of 1996, arrived at a precise count of 9,216 persons and suggested that approximately 25 percent were in shelters, almost 40 percent were on the streets, and 25 percent were in abandoned buildings. (The remaining 10 percent were in labor bunkhouses, halfway houses, hospitals, or jails.) In each count, the numbers of people found to be living in abandoned buildings were striking.

In terms of its demographic and diagnostic profiles, the homeless population in Houston closely resembles cross-sectional point-in-time samples drawn from other large cities. Interviews with a probability sample of 802 homeless adults in Houston conducted by researchers Paul Koegel and Greer Sullivan in 1996 (see Koegel et al. 2000) suggested that the homeless population was predominantly male (83 percent), young (mean age of thirty-eight), and neither married nor living with someone as though they were married (84 percent). They were also disproportionately nonwhite: Three-fifths were African-American, one-fifth were Hispanic or other, and the remaining one-fifth were white. Only 8 percent were homeless families, that is, currently had children in their care. On average, people had been homeless three times for a total of thirty-two months during the course of their lives. Slightly more than one-quarter were "newly" homeless, that is, had become homeless for the first time within the last year.

Like other point-in-time homeless samples, this Houston sample contained disproportionate numbers of people with serious mental illness and/or substance abuse. One-quarter were seriously mentally ill (10 percent were schizophrenic, and 15 percent had a major affective disorder—either clinical depression or bipolar disorder, otherwise known as manic depression), and slightly more than two-fifths had experienced either drug or alcohol dependence during the last year. More than half of those people with serious mental illness had co-occurring substance dependence. Most people were not receiving care for these disorders. Only 27 percent of homeless adults with serious mental illness had received mental health care during the year prior to the interview. Likewise, only 27 percent of those people with substance dependence had received residential substance abuse treatment during the last year. Since the time that these data were collected, services for both mental illness and substance abuse have been curtailed rather than expanded. For instance, the Mental Health and Mental Retardation Administration, the public agency responsible for serving the seriously mentally ill, has had to reduce its services by more than 30 percent. Similarly, the Houston Recovery Campus, the major drug treatment facility for the poor, has significantly cut back its services as part of a partial closure.

In contrast to cities such as New York, Philadelphia, and Los Angeles, which have large municipal shelter systems and/or voucher programs that temporarily house homeless individuals in hotels, Houston has relied primarily on private organizations to provide shelter and other subsistence services for its homeless population. According to the Homeless Services Survey conducted by the Coalition for the Homeless Houston/Harris County, in 2003 approximately 2,000 emergency shelter beds existed in the greater Houston area (an area larger than the city itself that includes four counties: Harris, Fort Bend, Montgomery, and Galveston), whereas 2,317 emergency shelter beds existed ten years earlier. One moderate-sized shelter closed since the 2003 survey, and several other major shelters have since reduced their numbers of emergency beds due to declining funding for this mode of shelter.

Clearly, emergency shelter capacity is not nearly enough to meet the needs of a population last estimated to be five times larger than capacity. Shelter capacity is consistent with the subsistence experiences reported by homeless adults in Houston. Koegel and Sullivan's 1996 survey suggested that as much as 39 percent of the homeless population in Houston spent each of the last thirty nights in places that weren't meant for sleeping—on the streets or in abandoned buildings, public transportation, their cars, or other such places. Fewer homeless—only 31 percent—had spent each of the last thirty nights in shelters or other places meant

for sleeping. The remaining 30 percent moved back and forth during the last thirty nights between shelters and places not meant for sleeping. Approximately 70 percent, then, had spent some time on the streets in the last month.

THE POLITICAL CLIMATE AND FUTURE TRENDS

Advocacy for the homeless in Houston has been spearheaded by the Coalition for the Homeless of Houston/Harris County, an organization established in 1983 to educate the public about issues related to homelessness, press for services for the homeless, and coordinate the many groups providing services to them. Although less political than some of its counterparts in other large cities, the coalition has been successful in effecting change despite the dearth of local revenue for homelessness programs, although the barriers the coalition faces remain considerable. Other local organizations have pressed for improved services for homeless individuals as well. For instance, Healthcare for the Homeless—Houston, which has an advisory council of twenty-eight agencies and aims to integrate health care efforts in the county, recently launched a bus service for homeless persons that aims to improve access to health services and related services.

In important ways, however, the outlook is not a rosy one for the homeless of Houston. In addition to facing inadequate service capacity and a continued dearth of affordable housing, the homeless are increasingly facing a new set of pressures resulting from active efforts to revitalize the downtown area. As revitalization efforts reclaim more and more of the central city, the traditional tolerance for homeless people in this area has been dissipating. A new civility ordinance, passed in 2002, criminalized "dumpster diving," "aggressive panhandling," and sleeping on the sidewalk during all but a few hours in the middle of the night. Pressure from residents, local business owners, and developers has similarly translated into increased enforcement of civility ordinances that target, for instance, loitering and other public behaviors that are common among the homeless. Moreover, efforts are underway to expand the civility ordinances to areas surrounding the central business districts. In a similar vein, homeless encampments once tolerated by authorities have increasingly been dismantled. These trends appear to be pushing more and more homeless people out of the traditional central city zone of tolerance and into the surrounding areas, where they are far more dispersed and isolated from the care and services that target them. Balancing competing interests and finding the resources necessary to effect significant change are challenges that will continue to confront those in Houston who are struggling to address this pressing problem.

—Paul Koegel and David S. Buck

Further Reading

Buck, D. S., & Easling, I. (2001). *Findings from the HHH Homeless Needs Assessment Questionnaire, 2001.* Houston, TX: Healthcare for the Homeless—Houston.

Buck, D. S., & Rochon, D. (2003). *Findings from the HHH Homeless Needs Assessment Questionnaire, 2003.* Houston, TX: Healthcare for the Homeless—Houston.

Coalition for the Homeless/Harris County. (2001). *March 2001: Homeless service demands 2001: An analysis of trends, services, and demographics.* Houston, TX: Coalition for the Author.

Coalition for the Homeless of Houston/Harris County. (2003). *Homeless service demands 2003: An analysis of trends, services, demographics.* Houston, TX: Author.

de Mangin, C. (2002, July 11, Star Edition). Signs posted along U.S. 59 to discourage panhandling. *Houston Chronicle* (p. 10).

Koegel, P., Sullivan, J. G., Jinnett, K., Morton, S., Jackson, C., & Miu, A. (2000). *Characterizing the homeless population in Houston.* Santa Monica, CA: RAND.

McKinsey & Company. (1989). *Addressing the problem of homelessness in Houston and Harris County.* Houston, TX: Author.

Ringheim, K. (1990). *At risk of homelessness: The roles of income and rent.* New York: Praeger.

Ringheim, K. (1993). Investigating the structural determinants of homelessness: The case of Houston. *Urban Affairs Quarterly, 28*(4), 617–640.

Weiher, G. R., Sen, L., Durand, J., & Williams, J. (1996). *An enumeration and needs assessment of the homeless of Houston and Harris County.* Houston, TX: Center for Public Policy, University of Houston.

Wenzel, S. L., Burnam, M. A., Koegel, P., Morton, S. C., Miu, A., Jinnett, K. J., Sullivan, J. G., et al. (2001). Access to inpatient or residential substance abuse treatment among homeless adults with alcohol or other drug use disorders. *Medical Care, 39*(11), 1158–1169.

HUNGER AND NUTRITION

Homelessness and problems gaining access to adequate food are closely related. Both are, in general, associated with poverty. Furthermore, because homeless people do not have adequate kitchen facilities, it is difficult for them to consume food items that need preparation, and many homeless people do not have family members close to them or other social supports that could provide them with food and shelter. In addition, homelessness itself can be a barrier to accessing public food assistance programs.

The two most important sources of food assistance for people experiencing homelessness in the United States are the U.S. Department of Agriculture (USDA) Food Stamp Program (FSP) and a network of private food assistance providers, often called the Emergency Food Assistance System (EFAS). The following sections discuss these two programs, providing statistics related to their services to homeless people and demographic characteristics of the homeless people using these services.

THE FOOD STAMP PROGRAM

The Food Stamp Program is the largest public food assistance program in the United States available to the homeless. Established in 1964, reenacted in 1997, and periodically reauthorized, it is the principal domestic food and nutrition assistance program that the USDA administers. During fiscal year 2002, the program served more than 19 million people in an average month at a total annual cost of over $18 billion in benefits. With its main purpose being "to permit low-income households to obtain a more nutritious diet . . . by increasing their purchasing power" (Food Stamp Act of 1977, as amended), the FSP is the only form of public assistance available nationwide to all households on the basis of financial need only, regardless of family type, age, or disability.

Households apply to the FSP at local offices. In general, each county within a state contains one or more food stamp offices. Families or individuals who meet certain financial and other eligibility criteria are certified by the local offices to participate in the program and are issued monthly food stamp benefits based on their household size and the net income they have available to purchase food. In the past, the benefits were issued as paper food coupons. In recent years, however, they have been issued increasingly as debit cards under "electronic benefit systems." Food stamp benefits can be used to buy food items at most food outlets nationwide. These outlets redeem the coupons for money at local banks, which are then reimbursed through the Federal Reserve System. Program benefits are paid for entirely by the federal government, while the federal and state governments share the administrative costs equally.

Unfortunately, homelessness is a significant deterrent to FSP participation for several reasons that include, but are not limited to, mental illness, transportation barriers, not having kitchen facilities, and difficulty in presenting the required documentation to qualify for the program. While there are no exact national estimates available for a recent period, various studies suggest that the FSP participation rate among the homeless remains at a low level. Data from a recent America's Second Harvest study reveal that only 11.5 percent of its homeless clients were receiving food stamps at the time they were interviewed, while the comparable figure for the overall America's Second Harvest client population was 29.8 percent (Kim, Ohls, and Cohen 2002). These findings suggest that access to the FSP among the homeless could be improved, though the study was not designed to be representative of the homeless population.

The overall number of FSP participants has dropped substantially in recent years. It is estimated that 8 million fewer people received food stamp benefits in 2002 than did in 1994. The most sudden drop occurred between 1996 and 1998. Although the strong economy played a major role in the decline, other factors were involved, since the proportion of poor people receiving food stamps dropped. Two of these factors were (1) reduced eligibility imposed by the 1996 welfare reform legislation, and (2) administrative practices that discouraged people leaving welfare from applying for food stamp benefits (Wilde et al. 2000).

There is other evidence of a decline in FSP participation among the users of EFAS. The America's Second Harvest report estimated that 30 percent of

the people who used its affiliated emergency food providers (for example, food pantries, soup kitchens, and emergency shelters) were receiving food stamps at the time of the interview in 2001 (Kim, Ohls, and Cohen 2002). The comparable figure reported in a similar America's Second Harvest study conducted in 1997 was 41 percent (America's Second Harvest 1998).

Legislative initiatives have taken place over the years to alleviate access problems among the homeless. Because of these initiatives, there are now the following special provisions in the FSP for people experiencing homelessness:

1. there is no requirement for a fixed address,
2. people are allowed to pick up the coupons at the food stamp office,
3. funding is provided for outreach to the homeless,
4. monthly reporting requirements are waived,
5. homeless people are allowed to use food stamps to purchase meals in restaurants, and
6. expedited services are available to assist people of very low income and few resources.

Other more specialized public programs through which certain groups of homeless adults and children may obtain food and nutritional services include the Special Supplemental Food Program for Women, Infants, and Children (WIC; a program specifically designed to address the nutritional and health needs of low-income infants and children, along with pregnant, lactating, and postpartum mothers); the Elderly Nutrition Program; the Child and Adult Care Food Programs; the National School Lunch Program; and the School Breakfast Program.

Despite the presence of such public programs, it appears that many low-income individuals, including people experiencing homelessness, are slipping through the public safety net. Instead, they are turning to the private network of hunger relief programs, such as food pantries and soup kitchens.

THE EMERGENCY FOOD ASSISTANCE SYSTEM

The Emergency Food Assistance System is a major source of nutrition services for low-income families and arguably the largest and most used source of food assistance for the homeless. The goal of EFAS is to help fill nutrition gaps for people who are not receiving food stamps or whose nutritional needs are not fully met by food stamps or other direct government assistance programs.

There are two general categories of organizations in EFAS: (1) those directly serving people, and (2) those serving other providers. Locally operated EFAS providers serve households directly, primarily through soup kitchens and food pantries. Emergency shelters, which are usually considered part of EFAS, were not included in this USDA study. Soup kitchens—sometime called "emergency kitchens"— are local facilities that provide prepared meals on-site for individuals and families who visit those facilities. Emergency shelters that provide meals for their residents or nonresident users are often considered part of EFAS, serving a function similar to that of soup kitchens. Food pantries, on the other hand, distribute grocery items that require further preparation (such as canned goods, cereals, rice, bread, and sometimes fresh fruits or meat) and other basic supplies for off-site use. A recent USDA study estimates that more than 5,000 soup kitchens and more than 38,000 food pantries were operating in the United States in 2001 (Ohls et al. 2001). They help working poor families increase their purchasing power for food, provide nutritious meals to low-income seniors and homeless people, and help those who have been excluded from the FSP and other direct government assistance programs. Food and funds for these local providers come from several sources, including individual and group donations, public funds, and surplus food through the federal Emergency Food Assistance Program.

EFAS also includes organizations that are not in direct contact with individual users of these services but that provide key support for the direct providers. These organizations include food banks, food rescue organizations, and emergency food organizations. Food banks are nonprofit, regional organizations that solicit, store, and distribute food from local producers, retail food sources, the federal commodity distribution program, and the food industry. It is estimated that there are approximately 400 food banks in the United States. Food rescue organizations play a role similar to that of food banks but focus on obtaining perishable foods, such as contributions and gleanings from farmers and surplus food from restaurants and other commercial food service facilities. Emergency food organizations operate in some, but not all, areas of the country and have a more specialized role, focusing on the distribution of government commodities to primarily to soup kitchens and food pantries. (In some states, the term *emergency food organization* is also used to include organizations that distribute commodities directly to households.)

America's Second Harvest, which is a national network of about 80 percent of the food banks, supports the system by acquiring food from national organizations, providing technical assistance and other services to the food banks and food rescue organizations, and representing the interest of the EFAS community in the national political process.

It is estimated that approximately 10 percent of the people who used food assistance facilities affiliated with America's Second Harvest in 2001 were homeless. The estimated number of people served by America's Second Harvest–affiliated facilities during a one-year period between spring 2000 and spring 2001 was 23 to 28 million. We thus infer that America's Second Harvest served more than 2 million homeless people in 2001 through its affiliated emergency food assistance facilities (Kim, Ohls, and Cohen 2002); This estimate is based on extrapolation of weekly estimates for a twelve-month period using the same turnover rate among the homeless as the overall EFAS client population.

Characteristics of the Homeless Served by America's Second Harvest–Affiliated EFAS

In this section, we present statistics of demographic characteristics and service utilization patterns among the homeless population. These statistics and patterns are based on the client data from the Hunger in America 2001 study.

The percentage of homeless people at emergency food programs that provide prepared meals (such as soup kitchens and emergency shelters) is greater than the percentage at those programs that provide grocery items (such as food pantries). This situation may be largely due to the lack of kitchen facilities available to the homeless population. More than three-quarters (76 percent) of the people served at America's Second Harvest–affiliated emergency shelters and more than a quarter (26 percent) of the kitchen clients are homeless. In comparison, less than 3 percent of the pantry clients are homeless.

Comparing the demographic characteristics of the homeless clients at the America's Second Harvest network providers with those of the overall America's Second Harvest client population, the data show the following:

- More than 80 percent of homeless clients are male (versus 38 percent among all America's Second Harvest adult clients).

- Fewer than 2 percent of homeless clients are age sixty-five or older (versus 20 percent among all America's Second Harvest adult clients).

- From 24 to 25 percent of America's Second Harvest adult clients, homeless or not, have a part- or full-time job.

- Only 11 percent of homeless clients are married or living as married (versus 32 percent among all America's Second Harvest adult clients).

- From 63 to 64 percent of America's Second Harvest adult clients, homeless or not, graduated from high school.

- From 12 to 17 percent of all America's Second Harvest adult clients, homeless or not, are of Hispanic origin.

- From 44 to 45 percent of all America's Second Harvest adult clients, homeless or not, are white.

- From 35 to 40 percent of all America's Second Harvest adults clients, homeless or not, are African-American.

- Some 34 percent of homeless clients report that their health is fair or poor (versus 45 percent among all America's Second Harvest adult clients).

In brief, a homeless client of America's Second Harvest network providers is likely to be a nonsenior living without a spouse and utilizing services at emergency shelters and soup kitchens.

PROGRAM RESULTS

Many private and public nutrition services provide food and other nutrition services to people experiencing homelessness. The USDA's FSP and the private sector's EFAS network, represented by soup kitchens and food pantries, are two major food programs available for low-income families and the homeless. Despite a number of legislative changes made to improve access to food stamps among the homeless, the percentage of homeless people receiving food stamps remains low. The private EFAS continues to serve an increasing number of low-income households, including homeless people.

—*Myoung Kim*

Further Reading

America's Second Harvest. (1998.) *Hunger in 1997: The faces and facts.* Chicago: Author.

Kim, M., Ohls, J., & Cohen, R. (2002). *Hunger in America 2001: National report prepared for America's Second Harvest.* Princeton: Mathematica Policy Research.

Ohls, J., Saleem-Ismail, F., Cohen, R., and Cox, B. (2001). *Providing food for the poor: Findings from the Provider Survey for the Emergency Food Assistance System study.* Washington, DC: U.S. Department of Agriculture, Economic Research Service.

Wilde, P., Cook, P., Gundersen, C., Nord, M., & Tiehen, L. (2000, June). *The decline in food stamp program participation in the 1990s.* Food Assistance and Nutrition Research Report No. 7. 28. http://www.ers.usda.gov/publications/fanrr7

I

◉ IMAGES OF HOMELESSNESS IN CONTEMPORARY DOCUMENTARY FILM

Contemporary documentary images of homelessness and poverty are rooted in early ethnographic studies, WPA interviews, and Depression-era newsreels, as well as advocacy-inspired art such as the photographs of Jacob Riis. Like their predecessors, later documentary images of homelessness are usually concerned with both the aesthetic and the political, often promoting public policy changes at the local or national level. Since 1980, more than four dozen documentaries have been produced about the crisis of the "new homeless" in America. Most seek to debunk myths about homeless people, addressing both the discrimination they face and the empowerment they can achieve, and acknowledging the common humanity of subject, filmmaker, and audience. In contrast to Hollywood films' preoccupation with male homelessness, documentary films often give due consideration to homeless families, youth, and women.

DOCUMENTING HOMELESS LIVES

There is no dominant face of homelessness in documentary film; the images are as diverse as the homeless population itself. Most documentaries explore the daily lives of homeless individuals, the communities they inhabit, and their encounters with shelter staff, social workers, law enforcement personnel, and advocates. Films such as *Down and Out in America* (1986), *Shadow Children* (1991), and *101 Rent Boys* (2000) reveal the daily routines, survival strategies, and living conditions of people who are homeless. In the short documentary *Repetition Compulsion* (1997), Ellie Lee uses anonymous animated images to illustrate audio testimony about the cycle of violence in the lives of homeless women. In contrast, Michel Negroponte takes a very subjective approach in *Jupiter's Wife* (1994), which traces the evolution of his own personal fascination with Maggie, a homeless woman living in New York City's Central Park. The film was shot with a VHS camcorder, and the narrative centers upon revelations about Maggie's history before homelessness. Both films raise important questions about the relationship between filmmaker and subject, which is particularly problematic when the subject lives under impoverished, unstable, and unsafe conditions.

A similar dilemma about the responsibilities of filmmaker and audience surfaces in *Streetwise* (1985), about homeless youth in Seattle. Both the filmmaker and the audience take on the role of a voyeur, watching the daily struggles of the youth to survive. The film chronicles their histories of abuse and neglect, and their experiences in a street community of prostitution, panhandling, and addiction. While the film has a scripted feel at times, the unexpected suicide of one of the youths, Dewayne, collapses the distance between subject, filmmaker, and audience. Director Martin Bell was one of the few mourners at the small funeral from which Dewayne's homeless friends were noticeably absent.

Other films, such as *The Homeless Home Movie* (1997) and *Dark Days* (2000), bridge the gap between filmmaker and subject by employing the homeless as film crew and permitting them to collaborate in the creative process. This is particularly evident in *Dark Days,* a black-and-white documentary about a community of people living in an abandoned Amtrak tunnel under Manhattan. Novice director Marc Singer filmed the underground community for more than a year, living and working among them. With the tunnel dwellers doubling as a film crew, Singer tapped into the city's electrical power and used a homemade camera dolly on an abandoned railway track to film a tracking shot of the homes in the community. The result is powerful aesthetic images, intimate interviews, and an informative glimpse at a unique community and the ethical questions it raises for society.

DOCUMENTARY AS ADVOCACY

Documentary filmmakers are often motivated by political and ethical concerns, hoping to have "an effect on attitudes, possibly leading to action" (Ellis 1989, 3). The primary goal for most documentaries about homelessness is to elucidate the common humanity and normality of the unhoused population. Other films take this one step further by examining bureaucratic inefficiencies, policy inconsistencies, the criminalization of homelessness, and the organization of homeless rights movements. Paula Rabinowitz, literature and film scholar, suggests that these "cultural representations can have political agency" (Rabinowitz 1994, 3).

Films such as *Takeover* (1990) and *Taylor's Campaign* (1997) focus on the issue of advocacy itself, illuminating the strength of grassroots and national homeless rights organizations and affordable housing movements. *Takeover* depicts the homeless

activists nationwide who draw attention to the affordable housing shortage by "taking over" vacant houses repossessed by the federal Department of Housing and Urban Development. The film emphasizes the varying faces of homelessness and the unifying desire to live in safety and dignity. Scenes of an anonymous burial in Potter's Field frame the film, suggesting the tremendous urgency of housing the homeless. Potter's Field is a public cemetery established on Hart Island in 1869, for the impoverished, indigent, and homeless residents of New York City. In *Taylor's Campaign,* Richard Cohen follows homeless activist Ron Taylor in his grassroots campaign for a seat on Santa Monica's city council, and the council's simultaneous attempt to outlaw programs providing food for the homeless in public parks. Through interviews with Taylor, members of the homeless community, volunteers and advocates, tourists, local residents, and politicians, Cohen weaves a complex narrative about discrimination against the local homeless population. For viewers, the result is often a deeper empathy for the homeless people of Santa Monica and greater awareness of the varying degrees of support for and condemnation of homelessness in the wider community.

EXPLOITATIVE IMAGES

Exploitative material on some Internet websites stands in sharp contrast to the general tone of empathy and advocacy in contemporary documentary films. Indeed, these sites raise questions about the regulation of public images and the rights of homeless people generally. While archival interviews and testimonies about homelessness on some websites are generally fair and informative, two sites are particularly notable for their abusive content. The author of Bumhunt.com encourages the public to "hunt" for the "world's dirtiest and most insane vagabonds" with a camera and submit the results to a collection of photographs and video footage of homeless people. Once posted on the website, these images are accompanied by humiliating commentary. The authors of another website, Bumfights.com, use it as a forum for the sale and distribution of their video of the same name. The video includes staged fights between homeless men and images of homeless people performing dangerous stunts for money. In addition to condemnation by homeless advocates, the producers of this site face various charges in civil and criminal court.

RESEARCH DIRECTIONS

Documentary film is a measure of the current faces of homelessness, and conveys important information about discrimination, advocacy, and localized experiences of homelessness in America. While there have been ample academic studies about documentary film focusing on poverty, there is still significant research to be done on those focusing on homelessness in particular.

Almost without exception, documentary films about homelessness are independently produced, and their distribution is often limited to film festivals, small art theaters, and public television broadcasts. Even critically acclaimed and award-winning films like *Dark Days* have relatively small audiences, and the political messages are not as accessible to the general public as they could, or perhaps should, be. Furthermore, while there have been ample academic studies about documentary film focusing on poverty, there is still significant research to be done on those focusing on homelessness in particular.

—*Amanda F. Grzyb*

See also Appendix 2: Filmography of American Narrative and Documentary Films on Homelessness

Further Reading

Ellis, J. C. (1989). *The documentary idea: A critical history of English-language documentary film and video.* Upper Saddle River, NJ: Prentice Hall.

Film links. (2004). The Homeless Search Engine. Retrieved April 13, 2004, from http://www.sparesomechange.com/search/engine/?find=Films

Nichols, B. (1991). *Representing reality: Issues and concepts in documentary.* Bloomington: Indiana University Press.

Rabinowitz, P. (1994). *They must be represented: The politics of documentary.* New York: Verso.

Renov, M. (1993). *Theorizing documentary.* New York: Routledge.

Rosenthal, A. (1980). *The documentary conscience: A casebook in film making.* Berkeley: University of California Press.

Sherman, S. R. (1998). *Documenting ourselves: Film, video, and culture.* Lexington: University of Kentucky Press.

Winston, B. (1995). *Claiming the real.* London: British Film Institute.

◉ IMAGES OF HOMELESSNESS IN NARRATIVE FILM, HISTORY OF

Homelessness is a prominent theme in American narrative film, from the earliest silent shorts to contemporary studio features. While homeless characters appear in every decade of film history, the most significant images are found in silent films from the 1890s to the mid-1930s, in films of the Depression era and its aftermath (1929–1941), and in films of the Reagan-Bush era (1980–1992). The earliest silent films often portray homeless men as lazy and criminal, but later films depict homelessness in a romanticized manner. During the Depression, public opinion about the homeless shifted to concern and empathy, and film images reflected this change. Contemporary films featuring homelessness are overwhelmingly comedies, either reinforcing dominant ideologies about success and individualism or critiquing the distribution of wealth and power in America.

THE TRAMP IN SILENT FILM

Early silent film shorts about homelessness are generally comedies that employ one of two "tramp" stereotypes: the menacing thief and trespasser, or the unsuspecting "layabout" who is tricked and humiliated. Such negative images are rooted in the antagonistic attitude towards the homeless that permeated American culture from 1870 to 1900, and reflect a fear and mistrust of homeless men. In the story repeated most often, a tramp attempts to steal food only to be caught and beaten by a cook or set upon by a dog. Variations on this narrative are found in *The Tramp and the Muscular Cook* (1898), *The Tramp Caught a Tartar* (1898), *The Tramp in the Kitchen* (1898), *The Ugly Tempered Tramp* (1900), *The Cook's Revenge* (1901), *Meandering Mike* (1901), and *Pie, Tramp and the Bulldog* (1901). Another popular theft narrative depicts a tramp who steals a baby bottle from an unsuspecting nurse or mother. This theme appears in *A Tramp's Dinner* (1897), *The Tramp and the Nursing Bottle* (1901), and *On a Milk Diet* (1902). Also common is the narrative about a tramp who secretly impersonates a woman's lover, only to be discovered in horror by the unsuspecting woman. Although intended to be humorous, this portrayal resonates with a particularly pernicious image of the homeless man as a sexual predator. This narrative is employed in *When We Were Twenty-One* (1900), *On the Benches of the Park* (1901), *Hubby to the Rescue* (1904), and *Poor Algy* (1905).

In *The Tramp's Unexpected Skate* (1901), a typical tramp humiliation comedy by Thomas A. Edison, two men attach a pair of roller skates on to the feet of a homeless man who is asleep under a tree. The tramp falls repeatedly while he attempts to run after the tricksters, who continue to taunt him. Another variation appears in *The Tramp and the Giant Firecracker* (1898), in which a sleeping homeless man is awakened abruptly when two boys explode a firecracker under his nose. Other notable humiliation films include *The Tramp's Last Bite* (1898), *Happy Hooligan April-Fooled* (1901), *The Sleeper* (1902), *The Golf Girls and the Tramp* (1902), and *The Tramp's Surprise* (1902). The common theme of these and the theft narratives is revenge: The homeless man is usually beaten, shamed, or punished.

Later silent films and early "talkies" break with disparaging images of homelessness and explore the pathos of the tramp as a tragic and romantic figure. Often the tramp character is a plot contrivance, used to symbolize an economic, emotional, or moral decline. Many of these films also explore the causes

Charlie Chaplin in his classic hobo costume in the 1920s–1930s.
Source: Bettmann/Corbis; used with permission.

for the displacement of their characters, and usually depict them as heartbreaking, wandering heroes. In *Smoldering Embers* (1920), a man becomes a tramp after his wife takes their baby son and runs away with another man. Many years later, the unfortunate tramp intervenes in his son's life without revealing himself. More images of the homeless tragic hero are found in *Buchanan's Wife* (1918), *The Innocent Cheat* (1921), and *The Limited Mail* (1925). The figure of the tramp also becomes a means of disguising a character's identity, thus creating convenient plot twists in longer films. In *Beggars of Life* (1928), the female protagonist disguises herself as a male tramp to escape murder charges. Similarly, in *Love Aflame* (1917) and *Miss Nobody* (1921), women impersonate tramps to flee the unwanted affections of a man. In *Pals First* (1918), *Blues Blazes* (1922), and *Love's Old Sweet Song* (1923), important men—the master of the house, a prizefighter, and a secret service agent, respectively—disguise themselves as tramps and reveal their true identities at the climax of the narrative. This period of film also represents a growth in the number of homeless women and children in film, including homeless girls in *Princess of Patches* (1917) and *The Five Dollar Baby* (1922) and a suicidal homeless woman in *The Docks of New York* (1928).

CHARLIE CHAPLIN'S "LITTLE TRAMP"

The introduction of Charlie Chaplin's "Little Tramp" persona in 1914 signifies the advent of an increasingly sympathetic and nuanced image of the homeless figure in silent cinema. The tramp appears in Chaplin's films from *Kid Auto Races at Venice* (1914) to *Modern Times* (1936). In *Down and Out, On the Road,* Kenneth Kusmer shows that Chaplin's tramp is analogous to the actual homeless population: "At different times he is shown living in a patchwork dwelling (*A Dog's Life* [1918]), sleeping in a homeless shelter (*Police!* [1916], *Triple Trouble* [1918], and *The Kid* [1921]), emerging from the undercarriage of a train (*The Idle Class* [1921]), and on many occasions pilfering for food to survive" (Kusmer 2002, 189). While not an entirely benevolent character, Chaplin's tramp is both comedic and sentimental, emphasizing the social inequities of the early twentieth century and the follies of the upper class. One of the most successful films to walk the line between slapstick and pathos is *The Kid,* a film that chronicles the tramp's adventures as he raises a homeless waif. In *Working-Class Hollywood,* Steven J. Ross suggests that "many early films presented poignant stories of immigrants and workers suffering at the hands of employers, politicians, and hypocritical clergy and civic leaders" (Ross 1998, 12), thus appealing to a predominantly working-class audience. Chaplin's brilliant parodies of the wealthy, most notably in *The Idle Class,* allowed him to expand his audience to the middle class as well.

THE GREAT DEPRESSION

Like the later silent films, Depression-era films also produced relatively congenial images of homelessness. Economic hardships had made poverty commonplace, and the homeless person was no longer an object of fear and ridicule. Kusmer writes, "The long-standing image of the lazy homeless person appeared less often, and the humorous tone of many newspaper stories about beggars and lodging-house residents was replaced, for the most part, by more prosaic factual accounts" (Kusmer 2002, 209). The dominant image of the homeless man diversified in the 1930s and 1940s, and homeless women, homeless children, and homeless communities were frequently represented in cinema. Films that feature homeless women include *Girl Overboard* (1929), *The Girl From Avenue A* (1940), and *Under Age*

(1941). In *Girls of the Road* (1940), a governor's daughter runs away to learn more about a group of girls living in a hobo jungle; she then raises public awareness about their plight. Similarly, a group of homeless boys are captives in a residential work camp in *Boy Slaves* (1939), and another band of homeless youth experience the hardships of transient life in *Wild Boys of the Road* (1933). *The Grapes of Wrath* (1940) chronicles the journey of a dispossessed migrant family across America. *The Courageous Dr. Christian* (1940) explores the issue of public housing for the homeless, and groups of homeless men come together to help rebuild destitute properties in *Friendly Neighbors* (1940) and *Mountain Rhythm* (1939). A notable exception to these films is Lewis Milestone's muddled musical comedy *Hallelujah, I'm a Bum* (1933). Al Jolson starred as Bumper, a happy and carefree homeless man who is the "mayor" of a large homeless community in Central Park. Speaking in rhyme and breaking into song with his fellow homeless friends, Bumper sings, "I find great enjoyment in unemployment."

Two of the most significant and influential films from this period are *My Man Godfrey* (1936) and *Sullivan's Travels* (1941). Directed by Gregory LaCava, *My Man Godfrey* is a screwball comedy about the relationship between a "forgotten man" and a wealthy family. In a memorable opening sequence, two wealthy sisters find Godfrey at a city dump and bring him back to an upscale hotel as the final item of a scavenger hunt. He becomes the butler for their dysfunctional family, and, as the moral compass of the film, he is exposed to their shallow, selfish, and wasteful ways. Although Godfrey is revealed to be a man of stature who has become homeless by choice after a failed love affair, he remains faithful to his fellow "forgotten men" and builds a nightclub at the dump where they can sleep and work. Godfrey explains to his friend, "The only difference between a derelict and a man is a job."

Like *Godfrey,* Preston Sturges's *Sullivan's Travels* satirizes the extravagance and arrogance of the wealthy, although it is markedly more complicated in form and content. The film makes use of many subgenres, including screwball comedy, drama, romance, social documentary, silent slapstick, and prison narrative. Its hero is John Sullivan, a famous director of comedies who now wants to make an epic drama about the suffering of the masses. In preparation for the film, he disguises himself as a homeless man and ventures off to explore the world of poverty and misery. However, he is closely followed by a group of handlers, reporters, and doctors who watch his every move. Sullivan does not speak to a homeless person once on screen during his travels; instead, the plight of the poor is represented through a montage of silent images of shelters, soup kitchens, trains, nights spent sleeping rough, and meals scavenged from garbage cans. It is not until Sullivan inadvertently experiences life on a chain gang that he realizes he has not "suffered enough," and that his films can only ease human misery with laughter, not with tragedy.

HOLLYWOOD AND THE "NEW HOMELESS"

Several decades later, the homeless population of the early 1980s inspired a series of comedies of varying commercial and critical success. Although the "new homeless" consisted of a growing number of women and children due to the detrimental public policies and massive cuts in social programs enacted by the Reagan and Bush administrations, Hollywood returned to the icon of single homeless male—but with a difference. Now he was predominantly characterized as a sage, imparting his wisdom to the wealthy in exchange for a place to sleep. In this view, the homeless are happy and resourceful teachers, catalysts for the growth of members of the upper class. Not since the early silent shorts had there been such a disparity between the actual homeless population and its representation in film.

Two of the most successful comedies of the 1980s—*Trading Places* (1983) and *Down and Out in Beverly Hills* (1986)—feature a homeless male protagonist who is virtuosic in his abilities. John Landis's *Trading Places* is one of the only narrative films to deal with the issue of race and homelessness. The opening credit sequence is a montage of images of white privilege and of predominantly African-American poverty and homelessness. Valentine, an African-American hustler and pan-

handler, is the "embodiment of criminality" (Nadel 1997, 35) for the wealthy white characters in the film. To settle a secret bet about genetic or environment causes for criminal behavior, the millionaire Duke brothers switch Valentine with Winthorpe, the manager of the Dukes' investment company. In turn, Winthorpe becomes homeless and penniless, later rescued by a prostitute. Winthorpe and Valentine discover the Dukes' scheme, then use trickery to take over the company shares and put the brothers out of business. Film scholar Alan Nadel suggests that all of the characters in the film—both rich and poor—are essentially criminals who reinforce the ideological goals of the Reagan administration. Far from the subversive comedy promised by the opening montage, *Trading Places* posits the notion that there can only be a happy resolution if the protagonists are millionaires.

Jerry, the central character in Paul Mazursky's *Down and Out in Beverly Hills,* also moves from homelessness to a millionaire's mansion. Like Godfrey in *My Man Godfrey* (1936), he joins a family afflicted with the pretensions and trivial preoccupations of the privileged class. Jerry is both brilliant and pragmatic, and helps each family member to discover true happiness. Yet, unlike Godfrey, he does not use his new connections to build a shelter for the homeless; he decides to stay with the wealthy family rather than returning to the streets. The "rags to riches" theme dominates other films as well. Many contemporary narratives have a pivotal transformation scene, in which the homeless character bathes and dresses like a "regular" person, symbolically moving out of the homeless condition. This sort of scene is only possible because the films introduce them dressed in a homeless "uniform" derived from stereotypical media images. Such "makeover" scenes are found in *Down and Out in Beverly Hills, Curly Sue* (1991), *The Fisher King* (1991), and *The Caveman's Valentine* (2001). In *Life Stinks* (1991), *Fisher King,* and *With Honors* (1994), the romanticized homeless protagonists help the housed characters discover what is truly important in life. The homeless condition is used as a critique of the materialistic and competitive aspects of American culture. Notably, there is more tension between the dramatic and comedic elements of these later films, and the result is often a muddled sentimentality.

David Riker's *The City* (1999) is a departure from the homeless comedies of the Reagan-Bush era. This independent drama, made with non-actors from the Latino immigrant community, consists of four vignettes about immigrant life in New York City. It is reminiscent of *Salt of the Earth* (1953), a drama about Mexican-American zinc miners in New Mexico who go on strike for equal treatment and safer working conditions. Both films avoid the use of homeless stereotypes, choosing instead to meditate on themes of home, displacement, community, nation, and discrimination. The climactic sequence in *Salt of the Earth* is the forced eviction of a mining family from a substandard company house. The entire community comes together to prevent the eviction, winning the strike in the process. Similarly, the final vignette in *The City* demonstrates the power of a cohesive and organized community to combat exploitation and confront the challenges of poverty.

RESEARCH DIRECTIONS

A film is often a measure of the fears and preoccupations of its era. The shifting images of homelessness in cinema provide a glimpse into the changing popular stereotypes, sympathies, and political concerns over the span of more than a century. While the cultural significance of the images of homelessness in film is clear, no comprehensive studies have been published on the subject. The topic requires extensive research in the fields of social history, film and video studies, and cultural studies.

—Amanda F. Grzyb

See also Appendix 2: Filmography of American Narrative and Documentary Films on Homelessness

Further Reading

Beach, C. (2001). *Class, language, and American film comedy.* New York: Cambridge University Press.

Holtman, L. (2000). *Media messages: What film, television, and popular music teach us about race, class, gender, and sexual orientation.* New York: M. E. Sharpe.

hooks, b. (1996). *Reel to real: Race, sex, and class at the movies.* New York: Routledge.

James, D. E., & Berg, R. (Eds.). (1996). *The hidden foundation: Cinema and the question of class.* Minneapolis: University of Minnesota Press.

Kusmer, K. (2002). *Down and out, on the road: The homeless in American history.* New York: Oxford University Press.

Lester, J. K. (1996). *Images that injure: Pictorial stereotypes in the media.* Westport, CT: Praeger.

Maland, C. (1989). *Chaplin and American culture.* Princeton, NJ: Princeton University Press.

McCaffrey, D. (Ed.). (1971). *Focus on Chaplin.* Englewood Cliffs, NJ: Prentice Hall.

Musser, C. (1990). *The emergence of cinema: The American screen to 1907.* Berkeley: University of California Press.

Nadel, A. (1997). *Flatlining on the field of dreams: Cultural narratives in the films of President Reagan's America.* New Brunswick, NJ: Rutgers University Press.

Platt, D. (1992). *Celluloid power: Social film criticism from* The Birth of a Nation *to* Judgment at Nuremberg. Metuchen, NJ: Scarecrow Press.

Quart, L., & Auster, A. (2002). *American film and society since 1945.* Westport, CT: Praeger.

Ross, S. J. (1998). *Working-class Hollywood: Silent film and the shaping of class in America.* Princeton, NJ: Princeton University Press.

Sloan, K. (1988). *The loud silents: Origins of the social problem film.* Urbana: University of Illinois Press.

Sklar, R. (1975). *Movie-made America: A cultural history of American movies.* New York: Vintage.

Turner, G. (1988). *Film as social practice.* New York: Routledge.

▣ IMAGES OF HOMELESSNESS IN NINETEENTH- AND TWENTIETH-CENTURY AMERICAN LITERATURE

One of the sustaining ideologies of the United States is that America is a home for the homeless, a nation built on immigration and migration. Therefore, it is not surprising that the mythology of the homeless figure is a significant part of the American cultural imagination, and that prominent images of displacement, exile, and drifting exist in every period of American literature. Homelessness is a central theme in some of the canonical works of nineteenth- and twentieth-century American literature, including the writings of Mark Twain, Stephen Crane, William Dean Howells, Theodore Dreiser, William Faulkner, John Steinbeck, William Kennedy, Toni Morrison, and Paul Auster. Homelessness emerges as a tacit social and political concern; a metaphor for subjectivity, race, and identity; a symbol of moral or social transgression and redemption; an icon for the challenges endured by the working class; and a portal for migration, travel, and adventure narratives. Although there are some notable exceptions, these texts often present contradictory images of homelessness, some offering oppressive tales of urban poverty, others romanticized stories of rural adventure.

Historically, representations of homelessness in literature, film, and popular media have shifted with changing attitudes about homelessness in America. Highlighting the changing vision of homelessness from the nineteenth century to the early twentieth century, the historian Kenneth Kusmer suggests that "while the image of the tramp changed and became more complex, its function as a mirror for the society's divisions and anxieties remained unaltered" (Kusmer 2002, 169). Literary conceptions of the homeless figure often consist of stereotypes or icons: "dangerous" outsiders and immigrants; sentimental orphans and runaways; romantic wandering hoboes, drifters, and heroes; "lazy" waifs; emblems of suffering; and representatives of contemporary street life. Furthermore, homelessness is a lens refracting the meaning of "America" and its connections to ownership, the constitutional right to property, vagrancy laws, and the relationship between landholders and civic empowerment. Images of the homeless not only reveal cultural and historical attitudes about homelessness, but also, by extension, the ideologies associated with notions of "home" as well.

SLAVERY AND HOMELESSNESS

Homelessness became a national issue during the economic recession of the 1870s, but the "wandering poor" have existed in America since colonial times. By the late 1700s, most provinces had passed vagrancy laws that were often used to incarcerate escaped or former slaves (Kusmer 2002, 17). For example, between 1823 and 1826, African-Americans made up close to 50 percent of those imprisoned for vagrancy in Philadelphia (Kusmer 2002, 24). Early works of African-American literature, such as slave

narratives, also reflect a preoccupation with home and homelessness, identifying cultural and historical ties to Africa *and* to America. Autobiography and critical writing have long suggested that being black in America often means negotiating what W. E. B. Du Bois called a "double-consciousness," an ontological homelessness.

Many early works of African-American literature reflect this "twoness" through complex themes of displacement. Texts such as Phillis Wheatley's "On Being Brought from Africa to America" (1773), Olaudah Equiano's *The Interesting Narrative* (1789), and Harriet Jacobs's *Incidents in the Life of a Slave Girl* (1861) are meditations on the intersections between slavery, freedom, national identity, home, and homelessness. Africa was the childhood homeland of Wheatley and Equiano, who were kidnapped and brought across the Atlantic on slave ships as children. Equiano's autobiographical narrative inhabits a space between Africa, America, and Europe, and the "middle passage" is an apt metaphor for this forced cultural transition. Equiano was homeless in the sense that he was without a single nation or a fixed national identity, straddling the culture of his childhood and the culture of the American and European powers that enslaved him.

Harriet Jacobs, who was born into slavery in America, had contradictory models for "home" in her life: her master's plantation, the house of her emancipated grandmother, and the abodes of her employers in the north. Yet, despite her access to various modes of shelter, Jacobs remains "homeless" as long as she is not free. In a chapter entitled "The Loophole of Retreat," Jacobs describes her ordeal as a fugitive after running away from her abusive master. For seven years, she hides in a tiny crawl space—the "garret"—above her grandmother's house, existing in the house but living apart from the "home" her family has created. After boring a small hole in the wall of her chamber, she is able to secretly watch her children grow up in the yard below her. When she finally does escape to "freedom" in the north, home still eludes her because the Fugitive Slave Act requires northerners to give runaway slaves back to their southern masters. For Jacobs, homelessness was defined by a lack of freedom, her experience as a fugitive slave, and the constant threats to her personal safety and liberty.

ORPHANS, RUNAWAYS, AND OPEN-AIR LIFE IN NINETEENTH-CENTURY LITERATURE

Living in the open air and a preference for rural environments were preoccupations in several subgenres of nineteenth-century American literature: the pioneer books, orphan tales, the "boy books," and various treatments of tramps. Homeless orphans were a particularly notable narrative preoccupation. They were popular, in part, because the sensational narratives include romantic child heroes who make their way in the world without the security of parental guidance and control. With its origins in British texts such as *Oliver Twist* (1837) and *Jane Eyre* (1846), the orphan theme was explored by many authors, including Henry James in *Watch and Ward* (1878) and *What Maisie Knew* (1897), and Mark Twain in *The Adventures of Huckleberry Finn* (1885).

Huck Finn, a seminal work of American fiction, narrates the adventures of Jim, a runaway slave, and Huck, a "homeless waif," as they drift down the Mississippi river on a raft. The state of homelessness, wandering from town to town, provides a setting for humor and adventure, but perhaps more importantly, it separates Huck and Jim from an existing set of cultural norms and practices. Before the journey begins, Huck and Jim witness the inversion of the traditional notions of "home" as a house becomes disengaged from its foundations and floats down the river towards them. Huck narrates, "Another night when we was up at the head of the island, just before daylight, here comes a frame house down" (Twain 1885/1987, 56). Some critics suggest that the act of homeless drifting on a raft creates a neutral space where Jim and Huck can explore a relationship that is not wholly determined by the institutions and laws of a slaveholding community. Within this framework, homelessness may allow Huck and Jim to style new notions of "home" and "family" in which Jim plays the role of Huck's father. Additionally, *Huck Finn* exemplifies the nineteenth-century interest in open-air life and rural adventure. A transient life, whether it is at a campsite in the forest, a cave in the canyons, or a raft on the river, can reflect romanticized notions of simplicity, purity, and a deep connection to nature.

Several novels chronicle the predicament of a young woman who is forced to find her own way in the world after becoming orphaned and homeless. For example, Susan Warner's *The Wide, Wide World* and E.D.E.N. Southworth's *The Hidden Hand* examine a female protagonist's struggle to survive in the world alone. Both novels are sentimental adventure stories with a heroine who has the freedom to explore the landscape of the nation. When Capitola, the protagonist in *The Hidden Hand,* finds herself alone and adrift in New York City, she disguises herself as a boy in order to survive on the streets. Her status represents not just poverty and desperation, but also a sense of freedom and an ingenuity usually reserved for male protagonists.

LATE NINETEENTH-CENTURY AND EARLY TWENTIETH-CENTURY URBAN HOMELESSNESS IN LITERATURE

Nineteenth-century and early twentieth-century images of urban homelessness differ dramatically from those of rural homelessness. Homelessness in an urban setting often situates the homeless man as a victim, a tragic figure of transgression and redemption. William Dean Howells's novels *The Undiscovered Country* (1880) and *The Minister's Charge* (1887) are "case studies of the descent of innocent people into the homeless class" (Kusmer 2002, 170). The motives of the authors of such texts are political and ethical as well as artistic. In *The Minister's Charge,* Lem Barker loses his money and ends up in a lodging house for homeless men; this predicament provides the reader with a glimpse at the degradations and inequities endured by the poor and homeless who do not have access to permanent housing.

The tragedy of urban homelessness culminates in the character of Hurstwood in Theodore Dreiser's *Sister Carrie* (1900), the paradigm of the homeless city dweller. Hurstwood's homelessness is characterized as a "fall" from a comfortable middle-class existence, and an inverted reflection of Carrie's social ascent. Hurstwood's transition from the privacy of his apartment to the public nature of the shelter is significant. Although such charities are accessible by the public, they are invisible to those who do not experience need. Dreiser writes, "Institutions and charities are so large and so numerous in New York that such things as this are not often noticed by the more comfortably situated" (1900, 357). Hurstwood's death in a temporary room is the culmination of his descent into poverty. He has lost every semblance of control in his life, and he commits suicide after uttering the seemingly impenetrable question, "What's the use?" (Dreiser 1900, 367).

IMAGES OF THE HOMELESS IMMIGRANT

As the homeless population grew in the 1870s and 1880s, the popular image of the homeless person consisted of an immigrant, an unassimilated foreigner, an alien "other." The stereotype of the "outsider" prevailed into the early twentieth century, regardless of the fact that by 1920 the majority of homeless people were native-born Americans. Likewise, preoccupations with class inequities were also an important concern for writers who explored the issue of home, work, and displacement in their texts. This theme was investigated in Jacob Riis's *How the Other Half Lives* (1890), Upton Sinclair's *The Jungle* (1906), and in multiple texts by Stephen Crane. Riis's text set the stage for images of poverty and homelessness that were both political statements and pedagogical tools used to educate the middle and upper classes about the abject living conditions in some urban centers.

In Crane's *Maggie: A Girl of the Streets* (1893), the tenements of the Lower East Side invert traditional notions of public and private, of familial care and abuse, and, ultimately, of home and homelessness. Writing in the naturalist tradition, Crane uses Maggie's fall into street life as a means to externalize her internal emotional state. Almost every scene at home centers upon the destruction of domestic space, violence perpetrated against the furniture, the hearth, and the bodies of the children. While the hearth is usually a place of family nurturing and sustenance, Maggie's hearth is usually barren and cold.

Crane writes, "The fire in the stove had gone out. The displaced lids and open doors showed heaps of sullen gray ashes. The remnants of a meal, ghastly, lay in a corner" (1893, 51). "Ruined" by a Bowery man, Maggie is eventually forced to leave her home and to move to the streets, where she works as a prostitute. Her initial forays into public life could be seen, as some critics have suggested, as threatening the racial and economic boundaries of the American social order. As a "pretty girl" in the Bowery (Crane 1893, 38), the character of Maggie invokes fear of miscegenation for the white middle-class reader. Ultimately, Maggie's status remains ambiguous and ends in suicide. She is eternally displaced, since she is both a representative of immigrant poverty and perceived as a threat to the physical boundaries that seek to contain it.

DEPRESSION-ERA IMAGES

At the beginning of the twentieth century, a romanticized version of the "tramp" began to compete with the earlier images of the homeless person as a pernicious outsider. Working class and anti-capitalist heroes began to emerge in vaudeville, popular music, and film. By the time of the Great Depression, the image of the homeless person was no longer a suspicious or romantic wanderer, but had been reclaimed by the working class as an emblem of economic suffering. In film, Charlie Chaplin established the character of the "little tramp," a homeless icon that embodies the image of the harmless, lovable hero who challenges industrialism and capitalist power structures. Chaplin's homeless icon is sentimental and comical, a clear departure from the predominantly negative images of the homeless in early twentieth-century film, media, and literature.

With their roots in turn-of-the-century writers such as Jack London and Josiah Flynt, writers such as Edward Dahlberg, Tom Kromer, and John Steinbeck documented Depression-era poverty and displacement. Tom Kromer's *Waiting for Nothing* (1934), written on the road while the author was homeless, is an autobiographical novella composed in first-person testimonial fashion. Form and content are married in the text, while the narrative about homelessness itself "wanders," and the episodic stories are without a plot-driven chronological logic. There is no explanation for how the protagonist became homeless, only the constant mantra "I am a hungry man" (1934, 13) or "I am cold" (1934/1986, 22). The first claim of any autobiographical narrative is "I am," and for Kromer's protagonist, subjectivity is based on a set of conditions—hunger, cold, fear— that are determined by his homeless status. Kromer's protagonist presents the reader with a set of techniques for survival on the road, reflects on the temptations of crime, and notes the individual and collective tragedies of the transient population. The survival options for the homeless population are also explored in the protagonist's experiences and observations, and include begging, squatting, hustling for food and shelter as a prostitute, bank robbery, giving up an infant, riding the rails, scams and cons, staying at a religious mission, starvation, and suicide. The protagonist's relationships are determined entirely by external circumstances, and characters that are important to the narrative in one chapter entirely disappear without explanation in the next. Kromer is also critical of religion and 1930s mission culture in particular, and the text offers an inversion of the traditional religious conversion narrative. There is no redemption or resolution, and with the specter of suicide throughout the text, Kromer suggests that the characters are indeed "waiting for nothing."

DRIFTERS, WANDERERS, ROMANTIC HEROES

The images of wandering, romantic heroes after World War II are rooted in the youthful orphan drifters of the nineteenth century such as Huck Finn, and the rail-riding "tramps" of the Great Depression such as Tom Kromer. Mid-twentieth-century itinerant characters are also the predecessors of the contemporary homeless autobiographical texts; both function with a predominantly male paradigm, and their stories are episodic adventures. Images of homelessness created by mid-century "beat" writers such as William S. Burroughs and Jack Kerouac continue to inspire fantasies of an open road and the drifter's "carefree" lifestyle. Such writers create romantic heroes who drift across city and countryside, imbibing drugs and alcohol, and looking for adventure. Unlike the overwhelming desperation and disenfranchisement found in Kromer's autobiographical fiction, Jack Kerouac's *On the Road* (1957) strikes a balance that captures the lost, rebellious, and exuberant liberation expressed in drifting, and the youthful excitement of the "beat generation."

William Kennedy's Pulitzer Prize–winning novel *Ironweed* (1983) modifies this characterization to create the wandering homeless antihero. Francis Phelan's homeless odyssey begins when he accidentally drops his son, resulting in his death. Rather than face his family after the tragedy, he takes to the road and creates a new life with a homeless woman named Helen. The novel begins with his return to Albany many years later and reveals the specters of memory and violence that haunt Francis, suggesting a past that is continuous with the present. For Francis, homelessness is not only a lack of permanence or a rooted existence, but it is also a symbol of his quest for redemption.

HOME AND HOMELESSNESS AS METAPHORS FOR RACE AND IDENTITY

In keeping with the theme of race, discrimination, and displacement running through eighteenth- and nineteenth-century African-American literature, twentieth-century depictions of racial difference often used the theme of homelessness or exile as a metaphor for subjectivity. Ralph Ellison's novel *Invisible Man* (1952) begins with a description of a nameless protagonist who squats in basement, siphoning power from Monopolated Light and Power to light his adopted home (Ellison 1952, 5). The narrator's homeless status emphasizes his disenfranchisement, an existence outside the community while simultaneously within it. He is "neither dead nor in a state of suspended animation," but his invisibility is a "state of hibernation" (Ellison 1952, 6). Similarly, in *Playing in the Dark* (1992), Toni Morrison suggests that America's canonical literature is a production that responds to a deeply vexed and parasitic relationship to the historically displaced population of African-Americans. For Morrison, African-

American characters are often displaced from traditional notions of home through their "double-consciousness," and their presence in novels by white authors are often a nameless catalyst for plot changes or representative of an American fear of blackness. She writes, "The very manner by which American literature distinguishes itself as a coherent entity exists because of this unsettled and unsettling population" (Morrison 1992, 6). White writers also explore race and subjectivity using homelessness. For example, all of the characters in Faulkner's *Light in August* (1932) are rootless outsiders in the town of Jefferson, and the "central theme [is] . . . the placelessness of persons who have, either by their own efforts or because of some twist of fate, become located in the margins of society" (Watkins 1994, 11). Over the course of the novel, the central character, Joe Christmas, shifts from orphan to runaway to drifter to squatter to fugitive. Another character, Byron Bunch, observes that Christmas "did not look like a professional hobo in his professional rags, but there was definitely something rootless about him, as though no town nor city was his, no street, no walls, no square of earth his home" (Faulkner 1932, 31). Christmas's homelessness has less to do with place, and more to do with racial and cultural identity. He has ambiguous racial origins; while his racial identity is not resolved in the novel, it is suggested that he is a biracial man who can "pass" for white. He drifts from town to town, between African-American and white communities, and details his eternal status as "marginal," as a suspected "foreigner." Jefferson's notions of white identity—and, by extension, of "home"—rely upon the contrasting depictions of blackness that permeate the text. Christmas's racial ambiguity and rootlessness is threatening to Jefferson, and it breaks "all the semiotic codes of society" (Snead 1986, 156).

CONTEMPORARY AND POSTMODERN FICTION

Postmodern fiction is particularly well suited to the theme of homelessness due to the contemporary preoccupation with silences, gaps, displacement, alienation, and paradox. Homeless metaphors are often a means to represent the "uncanny" (the German word *unhiemlich* literally means "un-home") to hypothesize an ontological homelessness or a fragmented subjectivity, or to explore nonlinear narrative. Images of homelessness are found in Don DeLillo's *Underworld* (1997) and Thomas Pynchon's *The Crying of Lot 49* (1966), and displacement is a recurring theme in texts by Cormack McCarthy, Toni Morrison, and Paul Auster.

In Paul Auster's *Moon Palace* (1989), the protagonist is a Columbia University student who runs out of money and ends up living rough in Central Park. His homelessness is a portal into a narrative that meditates on the American journey "west" and the myth of the frontier. In *Timbuktu* (1999), Auster returns to the theme of homelessness in more detail. The narrator of *Timbuktu* is Mr. Bones, the pet dog of a homeless man named Willy Christmas. The text represents displacement in a unique way, exploring three versions of America: one through the eyes of a homeless man with mental illness, another through the life of an immigrant urban boy, and the last through the narrative of a family living in the comforts of suburbia. While Willy may be homeless, Mr. Bones does not become "homeless" himself until Willy dies on the street. Therefore, the *experience* of homelessness—and its associated fears, trials, and loneliness—are introduced to the reader by the homeless dog, not the homeless man.

IMAGES OF HOMELESS WOMEN

In the late 1970s, the "new homeless" population exploded, an urban group dominated by women and children who were and remain disproportionately African-American and Latino. A contemporary literature that imagines homelessness as a predominantly male experience, while simultaneously remaining silent about homeless women, lacks the full expression of the gender variations of homeless experiences. Fiction about homeless women is rare, and autobiographies by homeless women are even rarer. The autobiographies that do exist are often collaborative efforts, with less focus on the traditional male autobiographies that chronicle homeless life as an episodic and adventurous narrative. The female autobiographies that do exist are often collaborative efforts, and they differ significantly from male autobiographies, which often chronicle homeless life as an episodic and adventurous narrative. Often, the only consistent forum for women's homeless narratives are oral histories and ethnographic studies such as Jonathan Kozol's *Rachel and Her Children: Homeless Families in America* (1988), Jennifer Toth's *The Mole People: Life in the Tunnels Beneath New York City* (1993), and Elliot Liebow's *Tell Them Who I Am: The Lives of Homeless Women* (1993).

RESEARCH DIRECTIONS

Images of homelessness are inseparable from the history of American literature and culture. The theme pervades American literature from the country's earliest days to the present. Yet, despite its role in literature and culture, homelessness is often combined with general studies of poverty in literature. As an independent theme, it remains relatively unexplored in scholarly work and literary criticism. There are also important connections to be made between the images of homelessness in literature and current research on areas such as realism and naturalism; First Nations People; the middle passage of slaves transported from Africa to America, slave narratives, and African-American migrations; globalization; Atlantic studies; and postcolonialism. Each of these areas of study emphasizes notions of home and displacement, and there are many intersections with the study of "homelessness" itself.

—*Amanda F. Grzyb*

Further Reading

Alger, H. (1895). *Adrift in the city.* New York: Street and Smith.

Allen, J. (2003). *Homelessness in American literature.* New York: Routledge.

Auster, P. (1989). *Moon palace.* New York: Penguin.

Auster, P. (1999). *Timbuktu.* New York: Picador USA.

Carey-Webb, A. (1992). Representing the homeless. *American Literary History, 4*(4), 697–708.

Crane, S. (1893). *Maggie: A girl of the streets.* New York: Norton.

Dreiser, T. (1900). *Sister Carrie.* New York: Norton.

Ellison, R. (1952). *Invisible man.* New York: Vintage.

Faulkner, W. (1932). *Light in August.* New York: Vintage.

Feied, F. (1964). *No pie in the sky: The hobo as American cultural hero in the works of Jack London, John Dos Passos, and Jack Kerouac.* New York: Citadel.

Flynt, J. (1899). *Tramping with tramps.* New York: Century.

Giamo, B. (1996). *The homeless of Ironweed: Blossoms on the crag.* Iowa City: University of Iowa Press.

Giamo, B. (1989). *On the Bowery: Confronting homelessness in American society.* Iowa City: University of Iowa Press.

Howells, W. D. (1884). *The undiscovered country.* Boston: Houghton Mifflin.

Jacobs, H. (1861). *Incidents in the life of a slave girl.* New York: Oxford University Press.

Kennedy, W. (1983). *Ironweed.* New York: Penguin.

Kerouac, J. (1991). *On the road.* New York: Penguin. (Original work published 1957)

Kromer, T. (1986). *Waiting for nothing and other writings.* Athens: University of Georgia Press. (Original work published 1934)

Kusmer, K. (2002). *Down and out, on the road: The homeless in American history.* New York: Oxford University Press.

London, J. (1907). *The road.* New York: Macmillan.

Morrison, T. (1992). *Playing in the dark: Whiteness and the literary imagination.* Cambridge, MA: Harvard University Press.

Riis, J. (1996). *How the other half lives: Studies among the tenements of New York.* Boston: Bedford.

Sinclair, U. (2002). *The jungle.* New York: W.W. Norton. (Original work published 1906)

Snead, J. (1986). *Figures of division.* New York: Methuen.

Steinbeck, J. (1976). *Grapes of wrath.* New York: Penguin Books.

Southworth, E. D. E. N. (1888). *The hidden hand or, Capitola the Madcap.* New Brunswick, NJ: Rutgers University Press.

Twain. M. (1987). *The adventures of Huckleberry Finn.* New York: Penguin. (Original work published 1885)

Ward, D. (1989). *Poverty, ethnicity, and the American city, 1840–1925: Changing perceptions of the slum and the ghetto.* Cambridge, UK: Cambridge University Press.

Warner. S. (1850). *The wide, wide world.* New York: Feminist Press.

Whalen, B. (1989). *Home and homelessness in the American imagination.* University of Dallas: Unpublished doctoral dissertation.

Watkins, R. (1994, Spring). "It was like I was the woman and she was the man": Boundaries, portals, and pollution in *Light in August. Southern Literary Journal, 26*(2), 11–24.

▣ IMAGES OF HOMELESSNESS IN THE MEDIA

After virtually ignoring the problem of homelessness for decades, the news media in the United States sharply increased its coverage during the early to mid-1980s. This increase, and its subsequent decline and plateau, offer a view of the changing image of homelessness in America. Assuming that the media play an important role in influencing public opinion and knowledge, then certainly this shifting amount, tone, and salience of media coverage of homelessness have affected the general public's views on this issue. The media may also influence policymakers both directly and indirectly through public opinion. Indeed, all of these factors are mutually influential.

MEDIA DEPICTIONS OF HOMELESSNESS: A HISTORICAL OVERVIEW

Homelessness in Western society has its roots in the urbanization of the early nineteenth century. From that time on, the theme of homelessness has received attention in popular literature, spanning the decades from Charles Dickens's *Oliver Twist* and Mark Twain's *The Prince and the Pauper,* to John Steinbeck's *Of Mice and Men,* as well as in motion pictures: Charlie Chaplin in *The Tramp,* and more recently Dustin Hoffman and Jon Voight in *Midnight Cowboy* and Dan Ackroyd and Eddie Murphy in *Trading Places.* Although such popular media have frequently depicted the homeless in stereotypical ways, from tramp to villain to purveyor of practical wisdom, it is relatively rare for a homeless protagonist to be portrayed in a strictly negative light.

In the decades before 1980, homelessness was infrequently covered in the news media. When references were made, they often depicted the stereotypical skid row derelict, an older, single, alcoholic male. However, starting in the early 1980s, the news media began to cover homelessness in detail and as a recognizable social problem distinct from poverty. Furthermore, a dramatic shift in labeling occurred in newspaper indexes around this time. The subject keywords "vagrant" and "vagrancy" began to be replaced by the somewhat more neutral "homeless" and "homelessness," a change that was virtually complete by the late 1980s. Indeed, the change parallels the shift in public perception of homeless people as tramps and hoboes to being, at least in part, victims of uncontrollable circumstances.

What prompted this turnaround in the early to mid-1980s? Several possible catalysts have been proposed. First, President Ronald Reagan's social program cuts during the recession of the early 1980s were a sharp departure from previous government policy. When Reagan's political opponents and activists for the homeless mobilized to fill the gap, they helped push the homelessness issue into the consciousness of those in the media. Second, as many American inner cities were developed and gentrified, the cheap hotels and flophouses in previously poor districts closed their doors, pushing large numbers of marginal people out. Third, the news media began to describe the situation of the homeless as a "plight," framing the problem more in terms of victimization than of personal failure. Fourth, widespread media coverage of the winter deaths of a number of homeless people (which mostly occurred during the winters of 1984 and 1985) vividly demonstrated the seriousness and urgency of this problem. Finally, Hands Across America, a 1986 charity event that involved more than 5 million people joining hands in a fund-raiser to combat homelessness, was extensively covered in the news media.

But after peaking in the late 1980s, coverage in the print news media began to decline, followed soon thereafter by a similar trend, albeit less pronounced, in network television news. If newspaper journalism indeed serves as the leading edge of the various news media, that trend was reflected here. Many topics do first appear in newspapers and are later picked up by broadcast media, and this was true of homelessness in the 1980s.

RECENT TRENDS IN MEDIA COVERAGE

Relatively few researchers have systematically examined the media's depiction of the homeless, and those few have reported mixed results. A review of *The New York Times* between 1980 and 1990 found that most articles on the subject covered policies and services for homeless persons, as well as their demographic features, while fewer than half mentioned either deviant characteristics or any cause of homelessness. James Power (1991) conducted a study of network television news media between 1982 and 1988 and concluded that most portrayals did not stigmatize the homeless. Power also noted that when the causes of homelessness were mentioned, they tended to center on societal factors.

Likewise, in analyzing national television evening newscasts and national magazines from 1986 to 1989, the Center for Media and Public Affairs found coverage generally sympathetic, with most stories focusing on local programs and services, or on the homeless people themselves, rather than on the roots of the problem. The stereotypic image of the unemployed male alcoholic was rare; images focused as frequently on families and children as on single males. As for the causes of homelessness, reporters were likely to address structural issues, such as housing market forces, rather than personal problems. When public reactions to the homeless were portrayed, almost 70 percent of them were characterized as compassionate.

Another analysis of television network news stories on poverty from 1981 to 1986 found that twice as many stories focused on individuals as on a broader societal context. Perhaps ironically, however, by featuring and personalizing homeless individuals, the media may actually have fostered a public perception of homelessness as rooted in personal, not societal, causes. In particular, portrayals of personal problems such as substance abuse and mental illness are likely to increase levels of stigmatization. This was the conclusion of a study that examined a series of well-publicized news stories in 1987 and 1988 about the involuntary institutionalization of Joyce Brown, a homeless mentally ill woman who claimed to be living on the streets of New York City by choice. At least one additional study of magazine and television news stories throughout the 1980s concluded that their general tone placed much of the blame for homelessness on the homeless themselves.

A closer look at two of the previously mentioned studies that reported sympathetic coverage reveals a disturbing trend over time. The analysis of television news media between 1982 and 1988 found that while the homeless were not usually stigmatized, the occurrence of negative portrayals appeared to be increasing. Also, compared to stories published in the *New York Times* between 1980 and 1983, those published from 1988 to 1990 tended to be more neg-

ative. Specifically, the later stories focused to a greater extent on the deviant characteristics of some homeless people; they were also less critical of existing programs and services' shortcomings. Consistent with these findings, some researchers and policy analysts have proposed that the late 1980s and early 1990s saw a negative shift in attitude both in the media and among society's other social elites—politicians in particular. However, a content analysis of editorial cartoons on the subject, which were published in two San Francisco newspapers between 1989 and 1992, did not support this view. It found that only 30 percent tended to blame homeless people for their own plight, while most appealed to the government to take responsibility for the problem.

Finally, another analysis of national television and radio news conducted by Rebecca Lind and James Danowski from 1993 to 1996 found very little reporting on homelessness overall (Min 1999). Among the small number of reports that were produced during these years, there were, however, many mentions of substance abuse, mental and physical illness, and criminality. Although few stories discussed the causes of homelessness, those that did were most likely to mention economic and societal factors. Overall, one might conclude that the content of the broadcast news reporting during this period of the early 1990s was rather "mixed."

MEDIA AND PROFESSIONAL COVERAGE IN THE UNITED STATES: SCOPE AND CONTENT

A recent study (Buck and Toro 2002) examined several relevant trends in coverage during the period 1972 to 2001. It focused on two areas: the general media—represented by four major newspapers: *The New York Times, The Washington Post, The Los Angeles Times,* and *The Chicago Tribune*—and the professional literature indexed in the PsycINFO database, which covers psychology and other social science, health, and mental health professions. The study sought, first, to document the volume of coverage of homelessness in both these categories; second, to describe the content of that coverage; and third, to determine whether and how the content had changed over this thirty-year span.

Portrayals of the homeless in the media have always been characterized by gross stereotyping. This magazine circa 1900 showing a homeless person being chased off by a dog hanging from a fence is typical for its time.

Source: Bettmann/Corbis; used with permission.

Consistent with previous research, they found minimal newspaper attention to the topic until around 1980. However, the period from 1981 to 1987 saw an explosion of coverage. Then it declined through the early 1990s, almost as steeply as it had risen a few years before. Finally, from the mid-1990s through 2001, newspaper coverage appeared to have reached a plateau, albeit with some fluctuation from year to year.

In the professional literature, homelessness was barely covered during the 1970s. In fact, this period of little interest continued until the mid-1980s, longer than it did in the newspapers. But professional coverage eventually rose as well, beginning to gather momentum by the late 1980s and peaking in 1992. It then decreased somewhat, though not as dramatically as the newspaper coverage, and leveled out from 1994 through 2001. Overall, the professional literature seems to parallel the trend in newspaper reporting, with less pronounced fluctuation and with a lag of about five years.

Next, the researchers analyzed content, randomly sampling about 500 of the newspaper articles and dividing the thirty-year span into four time periods: 1972–1980 (pre-interest), 1981–1987 (rise and peak), 1988–1993 (decline), and 1994–2001 (plateau).

The rise-and-peak period may be the most revealing. During this time, the four newspapers appeared in many respects to present the most sympathetic view of homeless people as compared to the years before and since. They reported frequently on mental illness as a factor, often focusing on deinstitutionalization and other possible structural causes of homelessness, and dramatically reduced their earlier depictions of the skid row alcoholic (most common during the "pre-interest" period). However, they tended not to discuss health services and long-term programs for homeless people, quite possibly because relatively few such programs yet existed; these topics were covered more positively in later periods. Overall, these data support the conclusion that media coverage has not simply become more negative toward homelessness in recent years, but that it has become more varied and, at the same time, more sophisticated. The fact that recent coverage included a greater number of topics may reflect the public's increased knowledge and understanding that homelessness is a complex social issue.

The study also analyzed a sample of about 300 professional journal articles indexed in PsycINFO. Due to this literature's slower "takeoff" in coverage of homelessness, the researchers conflated the first two time spans used for the newspaper sample, yielding three periods for analysis: 1972–1987 (pre-interest/early rise), 1988–1993 (rise and peak), and

1994–2001 (plateau). Some parallels with the news media were observed. The pre-interest/early rise period contained the most emphasis on mental illness and substance abuse and on inadequate policies and structural causes, corresponding roughly to the high level of similar news coverage during this period. During the rise and peak period (1988–1993), the professional literature focused more on long-term services for homeless persons, corresponding to the similar emphasis in the media from 1988 through 2001.

Seasonal Differences in Media Coverage

Apart from the broad trends described above, analyses of the American news media have consistently shown more reporting on homelessness during the fall and winter months. These seasonal differences are not surprising. Over the course of a year, even casual media observers will notice that interest in homelessness, and other disadvantaged groups such as the mentally ill, seems to be piqued during the holiday season. Every year, news stories tell how to give to those in the most need. Shelters and soup kitchens also report increased volunteerism during this time of the year. The media often cover such activities as human interest features during the holidays. While the seasonal spike in media coverage could be partly due to the onset of cold weather in many areas of the nation, it seems to reflect the sense that the holiday season can spark compassion and sympathy for the poorest members of society.

MEDIA AND PROFESSIONAL COVERAGE IN OTHER DEVELOPED NATIONS

In developed nations outside of the United States, very little systematic research has examined media coverage of homelessness. However, based on one study (2002) completed in Belgium (by Pierre Phillipot and his colleagues, as described below) and discussions by Buck and Toro (2002) with researchers studying homelessness in other European nations, it appears that such coverage has increased since the early 1980s. In the United Kingdom, the amount and timing of coverage has been somewhat similar to that seen in America. However, the sheer volume of coverage in the UK was not nearly as heavy as was seen in the United States during the mid-1980s. Like the United States, the UK saw a dramatic shift in political orientation in the 1980s (with the ascendance of Margaret Thatcher's conservatives) coinciding with a rise in coverage on homelessness. Media coverage in other major English-speaking nations, specifically Canada and Australia, started to become obvious a bit later, in the early 1990s.

The professional literature in English-speaking nations (especially the United Kingdom) began to mention homelessness a few years later than the increase seen in the United States. Coverage in both categories—news media and journal articles—rose much more recently in most other developed nations of the world, including France, Belgium, Italy, Spain, Germany, and Japan. A study by Pierre Phillipot and his colleagues in Belgium found results similar in many respects to those of the Buck and Toro study. Considering four major newspapers, three in French and one in Dutch, the Belgian researchers found a rise in coverage from the late 1980s to the mid-1990s, followed by an apparent decline since then. They also found a trend for more coverage in the fall and winter months.

WHY DOESN'T MEDIA COVERAGE MESH WITH PUBLIC OPINION?

Around 1990, some American media sources began to suggest that the public was tiring of the homelessness problem, and was even becoming hostile to homeless people. However, studies by Bruce Link and a research group led by Paul Toro that have examined public opinion polls from 1987 to 2001 have suggested that this "compassion fatigue" has been overstated by the media. According to these polls, the public seems to have a fairly accurate perception of the demographics of homelessness, and of its multiple causes, including structural ones. Such awareness may be a result of the widespread and generally sympathetic media coverage from the mid-1980s through the early 1990s.

So why have the media alluded to a "compassion

fatigue" among the public—and even displayed their own version of it (at least in terms of their overall coverage) during this time period? One explanation is that the media are influenced by the desire to cover "news" that tends to involve emotional (and often controversial) issues in order to attract the public's interest. Having covered homelessness extensively for several years in the late 1980s, perhaps those in journalism sensed the need to move onto other, more novel topics. Homelessness was no longer "news." Given that the media's attention to any particular subject tends to be very brief, the many years of sustained and intense interest in homelessness during the 1980s could, perhaps, be viewed as very unusual and impressive.

CAUSES, EFFECTS, AND INFLUENCES

The reciprocal interaction between those who work in the media and the sources of news stories (e.g., politicians, advocates, and interest groups) is vital in setting the media's agenda. This news agenda is important in that it is usually the public's primary source of information about issues at both the national and local levels. The public, too, depends on the news media as its primary source of information about issues at both the national and local levels. Although research suggests that media accounts may influence the public's attitudes, beliefs, and behaviors toward the homeless, a direct link is difficult to prove. Despite the media's ubiquity—for example, almost 98 percent of the respondents in a Nashville 1987 citywide survey had seen a news story on homelessness during the past year— other sources of information about homelessness, such as seeing a homeless person on the street, may be more salient to people than what they read in a newspaper or watch on the nightly news. Therefore, exposure to news on homelessness may bring this topic to mind without influencing what citizens actually think.

In any event, a change in the amount and focus of coverage of homelessness by the mass media can be expected to have policy implications. Social problems that receive wide and favorable media attention tend to be addressed with policy initiatives. For example, concurrent with the outburst of sympa-

thetic media attention, the Stewart B. McKinney Homeless Assistance Act became law in 1987. Alternatively, if media coverage decreases and/or adopts a harsher tone in the future, then policy decisions that reduce programs for homeless people may be more easily defended.

The amount and focus of scientific research may also influence policy decisions. Professional scientific and academic groups frequently engage with the media and politicians in order to help shape policy based on sound science, as well as to influence the direction of federal funding that is vital to conducting research. But these professionals may, like the public at large, be influenced by the media themselves. Indeed, the Buck and Toro data suggest that the rise in media coverage of homelessness in the mid-1980s may have contributed to a similar increase in professional interest in the subject a few years later.

Homelessness is often described as a continuum ranging from doubling up with family or friends to sleeping on sidewalks at night. Because of a lack of consensus on the definition of homelessness—and thus on its actual prevalence—politicians are forced to rely heavily on indirect sources such as public opinion surveys and media coverage in making policy decisions. Advocates tend to hold the broadest definitions of homelessness and government officials the narrowest, with social scientists presenting an array of possible definitions. Although there is no firm empirical data confirming that America's rate of homelessness rose sharply during the 1980s, it is widely believed that it did and, furthermore, that this rise was at least partly responsible for the subsequent spike in media coverage, professional interest, and political debate and action. In that case, a real-world trend actually sparked the interest. However, there is no clear evidence for a *drop* in the homelessness rate since 1987. Thus, the decrease in media interest in homelessness cannot be readily explained by a reduction in the problem itself.

AN UNCERTAIN FUTURE

Recent media coverage of homelessness seems to have gained in complexity, rather than simply becoming more negative, as some have suggested.

Furthermore, given the decline in the amount of coverage since the late 1980s, this decline has not yet had a discernable influence on public opinion; there is no evidence for general "compassion fatigue." The current relatively low plateau in media coverage does not appear to reflect lower public concern for the homeless, nor does it mirror the continuing fairly substantial interest among professionals.

With regard to homelessness, as with many other social problems, there seems to be a complex interplay of factors. In this case, the media, public opinion, policymakers, professionals—both researchers and service providers— and the actual prevalence of homelessness each influence the others. The media have clearly been a collective "player" here, and not just in a passive way. The media have, perhaps, pushed the public, professionals, and policymakers alike to consider the problem of homelessness. Moreover, the media's relative lack of concern in recent years has coincided with a lack of interest by policymakers; for example, homelessness was not mentioned in the presidential debates of 1996 and 2000. Perhaps, in time, the decline of media interest will also lead to a true decline of concern among the public. Of course, any rise or decline in public opinion and/or media coverage may or may not have an impact on the actual number of persons who actually are homeless or on how they are treated.

—Philip O. Buck and Paul A. Toro

Further Reading

Blasi, G. (1994). And we are not seen: Ideological and political barriers to understanding homelessness. *American Behavioral Scientist, 37,* 563–586.

Buck, P. O., & Toro, P. A. (2002). Media and professional interest in homelessness over the past three decades (1972–2001). Retrieved April 2, 2004, from http://sun.science.wayne.edu/~ptoro/medpap7.htm

Bullock, H. E., Wyche, K. F., & Williams, W. R. (2001). Media images of the poor. *Journal of Social Issues, 57,* 229–246.

Bunis, W. K., Yancik, A., & Snow, D. A. (1996). The cultural patterning of sympathy toward the homeless and other victims of misfortune. *Social Problems, 43,* 387–402.

Campbell, R., & Reeves, J. L. (1989). Covering the homeless: The Joyce Brown story. *Critical Studies in Mass Communication, 6,* 21–42.

Center for Media and Public Affairs. (1989). The visible poor: Media coverage of the homeless 1986–1989. *Media Monitor, 3*(3), 1–6.

Gilens, M. (1996). Race and poverty in America: Public misperceptions and the American news media. *Public Opinion Quarterly, 60,* 515–541.

Iyengar, S. (1990). Framing responsibility for political issues: The case of poverty. *Political Behavior, 12,* 19–40.

Lee, B. A., Jones, S. H., & Lewis, D. W. (1990). Public beliefs about the causes of homelessness. *Social Forces, 69,* 253–265.

Lee, B. A., Link, B. G., & Toro, P. A. (1991). Images of the homeless: Public views and media messages. *Housing Policy Debate, 2,* 649–682.

Link, B. G., Schwartz, S., Moore, R., Phelan, J., Struening, E., Stueve, A., & Colten, M. E. (1995). Public knowledge, attitudes, and beliefs about homeless people: Evidence for compassion fatigue. *American Journal of Community Psychology, 23,* 533–555.

McNulty, B. R. (1992). *Homeless and hopeless: Resignation in news media constructions of homelessness as a social problem.* Unpublished doctoral dissertation, University of Pennsylvania.

Min, E. (Ed.). (1999). *Reading the homeless: The media's image of homeless culture.* Westport, CT: Praeger.

Page, B. I., & Shapiro, R. Y. (1989). Educating and manipulating the public. In M. Margolis & G. A. Mauser (Eds.), *Manipulating public opinion: Essays on public opinion as a dependent variable* (pp. 294–320). Belmont, CA: Brooks/Cole.

Penner, M., & Penner, S. (1994). Publicizing, politicizing, and neutralizing homelessness: Comic strips. *Communication Research, 21,* 766–781.

Phillipot, P., Sempoux, F., Nachtergael, H., & Galand, B. (2002). Réflections sur le traitement médiatique de la problématique des personnes sans-abri [Reflections on media coverage on the problem of homelessness]. Unpublished manuscript, University of Louvain, Louvain-la-Neuve, Belgium.

Platt, S. (1999). Home truths: Media representations of homelessness. In B. Franklin (Ed.), *Social policy, the media and representation* (pp. 104–117). New York: Routledge.

Power, J. G. (1991). *Mass communication of otherness and identification: An examination of the portrayal of homeless people in television network news.* Unpublished doctoral dissertation, University of Southern California.

Shinn, M. (1992). Homelessness: What is a psychologist to do? *American Journal of Community Psychology, 20,* 1–24.

Snow, D., & Anderson, L. (1993). *Down on their luck: A study of homeless street people.* Berkeley: University of California Press.

Toro, P. A. (2003). *Research group on homelessness and poverty: Applying methods of the social sciences to the problems of homelessness and poverty.* Retrieved May 19, 2003, from http://sun.science.wayne.edu/~ptoro/

Toro, P. A., & McDonell, D. M. (1992). Beliefs, attitudes, and knowledge about homelessness: A survey of the general public. *American Journal of Community Psychology, 20,* 53–80.

Toro, P. A., & Warren, M. G. (1999). Homelessness in the United States: Policy considerations. *Journal of Community Psychology, 27,* 119–136.

▣ INDONESIA

Homelessness is still a relatively new concept in Indonesia. There is not yet a generally accepted definition, no accurate data are available, and little has been written about the topic.

The official Indonesian term for "homeless" is *tunawisma,* Old-Javanese for "no *(tuna)* home *(wisma)*." The Majlis Bahasa Brunei Darussalam–Indonesia–Malaysia (Brunei Darussalam–Indonesia–Malaysia Language Council) in 2000 adopted the word *ketunawismaan* as the translation of "homelessness" to be used in the three countries.

Another word often used to describe homelessness is *gelandangan,* which has the same meaning and connotation as the English word "tramp." *Gelandangan* is often used in combination with *pengemis* ("beggar"). In fact, a new word *gepeng* (combining *gela*ndangan and *peng*emis) has been coined and is often used in the context of operations to remove the homeless from places such as street intersections, where they are seen as an eyesore and a nuisance to motorists. Sometimes *gepeng* is used to describe psychiatric cases who wander about the city aimlessly. In the Social Welfare Act 6 of 1974, these people are grouped together with prostitutes, street children, and substance abusers under the label *penyandang masalah sosial* ("people suffering from social problems").

The Housing and Settlement Act 4 (1992), though acknowledging the housing shortage in Indonesia, makes no single mention of *tunawisma, ketunawismaan, gelandangan* or *gepeng.* The act sees housing more in terms of adequacy. The act recognizes the right of all citizens "to live in and/or to have the use of and/or to own an adequate house located in a healthy, safe, harmonious and orderly environment" (Housing and Settlement Act 4 [1992], Article 5[1]).

It defines adequate housing as "a house structure that, at least, meets building safety, minimum floor area and health requirements" (Housing and Settlement Act 4 [1992] Official Explanatory Note of Article 5[1]). A healthy, safe, harmonious, and orderly environment is defined as an environment that "meets spatial planning, land-use, ownership and service provision requirements" (Housing and Settlement Act 4 [1992], Official Explanatory Note of Article 5[1]). Thus, according to the act there are two aspects of adequacy: physical and legal.

Indonesia's 2000 national census divided the population into two main categories, namely, those "having a permanent place to stay" (*mempunyai tempat tinggal tetap*) and those "not having a permanent place to stay" (*tidak mempunyai tempat tinggal tetap*). According to the census guidelines, those who do not have a permanent place to stay include *tunawisma*s, boat crew, people living in houseboats/floating houses, and itinerant or nomadic communities (usually living in remote areas). The 2000 census results showed that out of the 203.4 million Indonesians, 3.2 million (1.6 percent) do not have a permanent place to stay.

LATENT HOMELESSNESS

In Indonesia, a squatter settlement is called *kampung liar.* This is a poor urban settlement that has developed on an unattended plot of land. Some *kampung liar*s are located on riverbanks, along drainage canals, along railway tracks and in station yards, and near marketplaces. Most of the inhabitants are migrants from rural areas or from smaller towns who moved to the city to earn a living. Their dwellings are made out of used nondurable material such as cardboard, plastic sheets, pieces of wood, and scrap metal.

Inhabitants of the *kampung liar*s work as waste collectors, itinerant vendors, *becak* (pedicab) drivers, construction workers, and other unskilled occupations. As they are considered as illegal residents, they are not able to obtain the all-important identity card *(kartu tanda penduduk* or KTP*),* which all Indonesians above the age of seventeen should possess. Consequently, they are in constant danger of being evicted.

The majority of people who actually live on the street and those who live under bridges, in the shade of large trees, or under overhangs of buildings more or less share the same characteristics of those living as squatters. A study conducted in Semarang, Indonesia's fifth most populous city (population 1.4 million), in 2001 showed that although their dwellings might be less permanent, just like squatters the street homeless also usually live in households, work in the same informal sector, and are not recognized as city residents.

Both squatters and street homeless people are often subject to raids. The more violent evictions usually happen to squatters because usually squatting involves the sensitive issue of land ownership. The land occupants usually refuse to be removed on the ground that they have been living there long before the land had any commercial value.

The raids against street homeless people are carried out primarily because they are seen as a nuisance or, using an expression often used by city officials, they "disturb the attractiveness of the city." The victims of these raids, unlike the squatters, usually do not resist. They see their displacement as being temporary (such as when there is a visiting dignitary or a national day celebration). After things have returned to normal, they usually can come back to their "homes." For the residents of *kampung liar*s, however, it is impossible to return to their demolished homes.

CAUSES: POVERTY AND DISREGARD FOR THE RIGHTS OF THE POOR

Under General Suharto's repressive rule (1966–1998), the government's basic policy was to promote economic growth and maintain political stability. With the help of foreign loans, the economy grew at an average rate of 7 percent annually, but Indonesia became one of the most indebted and most authoritarian countries in the world. To attract investments, the rights of workers were suppressed. Indonesian workers became the lowest paid in the region. Strikes were outlawed, and those who questioned the government's labor policy were dealt with severely.

The same pattern can be found elsewhere. Many people were forcefully evicted from their settlements because the land was needed for new office blocks, factories, or toll highways built by companies closely linked to the ruling elite. If residents resisted, their KTPs (if they had one) were revoked and, even worse, they were branded as "communists." Persons accused of being "communists" (though they were never put on trial) lost their right to vote and to run for public offices; they could not enter the civil service or join the military and could not start any business in the formal sector. This in effect deprived them of their civil rights and consequently many ended up being homeless.

Following the financial crisis of 1997, which caused the fall in value of many Asian currencies and of which Indonesia was the worst hit country, Suharto was forced to step down in May 1998. Since then, Indonesia has been struggling painfully to become a democracy. Nevertheless, forced evictions still happen because Indonesian cities are still administered by the same bureaucracy, considered by many to be high-handed, inefficient, and corrupt. The difference now is that the people are less afraid to fight for their rights.

—Tjahjono Rahardjo

Further Reading

Badan Pusat Statistik (BPS-Statistics Indonesia). (2000). Retrieved August 25, 2003, from http://www.bps.go.id/release/sp2000-sementara.pdf

Budiman, A. (1993). Stabilitas politik dan Pertumbuhan Ekonomi (Political Stability and Economic Growth). In INFID (International NGO Forum on Indonesian Development) (Ed.). *Pembangunan di Indonesia: Memandang dari Sisi Lain* (Development in Indonesia: Looking from another side), pp. 7–21. Jakarta, Indonesia: Yayasan Obor Indonesia and INFID.

Jellinek, L. (1991). *The wheel of fortune: The history of a poor community in Jakarta.* Sydney, Australia: Allen & Unwin.

Leach, M. (1998). *A roof is not enough: A look at homelessness worldwide.* Retrieved July 14, 2003, from http://www.shareintl.org/archives/homelessness/i_homelessness.htm

Majlis Bahasa Brunei Darussalam–Indonesia–Malaysia. (2000). Retrieved August 25, 2003, from http://dpb.gov.my/mab2000/Aktiviti/Pakar/s11perkot.pdf

Rahardjo, T. (2000). The Semarang environmental agenda: A stimulus to targeted capacity building among the stakeholders. *Habitat International 24*(4), 443–453.

Rahardjo, T. (2002). *The nature, extent, and eradication of homelessness in developing countries: Indonesia (CARDO/*

ESCOR Project R7905). Semarang, Indonesia: Centre for Urban Studies & Soegijapranata Catholic University.

Undang-Undang Republik Indonesia Nomor 4 Tahun 1974, tentang Ketentuan-ketentuan Pokok Kesejahteraan Sosial (Social Welfare Act 9/1992 of the Republic of Indonesia).

Undang-Undang Repunlik Indonesia Nomor 4 Tahun 1992, tentang Perumahan dan Permukiman (Housing and Settlement Act 9/1992 of the Republic of Indonesia).

United Nations Center for Human Settlements. (2000). *Strategies to combat homelessness.* Nairobi, Kenya: Author.

Yudohusodo, S., & Salam, S. (Eds.). (1991). *Rumah Untuk Seluruh Rakyat.* Jakarta, Indonesia: Yayasan Padamu Negeri.

◨ INTERNATIONAL NETWORK OF STREET NEWSPAPERS

The International Network of Street Newspapers (INSP) is an alliance of "social businesses" that aims to bring together and facilitate communication between street newspapers sold by homeless and unemployed people throughout the world. Based in Glasgow, United Kingdom, the INSP has a membership of almost fifty publications, with member papers in twenty-seven countries internationally, and a combined annual circulation of about 26 million copies worldwide. Operating on the philosophy that all profits produced by the sale of street papers should be used to provide social support for the homeless and unemployed, the INSP works to ensure that such people have the potential to earn an income and develop a positive outlook that will help them successfully merge into society.

The INSP is run by a secretariat, but a board comprising three member paper representatives is responsible for making executive decisions on behalf of the other members. The INSP holds an annual conference every year, organized by the secretariat, where members exchange information and ideas about their publications. Outside guest speakers are also invited to come and share their ideas and experiences. The goal of the conference is to provide a place where INSP members and other outside experts on poverty and homelessness can interact and communicate regarding important issues.

In its charter, the INSP lists seven main goals it seeks to achieve in order to be successful: (1) to help socially excluded people help themselves by providing them with means of earning an income and facilitating their reintegration into society through social support; (2) to use all post-investment profits to finance support for street paper vendors, the socially excluded, or social business; (3) to provide vendors with a choice in the media and campaigning on behalf of the socially excluded; (4) to create quality street papers that vendors are proud to sell and the public is happy to buy; (5) to exert social responsibility in business in terms of editorial, staff, vendor, and environmental policies—discouraging excessive spending on professional staff, with money instead being targeted toward vendor and vendor support; (6) to support prospective street papers that share a common philosophy and intend to sign the street paper charter; (7) to ensure that no charter paper shall enter the established area of an existing charter member. The INSP operates with these goals in mind and aims to provide the rights they detail to every one of its member publications.

PROJECTS

The INSP takes part in numerous projects outside of street paper publication, and information on several of its most notable projects follows:

- *Straatnieuws* is a street paper based in Utrecht, the Netherlands, that not only provides a means of communication between socially excluded people, but also organizes tours of the city led by vendor guides and provides opportunities for former homeless employees to give presentations in schools and other institutions. Sponsored by the Fund for Social Integration, the *Straatnieuws* project serves three main functions—to offer support to homeless people in giving public presentations, to provide training for homeless people in presenting and using multimedia, and to develop educational programs about homelessness for schools.

- *Novy Prostor* is a weekly publication that was started in Prague in 1999. Originally published once a month, *Novy Prostor* is now published weekly due to its increased popularity, and about 15,000 copies are sold every week in almost every major city in the Czech Republic. *Novy Prostor* provides a kind of literary community where homeless and formerly homeless people can remain in contact with others as they progress into full-time employment and obtain their own homes. *Novy Prostor*'s online counterpart, *1street*, provides virtual homes for the homeless under the motto, "Helping People Get On With Their Lives."

- The Homeless World Cup is an international function organized by the INSP and other international service agencies that was held in 2003 in Graz, Austria. International soccer teams and world-renowned players participated, and the tournament provided a place to inform a wider group of people about the issues surrounding homelessness.

- *The Big Issue Namibia* is a monthly street magazine that went into publication in 2002. The magazine aims to increase awareness of the unemployment epidemic in Namibia—60 percent of Namibians live below the poverty line—and address related issues. *The Big Issues Namibia* is sold primarily on the streets of Windhoek, Namibia, by homeless and long-term unemployed adults.

The INSP provides support to socially excluded members of society by publicizing and promoting street newspapers, as well as organizing informational conferences and publicity projects. As a nonprofit organization, the INSP acquires the majority of its funding through membership fees, street paper sales, grants, and donations, and puts this funding directly toward achieving the goals stated in its charter. More information on INSP membership and links to related organizations are available on the INSP website at www.street-papers.com.

—*Emily A. Colangelo*

▣ INTERNATIONAL UNION OF TENANTS

Founded in 1926 in Zurich, Switzerland, the International Union of Tenants (IUT) focuses on issues of poverty and homelessness by exploring them as they specifically apply to tenants. A nongovernmental organization with forty-eight member groups in forty-two countries, the IUT has one regional office in Prague, Czech Republic, which manages the member organizations in central and eastern Europe, and another in Tanzania, which manages members in East Africa (Tanzania, Kenya, Benin, and Uganda). The IUT remains in direct contact with and receives direction and guidance from the United Nations Economic and Social Council.

As stated on its website, the IUT's five main objectives in working for tenant rights are as follows: "(1) Cooperation between tenants through sharing information, (2) aiming to realize the right of everyone, both to good housing and to a sound and healthy residential environment, and to an affordable and fair rent, (3) residential/tenants democracy and a right to participation, (4) no discrimination with regard to sex, racial, ethnic, and religious backgrounds, and (5) the right to organize." The IUT regards housing as a basic human right, and its members feel strongly that housing issues need to be addressed on local, national, and international levels for progress and change to be made. The IUT sees housing as an essential component for providing provides people with a sense of security and peace.

To obtain its objectives, the IUT works in partnership with U.N. agencies, such as the U.N. Economic Commission for Europe and the U.N. Center for Habitat Studies, as well as with the International Federation for Housing and Planning, the Habitat International Coalition, the EU Network, and the European Housing Forum. The IUT disseminates information on housing issues on its website (http://www.iut.nu) and in its quarterly publication, *The Global Tenant* magazine.

CONFERENCES AND EVENTS

The IUT Board meets twice a year, and the IUT Congress meets three times a year to discuss important housing issues and developments in housing solutions. Annual conferences deal with issues involving poverty, homelessness, social welfare, housing policy, and demographic, social, political, and economic trends in relation to each of the topics.

Together, the IUT and the U.N. Economic Commission for Europe have formed the Committee on Human Settlements, which meets annually in Geneva,

Switzerland, to discuss topics related to providing adequate and affordable housing, such as urban renewal and housing modernization. Information on upcoming conferences and events is available at the IUT website, http://www.iut.nu.

—*Emily A. Colangelo*

◙ INTERVENTIONS, CLINICAL

Homeless people experience more ill health than the general population, and disabling health problems frequently contribute to homelessness. For instance, mental illnesses, substance use disorders, or chronic illnesses such as asthma or heart disease can make it difficult to sustain employment and maintain a home. In turn, homelessness itself can be quite dangerous to health. Exposure to the elements, poor diet, overcrowded sleeping accommodations, inadequate facilities for personal hygiene, and sexual and other assaults make homeless people particularly vulnerable to disease. They thus have a greater than average need for health care.

BARRIERS TO HEALTH CARE

In spite of their high need, homeless people frequently encounter great difficulty in obtaining health care. In the United States, some homeless people are enrolled in public programs such as Medicaid or Medicare, but most have no health insurance at all. Even in countries where in theory there is universal access to health care, dirty or unkempt people are often unwelcome in hospitals, clinics, and doctors' offices. Some health care providers have difficulty dealing sympathetically with patients who do not always behave in socially desirable ways. Clinics and offices may not be located in areas that are within the practical geographic range of a street person.

Personal factors may also present barriers to obtaining health care. For example, homeless people are often loners, so that there is nobody to encourage them to seek help when they need it or to urge them to follow up on recommendations from their health care providers. What is more, illness itself, coupled with low self-esteem and a sense of futility, erodes the motivation of homeless people and affects their ability to persist in seeking help for their problems. Fear or distaste for medical settings or health care providers may also constitute a barrier to seeking help.

INCREASING ACCESS

Because of the great need for health care and the barriers outlined above, it is important to make health care services for homeless people easily accessible. This access can be promoted in a number of ways. First, services can be provided at locations where homeless people can easily take advantage of them—for example, in a clinic at a site close to food programs, emergency shelters, and other facilities. The physical setting should be as welcoming as possible; many homeless people avoid large, imposing institutions. Providing walk-in services and same-day appointments also facilitates easier access to care for homeless people who may have to choose between getting food at a soup kitchen or keeping a clinic appointment. Health care can also be offered in other locations, such as shelters. Shelters are particularly appropriate for health screening, preventive services, and basic care for simple ailments. Mobile services have been employed in some places. Vans, trucks, or buses can be outfitted as mobile clinics and go to places where homeless people tend to congregate.

It is important to select a staff who not only are experts in their fields but also understand and accept the particular needs of homeless people; they also need to be flexible enough to cope with the eccentricities of some patients and innovative enough to provide services in unconventional ways if necessary. In addition, access can be facilitated by the use of outreach strategies. Workers from homeless health care programs can go out on the streets or into shelters or soup kitchens to meet people in as unthreatening a manner as possible. By listening closely and addressing basic needs, health care workers can create a trusting relationship and help get ill homeless people into care.

SERVICE INTEGRATION

Homeless people often face a bewildering set of problems. What is more, the problems are often interconnected, so that solving one problem depends on solving others. For example, a homeless woman may be pregnant and suffering from diabetes and alcoholism and may have just escaped from an abusive domestic situation and sought refuge in a shelter for battered women. She will need prenatal care, treatment for the diabetes that renders this a high-risk pregnancy, treatment for alcohol withdrawal and subsequent rehabilitation, possible treatment for injuries received from her abusive partner, and counseling to help her deal with the emotional trauma she has endured.

Thus a health care program for homeless people must include a variety of professionals who work closely together. Members of an interdisciplinary team can use their expertise and skills to plan, implement, and evaluate a plan of care. The best way to coordinate care is to have all these services and providers located in the same building. Where this is not possible, a case manager may facilitate integration.

Case management is a concept that has gained wide acceptance in the management of complex health care. A range of private and governmental agencies provides health and social services, and funding comes from numerous sources. A well-functioning person may have great difficulty finding a way through the maze of programs and agencies, and when a person is disabled, debilitated, or demoralized, the challenge can often be overwhelming. A case manager is a staff member who assists the person navigating through the multiple services. The case manager works closely with the primary care provider and other members of the interdisciplinary team to implement and reinforce the plan of care for the person who is homeless, making sure that the various needs are met.

HEALTH SERVICES FOR HOMELESS PEOPLE

The health services needed by homeless people can be divided into four main categories: primary care services, mental health services, substance abuse services, and a broad group of other specialized services that includes eye care, dental care, and podiatry as well as care specifically targeted to women, children, and youth.

Primary Care

Many health problems reported by homeless people could be treated with home remedies, over-the-counter medicines, a nutritious diet, rest in bed, or at the most, a visit to a family doctor. But all these measures are difficult or impossible for a homeless person. Primary health services are thus of central importance because they provide basic treatments for conditions that are complicated by homelessness, such as coughs and colds, bronchitis, stomach upsets, high blood pressure, skin rashes, varicose veins, sore feet, and arthritis. Homeless people are also more likely than others to suffer from serious diseases such as tuberculosis, hepatitis, and HIV infection.

Homeless people may also face several obstacles in following through with treatments because of their homeless condition. For example, obtaining medicines can be a major challenge to a person with no health insurance, as is the case with about 75 percent of homeless people. Homeless health care programs devise ways of obtaining medications for their patients by seeking special discounts or donations from drug manufacturers or pharmacies, or by fundraising and obtaining grants. Certain illnesses demand complicated treatments with several medicines, and keeping track of a dosage schedule can be difficult. It is therefore critical for health care providers to be aware of these constraints and to work with homeless people to design a viable medication plan. Health care providers also need to collaborate with soup kitchens and shelters to meet the food requirements of individual patients.

Prevention is an important element in primary care, no less for homeless people than for others. Prevention activities include screenings for chronic conditions and communicable diseases, well-child exams, immunizations, family planning, perinatal care, education, and health promotion. For homeless people, screening is focused on immunization status as well as on specific health problems like substance use, mental illness, diabetes, hypertension, tuberculosis, and HIV/AIDS.

Mental Health

Psychiatric disorders are more prevalent in homeless people than in the general population. It is convenient for the purposes of this discussion to consider mental disorders in two categories, "less serious" and "serious." The less serious disorders may be quite distressing and, in the short term, may interfere with the ability to cope with the everyday demands of life. These conditions include anxiety states and phobias, obsessive-compulsive disorders, transient depressions, and adjustment disorders (normal emotional responses to traumatic circumstances or events). These illnesses require treatment with medicines, other therapies, or counseling, which can be provided by appropriately trained staff in a homeless health care program.

The serious mental disorders are those that are long-lasting and disabling. They usually manifest themselves in adolescence or early adult life and have a major impact on a person's ability to cope and be successful in life. The two major categories of serious mental illnesses are the major mood disorders, and schizophrenia and related disorders. All of them require a lifelong commitment to treatment with medicines and often also need a variety of supportive and rehabilitative services.

Providing clinical services for people with mental illnesses thus requires a variety of skills and approaches. The first stage of treatment is engagement, but persuading someone of the need for treatment and the possibility of recovery can require much effort and patience from an outreach worker, or possibly a shelter provider or other person who recognizes the need. Sometimes the first person to recognize the need is a police officer. Many police departments provide training for their officers in the appropriate responses to mentally ill people on the streets. The second stage of treatment is evaluation, which requires a skilled clinician—a psychiatrist or psychologist—to make a careful diagnosis upon which a treatment plan can be based. This plan will often include appropriate medications, counseling or psychotherapy, and several supportive services. These services may be many.

Housing is of primary importance. Mentally disabled people have a variety of needs and preferences, so that ideally a range of housing options should be available. Some are quite able to take care of themselves and their own daily needs, but others will require special housing in a situation where other supports are available, including, for example, assistance with food preparation, with obtaining income entitlements, and with budgeting, laundry, and housekeeping. It is a function of case management to ensure that all these needs are met in the best way possible, given the preferences of an individual and the limitations of what is available. This is another reason why a homeless health care program needs to have close working relationships with other mental health and social services and programs in the area.

Substance Abuse and Dependence

Alcoholism and other drug dependencies are very prevalent among homeless people. Homeless health care programs must therefore provide access to a range of services for addicts. Treatment proceeds in several stages. Stage one involves motivation. People need to accept the reality of their addiction and the need for radical changes in their life; this is sometimes referred to as moving from a "contemplative" to an "action" level of motivation. Assisting a person to reach this new stage may take the combined efforts of many people.

Stage two is detoxification, which focuses on the physical aspects of withdrawal. Withdrawal from alcohol may be quite dangerous if not carefully supervised; withdrawal from opiates is less dangerous but involves a lot of physical discomfort, even pain. In the traditional "medical detox," which is supervised by doctors and nurses, medications are provided to minimize some of the more dangerous effects of withdrawal or to relieve some of the discomfort. Another, less expensive approach to helping addicts through withdrawal is called "social detox," which may be as effective as medical detox. A social detox program provides a high level of emotional and social support to help the alcoholic. Technically, detoxification is the simplest stage of the treatment process and lasts only about a week or less. However, few homeless health care programs are able to provide this service and must refer clients to substance abuse service programs in their local area.

The third stage of treatment is the most difficult, and it is here that most failures occur. This is the stage of rehabilitation, which requires an addict whose life has centered on the quest for alcohol or drugs to develop new patterns of behavior. Homeless health care programs make use of a number of approaches to assist their clients through this difficult process. Some type of residential program is needed, often with other recovering addicts, so that a group of residents can support each other in staying drug-free and sober. Mutual help organizations are very helpful for many addicts. The best known are Alcoholics Anonymous (AA) and Narcotics Anonymous (NA). AA/NA meetings are held in many different settings, sometimes within homeless health care facilities.

Many alcoholics and addicts are not yet prepared to take the action necessary to enter treatment. For these people, there are several "harm reduction" approaches that may be used to try to avoid some of the complications of the addiction. For example, clean needle exchanges for intravenous drug users help to reduce the incidence of blood-borne infections such as HIV, and "wet shelters" (shelters that do not require sobriety for admission) may help alcoholics avoid some of the dangers of sleeping on the street exposed to the elements.

Other Specialized Services

Additional health services provided to homeless people range from specialized care for women to dental and eye care.

Women's Health

Homeless women have special health care needs and problems whether they are single or part of a family. Family planning, pregnancy, and female genito-urinary problems are of particular concern to women. For example, pregnant women who are homeless are considered high risk due to the complications of homelessness, such as poor nutrition, exposure to trauma and communicable diseases, extremes in weather, stress, and lack of prenatal care.

Domestic violence is one of the most common reasons for women and their children becoming homeless. However, women living on the streets are often victims of sexual and/or physical assault, and those who are mentally ill or who are substance users are even more susceptible to attack. Social isolation compounds their emotional devastation. Substance use, anxiety, and depression are often part of the clinical picture for women who are homeless. Not surprisingly, they have high rates of posttraumatic stress disorder (PTSD).

The exchange of sex for food, housing, or drugs by homeless women can lead to sexually transmitted diseases and HIV/AIDS. Because homeless women may be reluctant to reveal substance use or an active sexual history to health care providers, screening for these communicable diseases can be challenging. Health care providers working with homeless women need to understand the paradigm of traumatic experience. By respecting the psychological and physical space of the women they care for, providers can forge a trusting relationship.

Children and Youth

Homeless children are hospitalized more frequently than other low-income children and they are more likely to be seen in hospital emergency departments. Upper respiratory infections, acute otitis media, lice, scabies, and diarrhea are common problems. These children are also more vulnerable to injuries because they live in less structured and less safe environments. Homeless children are more likely to have elevated blood lead levels due to their exposure to dust and dilapidated housing coupled with poor nutrition. Lead screening is an important preventive measure. Asthma rates are also high because of exposure to allergens, and the stress of homelessness itself may be an added trigger. Because of the transitory nature of their lives, it is not uncommon for homeless children to have had their immunizations delayed.

Homeless children are more likely to come from backgrounds with domestic violence, mental illness, and substance use and are more likely to exhibit aggressive behaviors and temper tantrums. Developmental screening of homeless preschool children has identified more developmental lags than are noted in the general population, and academic problems are common among school-age children.

Health care providers need to furnish homeless children with a "medical home" that includes not only primary health care but also access to subspecialty care, developmental and psychological evaluation and treatment, and access to an answering service 24 hours a day, 7 days a week. Acute care visits can be used as an opportunity to take a thorough medical, developmental, and psychological history as well as to provide a physical examination. Immunizations and screening for lead toxicity, anemia, visual problems, and hearing loss are a part of primary care for homeless children. Monitoring of growth and nutrition is also essential. To provide adequate health care to homeless children, health care workers need to forge strong links with service providers who work in family shelters. Health care workers can educate shelter providers on numerous topics, including communicable diseases, parenting skills, asthma triggers, safety precautions, and the preparation of healthy meals. Surveillance of health and safety conditions in shelters and other service sites will help homeless children avoid accidents and injuries and will also help prevent communicable diseases.

Homeless youth are sometimes called runaways, throwaways, or simply street kids. They suffer from illnesses directly related to a violent lifestyle on the streets, including trauma, substance use, psychiatric disturbances, skin infestations, sexually transmitted diseases, and HIV/AIDS, as well as from other chronic conditions that have been exacerbated by the lack of care. Young women who are homeless are also at high risk of pregnancy. Drop-in centers operating twenty-four hours a day in areas where homeless youth congregate can successfully engage this group into care. Availability of laundry facilities, food, telephones, and e-mail access combined with a low-demand approach, in which, for example, a youth may not have to give a name or other identifying information to obtain services, has proved successful in many communities. Conducting outreach during the night to areas where prostitution and drug activity operate is another useful way to engage homeless youth into care. All these methods depend on creating an open and friendly environment for youth that includes nonjudgmental attitudes by providers and a flexible service-delivery system.

Eye Care

Like many of the poor and underserved, homeless people lack access to specialty care for diseases of the eyes. Vision testing and annual eye examinations are integrated into primary health care, but after a problem has been identified, a patient may need an ophthalmology consultation. In some places, it has been possible to gain access for homeless people to specialty eye care by arranging referral agreements with local ophthalmologists and opticians. Some national retailers will donate glasses and services, and some private and corporate foundations have funded eye care.

Dental Care

People who are homeless experience high rates of oral diseases and lack access to dental services. Acute dental problems include caries, periodontal disease, and loss of teeth. Prevention is perhaps the most important element in dental health, in the form of good oral hygiene and proper nutrition accompanied by access to dental care. But homeless people often lack even the most basic tools of prevention—namely, a toothbrush, toothpaste, and water. They also have little control over the quality of their diet. Consequently, maintaining preventive oral health practices is very difficult.

Strategies for securing dental services include referring homeless people to dental schools, publicly funded dental clinics, or nonprofit organizations that provide free dental services. These referral relationships can be informal, or they can be formal contracts that ensure a certain level of dental services. Preventive oral health care can be provided within the primary care clinic by giving out toothbrushes and toothpaste. Providers can demonstrate how to brush teeth and explain the basics of oral health care. They can support homeless patients in their efforts by working with shelter providers to reinforce the oral health care message.

Podiatry

Foot problems in homeless people are compounded by long periods of walking and standing, by underlying chronic disease, and by a lack of proper footwear. Prolonged standing and walking can lead to venous pooling and swelling and can also exacerbate the condition of people with peripheral vascular disease, diabetes, and other chronic diseases. Although homeless people can often obtain used clothing, new shoes and socks are not usually easy to obtain. Wearing used shoes that do not fit correctly can cause blisters and other podiatric problems.

In many communities, podiatrists have volunteered to provide services at primary care clinics for homeless people. Linking with local podiatrists has made it possible for primary care providers to increase the access of their homeless patients to specialty foot care. Primary care providers can teach homeless people, especially those with diabetes, how to examine their feet, and can urge them to visit them immediately if they have open foot sores. Dispensing clean white cotton socks during a discussion about foot care can reinforce a health care message while providing tangible assistance.

Providing health care for homeless people is a complex task. Most large cities have special Health Care for the Homeless programs funded from public and private sources, that have developed high levels of expertise in addressing the needs of this population. At the national level, the National Health Care for the Homeless Council coordinates and supports these programs and, along with other like-minded bodies, advocates for policies to address poverty, end homelessness, and provide affordable health care for all citizens.

—*William R. Breakey and Laura Gillis*

Further Reading

Brickner, P. W., Scharer, L. K., Conanan, B. A., Savarese, M., & Scanlan, B. C. (1990). *Under the safety net.* New York: Norton.

Fosburg, L. B., & Dennis, D. L. (1999). *Practical lessons: The 1998 National Symposium on Homelessness Research.* Washington, DC: U.S. Department of Housing and Urban Development and U.S. Department of Health and Human Services.

McMurray-Avila, M. (1997). *Organizing health services for homeless people.* Nashville, TN: National Health Care for the Homeless Council.

Weinreb, L., Goldberg, R., Bassuk, E., & Perloff, J. (1998). Determinants of health and service use patterns in homeless and low-income housed children. *Pediatrics, 102,* 554–562.

Wood, D. L., Valdez, R. B., Hayashi, T., & Shen, A. (1990). Health of homeless children and housed poor children. *Pediatrics, 86,* 858–866.

▣ INTERVENTIONS, HOUSING

Housing interventions—both transitional and permanent—provide housing and services for homeless people, especially those people who have specific needs such as mental health and substance abuse treatment.

TRANSITIONAL HOUSING INTERVENTIONS

Transitional housing is time limited and typically provides services beyond food, shelter, and clothing. However, no consistent definition or model of transitional housing exists. Transitional housing programs vary greatly in the amount of time a person can stay (three months to twenty-four months or longer), services provided, physical structure (congregate settings to individual apartments), and admission criteria (e.g., some programs may be exclusively for people in substance abuse recovery).

Even the goals of transitional housing interventions can range considerably. In some cases, because of the limited supply of affordable permanent housing, transitional housing has emerged as an intermediate place to live for people who are waiting for permanent housing. In other cases, transitional housing has been designed to help people increase their chances of locating appropriate housing and become "housing ready." In these cases in particular, transitional housing is a step between a shelter and permanent housing for those who need a more structured setting with a range of services—including mental health, substance abuse, health, employment readiness, educational programs, and other services—before moving into permanent housing. In addition to offering an opportunity to work on clinical and self-sufficiency issues, these housing programs sometimes provide structured savings programs that help people save money for rental down payments and move-in costs.

Some communities are testing "transition in place" or convertible housing models, where intensive services are provided initially and gradually reduced and where the apartments become permanent dwellings for those people who proceed through the program successfully.

Experts have done little direct study of transitional housing, and no study has compared transitional housing with permanent housing. However, several studies have indicated that some homeless people, even those with multiple needs, can move directly to permanent housing and remain stable for considerable periods of time. Program providers need to understand when transitional housing is warranted and for what purposes (i.e., to provide interim housing for people who do not yet have access to permanent housing or to provide a place where people can become ready to live more independently on their own).

SUPPORTIVE HOUSING INTERVENTIONS

Supportive housing combines permanent housing with direct or arranged access to services to address the needs of formerly homeless people. Supportive housing is generally considered an option for those people who have either lived on the streets or in homeless shelters for long periods of time and/or who have needs that may best be served by services provided through their housing. Permanent housing options range from single-room occupancy (SRO) hotels (especially in large cities such as New York City) to scattered site apartments to home ownership. The physical structure of the housing is often determined by the housing stock available in the community and the funding that is available.

Services may be provided on-site or off-site and may be limited to basic case management services or may include health, mental health, substance abuse, and daily living supports. Providers use a variety of

models of case management but typically help a client obtain services as well as assist in daily living, such as assisting in money management, transportation, and problem solving. Supportive housing programs for people with a specific set of needs, such as people with severe mental illness or those with HIV/AIDS, may have a much broader and more intensive array of services on-site than do housing programs that serve a range of individuals.

Many supportive housing programs are funded by federal initiatives developed during the last ten to fifteen years. The largest programs, sparked by the Stewart B. McKinney Homeless Assistance Act and administered by the U.S. Department of Housing and Urban Development (HUD), include the Supportive Housing Program (SHP) and Shelter Plus Care (S+C). Funding also comes from federal Section 8 housing certificate and voucher programs and the Housing Opportunities for Persons with AIDS (HOPWA) program.

The Supportive Housing Program was created to combine housing and services for homeless people, especially people with special needs. The program funds four basic types of interventions: transitional housing for up to twenty-four months, permanent housing with support services for homeless permanently disabled persons, support services without housing for homeless people, and supportive housing.

Shelter Plus Care (S+C) provides rental assistance for homeless persons with disabilities, much like the permanent housing component of SHP. S+C rental assistance can be provided through tenant-based vouchers (vouchers that a person receives and can use for housing in the open market), sponsor-based vouchers, and project-based assistance (that provides the subsidies to the building) or SRO assistance. Services for those persons living in S+C housing are funded by other outside sources.

HUD's Section 8 program, not exclusively for homeless people, provides subsidies for housing, either directly to the tenant or to the landlord, and allows a household to pay only 30 percent of its income toward rent. The program is designed to let people rent market rate housing at an affordable cost. The difficulty, however, is that when housing markets are tight, landlords may be hesitant to accept Section 8 vouchers when they can get higher rents from people without vouchers.

HOPWA is also administered by HUD and provides funding for housing and services for persons with HIV/AIDS. This program is not funded by the McKinney Act and is not available solely to homeless people but rather is available to all low-income persons. HOPWA funds are used to support a range of services, from housing to medical assistance, as well as planning and development costs.

Foundations and other private groups have also helped foster the development of supportive housing programs. The Robert Wood Johnson Foundation, for example, has twice teamed with HUD to examine the relationship between providing housing and services for homeless persons and has also attempted to seed housing for specific groups of homeless people. The Program for the Chronically Mentally Ill and the Homeless Families Program combined Section 8 certificates with services for homeless people with severe mental illness and/or families with multiple problems, including long-term instability, domestic violence, and alcohol and drug abuse. Another important national contributor has been the Corporation for Supportive Housing (CSII), a nonprofit intermediary established in 1991 to expand supportive housing for special needs populations who are homeless or at risk of becoming homeless.

THE EFFECTIVENESS OF HOUSING INTERVENTIONS

Since the late 1980s, researchers have examined housing and its effectiveness for homeless people. Studies have ranged from rigorous randomized studies of specific supportive housing interventions to descriptive studies tracking people in housing over time.

As a whole, these studies indicate that housing with supports improves the residential stability of homeless people, including those with multiple disabilities and issues such as mental illness and substance abuse. However, people with both mental illness and substance abuse fare least well of all groups studied. In almost every study that examines stability over time, the majority of people receiving housing

(typically with supports) remain stably housed for at least one year. Studies have found no consistent change in other outcome areas, however, such as mental health functioning, self-sufficiency, or community adjustment.

Access to affordable housing, generally through some form of rental subsidy, appears to be an essential contributor to stability. Research has offered little guidance on the configuration of housing and services that is most effective for homeless people, although studies have shown that housing options increase stability. Surveys of people with severe mental illness, however, have found that mental health consumers prefer to have a choice in their housing and that they prefer to live alone (as opposed to in a group home). Some people may prefer community living, however, and others may prefer time to transition into more permanent housing options. A range of residential options, therefore, may be needed to meet the range of needs and preferences.

THE NATURE OF SUPPORTS AND SERVICES IN HOUSING

Researchers have done little direct study of the role that services and supports play in improving housing stability. A few studies have shown improvements in residential stability of people in both comparison and experimental groups but note greater improvements for those people in the groups that received more intensive services, particularly case management. In addition to case management and subsidies, assistance in finding and maintaining housing, although not directly studied, has reportedly been useful to people. Housing specialists or locaters, for example, can provide individualized attention and assistance in applying for housing subsidies, locating an appropriate apartment or house, traveling to see potential homes, and negotiating with landlords. They can also serve as advocates with landlords, reducing landlord concerns about rent payment and letting the landlord know that the potential tenant is linked to programs and supports in the community.

Evidence also shows that assistance during the transition process from being homeless to living in a home can be critical, especially for those people who have been homeless for long periods of time. Besides practical assistance, such as helping people obtain and move in furniture, more emotional support may be needed in the months after people leave the shelter or streets.

ISSUES AND CHALLENGES

Despite evidence that housing interventions can curb homelessness and increase residential stability, a critical shortage of housing continues. A large factor is the lack of affordable housing in general. Studies have consistently found a lack of affordable housing in almost every city and state in the nation, making it difficult for low-income persons to find decent, affordable housing even if they are fortunate enough to have a housing subsidy such as a Section 8 certificate.

Nonprofit groups such as CSH and others have made efforts to increase the affordable housing stock, especially for homeless people with special needs. These efforts, however, are difficult to fund and even more difficult to implement due to community opposition. Community opposition—NIMBYism ("not in my back yard")—is a challenge for any group who wants to increase the stock of affordable housing. Groups continue to be successful, but the process can be time consuming and expensive. Those groups who have been successful often credit their outreach efforts to the community before and throughout the development process.

Another challenge for developing and operating housing with supports is finding funds. Typically, multiple funding sources are required; these can require much time and effort to obtain and coordinate, slowing the development process. Those groups trying to build new housing with supports also face a tension between the short time frame of service funding, when money is typically provided on a year-to-year basis, and the longer time frame required to finance construction.

MAINTAINING THE STABILITY OF SUBSTANCE ABUSERS

Substance abuse appears to be the major reason why people drop out of supported housing. Although peo-

ple with substance abuse have shown increases in residential stability once provided with housing and supports, substance abuse continues to be identified as one of, if not the primary, cause of housing loss for formerly homeless people. This is particularly true for people who also have mental illness.

FUTURE DIRECTIONS

Housing with supports has been shown to be effective in improving the residential stability of homeless people, even those with multiple and long-term problems. A variety of housing programs has been shown to be effective for a range of individuals. Research should be done to identify those aspects of housing and supports that make the most difference and for whom.

On the other hand, a subset of homeless people apparently does not succeed in supported housing. Learning more about these people and the types of interventions that could improve their stability would be useful to providers who struggle to meet the needs of these people. Clearly we must learn more, but the evidence is overwhelming that people who have been homeless can live successfully in a wide range of supportive housing approaches. The great need for housing, coupled with this evidence, suggests that providers should maximize the housing stock available to them.

—Debra J. Rog and C. Scott Holupka

Further Reading

Abt Associates. (1997). *National evaluation of the Shelter Plus Care Program: Final report.* Rockville, MD: U.S. Department of Housing and Urban Development.

Barrow, S., & Zimmer, R. (1999). Transitional housing and services: A synthesis. In L. B. Fosburg & D. L. Dennis (Eds.), *Practical lessons: The 1998 National Symposium on Homeless Research.* Delmar, NY: National Resource Center on Homelessness and Mental Illness. Retrieved January 5, 2004, from http://aspe.os.dhhs.gov/progsys/homeless/symposium/10.htm

Center for Mental Health Services. (1994). *Making a difference: Interim status report of McKinney demonstration program for homeless adults with serious mental illness* (DHHS Publication No. [SMA] 94–3014). Rockville, MD: U. S. Department of Health and Human Services.

Dolbeare, C. N. (1996). *Homelessness in America.* Phoenix, AZ: Oryx.

Hurlburt, M. S., Wood, P. A., & Hough, R. L. (1996). Providing independent housing for the homeless mentally ill: A novel approach to evaluating long-term longitudinal housing patterns. *Journal of Community Psychology, 24*(3), 291–310.

Rog, D. J., & Gutman, M. (1997). The Homeless Families Program: A summary of key findings. In S. L. Isaacs & J. R. Knickman (Eds.), *To improve health and health care: The Robert Wood Johnson Foundation Anthology* (pp. 209–231). San Francisco: Jossey-Bass.

Rog, D. J., & Holupka, C. S. (1999). Reconnecting homeless individuals and families to the community. In L. B. Fosburg & D. L. Dennis (Eds.), *Practical lessons: The 1998 National Symposium on Homeless Research.* Delmar, NY: National Resource Center on Homelessness and Mental Illness. Retrieved January 5, 2004, from http://aspe.os.dhhs.gov/progsys/homeless/symposium/10.htm

Shern, D. L., Felton, C. J., Hough, R. L., Lehman, A. F., Goldfinger, S., Valencia, E., Dennis, D., Straw, R., & Wood, P. A. (1997). Housing outcomes for homeless adults with mental illness: Results from the second-round McKinney Program. *Psychiatric Services, 48*(2), 239–241.

Shinn, M., Weitzman, B. C., Stojanovic, D., Knickman, J. R., Jiminez, L., Duchon, L., James, S., & Krantz, D. H. (1998). Predictors of homelessness from shelter request to housing stability among families in New York City. *American Journal of Public Health, 88*(10), 1–7.

◉ ITALY

The differing estimates of the number of homeless that are constantly brought up in academic and political debate are, to a large extent, the result of the conceptual uncertainty that surrounds the definition of homelessness, and this focuses attention on the contrasting definitions that fight for prominence in the construction of the problem. The question is especially important in a country like Italy, where "borderline" cases or "hidden homelessness" is particularly frequent and where responsibility for policies for the homeless lies with local governments. Furthermore, no valid defining criteria have been established for the country as a whole at the national level.

HOMELESSNESS IN THE NATIONAL SETTING

Homelessness in Italy is essentially conceptualized as a problem of social marginalization. The social construction of the homeless is centered on the figure of persons referred to as being of "no abode" *(senza dimora)*. The accent is generally placed on the advanced stages of marginalization processes, and most often the term denotes the homeless characterized by multiple deprivations and by traits of desocialization. In these portrayals, the strictly housing component—not having housing—is not central. It is implied in the definition, but is only considered important as part of the multiple dimensions of the problems of the "no abode."

Persons without a home, but not characterized by these traits, tend to be classified differently. Different terms are used, such as *senza casa* (without a house) and *senza tetto* (without a roof). A sort of distinction is made between the two conceptual areas connected with the notion of homelessness: housing exclusion and social exclusion. This separation reflects and confirms an accentuated (traditional) division between housing policies and welfare policies.

The narrowness or the breadth of the different definitions adopted obviously determines estimates of the number of homeless. While the number of the "no abode" was estimated in 1994 at about 50,000 persons, when a broader definition of the homeless proposed by FEANTSA (European Federation of National Organisations Working with the Homeless) was used, estimates came to between 150,000 and 200,000 persons.

The conceptual uncertainty surrounding the definition of homelessness also affects definitions in the narrow sense of the term, those that identify the "no abode" or the "street homeless." Attempts to estimate the size of the phenomenon based on the opinions of service providers at the end of the 1990s put the number of the "no abode" at between 70,000 and 80,000. A survey-based estimate produced a much lower figure of 17,000 "no abode" (the population of Italy in 2001 was 57.0 million). Even when the definition of homeless is narrow, the types of people and the cases that are included can vary. For example, foreigners living in shacks, abandoned buildings, and ruins may be left out of the account as most do not fit the typical, conventional description of the "no abode." In the same way, Gypsies are generally not considered as being "with no abode," even when they are living in shacks or tents.

THE HOMELESS POPULATIONS

Despite the uncertainty over numbers, those who work with the homeless generally feel that there has been an increase since the end of the 1980s both of "no abode" and of other socially marginalized groups. Changes that have occurred in the composition of the homeless are similar to those occurring in other European Union countries: a fall in the average age, the appearance of female homelessness (although the social protection afforded to women in the fabric of society means that women are rarely explicitly homeless), and, more recently, an increase in homeless immigrants.

The new homelessness calls into question a whole variety of structural factors that lie behind the increase in social exclusion in industrialized countries: the breakup of traditional social relationships and the decline in their capacity for protection; the crisis of the family; insecurity in labor markets and new tensions in housing markets; and the crisis of the welfare state. Compared to other groups living in poverty, the "no abode" present specific characteristics. They suffer a greater degree of isolation, and they are less likely to be able to count on a robust network of support. Their health is worse than other groups due to alcohol and drugs and mental problems in particular; fewer of them are working; and they make greater recourse to insecure employment and to begging. They make less use of social services.

These factors are clearly visible in individual case histories. Most are characterized by such events as expulsion from the family, traumatic breakdown of the household, and so on. Recurrent circumstances include long-term unemployment, alcoholism, experience of prison or mental hospital, and institutionalization in childhood.

Individual case histories also show that the chain of events that leads to life on the street often happens to people who come from intrinsically fragile situations. Most persons living on the street come from poor backgrounds, often living in "extreme poverty," in many cases poverty that has been inherited from the family of origin. There is also the importance of cases of homelessness where the problems are mainly determined by sheer poverty, with no real processes of marginalization, and even more histories of homelessness with no desocialization traits and no loss of capabilities.

Homeless immigrants provide a clear example of a type of homeless that contradicts the prevailing construction of the phenomenon, which is centered on the figure of the "no abode." In most cases, homelessness among immigrants, often of the "street" variety, results from difficulties arising from being without documents, from difficulty in gaining access to housing markets, and from insecure employment. There is a high probability of immigrants suffering housing exclusion without serious elements of marginalization occurring and an even higher probability of them suffering housing exclusion without those features of personality destructuring that characterizes many "no abode." They are simply poor people without a home. For them, the lack of housing may be nothing more than a stage on the road to integration in a new society.

POLICY AND SERVICES

Apart from the prevailing construction of the problem, intervention for the homeless has suffered from the traditional limits of the Italian welfare system: the lack of a comprehensive system of protection and the little protection provided for adults who do not have a normal regular job, the high geographical variance of the coverage provided, and the discretionary nature of many welfare assistance measures. Notwithstanding significant progress in the policy framework in the late 1990s, all this still has a serious impact on intervention to help the homeless.

Responsibility for dealing with homelessness in Italy lies mainly with local government and with private welfare associations. Until 2000, there were no guidelines in the legislation establishing minimum standards of support across the country, and local authorities acted independently to provide their own degree of coverage and services for people suffering extreme poverty. Today, the coexistence of very heterogeneous models of intervention at the local level is a characteristic feature of policies for the homeless. The difference concerns the degree to which needs are covered and the criteria for access to services and accommodation.

There is a large gap between the north and south of the country in this respect. In the towns and cities of northern and central Italy, attempts to go beyond the traditional old-fashioned welfare approach based on emergency measures are more frequent and are often up to the same standards as the best European practices.

Nevertheless, even where substantial progress has taken place, this new innovative culture has not translated systematically into concrete initiatives, and the new services it has produced are insufficient quantitatively. Emergency-oriented policies are still the rule rather than the exception at the local level.

In the more innovative areas, the "no abode" now enjoy a full range of services: preventative services, emergency and crisis services, and rehabilitation services. Different types of shelter and accommodation services are provided to meet the differing needs of a very heterogeneous user base. Multidimensional, integrated action (action that integrates different types of resources such as health, personal relations resources, financial, training, and housing resources) is offered to help individuals to develop their own capacities for reintegration into society. Cooperation between local actors and integration of services (public, voluntary, and private welfare) are standard practice. Municipal administrations play a more active role here in formulating policies and promoting forms of coordination with welfare cooperatives and voluntary organizations.

IMPLICATIONS

The almost exclusive focus on the figure of the "no abode" places a question mark over the social construction of the problem in Italy. There is a risk with this concentration on extreme situations of conveying the idea that the field of homelessness can be "cut out" and separated from the broader processes that produce social and housing exclusion. There is also a related risk that the broader range of different types of housing exclusion are excluded from the debate

A homeless boy plays a tambourine for coins on a street frequented by tourists in Venice in July 2003.
Source: Karen Christensen; used with permission.

on homelessness and that housing exclusion is neglected when it is not accompanied by strong traits of social marginalization.

This narrow approach has a particularly distorting effect on policies in a country like Italy, where "integrated poverty" is widespread and cases of housing exclusion without social marginalization are particularly frequent. However, the attention to extreme situations and the biases mentioned above also occur in other countries. Italy provides examples of social construction problems that are to be found almost everywhere. More research is needed to clarify the factors that combine in the different types of homelessness and to compare the effects of policies based on different definitions of the phenomenon.

—*Antonio Tosi*

Further Reading

Commissione d'indagine sulla povertà' e l'emarginazione. (1993). *Rapporto sulle "povertà estreme" in Italia* [Report on "extreme poverty" in Italy]. Rome: Presidenza del Consiglio dei Ministri, Dipartimento Affari Sociali.

Commissione d'indagine sull'esclusione sociale. (2002). *Rapporto sulle politiche contro la povertà e l'esclusione sociale 1997–2001* [Report on policies to combat poverty and social exclusion]. (C. Saraceno, Ed.). Rome: Carocci.

Pollo, M. (1995). I senza fissa dimora in Italia [The no abode in Italy]. In G. Pochettino (Ed.), *I senza fissa dimora* [The no abode persons] (pp. 7–32). Casale Monferrato, Italy: Piemme.

Tosi, A. (1999). Homelessness and the housing factor: Learning from the debate on homelessness and poverty. In D. Avramov (Ed.), *Coping with homelessness* (pp. 103–126). Aldershot, UK: Ashgate.

Tosi, A. (2001). Access to housing in Italy. *Annual report to the Observatory on Homelessness.* Brussels, Belgium: Euro-pean Federation of National Organisations Working with the Homeless.

Tosi, A., & Ranci, C. (1994). Italy. *Report for the European Observatory on Homelessness.* Brussels, Belgium: Euro-pean Federation of National Organisations Working with the Homeless.

J

◉ JAPAN

In contemporary Japan, the word *homuresu*, derived from English, is the most commonly used term to refer to people who inhabit public spaces such as parks, train and subway stations, riversides, and shopping districts. The term came into use as unhoused people became more visible with the deepening of the Great Heisei Recession—the stagnation following the burst of Japan's economic bubble in 1992. The use of *homuresu* in the media, academia, and common conversation has replaced the somewhat more derogatory *furosha* ("wanderer") or *runpen* ("bum") used previously. However, noting the stereotype of America's homeless as lazy substance abusers who deplete public resources, many social science researchers, activists, and journalists in Japan have come to use the more precise terms of *nojukusha* ("person who sleeps outside") and *nojuku roudousha* ("laborer who sleeps outside").

HOMELESSNESS IN POST–WORLD WAR II JAPAN

Homelessness proliferated in Japan at the end of World War II, as American conventional and nuclear bombs devastated major urban areas and the country struggled to rebuild its economy. At this time, many families and lone survivors of the war created makeshift housing in parks and other unused public and private spaces. By the time the country entered its period of rapid economic growth (1960–1973), the level of homelessness had waned substantially. However, despite popular myth, homelessness never wholly disappeared—even as Japan enacted its postwar "economic miracle." Urban poverty and homelessness were largely confined geographically and socially to urban day-labor ghettos called *yoseba,* where unemployed men, many of them rural migrants, gathered in search of readily accessible employment, cheap housing, and camaraderie.

As the expanding manufacturing, shipping, and construction industries' demand for workers grew, a large pool of cheap and flexible labor was forming in *yoseba,* composed of men displaced from the declining agricultural and mining sectors, as well as the urban unemployed, persons disaffiliated from their families, the disabled, and former convicts. While many workers were reaping the benefits of Japanese-style labor management characterized by lifetime employment and seniority-based advancement, those pushed and pulled into *yoseba* had to continuously search for short-term work and housing, rendering their livelihoods susceptible to fluctuations in the economy. Levels of homelessness within *yoseba* increased with rising unemployment during the oil-driven recessions of the 1970s, though still not reaching the levels known later. Homelessness was

A homeless person sits with his possessions in a park in Tokyo in June 1995.
Source: Hashimoto Noboru/Corbis Sygma; used with permission.

largely short-term and generally confined to these districts. This limited form of homelessness, invisible to many, fueled a popular myth both at home and abroad that Japanese society was immune to the exploding problems of urban poverty and homelessness that the United States was facing.

This myth disappeared as the Heisei Recession, beginning in 1991, continued to stall the economy and homelessness proliferated in most major cities and suburban areas. In 2001, the Japanese national government estimated the size of its "literal" homeless population to be around 25,000 people, some staying in the handful of short-term public shelters, but the vast majority living in encampments in major urban parks, stations, riversides, and scattered about the periphery of downtown shopping and business districts. Although activists note that the limitations of counting such a mobile and often hard-to-find population render this number a lower bound estimate of the nations' homeless population, they have yet to be able to provide an alternative estimate. Homelessness is concentrated in major urban areas, with the homeless populations in Osaka and Tokyo making up over one-half of the nation's total. While the growth of homeless persons in these major cities appears to be leveling off, the numbers

in nearby suburban areas are on the rise.

Demographically, Japan's homeless population is primarily male, middle-aged, and blue-collar. Large-scale survey research among the homeless in major urban and suburban areas has found that the average age is about fifty-five years; over 95 percent are single men; and the great majority have worked in blue-collar occupations in the manufacturing and construction industries, with about one-half having day-labor experience through the *yoseba* system. Observational research has revealed that in comparison to their U.S. counterparts, Japan's homeless have lower rates of severe mental illness, due to the fact that Japanese policies do not deinstitutionalize the mentally ill. Rates of illicit substance abuse are also lower, although alcohol is widely used as a temporary antidote to the harshness of street life.

STRUCTURAL CAUSES OF THE RECENT INCREASE IN HOMELESSNESS IN JAPAN

While homelessness has increased sharply in Japan since the onset of the Heisei Recession, it has still not reached the scale observable in the United States. This has been due largely to the multiple economic and social buffers in Japanese society: lower levels of unemployment, poverty, and income inequality; lifetime employment, employee housing, and other benefits of the "institutionalized paternalism" of Japanese corporations; higher investment in public housing; persistent institutionalization of the mentally ill; the relative lack of systemic racism; and the tradition of "shared poverty" in multigenerational families and close-knit communities. However, many of these buffers have weakened under recent economic, demographic, and cultural changes, in good part due to the effects of globalization. The structural origins of the recent explosion of homelessness in Japan are generally understood by social scientists to be rooted in deindustrialization, economic stagnation, changes in employment practices, an aging workforce, competition for low-skill employment from immigrant workers, the decline of the traditional multigenerational household, and inadequate welfare protections. Although *seikatsu hogo*, Japan's version of social security insurance, is by law available to any citizen whose quality of life falls below certain cultural standards, in practice it has been allocated only to persons who are either over sixty-five years old or physically unable to work.

MEASURES TO ADDRESS HOMELESSNESS

The sizable growth in Japan's homelessness during the Heisei Recession has roused widespread concern among private citizens, policymakers, and social scientists. This concern has driven both a boom in research on homelessness and a growth of interest in measures that have been applied in other advanced economies to address the problem. In 1999, the national government made its first commitment to assist localities by providing funds for half of the cost to build and operate emergency and transitional shelters in four cities—Tokyo, Osaka, Yokohama, and Nagoya. In addition, legislation was adopted that enables community-based organizations to incorporate as nonprofit entities. With this change, private efforts to address homelessness have proliferated, expanding provision of shelter, food, clothing, and, to a much lesser extent, assistance in finding stable employment and housing. Largely replicating the American "continuum of care" model in which programs aim to address the limitations of individual homeless persons without addressing the structural problems of diminishing opportunities in

labor and housing markets, measures to address homelessness in Japan appear likely to merely manage the problem of mass homelessness rather than ameliorate it.

—*Matthew D. Marr*

See also Toyko

Further Reading

Aoki, H. (2000). *Gendai Nihon no toshi kaso: Yoseba to nojukusha to gaikokujin roudousha* [The urban underclass in contemporary Japan: *Yoseba*, the homeless, and foreign laborers]. Tokyo: Akashi Shoten.

Aoki, H. (2003). Homelessness in Osaka: Globalization, *yoseba*, and disemployment. *Urban Studies, 40*(2), 361–379.

Ezawa, A. (2002). Japan's new homeless. *Journal of Social Distress and the Homeless, 11*(4), 279–291.

Fowler, E. (1996). *San'ya blues: Laboring life in contemporary Tokyo*. Ithaca, NY: Cornell University Press.

Gill, T. (2001). *Men of uncertainty: The social organization of day laborers in contemporary Japan*. Albany: State University of New York Press.

Gill, T. (2001). A slowly dawning recognition. *Social Science Japan, 23*, 24–28.

Hagiwara, K. (2001). *Roujou seikatsu e to saru keirou—Heisei 11 nendo roujou seikatsu jittai chousa houkokusho kara* [Paths to street life—From the Tokyo metropolitan government 1999 homeless survey report]. *Shelter-less, 10*, 107–128.

Iwata, M. (2000). *Homuresu / Gendai shaka I / Fukushi kokka: "Ikite iku basho" wo megutte* [The homeless / Contemporary society / The welfare state: In search of a "place to live"]. Tokyo: Akashi Shoten.

Marr, M. D. (1997). Maintaining autonomy: The plight of the American skid row and Japanese *yoseba*. *Journal of Social Distress and the Homeless, 6*(3), 229–250.

Marr, M. D. (1999). Down and out in Kobe: Homelessness reshaped by economic and seismic upheaval. *Kyoto Journal, 41,* 59–65.

Stevens, C. S. (1997). *On the margins of Japanese society: Volunteers and the welfare of the urban underclass*. New York: Routledge.

Ventura, R. (1992). *Underground in Japan*. London: Jonathan Cape.

L

See Brazil; Cuba; Homelessness, International Perspectives on; Housing and Homelessness in Developing Nations; Latino(a)s

◙ LATIN AMERICA

See Brazil; Cuba; Homelessness, International Perspectives on; Housing and Homelessness in Developing Nations; Latino(a)s

◙ LATINO(A)S

Latinos are one of the fastest growing ethnic groups in the United States. The Hispanic population in the United States increased by more than 50 percent between 1990 and 2000 to 32.8 million, representing 12.0 percent of the total population. Youthfulness, birthrate, and levels of immigration have contributed to the growth of the Latino population. In 2000, 39.1 percent of the Hispanic population was foreign-born. Hispanic immigration to the United States has reached unprecedented levels and has dispersed across the nation, including states, regions, cities, and towns that previously had virtually no Latino residents. In addition, the diversity of national origin groups among the Hispanic population in the United States has increased. Latinos can be of any race and of more than twenty national origins. Emerging communities of Dominicans, Colombians, El Salvadorans, Nicaraguans, and Peruvians, for example, have added to the larger and more established communities of Mexicans, Puerto Ricans, and Cubans.

Hispanics are one of the poorest ethnic groups in the United States. Hispanics have high rates of poverty among full-time workers and working husbands in intact families with children. Latinos may suffer from the effects of economic downturns more than non-Latinos and benefit less from periods of economic growth. Low levels of educational attainment compound Hispanic socioeconomic vulnerability.

However, compared to other racial and ethnic groups, Latinos present a profile that sometimes appears counterintuitive and is not sufficiently explained by existing wisdom or scholarship. One of the most striking examples is in the area of health. This "epidemiological paradox" is a dominant theme in Hispanic health research. In the aggregate, compared to other racial and ethnic groups, Latinos have lower age-adjusted death rates in the face of higher risk factors for most causes of death, including heart disease, cancer, stroke, chronic obstructive pulmonary disease, pneumonia and influenza, and suicide. In the case of birth outcomes, for example,

in spite of high risk factors, Latina birth outcomes more closely resemble those of the non-Hispanic white and Asian/Pacific Islanders populations, which had higher income, more education, and better access to first-trimester care. None of this would be expected from the standard norms and models. (Hayes-Bautista 2002, 221)

When applied to Latino populations, established theoretical models that explain patterns and variations of illness and disease yield "results that are confusing, seemingly paradoxical, and of little use in creating policies and programs aimed at the Latino population" (Hayes-Bautista 2002, 216).

The growing need for Latino-based metrics and models is also evident in the study of homelessness. Hispanics and African-Americans have similar socioeconomic profiles, with, most important, high poverty rates. Yet studies have found that African-Americans are overrepresented and Latinos underrepresented among the homeless population. Researching Latino homelessness can contribute to the increased well-being of the Hispanic population, and the knowledge gained may also benefit the well-being of non-Latinos.

Understanding homelessness among Hispanics requires an especially nuanced conceptual and methodological framework that appropriately models a number of dimensions that determine within- and between-group variation. Latinos differ from each other in terms of national origin, citizenship status, race, and English-language proficiency. These factors may affect the dynamic of homelessness among Hispanics. This entry discusses and analyzes Latino homelessness. It presents an overview of homelessness among Hispanics, a discussion of the pan-Hispanic rubric, and an analysis of how social, cultural, and economic factors affect Latino homelessness.

COUNTING LATINO HOMELESS

Counting the homeless is a complex methodological and definitional issue because "the essential characteristic of homelessness is its transience, instability, and flux" (Burt, Aron, Lee, and Valente 2001, 2). There are bureaucratic and programmatic definitions of the phenomenon that complicate the issue. The "Shelter and Street" (S-Night) method utilized by the United States Census Bureau in the 1990 census is an example of the attempt to cope with the inherent problems in enumerating and statistically sampling the homeless. S-Night relied on an experimental research design to accurately account for the homeless in both the "streets" and "shelters."

Counting Hispanics

Counting Hispanics has become one of the most complicated efforts of the Census Bureau, ultimately necessitating the creation of a two-stage racial and ethnic identification classification. Question 5 on the 2000 census form established Hispanic ethnicity, and question 6 established racial identity. Another compromise in the 2000 census was in using the terms *Hispanic* and *Latino* interchangeably. In 2000, people of "Spanish/Hispanic/Latino" origin could identify as "Mexican," "Puerto Rican," "Cuban," or "other Spanish/Hispanic/Latino" (people who marked "other Spanish/Hispanic/Latino" had an additional space to write in their national origins, such as "Salvadoran" or "Dominican"). The question on Spanish/Hispanic/Latino origin was separate from the question on race. Hispanic origin is considered an ethnicity; therefore, Latinos may be of any race. Hispanics could identify from over twelve designated racial categories including "White," "Black/African American/Negro," "American Indian or Alaska Native," or "Asian or Pacific Islander."

Immigration and language also impede an accurate count of the Latino population. A substantial number of Hispanics are undocumented immigrants and are less likely to be counted in government figures. Many Latinos are unlikely to be fluent in English. Most are Spanish-speaking, but a substantial number speak indigenous Native American languages such as Quechua and Nahuatl.

The Latino Homeless Population

Fielding accurate counts of the Latino homeless population is a demographic challenge. However, some rigorous efforts have established reliable estimates. Based on the National Survey of Homeless Assistance Providers and Clients (NSHAPC), a comprehensive, longitudinal national data set on urban, suburban, and rural homelessness, in 1996 non-Hispanic whites comprised 52 percent of the U.S. poor adult population and 41 percent of all currently homeless clients. Non-Hispanic blacks comprised 23 percent of the U.S. poor adult population and 40 percent of all currently homeless clients. Hispanics comprised

20 percent of the U.S. poor adult population and 11 percent of all currently homeless clients. A 2000 census report estimated that the percent of the population in emergency and transitional shelters in 2000 was 33.5 percent non-Hispanic white, 40.4 percent non-Hispanic black, and 19.9 percent Latino. These two studies reflect the relative underrepresentation of Latinos in the homeless population.

Documenting the demographic profile of the Hispanic homeless population is further complicated by calculating what proportion of Latino homeless are immigrants. Although "some subset of the Latino homeless consists of immigrants . . . there is scant direct evidence on the immigrant share of the total" (Baker 1996, 133). Differences by subgroup (for example, Mexican versus Puerto Rican) and location (region, state, and locality) also vary the profile of the Hispanic homeless population.

THE "LATINO PARADOX"

Recognizing the need for caution in light of Latino demographic diversity, the preponderance of evidence suggests that as an aggregate, Hispanics demonstrate a paradoxical pattern of homelessness. Despite their socioeconomic position, Latinos are underrepresented among the homeless population in the United States. What factors explain this "Latino paradox"?

Demographic Differences between Latinos and Other Racial and Ethnic Groups

Demographically, Hispanics differ from non-Hispanic groups because of race, language, culture, and immigration. Variations occur among Hispanics by Latino subgroup, geography, nativity and citizenship status, race, and gender. The Asian-American population has a number of similarities to Hispanics. Asian-American communities are greatly affected by linguistic and cultural diversity because various national origin groups comprise the panethnic grouping. Immigration is also particularly salient within Asian-American communities. However, language operates differently for Latinos than for Asians. Although it is characterized by pronounced regional and national dialects, the Spanish language creates a homogenizing force that is lacking among Asian-Americans. For non-Hispanic whites and non-Hispanic blacks, race is a more inherently unifying characteristic than among Latinos. Non-Hispanic whites and non-Hispanic blacks are primarily native-born populations for whom immigration does not have the same effect as with Hispanics and Asian-Americans.

Age sets Latinos apart from other racial and ethnic groups. Hispanics are more likely to be under eighteen years old than non-Hispanic whites. The median age of Latinos in 2001 was the lowest of any racial and ethnic group at 26.2 years of age. In the same year, the median age was 36.9 for non-Hispanic whites, 30.3 for non-Hispanic blacks, 33.0 for Asian-Americans, 28.1 for American Indians or Alaska Natives, and 27.3 for Native Hawaiians and other Pacific Islanders. In addition, compared to other immigrants by region of birth, Hispanic immigrants were younger. In 2000, the median age of the Latin American foreign-born population was 35, compared to 39 years for those from Asia and 50 for Europeans.

Household composition for Hispanics differs from other racial and ethnic groups. Latinos are more likely to live in larger family households than non-Hispanic whites. In 2000, 20 percent of Hispanic families had three or more children compared to 12 percent of non-Hispanic black families and 9 percent of non-Hispanic white families. Fertility rates are higher for Latinos than for other racial and ethnic groups. For 2000, the projected total fertility rate, the number of births that 1,000 women would have in their lifetime based on birthrates, was 3,108 for Hispanics compared to 2,193 for non-Hispanic blacks and 2,114 for non-Hispanic whites.

Socioeconomic Differences between Latinos and Other Racial and Ethnic Groups

There are significant socioeconomic differences between Hispanics and other racial and ethnic groups. Latinos are generally the least educated of all racial and ethnic groups and have the highest dropout rates. Hispanics are more likely to be unemployed than non-Hispanic whites. Latinos tend to experience a systematic disadvantage in the labor market. Median income rates for Latinos are among the lowest ranking of any racial and ethnic group.

The level of residential segregation of Latinos is second only to non-Hispanic blacks. However, residential segregation has been steadily decreasing for non-Hispanic blacks but has increased for Hispanics. Home ownership rates are lower among Hispanics than non-Hispanic whites and non-Hispanic blacks. In part, this is due to the fact that immigrants are less likely to own a home than those who are native-born, but these differences in the rate of home ownership between natives and immigrants become negligible after ten years of residency.

Overall, Hispanics most closely resemble non-Hispanic blacks in their socioeconomic profile. Given their respective economic vulnerabilities, the rate of homelessness among the two groups should be comparable, yet they are not. The Latino paradox in homelessness may be simply the result of flawed sampling methods. Hispanics may be more heavily represented in street samples than in shelter samples, and undocumented immigration might deflate overall counts, but methodological deficiencies do not appear to sufficiently explain the Latino paradox.

Cultural Differences between Latinos and Other Racial and Ethnic Groups

Cultural differences have been assumed to explain the Latino paradox. Cultural values and behavioral norms are thought to increase Hispanics' sense of solidarity and maximize their social capital. The two most cited in the literature are "allocentrism," a sense of identity and commitment to collectives and groups rather than autonomous individuals, and "familism," loyalty and attachment to one's nuclear family and extended family. Hispanics are characterized as focusing on intergroup and intragroup harmony, avoiding conflict and confrontation, preferring closeness in interpersonal space, maintaining traditional male/female gender-role expectations, and having a flexible time orientation that prizes the "here and now" over the future. Most of these generalized cultural values and behavioral norms are typical not only of Hispanic culture but of "traditional"

societies in general. Many of these cultural values and norms are also similar to traits associated with the "culture of poverty" thesis. The culture of poverty thesis stresses the preeminent role of culture and behavior in intergenerational poverty and the failure of economic development and modernization in many non-Western societies (for example, the inability to delay gratification or the lack of individualism and competitiveness).

Arguably, "there is no commonly agreed-upon conceptual construct for Latino culture, although cultural-sensitivity curricula have attempted to reduce it to a dozen or so characteristics applied uniformly to all Latinos everywhere" (Hayes-Bautista 2002, 232). Cultural values and norms do not adequately explain the Latino paradox. The role of risk factors may be more explanatory.

Risk Factors

Risk factors can be grouped along three dimensions: individual characteristics (the prevalence of mental illness and substance abuse); structural influences (economic position, housing markets, public housing and shelter availability, and residential segregation); and "middle range" factors (social networks and social support).

The pervasive effects of mental illness and substance abuse have long been debated in the literature on homelessness. Similarly, there is the possibility that a greater prevalence of mental illness and substance abuse within a racial or ethnic group relative to others might be reflected in higher rates of homelessness. The evidence does not indicate that mental illness and substance abuse explain the Latino homelessness paradox. In fact, it tends to suggest that in comparison to non-Hispanic whites, Latinos and non-Hispanic blacks are quite similar in their epidemiological patterns of mental illness and drug abuse.

For the most part, Hispanics and non-Hispanic blacks do not differ enough in terms of their economic position to explain the paradox. Each group has high rates of unemployment and poverty. Compared to non-Hispanic whites, African-Americans and Latinos are both more likely to experience numerous episodes of homelessness and to be homeless with children. These similarities underscore the economic vulnerability of both groups.

There are differences in the area of housing that may contribute to the differential outcomes between Latinos and non-Hispanic blacks. Hispanics are more likely than non-Hispanic whites to inhabit physically substandard housing and to live in areas that have been most affected by overall population loss, disinvestments, and recurring issues of abandonment and blight. This is even more likely for non-Hispanic blacks. Non-Hispanic blacks rely on federal government housing supports more than Hispanics, but these supports have dwindled since the 1980s. Although rates of residential segregation for Latinos are the fastest growing of any group, non-Hispanic blacks still have the highest rates and tend to suffer the greatest amount of housing discrimination.

Differences in Social Networks between Latinos and Other Racial and Ethnic Groups

Differences in the structure of social networks (size, density, and diversity) and content of social support (emotional aid, and exchange of guidance, information, personal services, and material assistance) between Hispanics and other groups may explain the paradox. Compared to non-Hispanic whites, social networks among both African-Americans and Latinos are smaller, more kin-based, denser, and less diverse. There is some evidence, especially higher rates of overcrowding in housing units, that Hispanics use a wider range of housing arrangements within their networks than non-Hispanic blacks. Diverse housing arrangements (young adults living with parents, unrelated adults or multiple families within the same household, and older parents living with adult children) may lessen the reliance on shelters and increase avoidance of the street.

These differences between non-Hispanic blacks and Latinos in the use of social networks may be the result of their history and incorporation into the U.S. political and economic system. Non-Hispanic blacks have a longer history of involvement with civil rights–era social programming and the provision of govern-

ment services. As a result, these services may have enriched existing network resources. Lax enforcement of civil rights policies and the ongoing disinvestment in government service provision have depleted these resources within the social networks of non-Hispanic blacks. The variety of housing arrangements currently deployed by Latinos also operated among poor, urban non-Hispanic blacks to a greater extent in the past, but have been eroded by changes in public and social policy. Social networks among non-Hispanic blacks still play a vital role in coping with poverty and forestalling homelessness. Non-Hispanic blacks and Hispanics have a longer time gap between their last steady job and the onset of a current spell of homelessness than do non-Hispanic whites. This suggests a greater ability to avoid homelessness in periods of financial distress. The use of social supports plays a crucial part in this process.

Latino families and communities include immigrant members. Latino social networks differ from most racial and ethnic groups other than Asian-Americans because of their inclusion of immigrant ties. Immigration affects the majority of Hispanics' social networks. Immigrant social networks are well-developed sources of social support: "At both ends of the migration channel, kinfolk and hometown friends can greatly minimize those risks by providing loans, safe havens, and information" (Suro 1998, 34). Immigrant families and communities operate as income, resource, and information-pooling units that "raise capital, vouchsafe the investment's legitimacy, and, when it produces a profit . . . dividends in the form of remittances [are] sent home by the migrant" (Suro 1998, 34). The circulation of people and remittances makes Latino social networks transnational in scope.

Immigrant social networks make barrios (neighborhoods, or groups of neighborhoods, in which Latinos are the predominant population) important zones for newcomers and distinct from communities that are primarily native-born. Latinos demonstrate a high level of geographic mobility. Hispanics tend to "move constantly within a metropolitan area to take advantage of housing and work opportunities, and they constantly move back and forth to their home countries" (Suro 1998, 121). Under these conditions, place, family, and housing are highly unstable.

Mobility in the Hispanic community is facilitated and cushioned within the barrio. Immigrant social networks and social support make new labor and housing markets more manageable.

Latino Paradox or Latino Norm?

Race, language, immigration, and social networks make Latinos substantially different from other racial and ethnic groups. The appearance of paradoxical outcomes should not be surprising. The extent of these substantive differences calls into question the usefulness of the paradox metaphor. It may be more productive to shift the emphasis from the contradictory nature of the Hispanic profile relative to other racial and ethnic groups, to understanding the basis for baseline patterns of well-being among Latinos. This shift could generate data on the nature of Latino well-being and provide a conceptual model of Hispanic risk factors, facilitating the development of interventions and services, educational and training curricula, and policy models that better serve the needs of the Latino communities.

Hispanic health outcomes demonstrate the need for Latino-based norms and models. Generic categorizations do not sufficiently explain these outcomes. Notable exceptions to the epidemiological paradox underscore these limits. Hispanics are more likely to report being in fair or poor health than non-Hispanic whites of the same age group. Despite the lower age-adjusted death rates for a wide variety of illnesses compared to non-Hispanic whites, Latino death rates are higher for diabetes, HIV/AIDS, homicide and legal intervention, and chronic liver disease and cirrhosis. Some studies have found that Latino immigrants are at higher risk for tuberculosis and other infectious diseases and that they may engage in more health risk behaviors than non-Hispanic whites resulting in illnesses such as sexually transmitted diseases. This is particularly the case among Hispanic migrant workers. Migrant workers typically live and work in substandard, unsanitary, and transient conditions. Generally, compared to non-Hispanic whites, Latinos are more likely to experience hazardous social and physical environments in residence and work. The basic work of documenting Latino norms needs to occur and, once these are established, variations from these norms and the risk factors that cause them can be identified.

Acculturation

Many of the exceptions to the Latino epidemiological paradox are associated with the phenomenon of acculturation. Acculturation is the level of cultural assimilation or incorporation of an individual to a foreign or receiving society. The pattern exhibited in the paradox is most applicable to Hispanic immigrants, in particular those from Mexico, Central America, and South America. The pattern breaks down the longer immigrants reside in the United States. This suggests that as Latino immigrants become acculturated, protective factors dissipate. The behaviors and social networks associated with the traditional culture of their homeland are eventually adapted to, or replaced by, the behavioral norms of the host society (for example, diets change, and family ties may become less binding).

THE FUTURE

The experience of non-Hispanic blacks and their utilization of social networks and resources could provide a glimpse of the future of homelessness among Hispanics. Perhaps the Puerto Rican experience provides the most important clues to predicting the direction of Latino homelessness in the United States. When compared to other Latino groups, non-Hispanic whites, and Asian-Americans, Puerto Ricans generally rank lowest on such indicators as per capita and household income, unemployment and poverty rates, receipt of public assistance, labor force participation, educational achievement, and rates of home ownership. Puerto Ricans are the exception the Latino epidemiological paradox. The overall profile of Puerto Rican economic and social well-being closely resembles that of African-Americans and Native Americans.

Unlike other Latino national-origin groups, Puerto Ricans, even those who are island-born, are citizens of the United States. Puerto Rico maintains a separate language and distinct traditions from the

United States, yet it is one of the most Americanized countries in the Caribbean and Latin America. Because of citizenship status, geographic proximity, and familiarity with U.S. culture, the acculturation experience for Puerto Ricans is very different from that of most other immigrant populations. The currents of acculturation are strong within Puerto Rican culture. It is conceivable that at one time the deployments of social supports that are now characteristic of Hispanic groups that exhibit the paradox also operated to a greater degree among Puerto Ricans but were eroded by the forces of acculturation. In the wake of acculturation, the cultural strengths and social supports that appear to play a critical role in explaining the underrepresentation of Hispanics among the homeless population may be fundamentally altered. In the process, the paradox of Latino homelessness might fully unravel.

—Gregory Acevedo

Further Reading

Baker, S. G. (1994). Gender, ethnicity, and homelessness. *American Behavioral Scientist, 37*(4), 476–505.

Baker, S. G. (1996). Homelessness and the Latino paradox. In J. Baumohl (Ed.), *Homelessness in America* (pp. 132–140). Phoenix, AZ: Oryx Press.

Baumohl, J. (Ed.) (1996). *Homelessness in America*. Phoenix, AZ: Oryx Press.

Brown, E. R., & Yu, H. (2002). Latino access to employment-based health insurance. In M. M. Suárez-Orozco & M. M. Páez (Eds.), *Latinos remaking America* (pp. 236–253). Berkeley, CA: David Rockefeller Center for Latin American Studies, Harvard University/University of California Press.

Burt, M., Aron, L. Y., Lee, E., & Valente, J. (2001). *Helping America's homeless: Emergency shelter or affordable housing*. Washington, DC: The Urban Institute Press.

Gutiérrez, L., Yeakley, A., & Ortega, R. (2002). Educating students for social work with Latinos: Issues for the new millennium. *Journal of Social Work Education, 36*(3), 541–557.

Hayes-Bautista, D. E. (2002). The Latino health research agenda for the twenty-first century. In M. M. Suárez-Orozco & M. M. Páez (Eds.), *Latinos remaking America* (pp. 215–235). Berkeley, CA: David Rockefeller Center for Latin American Studies, Harvard University/University of California Press.

Hopper, K., & Milburn, N. G. (1996). Chapter 11: Homelessness among African Americans: A historical and contemporary perspective. In J. Baumohl (Ed.), *Homelessness in America* (pp. 123–131). Phoenix, AZ: Oryx Press.

Julia, M., & Hartnett, H. P. (1999). Exploring cultural issues in Puerto Rican homelessness. *Cross-Cultural Research, 33*(4), 318–341.

Katz, M. B. (1989). *The undeserving poor: From the war on poverty to the war on welfare*. New York: Pantheon Books.

Koegel, P., Burnam, M. A., & Baumohl, J. (1996). In J. Baumohl (Ed.), *Homelessness in America* (pp. 24–33). Phoenix, AZ: Oryx Press.

Lewis O. (1966). *La vida: A Puerto Rican family in the culture of poverty: San Juan and New York*. New York: Random House.

Massey, D. S. (1993). Latinos, poverty, and the underclass: A new agenda for research. *Hispanic Journal of the Behavioral Sciences, 15*(4), 449–475.

Massey, D. S., & Denton, N. A. (1993). *American apartheid: Segregation and the making of the underclass*. Cambridge, MA: Harvard University Press.

Melendez, E., Rodriguez, C., & Figueroa, J. (1991). Hispanics in the labor force: An introduction to issues and approaches. In E. Melendez, C. Rodriguez, & J. B. Figueroa (Eds.), *Hispanics in the labor force: Issues and policies* (pp. 1–24). New York: Plenum.

Painter, G., Gabriel, S., & Myers, D. (2000). *The decision to own: The impact of race, ethnicity, and immigration status*. Washington, DC: Research Institute for Housing America.

Rossi, P. H. (1988). Minorities and homelessness. In G. D. Sandefur & M. Tienda (Eds.), *Divided opportunities: Minorities, poverty, and social policy* (pp.87–115). New York: Plenum.

Snow, D. A., Baker, S. G., Anderson, L., & Martin, M. (1986). The myth of pervasive mental illness among the homeless. *Social Problems, 33*(5), 407–423.

Suárez-Orozco, M. M., & Páez, M. M. (Eds.). (2002). *Latinos remaking America*. Berkeley, CA: David Rockefeller Center for Latin American Studies, Harvard University/University of California Press.

Suro, R. (1998). *Strangers among us: Latino lives in a changing America*. New York: Vintage.

United States Bureau of the Census. (2001, March). *Census 2000 population characteristics: The Hispanic population in the United States*. Washington, DC: U.S. Government Printing Office.

United States Bureau of the Census. (2001, May). *Census 2000 brief: The Hispanic population*. Washington, DC: U.S. Government Printing Office.

United States Bureau of the Census. (2001, October). *Census 2000 special reports: Emergency and transitional shelter population*. Washington, DC: U.S. Government Printing Office.

United States Bureau of the Census. (2002, February). *Census 2000 brief: Current population survey: Coming to America: A profile of the nation's foreign born (2000 update)*. Washington, DC: U.S. Government Printing Office.

United States Bureau of the Census. (2002, August). *Census 2000 special reports: Racial and ethnic segregation in the United States: 1980–2000*. Washington, DC: U.S. Government Printing Office.

United States Bureau of the Census. (2002). Population section, Table 14, resident population by race, Hispanic origin, and single years of age; and Table 55, families by number of own children under 18 years old; Vital section, Table 72, projected fertility rates by race, origin, and age group. In *Statistical abstract of the United States* (pp. 16–17, 51 62). Washington, DC: U.S. Government Printing Office.

Wright, J. D., & Devine, J. A. (1992). Counting the homeless: The Census Bureau's "S-Night" in five U.S. cities. *Evaluation Review, 16*(4), 355–364.

▣ LEGAL ADVOCACY

Legal advocacy has been an integral part of efforts to prevent and alleviate homelessness in the United States. Legal advocacy has included legal aid (legal aid provided to the poor) to prevent homelessness, secure shelter and services, protect civil rights, and preserve and expand access to permanent housing. Legal advocacy has involved legal assistance for individuals as well as groups of similarly situated clients and community-based organizations; legal representation in judicial and administrative proceedings; and representation of clients before legislative bodies, administrative agencies, and the media.

Across the country, legal advocacy has been led by lawyers and legal staff representing local Coalition for the Homeless organizations and other advocacy groups, legal aid and legal services staffs, and the staffs of civil liberties and social justice advocacy organizations, with additional support from law school clinics and private law firm lawyers and paralegals working pro bono.

Beginning with the rise in homelessness in the 1970s, legal advocates in key urban areas—including New York, Boston, Los Angeles and other parts of California, New Jersey, Chicago, Florida, and Washington, D.C.—have been leaders in providing legal services to fight homelessness. Indeed, resourceful and creative strategies have been employed throughout the country by legal organizations and community advocates working together to stem the rising tide of homelessness and the resulting harm to homeless clients. Although by no means the only example of the kind of comprehensive legal services that can address homelessness, the Legal Aid Society in New York City illustrates the key role that legal advocacy can play in the fight to end homelessness.

THE LEGAL AID SOCIETY'S ADVOCACY IN NEW YORK

Founded in 1876, the Legal Aid Society is the oldest and largest law firm for low-income people. With offices in all five boroughs of New York City and with a combination of federal, state, local, and private funding, the society provides legal assistance in 300,000 cases each year involving civil, criminal, and juvenile rights problems. Even before the rise in homelessness more than two decades ago, in some sense the work of the Legal Aid Society—like that of other legal services programs—has always been focused on preventing homelessness by preserving access to housing, stopping evictions, securing income support and services, and enforcing civil rights. During the past two decades, the Legal Aid Society's Homeless Rights Project, its representation of the Coalition for the Homeless as retained counsel, and the Legal Aid Society's landmark affirmative litigation and innovative homelessness prevention work in neighborhood-based offices have exemplified what legal advocates across the country can do to address homelessness.

Several examples of legal advocacy to prevent homelessness illustrate what can be accomplished for clients.

The gap between income and rent costs is a primary factor in homelessness in this country. The minimum wage of $5.15 per hour, for example, is insufficient to cover housing costs (National Low Income Housing Coalition 2003). This gap is of particular concern as national and local "welfare reform" efforts have focused on moving people from "welfare to work," but low-wage employment income is inadequate to meet housing costs and avert homelessness. Study after study, however, has found that education and training provide access to higher-wage employment, which in turn provides increased ability to pay high housing costs. Litigation enforcing state "welfare reform" statutes to ensure access to such education and training brought by the Legal Aid Society and other legal advocates is therefore a key component of efforts to prevent homelessness (*Davila v. Turner* 1998; *Davila v. Turner* 1999).

Likewise, for people who must rely on public assistance, state welfare allowances to pay monthly rent bills are far below rent costs. In New York City, for example, the state welfare shelter allowance is less than half of what the U.S. Department of Housing and Urban Development has calculated private market rents to be. Litigation on behalf of clients faced with evictions and homelessness to enforce state statutes requiring that the public assistance shelter allowance be adequate to enable families to raise their children in homes is a critical element of efforts to end family homelessness (*Jiggetts v. Grinker* 1990; *Jiggetts v. Dowling* 1999).

Lack of legal representation in Housing Court eviction cases is another cause of rising homelessness. Although people have a judicially recognized right to counsel in cases in which they are accused of crimes, people have no judicially recognized right to counsel in civil cases in which the loss of housing and homelessness are at stake. In New York City, approximately 90 percent of tenants are unrepresented in Housing Court eviction cases, and more than 90 percent of landlords are represented. Not surprisingly, unrepresented tenants typically lose their eviction cases, whereas represented tenants are able to retain their housing. As part of relief in the Legal Aid Society's litigation on behalf of homeless families (*McCain v. Dinkins* 1994), New York City has implemented homelessness prevention legal services programs through which legal services organizations in

Privacy Rights versus Homeless Surveillance

The following privacy alert—released by the Electronic Privacy Information Center (EPIC) in October 2003—questions the Department of Housing and Urban Development's Homeless Information Management Systems (HMIS):

Eight civil liberties groups joined EPIC in opposing the Department of Housing and Urban Development's implementation of Homeless Information Management Systems (HMIS). HMIS are programs intended to track recipients of benefits in order to assess the number of persons receiving care, and to improve efficiency of services to the poor. While well intentioned, proposed mandatory guidelines for HMIS issued by the Department are highly privacy-invasive.

The proposed guidelines create information collection requirements that could be aggregated into a national homeless tracking system. Homeless shelters and other care providers would have to collect full legal names, dates of birth, Social Security Numbers, ethnicity and race, gender, veteran status, and the person's residence prior to program entry. In some cases, even more sensitive information would be collected, including disabilities, health status, pregnancy status, HIV status, behavioral health status, education, employment, and whether they have experienced domestic violence.

The groups argued that law enforcement, Secret Service, and national security access to the data was too broad. Police would be able to obtain access to this sensitive data without a warrant, and the Secret Service and agents of national security agencies could simply request access to the database without a requirement of any judicial oversight. Additionally, the aggregation of personal information raises risks that the homeless or disadvantaged could be located and subjected to politically motivated purges or forced removal.

The groups urged the agency to rewrite its HMIS guidelines in favor of a system where the homeless are enumerated through representative sampling or a "point in time" snapshot. Such alternative approaches are less expensive and require no collection of personally identifiable information. The groups also urged the agency to limit law enforcement, Secret Service, and national security access to personal information. Finally, the groups recommended a series of changes that would establish a framework of technical and procedural protections for individuals' data.

Source: Epic Alert. Retrieved October 10, 2003, from http://www.epic.org/privacy/poverty

New York City are paid to provide counsel to a specified number of tenants in Housing Court each year. The funding is the same emergency assistance funding stream that would otherwise be used to pay for shelter for families who are evicted from their homes. Through this program, the neighborhood offices of the Legal Aid Society have prevented more than 30,000 evictions during the past twelve years. When the program began, a state study had found that eviction prevention legal services programs such as this save at least $4 in averted shelter costs for every $1 of program cost. The U.S. Congress has also recognized the key role of innovative homelessness prevention programs that the Legal Aid Society and other legal advocacy groups have developed (Committee on Banking, Housing, and Urban Affairs, U.S. Senate 1990).

RIGHT TO SHELTER

More than twenty years ago, uncontested court testimony established that lack of shelter from the elements resulted in deaths from exposure on the streets of New York City and the loss of limbs due to hypothermia (*Callahan v. Carey* 1979). Likewise, a New York appellate court found that lack of shelter had caused homeless children and their families to sleep in public spaces in the city (*McCain v. Koch* 1986, 1987). Legal advocacy by the Coalition for the Homeless and the Legal Aid Society has been aimed at stopping this harm and securing protection from the elements for homeless people.

The first case nationally to obtain a right to shelter to secure protection from the elements for homeless people was *Callahan v. Carey*, which was filed on behalf of homeless men who sought to enforce legal obligations in the New York State Constitution and statutes requiring the provision of care to the needy. In the landmark *Callahan* consent decree (a judicial decree that sanctions a voluntary agreement between parties in a dispute) in 1981, the city agreed to provide shelter from the elements that complies with basic standards of habitability to homeless persons who meet the financial need standard for public assistance or who are "homeless by reason of physical, mental, or social dysfunction" (*Callahan v. Carey* 1979). The decree was negotiated for the Coalition for the Homeless by Robert Hayes, a private lawyer who had brought the litigation of counsel to the Legal Aid Society's pro bono program. Separate litigation had to be brought to extend the right to receive lawful shelter as protection from the elements to homeless women (*Eldredge v. Carey* 1983). Through a retainer arrangement with the Coalition for the Homeless, which funds staff at the

Legal Aid Society's Homeless Right Project, Legal Aid now serves as counsel to the Coalition for the Homeless for homeless men and homeless women.

Even after a right to shelter from the elements had been established for homeless men and women, litigation was still necessary to secure shelter for homeless children and their families. As a result of the Legal Aid Society's *McCain* litigation on behalf of families with children, court orders require the provision of shelter from the elements, the provision of shelter that meets basic standards of habitability, and the provision of essential services for homeless families, including permanent housing relocation services (*McCain v. Koch* 1986, 1987; *McCain v. Dinkins* 1994; *McCain v. Giuliani* 1997).

Extensive legal advocacy has frequently been necessary to secure critical services. Several examples illustrate the kind of legal advocacy that can significantly help homeless people.

Lack of public benefits leaves homeless people without the ability to meet basic needs and secure permanent housing or services. Litigation to secure access to public benefits can address this critical need (*Thrower v. Perale* 1987).

Access to medically appropriate shelter and services is also essential. For example, litigation by the Legal Aid Society on behalf of families with pregnant women, newborn babies, or medically frail children or adults has been required to secure such access (*Slade v. Koch* 1987).

The prevalence of asthma among homeless children in New York City has been even higher than that in neighborhoods with high numbers of children with asthma. Litigation by a coalition of legal advocates, including the Legal Aid Society, to enforce provisions of the federal Medicaid law requiring the early and periodic screening, diagnosis, and treatment of children has resulted in greater access to medical care for homeless children with asthma (*Dajour B. v. City of New York* 2001).

ADEQUATE ASSISTANCE AND SERVICES

Lead paint poisoning is still a significant health problem for children. Eliminating lead paint hazards in shelter facilities is therefore critical to protecting the health of children. The Legal Aid Society's litigation preventing placement of homeless children and their families in emergency housing with both lead paint and asbestos hazards (and requiring abatement of these conditions through a consent decree) is representative of this kind of legal advocacy (*Barnes v. Koch* 1987).

Maintaining the ability to attend school is also essential for homeless children. Litigation by Legal Aid on behalf of homeless children to obtain school transportation allowances has been necessary to enable homeless children to continue their education (*Fulton v. Krauskopf* 1986).

Securing access to permanent housing is clearly a crucial component of effective advocacy to alleviate homelessness. Judicial relief requiring the provision of permanent housing has been granted in the Legal Aid litigation on behalf of homeless children and their families as a remedy for governmental failures to provide sufficient temporary housing. Specifically, relief ordered in contempt proceedings requires the city to substitute permanent housing for shortfalls in temporary housing and to provide a sufficient amount of temporary and permanent housing (*McCain v. Dinkins* 1994). However, low-income people of color, including homeless New Yorkers, frequently encounter racial discrimination as a barrier to permanent housing. Legal assistance is an essential tool to stop such discrimination. For example, the Legal Aid Society litigated federal Fair Housing Act claims to end racial discrimination in the New York City Housing Authority's application process, which had resulted in unlawful apartment assignments based on race and segregated housing projects in certain parts of the city (*Davis v. New York City Housing Authority* 2002).

Legal advocacy can stop the breakup of families and the placement or retention of children in foster care because of lack of housing. For example, litigation on behalf of families whose children were languishing in foster care or were under threat of placement in foster care because of their families' lack of housing resulted in a court ruling finding it unlawful for a local social services district to place or retain children in foster care because of lack of housing. In contrast, a local social services district is legally obligated to provide temporary housing and permanent housing rent subsidies (*Cosentino v. Perales* 1989).

Studies have shown that domestic violence is a major cause of homelessness. Advocacy by Legal Aid on behalf of survivors of domestic violence has resulted in court orders directing the local social services district to refrain from denying shelter eligibility to families who would otherwise have no choice but to return to unsafe housing from which they had fled because of domestic violence (*McCain v. Giuliani* 1997, 1998, 1999, 2001).

Legal Aid Society representation of survivors of domestic violence before the New York City Council has also resulted in a local law prohibiting the denial of shelter to domestic violence survivors because of the lack of a police report or an order of protection or because the violence was perpetrated by someone other than an intimate partner (New York City Administrative Code §21–130).

CIVIL RIGHTS

Lack of a home frequently results in homeless people spending time in public spaces even when they have shelter placements. In many instances, local government attempts to portray non-criminal conduct such as sitting on a bench in an area open to the public as criminal when it involves a homeless person, whereas the same conduct by a non-homeless person would not normally result in a criminal sanction. Criminal penalties meted out in this way can act as a barrier to employment and housing when criminal background checks are conducted.

Legal advocacy can stop the most flagrant government conduct of this nature. For instance, on behalf of clients who had been arrested in the public areas of a train station pursuant to a loitering statute, the Legal Aid Society obtained a ruling that the statutory requirement that a person give a "satisfactory explanation of presence" in order to avoid arrest was unconstitutionally vague (*People v. Bright* 1988).

The Legal Aid Society's representation of homeless people before the New York City Council has also resulted in local laws prohibiting the use of barracks-style shelters for families, requiring that new shelter units be readily convertible to permanent housing and that any commercial hotel facilities used as emergency housing for families meet basic standards, including providing self-contained living units with bathroom facilities and cooking facilities (New York City Administrative Code §§21–124, 21–309).

Some of these provisions codified earlier court orders, and subsequent court proceedings enforced these provisions of the administrative code (*McCain v. Dinkins* 1990; *McCain v. Bloomberg* 2002).

In the end, the essential ingredient for all of these successful advocacy efforts has been the Legal Aid Society's representation of thousands of clients whose cases revealed systemic problems requiring legal advocacy.

—Steven Banks

See also American Bar Association Commission on Homelessness and Poverty; Homeless Court Program; National Coalition for the Homeless

Further Reading

Committee on Banking, Housing, and Urban Affairs, United States Senate. (1990, June 8). *National Affordable Housing Act* (Senate Report No. 101–316). Washington, DC: GPO.

National Coalition for the Homeless. (2003, August). *Illegal to be homeless: The criminalization of homelessness in the United States*. Retrieved December 26, 2003, from http://www.nationalhomeless.org/civilrights/crim2003/index.html

National Low Income Housing Coalition. (2003). *Out of reach 2003: America's housing wage climbs*. Retrieved December 26, 2003, from http://www.nlihc.org/oor2003

Court Cases

Barnes v. Koch, 136 Misc. 2d 96 (Sup. Ct. N.Y. Co. 1987).
Callahan v. Carey, Index No. 42582/79 (Sup. Ct. N.Y. Co. 1979).
Callahan v. Carey, N.Y.L.J., December 11, 1979, at 10 (Sup. Ct. N.Y. Co. 1979).
Cosentino v. Perales, 153 A.D.2d 812 (1st Dep't 1989).
Dajour B. v. City of New York, 2001 U.S. Dist. LEXIS 10251 (S.D.N.Y. 2001).
Davila v. Turner, N.Y.L.J., September 18, 1998, at 1 (Sup. Ct. N.Y. Co. 1998).
Davila v. Turner, N.Y.L.J., April 16, 1999, at 25 (Sup. Ct. N.Y. Co. 1999).
Davis v. New York City Housing Authority, 278 F.3d 64 (2d Cir. 2002).
Eldredge v. Carey, 98 A.D.2d 675 (1st Dep't 1983).
Fulton v. Krauskopf, 217 N.Y.2d 198 (1st Dep't 1986).
Jiggetts v. Dowling, 261 A.D.2d 144 (1st Dep't 1999).
Jiggetts v. Grinker, 75 N.Y.2d 411 (1990).
McCain v. Bloomberg, Index No. 41023/83 (Sup. Ct. N.Y. Co.) August 30, 2002 Order.
McCain v. Dinkins, Index No. 41023/83 (Sup. Ct. N.Y. Co.) June 1, 1990 Order.
McCain v. Dinkins, 84 N.Y.2d 216 (1994).
McCain v. Giuliani, 236 A.D.2d 256 (1st Dep't 1997).
McCain v. Giuliani, Index No. 41023/83 (Sup. Ct. N.Y. Co.) September 10, 1997 Order, March 17, 1998 Order, January 12, 1999 Order, January 31, 2001 Order.
McCain v. Koch, 217 A.D.2d 198, 205–06 (1st Dep't 1986), rev'd in part 70 N.Y.2d 109 (1987).
People v. Bright, 71 N.Y.2d 376 (1988).
Slade v. Koch, 135 Misc. 2d 283 (Sup. Ct. N.Y. Co. 1987), modified 136 Misc. 2d 119 (Sup. Ct. N.Y. Co. 1987).
Thrower v. Perales, 138 Misc. 2d 172 (Sup. Ct. N.Y. Co. 1987).

▣ LEGISLATION, PROGRAMS, AND POLICIES, U.S. FEDERAL

A range of federal programs is available to help homeless people. Some programs are targeted specifically to those who are homeless (labeled below as "homeless-specific"), while others are available to a broader group of low-income people, including those who are homeless (labeled as "mainstream"). This entry surveys the most important federal programs for homeless people: what the programs do, their size, and key issues and proposals for change. It covers programs that can provide housing for people who are homeless and those that are designed to lead to better incomes and access to supportive services for homeless people.

Homelessness policy can be divided into the three general functions that it serves: (a) managing the homelessness problem by taking care of people while they are homeless, (b) assisting people who are homeless to move back into housing, and (c) preventing people from becoming homeless in the first place. Existing federal programs and policies treat those three functions in declining order of importance. Federal programs concentrate on managing the problem and meeting the basic needs of people who remain homeless. There is, particularly recently, some focus of moving homeless people into permanent housing. There is little in the way of resources or incentives in federal policy specifically aimed at preventing homelessness.

To make progress toward ending homelessness, a much stronger focus on prevention is necessary, along with continued progress on rehousing people who are already homeless. The last part of this entry briefly examines proposals to meet those goals.

FEDERAL HOUSING PROGRAMS

Lack of housing is the common denominator for all homeless people, and it is the key to the prevention of homelessness. A number of federal programs address housing for low-income people, providing either funding for capital expenses such as construction and rehabilitation, or rent subsidies to cover ongoing costs of operating housing, such as maintenance, utilities, and security. What follows is a description of federal housing programs, all administered by the U.S. Department of Housing and Urban Development, of greatest importance to homelessness.

HUD McKinney-Vento Programs/Homeless Assistance Grants (Homeless-Specific)

The McKinney-Vento Homeless Assistance Act is the most important piece of federal legislation addressing homelessness. Originally passed in 1987, it established programs in a number of federal agencies. The four McKinney-Vento programs at the U.S. Department of Housing and Urban Development (HUD) are operated in a consolidated fashion, through what HUD terms the Homeless Assistance Grants. These grants provide over $1 billion per year to state and local governments, housing authorities, and private nonprofit programs.

For the last several years, the first $150 million of funding has been distributed to state and local governments by formula for the Emergency Shelter Grants program. Most of the rest is distributed through the "Continuum of Care" process. Under this process, homelessness providers in each community work together to describe their services, identify their needs, and rank the projects that they want funded. HUD provides funding based on the quality of the application, the need for homeless services, and the local rankings of individual programs. Funding can be used for permanent and supportive housing, transitional housing, and services. This process covers grants through the Supportive Housing Program, Shelter Plus Care, and the Section 8 Moderate Rehabilitation Single-Room Occupancy program.

For the last five years, Congress has required that 30 percent of all funding be used for permanent housing for homeless persons with disabilities. In addition, since the year 2000 Congress has provided specified funding to renew expiring Shelter Plus Care permanent housing grants. These measures express Congress's support for permanent supportive housing, a program model of subsidized housing combined with treatment and support services that has proven cost-effective in ending homelessness for people with chronic disabilities who have been homeless for long periods of time.

Housing Opportunities for Persons with AIDS (HOPWA) (Mainstream)

Several studies confirm that stable housing is one of the greatest needs of persons living with HIV/AIDS. Without stable housing, they cannot access the complex treatment and care vital to survival. The Housing Opportunities for Persons with AIDS (HOPWA) Program, administered by the Office of HIV/AIDS Housing at HUD, provides funding to eligible jurisdictions across the country to address the compelling housing needs of persons living with HIV/AIDS and their families. In fiscal year (FY) 2003, Congress appropriated $292 million for HOPWA.

Section 8 Housing Certificate Fund and Public Housing (Mainstream)

The Section 8 program pays rent for low-income households, primarily through vouchers. In a voucher system, a household pays 30 percent of its income for housing with the government paying the difference between that amount and the actual rent. Vouchers are primarily *tenant-based*, meaning that tenants receive vouchers and find housing on the private market that meets quality standards, does not cost more than the fair market rent, and is owned by a landlord who is willing to accept vouchers. There are over 2 million vouchers in use nationally.

Residents of public housing also pay 30 percent of their income for rent, but the units are owned and operated by local housing authorities. In 1999, the average wait for public housing was eleven months. In large cities, the wait is typically much longer, and some cities have closed their waiting lists.

The need for public and assisted housing is great. There are approximately 5 million households with worst-case housing needs. That means they receive no HUD assistance, have low incomes, and either pay more than half their income for rent or live in severely substandard housing. These households are at extreme risk of losing their housing and need affordable housing or rental assistance to reduce their risk of homelessness. The Section 8 and Public Housing programs currently combine to serve about 4.5 million households—less than half the need.

Community Development Block Grants and HOME Investment Partnerships (Mainstream)

There are several programs that support the production of affordable housing. Two of the largest are the Community Development Block Grant (CDBG) and HOME Investment Partnership, two block grant programs operated by HUD.

CDBG is a formula allocation to cities, counties, and states that can be used in a variety of ways to meet locally determined housing and community development priorities, including housing. However, most CDBG funding is used for activities other than housing, for example, economic development and public infrastructure. Current funding is $4.4 billion annually.

The HOME Investment Partnerships program is a block grant to states and cities for the sole purpose of increasing the amount of affordable housing. Communities can use the funds for housing construction, rehabilitation, and rental assistance. Roughly 40 percent of units are affordable to households with extremely low incomes (up to 30 percent of area median income). Current funding is $2 billion annually.

Section 202 Supportive Housing for the Elderly/Section 811 Supportive Housing for Persons With Disabilities

More than 7.4 million elderly households pay more than they can afford for housing. This includes 1.5 million very-low-income elderly people who pay more than half of their income in rent or live in substandard situations. Section 202 funds the construction, rehabilitation, and operation of housing for the elderly. Current funding is $783 million annually. Senior advocates estimate that nine seniors are on a waiting list for each Section 202 unit available.

People with disabilities are overrepresented among the homeless population. The need for housing for persons with disabilities has increased over the last several years. HUD's Section 811 program provides housing resources for people with disabilities. Current funding is $251 million annually.

SERVICES AND INCOME PROGRAMS

Of course, many homeless people need support services in order to survive and move into stable housing. In addition, they need income if they are to pay rent and become housed. The following are some existing programs to meet these needs.

Projects for Assistance in Transition from Homelessness (Homeless-Specific)

Projects for Assistance in Transition from Homelessness (PATH) allocates funds by formula to states to serve homeless people with serious mental illness. Eligible services include outreach, screening and diagnosis, habilitation and rehabilitation, community mental health services, substance abuse treatment, case management, residential supervision, and housing. The FY 1999 appropriation of $26 million served nearly 60,000 people. The program distributed $43 million in FY 2003.

*Grants for the Benefit of Homeless
Individuals (GBHI) (Homeless-Specific)*

The Grants for the Benefit of Homeless Individuals (GBHI) program enables the Department of Health and Human Services (HHS) to award funds to develop and expand substance abuse treatment and mental health treatment services for homeless people. Grants are awarded competitively. The program distributed $18 million in FY 2003.

According to HHS staff, the program has been very popular. For instance, in the FY 2001 grant cycle, only seventeen of eighty-eight qualified applicants received awards. Demand for this program is high because mainstream addiction and mental health programs often do not adequately serve homeless people. These mainstream programs may lack the full range of health, housing, and support services required to adequately help homeless people, particularly those who have co-occurring mental illness and substance abuse problems. GBHI grants help mainstream programs bridge these gaps.

*Runaway and Homeless
Youth Act (Homeless-Specific)*

The Family and Youth Services Bureau, in the Department of Health and Human Services Administration for Children and Families, administers the programs created by the Runaway and Homeless Youth Act. The three programs are the Basic Center Program, the Transitional Living Program, and the Street Outreach Program.

The Basic Center Program provides financial assistance to meet the immediate needs of runaway and homeless youth and their families, including emergency shelter, reunification when possible, food, clothing, counseling, and facilitating access to health care. The Transitional Living Program supports projects that provide long-term residential services to homeless youth ages sixteen to twenty-one for up to eighteen months. The Street Outreach Program provides funds to private, nonprofit agencies to engage in outreach efforts designed to serve runaway and homeless youth and move them off the streets. Notices of funding availability for the three programs

are made annually, and the grants are competitively awarded for a three-year period. The three programs together received $105 million in FY 2003, distributed in grants to local nonprofit providers.

*Education for Homeless Children
and Youth (Homeless-Specific)*

The Education for Homeless Children and Youth program (EHCY), operated by the Department of Education, ensures that homeless children are able to enroll, attend, and succeed in school. EHCY establishes liaisons between shelters and schools and provides funding for transportation, tutoring, and supplies. Congress appropriated $50 million for the program in FY 2003.

*Homeless Veterans Reintegration
Program (Homeless-Specific)*

The Department of Labor operates the Homeless Veterans Reintegration Program (HVRP) to provide job placement services to homeless veterans. Congress appropriated $18 million for HVRP in FY 2003, distributed through direct grants to local providers.

*Health Centers (Homeless-Specific
and Mainstream Components)*

The Consolidated Health Centers (CHC) program is a competitive grant program that funds health facilities in medically underserved areas. The goal of CHC is to ensure that people in high-poverty rural and urban areas, who traditionally have poor access to medical facilities, have adequate access to health care, especially primary care. The program is viewed as one of the major providers of health care for the roughly 40 million Americans who are uninsured.

The Healthcare for the Homeless (HCH) Program receives 8.6 percent of the CHC appropriation. HCH funds local clinics to provide health care and related services to homeless people. Services include primary, diagnostic, preventive, emergency medical, pharmaceutical, addiction, and mental health care. HCH also provides funding for intensive outreach, case management, and linkage to housing, income, and transportation. Because of limited funding, the HCH program is able to serve only one-seventh of the people expected to experience homelessness in a given year.

Substance Abuse Prevention and Treatment Performance Partnership Grant (Mainstream)

The Substance Abuse Prevention and Treatment (SAPT) Performance Partnership Grant is the primary source of federal funding for substance abuse treatment and prevention for many low-income individuals, including those experiencing homelessness. Funds are distributed by the Substance Abuse and Mental Health Services Agency (SAMHSA) and are allocated to states based on a formula. Current funding is $1,692,000 annually. States have broad discretion in how the funds are utilized. It is unclear how many homeless individuals have benefited from substance abuse services through this program.

Mental Health Performance Partnership Grant (Mainstream)

The Mental Health Performance Partnership Grant provides flexible funding to states to provide mental health services. The Substance Abuse and Mental Health Services Administration, located within the Department of Health and Human Services, distributes funds by formula. States can choose to spend the money on a variety of activities related to mental health. Current funding is $437 million annually.

Ryan White CARE Act (Mainstream)

The Ryan White CARE Act programs address the unmet health needs of persons living with HIV disease by funding primary health care and support services. The CARE Act reaches over 500,000 individuals each year, making it the federal government's largest program specifically for people living with HIV. Ryan White programs include Emergency Assistance ($619 million in FY 2003), Comprehen-

sive Care ($1,053,000), and Early Intervention ($198 million).

Battered Women's Shelters (Mainstream)

The Battered Women's Shelter program in the Department of Health and Human Services provides formula grant funding to support community-based groups operating shelters for victims of domestic violence. These shelters provide critical services to women and children fleeing violence in their own homes. Congress appropriated $126 million in FY 2003 for this purpose.

Supplemental Security Income (Mainstream)

Supplemental Security Income (SSI) provides monthly cash payments to low-income people with severe disabilities that prevent them from working and to low-income elderly people. The program is operated by the Social Security Administration. It is considered an entitlement, which means all people meeting the eligibility requirements receive benefits.

In its FY 2003 Appropriation for the Social Security Administration, Congress included $8 million for grants to organizations to provide outreach and application assistance for homeless people and other underserved populations.

Temporary Assistance for Needy Families (TANF) (Mainstream)

The Temporary Assistance to Needy Families (TANF) block grant program provides $16.5 billion in federal resources to states and is used along with state "maintenance of effort" funds to provide financial assistance and work supports for low-income families with children. In addition to providing the cash assistance and supports that can help families remain housed or move out of homelessness, state and federal TANF block grant resources have been used more directly to prevent and end homelessness through short- and long-term housing subsidies, services in supportive housing for homeless families and youth transitioning from foster care, and eviction prevention.

*Workforce Investment Act
(WIA) Reauthorization (Mainstream)*

The Workforce Investment Act of 1998 (WIA) consolidated various federal programs that were designed to help low-income people access employment training and supports. The legislation required the development of Workforce Investment Boards that made decisions regarding the use of the federal resources and directed the use of "one stop centers" intended to ensure that job training was easily accessible. Local boards are encouraged under the program to prioritize services to homeless people, among other groups.

FEDERAL POLICY TO PREVENT HOMELESSNESS

Three kinds of activities fall under the rubric of homelessness prevention:

Crisis intervention. Programs identify families facing immediate risk of loss of housing and provide emergency, one-time funds, sometimes along with eviction prevention services such as landlord–tenant mediation and legal services. Both the Emergency Food and Shelter Program at FEMA and the Emergency Shelter Grants program at HUD fund this kind of activity (although it is only a small part of ESG). Homelessness advocates agree that funding for EFSP should be increased from its current level of $153 million annually.

Discharge planning. Residential institutions can ensure that when individuals leave an institution, they are settled in housing that will be sustainable. Examples of such institutions include jails and prisons, foster care/child welfare group homes, inpatient mental health or substance abuse treatment facilities, and the military. McKinney-Vento was amended in 2000 to require that any public sector entity receiving Continuum of Care funds adopt protocols so that discharges from publicly funded institutions do not directly result in homelessness "to the maximum extent practicable and where appropriate." While this has had some impact, most believe that it provides incentives to the wrong party, that is, the local

homeless service system rather than the institutions that are discharging people into homelessness. New resources were made available to state child welfare systems in the Chafee Foster Care Independence Program to focus on preparing young people for exit from the foster care system. The Department of Justice (DOJ) has allocated $2 million to each state to develop programs to address prisoner reentry, and in its technical assistance activity, DOJ has involved HUD and the Interagency Council on the Homeless to include a housing focus and prevention of homelessness.

Accountability for housing stability. Large government-funded systems that care for groups of people can monitor housing stability among the groups they serve and take responsibility for improving it. Such systems can include TANF, the outpatient mental health system, the HIV/AIDS care system funded under the Ryan White CARE Act, and the Veterans Health Administration. SAMHSA has revised the method for reporting performance for two of its block grants. The Substance Abuse Prevention and Treatment Block Grant and the Mental Health Services Block Grant will now include performance measures. States will be required to set targets and report on their performance on several measures, which include housing status as a required element for mental health and a recommended element for substance abuse treatment. Technical assistance will be directed to states that are not meeting their targets. In addition, homeless veterans legislation has provided some tools for the Veterans Administration health system to prevent homelessness.

FEDERAL POLICY TO END HOMELESSNESS: FUTURE DIRECTIONS

In recent years, there have been many proposals to change policy to help end homelessness by strengthening support and encouragement for efforts to prevent homelessness; moving homeless people more quickly into housing; and generally improving housing affordability, incomes, and availability of support services for those near the bottom of the income scale. What follows is a brief summary of these ideas.

Prevention

For crisis intervention, the program tools described earlier appear to be adequately designed. Policy proposals in this area focus on expanding the amount of resources available and the level of coordination, with other programs designed to provide longer-term support once people are beyond the crisis stage.

For discharge planning, there are numerous proposals to provide incentives, along with funding, to residential systems such as prisons, foster care, and inpatient behavioral health treatment. Proposals focus on the housing needs of people leaving these systems. They have two priorities: (1) ensuring that adequate planning is done before an individual leaves the system, so that a place to live is available and that income is sufficient (whether through employment or government support) to pay the rent; and (2) expanding the range of housing options available. An example of the latter is a bill to create a tax credit to finance construction and rehabilitation of buildings to be used for residential programs for prisoners returning to their communities.

There are also proposals to improve accountability of mainstream programs for housing stability of the people they serve. The approach taken by SAMHSA, referred to earlier, could serve as a model for other block grants. Federal programs funding state and local welfare systems are prime candidates.

Rehousing

There are various proposals to use HUD and other homeless program funds as incentives to move homeless people more quickly back into housing. Most advocates agree, however, that this must be accompanied by measures to improve the availability of housing that is affordable to the lowest-income individuals. Proposals range from increasing the size of existing programs, such as Section 8 or the HOME program, to creating a new Housing Trust Fund. An important example of the latter is the National Affordable Housing Trust Fund Act of 2003 (H.R. 1102, in the 108th Congress), which would provide 1.5 million additional affordable housing units over the next ten years, using profits generated by a foreclosure insurance fund in a federal housing program as the initial source of capital.

—*Nan Roman and Steve Berg*

See also Fair Housing Laws; Low-Income Housing; Social Welfare Policy and Income Maintenance

Further Reading

Colton, K. W. (2003). *Housing in the twenty-first century: Achieving common ground.* Cambridge, MA: Harvard University Press.

Culhane, D. P., & Hornburg, S. P. (Eds.). (1997). *Understanding homelessness: New policy and research perspectives.* Washington, DC: Fannie Mae Foundation.

National Alliance to End Homelessness. (2002). *A plan, not a dream: How to end homelessness in ten years.* Retrieved December 29, 2003, from http://www.endhomelessness.org

U.S. Government Printing Office. (2002). *Meeting our nation's housing challenges: Report of the Bipartisan Millennial Housing Commission.* Retrieved December 29, 2003, from http://www.mhc.gov

▣ LIBRARIES: ISSUES IN SERVING THE HOMELESS

Libraries, especially public libraries, aim to serve the informational, educational, and recreational needs of *all* patrons. But libraries are not especially equipped for in-depth services or specialized treatment of individuals with special needs. Many of the varied needs of homeless individuals have been beyond the scope or intent of traditional library services, but that may be changing.

Library publications had little mention of homeless patrons prior to the late 1970s. Even then, such individuals were often decribed with euphemisms, in the context of the problems they seemed to cause (mostly hygiene-related) that brought complaints from other citizens. By the mid-1980s, several large libraries were reporting significant problems (again mostly hygiene-related) caused by patrons who seemed to have no other homes. Articles in the late 1980s often focused on policies designed to govern the behavior and hygiene of all patrons, including the homeless.

Then came a widely reported suit against a New Jersey public library (*Kreimer vs. Town of Morristown et al.)* in 1990, brought by a homeless man who alleged discrimination. The result of this case was a dramatic change throughout the nation (beginning in the early 1990s) in how library policies were written and in the treatment of patrons believed to be homeless.

In recent years, many libraries report successful programs for the homeless, as well as mutually profitable links with other community and governmental entities. However, the number of homeless using libraries continues to rise.

WHY DO MANY HOMELESS GRAVITATE TO LIBRARIES?

Imagine having no place of your own and being unwelcome at most businesses or other private establishments. Public places may be open to you, but parks and streets may be cold or dangerous, bus and train stations noisy and chaotic, museums and art galleries expensive or lacking places to rest for long. A logical candidate for a reasonably safe, warm in winter, cool in summer, and relatively quiet place to rest for hours undisturbed is the nearest public library.

There are about 16,000 U.S. public library facilities, many of these in urban areas, often proximate to community shelters. In addition to safety, comfort, and accessibility, public libraries offer such facilities and options as these:

- *Open Access.* Generally, the homeless cannot be turned away no matter their reason for being there, so long as they don't grossly violate the rules. They typically don't need an ID to get in and can use many of the library's services with anonymity. Many libraries are open during evening hours and on weekends.

- *Comfort.* Unlike the harder, plastic chairs available at some institutions, which are designed to speed people on their way, the library typically offers comfortable chairs that encourage long-term use.

- *Sanitation.* Clean restrooms are available not only for bodily functions but also for improvised bathing or washing, shaving, and brushing teeth.

- *Communication.* With ready access to the Internet via computer and a free e-mail address (available from services such as Hotmail or Yahoo), one can

easily surf the Internet or send and receive e-mail. This can provide an erstwhile "residence" for a homeless person.

- *Companionship.* Homeless "regulars" at the same library may well strike up friendships or form a sort of para-community of acquaintances; some even "network" information about shelters, meals, and so forth.

- *Entertainment.* A library patron can pass the time all day with newspapers, magazines, books, audios, etc.

Best of all, from the point of view of homeless people, is that all these services are free. If libraries didn't close for the night, many homeless individuals would never leave except to get food. And when a downtown library does close, typically a homeless shelter is not far away.

How Extensively Do the Homeless Use Libraries?

Specific numbers are not widely reported, but library use by homeless people seems to have become a recognizable "problem" after the deinstitutionalization of the 1960s and 1970s, and it has grown constantly since then. The virtual disappearance of vagrancy laws (or their lessened enforcement) has added considerably to the numbers of individuals who are in libraries because they have nowhere else to go. As Michael Stoops, an organizer for the National Coalition for the Homeless in Washington, has said: "Libraries have become de facto day centers for the homeless" (Furtado 2002, 1A).

PROBLEMS IN SERVING THE HOMELESS

The American Library Association's views on service are characterized by an article published in its official journal, *American Libraries.* In "12 Ways Libraries Are Good for the Country" (1995, 1114), the second ideal listed is that libraries break down barriers—in particular, that libraries serve the homeless (among five other special categories of patrons).

Many homeless patrons expect no more and no less than any other citizen; they maintain behavior, appearance, and hygiene standards that meet reasonable library requirements. Such individuals may be present in a library for many years without causing any significant problem or accommodation.

However, some homeless patrons are very demanding and seem to expect more than "regular" citizens. Many of them enter the facility with heightened defenses and manifest correspondingly offensive behavior, appearance, and hygiene—often citing laws or threatening litigation if anything is not to their satisfaction and causing serious problems in libraries.

Specific Problems

It is appropriate and important to acknowledge that the influx of homeless individuals into library facilities has caused problems in the past and present. The relationship between libraries and the homeless will continue to be problematic as long as library facilities are used for purposes not intended or for services not reasonably available, and as long as legitimate needs of the homeless are not being met by other, more appropriate agencies in those communities.

This entry discusses homeless "problems" that relate to manifestations of those who are mentally ill, the misbehavior and conditions of certain individuals, and other problems typically created in libraries.

Manifestations of Those Who Are Mentally Ill

The estimated proportion of homeless people who are mentally ill ranges from about 33 percent to 40 percent. Of all the types of homeless patrons generating problems within the library, mentally ill clients typically cause the greatest concern—generating apprehension and uncertainty about how to respond, not only among other patrons but among staff as well. It is important to remember that there are many different types of mental illness, each of which poses a different level of risk in a library setting.

Low Risk. Neurotics include people with obsessive thoughts and compulsive behaviors. They may express a good deal of anxiety and seek an outlet for that anxiety in endlessly repeating specific compulsions, such as writing and leaving odd notes all over the library. They may be annoying nuisances but are unlikely to pose much risk to others. The same holds true for individuals who are mentally retarded, unless they become agitated (perhaps as a result of being teased or provoked). Usually just reassurance and guidance on the rules of the library are required.

Moderate Risk. Simple schizophrenics with delusional ideas or hallucinations may frighten others but generally tend to be loners and do not instigate violence. When upset, they may lose self-control and could accidentally harm themselves or others. The same is usually true of people with the lesser personality disorders, though when inebriated with alcohol or illegal drugs they have more potential for violent action in response to perceived threats, real or not. Having a backup staff person is a good idea when confronting such a case.

High Risk. Paranoid people, including paranoid schizophrenics, with their delusions of grandeur and persecution, can definitely pose a high risk. They may work other patrons or staff members into their delusional worlds as enemies whom they must attack first, fearing they themselves are under attack. Psychopaths and others with severe personality disorders may also become dangerous because they have little regard for who may be hurt in their wake and fail to respond realistically to the normal social forces that keep most people in line. A library staff member dealing with such an individual should alert library guards and/or police.

That said, it is important to realize and remember that just because an individual's appearance or manner may *seem* threatening does not necessarily mean the person is mentally ill. Furthermore, it does not necessarily mean he or she actually *is* a threat of any kind.

Misbehavior and Conditions Associated with Homelessness

Many homeless patrons use library facilities for years without causing any particular problems or requiring any special accommodations. However, some individuals (including those who are homeless) cause problems in libraries by panhandling, intimidation (intended and unintended) of employees or other patrons, overt harassment of staff or patrons, or other aggressive words or actions.

The belongings of many homeless individuals create special problems in libraries. Large bags or boxes (and even luggage) are often hauled around the building. These take up additional space in facilities that may already be crowded; furthermore, the belongings may present their own disagreeable smells and related hygiene problems. Since most libraries do not generally inspect a patron's belongings without cause, they likewise will not typically search the belongings of homeless individuals. With today's awareness of security issues (related to bombs, terrorism, etc.), containers with unknown contents may be presumed to be potential threats. Furthermore, belongings left unattended for any significant time may cause a hurried visit from fire or security officials (and even bomb squads). Libraries in Tacoma and Seattle are among those that have passed restrictions against "bedrolls, big boxes, or bulky bags" (Cronin 2002, 46).

Intimidation and harassment are typically reported when the homeless stare at employees or patrons (sometimes for hours at a stretch) or follow employees or patrons into the stacks or throughout the facility. There have even been cases of homeless individuals "stalking" library employees. Also reported are homeless individuals dominating the time and attention of employees or patrons or otherwise posing excessive demands on their services.

There are also reports of homeless patrons engaging in arguments (with one other or with other non-homeless patrons). Some of these exchanges escalate into actual fights, causing injuries. In 1998, one homeless man shot another, who ran inside the public library in Berkeley, California; the shooter followed and pointed his pistol at an employee before being arrested by police. The homeless shooter was a "regular" visitor to that facility.

America's Libraries and the Homeless

The American Library Association's fact sheet "America's Libraries and the Homeless," excerpted below, details how libraries are serving homeless patrons.

Promoting equal access to information for all people, including homeless and low-income people, is the number-one priority of the American Library Association (ALA).

Many librarians play a leadership role in addressing the problem of homelessness in their communities by working in cooperation with other agencies and by providing direct services such as special reading collections in shelters for the homeless, literacy programs and information and referral services.

Examples of how libraries serve the homeless:

- A "Street Card" listing services such as food, health, shelters, winter services, legal aide, welfare and employment was created by the Baltimore (Md.) County Public Library in cooperation with the Baltimore County Coalition for the Homeless.
- The Multnomah County Public Library in Portland, Ore., and Milwaukee (Wis.) Public Library received federal grants to create reading rooms in centers for the homeless.
- The San Francisco Public Library provides library cards to the homeless as well as those with permanent addresses. The library provides extensive programming for children, including storyhours and films, at city shelters for the homeless. The Free Library of Philadelphia operates a similar program.
- The Special Services and Manhattan branch offices of The New York Public Library operate projects for the homeless in welfare hotels, motels and day-care shelters. Services include special reading collections, educational and cultural programs, parenting workshops and volunteer readers who read stories to children.
- The Cumberland County Public Library in Fayetteville, N.C., operates an information and referral service, ACCESS, recognized as the central information and referral agency for the county. Many other libraries, including the San Diego Public Libraries and Memphis/Shelby County (Tenn.) Public Library and Information Center, operate referral services that aid the homeless.
- Many libraries, including the San Francisco and Milwaukee Public Libraries, sponsor or participate in literacy programs that benefit the homeless.

Source: "America's libraries and the homeless." (n.d.) American Library Association Fact Sheet. Retrieved October 17, 2003, from http://www.ala.org

Though apparently rare, there have even been library murders by a homeless person. In 1993, two librarians were murdered at the Sacramento Public Library by a homeless man, who was later killed by police when he aimed at them from the Central Library's rooftop.

Other Problems Related to Homeless People in Libraries

In a widely reported example in late 1984, the Ann Arbor (Michigan) Public Library instituted new policies with relatively comprehensive guidelines about various negative behaviors that would "interfere" with or "disturb" other patrons in their use of the facility. Various media accounts focused on the rules against offensive hygiene and sleeping, thereby framing the policies as crafted to exclude the homeless. The American Civil Liberties Union warned the library that such regulations could be discriminatory. Librarians from other systems expressed views on both sides of the matter: Some favored rules, others favored unrestricted access.

In mid-1987, the five-year-old central public library in Dallas made headlines with shocking statistics: From 100 to 200 homeless people were sitting or sleeping inside on moderate weather days, but often double those numbers did so in inclement weather. During its first year of operation, dozens of chairs had been ruined by stains and urine. The director was quoted as expressing concern over the rights of the homeless, but he also noted the serious problems caused by offensive smells, stains to furnishings, and related hygiene matters. Some fifteen years later, this library continued to report problems with homeless citizens using the facilities as "daily camping grounds and living quarters" ("Dallas Cracking Down on Homeless in Libraries" 2003). Similar problems with homeless in libraries were reported in many major U.S. cities during the 1980s and 1990s.

Why are these situations with homeless patrons in libraries considered problems? They significantly add to employee stress and complicate the working environment.

Dealing with the homeless daily tends to arouse negative feelings in employees, leading to high turnover or a decline in morale. . . . Listening to complaints about the homeless, yet being unable to do anything about them, is stressful. (Shuman 1996, 13)

Also, they may have the effect of "running off" other patrons who do comport themselves properly. Furthermore, there may be fears concerning public safety, such as possible infections and/or communicable diseases resulting from contact with the stains and residue. Finally, there are sufficient examples to establish actual or potential danger. However, it is important not to assume that a person is homeless simply because he or she is disheveled or carries many belongings. Conversely, a person may still be homeless even if he or she does not "look" that way. Appearances are often not the determining factor.

PROGRAMS AND APPROACHES FOR HELPING THE HOMELESS

"Promoting equal access to information for all people, including homeless and low-income people, is the number-one priority of the American Library Association (ALA)," according to the ALA's fact sheet "America's Libraries and the Homeless." The ALA's strongly stated position suggests that librarians work in cooperation with other agencies "and by providing direct services."

Referrals and Other Traditional Library Services

Assistance to any client group must logically be balanced by available resources, but most libraries already have services of particular benefit to the homeless. These services include special reading collections in shelters (e.g., in Tulsa City-County Library System in 1987 and by Portland's Multnomah County Public Library in 1988) and permitting homeless people to obtain library cards. In 1994, the Denver Central Library was registering homeless patrons by issuing borrower's cards if it could "confirm a shelter or even a temporary motel address." In 2002, the Los Angeles Public Library held a pilot program aimed at helping homeless children to familiarize them with available library services.

Some libraries provide traditional listening stations; others have videos available for viewing on the facilities' VCRs. DVDs and players are also accessible in some libraries.

Helpful services for the homeless include job placement information and referral, literacy assistance, and GED preparation and English as a Second Language (ESL) resources. Referrals to available community agencies can be valuable, especially information on the locations (and hours) of meals, showers, cots, and so on. It is important to update this information periodically, including any special requirements the agencies have for eligibility or access. In addition to referrals to services, some librarians have provided more specific assistance, including actual facilitation, transportation, or other direct help.

Computers and Internet Access

According to Urban Library Council estimates, about 90 percent of all U.S. urban libraries offer Internet access to the public.

> In these libraries is where the homeless are most often tapping into the Internet. . . . [This] has increased the popularity of the library as a refuge for the homeless. So the issue of the homeless accessing the Internet is inextricably tied to the larger issue of the homeless' use of the public library. (Montz 1996, para. 1)

Availability of computers—particularly for Internet access—has added a significant dimension to the services libraries offer to homeless patrons. In 1998, the Gates Library Foundation launched a $400 million commitment to provide computers to public libraries all over the nation. Billed as "the largest gift to U.S. public libraries since that of Andrew Carnegie," (Gordon et al. 2003, 44), as of 2004 the Gates program had brought computer systems into the majority of U.S. public libraries—donating a total of 40,000 computers since 1997 to some 10,000 facilities. The Gates program has focused on the needs of the disadvantaged, the "have-nots," and the impoverished. Even if the homeless are not named specifically, they certainly may be described in some of those groupings.

One notable homeless man named Kevin Michael Barbieux launched his own website, TheHomeless

Guy.net, which he reportedly started operating from the downtown Nashville Public Library in 2002. The site includes Barbieux's own "blog" (a web log or diary) and links to useful or interesting sites (including blogs written by other homeless people). Most libraries with technology centers (special areas for computers) also provide instruction and training classes for the public, including interested homeless patrons. Among popular recent Internet features are online games, instant messaging, chat rooms, blogs, online music, and even streaming video clips.

LIBRARY POLICIES

Undoubtedly the most significant legal case affecting U.S. library access policy is *Kreimer vs. Town of Morristown et al.* (1992).

Legal Issues and the Kreimer Case

Responding to complaints about homeless patrons in 1989, the Joint Free Library of Morristown, New Jersey, adopted policies specifying standards of behavior, dress, and hygiene. One of the alleged offenders, Richard Kreimer, was subsequently barred. The ACLU intervened on his behalf; the library's policies were modified, and Kreimer was readmitted. The library believed he still violated their rules, and Kreimer filed suit in 1990. Kreimer alleged the library's new policy discriminated against the homeless; in turn, the library alleged Kreimer's behavior and hygiene were too offensive.

In 1991, a U.S. District Court judge ruled the library had violated Kreimer's rights, in part because their policies were "unacceptably vague and overbroad." This ruling split the library profession: Part of the national association sided with Kreimer, even to the point of filing an amicus brief; the New Jersey state library association filed a brief supporting Morristown. Kreimer was interviewed on network television, and his story ran in prominent national publications.

The library appealed, and the court judgment for the plaintiff was overturned in 1992, when the appeals court ruled that the library's rules were constitutional. (However, the library's insurance carrier had already settled with Kreimer in the amount of $80,000. Among the issues raised by the Kreimer case were (1) access itself (as a First Amendment right); (2) possible discrimination against a defined group of people; and (3) whether employees might vary quality of services based on perceptions of the client's status.

Stuart Comstock-Gay, then executive director of the Maryland ACLU in Baltimore, reviewed the Kreimer case a couple of years later and offered the following conclusions (Comstock-Gay 1995, 33–35):

- Libraries "can and should" enact a code of conduct. The criteria are "conduct, or behavior, not appearance or speech." Libraries must let everyone know "what behavior is acceptable in your library and what behavior is unacceptable."

- Conduct rules "must be applied in a nondiscriminatory way."

- Objective "due process standards must be met in applying the conduct rules." Interpretations, where necessary, should be "based on what a reasonable person would consider" to be a violation.

- Any library limit on patrons' "right to receive information is on dangerous ground." Any rules "must meet important objectives of the library and must leave open alternative channels for receiving the library's information."

- Most anti-loitering laws "have been struck down across the country because they are unconstitutionally vague."

- Although the court "upheld rules banning odorous patrons . . . [libraries must] pass such rules carefully and apply them fairly."

- The emphasis in these rules is "conduct . . . protecting the patrons' right of access to information."

- The library rules should be "clearly posted or readily available in handouts."

Community Resources

Besides human resources, the library has facilities (space), furnishings, equipment, and materials of many types and formats. The extent (or limit) of these resources may affect the kinds of services a given library provides. But all services provided should be available to all patrons who abide by the policies.

The media may play a significant role in shaping public expectations. The image of the homeless is often characterized in extremes: either as aggressor (or even criminal)—suggesting stricter treatment, or given "victim" status—suggesting more library tolerance. Local governmental entities (city council, county commission, etc.) may have an impact on library policies, especially if the plight of the homeless becomes a campaign political issue or an administration's focus.

Other community factors come into play as well. For example, what is the local police department's approach to the homeless? Are they arrested for trespassing . . . or are they transported to shelters? How do library board trustees feel homeless patrons should be treated? As tax-supported entities, the library's policies should reflect the community's commitment to service and its compassion for those typically underserved; policies must also address legitimate complaints of employees and other patrons.

LIBRARY DILEMMA

Not all librarians (or citizens) agree about the proper roles for libraries in helping the homeless who enter their facilities. As librarian Jane Montz has said,

> Libraries must balance the rights of each individual to equal access with the right of the public to a library which is free to carry out its primary mission. Today's urban library must continually balance the rights of the homeless to equal access against the rights of the other patrons who object to the drain on library resources created when the homeless take up residence in the library. (Montz 1996, para. 3).

To help librarians take up this challenge, the ALA has several entities that focus on needs of the homeless. These include the Hunger, Homelessness, and Poverty Task Force of the Social Responsibilities Round Table, and the Subcommittee on Library Services to Poor and Homeless People of the Office for Literacy and Outreach Services, among others.

In 1989, one library (in Haverhill, Massachusetts) had widely reported plans for a special homeless room as part of its projected $5.7 million construction project. While this is occasionally still cited as fact, the room itself was not included in the Library's project—completed in 1997—for funding reasons (among other considerations).

What would result from further library involvement, such as the creation of a "homeless room"? Would more "direct" library involvement lessen the problems caused (in libraries) by some homeless? Or would it merely place greater demands on the staff and dilute the library's purpose (and resources)?

What may libraries reasonably expect of the homeless? No more and no less than other patrons. Homeless individuals should obey library policies and follow standard procedures; they should exhibit civil and sane behavior with employees and other patrons; their hygiene must meet certain reasonable requirements for the health and safety of employees and other patrons.

RECOMMENDATIONS FOR THE FUTURE

Libraries must avoid extremes in their policy, enforcement, services, and treatment of homeless patrons. Libraries must not have discriminatory policies that focus on appearance or perceived attitudes of patrons; must not invoke excessive restrictions on practices of homeless; must not strictly enforce regulations (even those that are reasonable) against homeless, while ignoring similar conditions among other patrons. Conversely, libraries must not ignore the effects of improper behavior or hygiene by the homeless, when it creates an unsatisfactory environment for the safety and comfort of other patrons. Libraries must not allow any "group" of patrons (including the homeless) to seem to "take over" the facility or run roughshod over employees. Libraries should not allow a situation to develop where most "other" patrons cease their use of the facility because of a clientele that seems prevalent.

The best route is for libraries to have reasonable, clear, specific, legal policies in place (for patron behavior, conduct, apparel, hygiene, belongings, etc.); apply these policies fairly, to all patrons, regardless of their perceived status; and equip employees with information and training necessary to ensure reasonable consistency of treatment for all

patrons. Furthermore, libraries would be wise to establish (or reinforce) contact with appropriate community service agencies that could provide direct services to the homeless and try to get representatives of those agencies to visit the library periodically to distribute information about their services and even to make contact with library patrons known to be homeless.

—Jeffrey L. Salter and Charles A. Salter

Further Reading

Abramson, I. (2003, January). A haven for homeless kids. *School Library Journal, 49*(1), 41.

America's libraries and the homeless. (n.d.). American Library Association Fact Sheet. Retrieved October 17, 2003, from http://www.ala.org

Comstock-Gay, S. (1995, February). Disruptive behavior: Protecting people, protecting rights. *Wilson Library Bulletin, 69*(6), 33–35.

Cronin, B. (2002, November 15). What a library is not. *Library Journal, 127*(19), 46.

Dallas cracking down on homeless in libraries. (2003, October 17). *Library Journal.* Retrieved October 17, 2003 from http://www.libraryjournal.com

Eberhart, G. M. (1998, September). Pistol-wielding man gives Berkeley PL a scare. *American Libraries, 29*(8), 16.

Furtado, C. (2002, December 23). For homeless, the Internet is a link to jobs and loved ones. *Miami Herald*, p. 1-A.

Gaughan, T. M. (1991, October). Morristown PL homeless case generates nationwide attention. *American Libraries, 22*(9), 830–831.

Gordon, A. C., Gordon, M. T., Moore, E., & Heuertz, L. (2003, March 1). The Gates legacy. *Library Journal, 128*(4), 44–48.

Grace, P. (2000, May). No place to go (except the public library). *American Libraries, 31*(5), 53–55.

Haverhill's library plus. (1989, January 29). *Boston Globe*, p. A-22.

Homeless man's stalking results in action against employer. (2000, June). *Library Administrator's Digest, 35*(6), 42.

Jacobson, S. (1987, June 8). Library attracts homeless: Street people napping, washing at downtown facility. *The Dallas Morning News*, p. 1-A.

Kornblum, J. (2002, October 3). A homeless guy finds a refuge on the Internet. *USA Today*, p. 10-D.

Kreimer vs. Town of Morristown et al, 958 F2d. 1242 (3d Cir.), 1992.

Libraries facing up to reality: homeless, restroom users, violence pose challenges. (1996, January 7). *The Dallas Morning News*, p. 1-A.

Martinez, M., & Sjostrom, J. (1995, March 5). Homeless find refuge in public libraries. *Chicago Tribune*, p. 1 (Metro).

McCook, K. (2000, May). Ending the isolation of poor people.

American Libraries, 31(5), 45.

Montz, J. (1996). *Internet Access for the Homeless.* Retrieved October 7, 2003, from http://www.nortropic.com/lis341 /jmontz/access.htm

Morris, E. (1987, June 24). Dealing with "problem patrons"— Public library faces persistent dilemma. *Atlanta Constitution*, p. 1-C.

Pearson, L. R. (1988, April). Public libraries find ways to serve urban homeless. *American Libraries, 19*(4), 250–252.

Responding to homeless, Tacoma PL limits packages. (2002, May 30). *Library Journal.* Retrieved November 3, 2003, from http://www.libraryjournal.com

Salter, C. A., & Salter, J. L. (1988). *On the frontlines: Coping with the library's problem patrons.* Englewood, CO: Libraries Unlimited.

Salter, C. A., & Salter, J. L. (1996). Mentally ill patrons. In B. McNeil & D. J. Johnson (Eds.), *Patron behavior in libraries: A handbook of positive approaches to negative situations* (pp. 18–43). Chicago: American Library Association.

Schneider, C. (2003, March 15). Nowhere to call home: Marietta's library is a warm, familiar place to the homeless, and here they rub shoulders with regular folks. *Atlanta Journal-Constitution*, p. H-1.

Scott, J. (1993, August 10). No longer a refuge for readers: Libraries are trying off-duty police, security cameras to counter rising crime. *Los Angeles Times*, p. A-1.

Serving the homeless in Denver. (1995, April). *Library Administrator's Digest, 30*(4), 27.

Shuman, B. A. (1996). Down and out in the reading room: The homeless in the public library. In B. McNeil & D. J. Johnson (Eds.), *Patron behavior in libraries: A handbook of positive approaches to negative situations* (pp. 3–17). Chicago: American Library Association.

Silver, J. (1996, Winter). Libraries and the homeless: caregivers or enforcers. *The Katharine Sharp Review, No. 2.* Retrieved October 7, 2003 from http://alexia.lis.uiuc.edu

Simmons, R.C. (1985, Fall). The homeless in the public library: Implications for access to libraries. *Reference Quarterly 25*, 110–120.

Smelly people barred from Ann Arbor PL. (1985, February 1). *Library Journal, 110*, 19.

12 ways libraries are good for the country. (1995, December). *American Libraries, 26*(11), 1113–1119.

Two librarians slain at Sacramento PL. (1993, June). *Wilson Library Bulletin, 67*(10), 20.

▣ LIMINALITY

Liminality, a term borrowed from cultural anthropology, refers to various states of passage through which designated members of a culture travel at specified times of transition. For the duration of passage, such people are "betwixt and between," suspended between the old roles they leave behind and the yet-to-be-shouldered demands of a new identity. Occupying no fixed position, they are considered dangerous, and special precautions are taken to segregate them from ordinary social life. Deputized guides are provided to expedite the transition process and serve as mentors.

THE EXPERIENCE OF LIMINALITY

In traditional societies, initiation rites exemplify ceremonies of liminality. But many cultures make similar provisions for other critical transition periods, such as entering marriage, assuming leadership, taking religious vows, apprenticing in a profession. Even in their modern embodiments, a number of distinctive features are apparent. Such passages are usually undertaken in secret or ritually segregated settings, entail taxing ordeals, and are supervised by expert guides. During this time, the usual social markers of distinction are erased — a "leveling" process that, along with the experience of shared suffering, encourages intense and enduring bonds of solidarity among initiates. But no matter how rigorous the ordeal or sublime the camaraderie experienced en route, the expectation is that the initiate will return to ordinary life and take on new responsibilities.

In a more extended sense, the distinctive blend of peril and privilege that liminality offers may apply to people who voluntarily remove themselves from the sway of convention for a time. Pilgrimages, religious revivals, secular festivals, even wilderness treks and corporate retreats: Participants in all of these briefly suspend responsibility and court uncertainty; all do so with the expectation of a return to normality. Crises, too, may usher in liminal periods. Consider the suspension of routine that follows natural disasters (epidemics, floods), civil disturbances (wars or revolutions), or private misfortunes (a death in the family). Finally, sociologists remind us that the experience of illness may be exploited (consciously or not) for its liberating potential in relieving the afflicted person from the demands of ordinary life.

All such states share a few core elements: suspension of the rule of the commonplace; mixing with unfamiliar others in strange settings and often mobile circumstances; and a heightened sense of uncertainty, of things being unfinished. It is this last property of indeterminacy—the fact that the process sometimes takes place without experienced guides in poorly marked and badly mapped territory—that makes liminality relevant to students of homelessness.

On occasion liminality stalls, the return fails to take place as projected, and the transitional period becomes extended. Should this persist, the built-in expectation of a return (on the part of both voyager and awaiting community) can weaken, eventually giving way to a routinization of the displacement itself. A kind of forgetfulness sets in: The tug of broken ties and foregone appointments weakens and the becalmed voyager finds a substitute normalcy beckoning. This was precisely the concern of critics who warned of the "demoralizing" effects of municipal lodging houses on the newly unemployed of the Progressive Era and, later, of researchers who charted the hazards of "shelterization" in the congregate relief warehouses of the Great Depression. In each case, the worry was that what had begun as a moratorium on business as usual had been transformed into a way of life in its own right. Nor were these unprecedented concerns.

In the momentous dislocations of the late Middle Ages, for example, various outlaw groups were able to contrive a livelihood out of the rigors of social ostracism. In the process, what began as haphazard makeshifts were transformed into durable institutions. The Franciscans and other mendicant orders trace their origins in this fashion: Begun as protest movements against the extravagances of the established church, they were eventually institutionalized (and co-opted) as part of its official embrace of the doctrine of poverty. More colorful still, the bands of "wandering scholars" who traversed the circuit of monasteries in the fourteenth century managed to turn liturgical mischief into an unruly livelihood, performing ribald parodies of ecclesiastic hymns in exchanges for a night's lodging and meal (Waddell 1961/1927). (Eventually, an unamused church hierarchy cracked down on the practice.) Gypsies over the ages have survived on the edges and in the interstices of settled life.

When displacement is routinized, but the sense of being suspended betwixt and between endures, liminality becomes a social and cultural *limbo*. Traditionally, that term refers to the celestial holding mechanism invented by Catholic theologians as a necessary adjunct to the doctrine of redemption. (Limbo was reserved for those souls born too early in history— righteous pagans—or dying too early in life—unbaptized infants—to be held accountable to the test of confessing Christ as savior.) Unlike stalled liminality that manages to invent a socially acceptable alternative destination, limbo describes a state of suspended resolution, an anomalous way station for those with nowhere else to go. Downsized corporate executives embody a "living contradiction" of the American promise: talented managers out of work. Unless comparable positions open up in the market or in public employ, their predicament may persist without ever being resolved—they remain in "limbo."

OTHER POSSIBILITIES

Liminality intersects with homelessness when the dislocations occur at critical transitions, like the move of single mothers to set up independent households. But liminality also opens two other possibilities. First, it can give birth to new livelihoods. What begins as a way station en route to established roles can be institutionalized, in the process becoming part of the abeyance process proper. This institutionalization may happen directly, as with the normalization of the extended unemployment of the high school adolescent; or at one remove, as with the burgeoning not-for-profit shelter and service industry established to manage homelessness as a durable social problem. Second, although liminal passage is usually undertaken for specific reasons, in known territory, with every expectation of return, that cultural process may be upset and the markers dislodged. When that happens, the stage is set for forced improvisation. In America in the late twentieth century, life-course transitions in general have become more individualized, less bound to strategic family decisions, less subject to custom's scripting.

As liminality become riskier and more easily derailed, its casualties may find their way into the ranks of the officially homeless.

—*Kim Hopper and Jim Baumohl*

Further Reading

Jusserand, J. J. (1920). *English wayfaring as a way of life in the Middle Ages,* rev. ed. London: Ernest Benn.

Modell, J. (1989). *Into one's own: From youth to adulthood in the United States, 1920–1975.* Berkeley: University of California Press.

Ringenbach, P. T. (1973). *Tramps and reformers, 1873–1916.* Westport, CT: Greenwood.

Turner, V. (1974). *Dramas, fields, and metaphors.* Ithaca, NY: Cornell University Press.

Turner, V. (1985). *On the edge of the bush.* Tucson: University of Arizona Press.

Waddell, H. (1961). *The wandering scholars.* New York: Doubleday. (Originally published 1927)

▣ LITERATURE, HOBO AND TRAMP

The literature of the hobo and tramp, and of the homeless in general, is rich and varied, featuring the work of some of America's greatest authors—Jack London, Stephen Crane, Theodore Dreiser—as well as lesser-known writers such as Tom Kromer. The great theme, or tension, of the literature about homelessness is the conflict between the romantic appeal of the road and the brutal realities of the vagabond life. Indeed, all of the authors discussed here can be placed along this continuum.

There are other related tensions as well. Writings about rural homelessness tend to be romanticized, while those of the urban homeless tend toward social realism. Some writers happened to be homeless themselves, while others became homeless in order to write about their experiences. In general, writers who were "indigenously" hoboes or homeless, such as Kromer, do little to portray their experiences in any sort of romantic fashion, while those who have chosen homelessness, like London, bring a sense of hope and adventure to their accounts—a veneer that inevitably wears thin, however, with the length of time spent on the margins.

ROMANCE OF THE FRONTIER

Oh highway . . . you express me
better than I can express myself!

—"Song of the Open Road,"
Walt Whitman (*Leaves of Grass,* 1855)

Leaves of Grass was published just a decade before the tramp and hobo era began in earnest after the Civil War. In *Leaves*—"I inhale great draughts of space/ The east and west are mine, and north and/the south are mine"—Whitman celebrates the second chance of the New World, the "free original life there . . . simple diet and clean and sweet blood . . . litheness, majestic faces, clear eyes and perfect physique there . . . immense spiritual results." In the 1860s and 1870s, the simultaneous opening of the Western frontier, growth of the railroad, and rapid transition of the United States from an agricultural to an industrial economy created a volatile society which, in the words of the historian Stephan Thernstrom, made "a hero of the man on the road, heading for the Great West or the Great City" (Thernstrom 1964).

Although Whitman wrote only incidentally about tramping, his free-roaming, liberated spirit hovers over virtually all later writings about the itinerant life, from the tramp letters of William Aspinwall to Jack Kerouac's *On the Road.* Even when the monotony and brutality of the vagabond experience sets in, that spirit often survives. William Aspinwall, a Civil War veteran and longtime tramp, was among the first to file literary dispatches from tramp world. He was commissioned in this exercise by John McCook, a rector and instructor in foreign languages at Trinity College in Connecticut, who published a series of letters from Aspinwall in 1901 and 1902. While Aspinwall decries his periods of intemperance and describes the dangers of riding the rails, he largely champions the freedoms of the vagabond life and its natural pleasures. In words sometimes oddly spelled, he is more likely than not to defend his ilk:

It is all very well for . . . member of Congress to abuse us as idle drifters and drunken bums and hobos. . . . You must remember our vocation is somewhat exciting, but not pleasant, ennobling nor renumerative . . . Often I have heard professional men say what does the hobo know about work. About as much or more than the proffessional men at the same time. (Aspinwall in an entry dated 1890–1826)

A series of early writers softened the public image of tramps and hoboes for a concerned public. As a recent Princeton graduate, Walter Wykoff described his experiences as an unemployed laborer in a beautifully written two-part volume, *The Workers: A Study in Reality* (1897, 1899). In it, he identifies with, and describes, the itinerant class. William Dean Howells, the influential editor of the *Atlantic,* wrote a series of novels—*The Undiscovered Country* (1880), *The Minister's Charge* (1887), *A Hazard of New Fortunes* (1890), *A Traveler from Altruria* (1894)—depicting the descent of middle-class people into homelessness, or encounters with beggars which call into question bourgeois assumptions about the deserving and undeserving poor. Josiah Flynt, himself a hobo, wrote a series of essays anthologized into *Tramping with Tramps* (1899), the first direct accounts of the vagabond life that were widely read. While deeply ambivalent about his subject—Flynt injects a tone of nagging moralism throughout—these were among the first popular accounts that were informed by actual experience of tramping, and in that manner served to ease the public's paranoia about the violent capacities of the homeless class.

Jack London was the first prominent writer to be smitten by the allure of the roaming life. In *The Road,* he describes a chance meeting, while swimming, with a group of "Road Kids." The almost foreign language they spoke, and the apparent lack of rules by which they lived, fascinated him. He quickly joined them and immediately aspired to be a "Profesh," a professional tramp, whom he believed to be

Catching Your First Train

One time in a bar, under the Truman Street Bridge, I got the idea that I wanted to catch a train. I didn't care where it went, I just wanted some adventure in my life before I got too old to get around. It just so happened that a main line was less than 500 feet away from the bar's door. It was around midnight, and I was pretty liquored up, so when I made the final decision to catch a train, I didn't have far to go.

Sitting at the bar, half listening to what was going on around me, and half to a train horn that might blow at any time, I finally heard it. The blowing of an air horn telling me that a train was coming down the tracks. I quickly finished my beer and then went outside. I never took a thought at what I might do, when I got to where I was going, if I got there at all. The "Jug Of Youth And Courage" told me I could make it anywhere! Hadn't I watched the trains from my Spruce Tree? And after my studying the trains for as long as I did, with my friends Mogan David, and Jim Beam, didn't I know everything there was to know about how trains moved? After all I had even seen some hoboes do it. Right! Besides the caged beast of travel was wanting to get out.

I waited in the shadows of the alley behind the bar as the Mars Light of the lead unit passed by me. The roaring of the big diesel engines and the squealing of the brakes and the sounds of the tracks, clack-clack! Clack-clack! made my heart pump faster. Just the idea of adventure gave me a rush. All this power that was passing me by, and I was going to harness it, by riding it. The train was doing around 20 mph when I decided to make my move. All I had to do was run along it, grab the ladder and pull myself up. Right? I ran as fast as I could alongside the train, and for a brief moment I thought that I was matching the speed of the boxcar. I grabbed for a run on its ladder.

Wake Up Call! I was thrown about 15 feet away. But I wasn't the kind of person to give up. After the third time of eating ballast, and getting my arms nearly jerked out of their sockets I figured that I would try it again another day. In retrospect I'm glad that I was thrown away from the train instead of under it. It was a few years later when I was to try and this time succeed in riding a train.

Source: Arkansas Traveler. Personal communication to David Levinson, March 9, 2002.

"the aggressive men, the primoridial noblemen, the blond beasts so beloved of Nietzche" (1970, 173). Throughout *The Road,* London contrasts the tough, daring Frontier West with the pallid, effete East. He sums up his adventure:

> I lay on my back with a newspaper under my back for a pillow. Above me the stars were winking and wheeling in squadrons back and forth as the train rounded curves, and watching them, I fell asleep. The day was done—one day of all my days. Tomorrow would be another day and I was young.

Jim Tully, one of the best known of the tramp memoirists, wrote first in *Beggars of Life* (1924,

11–12) about the harshness of his experience: "At times I cursed the wanderlust that held me in its grip," he wrote, but then added, " . . . while cursing, I loved it. For it gave me freedom undreamed of in factories." He characterized his first two weeks on the road: "I was going somewhere. Over to the next valley were life and dreams and hope. Monotony and the wretched routines of the drab Ohio town would be unknown. I was at last on the road to high adventure."

FOLKLORE OF THE ROAD

While little documentary evidence of the folklore of hobo life endures, it was a vital part of the enduring appeal of the road. Many hoboes and tramps were self-styled poets and raconteurs who told tall tales, recited lyrics, and sang songs in camps, boxcars, and "hobo jungles." According to Richard Wormser, many hoboes knew the poems of Kipling and Tennyson by heart. Harry Kemp, who carried a copy of Keats with him everywhere, became famous as the "tramp poet," a career he fashioned out of his early itinerant life. Many of the poems and songs shared by hoboes were about the idyllicized pleasures of hobo life, smoking and eating, sitting around the campfire, camaraderie on the road, and riding the rails, as conveyed in the titles of popular songs: "One More Train to Ride," "Sitting Around Our Little Fires," "The Last Hobo," "Early Morning Train," and "Catchin' Out for Freedom."

In addition, many hoboes were self-educated, widely read in politics and economics, and particularly well-versed in Karl Marx and other socialist writers. The political leanings of many hoboes were capitalized upon by radical labor unions, such as the Industrial Workers of the World, founded in 1905. By 1910, the I.W.W, or "Wobblies," began an aggressive campaign to recruit hoboes to their cause. Among their recruiting techniques were street theater and labor songs. Members of the I.W.W. included talented songwriters such as Joe Hill, T-Bone Slim, and Ralph Chaplin. These songs were collected in *The Little Red Song Book,* which at the height of the Wobblies' influence was carried by hobos all over the West. The most popular ballad of all was "Hallelujah, I'm a Bum."

> Oh why don't you work
> Like other men do.
> How the hell can I work
> When there's no work to do?
> Hallelujah, I'm a bum.
> Hallelujah, bum again.
> Hallelujah, give us a handout
> To revive us again.
>
> —Kornbluth 1964

Other musical forms, such as railroad work songs like *Casey Jones* and *John Henry,* became part of the hobo tradition. The blues also captured the African-American experience, particularly the journey from the rural south to the industrial north. Important artists were Robert Johnson, Lightning Hopkins, and Blind Lemon Jefferson, who himself was at times homeless, and reportedly died of exposure in Chicago in 1929.

In 1915, when Joe Hill was executed for killings to which he was never legitimately linked, his legend, and the legend of the Wobbly protest songs, was sealed. Hill's most enduring song was "The Preacher and the Slave," which lambasted the hypocrisy of the missions that served the homeless in exchange for their conversion to Christianity:

> Long-haired preachers come out every night
> Try to tell you what's wrong and what's right
> But when asked how 'bout something to eat
> They will answer you in voices so sweet.
> You will eat by and by,
> In that glorious land above the sky;
> Work and pray, live on hay
> You'll get pie in the sky when you die.
>
> —Hill 1996, 36

BITTER EXPERIENCE

A darker vision of the itinerant life was informed by a near endless tide of newspaper articles during the depressions of the 1870s and 1890s, when the numbers of tramps and hoboes grew into the millions.

Their headlines, a mixture of fact and fiction, decried the "Tramp Menace" and portrayed tramps and hoboes as violent, lazy, and ready to riot and pillage at any moment. Yale professor Francis Wayland famously called the tramp a "lazy, shiftless, sauntering or swaggering, ill-conditioned, irreclaimable, incorrigible, cowardly, utterly depraved savage" (Wayland 1877, 113).

While these demonizing characterizations were used, more often than not, to fuel the flames of popular hysteria and sell newspapers, the more difficult realities of the homeless life began to appear in the homeless literature of the twentieth century.

Even Jack London, reflecting on his sojourn as a tramp in his essay "What Life Means to Me" (1905), soberly characterized his experience in terms far different from the larger-than-life, heroic visions of *The Road:*

> I became a tramp. . . . I was down in the cellar of society, down in the subterranean depths of misery about which it is neither nice nor proper to speak. I was in the pit, the abyss, the human cesspool, the shambles and charnel-house of our civilization. This is the part of the edifice of society that society chooses to ignore.

Theodore Dreiser employed his own experience of near homelessness—down and out as a young man, he was a resident at the Mills Hotel, a New York City lodging house—to inform his description of one man's fall into homelessness and despair in his 1901 masterpiece *Sister Carrie*. George Hurstwood, through a series of disastrous but quite ordinary missteps, falls from being a complacent member of the professional class to being unemployed. In a meticulous and brutal social realist style, Dreiser dissects Hurstwood's new existence as a denizen of Bowery flophouses and soup lines, and then his eventual suicide. Hurstwood's tragedy is particularly unsettling because it shows how the comfortable bourgeois world and the abyss he eventually occupies are not far removed from one another. Two short pieces of journalism by Stephen Crane explore the grim truths of typical Bowery scenes. Published in the *New York Press* in 1894, "An Experiment in Misery" depicts a night in a flophouse. In "The Men in the Storm" (1894), a crowd

of anonymous men stand in a blizzard waiting for a shelter's doors to open.

The preeminent example of "native" homeless writing is Tom Kromer, whose writing and life are shrouded in mystery. Kromer was a homeless man who produced one book, *Waiting for Nothing* (1935), which was championed by Dreiser, and an unfinished novel. Each chapter of *Waiting for Nothing* describes a different aspect of homeless life, each more brutal than the last: illness, insanity, the bread line, the flophouse, death on the rails. The tone of the book is set by its dedication: "To Jolene, who turned off the gas." With a realistic, minimalist style worthy of Samuel Beckett, *Waiting for Nothing* represents the harrowing antithesis of Whitman's poetic raptures. Here Kromer describes a winter day:

> It snows. It melts as it hits, and the slush is inches thick on the pavement. The soles of my shoes are loose. The right one flops up and down as I walk. This morning I tied it to the toe of my shoe with a string, but the string wore through in an hour. Tomorrow I will tie it up with a piece of wire. It will stay a week if I tie it up with a piece of wire. My shoes are filled with water. I can feel it oozing through my toes as I walk. I walk and I can see the bubbles slosh from the soles. I am chilled to the bone. I pull my coat collar up around my ears, but it does no good. The chill comes from my soggy feet and the wind that howls around the corners. Besides, my coat is thin. I bummed it from an undertaker. The stiff that owned it croaked in the park with T.B. There's still a smudge of blood on the sleeves from the hemorrhage. I could have had his pants and shoes, too, but they were worse than mine. This coat is my Christmas present. For this is Christmas Eve. (1935, 77)

MID- TO LATE-TWENTIETH CENTURY WRITERS

Varying aspects of homelessness in the last half of the twentieth century are described by Ralph Ellison's *Invisible Man* (1952), Dorothy Day's *Long Loneliness* (1972), and Joseph Mitchell's *Joe Gould's Secret* (1965). Recent books that capture the greater diversity of homelessness in the 1980s and 1990s are Ted Conover's *Rolling Nowhere* (1984), Lars Eighner's *Travels with Lisbeth* (1993),

Lee Stringer's *Grand Central Winter* (1998), Colum McCann's *This Side of Brightness* (1998), and Nathaniel Lachenmeyer's *The Outsider* (2000). Conover describes the remnants of hobo railroad culture, Stringer and Eighner the realities of addiction and homelessness, McCann the lives of people living in the tunnels under Manhattan. Lachenmeyer, who retraced the steps of his mentally ill father, captures the nature of having a severe psychiatric illness and being homeless in the era of deinstitutionalization.

REALISM AND ROMANCE

The themes of realism and romance have competed throughout the history of writings about homelessness in America. These themes are captured most poignantly in the most famous of all Western hobo ballads, "The Big Rock Candy Mountain," which depicts a wanderer's vision of heaven and imparts equally both the hope and the brutality of life on the road:

In the Big Rock Candy Mountain

You never change your socks

And little streams of alcohol

Came a-trickling down the rocks

The boxcars are all empty

And the railroad bulls are blind

There's a lake of stew and whiskey too

You can paddle all around 'em in a big canoe

In the Big Rock Candy Mountain.

—*Charles Barber*

Further Reading

Allsop, K. (1967). *Hard travellin': The hobo and his history:* New York: New American Library.

Aspinwall, W., to J. McCook (1895). *The social reform papers of John James McCook.* Hartford, CT: The Antiquarian and Landmarks Society.

Bruns, R. A. (1980). *Knights of the road: A hobo history.* New York: Methuen.

Crane, S. (2000). *Maggie: A girl of the streets and other tales of New York.* New York: Penguin Books.

Dreiser, T. (1900). *Sister Carrie.* Boston: Houghton Mifflin.

Kornbluth, J. L. (1964). *Rebel voices: An I. W. W. anthology.* Ann Arbor: University of Michigan Press.

Kromer, T. (1986). *Waiting for nothing and other writings* (A. D. Casciato & J. L. West III, Eds.). Athens: University of Georgia Press.

Kusmer, K. L. (2002). *Down and out, on the road: The homeless in American history.* New York: Oxford University Press.

Lomax, A., & Lomax, J. A. (1934). *American ballads and folk songs.* New York: Macmillan.

London, J. (1909). *Revolution and other essays.* New York: Macmillan.

London, J. (1970). *The road.* (Introduction by K. Hendricks.) Santa Barbara, CA and Salt Lake City, UT: Peregrine.

McCook, J. J. (1890–1926). *The social reform papers of John James McCook.* Available on Microform in Yale University Library.

Songs from the *Little Red Book Song Book.* http://www.bloomington.in.us/~mitch/iww/lrs.html

Thernstrom, S. (1964). *Poverty and progress.* Cambridge, MA: Harvard University Press.

Tully, J. (1924). *Beggars of Life.* New York: Grosset & Dunlap.

Wayland, F. (1877). *The tramp question: Conference of boards of public charities proceedings.*

Wormser, R. (1994). *Hoboes: Wandering in America, 1870–1940.* New York: Walker.

Wykoff, W. (1897). *The workers: A study in reality: The east.* New York: Scribner's.

Wykoff, W. (1898). *The workers: A study in reality: The west.* New York: Scribner's.

▣ LITERATURE ON HOMELESSNESS

See Appendix 1: Bibliography of Autobiographical and Fictional Accounts of Homelessness; Appendix 4: Documentary History of Homelessness; Autobiography and Memoir, Contemporary Homeless; Images of Homelessness in Nineteenth- and Twentieth-Century American Literature; Literature, Hobo and Tramp; Media

▣ LONDON

The United Kingdom is a welfare state, and discussions of the causes of homelessness in London are generally framed by a debate over two welfare regimes (1979–1997 and 1997–2002). This is because the ideological shifts from Conservative to Labour governments have a significant impact on the

Applying to Be Registered as Homeless in London

To create a book that newcomers to London could use as a bible to understanding a complex city, John Grounds edited London: A Living Guide *(1990). Grounds was especially concerned about what he termed "rocketing" homelessness and vagrancy and included an extensive chapter on housing options in London. Below are excerpts from the information provided about applying to be "registered" as homeless in London.*

If you are a single person without children or a couple without children you have very little chance of being housed by the council unless you have special needs (see below).

If you are homeless or about to become so go to your local Homeless Persons Unit at the council Housing Department or ring Housing Advice Switchboard.

You are considered to be homeless if you are at the present time without a home or if you are threatened with being in that situation within twenty-eight days.

If it is agreed that you satisfy the conditions listed in the Homeless Persons Act, the local council has a duty to find you accommodation. . . .

If you are coming out of hospital or prison, a social worker or probation officer should help you apply to the council.

It is necessary to satisfy *all* the following conditions in order to be legally homeless.

1. You must be considered to have a "priority need." In order to satisfy this condition you must fit into one of the following categories.

   You or someone you live with have children aged under 16.

   You are a pregnant woman.

   You have an elderly or disabled dependant.

   You are an elderly or disabled or mentally ill person.

   You have been made homeless by an emergency such as fire or flood.

Victims of domestic violence or victims of sexual exploitation especially women, who have been forced to move out of their home, even if they are not theoretically 'homeless,' are also usually treated as homeless by the council. The usual course of action is for such people to be referred to a refuge.

2. You must not be intentionally homeless. If you are considered to be "intentionally homeless,' that is you have left accommodation of your own accord and not for one of the reasons listed in the Act, or have been asked to leave for such things as nonpayment of rent, the council is only likely to give you temporary accommodation.

3. You must normally live in the area to which you are applying for accommodation or have some direct local connection.

If you fulfill *all* these conditions you *must* be offered accommodation by the council. If you only satisfy one or two, you might only be given advice on finding somewhere to live. . . .

If you are a refugee, you may well qualify as homeless but you will need to contact one of the specialist advice agencies listed in this chapter.

If a council home is not available immediately, as is quite likely to be the case, you may be put into temporary accommodation such as a bed and breakfast hotel, hostel or house waiting for improvements to be made.

Source: Grounds, John. (Ed.). (1990). *London: A Living Guide* (pp. 212–213). London: Unwin Paperbacks.

levels of provision for the homeless. These changes also influence the conceptualization and interpretation of the causes of homelessness.

Under both regimes, the causes of homelessness in London have been largely linked to *structural issues,* that is, poverty, unemployment, and a shortage of affordable housing. While this linkage is well-documented and rooted in the dominant research tradition, surprisingly little systematic work has been conducted to explore the effects of structural issues on the rates of homelessness (see Kemp, Lynch, and Mackay, 2001).

EARLY RESEARCH

The earliest research into the causes of homelessness in London was initiated by the London City Council (1961) in response to an increase in assistance appli-

An Encounter with a Homeless Girl in Central London, circa 1990

The deep hollow pull of the wind was something different that night, whispering on every rough mortared ledge and tossing the tops of the plane trees in the Embankment Gardens, their bright patchy bark just visible in the dusk. I picked up my step, down Villiers Street on the east side of Charing Cross Station.

Under the sounds of the city, out of the darkness, a soft voice caught me, "Can you . . ." It trailed away, and I stopped, so startled that I forgot my mission. At first I couldn't see, but as I stepped out of the light from the Strand I saw a dark doorway, dull brass knocker long unused. There, in the shadows, with her long print skirt making a pattern over the steps, sat a young woman. Her eyes were still and steady, and she had a tiny red stone set into her nose, blond hair cut at chin level. Her face was round and soft, very pale, and she had those rosy English cheeks that undo the dignity of young solicitors and stockbrokers.

I never gave money to beggars. I knew the drill, from travel books, but it was really because I was so short of money myself, carefully counting out enough for bus fares and babysitters, and adding up items as I went through the grocery store to make sure I would have enough not to have to put things back after my bill was rung up. Things were getting worse now, too, with mortgage rates sky high and the children needing shoes every six weeks.

But something about this woman-child stopped me cold. She was in such an impossible spot, not up by the station where there were plenty of people in a hurry, people with guilty consciences, perhaps, for profiting under Maggie Thatcher while homeless people reappeared on London's streets. She didn't seem to know the basic rule of real estate: location, location, location. She was so very young.

I shifted the bag of bread and found my purse. I began to pluck out a pound but found myself tipping the wallet over, into my hand, and then leaning forward to pour all of it, every penny, into her cautiously outstretched hand.

She breathed a husky "thank you," and looked down at her hands, now resting together in her lap, holding the change. I smiled awkwardly. I had to go. I couldn't linger, and I didn't know what to say.

Source: Christensen, Karen. *A Smaller Circle.* Unpublished account.

cations (see Pleace and Quilgars, 2003). In 1948, the Council became responsible for welfare support, including rehousing homeless people, but as Nicholas Pleace and Deborah Quilgars (2003) report, research findings and lobbying efforts caused homelessness to be redefined as a housing issue and no longer directly tied to welfare as before. As a result, Local Authorities received statutory responsibility to house homeless people under the Homeless Persons Act (1977).

DEFINING HOMELESSNESS

In the United Kingdom and in London, homelessness is defined in statute. However, because a wide range of personal circumstances may result in homelessness, no single definition has been employed in the literature. In fact, the bulk of research on homelessness goes beyond the legal definition and includes a combination of the following: (a) rooflessness (i.e., street homelessness, also called "rough sleeping");

(b) living in an emergency or temporary accommodation for homeless people (i.e., hostels or night shelters); (c) living long-term (a year or more) in an institution because no other accommodation is available; (d) living in a bed-and-breakfast or similar accommodation that is an expensive solution to housing homeless people; (e) living informally with friends, or under notice to quit, or squatting; (f) living in intolerable physical conditions, including overcrowding, sharing sleeping arrangements, or not actually having a bed to sleep on; and (g) involuntary sharing (e.g., an abusive relationship) (see Fitzpatrick, Kemp, and Klinker, 2000; also see Anderson & Christian, 2003).

SOME RESPONSES TO HOMELESSNESS

During the 1980s and 1990s, there was an increase in the estimated number of people sleeping "rough" on the streets of London (Fitzpatrick, Kemp, and Klinker, 2000). A number of large-scale studies investigated this, and their results improved our understanding of the causes of individual and family homelessness and highlighted problematic issues related to service provision. (Anderson, Kemp, and Quilgars, 1993; Drake, O'Brien, and Biebuyck, 1981; O'Callaghan et al., 1996). The main gaps identified by this research suggested the need for a more finely tuned policy and for a greater coordination of providers.

To close these gaps and to reduce the number of homeless people in central London, particularly those sleeping rough, a program called the Rough Sleepers Initiative was designed. It was implemented in three phases (phase 1: 1990–1993; phase 2: 1993–1996; phase 3: 1996–2000). Within this policy framework, the government and several voluntary organizations established a network of services for homeless people. To coordinate this network, the government formed the Rough Sleepers Unit (RSU); the Office of the Deputy Prime Minister is now responsible for coordinating responses to homelessness.

WHERE ARE WE GOING?

Over the past few decades, the United Kingdom has moved away from seeing homelessness as either a structural social problem or an individual failure and now takes the view that homelessness arises from an interaction between the social structure and an individual's circumstances (Anderson and Christian, 2003). However, despite more sophisticated policy goals, homelessness remains a serious problem. While at first the shift in research focus might suggest a return to a personalized, individual explanation of homelessness, it actually reflects the comprehensiveness of research into homelessness and may even begin to make a case for the need to reconceptualize some of these microlevel issues. This is not to negate the idea that homelessness is a housing problem, but rather to develop a better understanding of the causes of homelessness in order to provide a more robust framework for exploring its overall effects.

—*Julie Christian*

Further Reading

Anderson, I., & Christian, J. (2003). Causes of homelessness in the UK: A dynamic analysis. *Journal of Community and Applied Social Psychology, 13*(2), 105–118.

Anderson, I., Kemp, P., & Quilgars, D. (1993). *Single homeless*

A homeless man on a London Street in July 2003 has set up for the day with a carpet, food and drink, and a drum.
Source: Karen Christensen; used with permission.

people. London: HMSO.

Drake, M., O'Brien, M., & Biebuyck, T. (1981). *Single and homeless.* London: HMSO.

Fitzpatrick, S., Kemp, P., & Klinker, S. (2000). *Single homelessness: An overview of research in Britain.* Bristol, UK: Policy Press.

Greve, J. (1964). London's homeless. *Occasional Papers on Social Administration, 10.* London: G. Bell & Sons.

Kemp, P., Lynch, E., & Mackay, D. (2001). *Structural trends and homelessness: A quantitative analysis.* Edinburgh, UK: Scottish Executive Central Research Unit.

O'Callaghan, B., & Dominian, L., with Evans, A., Dix, J., Smith, R., Williams, P., & Zimmeck, M. (1996). *Study of homeless applicants.* London: HMSO.

Pleace, N., & Quilgars, D. (2003). Leading rather that being led? Research on homelessness in Britain. *Journal of Community and Applied Social Psychology. 13*(2), 187–196.

▣ LOS ANGELES

Widespread homelessness in times of economic prosperity is a relatively recent occurrence in Los Angeles, dating only from the late 1970s. While a number of missions, principally serving alcoholics, have existed for over a century in the city's downtown "skid row" district, there were few, if any, secular homeless shelters in Los Angeles County before 1980. In the early 1980s, secular nonprofit social service organizations—both established and new ones—began creating shelters and other programs to

Tipper Gore with the New Directions Men's Choir (a homeless veterans group) at the opening of a photography exhibit in Los Angeles in July 2000.
Source: Erwitt Misha/Corbis; used with permission.

meet the needs of the "new homeless." In 2000, there were an estimated 153 agencies with 331 shelter programs providing 13,632 beds.

HOMELESSNESS: DEFINING FEATURES

The commonly cited federal Stewart B. McKinney Homeless Assistance Act of 1987 generally defines a homeless person as "an individual who lacks a fixed, regular, and adequate nighttime residence"; it excludes persons in prison or jail. This definition of homelessness has been subject to interpretation, particularly with regard to people who must imminently leave their own home, or that of a friend or family member, and have no other place to live. The U.S. Department of Housing and Urban Development (HUD), the government agency that administers most federal homeless programs, currently considers those facing a one-week deadline to be homeless.

LOS ANGELES'S HOMELESS POPULATION

Estimates of the city's number of homeless people vary, due in part to methodological variables such as differing definitions of homelessness and count time frames, as well as to the inherent difficulty of locating homeless persons. Given these limitations, current research suggests that the nightly homeless rate in Los Angeles is between 0.76 and 1.1 percent of

the population, or an estimated 71,000 to 102,000 people. In 2002, the Los Angeles Homeless Services Authority (LAHSA) estimated that 74,900 people—comprising 59,920 singles and 14,980 family members—were homeless each night.

Geographic Distribution

Los Angeles County, with 4,081 square miles, 88 incorporated cities, nearly 10 million people, and a 2002–2003 budget of approximately $16.4 billion, has a population larger than that of most states in the nation—all but eight, in fact. Its largest city, Los Angeles itself, contains 470 square miles with roughly 3.7 million people. Homeless persons can be found throughout the county, with concentrations of single persons found particularly in downtown Los Angeles, Santa Monica, and Hollywood. The city of Los Angeles is estimated to have 46 to 49 percent of the county's homeless population.

Demographics

On any given night, an estimated 66 to 85 percent of homeless people are single individuals. But over the course of a year, fully half of the total population that has experienced homelessness is composed of families. This variation is primarily due to two factors. First, families are typically homeless less frequently, and for shorter periods, than are single individuals. Second, as a consequence, more families move in and out of homelessness, while the pool of single individuals remains relatively constant.

Among homeless single persons generally, 70 to 80 percent are male and the average age is about forty years. Families are characteristically headed by a single female parent. Nationally, the average homeless family has 2.2 children. Unaccompanied youth, clustering in the Hollywood area, make up a small but significant percentage of homeless single individuals, with estimates hovering at around 6,000 to 8,000 young people.

Overall, African-Americans are disproportionately represented among the Los Angeles homeless population, particularly in the "skid row" district; Latinos are underrepresented; and whites roughly mirror their representation within the overall county population.

Veterans are thought to account for approximately 23 percent of the adult homeless, nearly twice their representation in the general population.

The incidence of both substance abuse and mental illness is higher among homeless persons than in the overall population, particularly for single individuals.

CAUSES OF HOMELESSNESS

Researchers, government agencies, and policy experts typically cite a variety of causes for homelessness in Los Angeles, often focusing on the interplay of a multiplicity of local, regional, national, and global economic and social factors. Commonly noted components include poverty and dramatically rising housing costs in the region, the loss of manufacturing jobs in southern California and the nation as a whole, the limited availability of housing for low-income households, changes in the welfare and social service systems, a growing income gap between wealthy and poor Americans, substance abuse, mental illness, and shifting family structures.

Affordable housing is indeed scarce. In 2003, the fair market rent for a two-bedroom apartment in Los Angeles was $967, representing 83 percent of the gross pay for a full-time, minimum-wage worker. A median-priced Los Angeles home in the third quarter of 2002 cost $304,600.

THE FUTURE

It is unlikely that many of the factors that have created homelessness in Los Angeles will abate in the near future. Much of the projected job growth in the region centers on low-paying service employment. Housing costs, the largest single element in most household budgets, are not expected to fall. Real wages for low-income workers declined between 1990 and 2000, while the county's poverty rate remains higher than either California's or the nation's. Mirroring efforts in other parts of the county, LAHSA and the Los Angeles County Coalition to End Hunger and Homelessness have begun

developing a ten-year strategic plan to end homelessness in Los Angeles.

—Paul Tepper

Further Reading

Institute for the Study of Homelessness and Poverty. (2000, June). *Who is homeless in Los Angeles.* Retrieved November 15, 2002, from http://weingart.org/institute/research/facts/pdf/JusttheFacts_LA_Homelessness.pdf

Interagency Council on the Homeless. (1999, December). *Homelessness: Programs and the people they serve.* Retrieved November 15, 2002, from http://www.huduser.org/publications/homeless/homelessness/contents.html

Interagency Council on Homelessness. (2002). Retrieved November 15, 2002, from http://www.ich.gov/

Los Angeles Homeless Services Authority. (2002). Retrieved November 15, 2002, from http://www.lahsa.org

Shelter Partnership, Inc. (n. d.). Retrieved November 15, 2002, from http://www.shelterpartnership.org

Sommer, H. (2001, January). *Homelessness in urban America: A review of the literature.* Institute of Governmental Studies Press, University of California at Berkeley. Retrieved November 15, 2002, from http://www.weingart.org/institute/research/other/pdf/HomelessnessUrban%20America.pdf

Wolch, J., & Dear, M. (1993). *Malign neglect: Homelessness in an American city.* San Francisco: Jossey-Bass.

LOW-INCOME HOUSING

Homeless people are distinguished from everyone else by their lack of housing. Understanding and solving homelessness in the United States require knowledge of U.S. housing policy and intervention in the U.S. housing market. Although the majority of people in the United States are well housed, approximately 14.4 million households (14 percent of all households) have critical housing problems, defined as paying more than one-half of their income for housing or living in overcrowded or substandard housing or being homeless.

A deficit of 2 million housing units exists between the number of renter households in the bottom income quintile (one-fifth) and the number of rental housing units they can afford (using the housing affordability standard of no more than 30 percent of income). As recently as 1970, the United States had a small surplus of housing units that the lowest-income households could afford. The rise of contemporary homelessness in the United States in the 1980s and 1990s coincided with the growing gap between the lowest-income households and the rental housing units they can afford. Expanding the supply of affordable housing is the fundamental solution to homelessness.

Although the housing sector remains one of the mainstays of the U.S. economic system, the market alone cannot provide housing for the lowest-income households in the United States. This is a market failure, and public intervention is required to close the housing gap. Since enactment of the United States Housing Act of 1937, the federal government has made substantial investment in the building and subsidizing of housing for low-income people. However, since the late 1970s the federal government has reduced its investment considerably. Federal budget authority for all low-income housing programs was $80 billion in 1978; by 2003 it was $30 billion.

FEDERAL LOW-INCOME HOUSING PROGRAMS

The major federal low-income housing programs are administered by the Departments of Housing and Urban Development (HUD), Agriculture (USDA), and Treasury. HUD and USDA programs are funding through direct spending that is subject to the annual federal appropriations process. The Low Income Housing Tax Credit (LIHTC) is a tax expenditure program, which means that it provides tax breaks to investors and therefore the U.S. Treasury foregoes revenue that would otherwise be collected. LIHTC is administered by the U.S. Department of Treasury. No federal housing program assures anyone an entitlement to housing. Indeed, only about one-fourth of households whose low incomes make them eligible for federal housing assistance actually receive any. Lengthy waiting lists exist for housing assistance in most communities.

Several HUD programs—including Public Housing, Section 8 Project-Based and Housing Choice Vouchers, Section 202 Housing for the Elderly and Section 811 Housing for People with Disabilities, and McKinney-Vento Homeless Assistance Programs—are governed by the "Brooke" rule, named

for former Senator Edward W. Brooke (R-MA), who wrote the legislation enacting this provision. The Brooke rule provides that the tenants' share of rent is 30 percent of their adjusted income (with some variations) and that federal subsidies make up the rest of the monthly rent up to a specified level. Thus, a household's rent can go up and down as the household gains or loses income. This core feature of most federal housing programs is what ensures housing stability for low-income people whose earnings can fluctuate and who are most vulnerable to periods of unemployment or underemployment.

Public Housing

Public housing is the oldest federal housing program, created in the U.S. Housing Act of 1937. Public housing is owned and operated by public housing agencies (PHAs), which are chartered by states. Their boards are appointed by state or local elected officials, and their funds flow directly from HUD. About 3,400 public housing agencies operate about 1.2 million units of rental housing. The housing subsidies are attached to the housing units for which low-income households apply and for which they are screened for eligibility.

Public housing has not expanded since the early 1970s, and most public housing is aging housing stock. Although PHAs receive both capital and operating funds from HUD each year, an estimated $20 billion backlog exists in needed capital improvements in public housing, leading to deferred maintenance and physical deterioration. Congress created HOPE VI (Housing Opportunities for People Everywhere) in 1992 to revitalize severely distressed public housing. HOPE VI has been the only source of funds for the development of new public housing in recent years, but nonetheless it has resulted in the loss of tens of thousands of units of public housing as obsolete housing has been demolished but not replaced. Although HOPE VI is acclaimed for its neighborhood revitalization and innovative design qualities, most units built through HOPE VI are occupied by people with incomes that are higher than those who have been displaced. HOPE VI is sharply criticized by low-income housing and homeless advocates for contributing to the loss of low-income housing and to homelessness. In 2003, President George W. Bush proposed ending HOPE VI, but members of Congress from both parties disagreed, and the program will continue at least another year, although at a significantly reduced appropriation.

Section 8

President Richard M. Nixon placed a moratorium on public housing in 1974, and Congress enacted the Section 8 program (Section 8 of the U.S. Housing Act of 1937 as amended) in its place. Section 8 created both a project-based and a tenant-based program. The project-based program provided grants and federally insured mortgages to private developers to build new housing or to substantially rehabilitate multifamily housing. In addition, operating subsidies were (and continue to be) provided to make up the difference between 30 percent of a tenant's adjusted income and the contracted rent. Initial contracts required that the housing be operated as affordable housing for twenty years. As these contracts began to expire in the 1990s, many owners opted out of the program, threatening the housing stability of the existing tenants. Congress has enacted various legislations to keep owners in the program, to contain costs, and to protect displaced tenants; these legislations have slowed but by no means stopped the loss of these housing units.

The tenant-based program of Section 8 continues today in the form of housing choice vouchers, which are administered by PHAs to which low-income households apply. Once approved for a voucher, a household shops for rental housing in the private market with an upper limit on cost and a minimum standard of quality. A key attribute of vouchers is their portability, which gives tenants the option to move if they are dissatisfied with their housing or if they want to relocate. In recent years voucher holders have had increasing difficulty using vouchers, that is, finding places to rent in the allotted time, because of the growing shortage of housing stock affordable with vouchers. Landlords also decline to rent to voucher holders, perhaps because they do not want to

deal with the PHA bureaucracy or because they object to voucher holders as a class of people. In some cases discrimination against voucher holders is illegal because it is a proxy for racial or another form of illegal discrimination. In a few jurisdictions landlords are not permitted to reject voucher holders based on source of income, but there is no federal prohibition. Approximately 2 million vouchers are funded today. In recent years adding new vouchers to HUD's annual appropriation was the primary way that federal low-income housing assistance has been expanded, but that has not been the case since the beginning of the George W. Bush administration. Some vouchers are specifically designated to assist homeless people or people with disabilities, who may or may not be homeless.

Sections 202 and 811

Two other smaller HUD programs serve elderly (Section 202) and disabled people (Section 811). In both programs HUD makes grants to nonprofit housing organizations to build housing and provides operating subsidies that allow residents to pay only 30 percent of income. Both programs continue to add new units each year. The 202 program, enacted in 1959, has produced 380,000 units; the 811 program was enacted in 1990 and has produced 18,000 units. Some 811 funds are used to finance the development of permanent, supportive housing for people with disabilities who have been homeless. Further, Section 811 has a voucher component that serves 10,000 households.

McKinney-Vento Homeless Assistance

The McKinney-Vento Homeless Assistance programs administered by HUD have made some contributions to low-income housing development through the Single Room Occupancy (SRO), Shelter Plus Care, and Supportive Housing funds. All SRO and Shelter Plus Care programs and some Supportive Housing funds support permanent housing. Advocates have argued that once permanent housing is developed using the McKinney-Vento funds, the funds needed to renew the subsidies should be transferred to the HUD Section 8 program because the residents are no longer homeless and their housing assistance should not come out of limited homeless assistance funds. The operating subsidies for the SRO program have been so transferred, but the Shelter Plus Care and Supportive Housing programs are still funded through McKinney-Vento.

In recent years, Congress has required that 30 percent of all McKinney-Vento funds be used for permanent housing through these three programs. Although all advocates support the development of permanent housing, some object to reliance on McKinney-Vento funds for this purpose because it reduces the amount of funding available for emergency and transitional homeless services. Another source of disagreement among homeless service providers and advocates is the requirement that the 30 percent permanent housing set aside in the McKinney-Vento program be used exclusively for supportive housing for people with disabilities. All McKinney-Vento funds that can support permanent housing development are distributed by the Continuum of Care process, which engages local citizens in ranking priority projects, but with HUD making final decisions about which projects are funded.

HUD Block Grants

HUD operates three block grants through which funds are distributed to states and localities on a formula basis and used for permanent low-income housing. Although HOPWA (Housing Opportunities for People with AIDS) funds can be used for other than permanent housing purposes, HOPWA also pays for rent subsidies as well as development of community-based residences for people with AIDS. The HOME Investment Partnership Program, enacted in 1990, is the largest source of HUD funds for affordable housing development. HOME dollars can be used for new housing production, rehabilitation, down payment assistance, and tenant-based assistance. The Community Development Block Grant (CDBG) is the most flexible of the block grants and can be used for a wide range of activities, including housing development. However, virtually no CDBG funds are used for rental housing that is

affordable to the lowest-income families. Because these are block grants, decisions about how to spend HOPWA, HOME, and CDBG funds are made by state or local governments. HUD requires that the decisions be made in a collaborative process with citizens and experts and that spending be based on local housing needs. A jurisdiction's housing needs assessment and other required planning processes are submitted to HUD as the Consolidated Plan, which serves as the CDBG and HOME application each year.

Section 515 Rural Rental Housing

Administered by the Rural Housing Service division of the U.S. Department of Agriculture, the Section 515 program (Section 515 of the Housing Act of 1949) provides very low interest loans to finance the development of modest rental housing for very low-income people in rural communities. Funds for the 515 program have dwindled in recent years. Further, as with Section 8 project-based housing, 515 owners are prepaying their mortgages, thereby ending the requirement that the housing continue to be rented to low-income people.

Low Income Housing Tax Credit (LIHTC)

Enacted in the Tax Reform Act of 1986, the Low Income Housing Tax Credit (LIHTC) serves as the major source of equity for the production of low-income rental housing in the United States today by providing investors in eligible affordable housing developments with a dollar-for-dollar reduction in their federal tax liability. Each state receives an annual allocation of LIHTCs from the U.S. Department of Treasury on a per capita basis. State housing finance agencies award the credits to low-income housing developers through a competition based on Qualified Allocation Plans (QAPs) that articulate federal and state preferences for how the funds will be used. Developers rarely have sufficient tax liability to use the LIHTCs directly, so they sell them to corporations, which make up 98 percent of all LIHTC investors. LIHTC has assisted in the development of more than 1 million housing units since enacted. LIHTC units must be initially affordable to people with incomes below either 50 percent or 60 percent of the area median. Only with additional subsidies to the tenants can LIHTC units be affordable for the lowest-income people.

STATE AND LOCAL LOW-INCOME HOUSING PROGRAMS

Although federal funds are the major source of funds for low-income housing development by far, on a lesser scale, many state and local governments have allocated their own funds for housing programs. One increasingly important source of state and local government investment in low-income housing development is housing trust funds. Approximately 280 state and local governments have created housing trust funds, usually with dedicated sources of revenue. Housing trust funds vary considerably in whom they assist and which uses are eligible. Their collective value is about $750 million a year, considerably less than the $30 billion spent by the federal government.

MAJOR ISSUES

Income Targeting

Income targeting is the term for policies concerning the allowable income levels for people who live in low-income housing. In federal housing policy, households with incomes at or below 80 percent of the area median income (AMI) are considered low income. Very low income is defined as 50 percent of AMI, and extremely low income is 30 percent of AMI. These amounts vary considerably from community to community. For example, the AMI in San Francisco in 2003 was $91,500 a year, whereas Laredo, Texas, had an AMI of $32,700. Thus, extremely low income in San Francisco was $27,450 a year or the equivalent of full-time work at $13.20 an hour; in Laredo, it was $9,810 or the equivalent of full-time work at $4.72 an hour, less than the minimum wage.

For many years, when a vacancy occurred in public housing or a housing voucher became available, those with the most serious housing problems, including having no housing at all, were at the top of the waiting list. This practice came under considerable criticism for concentrating the poorest people in public and assisted housing. Major legislation in 1998 set limits on the number of extremely low- and very low-income households who could live in public or assisted housing, in effect reducing access to the most affordable housing for those with the most serious housing problems.

Income targeting restrictions also limit the usefulness of HOME- and LIHTC-financed affordable housing units in addressing homelessness. Eligibility for such housing is geared to the middle and upper tiers of the households who are low income, who are generally of higher income than most homeless people. The only way that housing produced with these funds can be affordable to the lowest-income households is with additional operating subsidies that are tied to the unit or that come with a tenant such as a housing voucher.

NIMBY-ism

NIMBY stands for "not in my backyard" and describes resistance to the location of low-income housing by people who object to its presence in their neighborhoods. It is a major impediment to the development of low-income housing. Zoning and land use policy in general are the purview of local government. Unless a location for a proposed development is zoned "by right" to allow multifamily housing or group homes where several unrelated people share the same house, the developer must seek special permission, usually called a "special use permit," from the local government to build on that site. The special use permit process triggers community review that frequently results in community opposition. Even in cases where the proposed housing can be located by right with no requirement for a special use permit, neighbors have taken legal and other actions to prevent such development. The ostensible reasons for resistance often begin with fear of lost property values or overcrowded schools, but reasons have also been expressed as fear of the people who will live in the housing. Fair housing laws make it illegal to discriminate against people on the basis of race, disability, family status, and other protected statuses, but someone must be willing to assert illegal discrimination and be willing to file suit for fair housing protections to be helpful. Low-income housing developers may not have the resources to sue, or they may not want to generate the bad feelings in the community where they have to work, so NIMBY-ism frequently goes unchallenged.

Renting versus Owning

A major source of debate in federal policy and local practice is the preference for low-income housing to be owner-occupied, single-family owner homes over apartments and other forms of rental housing. The role of home ownership in the accumulation of assets in the United States has been promoted in recent years as an important antipoverty strategy. Market and policy forces have fueled growth in home ownership among low-income people, especially among racial minorities. This idealization of home ownership has led to a backlash against rental housing as a less desirable form of housing, which contributes to NIMBY-ism as well as the allocation of scarce public resources for down payment assistance, low or no interest mortgages, and other home owner subsidies. Although home ownership can be economically preferable for some low-income people, for many others, including most people who are homeless, it is not the right form of housing. The emphasis on home ownership limits the development of low-income housing that can serve people who are homeless.

THE FUTURE

The future of low-income housing policy and programs—both the sustainability of existing programs and the potential of new public investment—depends on federal budget decisions. The return of the federal budget deficit with tax cuts and new spending priorities leaves scant resources for addressing the shortage of affordable housing for the lowest-income households. Nonetheless, experts recognize the need for new production resources. Building on the lessons learned from state and local housing trust funds, a proposal to establish a national housing trust fund and similar ideas are attracting grassroots support and gaining the interest of federal policymakers.

—*Sheila Crowley*

Further Reading

Brooks, M. (2002). *Housing trust fund progress report 2002: Local responses to America's housing needs.* Washington, DC: Center for Community Change.

Daskal, J. (1998). *In search of shelter: The growing shortage of affordable rental housing.* Washington, DC: Center on Budget and Policy Priorities.

Dolbeare, C. N., & Crowley, S. (2002). *Changing priorities: The federal budget and housing assistance 1976–2007.* Washington, DC: National Low Income Housing Coalition.

Joint Center for Housing Studies of Harvard University. (2003). *The state of the nation's housing.* Cambridge. MA: Author.

Lipman, B. J. (2002). America's working families and the housing landscape 1997–2001 [Special issue]. *New Century Housing, 3*(2). Retrieved December 10, 2003, from http://www.nhc.org/nhcimages/HAWF4.pdf

Millennial Housing Commission. (2002). *Meeting our nation's housing challenges: Report of the bipartisan Millennial Housing Commission appointed by the Congress of the United States.* Washington, DC: Author.

National Low Income Housing Coalition. (2002). *The NIMBY report: Using civil rights laws to advance affordable housing.* Washington, DC: Author.

National Low income Housing Coalition. (2003). *Advocates' guide to housing and community development policy.* Washington, DC: Author.

Retsinas, N. P., & Belsky, E. S. (Eds.). (2002). *Low income homeownership: Examining the unexamined goal.* Cambridge, MA: Joint Center for Housing Studies of Harvard University.

Technical Assistance Collaborative. (2003). *Priced out in 2002.* Boston: Author.

M

MARGINALITY

Many social scientists consider homelessness to be a form, if not the prototype, of marginality. Marginality is sometimes confused with social exclusion from a dominant social order and from an institutionalized system of material and symbolic exchange, such as the formal labor market and families. However, marginality is best understood as a state or a series of situations between social exclusion and social integration. This definition is found in many theoretical perspectives that nevertheless imply different causes and mechanisms of marginality.

FUNCTIONAL SOCIOLOGY: MARGINALITY AS WEAK SOCIAL INTEGRATION

U.S. homelessness is often analyzed within a functionalist framework—a theory that analyzes social phenomena in terms of the part they play for the society as a whole. Following the French sociologist Emile Durkheim (1858–1917), a founder of positivist sociology, which posits the social world as a system of causal relationships between realities that can be observed and treated like scientific facts, marginality was considered a form of deviancy from a society's norms and a by-product of weak social integration. Sociologist Robert K. Merton (1910–2003) elaborated a modified functionalist theory of devi-

ancy that included different types of marginality. Skid row homeless were the prototype of one type called "retreatism." Although socialized to aspire to hegemonous (relating to influence) goals, retreatists lack the means of achieving them. They retreat from society by rejecting the goals, the means to achieving them, and dominant norms. Sociologists Richard A. Cloward and Lloyd E. Ohlin further observed that retreatists lack the know-how of illicit subcultures and thus reject both licit and illicit means to reaching that to which they aspire.

U.S. studies of skid row during the 1960s and 1970s illustrated the functionalist perspective. They characterized the homeless, most of whom were men and actually domiciled in flophouses and other so-called disreputable dwellings, as deviant, anomic (relating to social instability resulting from a breakdown of standards and values), and alienated from dominant social institutions. Among the best-known studies were those of the Columbia Bowery Project in New York City. Howard Bahr and his colleagues tested the disaffiliation thesis, or the idea that homeless persons have an attenuation (reduction), if not a veritable absence, of ties with mainstream institutions (family, work, religion, etc.). These studies defined marginality in relation to middle-class social organizations, such as Rotary Clubs, boards, and advisory committees. Yet, on many disaffiliation measures, homeless men turned out to be not very different from working-class controls. In fact, the differences between non-homeless poor and wealthy men were much greater on most measures than those between the homeless and the non-homeless poor. This similarity between marginal (homeless) and poor men suggests tenuous borders. However, paradoxically, by ignoring similarities between the social relations of homeless persons and those of non-homeless persons, these representations reinforced the image of marginality as exclusion from society rather than as structured by it.

Belonging to a nuclear family was also a criterion by which marginality was measured. These skid row studies found attenuated bonds of kinship and sometimes total loss of family ties. However, researchers during the 1980s and 1990s often ignored the evidence of family ties in their own studies. They interpreted marital status as a proxy for having a family, termed single-parent households from which some homeless originated as "a euphemism" for family, or described mothers living in shelters for singles as "single," "without family," or "disaffiliated." At the same time, homeless men on Manhattan's Bowery but also other types of homeless—women in shelters and homeless persons with psychiatric disabilities—were found to have varying degrees of family connections. In fact, the degree of marginality experienced by a homeless person is shaped by gender, ethnicity, age, and structural characteristics, such as social class. Thus, some African-American and Puerto Rican women in New York City shelters for "singles" keep family together by "fostering out" their children to relatives, then taking them back when they find housing again. On the other hand, young, severely psychiatrically disabled homeless men with patterns of frequent circulation between housing arrangements may be totally estranged from their families, maintaining the delusion of a "substitute" family. That marginality can be a state and not an end product is supported by longitudinal studies of the circulation of homeless between states of domiciled poverty, makeshift arrangements (such as doubling up with family, staying with friends), and the streets or shelters.

More anthropologically oriented studies of homelessness presented an alternative to the disaffiliation thesis. In 1923, sociologist Lars Anderson had already described the normative characteristics of homeless men within their own subcultures. During the 1970s, proponents of the "social enculturation/ replacement" thesis recognized that homeless men were stigmatized by mainstream society and experienced isolation from it. However, they argued that homeless men on skid rows reestablished social ties in an "ecologically appropriate" manner, with small, highly active but fluid networks, such as those focused on drinking. Like marginal rural migrants in Latin American cities, those homeless persons who are disconnected from the formal labor market may be integrated into precarious institutions, such as the informal economy, squats (empty buildings occupied by squatters), and shantytowns.

POLITICAL ECONOMY: MARGINALITY, CAPITALISM, AND GLOBALIZATION

For Marxists and political economists, marginality is a product of capitalist penetration in Third World countries, the destruction or displacement of jobs through deindustrialization and globalization, and the maintenance of surplus populations in industrialized and postindustrial countries. This perspective is relevant to homelessness in at least two ways.

Sociologist Saskia Sassen demonstrates how the global economy simultaneously creates sites of centrality and marginality. It materializes in strategic places along a geographic grid that cuts across national and regional boundaries. A transnational urban system, including "global cities," accommodates financial markets and their necessary support systems (information, banking, public relations, etc.). Vast territories within national boundaries meanwhile become increasingly peripheral and excluded from the major processes that fuel growth in the new global economy. This territorial inequality is accompanied by the rift between highly paid, highly educated workers necessary to finance and its support system and low-paid, low- or medium-skilled workers. Finally, within cities, a second rift occurs. Resources are focused on metropolitan business centers, downtowns, and the residential neighborhoods of the multinational workers, whereas peripheral, low-income neighborhoods experience resource shrinkage. As a result, communities break down, housing becomes scarce, and more low-paid workers and their families become vulnerable to homelessness.

Social scientists Kim Hopper and Jim Baumohl have borrowed the notion of "abeyance" (suspension) from Ephraim Mizruchi's theory of marginality and applied it to homelessness. When work and other status positions are scarce, a number of social institutions and arrangements "warehouse" redundant populations. They keep them out of the labor force while controlling their potential threat to the social order. This resonates with the Marxist idea of a reserve labor army. Abeyance works through marginal institutions such as shelters, religious orders, or countercultural movements that are thus functional equivalents of work, yet uncompetitive with mainstream labor. Framing homelessness in terms of abeyance redirects attention both to non-homeless institutions (e.g., hospitals, the military) and informal practices (e.g., "fostering out" children) that absorb the homeless and potentially homeless.

HISTORICAL SOCIOLOGY: THE SOCIAL STRUCTURING OF HOMELESSNESS

Sociologist Robert Castel's monumental history of economic marginality and the responses to it bridges theories of social integration and a neo-Marxist perspective. The marginalization of the homeless is socially produced through the way society organizes work and distributes roles and statuses. From the fourteenth through the eighteenth century, vagabonds in Europe belonged to a larger category of marginal people that included beggars, criminals, prostitutes, rogues, and marauders. They shared characteristics, such as (1) surviving through expediency (begging, swindling) outside systems of regulated work and common production of wealth; (2) seeking opportunities through mobility or settlement in devalued spaces (fallow land, edges of cities, etc.); (3) being disaffiliated from their communities of origin; and (4) maintaining atypical social relations, with their own hierarchies, slang, common law marriages, and so forth that reversed the dominant norms.

Vagabonds during this period came from the rural poor or the strata of unprotected, unregulated city jobs (i.e., outside the corporations). In most cases, a marginal status was a necessity, not a choice. However, as their marginalization intensified, vagabonds became dissocialized and replaced their attachments with less stable, often dangerous ones.

Castel hypothesizes that when marginals become a large enough group—a deviant majority, so to speak—they constitute a factor of social change through the pressure they exert on a society where they don't fit. Thus, in France and England, marginals reintegrated into mainstream society by becoming part of the workforce of the first large factory complexes during the Industrial Revolution.

CULTURALIST ANTHROPOLOGY: MARGINS BEYOND CLASSIFICATION

According to British anthropologist Mary Douglas, margins are those social spaces in which traditional ways of classifying things and people no longer work. The culturalist perspective has been used to understand how U.S. researchers classify homeless people and analyze homeless outreach work. Outreach workers and homeless people encounter one another at a borderland between their respective worlds. Outreach workers must often suspend their usual ways of understanding (the mental structures that shape their culture) at the cost of anguish and disorientation. On the other hand, they sometimes erroneously assume that the person encountered shares their worldview. For example, they may not see that crossing back over into mainstream society runs the risk of breaking up the networks and other resources on which homeless persons depend. They can leave behind their stigmatized identity when they cross the border. However, they court the danger of acquiring not full citizenship (rights, responsibilities, strong connections to mainstream institutions) but only another marginal status as second-class citizens with fragile connections to institutions, rights, and responsibilities.

SYMBOLIC INTERACTIONISM: THE DYNAMICS OF SOCIAL MARGIN

Social interaction— the focus of sociologists in the symbolic interactionism tradition, which considers that reciprocal action between individuals and the meanings they attribute to those actions are the basis of social phenomena—is a dynamic process. The interactionist concept of social margin has proved useful to understanding homelessness as a process rather than merely a status. Sociologist Jacqueline Wiseman defined social margin as

> the amount of leeway a person has in making errors on the job, buying on credit, or stepping on the toes of significant others without suffering such serious penalties as being fired, denied credit, or losing friends or family. Where a person is well-known and considered to have likeable traits, there exists social margin to have some unpleasant characteristics as well. (Wiseman 1979, 223)

In the homelessness context, social margin is the possibility of drawing on resources, relationships, and personal attributes to survive in or move beyond a marginal situation. Like the "forms of capital" in the theory of the French sociologist Pierre Bourdieu (1930–2002), and particularly his notion of symbolic capital (symbolic resources such as honor and prestige), social margin is both cumulative and "graduated like the possession of riches." The more one has, the more one can obtain. Social margin is a relative concept because it depends on the norms and values relevant to a particular setting.

Social margin and marginality work in opposite directions: The narrower one's social margin, the more marginal one is. Social margin is useful for examining social differentiation among homeless people, as well as between groups in the social structure. In a study by sociologist Steven Segal and his colleagues, young vagrants in California looked down on mentally ill street people they labeled "space cases." The latter possessed narrower social margin: fewer material resources, less social interaction, and negative personal attributes, such as undependability and unpredictable behavior. Homeless persons with psychiatric disabilities in New York City were far more likely to get into housing if they had more social margin, defined by a higher percentage of non-marginal persons in their social network and a higher social class background. One implication of these findings is that the breakup of

communities and networks of origin (through urban and economic processes or the nature of social services) needs to be addressed. Social margin may help understand how a segmented homelessness service system responds to certain people (families, those with psychiatric disabilities, battered women, etc.) while marginalizing others (the "generic" homeless).

SOCIAL ECOLOGY: HOMELESSNESS AND MARGINAL SPACE

Cultural geographers and sociologists in the social ecology tradition define homelessness in relation to marginal space. What distinguishes homeless persons from socially integrated members of society is not so much the former's lack of property rights as the functional value of the space they are obliged to occupy. That value is determined by the "host" community. As sociologists David Snow and Leon Anderson observed in their study of street people in Austin, Texas, "the critical question is not who owns the property or whether it is public or private land, but whether it is of importance for domiciled individuals" (Snow and Anderson 1993, 103). Space is classified on a continuum from prime (routinely used by the domiciled for residential, commercial, recreational, or symbolic purposes) to marginal (of little value to regular citizens, such as abandoned buildings, alleys, vacant lots, or impoverished residential areas).

Marginal space can be ceded intentionally and unwittingly to the powerless and propertyless. However—and this resonates with the abeyance view of marginality—space can also be made available in a way that controls and contains homeless populations. This happens when interstitial spaces—spaces under highway abutments, degraded parks, abandoned lots—are occupied by homeless persons.

However, marginal space can also be reconstituted as prime space through gentrification (a process of renewal and rebuilding), redevelopment, or informal homesteading, for example, by artists. Homeless or marginally domiciled persons are thus displaced by higher-income groups, as has happened in New York City during the past three decades. Paradoxically, homeless persons are then forced to seek resources in prime areas, a process that renders them at once more visible and more vulnerable, without changing their marginal status.

RESEARCH DIRECTIONS

Marginality may have outlived its usefulness as a concept for understanding and responding to homelessness, especially as a global phenomenon. One useful perspective is offered by European scholars, for whom homelessness is one possible outcome of an accumulation of handicaps that marginalizes people from collective and professional life. Thus, homelessness is not isolated, or conceptually marginalized, from other forms of social and economic precariousness. Another approach might examine what could be termed "civic marginality." French scholars have begun tracing the changing civic status of homeless persons throughout European history along these lines. For example, during the fourteenth century, vagabonds, such as beggars and the poor more generally, commanded dignity; they were seen as the image of God. When war and social transformation displaced thousands during the next centuries, wanderers and other homeless lost this dignity. Today, some European countries are moving toward the elimination of marginal legal status for homeless people by recognizing basic citizenship rights instead of specific categories reflected in laws on begging, vagrancy, or vagabondage, and administrative requirements for a local address. This perspective on homelessness and marginality joins wider concerns in the area of poverty and welfare that focus on the struggle for recognition as a central building block of civic society.

—*Anne M. Lovell*

Further Reading

Anderson, N. (1923). *The hobo.* Chicago: University of Chicago Press.

Avon-Soletti, M.-T. (Ed.). (2002). *Des vagabonds aux S. D. F. Approches d'une marginalité* [From vagabonds to the homeless: Perspectives on marginality]. Saint-Etienne, France: Publications de l'Université de Saint-Etienne.

Bahr, H. M. (1973). *Skid row: An introduction to disaffiliation.* New York: Oxford University Press.

Bourdieu, P. (1986). The forms of capital. In J. G. Richardson (Ed.), *Handbook of theory and research in the sociology of education* (pp. 241–258). New York: Greenwood Press.

Castel, R. (1995). *Les métamorphoses de la question sociale* [Metamorphoses of the social question]. Paris: Fayard.

Cloward, R. A., & Ohlin, L. E. (1960). *Delinquency and opportunity: A theory of delinquent gangs.* Glencoe, IL: Free Press.

Cohen, C. I., & Sokolovsky, J. (1989). *Old men of the Bowery: Strategies for survival among the homeless.* New York: Guilford Press.

Duncan, J. S. (1978). Men without property: The tramp's classification and user of space. *Antipodes 10,* 23–34.

Durkheim, E. (1982). *Rules of sociological method.* New York: Free Press. (Original work published 1895)

Hopper, K., & Baumohl, J. (1994). Held in abeyance: Rethinking homelessness and advocacy. *American Behavioral Scientist, 37,* 522–552.

Lomnitz, L. A. (1977). *Networks and marginality: Life in a Mexican shantytown.* New York: Academic Press.

Lovell, A. M. (1992). *Marginal arrangements: Homelessness, mental illness and social relations.* New York: Columbia University Press.

Lovell, A. M. (2001). Les fictions de soi-même ou les délires identificatoires dans la rue [Romancing the self: Delusional identities on the street]. In A. Ehrenberg & A. M. Lovell (Eds.), *La maladie mentale en mutation: Psychiatrie et société* [Mental illness under transformation: Psychiatry and society] (pp. 127–161). Paris: Odile Jacob.

Lovell, A. M., & Cohn, S. (1998). The elaboration of "choice" in a program for homeless persons labeled psychiatrically disabled. *Human Organization, 57,* 8–20.

Merton, R. K. (1948). *Social theory and social structure.* Glencoe, IL: Free Press.

Mizruchi, I. H. (1983). *Regulating society: Marginality and social control.* New York: Free Press.

Park, R. E. (1928). Human migration and the marginal man. *American Journal of Sociology, 33,* 881–893.

Paugam, S. (Ed.). (1996). *L'exclusion: L'état des savoirs* [Exclusion: State of the art]. Paris: La Découverte.

Perlman, J. E. (1976). *The myth of marginality: Urban poverty and politics in Rio de Janeiro.* Berkeley and Los Angeles: University of California Press.

Rowe, M. (1999). *Crossing the border: Encounters between homeless people and outreach workers.* Berkeley and Los Angeles: University of California Press.

Sassen, S. (2000). *Cities in a world economy.* Thousand Oaks, CA: Sage.

Segal, S. P., Baumohl, J., & Johnson, E. (1977). Falling through the cracks: Mental disorder and social margin in a young vagrant population. *Social Problems, 24,* 387–400.

Snow, D. A., & Anderson, L. (1993). *Down on their luck: A study of homeless street people.* Berkeley and Los Angeles: University of California Press.

Sosin, M. R., Piliavin, I., & Westerfelt, H. (1990). Towards a longitudinal analysis of homelessness. *Journal of Social Issues, 46,* 157–174.

Wiseman, J. P. (1979). *Stations of the lost: The treatment of skid row alcoholics.* Chicago: University of Chicago Press.

◉ MEDIA

See Appendix 3: Directory of Street Newspapers; Images of Homelessness in the Media; Photography; Public Opinion; Street Newspapers

◉ MEN

See Bowery, The; Chicago Skid Row; Great Depression; Literature, Hobo and Tramp; Skid Row Culture and History; Veterans

◉ MENTAL HEALTH SYSTEM

Most homeless people are burdened by unmet needs for mental health services. To meet these needs effectively, the planning and delivery of such services demand attention to the needs and characteristics of the homeless, in particular their mental health status, access and barriers to care and support, and the integration of other needed services, especially housing.

INCIDENCE AND PREVALENCE OF MENTAL ILLNESS AMONG THE HOMELESS

The 1996 National Survey of Homeless Assistance Providers and Clients was based on a statistical sample of seventy-six metropolitan and non-metropolitan regions, including small cities and rural areas. The survey found that 86 percent of homeless persons had experienced at least one alcohol, drug, or mental health problem in their lifetime, with 57 percent having had problems with mental health, 62 percent with alcohol, and 58 percent with drugs. In the previous month, two-thirds of the homeless persons surveyed had experienced at least one alcohol, drug, or mental health problem; 39 percent had problems with mental health, 38 percent with alcohol, and 26 percent with drugs. The survey also found that one-third of homeless adults suffered at that time from current serious psychiatric illness, including schizophrenia and affective, personality, and character disorders (Burt et al., 1999). Another study of a similar population found that one-third had substance abuse disorders, including 17 percent with dual diagnoses of serious mental illness and chronic substance abuse. Such dual diagnoses pose a challenge to those seeking to develop services that adequately address both needs (Drake et al., 2001).

MENTAL HEALTH CARE FOR HOMELESS PERSONS

During the latter half of the twentieth century, deinstitutionalization, the process of replacing long-stay psychiatric hospitals with smaller, less isolated community-based alternatives substantially changed the way most communities in the United States provided mental health services (Bachrach, 1996). This process of closing down or reducing the size of state hospitals was implemented primarily in the 1970s but continues into the present. The extent of the shift that occurred in the locus of care is illustrated by the change in the resident populations of state and county mental hospitals: From a peak in 1955 at 558,922 patients (339 per 100,000 population), the total had declined by 1998 to 57,151 patients (21 per 100,000) (Mechanic, 1999; Lamb & Bachrach, 2001). Unfortunately, the release of public mental hospital patients most often occurred without alternative community-based mental health services yet in place (Mowbray, Grazier, & Holter, 2002).

Some writers have posited that deinstitutionalization was the primary cause of homelessness from the 1950s into the 1980s (Isaac & Armat, 1990). Several studies have documented that a significant number of patients in mental institutions, particularly in state mental hospitals, were or have been homeless, and that a large proportion of discharged patients became homeless (Lindblom, 1991). However, other research has suggested that several structural factors contributed to the growth in homelessness among individuals with mental illness, including a shortage of affordable housing and a growing proportion of persons living below the poverty rate (O'Flaherty, 1996; Rossi, 1989). Still, it is important to note these latter factors did not come into substantial play until after the first waves of deinstitutionalization had already been largely completed.

CREATION OF COMMUNITY-BASED MENTAL HEALTH SERVICES

The primary programmatic response to deinstitutionalization and the consequent need to serve people with serious mental illness in the community has been the development of case management, the process of integrating the various facets of a client's care across an often fragmented service system. Case management is an alternative to hospitalization that, when correctly implemented, has proven to be effective in maintaining people in the community. However, community-based services have often been criticized for poor implementation and for their failure to facilitate access to the necessary continuum of care for many clients. The failure to create integrated services has meant that the mentally ill or substance-abusing homeless have faced even greater barriers to access and utilization of services.

BARRIERS TO MENTAL HEALTH TREATMENT

Given the high prevalence of mental illness and substance abuse among homeless people relative to the general population, it is not surprising that more than half of the hospital admissions of homeless people (51.5 percent) are for the treatment of these issues (Salit et al., 1998). Between 15 and 44 percent of homeless adults have had a previous psychiatric hospitalization (Koegel, Burnam, & Farr, 1988). A number of studies have established that despite the high prevalence of current mental illness and prior psychiatric hospitalization, most homeless persons do not use existing outpatient mental health and substance abuse systems of care. Gelberg and Arangua (2001) summarized a number of barriers experienced by homeless persons trying to access mental health and substance abuse treatment. They noted that one-half to two-thirds of the homeless population have no health insurance; accessible and affordable trans-

portation is often unavailable; homeless individuals spend an inordinate amount of time each day meeting their basic needs for food and shelter, leaving little time or energy to follow a prescribed treatment plan; the psychological distress experienced as part of homelessness acts as a barrier to obtaining services and often causes paranoia, disorientation, and distrust of the mental health system; and homeless persons often sense that they are unwanted and thus anticipate disrespectful, if not hostile, treatment from caregivers.

THE FEDERAL GOVERNMENT'S ROLE IN PROVIDING MENTAL HEALTH SERVICES TO THE HOMELESS

The Community Support Program (CSP) was initiated by the National Institute of Mental Health (NIMH) in 1977 as a response to the shift from large state institutions to community-based mental health care for persons with severe mental illness. In 1986, NIMH designated homeless persons with severe mental illness as a priority population for CSP service demonstration projects. The first direct congressional effort to provide health services to the homeless was through the Health Care for the Homeless program (HCH), begun in 1985 by the Robert Wood Johnson Foundation and covered under the Stewart B. McKinney Homeless Assistance Act of 1987. Although the HCH program targeted certain medical conditions (tuberculosis, hypertension, peripheral vascular disease, diabetes, and seizure disorders), 28 percent of patient encounters were for mental health and substance abuse treatment.

The McKinney Act established a range of programs to assist homeless persons. Title VI contains two provisions pertaining to services to homeless persons with mental health and substance abuse problems, the implementation of which are overseen by the Center for Mental Health Services of the Substance Abuse and Mental Health Service Administration. The first provision, now known as Projects of Assistance in the Transition from Homelessness, or PATH, sets aside funds to implement services for homeless persons with mental illness. (It was formerly known as the Mental Health Services for the

Homeless Block Grant.) Covered services include outreach, case management, community mental health and substance abuse services, including referral to inpatient treatment, and supportive services in residential settings. The McKinney Act's second provision (Section 612) funded two demonstration programs, one for mental health (the Demonstration Program for Homeless Adults with Serious Mental Illness) and one for substance abuse (Community Demonstration Grant Projects for Alcohol and Drug Abuse Treatment of Homeless Individuals).

In 1992, a Federal Task Force on Homelessness and Severe Mental Illness issued a report, *Outcasts on Main Street*, which suggested that a system of care should be developed to adapt the Community Support Program (CSP) to the special needs of the homeless. In the same year, NIMH was reorganized, leading to the establishment of the Center for Mental Health Services (CMHS). The center's mandate was to play a leadership role in delivering mental health services, generating and applying new knowledge, and establishing national mental health policy. CMHS is a component of the Substance Abuse and Mental Health Services Administration (SAMHSA) of the U.S. Department of Health and Human Services.

CMHS also initiated Access to Community Care and Effective Services and Supports (ACCESS), a $17 million, five-year, eighteen-site demonstration program designed to evaluate strategies intended to foster cooperation among agencies and reduce service system fragmentation for individuals who are homeless and mentally ill (Randolph et al., 1997). The McKinney Act was amended to consolidate the two previously separate demonstration programs into ACCESS. Incorporating the lessons of CSP and the Robert Wood Johnson Foundation Program on Chronic Mental Illness into its design, ACCESS combined system development strategies with assertive community treatment services. In its first three years of operation, 11,857 individuals were contacted, 80 percent of them in existing shelters, soup kitchens, or treatment programs, with the remainder living on the street. Evaluation of the program found that housing outcomes were improved

through greater service system integration (Rosenheck et al., 1998).

ISSUES IN SERVICE PROVISION

In a review of the McKinney Homeless Research Demonstration Programs, Breakey and Thompson (1997) identified four major stages in providing mental health services for homeless persons with severe mental illness. First, it is necessary to engage individuals and gain their confidence so that they will enter treatment. This process is complicated by the reluctance of people to seek help, distrust of the mainstream mental health system, and lack of insight into the fact that they are ill. Outreach services have thus emerged as an indispensable precursor to motivating potential clients to accept basic services and case management.

Second, providing a range of basic services can function as an engagement strategy in and of itself. A needs survey of shelter users in New York City found that mental health services were ranked far lower on the list than housing, food, clothing, and money (Herman et al., 1993). Third, once individuals are clinically stable and reliably housed, they can be transitioned to mainstream services, thereby freeing up the limited resources of programs targeting more needy homeless clients. Fourth, individuals are integrated into the general community with regular housing and other necessary supports. At this point, the person moves out of all programs that target the homeless, instead relying on ongoing community-based programs already in place. The success of this step depends upon the existence of adequate services and the willingness of programs to accept and retain potentially reluctant clients.

MODELS OF CARE

After proving effective through a process of demonstration and evaluation, several approaches serving this population have been labeled as "evidence-based."

Critical Time Intervention

Designed to prevent homelessness by enhancing continuity of care for persons in transition from a shelter to community living, the critical time intervention (CTI) model is a nine-month case management program. It was initially available to shelter users who had already acquired housing in the community, and was intended to supplement and provide a link to existing community services. Over an eighteen-month follow-up period, those receiving CTI spent an average of thirty nights homeless, compared to ninety nights for those receiving the usual services (Susser et al., 1997). Further, CTI participants had greater reductions of negative psychiatric symptoms (Herman et al., 2000). Overall, CTI has been found to be cost-effective in reducing homelessness relative to usual services (Jones, Colson, Holter et al., 2003).

The CTI model is currently being tested with individuals reentering the community from institutional settings such as state hospitals and jails. Since CTI works by facilitating access to existing mental health and housing services, its success depends in large part on an established system of care that provides mental health services appropriate for the homeless. For this reason, it may be more likely to be successful in urban centers, where service networks are denser, rather than in rural areas.

Assertive Community Treatment

In the 1960s, assertive community treatment (ACT) was begun in response to the "revolving door" phenomenon: Persons being discharged from state institutions into the community were soon being reinstitutionalized. Using a multidisciplinary, team-based approach, ACT provides comprehensive community-based treatment and services on a continuous and often long-term basis (Stein & Test, 1980). ACT teams provide "hands-on" services, as opposed to traditional case management wherein services are often contracted from other providers. The program, which has been replicated nationally, has been found to reduce the need for hospitalization, as well as to improve clients' clinical status and community functioning (Burns & Santos, 1995; Ziguras & Stuart, 2000). ACT has also been adapted to meet the needs of the homeless mentally ill through the inclusion of consumer advocates and a family outreach worker, as well as by transferring clients to other services

after twelve months of treatment when clinically appropriate (Dixon et al., 1995; Rosenheck & Dennis, 2001). In Baltimore, Lehman and colleagues (1997) found that an ACT program serving homeless clients reduced hospitalizations, increased housing stability, and produced clinical improvements. In following 1,617 homeless clients of the ACCESS program who received ACT services, Rosenheck and Dennis (2001) found that persons could be discharged or transferred from ACT teams to other mainstream services without any significant adverse impact on their improved mental health status, reduced substance use, or their ability to maintain housing and employment.

Choices

The "Choices" program, located in New York City, was also funded under the McKinney Homeless Assistance Act. The program was aimed at street-dwelling homeless persons, allowing them immediate access to basic needs for food and clothing, case management-coordinated services, and a continuum of care. Named for its approach allowing participants an active role in the decision-making process for treatment and rehabilitative services, Choices is composed of four components: (1) outreach and engagement, (2) a low-demand drop-in center, (3) a ten-bed respite housing unit, and (4) community-based rehabilitation. An evaluation of the program found that participants had better housing outcomes and improved quality of life compared with a control group receiving standard treatment (Shern et al., 1997).

The Mental Health Linkage Intervention Model

The Mental Health Linkage program (Mowbray et al., 1992) utilized a street outreach team of mental health workers with the goal of helping people gain independent housing in the community, providing them with the support necessary to maintain a residence, and, once housed, to transition to ongoing community mental health and social services. An evaluation of the program in two locations found that it produced significantly better housing outcomes (Bybee, Mowbray, & Cohen, 1995).

*The Veterans Administration's Homeless
Chronically Mentally Ill Veterans Program*

Operated by the U.S. Veterans Administration, this
program was established in 1987 in forty-three sites
around the United States, providing outreach, case
management, and residential treatment for chronically
ill veterans. An evaluation that used data from nine of
the sites suggested that the program was effective in
reducing homelessness among participants, as well as
improving their clinical status and social adjustment
(Rosenheck, Frisman, & Gallup, 1995).

*Integrated Treatment for Mental Health
and Substance Abuse Disorders*

Research and practice have consistently documented
the difficulty in serving homeless persons with concurrent mental health and substance abuse disorders
(Drake et al., 1998). In response, treatments have been
developed that combine elements of interventions for
dual disorders within the context of a primary treatment relationship or service setting. The critical components for integrated treatment include staged
interventions, assertive outreach, motivational interventions, simultaneous interventions, risk reduction,
tailored mental health treatment, tailored substance
abuse treatment, counseling, and social support. The
approach advocates a comprehensive, longitudinal
view of remission and recovery, and addressing "real-
life" issues with cultural sensitivity and competence
(Drake et al., 2001). Studies have indicated that substance abuse among this population does not improve
in the absence of specific dual-diagnosis interventions
(Morse et al., 1992). Integrated treatment targeting
both disorders has demonstrated superior outcomes in
reducing homelessness, alcohol and drug use, and the
severity of mental health symptoms (Morse, 1999).
However, Drake and colleagues (1993, 1998) have
found that even when treatment is integrated, successful outcomes may take three to four years to achieve.

Housing and Transitional Services

Housing is obviously a primary goal of services to
any homeless population, especially for those suffering from serious mental illness. Recent studies have
shown that specialized housing programs have some
success in placing and maintaining persons who are
homeless and mentally ill in appropriate housing,
although such programs have more difficulty housing the street-dwelling homeless than those transitioning from homeless shelters (Rosenheck, 2000).
Most studies report that simply housing people did
not necessarily lead to improvement in their symptoms or functioning (Rosenheck, 2000).

A GROWING TREND: HOMELESS FAMILIES

Since the early 1980s, families with children have
made up the fastest-growing segment of the homeless population, comprising 41 percent of the overall
totals (U.S. Conference of Mayors, 2002). The typical homeless family is headed by a single mother in
her late twenties with two children, both under six
years old (Rosenheck, Bassuk & Salomon, 1999).
Incomes of homeless families are significantly
below the poverty level. In a study of sheltered and
poorly housed children and families conducted in
western Massachusetts, Bassuk and colleagues
(1996) found that children old enough to be aware of
their social environment began to develop mental
health and behavioral problems, with 21 percent of
preschoolers and 32 percent of children aged nine
through seventeen experiencing serious emotional
problems. In addition, the typical shelter's structured
rule system tends to increase stress and undermine
parenting and the family authority patterns (Thrasher
& Mowbray, 1995).

Compared to the general female population, mothers of homeless families have higher rates of lifetime
depression, posttraumatic stress disorder, suicidal
tendencies, and substance abuse (Rosenheck et al.,
1999). These findings are especially troubling in that
Bassuk and colleagues (1996) report that the most
potent predictor of emotional and behavioral problems in homeless children was the mother's level of
emotional distress. A system of care for families
needs to take an integrated approach that attends to
the well-being of the entire family unit. To date, the
programmatic response to the mental health needs of
homeless families has been to develop adjunct serv-

ices as components of family shelters and transitional housing programs. These are a good start, but data indicate that more emphasis should be placed on permanent, affordable housing with case management and other services available to families on an ongoing and as-needed basis. Much more research is needed on the numbers and needs of homeless children (Burt et al., 2001).

THE ROAD AHEAD

By most definitions, a society's least fortunate and most vulnerable group of people would include those who are both homeless and mentally ill. The models discussed in this chapter have demonstrated effectiveness in improving housing and other outcomes for this group. Effective strategies exist to address the problems of those who are homeless with alcohol, drug, and/or mental health problems; "what is lacking clearly are the political will and concomitant resources" to implement them (Burt et al., 2001).

In addition, a central problem of deinstitutionalization—the lack of coordination between the systems of community-based care—continues to compromise the mental heath system and contribute to the continuing lack of stable housing for individuals with serious mental illness. The ACCESS demonstration program showed that system integration leads to better housing outcomes and that, conversely, a fragmented system makes it hard to access and maintain stable housing. Breakey and Thompson (1997) suggest that the mental health system would be better served by a formal integration of evidence-based practices, rather than by launching a series of new and independent categorical programs that may exacerbate rather than ameliorate problems in the long run by further fragmenting service options. Even if such new programs do improve short-term outcomes for specific subgroups, such as the homeless, they may exacerbate rather than ameliorate problems in the long run by further fragmenting service options.

—*Mark C. Holter and Carol T. Mowbray*

Further Reading

Bachrach, L. L. (1996). Deinstitutionalization: Promises, problems, and prospects. In H. C. Knudsen & G. Thornicroft (Eds.), *Mental Health Service Evaluation*. Cambridge, UK: Cambridge University Press.

Bassuk, E., Weinreb, L. F., Buckern, J. C., Browne, A., Salomon, A., & Bassuk, S. (1996). The characteristics and needs of sheltered homeless and low-income housed mothers. *Journal of the American Medical Association, 276,* 640–646.

Breakey, W. R., & Thompson, J. W. (1997). *Mentally ill and homeless: Special programs for special needs.* Amsterdam, The Netherlands: Harwood Academic.

Breakey, W. R., & Thompson, J. W. (1997). Psychiatric services for homeless people. In W. R. Breakey & J. W. Thompson (Eds.), *Mentally ill and homeless: Special programs for special needs.* Amsterdam: Harwood Academic.

Burns, B. J., & Santos, A. B. (1995). Assertive Community Treatment: An update of randomized trials. *Psychiatric Services, 46*(7), 669–675.

Burt, M., Aron, L., & Lee, E. (2001). *Helping America's homeless: Emergency shelter or affordable housing?* Washington, DC: Urban Institute Press.

Burt, M., Aron, L., Douglas, T., Valente, J., Lee, E., & Iwen, B. (1999). *Homelessness: Programs and the people they serve.* Washington, DC: Interagency Council on Homelessness.

Bybee, D., Mowbray, C. T., & Cohen, E. (1995). Evaluation of a homeless mentally ill outreach program: Differential short-term effects. *Evaluation and Program Planning, 18,* 13–24.

Dixon, L. B., Krauss, N., Kernan, E., Lehman, A. F., DeForge, B. R. (1995). Modifying the PACT model to serve homeless persons with severe mental illness. *Psychiatric Services, 46*(7), 684–688.

Drake, R. E., Essock, S. M., Shaner, A., Carey, K. B., Minkoff, K., Kola, L., Lynde, D., Osher, F. C., Clark, R. E., & Rickards, L. (2001). Implementing dual diagnosis services for clients with severe mental illness. *Psychiatric Services, 52*(4), 469–476.

Drake, R. E., Mercer-McFadden, C., Mueser, K. T., McHugo, G. J., & Bond, G. R. (1998). Review of integrated mental health and substance abuse treatment for patients with dual disorders. *Schizophrenia Bulletin, 24*(4), 589–608.

Gelberg, L., & Arangua, L. (2001). Homeless persons. In R. M. Andersen, T. H. Rice, & G. F. Kominski (Eds.), *Changing the U.S. health care system: Key issues in health services, policy, and management* (2nd ed., pp. 332–386). San Francisco: Jossey-Bass.

Herman, D., Opler, L., Felix, A., Valencia, E., Wyatt, R. J., & Susser, E. (2000). A critical time intervention with mentally ill homeless men: Impact on psychiatric symptoms. *Journal of Nervous & Mental Disease, 188*(3), 135–140.

Herman, D. B., Struening, E. L., & Barrow, S. M. (1993). Self-assessed need for mental health services among homeless adults. *Hospital and Community Psychiatry. 44*(12), 1181–1183.

Isaac, R. J., & Armat, V. C. (1990). *Madness in the streets.* New York: Free Press.

Jones, K., Colson, P., Holter, M. C., Valencia, E., Lin, S., Wyatt, R., & Susser, E. (2003). Cost-effectiveness of the Critical Time Intervention in reducing homelessness. *Psychiatric Services, 54*(6), 884–890.

Koegel, P., Burnam, M., & Farr, R. (1988). The prevalence of specific psychiatric disorders among homeless individuals in the inner city of Los Angeles. *Archives of General Psychiatry, 45*, 1085–1092.

Lamb, H. R., & Bachrach, L. L. (2001). Some perspectives on deinstitutionalization. *Psychiatric Services, 52,* 1039–1045.

Lehman, A. F., Dixon, L. B., DeForge, B. R., et al. (1997). A randomized trial of assertive community treatment for homeless persons with severe mental illness. *Archives of General Psychiatry, 54,* 1038–1043.

Lidz, C. W. (1998). Coercion in psychiatric care: what have learned from research? *Journal of the American Academy of Psychiatry and the Law, 26*(4), 631–637.

Lindblom, E. N. (1991). Toward a comprehensive homeless-prevention strategy. *Housing Policy Debate, 2,* 957–1025.

Mechanic, D. (1999). *Mental health and social policy: The emergence of managed care.* Boston: Allyn & Bacon.

Morse, G. (1999). A review of case management for people who are homeless: Implications for practice, policy, and research. In L. B. Fosburg & D. L. Dennis (Eds.), *Practical lessons: The 1998 National Symposium on Homelessness Research.* Delmar, NY: National Resource Center on Homelessness and Mental Illness.

Morse, G., Calsyn, R. J., Allen, G., Tempelhoff, B., & Smith, R. (1992). Experimental comparison of the effects of three treatment programs for homeless mentally ill people. *Hospital and Community Psychiatry, 43,* 1005–1010.

Mowbray, C. T., Cohen, E., Harris, S., Trosch, S., Johnson, S., & Duncan, B. (1992). Serving the homeless mentally ill: Mental health linkage. *Journal of Community Psychology, 20,* 215–227.

Mowbray, C. T., Grazier, K. L., & Holter, M. C. (2002). Managed behavioral health care in the public sector: Will it become the third Shame of the States? *Psychiatric Services, 53*(2), 157–170.

O'Flaherty, D. (1996). *Making room: The economics of homelessness.* Cambridge, MA: Harvard University Press.

Randolph, F., Blasinsky, M., Leginski, W., Parker, L. B., & Goldman, H. H. (1997). Creating integrated service systems for homeless persons with mental illness: The ACCESS program. *Psychiatric Services, 48*(3), 369–373.

Rosenheck, R. (2000). Cost-effectiveness of services for mentally ill homeless people: The application of research to policy and practice. *American Journal of Psychiatry 157*(10), 1563–1570.

Rosenheck, R., Bassuk, E., & Salomon, A. (1999). Special populations of homeless Americans. In L. B. Fosburg & D. L. Dennis (Eds.), *Practical lessons: The 1998 National Symposium on Homelessness Research.* Delmar, NY:

National Resource Center on Homelessness and Mental Illness.

Rosenheck, R., & Dennis, D. (2001). Time-limited assertive community treatment of homeless persons with severe mental illness. *Archives of General Psychiatry, 58*(11), 1073–1080.

Rosenheck, R., Frisman, L., & Gallup, P. (1995). Effectiveness and cost of specific treatment elements in a program for homeless mentally ill veterans. *Psychiatric Services 46,* 1131–1139.

Rosenheck, R., Morrissey, J., Lam, J., Calloway, M., Johnsen, M., Goldman, G., Calsyn, R., Teague, G., Randolph, F., Blasinsky, M., & Fontana, A. (1998). Service system integration, access to services and housing outcomes in a program for homeless people with mental illness. *American Journal of Public Health 88*(11), 1610–1615.

Rossi, P. H. (1989). *Down and out in America.* Chicago: University of Chicago Press.

Salit, S. A., Kuhn, E. M., Hartz, A. J., Vu, J. M., & Mosso, A. L. (1998). Hospitalization costs associated with homelessness in New York City. *New England Journal of Medicine, 338,* 1734–1740.

Shern, D. L., Tsemberis, S., Winarski, J., Cope, N., Cohen, M., & Anthony, W. (1997). A psychiatric rehabilitation demonstration for persons who are street dwelling and seriously disabled. In W. R. Breakey & J. W. Thompson (Eds.), *Mentally ill and homeless: Special programs for special needs* (pp. 119–147). Amsterdam: Harwood Academic.

Steadman, H. J., Dennis, D. L., Gounis, K., Hopper, K., Roche, B., Swartz, M., & Robbins, P. (2001). Assessing the New York City involuntary outpatient commitment program. *Psychiatric Services 52,* 330–336

Stein, L. I., & Test, M. A. (1980). Alternate to mental hospital treatment: I. Conceptual model, treatment program, and clinical evaluation. *Archives of General Psychiatry, 37,* 392–397.

Susser, E., Valencia, E., Conover, S., Felix, A., Tsai, W., & Wyatt, R. J. (1997). Preventing recurrent homelessness among mentally ill men: A "Critical Time" intervention after discharge from a shelter. *American Journal of Public Health 87*(2), 256–262.

Thrasher, S. P., & Mowbray, C. T. (1995). A strengths perspective: An ethnographic study of homeless women with children. *Health & Social Work, 20*(2), 93–101.

Torrey, E. F., & Kaplan, R. J. (1995) A national survey of the use of outpatient commitment. *Psychiatric Services, 46,* 778–784.

U. S. Conference of Mayors. (2002). *A status report of hunger and homelessness in America's cities.* Washington, DC: Author.

Ziguras, S. J., & Stuart, G. W. (2000). A meta-analysis of the effectiveness of mental health case management over 20 years. *Psychiatric Services 51*(11), 1410–1421.

▣ MENTAL ILLNESS AND HEALTH

The upsurge of homelessness in the United States and other western countries since the late 1970s has stimulated a new level of concern about mental illness in homeless people. In earlier times, the chronic alcoholic stereotype often pervaded discussions of homelessness, leading to negative labels such as "wino" and "skid row bum." The more recent focus on mental illness in homeless people was occasioned by their high visibility since the 1980s in major American and European cities, and by the public perception that many homeless people were seriously disabled by mental illness. There was concern that these high numbers were a result of the policies of deinstitutionalization that dominated mental health care since the 1970s.

For more than a century, Americans have generally accepted that the care and treatment of people with serious mental illnesses is a public responsibility. Until the middle of the twentieth century, this responsibility was largely met through state mental hospitals, which cared for steadily growing numbers of severely disabled psychiatric patients. The number peaked in 1955, when state and county mental hospitals housed 560,000 patients. Since then, there has been a movement toward treatment in community-based programs, a trend motivated partly by medical advances and a new philosophy of mental health care, but also by humanitarian and civil rights considerations and the political goal of reducing the huge maintenance costs of public institutions. Deinstitutionalization policies sought to provide care largely on an outpatient basis, with a range of treatment, support, and rehabilitation services for people whose ability to function independently might be severely limited. This task has proved to be costly and complicated. Nevertheless, hundreds of thousands of severely mentally ill people who in a previous era would have been institutionalized indefinitely are now living in community settings.

Community mental health services are provided under local auspices, but unfortunately only a few localities have managed to provide an adequate array of services for the most severely disabled. For some of these people, when family or community supports fail, or when the illness itself hinders good use of available services, homelessness has been the result.

THE EXTENT OF THE PROBLEM

Concern about homelessness and the search for policies to address the needs of homeless people have prompted a series of research studies in American and European cities to discover what proportion of homeless people are mentally ill.

The simplest, but also the crudest, measure of the prevalence of serious mental illness is to ask homeless people if they have ever been admitted to a psychiatric hospital for treatment. When this question is put to clients of homeless shelters, about one-third of the respondents typically report such a hospital admission. This provides a rough approximation, but it does not identify those persons who may be ill but untreated, or those who have had treatment, but not in a hospital. It is also likely to underestimate the numbers, because for a variety of reasons people may not wish to disclose their history of hospitalization.

More informative data can be obtained by surveys that use standard methods to examine the mental health status of shelter residents or other homeless subgroups. A study of this sort must use rigorous scientific methods to obtain valid data. It requires careful sampling of the population, well-designed interview instruments, and trained interviewers, ideally with clinical backgrounds. With a clinical diagnosis for each person examined, the investigator can estimate the prevalence of mental illness in the population from which the sample was selected. Such studies have confirmed that a very high proportion of homeless people suffer from some type of mental, emotional, or substance use disorder. These range from mild and understandable substance abuse, depression, anxiety, or phobias to life-threatening alcohol-related illnesses, suicidal depression, or severely disabling schizophrenia. Many individuals show signs of more than one of these. In fact, only a small fraction of homeless people contend with no emotional, mental, or substance abuse problems at all.

A careful survey of single homeless people in Baltimore, Maryland, in the 1980s revealed that

42 percent of men and 49 percent of women had a major mental illness such as severe depression or schizophrenia. In addition, 75 percent of men and 38 percent of women had histories of alcohol or drug abuse currently or in the past (Breakey et al., 1989). About 25 percent of both sexes had what is sometimes referred to as a "dual diagnosis"—both a serious mental illness and a substance use disorder.

The findings in Baltimore are very similar to those of other careful diagnostic studies of comparable homeless groups in other cities in North America, Europe, and around the world. Each city has its own characteristics, but overall the findings are parallel. For example, in the 1990s a study of homeless single men in Munich found that, currently or previously, 37 percent had a major mental illness, and 73 percent were dependent on alcohol. Overall, the prevalence of psychiatric disorders was double that in the general population; for psychoses, the most disabling illnesses, the rate was seventeen times higher (Fichter and Quadflieg, 2001).

Mental illnesses vary widely in severity and impact. Many people with bipolar illness, for example, lead successful and productive lives with appropriate treatment and the support of family and friends. Others have great difficulty coping with the demands of everyday life and need extensive help from family or professionals to live a decent, community-oriented life. The term *severe mental illness* designates those who have been ill for an extended period and whose level of functional impairment qualifies as disability. About 15 to 20 percent of homeless people meet these criteria, in contrast with an estimated 1 percent in the general population. These people are of primary concern to mental health authorities and community programs because of their greater needs for treatment, support, and rehabilitation.

Such illnesses can often impair the sufferers' ability to work or to be resourceful in seeking solutions to their problems. In one popular but ill-informed view, people with mental illness represent a danger or a threat, but in reality they are more often passive than aggressive, more likely to suffer through self-neglect or suicide than to hurt another person.

These descriptions are often applied to single adult homeless people—"street people," "bag ladies," and the typical residents of missions and shelters. However, any city's homeless population is far from homogeneous; indeed, its subgroups may vary widely. One large group is made up of homeless families. In most cases, these are single-parent families: mothers and children. Most of these mothers are between eighteen and thirty years old, and many have fled abuse or domestic violence to seek refuge on the streets or in a shelter. They often come from highly unstable circumstances: Many have changed residences several times in the year before becoming homeless. Although not much more likely than the general population to have severe mental illnesses such as schizophrenia or bipolar disorder, these mothers do have high levels of depression, anxiety, and substance abuse. In some cases, these symptoms form a pattern called posttraumatic stress disorder (PTSD), wherein abuse or trauma has persisting emotional effects.

MENTAL ILLNESS AS A RISK FACTOR FOR HOMELESSNESS

For most homeless people with serious mental illnesses, the illness predated the loss of the home. That alone is not enough to cause homelessness, however; a combination of factors is needed. Three basic factors usually contribute to a slide into homelessness, regardless of the person's mental health: poverty, disaffiliation, and personal vulnerability. The role of *poverty* is obvious: homeless people are the poorest of the poor, and affordable housing for low-income people can be scarce. *Disaffiliation* is a lack of those relationships that provide support for individuals in times of trouble: family, friends, neighbors, coworkers, religious congregations, and so on. Homeless people have fewer such relationships and often describe themselves as loners. *Personal vulnerabilities* of many kinds impair coping abilities and increase the risk of homelessness: unemployment, abuse, illness, disability, or addiction.

People with severe mental illnesses frequently score high on each of these three risk factors. They are poor because they lack the capacity to sustain employment, perhaps because they are disabled. In the United States, disability entitles a person to financial support provided through Social Security's Supplemental Security Income (SSI) program. The application process can be arduous, however, and help comes in the form of a sub–poverty level monthly payment, barely enough for subsistence. People who function poorly, for example in budgeting, often find it impossible to make ends meet and to pay for even minimally acceptable lodging. Disaffiliation can compound problems for people with mental illnesses. In some cases, they experience delusions—unrealistic, idiosyncratic beliefs that may have a paranoid, suspicious content; the person may perceive some type of persecution or victimization, for example. Delusional thinking may lead the sufferer to withdraw from friends, neighbors, and family members, or even to leave home, preferring to face the dangers of life on the street over the imagined dangers of the delusions. Meanwhile, those close to the sufferer may be disturbed or frightened by the symptoms, such as the negativity and irritability of a depressed person, or the grandiose hyperactivity of a person in a manic episode. This, added to society's persistent stigmatizing attitudes toward mental illness, may lead them to avoid contact or withdraw from the person. This loss of support leaves the sufferer with even fewer coping resources in times of trouble.

The effects of the illness itself render the person vulnerable. Mental illness saps the ability to be resilient and resourceful; it clouds thinking, impairs judgment, and leads to attitudes of pessimism and defeat. It also increases the risk for dependency on alcohol or other drugs. In many programs for severely mentally ill people, 35 to 40 percent also have substance use disorders, which compound their disabilities and further strain their fragile financial resources.

For all these reasons—the effects of poverty, the stigma and social isolation, the disabling effect of the illness, and the added vulnerability resulting from alcohol or drug use—people with mental illnesses are at greater risk of becoming homeless than most other people.

HOMELESSNESS AS A STRESSOR

Homelessness, in turn, has an adverse effect on mental health. Homeless people are at the lowest extreme of the economic scale. A person who arrives in this predicament often experiences it as shameful, a sign of personal failure. Often it is a result of a series of circumstances that are traumatic in themselves: loss of a job or a relationship; physical, emotional, or sexual abuse; eviction; imprisonment; or a disaster such as a flood or house fire. Thus a newly homeless person may already be in an emotionally vulnerable state—depressed, frightened, frustrated, or angry. To make matters worse, public agencies may subject them to humiliating and tedious bureaucratic procedures in an attempt to address their needs. Moreover, many homeless people, especially women, are at high risk of being robbed, beaten, or abused. They may find themselves in "shelter" settings that are themselves dangerous, while the alternative, sleeping on the streets, is even more risky. Thus the stress is increased, and it is easy to understand how anxiety, worry, fear, depression, sleeplessness, aggression, and substance abuse may result.

DUAL DIAGNOSIS

Alcohol and other drug dependencies are extremely common in homeless populations, and people with serious mental illnesses are not immune. Surveys have indicated that as many as 25 percent of single homeless people can be dually diagnosed with both a mental illness and a substance use disorder. In some cases, people report their use as an attempt to "self-medicate" and ease their symptoms, but more often it can be better interpreted as a result of boredom, diminished self-control, or a mistaken attempt to improve self-esteem and sociability. Addiction can often play an important role in the slide into homelessness; it has been clearly shown that those suffering from both problems are at even greater risk.

PROVIDING CARE AND TREATMENT

Providing for the needs of homeless people who are mentally ill presents challenges to mental health services. Such people have fallen through the cracks in the systems that are meant to support them; many sufferers do not grasp that they are ill and need treatment. They may have an aversion to psychiatric care, perhaps due to traumatic past experiences with doctors or hospitals. In some cases, the fear or paranoia symptomatic of their illness may deter them from seeking help, or social stigma may make them reluctant to accept appropriate treatment even if it is available. Mental health service providers often must go to extra lengths to engage them and address their often complex needs.

In many places, special health centers and mental health programs now address the needs of homeless people, using skills and therapeutic approaches appropriate for this population. Such programs often must reach out to mentally ill people wherever they are, on the streets or in shelters, to facilitate their entry into treatment. Then they must help with basic needs, such as shelter, food, and financial support, while providing clinical evaluation and treatment that is affordable and offered with sensitivity. The aim is that in due course, the person should move beyond the homeless health care program and be fully integrated into existing community service systems.

Even more carefully designed treatment is needed for those people dually diagnosed with both a mental illness and a substance use disorder. The two problems demand different approaches, and indeed have given rise to two entirely different treatment systems in America—systems with their own philosophies, treatment approaches, and cadres of professionals. Bringing these two systems together in the service of a person who needs both can be challenging. In recent years, as this problem has been better understood, and the need for well-integrated treatment planning has been appreciated, many localities have established programs that offer a coordinated approach, sometimes referred to as MISA (Mental Illness/Substance Abuse) programs.

HOMELESS FAMILIES

Homeless families constitute a group of particular concern. As noted above, in most cases these families consist of a mother and one or more young children. The mothers' mental health problems reflect the chaotic environments from which they often come. These young women often describe patterns of abuse and fractured relationships dating from their childhood. The circumstances of their becoming homeless add to their current distress. Depression and anxiety are common. Many have experience with drug and alcohol abuse in the past, and some continue their dependence. Many exhibit personality disorders—long-standing patterns of emotional and behavioral difficulties that have disrupted their lives and impaired their ability to cope. These mothers need help in a variety of ways. If they are depressed or anxious, they will benefit from appropriate medicines and therapies. If they have been victims of abuse, they will need support, counseling, and advice. If they are drug dependent, they will need appropriate drug treatment.

However, the family must be viewed as a unit. The mother may need help with child care and parenting skills, and the needs of the children must also be addressed. A home and family provide security that is essential for a child's intellectual and emotional maturation. Without a secure home, and with the implicit threats of shelter life or transient situations, children are at high risk for anxiety and depression. At key times for the growth of mental and social skills, major disruptions can lead to developmental delays. In one common scenario, as a homeless family moves frequently, the child is forced to move from school to school, with disastrous results. Children in poverty frequently describe being victims of, or witnessing, abuse and violence.

Meeting these children's needs involves, first, working with the mother to create an environment for the child that is as warm, safe, stable, and supportive as possible. This requires helping her find accommodation in a family shelter program initially, and then moving towards permanent housing. The child's developmental needs can be addressed by school or preschool programs that nurture social, language, and cognitive skills. Localities should make special provisions to keep a homeless child in one consistent school even if the family is forced to move to a new neighborhood. In many cases, addressing these family and environmental problems will relieve much of the distress suffered by homeless children. However, if significant depression or anxiety persists, the children may require specific therapy or treatments such as antidepressant medications.

HOMELESS YOUTHS

Adolescents on their own on the streets constitute another group of great concern. Homelessness at this age indicates a major breakdown in the normal protective and supportive role of the family. Such youths frequently describe family histories of conflict, child abuse, parental separation, and substance use. Some migrate to metropolises from elsewhere, but most in fact do not move far from their familiar surroundings. They tend to seek the anonymity a city provides and live dangerous lives in environments characterized by substance abuse, prostitution, and violence. Research studies have documented high rates of psychiatric disorders, suicide attempts, substance use disorders, and other diseases.

Major mental illnesses often have their onset in adolescence, although this fact may not be recognized by the individual or by others until later. For some youths, it is the early onset of psychiatric illness that contributes to disruptions in relationships and behaviors that ultimately end in homelessness. Depression in adolescents, as in adults, may manifest itself as irritability or "difficult" behavior and "self-medication" with alcohol or drugs; declining school performance is also typical. These behaviors, especially where family coping resources are stretched, can lead to breakdown of relationships and flight or eviction. Other youths develop antisocial conduct patterns, possibly as a result of years of faulty parenting and possibly related to constitutional factors within the person.

Understandably, psychiatric disorders can easily develop under the harsh conditions of street life. Youths are extremely likely to become involved in substance abuse if not already so involved; they are also at high risk for violence, sexual exploitation, and exposure to sexually transmitted diseases, including HIV/AIDS. Anxiety, insomnia, demoralization, and depression are natural outcomes.

Treatment services therefore must take a multi-faceted approach. Great skill may be required to gain the confidence and cooperation of youths who are wary of adult authority and institutions. Services may be more acceptable if offered in a drop-in center or similar place geared to the needs of youths.

Without acceptable residential arrangements to get them off the street, therapeutic efforts will be largely in vain. General medical care, substance abuse treatment, and psychiatric treatments are also often needed. Educational or vocational training opportunities may also help the young person get back on track towards a more healthy, community-oriented life. Providing and coordinating services such as these is a formidable challenge, but case management approaches have been used with good effect.

—*William R. Breakey*

See also Deinstitutionalization; Mental Health System

Further Reading

Baumohl, J. (Ed.). (1996). *Homelessness in America*. Phoenix, AZ: Oryx Press.

Breakey, W. R., Fischer, P. J., Kramer, M., Nestadt, G., Romanoski, A. J., Ross, A., Royall, R. M., & Stine, O.C. (1989). Health and mental health problems of homeless men and women in Baltimore. *Journal of the American Medical Association, 262*(10), 1352–1357.

Federal Task Force on Homelessness and Severe Mental Illness. (1992). *Outcasts on Main Street*. Washington, DC: Interagency Council on the Homeless.

Fichter, M. M., & Quadflieg, N. (2001). Prevalence of mental illness in homeless men in Munich, Germany: Results from a representative sample. *Acta Psychiatrica Scandinavica, 103*(2), 94–104.

Fischer, P. J., & Breakey, W. R. (1991). The epidemiology of alcohol, drug, and mental disorders among homeless people. *American Psychologist 46*, 1115–1128.

Herman, D. B., & Susser, E. S. (1998). *Homelessness in America: A collection of articles from the American Journal of Public Health*. Washington, DC: American Public Health Association.

Robertson, M. J., & Greenblatt, M. (1992). *Homelessness: A national perspective*. New York: Plenum Press.

Robertson, M. J., & Toro, P. A. (1999). Homeless youth: Research, intervention and policy. In Fosberg, L. B., & Dennis, D. L. (Eds.), *Practical lessons: The 1998 National Symposium on Homelessness Research*. Washington, DC: U.S. Department of Housing and Urban Development and U.S. Department of Health and Human Services.

◫ MINNEAPOLIS AND ST. PAUL

Beginning in the early 1980s, retail merchants, workers, and residents of Minneapolis and St. Paul

A Twin Cities Success Story

MINNEAPOLIS (ANS)—Michael Frost has a life story similar to that of many homeless men and women. A Vietnam veteran recovering from alcoholism, with few work skills, he lost his job two years ago, fell behind on his rent and ended up in the Union Gospel Mission in St. Paul.

What distinguishes Frost, 48, from the estimated 12 million adults who have experienced homelessness is his good fortune in eventually finding housing, getting another job and receiving the support services he needs through an organization called the Supportive Housing Corporation.

The corporation was established in 1991 with grants from the Pew Charitable Trusts and the Ford and Robert Wood Johnson foundations. In the last nine years, the group has worked with developers, housing rehabilitation specialists and social service agencies to open 9,100 living units that are linked to treatment and job services for people who are not only homeless but also have physical, drug dependency or mental health disabilities.

Determining an accurate count of the homeless nationwide has proved elusive. Because homelessness is often a temporary condition, many experts say counting the number of people who are homeless at a given point in time is not particularly accurate. Perhaps the most widely cited statistic of this kind is 500,000, tallied by researchers at shelters, soup kitchens and on the street in one week in 1988.

A better study, many say, was compiled in 1995 by Bruce Link at Columbia University. In this study 12 million adults were found to have been homeless at some point in their lives; 6.6 million between 1989 and 1994.

What is clear is the high percentage of homeless men and women who are handicapped physically and mentally. In "The Forgotten Americans," released by the Department of Housing and Urban Development last December, 46 percent of 4,200 homeless men and women surveyed had a chronic health problem, such as cancer or arthritis. Thirty-nine percent had a mental illness, 38 percent had an alcohol dependency and 26 percent had a drug problem.

It's this one-two punch of homelessness and disability that the Supportive Housing Corporation seeks to address. Its projects run the gamut from Times Square, a 652-unit converted welfare hotel in New York City, to a single-family home in a Minneapolis suburb. But they all share a holistic management approach that focuses not just on the issue of reliable shelter but on the underlying causes of a person's homelessness.

"You can't just offer somebody who's mentally ill the keys to an apartment and say good luck," said one advocate. "We are dealing with very fragile people who are the least able to access all of the (agency) bureaucracies. In supportive housing, the skein of tangled systems has been untangled. Whatever they need is easily accessible."

At the Alliance Apartments in Minneapolis, a 124-unit facility for single adults, Frost has the support of an employment counselor, who helped him get a full-time job as a janitor at the Mall of America, a housing director, individual case managers and Donald Jackson, who does just about everything else.

"Sometimes people just need to talk to somebody to develop a direction," said Jackson, whose official title is community developer. He works hard at creating a feeling of family and unity, which residents have been hard-pressed to find elsewhere. Dances are organized to develop social skills. Monthly ceremonies are held to recognize small but important victories like getting a job, donating a needed service or maintaining sobriety.

Staying sober is important at the Alliance. With a waiting list of 500 people, the complex doesn't give second chances to newcomers who fall off the wagon. They must leave, sober up and reapply. Then they're in potential competition with 5,542 other homeless people in Minnesota estimated to have one or more disabilities.

Joyce Givens has every intention of maintaining sobriety. Disabled by asthma and arthritis, Givens is also recovering from drug addiction. After spending time in a treatment facility, she moved in with a relative but feared that easy access to illicit drugs in that household would tempt her. She moved into the Alliance a year ago and now works in the building's cooperative kitchen.

"It's a place where you can get your thinking going on, and think about your future and get a job," said Givens, who is 42. "People sit down and talk with you. They explain what's going on. We are like family. I feel comfortable when I'm here and I feel good when I cook."

Studies from both the federal government and the corporation show that coupling housing for the homeless with job and treatment services is far less expensive in the long run than individual services provided by multiple agencies. In Minnesota, a survey of 157 people in supportive housing in four

Source: Mieke H. Bomann, "Success with Homeless Means Providing More than Just Roof," American News Service, n.d.

began to notice increasing numbers of homeless adults in the downtown business districts. Independently but almost simultaneously, both cities convened task forces to investigate. In 1984, each task force commissioned a survey of homelessness, which found that most homeless individuals were adult males, often chronic alcoholics, and that their numbers were slowly increasing due to the demoli-

counties found that before they entered the program, these homeless men and women together cost the state $340,000 a month. Once in supportive housing, their combined monthly costs dropped to $215,000.

"People who are not able to maintain their housing are high users of very expensive public institutions, like shelters, detox, jails, state hospitals and emergency rooms," said Mari Moen, program director of the corporation in Minneapolis. "They have a poor quality of life, but it's very expensive to serve them."

Nevertheless, getting financial and social support for this relatively new approach to homelessness has proved difficult. While cheaper in the long run, supportive housing is expensive up front. It takes a long time to get the various financing and service agencies together, making it unpopular with politicians operating on election schedules. And in an age of unprecedented plenty, homelessness is simply not a burning social issue for many Americans, providers say—until it arrives in their neighborhoods.

Siting any kind of social service facility in established communities often proves controversial. But by working with neighborhood groups and pointing to on-site or on-call treatment providers, the group says it has lessened opposition. "What helps is that you emphasize property management and a service agency accountable for what goes on," Moen said.

The tangible successes of supportive housing projects will ultimately fuel their popularity, said Moen. While getting the financing together for the Alliance was time-consuming and included development tax credits, federal rent subsidies, and funding from the Department of Veterans Affairs, the city and the county, she said, more and more people realize the status quo simply isn't working.

At corporation projects, very few residents get evicted, Moen said. Those who do move out generally do so for positive reasons, like a good job that puts them over the annual income limit and allows them to afford even better housing.

Frost hopes to be one of those. In March he plans to begin studying to be a truck driver and looks forward to earning in excess of $20,000 a year. "They gave me the push, the kick in the butt to get a job," secure housing, and the incentive to stay sober, Frost said of the team at the Alliance. "This is a good approach."

tion of low-cost hotels and flophouses. At the time, family homelessness was virtually unknown, largely because homeless adults with children were able to receive immediate vouchers for temporary accom-

modations from the emergency service departments in both cities.

Beginning in 1985, the Minnesota Department of Economic Security began to conduct quarterly counts of persons living in emergency shelters. The first count, conducted in August of that year, found 538 homeless individuals using shelters in Minneapolis and 254 in St. Paul. Approximately half of those were adult men, one-quarter were adult women, and one-quarter were children. Twenty-eight children were reported as homeless and on their own, unaccompanied by any adult.

The first face-to-face surveys in homeless shelters, conducted by Wilder Research Center in St. Paul and the Hennepin County Office of Planning and Development in Minneapolis, found that more than half of all shelter residents were white, 25 percent were American Indian, and 16 percent were African-American. Only 8 percent of shelter clients were married, and only about 5 percent of residents had children with them.

In sum, during the mid-1980s the average homeless shelter user in the Twin Cities was thirty-five years old, white, and male, whose most recent fixed address was in Minneapolis or St. Paul. Only 15 percent of shelter users had moved from another state. About 15 percent of homeless adults were employed, and less than 5 percent had substantial part-time or full-time work.

During this time, homeless shelters were considered unsuitable for families by both county and private agencies. Typically, they diverted families to other accommodations—providing vouchers for a night at a hotel or small-scale family emergency housing, for example. Nonetheless, faced with families' rising demand for emergency shelter in the last half of 1983, Minneapolis created the area's first ongoing accommodation specifically for homeless families.

The St. Paul survey, first conducted in 1984 and repeated in 1986 and 1989, asked additional questions about physical and mental health. The 1984 study found that 43 percent of those surveyed had chronic physical health problems and 30 percent reported mental health problems, including 19 percent who had been hospitalized for mental health conditions. In addition, 30 percent reported chemical dependency problems, and 43 percent had been in a detoxification center within the past six months. This paralleled a similar finding in Hennepin County, where some 40 to 45 percent of homeless men were chronic alcoholics.

On the heels of these surveys, the initial task forces made several recommendations. These included an increase in the use of public/private partnerships to develop housing projects, including more transitional housing, the employment of outreach workers to help homeless adults apply for public assistance, the development of employment assistance programs based in drop-in centers and homeless shelters, and better access to basic health needs such as bathing and shower facilities and medical outreach assistance.

RECENT TRENDS

By the year 2000, the picture of homelessness in the Twin Cities had changed dramatically. A single-night survey in October showed that the entire metropolitan area was sheltering 1,443 men, 1,560 women and 2,418 children. This represented an overall increase of 36 percent over the previous survey in October 1997; the number of children had increased fivefold in the previous decade. Half of the children were under age six, and 40 percent of the parents with school-age children reported at least one child with significant learning or school-related problems. Although battered women still represented approximately one-quarter of all homeless women in the Twin Cities, their episodes of homelessness were lasting longer, often three months or more.

The October 2000 survey showed other significant changes. Approximately 44 percent of all area homeless people were now working, with 24 percent employed full-time. And while people of color made up less than 10 percent of Minnesota's adult population, they comprised 74 percent of homeless adults, with the majority now African-American and American Indian. In addition, the number of persons with serious or persistent mental illness, including those diagnosed within the past two years or recently institutionalized, had grown to 37 percent of the home-

less population. The housing situation had also changed. Although transitional housing programs now outnumbered emergency shelters in the metro area, the number of persons turned away from shelters on a single night hovered between 400 and 500 in Minneapolis and between 150 and 200 in St. Paul. The 2000 survey also showed some successes in local efforts to ensure continuity in children's schooling. Eighty-seven percent of parents reported that their children had attended school on the day of the survey. However, the waiting period for homeless families to find more stable housing had increased from one month to three months since the 1991 survey, and the number of homeless youth on their own exceeded 200 each night.

SERVICES

A large and diverse array of organizations provide services and advocacy for people experiencing homelessness in the Twin Cities. Wilder Research Center's recent survey of the region's temporary and permanent supportive housing programs found about 150 such programs. These ranged from "emergency overflow" bedding in intake offices to domestic violence shelters, and from emergency voucher programs to permanent supportive housing programs. Altogether, these programs can house more than 6,000 people on any given night.

Both Hennepin (Minneapolis) and Ramsey (St. Paul) counties have active shelter or homeless advisory boards. These bodies have recently been created to help coordinate efforts to address the needs of the homeless. The broader Twin Cities seven-county metro area includes six "Continuum of Care" regions, whose committees oversee activities related to the federally funded McKinney-Vento programs. Efforts are currently underway to bring these committees together to coordinate and strengthen the region's overall approach to the problem of homelessness.

Evaluations by Wilder Research Center (and others) of Twin Cities area transitional and supportive housing have shown that these programs are achieving some success. Transitional programs that have lasted a year or longer have been able to move participants into various types of housing, almost all subsidized, with success rates of between 60 and 70 percent. On the other hand, the number of supportive housing programs, particularly for persons with physical disabilities or mental health problems, has not come close to meeting the demand. The number of homeless persons with serious mental illness has climbed consistently in each survey since 1991.

Analysis of the 2000 survey also pointed to a substantial subset of the homeless population for whom the lack of affordable housing alone might be the barrier to a stable living situation. A major push by local and state government and private organizations to increase the supply of affordable housing has yet to make a significant dent in the small amount of housing that is affordable to low-income households, including low-wage workers.

In the summer of 2004, the final results of a 2003 survey of homelessness will be released. Researchers expect to learn more about the impacts of the recently expired time limits on welfare benefits and of the substantial state budget cuts that are affecting prevention, child welfare, and emergency and transitional shelter programs. Few local observers expect that the 2003 survey will show significant improvement in the homelessness situation in the Twin Cities metropolitan area.

—*Greg Owen*

Further Reading

Chase, R., Helmsetter, C., & Hendricks, S. (2002, July). *Emergency shelters, transitional housing, and battered women's shelters in Ramsey County: Data collection project, 11th annual report.* Saint Paul, MN: Wilder Research Center. Retrieved August 18, 2003, from http://www.wilder.org/research/reports/pdf/ramseyshelter7-02.pdf

City/County Task Force on Homeless Families. (2001, May). *Report on Homeless Families.* Minneapolis, MN: Hennepin County Office of Planning and Development. Retrieved August 18, 2003, from http://www.co.hennepin.mn.us/opd/htf/HTFMay2001/HTFMay2001.htm

Hart-Shegos, E. (2000, December). *Financial implications of public interventions on behalf of a chronically homeless family.* Minneapolis, MN: Family Housing Fund. Retrieved August 18, 2003, from http://www.fhfund.org

Minnesota Department of Children, Families, and Learning. (2002, May). *Quarterly Shelter Survey.* Saint Paul, MN: Author. Retrieved August 18, 2003, from http://www.dhs.state.mn.us/cfs/oeo/qss.htm

Wilder Research Center. (1998, February). *Minnesota's fifth year experience with supplemental assistance for facilities to assist the homeless (SAFAH).* Saint Paul, MN: Author.

Wilder Research Center. (2001, August). *Homeless adults and children in Minnesota.* Saint Paul, MN: Author. http://www.wilder.org/research/topics/homeless/statewide2001/index.html

Wilder Research Center. (2001, September). *Homeless youth in Minnesota.* Saint Paul, MN: Author. Retrieved August 18, 2003, from http://www.wilder.org/research/topics/homeless/statewide2001/index.html

Wilder Research Center. (2003, February). *Addressing homelessness: A needs assessment and plan for the seven county metro area.* Saint Paul, MN: Author. Retrieved August 18, 2003, from http://www.wilder.org/research/reports.html?summary=1030

◙ MISSIONS

See Association of Gospel Rescue Missions; Bowery, The; Chicago Skid Row; Great Depression; Shelters; Skid Row Culture and History

◙ MOBILITY

Human mobility occurs on many scales. It ranges from migration, which involves a permanent or semipermanent change of residence, to everyday, short-term, often cyclical circulation such as commuting from home to work. A high rate of mobility has traditionally been a defining characteristic of homeless individuals—from the continental wanderings of nineteenth-century "vagrants," "transients," and "tramps" to the involuntary displacement of the "new homeless" from prime public urban spaces in the 1990s. In the words of Jon May (2000, 737), "It is clear that the experience of homelessness cannot be considered apart from the experience of movement—of varying kinds and at a variety of scales."

Geographers, sociologists, anthropologists, and others have focused on a variety of related topics. The focus here is on three key issues: the changing ways in which academics have defined homelessness in terms of mobility, the links between homeless mobility and survival, and the methodological challenges researchers face in understanding these patterns.

MOBILITY AS A DEFINING FEATURE OF HOMELESSNESS: A HISTORICAL REVIEW

For 150 years, academics have considered mobility as a key feature of homelessness, often discerning patterns and types of homelessness through this feature. Following these definitions over time offers a way to understand the shifting relationship between mobility and other conditions of homelessness.

Within the United States, the issue of homelessness in general, and homeless mobility in particular, became especially prominent in the 1860s and 1870s. The disruptive effects of the Civil War, large-scale immigration, boom-bust economic cycles, the growing popularity of the railroad and the subsequent opening of the Western frontier—all created a highly visible group of homeless individuals, primarily men, alternatively known as "hoboes," "tramps," "bums," and the like. Although definitions varied, all focused on mobility and work: "The hobo was a migratory worker, the tramp a migratory non-worker and the bum a non-migratory non-worker" (Cresswell 2001, 49). These designations were frequently conflated, however, as the "tramp crisis" of the 1870s produced a strong moral, social, and legal backlash against anyone who appeared transient. Transiency became a crisis in the 1870s, a result of growing numbers of highly mobile and seemingly unattached men. This backlash was based on the widely held perception that "mobility appears to involve a number of absences—the absence of commitment, attachment and involvement—a lack of significance. The more widespread associations of mobility with deviance, shiftlessness and disrepute come to mind" (Cresswell 2001, 15).

With the gradual closing of the Western frontier, homeless individuals began to pool in the nation's large urban centers in areas known as "skid rows." By the early 1900s, the tramp problem was coming under intense academic scrutiny, concomitant with the rise of the social sciences. The most prominent of these early efforts to categorize the homeless was Nels Anderson's *The Hobo* (1923), in which Anderson employed two familiar criteria: mobility and work. To measure mobility, he used Chicago's "main stem" (skid row) area as a point of reference as a major node for nationwide and regional movements. Five categories emerged: the seasonal worker, hobo, tramp, bum, and homeguard. The first three were particularly mobile. The seasonal worker moved between summer labor in the countryside and winters in the city. The hobo was less temporally and spatially consistent, usually moving wherever and whenever employment was available. The tramp simply enjoyed the experience of traveling. Homeguard refers specifically to men who rarely left Hobohemia (another term for skid row) and worked intermittently. Many were former migratory men who decided to "settle down." The bum was not only immobile, but congenitally unemployable and without any visible means of support.

Anderson's criteria would shape subsequent categorizations of the homeless, many of which became inordinately complex and convoluted as social conditions shifted. By the 1950s, skid rows no longer contained highly mobile, employable men; rather, they were primarily inhabited by a dwindling pool of immobile men who cycled between the street and a host of local institutions, including mission halls, jails, and shelters. Indeed, the defining features of homelessness were changing. Academics' earlier focus on mobility—especially work-related *inter-urban* migration from city to city—now shifted to personal disaffiliation at the *intra-urban* level, within a given city.

By the early 1980s, the composition of America's homeless population was again changing with the rising tide of newly homeless groups, including women, teenagers, deinstitutionalized patients, Vietnam veterans, and a greater proportion of minorities. For instance, many newly released mental patients drifted towards inner-city zones of dependency, where they found a reservoir of services, cheap housing, and a modicum of social acceptance. However, as the ranks of the "new homeless" swelled, traditional skid rows were coming under attack, threatened by urban redevelopment and the demolition of affordable single-room occupancy (SRO) housing. With the physical erosion and outright dissolution of many skid rows, the new homeless became less rooted and more mobile, and thus more visible.

Their new visibility in public spaces generated a virulent backlash among other citizens. By the 1990s, policymakers were passing a series of anti-homeless ordinances, against panhandling, sleeping outdoors, and erecting encampments, for example. These were designed to reduce the presence of the homeless in prime urban spaces, either through outright banishment or, at the very least, physical containment. As Mike Davis (1990, 236) noted, the backlash in Los Angeles

> turned the majority of the homeless into urban bedouins. They are visible all over Downtown, pushing a few pathetic possessions in purloined shopping carts, always fugitive and in motion, pressed between the official policy of containment and the increasing sadism of Downtown streets.

In-depth research into the movement patterns of homeless individuals in Los Angeles suggested that those patterns were fairly predictable, were not always voluntary, and had less to do with individual preferences than with the availability and location of resources. Moreover, mobility was shown to be linked to a person's coping abilities and awareness of "homeless social connections, the availability of urban resources, and the broader contextual factors that shape access to welfare benefits, jobs, housing, and other critical human services" (Wolch, Rahimian & Koegel 1993, 159). Less systematic studies of mobility also flourished during this period, part of a surge in general academic interest in homelessness. These studies related to a wide variety of issues: the ways in which mobility fostered social networks; how mobility intersects with resistance to the social control of institutions; and the relationship between mobility and broader geographies of service provision, including public shelters.

Far from random, homeless mobility in the 1990s was largely shaped by the geography of human service providers such as drop-in centers, shelters, and transitional housing. The destruction of many skid row districts notwithstanding, most homeless services are channeled to poorer, heterogeneous inner-city neighborhoods through opposition from wealthier, better organized communities. As a matter of survival, many homeless people continue to tie their movements to these service locations, whether on a permanent or cyclical basis.

A MATTER OF SURVIVAL

How does mobility help or hinder everyday survival for the homeless? Is it a positive or a negative in the struggle to secure basic needs such as shelter, food, health care, hygiene, privacy, and security? According to Rahimian, Wolch, and Koegel (1992), as well as Dear, Wolch, and Wilton (1994), mobility serves as an adaptive coping mechanism, a way to escape stress, boost material well-being, and improve quality of life. Moreover, mobility is positive in that it represents some measure of autonomy. For instance, Jacqueline Wiseman (1970) noted that in the 1960s, skid row men creatively used mobility to stitch together a stable mode of survival. On the inter-urban scale, the 1996 National Survey of Homeless Assistance Providers and Clients found that 46 percent of its clients had moved since their current homeless episode began. Most relocated in a deliberate effort to improve their lives—to look for a job or share quarters with friends or relatives, for example (Interagency Council 1999, 4-1).

Conversely, other researchers have noted the disadvantages of frequent mobility. Especially when involuntary, moving can drain a person's energy and coping resources, leaving insufficient time to satisfy basic needs such as medical attention. Erratic and continuous moves can isolate and alienate the person from any sort of stable residential community. Individuals may also run the risk of becoming dependent on institutions. As they "develop routines based on the availability of services . . . [they become] accommodated to street life rather than directed toward disengagement [from it]" (Snow and Anderson 1993, 283). In these cases, individual agency is trumped by the challenges of the larger environment.

In the worst cases, the ill effects of hypermobility are combined with institutional dependency, leaving homeless mentally ill people cycling across a variety of unrelated, arbitrary, and inappropriate settings. They find themselves drifting through scattered venues that make a proper continuum of care impossible. Worse, these people may entirely lack the treat-

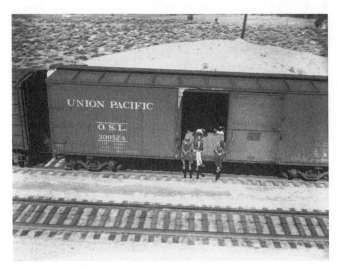

Hoboes in a train yard in southern California in 1934.
Source: Bettmann/Corbis; used with permission.

ment they need, whether for substance abuse, mental health problems, or both. As institutionalized cycling becomes a way of life, the homeless become institutionally dependent, adapting to the rhythms of these settings. For instance, some homeless will adapt to the short- and long-term time limits of shelters, ensuring that they stay the maximum amount of time and return as soon as possible to the same shelter (usually a year later). The accumulation of this trend may be seen in the fact that the Los Angeles County Jail was arguably the largest mental "hospital" in the United States in 1998.

METHODOLOGICAL CHALLENGES

The study of homeless mobility is inherently challenging: Movements that are difficult to track are even more difficult to understand. The research literature, therefore, traditionally relies heavily on cross-sectional surveys—those based on a single point in time. But such surveys tend to obscure the fact that homelessness may not be an end state, but rather a condition through which individuals move in and out. Longitudinal approaches—those spanning a longer time period—are better suited to the task. Not only can researchers track movements over time, rather than relying on retrospective accounts, they can also build more effective research relationships. More than a "snapshot" interview, a longitudinal approach

helps situate a person's decisions, strategies, and patterns as part of a larger suite of coping techniques. Further, a longitudinal approach can help place a given encounter or event in a more meaningful context. For example, what might initially appear to be self-defeating behavior can be placed into a broader context of long-term survival. Unfortunately, longitudinal methods are time-consuming and expensive, and attrition can be a major impediment.

Using longitudinal tracking methods in settings ranging from shelters to street corners, Snow and Anderson (1993) were able to better understand the relationship between mobility and various stages in personal adaptations to homelessness. For the recently homeless, mobility only deepened their disorientation. But for those who had adapted to the streets, mobility represented a lifestyle—whether for tramps (highly migratory and independent) or bums (more stationary and dependent). Using a qualitative, biographical approach to his study of homeless men, May focused on the generally ignored issues of "how much or why homeless people move or what the experience of such movement might be" (2000, 755). In his findings, May revealed the different meanings of mobility, ranging from homelessness as a transitional state to the situation where the individual sees mobility as entirely natural, having never really had a "home" to begin with.

RESEARCH DIRECTIONS

While much about homeless mobility has been examined, there remain a variety of unmet research needs. First, there is a critical lack of large-scale, longitudinal data in both intra-urban settings, for those who drift within a single city, and especially in inter-urban settings, for those who move from city to city. Second, relatively little is known about what motivates homeless people's movement patterns, how they experience those patterns, and how they might differ by race, gender, age, and mental ability. Finally, the public costs of involuntary mobility among the homeless—especially when it involves incarceration and/or hospitalization— need to be systematically traced.

—Geoffrey DeVerteuil

Further Reading

Anderson, N. (1923). *The hobo*. Chicago: University of Chicago Press.

Bahr, H. (1973). *Skid row: An introduction to disaffiliation*. New York: Oxford University Press.

Butterfield, F. (1998, March 5). Prisons replace hospitals for the nation's mentally ill. *The New York Times*, p. A1.

Cresswell, T. (2001). *The tramp in America*. London: Reaktion Press.

Davis, M. (1990). *City of quartz*. New York: Vintage Press.

Dear, M., & Wolch, J. (1987). *Landscapes of despair*. Princeton, NJ: Princeton University Press.

Dear, M., Wolch, J., & Wilton, R. (1994). The service hub concept in human services planning. *Progress in Planning, 42*, 179–267.

Hopper, K., Jost, J., Hay, T., Welber, S., & Haughland, G. (1997). Homelessness, severe mental illness, and the institutional circuit. *Psychiatric Services, 48*, 659–665.

Interagency Council on the Homeless. (1999). *National survey of homeless assistance providers and clients*. Washington, DC: White House Domestic Policy Council.

Kozol, J. (1988). *Rachel and her children*. New York: Crown.

Law, R. (2001). "Not in my city": Local governments and homelessness policies in the Los Angeles metropolitan region. *Environment and Planning, C 19*, 791–815.

May, J. (2000). Of nomads and vagrants: Single homelessness and narratives of home as place. *Environment and Planning, D 18*, 737–759.

Mitchell, D. (1997). The annihilation of space by law: The roots and implications of anti-homeless laws in the United States. *Antipode, 29*, 303–335.

National Law Center on Homelessness and Poverty. (1999). *Out of sight—out of mind? A report on anti-homeless laws, litigation and alternatives in 50 United States cities*. Washington, DC: National Law Center on Homelessness and Poverty.

Ogden, P. (2000). Mobility. In R. J. Johnston, D. Gregory, G. Pratt, & M. Watts (Eds.), *The dictionary of human geography* (pp. 460–461). London: Blackwell.

Rahimian, A., Wolch, J., & Koegel, P. (1992). A model of homeless migration: Homeless men in skid row, Los Angeles. *Environment and Planning, A 24*, 1317–1336.

Rossi, P. (1989). *Down and out in America: The origins of homelessness*. Chicago: University of Chicago Press.

Rowe, S., & Wolch, J. (1990). Social networks in time and space: Homeless women in skid row, Los Angeles. *Annals of the Association of American Geographers, 80*, 184–204.

Snow, D., & Anderson, L. (1993). *Down on their luck: A study of homeless street people*. Berkeley and Los Angeles: University of California Press.

Snow, D., Anderson, L., & Koegel, P. (1994). Distorting tendencies in research on the homeless. *American Behavioral Scientist, 37*, 461–475.

Spradley, J. (1970). *You owe yourself a drunk: An ethnography of urban nomads*. Boston: Little, Brown.

Takahashi, L. (1998). *Homelessness, AIDS, and stigmatization: The NIMBY syndrome in the United States at the end of the twentieth century*. Oxford, UK: Clarendon Press.

Wiseman, J. (1970). *Stations of the lost: The treatment of skid row alcoholics*. Englewood Cliffs, NJ: Prentice-Hall.

Wolch, J. (1980). Residential location of the service-dependent poor. *Annals of the Association of American Geographers, 70*, 330–341.

Wolch, J., & DeVerteuil, G. (2001). New landscapes of urban poverty management. In J. May & N. Thrift (Eds.), *Time-Space* (pp. 149–168). London: Routledge.

Wolch, J., Rahimian, A., & Koegel, P. (1993). Daily and periodic mobility patterns of the urban homeless. *The Professional Geographer, 45*, 159–169.

▣ MONTREAL

In Montreal, as in most large urban centers, homelessness is not a recent phenomenon. Historically, it appeared as early as the mid-nineteenth century and grew throughout the twentieth. Various factors account for this increase: the population explosion that occurred in the nineteenth century, rural population movements resulting from hardship and industrialization, waves of immigration from Europe, economic crises, and changes in the organization of work (Aranguiz and Fecteau 1998).

The initial social response to the problem of homelessness was essentially a charitable one. Originally, aid came from the clergy, religious communities, and the private sector. The services provided— soup kitchens, almshouses, shelters, clothing depots, and so forth—were intended to meet basic needs and were aimed at poor individuals and families. Meanwhile, the number of shelters grew rapidly: By about the 1890s, there were close to a dozen overnight shelters in Montreal alone.

For almost forty years, the phenomenon was relatively invisible and the available resources remained more or less constant. There was little community interest in the issue. Then, with the crises of the 1970s, the number of poor people began to rise steadily, as did the number of homeless. Indeed, although Montreal is the second largest city in Canada, with an average income of nearly Can$30,000, it now has one of the highest poverty rates in the country. The picture is the same as it is in most industrialized countries: transformation of the employment situation (with rising unemployment, more unstable jobs, and dwindling purchasing power), tightening of policies on support for those most in need (through benefit cuts and stricter controls), and reduced access to affordable housing (social housing, rooming houses, small hotels) as a result of real estate speculation. The phenomenon of homelessness itself has grown relentlessly, with the homeless becoming increasingly visible. Whereas in the mid-1980s, the number of homeless in Montreal was estimated to be between 10,000 and 15,000, a recent study put the count at 28,214, of whom 12,666 had been genuinely without shelter during the previous twelve months (Fournier 2000). The number of community resources staff available to help the homeless now varies between 150 and 200 for the Montreal area alone.

FEATURES OF CONTEMPORARY HOMELESSNESS IN MONTREAL

As well as an increase in the number of people affected, the last decade has also seen major transformations in the phenomenon of homelessness. Of these, the most important are changes in the homeless population and a worsening of individual circumstances.

The classic figure of the homeless person, as a disturbed, isolated, alcoholic man living on the street, has been replaced by a more varied picture. All ages, younger and older, are now represented. The situation with regard to elderly homeless people is disquieting. It can be interpreted in the light of an aging population, increasing isolation, transformation of the family, and policy changes on government support for the very poor. The more visible phenomenon of street youth is also on the rise. While the "summer getaway" notion may explain the behavior of some of these young people, studies clearly show that this is a social phenomenon and cannot be reduced to an adolescent whim or a passing fad.

The female component of Montreal's homeless population has grown at a surprising rate. While women accounted for 15 percent in 1989, by 1996 they made up 20 percent of the homeless population, and the figure has risen steadily since then (Fournier 2000). Female homelessness is indicative of the problems of exclusion some women experience, such as spousal violence, prostitution, psychiatric illness, and problems with the police. We would also draw attention to a notable feature of the Montreal situation: the near absence of homeless families (due to state child protection practices) and aboriginal peoples (present in the homeless population in Western Canada).

Another problem, in addition to the familiar ones associated with homelessness (mental health problems, addiction, problems with the police), is the deterioration of homeless people's physical and mental health. Comorbidity (the combined presence of multiple problems) renders assessment, intervention, and referral to appropriate services more complex. To the list of familiar factors, new ones have now been added, such as HIV/AIDS, hepatitis, multiple addictions, cognitive impairment, violence, and suicide (Laberge 2000).

THE FIGHT AGAINST HOMELESSNESS

Although they may not always converge on objectives and strategic choices, a diverse group of players have been working together on the problem of homelessness for many years. This unique joint effort is one of the defining features of the Montreal situation, since intervention in urban centers still tends to be fragmented. The "Montreal model" is characterized by a political framework, a network of public and community services, and a partnership with the research and educational community. In 1992, homelessness featured on the political agenda as a public health problem. The Quebec government's *Health and Welfare Policy* defined the prevention of homelessness, the alleviation of its consequences, and the reintegration of the homeless into the community as priority objectives. Such an approach highlights the transversality of the problems encountered and the need for a concerted, global response to complex situations.

The growing importance of this issue heralded a

new phase in the organization of existing services. The *Réseau d'aide aux personnes seules et itinérantes de Montréal* (RAPSIM; assistance network for single itinerant persons of Montreal) brings together some sixty organizations, mainly community groups, which provide a range of services (referrals, housing, drop-in centers, street work, supportive care, community follow-up, etc.). RAPSIM acts as a liaison between the various resources and represents them before the government authorities. On the institutional side, the *CLSC des Faubourgs* (a CLSC, or *Centre local de services communautaires*, is a local community service center) was the first establishment in Quebec to be granted a specific mandate to address the issue of homelessness (in 1990) and to set up multidisciplinary teams that work jointly with the various milieus. During the same period, a research group bringing together academic, community, and institutional partners was set up to develop a research program that would provide a clearer picture of the homelessness phenomenon. The *Collectif de recherche sur l'itinérance, la pauvreté et l'exclusion sociale* (CRI; collective for research on homelessness, poverty, and social exclusion) thus came into being in 1992. Since then, it has conducted more than one hundred studies on various aspects of what it means to be homeless, intervention practices, and the effects of certain social policies. These studies, integrated with university research programs, are aiding decision makers, practitioners, and political stakeholders alike.

—Shirley Roy and Roch Hurtubise

Further Reading

Aranguiz, M., & Fecteau, J-M. (1998). Le problème historique de la pauvreté extrême et de l'errance à Montréal, depuis la fin du XIXe siècle [Poverty and urban homelessness since the end of the nineteenth century]. *Nouvelles pratiques sociales, 11*, 83–98.

CLSC website. http://www.clscdesfaubourgs.qc.ca

CRI website. http://www.unites.uqam.ca/CRI

Fournier, L. (2000). *Enquête auprès de la clientèle des ressources pour personnes itinérantes des régions de Montréal-Centre et de Québec* [Survey of homeless people from Montreal and Quebec]. Québec City, Québec: Institut de la statistique du Québec.

Hurtubise, R., Roy, S., & Bellot, C. (2003). Youth homelessness: The street and work: From exclusion to integration. In L.

Roulleau-Berger (Ed.), *Youth and work in the post-industrial city of North America and Europe* (pp. 395–407). Boston: Brill Leiden.

Laberge, D. (Ed.). (2000). *L'errance urbaine* [Urban homelessness]. Sainte-Foy, Québec: Éditions MultiMondes.

Roy, S. (1995). L'itinérance, forme exemplaire d'exclusion sociale? [Homelessness as social exclusion]? *Lien social et politiques-RIAC, 34*, 73–80.

Thibaudeau, M-F., & Denoncourt, H. (1999). Nursing practice in outreach clinics for the homeless in Montreal. In M. J. Stewart (Ed.), *Community nursing: Promoting Canadians' health* (pp. 443–460). Toronto, Ontario: Harcourt Canada.

MUMBAI (BOMBAY)

Half the population of Mumbai (formerly known as Bombay), India's largest city and also its commercial capital, is either homeless or lives in informal or semi-permanent housing. According to official government estimates in the 2001 census of India, out of the 11.9 million people living in Mumbai—a city on India's west coast spread over 437 square kilometers—5.8 million people live in shanty towns or slums, or on pavements.

Not all these people are poor according to the definition of poverty set by the Indian government. Many have part-time or full-time jobs. But they cannot afford formal housing. As a result, they are forced to squat on open, vacant plots of land, on sidewalks, by the side of railway tracks, on buffer land near the airports, alongside canals, and even in abandoned water pipes.

DEGREES OF HOMELESSNESS

These 5.8 million people can be divided into groups representing different degrees of homelessness. The first and most severely affected group is of people who sleep out in the open without any cover—on park benches, on the beach, on the pavement, on a road divider, on a railway platform, or at a bus stop. Such people survive on daily wages, possess only the things they can carry, and are constantly on the move as they are never permitted to remain in the same spot for long. Either the municipal demolition squad or the police ensure that they are chased away.

The second category of homeless consists of "pavement dwellers" or people who have set up house on sidewalks. These people build a small lean-to, usually made of a plastic sheet or tarpaulin supported by bamboo poles. A wall running along one side of the pavement serves as the back wall of this structure. There are almost 20,000 households who live under these conditions. Many of them have occupied the same spot on a pavement for several decades. Every once in a while, a "demolition squad" from the local municipality removes these structures. But because these sidewalks are not policed to ensure that no one squats on them, the same people usually return and occupy their original patch.

The third category of homeless consists of people who lead an equally precarious existence as the pavement dwellers but live in a slightly better quality shelter. These are people who have discovered vacant land along the railway tracks. Mumbai has two commuter railway lines that run from the north of the city to its southern tip. Thousands of families discovered that no one policed the vacant land along these tracks. So they set up homes, first temporary shelters and before long small homes made of brick and mortar. However, even if they have a better quality of shelter than the pavement dwellers, their lives are equally insecure. As with pavements, the railways attempt to clear this land by sending in bulldozers. And the families, whose only "home" is crushed in the process, have no alternative but to save what they can and try to find another spot on which they can squat. At last count, there were over 23,000 households living along Mumbai's railway tracks.

The fourth category consists of people living in "regularized" slums—shanty towns that the government accepts because they are built on land not immediately needed for any other purpose. Given its inability to provide an alternative, the government has "regularized" many such slums by providing the residents basic infrastructure, such as common taps and toilets. Slum residents are expected to improve their homes with their own money. As a result, the city is dotted with these disorganized low-rise settlements housing millions of people. However, the basic services provided to them are minimal;

according to one survey, an average of ninety-eight persons share one toilet.

THE CRISIS

Why has a city like Mumbai, one of the richest in India in terms of the income it generates, reached this crisis point? There are several reasons. Mumbai grew from a port city to one of the most important industrial and manufacturing centers in India in the nineteenth century. It had scores of textile mills and industrial units. Workers for these factories and for the port, which was one of the busiest in India, were drawn from many parts of the country. The city government built some low-cost housing in the nineteenth century and early twentieth century to accommodate these workers. However, by the time India gained independence from the British in 1947, the need for housing far exceeded the supply.

This was a time when many cities in India, including Bombay, experienced an unnatural surge in their population as thousands of families displaced by the partition of India into India and Pakistan streamed in. From 1941 to 1951, the population grew exponentially because of this influx. The supply of housing could not keep up with the demand. An economy of shortages also resulted in land speculation. People with money invested in land and kept it vacant in the hope of selling when prices were high. As a result, millions of people found that even the housing that existed was beyond their reach.

INEVITABLE SLUMS

The growth of slums was an inevitable consequence of this state of affairs. As people came into the city from the countryside, they found work but found nowhere to live. Before long, they began squatting on vacant land. A money-strapped government could not build low-cost housing to meet this need, and the private land speculator was not interested in the low end of the market.

In 1976, the government tried to deal with land speculation by enacting a law that set a limit on the amount of land an individual could own in urban areas. Excess land was taken over by the government. But this law worked only on paper; in fact, much of this excess land had already been occupied by the homeless. Shifting them was politically impossible as political parties cultivated them as captive vote banks.

TACKLING HOMELESSNESS

Over the last fifty years, several efforts have been made to tackle homelessness. The government first resorted to the demolition route—that is, removing the poor and homeless from occupied land. But people came back when the government was not looking. The second strategy was slum improvement, where the government provided water and electricity but no security of tenure. This was followed by slum upgradation, through which people were allowed to improve their shelter.

In 1995, the government launched a slum redevelopment scheme. This consists of allowing slums to be redeveloped on the same land where they are situated, if this land is not required for any public purpose. The slum residents are temporarily relocated, the land is leveled, and high-rise structures to accommodate the slum residents are built. On the land freed in the process, other structures—such as shops or high-end housing—are constructed to subsidize the cost of construction. On paper, the scheme appeared workable. In fact, it has been unsatisfactory, and the problem of homeless and slums continues to remain an acute and pressing one for the city.

—*Kalpana Sharma*

Further Reading
Census of India. (2001). Series-28, paper-2: Rural-Urban distribution of population. Maharashtra, India: Director of Census Operations.
Dossal, M. (1995). Signatures in space: Land use in colonial Bombay. In S. Patel & A. Thorner (Eds.), *Bombay: Metaphor for modern India* (pp. 89–99). New Delhi, India: Oxford University Press.
Panwalkar, P. (1995). Upgradation of slums: A World Bank programme. In S. Patel & A. Thorner (Eds.), *Bombay: Metaphor for modern India* (pp. 121–142). New Delhi, India: Oxford University Press.
Patel, S., & Masselos, J. (2003). *Bombay and Mumbai: The city in transition.* New Delhi, India: Oxford University Press.
Patel, S., & Sharma, K. (1998, October). One David and three Goliaths: Avoiding anti-poor solutions to Mumbai's transport problems. *Environment and Urbanization, 10*(2), 149–159.
Seabrook, J. (1987). *Life and labour in a Bombay slum.* London: Quartet Books.
Sharma, K. (2000). *Rediscovering Dharavi: Stories from Asia's largest slum.* New Delhi: Penguin Books India.
Swaminathan, M. (1995, April). Aspects of urban poverty in Bombay. *Environment and Urbanization 7*(1), 133–143.
Verma, G. D. (2002). *Slumming India: A chronicle of slums and their saviours.* New Delhi, India: Penguin Books.

▣ MUNICIPAL LODGING HOUSES

During the second half of the nineteenth century, shelter for the homeless in such cities as New York, Chicago, and Boston was a jumble of makeshift arrangements: evangelical missions, professional charity lodges, seamen's "snug harbors," and, above all, police stations. The latter, an interesting example of the social welfare functions of urban police forces at that time, had steadily descended into notoriety. Conditions were spartan and often overcrowded: Floor space or rough planks were distributed nightly on a first-come-first-served, no-questions-asked basis. As the century drew to a close, the large-scale forces shaping the size and constituency of their clientele became increasingly hard to ignore—widespread unemployment, the growth of a more aggressive species of homeless man (the tramp), and the lure of the road for young men not yet ready to shoulder the burden of adult responsibilities. The haphazard accommodation of the police stations proved no match for such challenges. Those challenges, coupled with the stubborn ill repute of the stations themselves (and the protests of police who shared the quarters), spelled the demise of stations as shelters.

Prodded by the charity establishment, municipal lodging houses were the thinking person's successor to the police station. Opened at the turn of the twentieth century, municipal lodging houses essentially functioned as satellite facilities of the still-thriving almshouses. The most obvious change from the stations was the newly imposed discipline of the municipal lodging houses, a discipline they borrowed in part from the "wayfarers' lodges" established shortly before by charity reformers. Municipal lodging houses were not unconditional shelter. They offered a decent night's sleep, usually preceded by a thorough shower and fumigation of a client's clothes, in exchange for some small amount of work (ranging from doing chores around the facility to splitting wood or smashing rock in quarries). When the homeless were faced with such requirements, shelter demand plummeted. Police stations had been putting up unprecedented numbers by the nineteenth century's end (150,000 annually in New York, 93,000 in Chicago). Under the strict regime of the municipal lodging house, demand fell by 60 percent in New York and 82 percent in Chicago. Where the former residents of the stations went and how they fared are not known. What is known is that cyclical depressions continued to deposit huge numbers of vigorous working-age men—men whose primary complaint was that they couldn't find a job—at the doors of public shelters well into the twentieth century.

Not just large cities had such facilities. On a journalistic tour of homeless shelters in 1909–1910, Edwin Brown visited municipal lodging houses in Pueblo, Colorado; Kansas City, Missouri; Louisville, Kentucky; and Washington, D.C. He found no notable differences in the quality of shelter provided or the dignity with which the offer of shelter was made. Brown described himself (much as Charles Barnes would at about the same time in New York City) as "embittered" at the treatment and especially at the unfair terms of trade—hard work for shabby lodging and coarse food—but grateful that even this rude shelter was available.

TWO TYPES OF CLIENTS

The differences in clients complicated the mandate of municipal lodging houses and frustrated their champions. Lodging had been viewed as only part of the new institution's mandate. From the outset, reform-minded administrators were as dedicated to rehabilitating clients and returning them to productive labor as they were to rationalizing procedures. The objective, as they saw it, was to maintain such

displaced men in as dignified and industrious a manner as possible to avoid the contaminating effects (or "demoralization") of being lodged in the company of men ("vagrants") who had essentially given up on respectable life. Such an objective faced obvious difficulty when the primary impediment to employment was not want of effort but rather scarcity of jobs.

Here then was a central quandary, one clearly perceived by the institution's ablest administrators by the end of the Progressive Era (1918 or so): The municipal lodging house was both a transient way station for men temporarily dislodged by the labor market and a repository of last resort for institutional cast-offs and the independent-minded poor whose self-respect could not tolerate consignment to the almshouse. (One thinks of the elderly man, interviewed by Barnes in 1914 on the streets of New York, who simply could not reconcile himself to the reality that he had outlived his productive potential—that there was no work available, however mean, that he might be able to do—and so continued to avoid the almshouse for which he was otherwise qualified.) Historian Ken Kusmer (2001) also remarked on the "rebellious quality of many young vagabonds," noted by contemporary students of the problem, and the special difficulties that such men presented for routinized shelter. The problem for the administrators was that the rehabilitative program needed to sustain or retrain the latter group was totally at odds with the employment clearinghouse that the temporarily jobless so obviously needed. In that event both groups were ill served.

VARIED CONDITIONS

Across the country, conditions in municipal lodging houses varied markedly in the 1920s: Some enforced length-of-stay restrictions; some shut down seasonally. Some cities (Philadelphia and most cities in the South) had no such facilities at all. Some facilities, spurred by reformist social workers, eliminated the work requirement; others reinstated or modified it to make it somewhat less onerous (clearing up parks instead of chopping wood). However, food quality was poor, amenities were few, and rules were firmly enforced (e.g., early morning wake-up and ejection from the facility).

Eventually municipal lodging houses were casualties of Depression-era homelessness, or rather of the spectacular success of the domestic war effort in emptying shelters. During the postwar period, shelter functions either devolved to charitable organizations or religious organizations (some of which had been around since the late nineteenth century). Those lodging houses that did survive underwent a rehabilitation of their own—the New York City Municipal Lodging House was first moved to the Bowery area and then renamed the "Shelter Care Center for Men." As late as the early 1980s, however, old-timers still referred to it as "the Muni."

—Kim Hopper

Further Reading

Anderson, N. (1923). *The hobo*. Chicago: University of Chicago Press.

Anderson, N. (1932). *Report on the Municipal Lodging House of New York City*. New York: Welfare Council.

Depastino, T. (2003). *Citizen hobo*. Chicago: University of Chicago Press.

Kellor, F. (1915). *Out of work*. New York: Putnam's.

Kusmer, K. L. (2001). *Down and out, on the road*. New York: Oxford University Press.

Monkkonen, E. H. (1981). *Police in urban America, 1860–1920*. New York: Cambridge University Press.

Rice, S. A. (1922). The failure of the Municipal Lodging House. *National Municipal Review, 11*, 358–362.

Ringenbach, P. T. (1973). *Tramps and reformers, 1873–1916*. Westport, CT: Greenwood.

Solenberger, A. W. (1911). *One thousand homeless men*. New York: Russell Sage.

Sutherland, E. H., & Locke, H. J. (1936). *Twenty thousand homeless men*. Chicago: J. B. Lipincott.

N

▣ NAIROBI

There is no basic necessity that surpasses that of shelter. According to Universal Declaration of Human Rights Article 25, "Everyone has the right to a standard of living adequate for the health and well-being of himself and of his family, including food, clothing, housing and medical care and necessary social services" (www.un.org/Overview/rights.html). These are a must for any life to continue.

BRIEF HISTORY

In the traditional African setup, families lived in clustered homesteads headed by a clan elder. A clan was a group of families who shared close blood relations, especially through marriage. Land, though communally owned, was a prime sign of wealth and therefore regarded highly. It was inherited from generation to generation. After marriage, a man proved his worth by providing for the family. This included a comfortable house to live in.

The practice, however, changed with the colonization of Africa by the Europeans in the late 1880s. In Kenya, Africans were forced off their land and instead settled in concentrated camps where they were hired by the European settlers to provide cheap labor. The massive displacement of indigenous populations for the establishment of colonial economic and political structures was to become a critical issue in the post-independence political settlement. It contributes to the current land problems in sections of the country that saw the settler community assert their sovereignty over land occupied by indigenous people. The settler community introduced the land acts and the tenure system, under which Africans were required to buy land that was originally theirs. As a result, not many Africans could afford this, especially after spending years in the forests fighting for independence. Most ended up landless and squatters who built on government and individuals' farms after occupying the land by force. To date, there are still forcible evictions from these. A commission to review land issues was formed in May 2000 and headed by Charles Njonjo, a former cabinet minister of Kenya. The findings, released in 2003, recommended an overhaul of the lands ministry and advocated for the cancellation of all title deeds for "grabbed land." A subsequent commission has been established to report on how the findings should be implemented.

SLUMS AND SQUATTERS

As years progressed, the problem of landlessness became more entrenched. Many families now live in urban slums where the majority of the occupants know no other home. In Nairobi, for instance, over

60 percent of the entire population lives on a paltry 5 percent of the land, occupying poorly and cheaply constructed temporary shacks in slum areas. Most of these slums are cut out of the main water, sewerage, and sanitation and health services. Occurrences of robbery, violence, rape, stabbing, and shooting are disturbingly frequent. The inhabitants are financially poor and usually malnourished and rarely get access to quality education.

Still others cannot afford even these simply constructed shanties. They now live on the streets of Nairobi. They live on begging and leftovers thrown into dustbins from the various restaurants and hotels within the city. Their places of abode are plastic and papers laid on the pavements of Nairobi streets. Most are orphans or from single-parent families who can't afford even a single meal any day. With the rampant spread of HIV/AIDS, thousands of children are orphaned daily, and when these children grow up, they raise their own families on the streets, and the vicious cycle continues. These children are fed on almost rotten food, sleep on the hard and cold pavements, and are used by their parents to supplement earnings by begging. They also engage in risky sexual behaviors very early in life. Their lives are continually at risk as they have to fight daily to survive. Most will be seen sniffing glue and smoking marijuana as early as age four or five.

SERVICES AND LOCAL EFFORTS

Kenyans voted a new government in the 2002 general elections. Kenyans had been under Kenya African National Unity's (KANU) rule for over forty years. The KANU government played a minimal role in alleviating the problem of landlessness and subsequent homelessness. In both 1992 and 1997 election years, Kenya witnessed politically instigated land clashes in both the Rift Valley and the coast provinces. Kenyans therefore feel this is a time of great change and expectations, a time of physical reconstruction and realignment of national priorities, including the slums upgrading project. The slums upgrading project was started by the KANU government. It was designed to construct low-cost stone and brick houses to be rented out to tenants. These would

have electricity as well as piped clean drinking water. The initial beneficiary slum was the sprawling Mathare 4A in Nairobi's Kasarani Division. The project was jointly funded by the governments of Kenya and Germany, with supervisory roles played by the Catholic church alongside other institutions of civil society. Initially there was a hue and cry with most tenants fearing the government's role in it. Ultimately the project came to naught, and the German government withdrew support, citing lack of cooperation and transparency from its Kenyan counterpart.

Civil society, however, played a sterling role in sensitizing people to their rights, especially with respect to land. Some like the Pamoja Trust, a nongovernmental organization, helped organize villagers to collectively agitate for the ownership of the land they occupied. They represented victims of forceful eviction in the courts. They also helped communities initiate saving schemes to enable them build decent houses.

The Nairobi Central Business District Association has supplemented government efforts in improving security by establishing nongovernmental police structures within the city. The association also encouraged the Nairobi City Council to improve service delivery commensurate with the huge service charges (taxes) paid by the residents. These were services such as garbage collection, clean and efficient water supply, security, and lighting.

INTERNATIONAL PROGRAMS

The fact that Nairobi houses UN-HABITAT (the United Nations Human Settlements Programme) makes a statement about international interest in addressing the problem of urbanization and housing in Africa. Sadly, however, human settlements in developing countries, especially in Africa, have continued to be negatively affected by numerous calamities including civil strife and high poverty levels, and more recently HIV/AIDS and drug abuse.

The new NARC (National Rainbow Coalition) administration has made a serious commitment to carry out the slum upgrading project. Plans and negotiations between the government and funding agencies, with UN-HABITAT prime among them, are underway. According to Public Works, Roads, and Housing Minister Raila Odinga, the government will be constructing 450,000 housing units every year. At the top of the list is the sprawling Kibera slum in Nairobi's Langata Division, which is also Mr. Odinga's parliamentary constituency. Indeed, the government has set aside land along the Athi River to relocate the residents of Kibera to clear room for the project's new construction. In 2002, the Africa Medical Research Foundation organized charity events to help construct latrines for the residents of Kibera. The project was dubbed "flying toilets" in reference to the style used by the residents to get rid of human feces. Normally, owing to fact that latrines are few in Kibera and also that due to insecurity residents dare not step out of their houses at night, they relieve themselves on pieces of polyethylene at night and throw these away very early in the morning onto garbage heaps. Hence the name "flying toilets." Kibera is home to more than half a million residents with more than one hundred persons sharing a single pit latrine.

THE FUTURE

The NARC government's seriousness in dealing with the housing problem appears to be as a commitment to providing a lasting solution. The fact that residents in Kibera will be relocated soon will provide a precedent to other slum dwellers and hope for the realization of a dream they have lived with for so long.

During the nineteenth session of UN-HABITAT's Governing Council in Nairobi in May 2003, member states reiterated their governments' continued support for efforts to combat the lack of secure housing. The agency's 2004–2005 agenda includes creating a division to work on human settlements financing. The fact that over 800 delegates managed to reach consensus so quickly is an indication that governments from both the developing and the developed countries are fully committed to doing something about inadequate housing and urbanization.

—*Maurice N. Wamiti*

Further Reading

Global Campaign on Urban Governance. (n.d.). Retrieved May 16, 2003, from http://www.unhabitat.org/campaigns/governance

Human rights message. (1999). Stockholm, Sweden: Ministry for Foreign Affairs.

Shack/Slum Dwellers' International (SDI). (n.d.). Retrieved May 16, 2003, from http://www.sdinet.org

Welcome to Mji wa Huruma village, the first slum on the internet! Hamjambo! (2000). Retrieved May 16, 2003, from http://www.pips.at/huruma

◉ NATIONAL ALLIANCE TO END HOMELESSNESS

The National Alliance to End Homelessness (NAEH) is a nonprofit organization that seeks to ally other nonprofit, public, and private organizations in an effort to completely eradicate homelessness in the United States. The NAEH feels confident that this goal is absolutely attainable given that some $2 billion annually goes into programs fighting homelessness in the United States. The NAEH also, however, stresses that much more than money and resources are required to bring about change—education, advocacy, and activism on the part of American citizens are also needed.

At the heart of the Alliance's campaign lies the "Ten Year Plan to End Homelessness," which focuses on more specific issues such as housing, earnings, and services, and lays out four distinct steps that must be taken to ensure an end to homelessness in the next ten years. These steps are as follows:

1. *Plan for outcomes.* This translates into better collection of homelessness data at the local level as well as planning for an outcome that puts an end to homelessness altogether instead of simply reducing the rate of homelessness in the United States.

2. *Close the front door.* The homeless assistance program needs to be made more effective, which will in turn defer responsibility from other systems, such as welfare and health care, and drive down costs for those who are unable to afford these types of aid. This will ensure that new homeless people are not continually replacing those who have received help.

3. *Open the back door.* This idea suggests a housing-first approach: permanent supportive housing provided for the homeless in a timely fashion. People

need to be provided with housing quickly instead of lingering on the streets for long periods of time until they can be squeezed in wherever they fit.

4. *Build the infrastructure.* This idea is based on three fundamental principles in the fight against homelessness: The supply of affordable housing must be increased, incomes must be adequate enough to pay for necessities such as food and shelter, and people must be able to receive the services they need.

The Alliance feels strongly that if America's communities, organizations, and leaders work together to put these four steps into motion, homelessness can be a thing of the past within a decade, but advocacy among American citizens is equally essential in achieving this outcome. The more people who are informed and educated about homelessness legislation and policies, and the more people who are committed to ending homelessness, the more likely it is that America's leaders will make the most logical and worthwhile decisions concerning the issue.

RECENT AND ONGOING PROJECTS

There are three major projects whose creation and implementation the NAEH has been responsible for during the last few years: "Housin' 2000" and "Homeless to Harvard," both partnership projects, and the formation of their own Alliance Action Network. "Housin' 2000," a joint effort between the NAEH and the Fannie Mae Foundation, combined the knowledge and resources of students in more than ninety Washington, D.C., area schools with the interests of the "Housin' 2000" staff in order to develop age-appropriate educational materials to help youths learn the facts about homelessness and the ways in which they can become positively involved in the fight to end it. Age-specific factsheets for students from kindergarten to high school, developed as part of the "Housin' 2000" project, are accessible on the NAEH website.

"Homeless to Harvard" is an educational toolkit including worksheets, discussion-inspiring activity ideas, and a teachers' guide that can be distributed to high school educators and guidance counselors. The toolkit was designed in 2003 through the combined

efforts of the NAEH, Girls, Inc., and Lifetime Television with the goal of increasing awareness of homelessness issues and advocacy for a solution among teenagers and young adults. "Homeless to Harvard" worksheets and teachers' guide are also available for download on the NAEH website.

The Alliance Action Network is a division of the National Alliance to End Homelessness that allows organizations to join together with the NAEH in order to combat homelessness. By becoming a member of the Alliance Action Network, an organization takes on the responsibility of working to make an impact on the homelessness epidemic by communicating and building relationships with policymakers and garnering media attention with regard to homelessness issues and solutions. The Action Network's main areas of concern and focus are welfare, affordable housing, permanent supportive housing, families, youth, child welfare, mental health, substance abuse, domestic violence, corrections, and employment policy. Organizations can join the Alliance Action Network on the NAEH website.

PUBLICATIONS AND RESOURCES

The National Alliance to End Homelessness has also produced numerous publications and resources for those who are eager to learn more about one of America's most widespread issues, many of which are available at the NAEH website (www.endhomelessness.org). These resources include *The Ten Year Plan to End Homelessness* (2000); *Ten Essentials Toolkit* (2003), and a weekly e-mail newsletter *Alliance Online News.*

—*Emily A. Colangelo*

NATIONAL CENTER ON FAMILY HOMELESSNESS

The National Center on Family Homelessness (NCFH), located in Newton Center, Massachusetts, is a nonprofit organization working toward permanent solutions for problems that homeless families face in the United States. The organization's mission statement is as follows:

> The National Center on Family Homelessness is working to end family homelessness in America. We design, pilot, and evaluate innovative programs and services that provide long-term solutions for homeless families across the country. We share our knowledge by educating service providers, policymakers, and the public. (www.familyhomelessness.org/about_us/whoweare.html)

ORGANIZATIONAL STRUCTURE

The NCFH is organized around a nucleus of three divisions: Research and Evaluation, Program Design and Implementation, and Policy and Public Education. Research and Evaluation efforts identify important family homelessness issues and areas that require the most immediate attention, and help clinicians, providers, and philanthropists create programs that will ultimately rectify these issues. Research and Evaluation is also responsible for conducting research, evaluating the effectiveness of NCFH programs, and presenting important information through the media.

The Program Design and Implementation Division develops and executes programs to aid and better serve homeless families. These programs have helped activate services such as day care and preschool programs for children, family support systems, family violence initiatives, health care, and programs to help families remain in permanent housing available to poor and homeless families nationwide. This division also provides technical and organizational support to smaller program directors and helps them establish connections and communications to ensure that programs in local communities remain active and in place.

The Policy and Public Education Division is responsible for distributing information acquired through research and program activities to important and influential people such as policymakers, providers, philanthropists, advocates, and media VIPs. This increases the national awareness of homeless families' needs and improves the effectiveness of both current and future policies, programs, and services.

PROGRAMS

Since 1988, the NCFH has made 270 program grants in thirty-six states, providing a total of $58 million. These programs have provided services for thousands of poor and homeless families. A few of the NCFH's most recent and successful programs are as follows:

KIDSTART. The KIDSTART program begins with a person called a "Kidstarter"—a trained case manager who works to bring together families and services and advocate on their behalf. The Kidstarter begins by visiting local health centers, child care programs, homeless shelters, and soup kitchens in order to locate poor or homeless families with young children. Once a family is located, the Kidstarter conducts an evaluation of the family, particularly the children. Common steps for evaluation include screening children for developmental delays and lead poisoning, determining medical needs such as immunizations and dental checkups, and judging the necessity of mental health, play, or speech therapy. The Kidstarter then works with the parents to develop a plan that builds the family's strengths and identifies its weaknesses; this plan serves a dual purpose to make sure the family receives the services it needs, and to teach parents to be their own advocates for their family. The ultimate goal of KIDSTART is to identify homeless children, provide them with services they need, and increase society's awareness of the struggles that they face.

KIDSTART/Success by 6. This program combines the efforts of the NCFH's KIDSTART program and the United Way of America's (UWA) Success by 6 by affording communities located in Miami, Florida; Racine, Wisconsin; Salt Lake City, Utah; and Washington, D.C., an opportunity to remedy mental, physical, social, and emotional problems facing homeless children by supporting KIDSTART programs in their own communities. The "Success by 6" aspect of the project works to ensure that these problems are solved so that every young child is fully prepared to begin schooling.

Seeking Safety. Using funding from the Richard Smith Foundation, the NCFH has developed Seeking Safety as a group treatment program for poor and homeless women in the Boston area who suffer from posttraumatic stress and substance abuse disorders. The Seeking Safety staff are professionals in the field of interpersonal and community violence and its effects on the lives of poor women and children.

The Birth Circle. Based on midwife tradition and partly on John Kabat-Zinn's work on the effects of meditation and yoga on pain control, this program was funded by the Nathan Cummings Foundation and developed in order to teach homeless pregnant women ways to manage stress, improve physically and psychologically, and increase self-confidence, self-efficacy, and attitudes; it also provided prenatal education, parenting classes, and supportive relationships to young mothers who might be isolated from friends and family. The program involved yoga, meditation, breathing and visualization exercises, guided imagery, and expressive art and movement therapies. Groups led by a certified midwife and yoga instructor met once a week for two hours at St. Mary's Infant and Women's Center in Dorchester, Massachusetts, a center that provides residential services for homeless women and children. The goal of the program was to help women develop a sense of togetherness with each other through sharing the meaningful experience of pregnancy and birth.

"When I Was Six." An exhibit displayed at public forums, "When I Was Six" features the life stories and photographs of young mothers who are currently or were recently homeless and who were victims of family violence at a young age. The exhibit is displayed at forums up and down the east coast of the United States to increase awareness about issues of violence and homelessness, encouraging communication and problem solving between social service systems, and reaching out to others who have experienced or are experiencing violence in their own lives.

The Family Stabilization Program. Funded by the Annie Casey Foundation, this four-year project began in 1991 and gave a total of $750,000 to homeless family stabilization programs in Huntsville, Alabama; Bronx, New York; Yakima, Washington; and Portland, Oregon. This program was a joint effort on the part of the NCFH and UWA that was inspired by research published in the 1980s concern-

ing the harmful effects of homelessness on child development. By the end of the grant period, September 1995, 1, 587 families and 2, 761 children had been helped.

Tomorrow's Child. A 1990 partnership with the Ronald McDonald Children's Charities, Tomorrow's Child was a project that worked to assess and service the needs of homeless pregnant mothers and their children in three major U.S. cities. Agencies in Baltimore, Maryland; Oakland, California; and Portland, Oregon, received a total of over $700,000 toward providing mothers with important services such as prenatal and pediatric health care, health education, substance abuse treatment, and aid in locating residency.

The National Center on Family Homelessness regularly releases information and news about its activities to ensure that the public remains aware of the issues that face homeless families, especially women and children. NCFH research findings appear in such publications as the *Journal of the American Medical Association, Scientific American,* and the *American Journal of Public Health.* The NCFH also periodically publishes reports about its work and *The President's Report,* sent out twice a year to update supporters of the organization and other interested parties. Further information about the National Center on Family Homelessness is available on the NCFH website, www.familyhomelessness.org.

—Emily A. Colangelo

◉ NATIONAL COALITION FOR THE HOMELESS

One of the largest organizations fighting homelessness in the United States, the National Coalition for the Homeless (NCH) focuses its efforts on four major areas of concern surrounding the issue— housing justice, economic justice, health care justice, and civil rights. The organization's strategies include grassroots organizing, public education, and policy advocacy. The NCH's primary goal is to end homelessness altogether, and it not only proposes ideas for achieving this goal but also puts these proposals into action within the organization itself. Of the NCH's thirty-eight-member board, 30 percent are homeless and/or formerly homeless men and women.

As a component of grassroots organizing, the NCH allies with and aids many local and state organizations in the fight against homelessness by providing them with a range of resources such as technical assistance, written materials, and training. The NCH also works to employ and empower homeless people to ensure that their voices and opinions are heard by the public and by influential policymakers. In terms of policy advocacy, the NCH worked to pass the Stewart B. McKinney Homelessness Assistance Act in 1987, and the organization continues to provide funding for programs related to the McKinney Act, such as emergency shelters, health care, and education for the homeless. In addition, the NCH actively engages in new and developing struggles for policies such as a proposed Homeless Voter Registration Act, which would allow homeless people to exercise their civil right to vote.

To increase public education and awareness, the NCH publishes reports and fact sheets, as well as a seasonal newsletter, *Safety Network,* which provides updates on policies and legislation regarding homelessness at local, state, and national levels and reports on current and upcoming events such as conferences and projects. The NCH frequently attends these conferences and workshops in order to answer any questions the public might have regarding their efforts and progress.

PROJECTS

Of the more than fifteen projects the organization is currently involved in, some of the most notable are as follows:

- *The "Bringing America Home" Campaign.* This campaign was founded to meet the need for public education, grassroots organizing, and support for progressive policies and legislation. It promotes the belief that people need—and are entitled to— affordable housing, a living wage, health care, education, and protection of civil rights.

- *The National Homeless Civil Rights Organizing*

Project. This project is a nationwide, locally based effort to protect the often-overlooked civil rights of the homeless. The goal of the project is to increase public awareness of the abuse homeless people face at the hands of public officials, and the project ultimately aims to use videotaped accounts of abuse as the foundation for a counter-campaign against anti-homeless laws.

- *Rapid Response Network.* This network identifies and publicizes violations of homeless civil rights, focusing on such important issues as poverty, homelessness, and the ever-increasing use of the prison system to limit people's social and economic growth.

- *The Homeless Voting Rights Project.* This project serves as a model for a "State Homeless Voter Registration Act," which will ideally be the basis for future homeless voting laws. The homeless are often denied voting rights because of policies stating that a voter must have a mailing address in order to register. This project seeks to rewrite these policies so that all American citizens will have the opportunity to exercise their civil right to vote.

- *The Educational Rights Project.* Most parents of homeless children are unaware that their children are entitled to a public education by law. As a result, many homeless children fail to receive a much needed and/or desired education. The goals of the Educational Rights Project are to inform homeless families of their children's rights to an education, to inform schools and educators about the rights of homeless children, and to distribute an information packet on the educational rights of homeless children in shelters across the country to ensure that the children of homeless families can attend school.

- *The Hate Crimes Prevention Project.* The homeless are frequently victims of hate crimes in America, and the NCH seeks to eliminate the incidence of these hate crimes altogether by working with current and proposed legislation to combat them. As part of the Hate Crimes Prevention Project, the NCH requests that Congress conduct a General Accounting Office (GAO) investigation into the details of where, how, and why these violent acts take place.

- *Universal Living Wage.* The Universal Living Wage project works to establish economic justice across all social classes by ensuring a forty-hour workweek for all workers and by developing a minimum wage dependent upon local housing costs so that all workers can have access to decent, affordable, permanent housing. This will help solidify minimum wage workers' rights to basic economic and social privileges.

LeTENDRE EDUCATION FUND FOR HOMELESS CHILDREN

In addition to these broad-scope projects, the NCH provides a different kind of aid to those in need. Established in 1998, the LeTendre Education Fund for Homeless Children provides monetary assistance in the form of scholarships for students who are or once were homeless. The $1,000 scholarship is awarded annually to students who have demonstrated academic achievement and may be used for college tuition or other related educational expenses. A minimum of two scholarships are awarded to deserving students each year.

The National Coalition for the Homeless has combined all its efforts into one large endeavor that it hopes will cure the United States of one of its largest and most serious ailments by offering both social and monetary support to those in need. For more information on the NCH, visit the organization's website at www.nationalhomeless.org.

—*Emily A. Colangelo*

▣ NATIONAL RESOURCE CENTER ON HOMELESSNESS AND MENTAL ILLNESS

The National Resource Center on Homelessness and Mental Illness is the only national center specifically focused on the effective organization and delivery of services for people who are homeless and have serious mental illnesses. Policy Research Associates, Inc., in Delmar, New York, has operated it since 1988 under contract to the Center for Mental Health Services (CMHS) of the Homeless Program Branch of the U.S. Substance Abuse and Mental Health Services Administration. The Resource Center provides technical assistance and compre-

hensive information on the treatment, housing, and support service needs of people who are homeless and have serious mental illnesses.

BACKGROUND AND MISSION

While only 4 percent of the U.S. population has serious mental illness, the rate among the homeless is five to six times higher. People with serious mental illnesses are homeless more frequently and for longer periods than other homeless subgroups; many have been on the streets for years. Their diagnoses include the most personally disruptive and serious mental problems, including severe and chronic depression, bipolar disorder, schizophrenia, schizoaffective disorders, and severe personality disorders. Their symptoms are often active and untreated, making it extremely difficult for them to meet basic daily needs for food, shelter, and safety; they may also cause distress to those around them.

Serious mental illness is found among all subgroups, but its forms and the implications for those offering support vary greatly. Among single homeless adults, the prevalence of serious mental illness is between 25 and 33 percent, with as many as half of these also having a co-occurring substance use problem. This latter subgroup tends to be more difficult to reach and engage in services, and is more often chronically homeless. They have more physical health problems, resulting in greater use of inpatient care and higher mortality rates. Compromising their ability to escape homelessness is their difficulty gaining access to and retaining affordable housing. In addition, they are impoverished, and many are not receiving benefits for which they may be eligible.

Research and practice have provided a substantial amount of information on what services and practices are effective in ending homelessness for people with serious mental illness. Essential services include outreach and assessment, integrated mental health and substance abuse treatment, health care, income support, emergency shelter, and transitional and permanent supportive housing. Discharge planning helps people leaving institutions find housing, mental health, and other community services that often prevent homelessness during such transitions. Ideally such planning should begin upon entry into an institution, should be done in consultation with the individual, and should be ready for implementation upon discharge. Providing short-term intensive support services immediately after discharge from hospitals, shelters, or jails has proven effective in preventing recurrent homelessness during the transition to other community providers.

Central to the success of support efforts is the use of evidence-based and best-practice models for services, treatment, and the prevention of homelessness. Establishing partnerships with federal agencies, state and local governments, and public and private agencies to reduce barriers to services and increase resources and funding, and conducting research that addresses important gaps in knowledge are also key to addressing homelessness.

The Center for Mental Health Services' Homeless Program Branch has been at the forefront of federal efforts to break the cycle of homelessness by administering programs aimed at identifying approaches that work, by providing access to community care and effective mental health services, and by encouraging communities to integrate services to better meet the multiple needs of people who are homeless. The Branch also funds the contract to operate the National Resource Center on Homelessness and Mental Illness. The Resource Center's activities in turn enable CMHS to facilitate service systems change through field-based knowledge development, synthesis, exchange, and adoption of effective practices.

ACTIVITIES AND SERVICES

Resource Center staff provide information and targeted technical assistance to researchers, service providers, policymakers, and other interested parties about the implementation of effective systems integration strategies, as well as about the mental health treatment, housing and support needs of the people who are homeless. Staff perform a number of specific tasks and activities aimed at providing this critical link between emerging knowledge and everyday practice in the field.

Workshops and Training Institutes

The Resource Center arranges and offers workshops and training institutes on topics that identify and synthesize promising trends and practices in the field, and that assist communities and other groups in adopting best-practice approaches. The Center hosts a biannual national training conference on homelessness, mental illness, and substance use disorders. It also trains psychiatrists, psychiatric residents, and other mental health professionals to work with people who are homeless and have mental illnesses as part of the American Psychiatric Association's Annual Institute on Psychiatric Services.

Targeted Technical Assistance

Resource Center staff and consultants assess the need for technical assistance, then provide it as needed to CMHS and other federal agency grantees and service providers. CMHS grantees receive the highest priority for assistance. Technical assistance is provided on multiple topics related to homelessness and mental illness, including prevention, outreach, treatment, and supportive services and housing options. Resource Center staff and consultants not only deliver technical assistance to individual sites, but also are knowledgeable of the technical assistance and support needs of cross-site coordinating centers. Staff and consultants have recognized that while some issues faced by grantees require targeted technical help, for example, through on-site consultation, others may be common to multiple grantees or initiatives and thus require a broader activity—a training opportunity, for example.

Publications

The Resource Center assists in the development of a variety of referral lists, fact sheets, publications, and other materials to assist researchers and other interested parties. These are written by experts on topics not adequately addressed in the literature. Among its publications are a series of fact sheets on homelessness and mental illness and a guidebook on employment for persons with serious mental illness who have been homeless. The Resource Center has also completed a draft blueprint for services for people who are homeless and have mental illness and/or co-occurring substance use disorders. *Access,* an informational letter to the field, is published up to four times per year and contains information on innovative and effective service and housing programs, funding opportunities, and updates on policy initiatives. In addition, the Resource Center's referral list, *National Organizations Concerned with Mental Health, Housing and Homelessness,* is revised and distributed annually.

Resource Database

The Resource Center developed and maintains an extensive resource library of the literature in the field. A database of nearly 8,000 items related to homelessness and mental illness is available for customized searches on any related topic by Resource Center staff or online through the Center's website. The database is updated regularly to ensure that it contains new publications and materials in the field, as well as relevant historical information. The Resource Center also publishes annotated bibliographies on more than thirty topics related to homelessness and mental illness. These are available in hard copy and through the website.

Information Requests

The Resource Center handles more than 1,000 requests for information per year from researchers, students, service providers, consumers, government agencies, and the general public. Sometimes they are routine requests for general information, while others require database or web searches, customized annotated bibliographies, or other specific information.

The Resource Center also maintains an extensive website at www.nrchmi.samhsa.gov. One of its key features is the ability to access and search the Center's information resource database online. The site is updated regularly to ensure the most current information is available to users, including the latest information on funding and technical assistance opportunities, new publications, and training oppor-

tunities. The site also includes links to downloadable versions of new publications, to other sites of interest, and to registration brochures and information for training conferences and events.

—Jillian M. Price and Francine Williams

Further Reading

Burt, M. R., Aron, L. Y., Douglas, T., Valente, J., Lee, E., & Iwen, B. (1999). *Homelessness: Programs and the people they serve.* Washington, DC: Interagency Council on the Homeless.

Burt, M. R., Aron, L. Y., Lee, E., & Valente, J. J. (2001). *Helping America's Homeless.* Washington, DC: Urban Institute Press.

Federal Task Force on Homelessness and Severe Mental Illness. (1992). *Outcasts on Main Street.* Washington, DC: Interagency Council on the Homeless.

Fosburg, L., & Dennis, D. (Eds.). (1999). *Practical lessons: The 1998 National Symposium on Homelessness Research.* Washington, DC: U.S. Departments of Health and Human Services and Housing and Urban Development.

NETHERLANDS

Compared with other countries, the Netherlands has a relatively minor homelessness problem, although homelessness has increasingly become an issue since the 1980s. Whereas the number of homeless people was estimated at 15,000 during the 1960s, during the 1980s and 1990s the estimated number was increasingly higher, and experts feared that by 2000 the number would increase to 50,000 out of a total population of almost 16 million. Politicians and other citizens were shocked.

For years, debate focused on whether the problem of homelessness had merely become more visible because of the concentration of homeless people in city centers or whether the problem had actually worsened. Even today, we cannot answer this question with hard figures because in the Netherlands, no reliable data are available on the number of homeless persons. However, registration data of homeless shelters indicate that during the last few years the number of applications has risen and that the number of people who have been turned away because of lack of shelter capacity has also increased. The Salvation Army has estimated that there are 60,000 homeless persons in the Netherlands. Another study estimated 15,000 homeless persons. However, these estimates are based on different definitions of homelessness and have been calculated by different methods.

Homelessness is a relatively minor problem in the Netherlands probably because of the relatively high levels of social services, such as housing for lower-income groups, social benefits systems for the unemployed and disabled, and the National Health Service. The moderate degree of homelessness in the Netherlands, however, does not lessen the serious nature and the relative persistency of the problem. Undeniably, homeless persons are more visible on the streets today than they were twenty years ago. Few homeless people have simple problems, such as merely lacking accommodation or having financial troubles. The problems of the homeless are almost always complex and distributed across practically all areas of life. However, few homeless children or entire families end up living on the streets. The social security system and other social services prevent persons with simple problems from becoming homeless in large numbers.

PROFILE OF HOMELESS PEOPLE

During the past twenty years, a variety of types of socially vulnerable and homeless persons have appeared in shelters and on the streets in the Netherlands. These types include homeless young people, abused women, hard drug addicts, and former delinquents. These types have different profiles regarding age, male-female relationship, education, ethnicity, and socioeconomic background, as well as process of marginalization that they went through.

What they have in common are having to face multiple, complex problems and having to function on the margins of society. However, their skills and potential

Table 1. Homelessness History and Sleeping Locations

	The Hague Homeless N = 103[1]	Utrecht Homeless N = 150	Amsterdam Homeless N = 212	Rotterdam Homeless N = 112	National Homeless N = 500
Duration of homelessness					
Less than 1 year	20%	26%	33%	21%	18%
1 to 5 years	44%	74%	33%	47%	42%
5 to 10 years	20%	–	13%	33%	18%
10 years or more	17%	–	12%	–	22%
Sleeping locations					
Number of nights	15+ nights last month	15+ nights last month	1+ nights last month	13+ nights last month	1+ nights last 3 months
Street	41%	42%	26%	14%	55%
Night shelters	22%	35%	33%	37%	72%
Semipermanent residence for homeless people	3%	–	–	18%	–
With friends or family	22%	5%	–	3%	–
Other	10%	15%	42%[2]	26%	–

[1] N = Total sample
[2] Includes staying with family or friends

to recover and rejoin society also vary considerably. Some—after a short stay in a shelter—manage to live on their own again. Others are obliged to stay at shelters longer or permanently. Not all types can be portrayed here, so only the most deprived homeless will be examined using studies conducted between 1998 and 2002 in the larger cities of the Netherlands—Amsterdam, Rotterdam, Utrecht, and The Hague—and a recent national study covering twenty cities.

SOCIAL DEMOGRAPHICS AND HISTORY OF THE HOMELESS

Most homeless people in the Netherlands are male, in their late thirties, have never married, and live alone. This profile is consistent both nationally and locally. (See Table 1.) In the national study sample, 87 percent were male, 70 percent had never married, and a further 24 percent were divorced. The average age was thirty-nine for men and thirty-seven for women, and the majority (85 percent) were between twenty-five and fifty-five. The average age and gen-

Table 2. Educational Level and Sources of Income

	The Hague Homeless N = 103	Utrecht Homeless N = 150	Amsterdam Homeless N = 212	Rotterdam Homeless N = 100	National Homeless N = 500
Highest educational level					
Basic or no education	51%	51%	37%	40%	29%
Secondary education	33%	34%	38%	53%	53%
Higher education	15%	15%	17%	7%	18%
Sources of income					
Time period	Past year	Last Month	Past 7 days	Past year[7]	Not specified
Work[1]	36%	25%	–	19%	27%
Welfare benefits[2]	84%	70%	65%	72%	76%
Illegal activities[3]	52%	33%[5]	–	2%	19%
Other[4]	33%	25%[6]	–	7%	10%

[1] Work includes both legal and semilegal work

[2] Unemployment and other benefits, disability allowance, pension

[3] Stealing, burglary, prostitution, begging, and so forth

[4] Income from partners/family, gifts, grants

[5] Excludes prostitution

[6] Includes prostitution

[7] Refers to only main income past year

der of the respondents in the other samples—namely Rotterdam, Amsterdam, Utrecht, and The Hague—were similar (respectively, forty-two, forty, thirty-eight, and thirty-seven years old and 90 percent, 88 percent, 92 percent, and 80 percent male).

Average duration of homelessness varied from three and one-half to six years. The shortest duration was among the Rotterdam homeless sample (3.5 years), followed by The Hague homeless (4.9 years), the Utrecht homeless (5.6 years), and the national homeless sample (6.0 years). The vast majority of the homeless in these studies consisted of the long-term homeless. The percentage of short-term homeless (duration of less than one year) was one-fifth to one-third.

EMPLOYMENT, EDUCATION, AND INCOME

The majority of homeless people in the Netherlands do not have jobs. A substantial number once worked at unskilled labor, and most of them were not very successful in school or dropped out early. These facts are much evident in the studies reviewed. (See Table 2.) In the samples, 29 to 51 percent completed only elementary school. The studies also show that for the majority of homeless respondents, the main source of income was welfare benefits. Seventy-five percent of the sample in the national homeless study were on welfare benefits; across the cities studied, the percentage ranged from 65 to 84. Income from illegal activities showed wide variation across the studies. Approximately one in five in the national sample had income from illegal activities, compared with one in three in the Utrecht sample and one in two in The Hague sample. This variation could be a result of the varying time periods of the reporting by respondents. The study in The Hague asked respondents to report income of the past year, whereas the national study asked for only the current period.

Although many homeless people receive welfare benefits, they encounter problems in obtaining such benefits. Many also have to use part of their allotment to pay fines or debts, for instance, to the National Institute for Social Insurance, housing associations, or the National Health Service. Life on the street is not cheap, and an addiction to alcohol or drugs causes many homeless people further financial difficulties: a chronic shortage of money or real poverty. The customer fee charged for a stay in a shelter prevents some homeless people from using that service. The cost of staying in a shelter would, in combination with paying off debts and fines, reduce disposable income to a pittance. In addition, quite a few shelters obligate clients to have their budget and expenses supervised.

SOCIAL NETWORKS

Social networks are generally weak among homeless people. An unflattering portrayal presents a homeless person as a socially handicapped loner. However, in the long term, relationships with family, other relatives, and friends seem to be replaced by relationships in the homeless group. The longer homelessness persists, the more difficulty homeless people have in sustaining relationships with people outside the homeless group. However, data on contacts with relatives and friends are contradictory. According to Deben and associates (1992) only 8 percent of the homeless people in their sample maintained contacts outside the homeless group: They visited relatives or friends once in a while or stayed with them overnight. Research on homeless people in the city of Groningen confirmed the lack of contacts. However, the studies in Amsterdam and Rotterdam established that the majority did have contacts with relatives or friends outside the homeless group. Similarly, in The Hague study, respondents reported that during the past year they had had contacts with family and friends once a month or less on average. The national study also showed that 60 percent of the sample were still in contact with relatives—parents and siblings—although 40 percent had lost contact. Of course, merely being in contact does not say much about the quality of these relationships. Often the relationship with relatives and friends is a sensitive issue.

With regard to relationships, 17 percent of the national sample reported having a fixed partner currently. Similarly, 14 percent of the Utrecht sample reported having had a partner, and 8 percent of the Rotterdam sample reported having had a partner during the last month. These partner relationships among homeless persons are considered to be unstable. The insecurities of homelessness do not offer a firm base for long-term relationships, according to Doorn (1994). Many homeless people feel that the lack of intimacy and sex is a major deprivation. The feeling of loneliness is much present. Homeless people support each other as much as they can in order to survive, but they do not support each other much in terms of trying to build a new life. Contacts can even have a negative effect on building a new life.

PHYSICAL CONDITION

The physical condition of homeless people is poor, and that of homeless people is worse than that of the average homeless population using shelters. Homeless people have more health problems—such as bronchial, dermatological, gastrointestinal, and neurological disorders and infectious diseases—than the general population. Use of medication is high. Causes of the poor physical condition include poor nutrition, alcohol and drug use, excessive smoking, poor hygiene, and neglected health problems. Not all homeless people have health insurance and access to medical care. Some do not receive welfare benefits and therefore cannot obtain health insurance. Those who do receive welfare benefits often have outstanding debts and therefore cannot afford to pay for health insurance. In the studies reviewed, 25 percent to 30 percent of the homeless did not have health insurance.

PSYCHIATRIC DISORDERS, SUBSTANCE USE, AND ADDICTION

With the data available, one cannot estimate the prevalence of psychiatric disorders among the homeless population in the Netherlands. However, two of the studies in Utrecht and The Hague—did report two mental health disorders (depression and schizophrenic disorders) using standardized measurement instruments. The data report the prevalence of schizophrenia and other psychotic disorders of respondents during the past six months.

In Utrecht, 33 percent of the homeless sample were reported to have depression, and 15 percent had a schizophrenic disorder. In The Hague sample, the six-month prevalence of depression was 29 percent and a much lower prevalence of 5 percent of a schizophrenic disorder. Dual diagnosis (psychiatric disorders in combination with alcohol or drug addiction) was 24 percent in The Hague and 26 percent in Utrecht. Percentages of homeless people with dual diagnosis in the other studies varied from 25 percent to 30 percent.

Of the national homeless population, 10 percent used neither hard drugs nor excessive alcohol. More than 33 percent used hard drugs but not excessive alcohol. Eighteen percent used alcohol in addition to hard drugs, and 17 percent used excessive alcohol exclusively. In Utrecht, Reinking, Kroon, and Smit (1998) found hard drug use in 58 percent of the homeless population. A relationship was established between using drugs and sleeping outdoors and being of relatively young age and having legal problems and an antisocial personality disorder. According to Korf and associates (1999), addiction was one of the largest problems for people sleeping on the street in Amsterdam. Among individuals staying in facilities for homeless people, 57 percent were addicted to alcohol and/or drugs, and 33 percent were addicted to drugs only. In Rotterdam, one out of four homeless people drank alcohol daily, and one out of six used hard drugs such as heroin and/or cocaine daily.

SHELTER AND ITS DEVELOPMENT

Unlike today, care for the homeless in the past was conveniently arranged in three types of shelters—boarding houses for homeless persons, hostels, and day-care centers—and these provided shelter and protection that was termed "bed, bath, and bread." Since the mid-1980s, a broad range of social services has developed. Social service providers continue the goal of providing more support at the "front door" (prevention) and at the "back door" (reintegration and recovery). In addition to shelters, a growing number of other service providers, such as mental health care and drug addict treatment, have initiated this goal under the motto that "prevention is better and easier to achieve than curing." Social service providers want to prevent people from entering a downward spiral and being forced to give up their homes. To facilitate the transition from shelter living to supported independent living, so-called annex residential units and intermediate services were developed, sometimes as part of a short-term experiment, sometimes as part of an institution. In addition to the classic shelter, homeless individuals can now avail themselves of projects for budget management, housing projects with supported living and after care, formal and informal support systems and buddy projects, medical care and sick bays (places for the sick or injured), pastoral care, social security projects, and day activity and labor projects. Consumer-operated projects such as night shelters, employment agencies, and computer courses have also added to the service delivery continuum. Whereas in the past, shelters were intended for all homeless persons—one size fits all—today specific facilities increasingly are being created for specific groups. Social pensions (accommodations) for homeless persons with severe mental disorders were created in the mid-1990s, and then the first pensions specifically for homeless young people appeared as well. More recent are pensions for homeless women and for homeless hard drug addicts; shelters for older homeless persons and homeless alcoholics also are planned. Often, further differentiation is made within the offer for a specific group. For example, in larger cities heroin is provided to a restricted number of chronic addicts under strict medical supervision.

EXPANSION OF CAPACITY AND SHIFT OF SCALE

Homeless shelters are changing rapidly and expanding in the Netherlands. The residential capacity of shelters increased from 4,502 places in 1999 to 5,768 in 2001, an expansion of more than 25 percent. During the past few years, the number of shelter places increased in particular in the social pensions, day and night shelters, and sick bays. As stated earlier, registration data indicate a continuous increase of applications, and because of a lack of places, homeless people are still being turned away. Residential care is at risk of becoming clogged, partly because of the longer average stay of homeless persons.

POLICY

Government policies regarding shelter for the homeless also underwent major changes during the past ten to fifteen years in the Netherlands. An important change was the decentralization of policy responsibility from the national government to a number of so-called center municipalities created by the government. Since 1994, more than forty large- and medium-sized municipalities have been responsible for policy and practice of homeless shelters in their regions. Since then, subsidies for shelters no longer come straight from the government but rather come from center municipalities. Center municipalities must consult with local councils within their regions on spending these subsidies from the national Ministry of Health, Welfare and Sport (VWS).

Many policy areas now exist for the homeless: major city policy, poverty policy, safety policy, OGGZ (Public Mental Health Care) policy, policy for informal (social) shelters, drugs policy, and so on. Both at the national level and local level, several departments are involved. Cooperation between all these civil servants leaves much to be desired. At both levels, people are at cross-purposes and efforts are frustrated.

The input of homeless people on the development and evaluation of policy and practice is rather restricted in the Netherlands. Not until 1984 was an association created that developed into the Landelijke Vereniging Thuislozen (LVT) (National Association of Homeless Persons). This is a client organization of limited means. A number of consumer-operated services exist, but generally speaking they must function with few subsidies. However, homeless people are increasingly demanding a greater say in institutional policy. Although many institutions for the homeless have clients' councils now, in practice participation has not fully developed. Only 25 percent of the center municipalities named clients' representatives as consultation partners in 2001. At this level, too, homeless people's input is modest.

The increase of social services for the homeless indicates more financial means; government funds for shelters have increased approximately 40 percent during the past ten years. In 2001, these funds were combined with those for drug addiction treatment. In 2002 VWS made available 177 million euros (US$217 million for these combined funds. During the past few years, VWS, urged by Parliament, made additional funds available to improve labor conditions of workers and shelter quality, among other goals. Since 2000, additional funds have been issued by the Ministry of Home Affairs to develop 24-hour shelters and address the problems caused by homeless persons on the streets. In 2002, these funds amounted to 12 million euros (US$15 million). However, the majority of center munici-

palities feel that funding by the government is not sufficient, and they supplement this funding by means of the city treasury.

In summary, shelters for the homeless are quite active in the Netherlands. In 2003, a policy study at the national level was conducted by all departments involved in the problem of homelessness. This study identified the bottlenecks in the system of social (informal) shelter and produced policy variations for a more effective service delivery. Proposals include the following:

- Dealing with clogging of the shelter sector
- Preventing in-flow of ex-delinquents by providing better care after detention
- Using intensive forms of case management to be better able to guide people toward other services, thus also promoting through-flow
- Using better housing distribution and accommodation allocation
- Preventing problematic debt accumulation of vulnerable groups in society and allowing more effective debt restructuring
- Reflecting on the use of force and coercion in the shelter sector to counteract nuisances caused by certain groups of homeless persons
- Enhancing the direction role of center municipalities
- Monitoring the effects of modernization of the Exceptional Medical Expenses Act for the quality of care offered the homeless
- Investing in the knowledge infrastructure and information services by establishing local monitors in center municipalities

—Lia van Doorn and Judith Wolf

Further Reading

Bettonvil, A. (1997). *Dichter bij huis* [Closer to home]. Utrecht, Netherlands: Federatie Opvang.

Bruin, D. de, Meijerman, C. (2003). *Zwerven in de 21e eeuw. Een exploratief onderzoek naar geestelijke gezondheidsproblematiek en overlast van dak- en thuislozen in Nederland* [Homelessness in the twenty-first century. An exploratory study into mental health problems of and nuisance caused by homeless persons in the Netherlands]. Utrecht, Netherlands: Centrum voor Verslavingsonderzoek.

Daly, M. (1996). *Homeless: Policies, strategies, lives on the street.* London/New York: Routledge.

Deben, L., Godschalk, J., & Huysman, C. (1992). *Dak-en thuis-lozen in Amsterdam en elders in de Randstad*. [Homeless people in Amsterdam and elsewhere in the urban agglomeration of Randstad (western Holland)]. Amsterdam: Centre for Metropolitan Research, University of Amsterdam.

Doorn, L. van (2002). *Een tijd op straat. Een volgstudie naar ex-daklozen in Utrecht (1999–2000)*. [Time on the streets. A monitor study into former homeless people in Utrecht]. Academic Utrecht, Netherlands: Nederlands Instituut voor Zorg en Welzijn/NIZW [Netherlands Institute for Care and Welfare].

Doorn, L. van. (1994). Wegwijs: een etnografische studie naar dak-en thuislozen [Streetwise: An ethnographical study into homelessness]. Utrecht: NIZW.

Ewijk, H. van, & Kelder, T. (1999). *Who cares? An overview of the Dutch system of health and welfare*. Utrecht: NIZW. Retrieved January 15, 2004, from http://www.nizw.nl/nizwic

Feiter, H.J. de & H. Radstaak (1994). Homelessness in the Netherlands. *Trends and Developments*. Brussels, Belgium: FEANTSA.

Fleurke, F., Jochemsen, M., Montfoort, A. van, & de Vries, P. J. (2002). *Selectieve decentralisatie en de zorg voor kwetsbare groepen* [Selective decentralization and the care for vulnerable groups]. Amsterdam: Vrije Universiteit.

Hoogenboezem, G. (2003). Wonen in een verhaal. *Dak- en thuisloosheid als sociaal pension* [Living in a story. Roof-lessness and homelessness as a social boarding house]. Utrecht, Netherlands: de Graaff.

Korf, D.J., Diemel, S., Riper, H., & Nabben, T. (1999). Het volgende station. *Zwerfjongeren in Nederland* [The next station. Homeless young people in the Netherlands]. Amsterdam: Thela Thesis.

Menger, R., Jezek, R., & Wolf, J. (2004). Eens was ik één van jullie [Once I was one of you]. In: Nuy, M. et al. (Ed.). Wanorde in een mensenleven [Disorder in a human life]. Amsterdam: SWP.

Reinking, D., Kroon, H., Smit, F. (1998). *Opgevangen in Utrecht: Dakloosheid en zelfverwaarlozing in de regio MW-Utrecht* [Shelter in Utrecht: Homelessness and self-neglect in the region of mid-western Utrecht]. Utrecht: Trimbos-instituut.

Wolf, J. (1997). Client needs and quality of life. *Psychiatric Rehabilitation Journal, 20*(4), 16–24.

Wolf, J., Elling, A., & de Graaf, I. (2000). *Monitor Maatschap-pelijke Opvang. Deelmonitoren Vraag, Aanbod en Gemeentelijk Beleid* [Monitor for social shelter. Sub-monitors supply, demand and municipal policy]. Utrecht, Netherlands: Trimbos Institute.

Wolf, J., Nicholas, S., Hulsbosch, L., Pas Te, S., Hoogenboezem, G., & Van Oort, M. (2003). *Monitor Maatschappelijke Opvang. Jaarbericht 2003* [Monitor social shelter. Annual report 2003]. Utrecht, Netherlands: Trimbos Institute.

◉ NEW YORK CITY

From the end of World War II through the mid-1970s, the typical homeless individual in New York City was an older "derelict" man suffering from alcoholism and related problems. Such men typically lived in single-room occupancy (SRO) hotels, flophouses, and missions in the city's Bowery district. Beginning in the middle of the 1970s and greatly accelerating in the 1980s, however, New York's homeless population underwent a substantial transformation.

Following the recession of the early 1980s, thousands of residents found themselves relying on the city for basic shelter. In 1980, New York City sheltered 2,000 people on any given night; a decade later, that number had risen more than tenfold. While the number of people relying on public shelter declined during the economic boom of the 1990s, the period following the events of September 11, 2001, and the subsequent downturn in the economy has seen record increases in the city's homeless population. Still, the official figures can be misleading. Since many people are sheltered only briefly, the number of homeless New Yorkers in any given year far exceeds the number on any single night. Moreover, with hundreds of thousands of city residents marginally housed or living "doubled up" with family and friends, a definition of homelessness that is limited to those living on the streets, in public spaces, and in publicly supported shelters and transitional housing understates the nature of the problem.

A homeless man on a Sunday morning in October 2003 in the Soho neighborhood of southern Manhattan.
Source: Karen Christensen; used with permission.

While New York City does not have the nation's highest rate of homelessness, it does have the greatest *number* of homeless people in a given metropolitan area. In 2003, nearly 40,000 were sheltered on any given night. Such figures, however, undercount the number of homeless. Seventy-five percent of shelter users are in families, while many singles do not use the shelter system at all.

Homeless New Yorkers are overwhelmingly African-American or Latino, and most have lived in New York for much, if not all, of their lives. Problems of substance abuse and mental illness are common among homeless singles, especially women and the long-term homeless; such problems are less prevalent among those in families.

CAUSES

Although several factors contributed to the rise in homelessness in the 1980s, the economic downturn was one primary cause. Another was the decline in purchasing power among the poor, due to wages and public benefits that did not keep pace with rising housing costs. Changes in federal legislation left many previously eligible New Yorkers ineligible for welfare, food stamps, and Social Security disability payments.

Furthermore, the availability of low-cost housing units declined. Changes in city policies resulted in the loss of SRO housing. Arson and abandonment further reduced availability and also resulted in the city becoming landlord to thousands of rental units. New construction of federally funded public housing projects ceased. Publicly supported housing, in the form of the New York City Housing Authority, had a ten-year waiting list. The federal Section 8 housing program was greatly scaled back in the 1980s. The

Housing Works: A Unique Service Provider

Housing Works is a nonprofit organization that is the largest minority-run AIDS services provider in the United States, offering housing, health care, advocacy, job training, and supportive services for homeless people living with HIV/AIDS in New York City. Housing Works is unique because it focuses its efforts specifically on aiding people of color who have been diagnosed with HIV and who also suffer from other health complications, such as mental illness or chemical dependency. What makes Housing Works truly special, however, is the way in which they raise funding for their services.

Housing Works runs both a posh used book café and a handful of trendy thrift shops in New York City, with profits going directly to Housing Works programming and services. The Housing Works Used Book Café is home to 45,000 new, used, and rare books and records, and a café that serves sandwiches, wraps, soups, salads, fine coffee and teas, beer, wine, and desserts. The Used Book Café hosts special events, including live music and readings, and its classic library atmosphere, complete with twenty-foot ceilings, mahogany-paneled balconies and spiral staircases, has hosted numerous film shoots. For years the Café has served as the arena for parties of the New York City literary community, celebrating book releases and holiday festivities. The nationally renowned magazine, The New Yorker, rents space in The Café twice a year.

Housing Works Thrift Shops are known as New York's number one source for new and secondhand designer clothing, housewares, furniture, antiques, and art donated by inhabitants of New York City and sold at the lowest possible prices. Housing Works Thrift Shops can be found in four different locations throughout New York City, and volunteers at each of these locations work as sales associates and provide donor and customer services. All of the proceeds from the thrift shops go directly to support Housing Works programs. The shops also provide job training for clients, along with donated furniture and clothing needed by clients.

Housing Works uniquely uses high style to raise funds, bringing more than meets the eye to disadvantaged people in New York City.

—Emily A. Colangelo

vacancy rate for low-rent units was less than 2 percent throughout this period.

Other trends exacerbated the problem. In the 1960s and 1970s, many people housed in psychiatric facilities were "deinstitutionalized" to community-based supports that never materialized. Both the AIDS and crack epidemics also contributed to the homeless crisis. Significant numbers in each of these groups found themselves unemployed, sick, or without financial support from family members, and were therefore unable to sustain their housing. While other cities had similar trends, New York experienced them earlier, and on a larger scale, than most.

This illustration shows men sleeping in a five-cent-a-night lodging house on the Bowery in the late nineteenth century.

Source: Bettmann/Corbis; used with permission.

POLICIES AND PROGRAMS

Policies and programs have been shaped primarily by state regulations and a series of court decisions and consent decrees resulting from litigation initiated by advocacy groups. The landmark *Callahan v. Carey* legal case, filed in 1979 and settled by consent decree in 1981, required the city to provide shelter to all homeless men who requested it, and determined minimum health and safety standards for shelters. The right to shelter was later extended to women (*Eldredge v. Koch* 1982) and families with children (*McCain v. Koch* 1986). Since then, almost every dispute between city officials and advocates for the homeless has been settled within the judicial system.

In the mid-1980s, large city-run shelters and armories for homeless singles, and privately owned welfare hotels for families predominated. These costly facilities attracted widespread public attention to dirty and dangerous conditions. Over the next decade, the city shifted management of shelters for both singles and families to contracted nonprofit agencies. Welfare hotels for families were replaced by apartment-style "Tier II" shelters run by nonprofits. In the late 1980s, the city made use of more than sixty welfare hotels; by the mid-1990s, it placed families in fewer than ten hotels. Congregate shelters for singles, with hundreds of cots, were replaced by smaller facilities with semi-private sleeping quarters. The remodeled shelters and Tier IIs offered a broader array of supportive services, including assistance with permanent housing placement.

In the early 1980s, New York City spent less than $10 million a year on services for the homeless. By 1993, that figure had risen to over $500 million. To combat the homelessness problem and the high costs associated with it, the city increased permanent housing options. These included a variety of incentives for landlords to rent apartments to homeless people and a dramatic increase in publicly funded housing construction. Rent subsidy programs and supportive housing facilities for special needs populations were also introduced. By the early 1990s, however, the city realized that substantial improvements in shelters (including the speedy transition from shelters to permanent housing for families) had created the unanticipated effect of drawing more people, especially families, into the system—families who were previously doubled up with others or who were living in substandard housing. The city responded with new policies that created disincentives to shelter entry.

Most recently, in response to record numbers of shelter users, ambitious city policies have been expanded, including increases in housing vouchers and permanent apartments for homeless people. In addition, advocates and city officials agreed to the creation of an independent council on homeless families that would both reexamine existing policies toward this population and try to prevent future court cases by mediating disputes.

—*Beth C. Weitzman and Sean N. Fischer*

Further Reading

Berck, J. (1992). *No place to be: Voices of homeless children.* New York: Houghton Mifflin.

Coalition for the Homeless. (2003). Retrieved February 13, 2003, from http://www.coalitionforthehomeless.org

Legal Aid Society of New York. (2003). Retrieved February 13, 2003, from http://www.legal-aid.org

Kozol, J. (1988). *Rachel and her children: Homeless families in America.* New York: Crown.

Morton, M. (1995). *The tunnel: The underground homeless of New York City.* New Haven, CT: Yale University Press.

Morton, M. (2000). *Fragile dwelling.* New York: Aperture.

New York City Department of Homeless Services. (2003). Retrieved February 13, 2003, from http://www.nyc.gov/html/dhs/home.html

Stringer, L. (1998). *Grand Central winter: Stories from the street.* New York: Seven Stories Press.

Toth, J. (1993). *The mole people: Life in the tunnels beneath New York City.* Chicago: Chicago Review Press.

◙ NIGERIA

Within a national population of about 102.5 million, the homeless in Nigeria include

> those displaced as a result of disasters like floods, erosion, riots, fires as well as those displaced by public acquisition of land; tenants and owner-occupiers in sub-marginal living conditions in cities and villages; the disabled, the wandering psychotic as well as vagabonds who require rehabilitation and shelter; refugees/illegal immigrants; able bodied beggars; those sleeping under bridges, pavements, roadside curbs; those who lack real homes in the sense of it; social lepers (these are destitute, orphans, the jobless and poverty stricken ones with no place to lay their heads, no salary and no helper). (Labeodan 1989, 77; UNCHS 2000, 50)

MANIFESTATION

Homelessness is manifested in overcrowded slum accommodations; houses built on stilts especially in riverine areas, swamps, and floodplains; pavement dwellings; and informal settlements.

Olusola Labeodan's study (1989) in Ibadan, Nigeria, revealed a sample count of about 15,700 people homeless. The homeless found in the study slept on road curbs and pavements, inside old train coaches and public transport buses, and in front of closed market stalls. It was found that night guards harbor some of these homeless persons under the pretext that they too are guards. The homeless people play cards till about 2 a.m. and then sleep on benches or tables. In the morning, they go begging for alms or work as load carriers.

There are no national statistics or data on the number of homeless people or people living in marginal situations in Nigeria. About 10 percent (author's guess estimate) of the population are street homeless and are referred to as *omo gutter* ("gutter child"; *omo* is used as street slang to mean a child, youth, or adult who is homeless) or *omo asunta* ("child that sleeps outside/on the street"). Some of them are destitute, mentally ill, beggars, touts, area boys (dropout, street youths and adults in their twenties and thirties who engage in crime and illegal activities and are social misfits), *agberos* ("motor park touts," who are chronically homeless), *alabarus* ("porters in the market places"), and *omo abe gada* ("someone who sleep under the bridge/under bridge user"). On the other hand, about 70 percent (author's guess estimate) of the population live in slums or substandard housing. Ajakaiye (2000) affirmed that the proliferation of informal settlements and slums of despair is not likely to stop.

ANTECEDENTS

Homelessness in Nigeria is attributable to economic, political, social, and cultural factors, which are intertwined with the lopsided distribution of resources and wealth among the population. The antecedents of homelessness include a mismatch between supply and demand for housing, internal migration, increasing urbanization and population growth, obsolete housing stock, and unemployment. Further factors have been land issues, including local resistance against authorities in their bid to take possession of land and develop in spite of the 1978 Land Use Decree; cumbersome procedures for land acquisition; high cost of providing infrastructure on land; high cost of securing land and of settling compensation demands; and delays in the release of funds by government to housing authorities for land acquisition and settlement of compensation.

Poverty and its consequences also loom as antecedents for homelessness. About 75 percent of the working population earns less than US$1.00 a day, so many people simply cannot afford to pay rent, let alone to purchase their own dwellings. There is limited access to housing finance and heavy reliance on sweat equity, social capital, savings, and cooperatives. Poverty is further exacerbated by the International Monetary Fund's Structural Adjustment Program's liberalization policies and privatization resulting in job loss and retrenchment, subsequently pushing people to the brink of homelessness.

The land tenure system, which has altered the traditional rule of succession to land, and the cumbersome nature of the mortgage system also partly contribute to the marginal living conditions of about 70 percent of Nigerians. Poor housing is yet another significant factor. The 1991 National Housing Policy aimed to ensure that all Nigerians own or have access to decent housing accommodation at affordable cost by the year 2000. The policy also indicated that 700,000 housing units needed to be constructed annually. Only 20 percent of Nigerians occupy dwellings with more than one room. In urban centers, about 90 percent of the households live in one-room dwellings, while 73 percent of the rural population live in one-room dwellings.

GAME OF NUMBERS

Housing intervention in Nigeria has been a game of numbers, that is, the quantity (how many houses would be built, and how much funding is made available) rather than the quality of houses. The game of numbers has become evident since the beginning of the national development plans and it still continues today. In the First (1962–1968) and Second (1970–1974) National Development Plans, housing provision was grouped with town and country planning for funding. During the Third National Development Plan (1975–1980), an allocation of $19 million was made to the housing sector to generate 202,000 housing units for low- and middle-income families. The Nigerian Building Society was changed to the Federal Mortgage Bank of Nigeria with an initial capital of $1.2 million. The Fourth National Development Plan (1981–1985) was aimed at attaining optimum housing development in the country, according to Onibokun (1985), through direct construction of 200,000 housing units by the

government, allocation of $174,000 for housing development through the Urban Development Programmes, and introduction of the Infrastructure Development Fund (IDF) for financing urban development projects in 1985.

In 1986, the Sites and Services Programme was introduced, and there was a major change in macroeconomic and sectoral policies of the government as a result of the introduction of the Structural Adjustment Program (SAP). International Monetary Fund Investment in housing was inhibited during the SAP period by the high rate of default in loan repayments and delays in the release of funds by the government, the prohibitive cost of construction in terms of building materials and equipment costs, the cost of labor, and inadequate funds from government to pay construction costs. Government programs and policies aimed at housing development, by and large, were ineffective and inadequate. Most of these low-income and low-cost houses were not completed, were poorly constructed, or were not habitable. For example, the government was expected to build 121,000 housing units between 1994 and 1995 to address the housing shortage; only 1,014 houses were completed (Central Bank of Nigeria 1990–1998).

The actual achievements in terms of adequate housing delivery have been minimal, and the game of numbers persists. About 5 million new housing units are required to meet the existing and future housing needs in urban areas, and about 3.2 million are needed in rural areas.

STRATEGY

To remedy housing provision problems in the country, the 1996–2002 National Rolling Plans identified the following strategies:

- Establishment of appropriate institutional framework to facilitate effective planning and housing development
- Restructuring of all existing public housing delivery institutions
- Mobilization of private-sector participation
- Provision of a conducive environment that encourages the establishment of more mortgage

institutions and stronger local government involvement; research into the use of locally produced building materials; and relevant policies and proper financial facilities to come up with housing designs that medium-income households can afford over a twenty-five-year loan repayment period.

RESEARCH PRIORITY

The homelessness enigma is rife among the low-income and economically weaker sectors of the population, and poverty is a major factor contributing to the prevalence of homelessness. Slum conditions and overcrowding proliferate in the cities with adverse effects on sanitation and health.

There are no data on the number of homeless people. As Professor Tunde Agbola asserts, "There is not much interest in this area, there has been no information and/or research on homelessness in Nigeria and there is no research funding for such an issue" (personal communication, 4 March 2003). Research and up-to-date statistics and information data banks are pivotal to planning and policy for the homeless in Nigeria. Thus, as a matter of priority, nationwide research to document the nature, number of people affected, and characteristics of homelessness is very pertinent.

—*Olusola Olufemi*

Further Reading

Ajakaiye, O. (2000). Welcome address by the director general, NISER, workshop on contemporary issues in human settlements development. In F. Olokesusi & R. Adebayo (Eds.), *Contemporary issues in human settlements development* (pp. 149–151). Ibadan, Nigeria: New World Press.

Ajakaiye, O., & Falokun, G. (2000). Economic implications of housing provision in Nigeria during the 2000–2010 rolling plan period. In F. Olokesusi & R. Adebayo (Eds.), *Contemporary issues in human settlements development* (pp. 21–42). Ibadan, Nigeria: New World Press.

Centre for Settlements Studies and Development. (1992). *Ameliorating the impact of Structural Adjustment Programme (SAP) on housing and environmental development in Nigeria: Policy options*. A policy paper stemming from a research/workshop project undertaken by CASSAD with financial assistance from the Friedrich-Ebert Foundation of Germany.

Central Bank of Nigeria. (1990–1998). *Annual report and statement of accounts*. Abuja, Nigeria: Author.

Federal Republic of Nigeria. (1997). *Vision 2010 Main Report*. Abuja, Nigeria: Author. Retrieved August 12, 2003, from http://nigeriaworld.com/focus/documents/vision2010.html

Labeodan, O. (1987). *The homeless in Nigeria: The Ibadan case study*. Ibadan, Nigeria: Nigerian Institute of Social and Economic Research.

Labeodan, O. (1989). The homeless in Ibadan. *Habitat International Journal, 13*(1), 75–85.

National Population Commission. (1996). *National population census report*. Abuja, Nigeria: Federal Republic of Nigeria, Federal Secretariat Complex.

National Population Commission. (1998). *National rolling plan: 1996–1998* (Vol. 1). Abuja, Nigeria: National Population Commission and Federal Republic of Nigeria, Federal Secretariat Complex.

National Population Commission. (1999). *National rolling plan: 1997–1999* (Vol.1). Abuja, Nigeria: National Population Commission and Federal Republic of Nigeria, Federal Secretariat Complex.

National Population Commission. (2000). *National rolling plan: 1998–2000* (Vol.1). Abuja, Nigeria: National Population Commission and Federal Republic of Nigeria, Federal Secretariat Complex.

Okpala, D. C. I. (1980). Accessibility distribution aspects of public urban land management: A Nigerian case. *Habitat International Journal, 4*(4–6), 593–609.

Olufemi, O. (1993) *Institutional housing finance in Nigeria: A case study of the Property Development Corporation of Oyo State* (Monograph Series No. 6). Ibadan, Nigeria: Nigerian Institute of Social and Economic Research.

Onibokun, P. (1985). *Housing in Nigeria: A book of readings*. Ibadan, Nigeria: Nigerian Institute of Social and Economic Research.

Philips, A. (1997). *Population and development: 1998–2010* (Monograph Series No. 16). Ibadan, Nigeria: Nigerian Institute of Social and Economic Research.

United Nations Centre for Human Settlements (UNCHS). (2000). *Strategies to combat homelessness* (Series of Publications in Support of the Global Campaign for Secure Tenure No. 03/2000). Retrieved August 12, 2003, from http://www.unhabitat.org/en/uploadcontent/publication/HS-599.pdf

OLDER HOMELESS PERSONS

In the United States, older homeless persons—those age fifty and over—often seem invisible. Public policy generally focuses on younger homeless people or on social categories in which the aging are subsumed without special notice, such as disabled individuals and veterans.

For purposes of studying homeless populations, researchers have set the aging marker at anywhere from age forty to sixty-five. However, a growing consensus holds that the "older homeless" should be defined as age fifty and over. Indeed, at that age, many homeless persons look and act ten to twenty years older.

Although the proportion of older persons among the homeless has declined since the 1980s, their absolute number has grown. (As for the actual percentage of aging Americans who are homeless, estimates vary widely—from about 3 to 28 percent—due to heterodox methods and definitions of aged status.) In any case, the proportion of older homeless persons can be expected to increase dramatically as more baby boomers turn fifty. Thus, with an anticipated doubling of the fifty-and-over population by about 2030, a comparable increase in the number of older homeless persons is likely. The current low estimate of 60,000 would grow to 120,000, while the high estimate of 400,000 would mushroom to 800,000.

FACTORS CONTRIBUTING TO HOMELESSNESS IN OLDER PEOPLE

Homelessness generally results from a concurrence of conditions, events, and risk variables. The flow chart in Figure 1 depicts these factors in four categories, summarized below.

- Personal risk factors may accumulate over a lifetime. Except in the case of extremely vulnerable individuals, homelessness is likely to occur only when several of these personal risk factors coexist.

- Systemic factors play a critical role. In most instances, such variables as the availability of low-cost housing and the income to pay for it are the ultimate determinants of homelessness.

- Enculturation factors—that is, a person's adaptation to the street or shelter—may further sustain and prolong homelessness.

- Programmatic factors can prevent or terminate homelessness, depending on the timeliness, quality, and availability of the service intervention.

Individual Risk Factors

The principal risk factors found to increase vulnerability to homelessness among older individuals are described below, based on studies conducted in the period from 1983 to 1998.

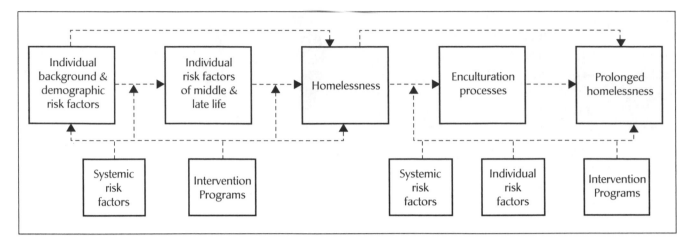

Figure 1. Model of Homelessness and Aging

Gender: The ratio of older homeless men to women is approximately 4:1.

Race: African-Americans are overrepresented among older homeless populations—and they are even more so among their younger counterparts.

Fifty to sixty-four age range: Because of the entitlements available to persons at age sixty-five, the risk of homelessness drops at that age. Indeed, the proportion of elders over sixty-five among the homeless is roughly one-fourth of their representation in the general population. Conversely, persons between fifty and sixty-four are overrepresented among the homeless, close to double their representation in the general population.

Extremely low income: Older homeless persons are likely to come from poor or near impoverished backgrounds and to spend their lives in similar economic status. More than three-fifths worked in unskilled or semi-skilled occupations. Median current income is roughly one-half the poverty level.

Disruptive events in youth: About one-fifth of older persons have had disruptive early life events such as the death of parents, placement in foster care, and so forth. Similar rates hold for younger homeless persons as well.

Prior imprisonment: Roughly half of older men and one-fourth of older women report prior incarceration.

Chemical abuse: Although the prevalence of alcoholism varies, older men have rates about two to four times higher than do older women, and older men have higher rates than their housed age peers. Illicit drug abuse falls off sharply in homeless persons over fifty, but this may increase with the aging of the younger generation of heavy drug users.

Psychiatric disorders: Levels of mental illness have been found to be consistently higher among women than men, with psychosis more common among women and depression equally prevalent, or slightly more prevalent among men. Studies in New York City have found that 9 percent of older men and 42 percent of older women displayed psychotic symptoms, whereas 37 percent of men and 30 percent of women exhibited clinical depression. Levels of cognitive impairment ranged from 10 to 25 percent, but severe impairment occurred in only 5 percent of older homeless persons, which is roughly comparable to the general population.

Physical health: Older persons suffer from physical symptoms at roughly 1.5 to 2 times the level of their age peers in the general population, although their functional impairment was no worse.

Victimization: Both younger and older homeless report high rates of victimization. Studies have found that nearly half of older persons had been robbed and one-fourth to one-third had been assaulted in the past year. One-fourth of older women reported having been raped during their lifetime.

Social supports: Social networks of older persons are smaller (about three-fourths the size of their age peers') and more concentrated on staff members from agencies or institutions. They are more likely to involve material exchanges such as food, money, or health assistance; to entail more reciprocity; and to have fewer intimate ties. Although not utterly isolated, older homeless persons lack the diverse family ties that characterize their age peers in the general population. Only 1 to 7 percent are currently married, versus 54 percent among their age peers. Nevertheless, various studies have found that about one-third to three-fifths of older homeless persons believe that they could count on family members for support.

Prior history of homelessness: One of the key predictors of prolonged and subsequent homeless episodes is prior history of homelessness. Durations of homelessness are substantially higher among older men than older women.

Other Risk Factors

Once a person becomes homeless, evolution into long-term homelessness involves an enculturation process in which the individual learns to adapt and survive in the world of shelters or streets. Shelter life may foster this enculturation in several ways. First, "shelterization"—adapting to the group lifestyle and organization of homeless shelters—may replicate earlier military or prison experiences for some men, while others develop a type of "learned helplessness." Second, shelters may be a rational choice based on safety and stability, especially for women. Third, they offer a new social support system; residents typically consider about one-third of their shelter or flophouse comrades to be "intimates."

Furthermore, certain older persons (men, the mentally ill, and those with prior homeless episodes in particular) are more apt to remain homeless for extended periods, a trend most likely reflecting impediments at the personal and systemic levels.

The two principal systemic factors that create homelessness are lack of income and lack of affordable housing. Even in cities with adequate housing supplies, it may be out of reach for the poor, because of poor-quality jobs, unemployment, and low incomes. Conversely, in cities where incomes may be higher and jobs are more plentiful, tight rental

markets stemming from middle-class pressures and escalating living costs also make housing less available to lower-income persons. Both of these conditions can push some people over the edge into homelessness.

Programmatic factors that negatively affect interventions for older homeless persons include limited availability of housing alternatives or in-home services for disabled older adults, agency staff who lack motivation or skills to assist older persons, and an absence of outreach programs that target older adults.

Although it is now recognized that most older homeless persons do *not* suffer from severe mental illness, the closing of mental hospitals ("deinstitutionalization") has been often cited as playing a critical role in causing homelessness. But evidence suggests that it does not exert such a direct effect. There is usually a time lag between a person's discharge from a psychiatric hospital and subsequent homelessness, and many mentally ill homeless people have never been hospitalized. Mental illness may indeed contribute to homelessness, especially among older women. But it is also apparent that the over-representation of the mentally ill among homeless persons more accurately reflects systemic factors such as inadequate entitlements and a scarcity of appropriate housing.

Triggers for Homelessness

The research literature has often dichotomized homelessness among older adults as resulting either from a long "slide" accelerated by an accumulation of events or risk factors over time, or from a "critical juncture" in which a crisis compels the person to leave his or her residence. However, many cases involve both: first a cumulative series of events or risk factors, then one final event that triggers true homelessness. Martha Sullivan's study in New York City found that older women had experienced an average of three major life events or crises over a period of one to five years preceding their homelessness.

Specific proximal causes (direct "triggers") of homelessness among older persons depend largely upon the person's age when first becoming home-

An older homeless man rests in the entrance way to a train station in London, England, in July 2003.

Source: Karen Christensen; used with permission.

less. In Britain, Maureen Crane drew three conclusions from a study of older homeless people. For those who first became homeless in early adulthood, homelessness was triggered by a disturbed family home, or by discharge from an orphanage or the armed services. For those who first became homeless in midlife, triggers included the death of a parent, marital breakdown, and a drift to less secure transient work and housing. Late-life homelessness often followed the death of a spouse, marital breakdown, retirement, loss of accommodation tied to employment, or the increasing severity of a mental illness.

It has been noted that for women in general, homelessness is apt to be triggered by failures or crises in family life, whereas for men it is more closely linked to occupational failures. While older men commonly have long histories of homelessness, older women are more often driven to it by a crisis in later life.

INTERVENTION STRATEGIES

Older homeless persons are a heterogeneous population. In Britain, for example, Anthony Warnes and Maureen Crane identified seven subtypes based on where they slept, their use of hostels and day centers, and whether they worked, used alcohol, had psychiatric illness, received benefits, moved frequently, or

had been rehoused in the past. Such diversity is worth keeping in mind when devising intervention strategies.

Three key points are particularly noteworthy with respect to such strategies. First, because these older homeless are perhaps the most heterogeneous of homeless subgroups—with broad differences in health, cognitive status, and length of homelessness, for example—interventions must be even more individualized than in younger populations. Second, interventions are possible at any point in the model shown in Figure 1: at the distal level (that is, in early and midlife), the proximal level (addressing immediate triggers for homelessness), and subsequent to becoming homeless. Third, in contrast to the self-sufficiency model used for younger persons—that is, moving from transitional supported residential situations to independent living—it may be more profitable to consider various types of permanent supported living arrangements for more vulnerable older persons.

However, unless new statutory interventions are forthcoming, the number of older persons at risk for homelessness will surely increase in tandem with the general population over age fifty. Unfortunately, many individual risk factors—such as previous incarceration, history of disrupted marriages, likelihood to be living alone, lifetime of low-income occupations, and greater use of illicit drugs—are the product of social forces that have left an indelible imprint on the postwar generation.

OPTIONS FOR PROGRESS

Despite these ominous signs, a dramatic increase in aging homeless persons may be forestalled by various statutory and service initiatives such as the following.

Legislation must be passed to improve income supports for suitable housing, especially in geographic areas where relatively low-cost housing is available. In areas where income and employment levels may be higher but affordable housing is scarce, legislation should focus on developing more inexpensive housing.

Policy must address the needs of the fifty-to-

A Dying Neighborhood Turns Around

MILWAUKEE (ANS)—When nursing home administrator Cordelia Taylor began to feel the corporate office was more concerned with the bottom line than quality care, she fumed to her husband.

His response: quit complaining and start your own.

So they left their dream home in an affluent suburban area and returned to their old neighborhood in Milwaukee's inner city, which had become one of the city's poorest and most violent, to start Family House, a licensed nonprofit community-based residential facility whose mission is to prevent people from being institutionalized and to give them a family living experience.

Now she provides a home for the homeless, the poor and others who have no place else to turn, regardless of the effect on her bottom line. Her only criteria: residents must be at least 55 years old, must not use alcohol or illegal drugs and must not be violent.

In the nearly dozen years since the first eight residents moved into Family House, Taylor has bought and added seven more group homes along her side of the street to serve 42 residents; started a community medical clinic that is doubling its space after just one year; provided a place for youngsters to study after school; and is leading the charge to revitalize this once pleasant neighborhood.

"It was terrible at first," Taylor said of the decaying neighborhood where drug dealers lived in boarded-up buildings. "When we left the central city, the area I lived in, it was not this way. My old neighborhood had done a 180-degree turnaround."

Most of Taylor's old neighbors had left the area, abandoning it to drug dealers and gangs. Those who were left were "scared to death," she said.

Others were unwilling to battle drug dealers, but they encouraged Taylor, who testified against dealers and confronted them on the street. She also saw that an unlicensed tavern at the end of the block, the scene of violent and unlawful behavior, was shut down. She is now negotiating to buy that building to open a community center with after-school activities and classes in parenting, budgeting and job training.

The medical clinic, which will be expanded to double its current three examination rooms and other offices, is open four days a week to the entire community, said Patrick Taylor, Taylor's youngest son, who is the clinic's administrative assistant.

"We're going to get more doctors and help more people," he said.

The clinic works in partnership with the Medical College of Wisconsin, Patrick Taylor said. "We have an agreement where their physicians come into our facility and work as a satellite," he said.

Family House's eight residential buildings now house 42 residents grouped together based on their physical abilities. In one building, staff members simply clean, see that the doors are locked at night and ensure that residents get their proper medications, while in another, staff are there 24 hours a day as in a skilled nursing home.

Each resident is offered a private room, though some prefer the company of a roommate, Cordelia Taylor said.

Residents are encouraged to garden in the home's raised garden beds and to volunteer working with neighborhood children. But sometimes it takes a while for them to feel at home, she said.

"When they first come in, they are very suspicious because these are people who have had good reasons to be suspicious; they're from the street and they've had to stay awake at night to stay safe," Taylor said.

Old habits die hard, and some continue for a while to stay up all night and sleep during daylight, keeping personal belongings with them at all times and hoarding food, she said.

"Once they learn that you are going to do what you say you're going to do, they slowly come out of their shell, and they are some of the most pleasant, happiest people you would want to be around," Taylor said.

Family House relies on its residents' ability to pay—even if it's nominal or nothing—and donations from faith-based groups, foundations and individuals. She will not accept city or state small-business money with strings attached.

"Since we are a mission and since God did not give me this for political reasons, I am not involved in politics," she said. "I don't want anybody to come in and tell me who I can take care of and say, 'This person can't pay so you can't keep them.' I want to be able to take care of people without someone telling me how I have to do it."

Source: "One Woman's Determination Turns Dying Neighborhood Around," American News Service, n.d.

sixty-five age group with health and other safety-net supports. Compared with their younger counterparts, they may have difficulty securing employment if they are laid off, they have more physical problems, and they are more apt to experience the death of a spouse and losses in close social ties.

Where legislation exists to provide assistance, benefits must be easily secured. Older persons who are eligible for benefits often do not obtain them, and those who do may not obtain the maximum allowable amounts. Judicial and administrative actions may be needed to enforce existing statutes.

Mentally ill homeless persons often need case managers who can help them secure entitlements and housing and link them to appropriate medical, psychiatric, or substance abuse treatment. Several demonstration projects have shown this to be valuable. Although not specifically targeted to older homeless persons, all of them included persons over age fifty.

Greater emphasis must be placed on preventing homelessness by early identification and help for people at risk. Effective systems of support should enable people to manage in independent or supported housing and should help prevent relinquished tenancies and evictions. Extant laws which may unintentionally foster homelessness should be changed. For example, persons in public housing or who receive federal Section 8 rent subsidies are prohibited from sharing their apartment with nonfamily members. Thus, if a family member dies or moves away, the remaining person may be unable to pay the rent.

Better reviews of condemned or uninhabitable buildings are needed, to ensure that the eviction of current tenants is not leading to other uses for the properties. Older persons are especially vulnerable to such issues since a disproportionate number live in declining neighborhoods with many dilapidated buildings. Government agencies in charge of formally condemning buildings could be required to institute mechanisms for providing transitional assistance to tenants. "Early warning" systems need to be created to identify vulnerable people who are not coping at home—before rent arrears and other problems accumulate and eviction proceedings commence. In the United States, efforts to prevent homelessness include legal assistance projects to help forestall evictions, cash assistance programs to assist with rent arrears, and direct landlord payments and voucher systems to ensure that tenants can cover their rents.

At the service level, there has been a paucity of programs for homeless and marginally housed older persons. Age-segregated drop-in social centers coupled with outreach programs have been shown to be useful with this population. Unfortunately, while many agencies proclaim an official goal of rehabilitating homeless persons and reintegrating them into conventional society, the bulk of their energies go into providing accommodative services that simply help them survive from day to day.

For extreme cases, help may be provided by a mobile unit of the type developed by Project Help in New York City to involuntarily hospitalize persons. Used judiciously and with awareness of civil rights, such units can assist those elderly homeless who are suffering from moderate, severe, or life-threatening mental disorders.

Finally, advocacy is important. For example, in Boston, the Committee to End Elder Homeless consists of a coalition of public and private agencies working to provide options for this population.

The imminent burgeoning of the aging population will result in a substantial rise in at-risk persons. Prevention of homelessness among older persons will depend primarily on addressing systemic and programmatic factors.

—*Carl I. Cohen*

Further Reading

Cohen, C. I. (1999). Aging and homelessness. *The Gerontologist, 39,* 5–14.

Cohen, C. I., Ramirez, M., Teresi, J., Gallagher M., & Sokolovsky, J. (1997). Predictors of becoming redomiciled among older homeless women. *The Gerontologist, 37,* 67–74.

Cohen, C. I., & Sokolovsky, J. (1989). *Old men of the Bowery: Strategies for survival among the homeless.* New York: Guilford Press.

Cohen, C. I., Sokolovsky, J., & Crain, M. (2001). Aging, homelessness, and the law. *International Journal of Law and Psychiatry, 24,* 167–181.

Crane, M. (1999). *Understanding older homeless people.* Buckingham, UK: Open University Press.

Hecht, L., & Coyle, B. (2001). Elderly homeless. A comparison of older and younger adult emergency shelter seekers in Bakersfield, California. *American Behavioral Scientist, 45,* 66–79.

Keigher, S. M. (1991). *Housing risks and homelessness among the urban elderly.* New York: Haworth Press.

Sullivan, M. A. (1991). The homeless older woman in context: Alienation, cutoff, and reconnection. *Journal of Women and Aging, 3,* 3–24.

Warnes, A., & Crane, M. (2000). *Meeting homeless people's needs. Service development and practice for the older excluded.* London: King's Fund.

▣ OUTREACH

The Federal Task Force on Homelessness and Severe Mental Illness has recognized outreach as the first and most critical component of any program serving a homeless population (Interagency Council on the Homeless 1994). Often conducted in a variety of nontraditional settings, outreach is the first step in developing relationships with some of the most disenfranchised people in America's communities. It is a process of linking people who are homeless to services and resources they want and need. The goal of outreach is to establish a personal connection that will provide the spark for the journey back to a vital and dignified life as part of the community (Winarski 1994). Outreach services are critical to ensuring survival in perilous living conditions and to supporting the person's reintegration to mainstream culture.

KEY FEATURES OF OUTREACH

Homeless people are a diverse group, but they share characteristics that contribute to the need for outreach, including poor physical or mental health, substance abuse problems, a history of negative experiences with service providers, fragmented relationships with family and significant others, and histories of trauma and/or neglect (Interagency Council on the Homeless 1994). Disorientation, mistrust, fear of rehospitalization, lack of motivation, and language problems contribute to the experience of isolation. It is not uncommon for people to be aware of their many needs and to want assistance, and yet still refuse to use available services. Many have also experienced multiple losses, including losses of fundamental cultural roles—as parent, spouse, worker, involved citizen (Winarski 1998). In addition, mainstream programs can present barriers to service utilization (Rog 1988). For all of these reasons, out-

reach services are needed to meet homeless people on their own turf and to address their unique needs with patience, perseverance, and respect.

Location of Outreach Services

Reaching homeless individuals and street dwellers, in particular, requires engaging them wherever they may live. Outreach may occur as part of a mobile intervention effort, in which staff seek out homeless persons in street locations such as under bridges or in doorways, in rural locations such as riverbanks or barns, in public facilities such as libraries or bus stations, and in institutions such as hospitals or jails. Mobile outreach staff typically work in pairs or teams and often use vans, bicycles, or go on foot to seek out places where homeless persons reside. Fixed-site outreach takes place at program sites where large numbers of homeless persons may congregate. These include drop-in centers, soup kitchens, and shelters. By establishing a presence in these facilities, outreach staff have access to a greater numbers of clients. Outreach programs often combine mobile and fixed-site approaches to reach the broadest range of individuals in need and to better coordinate services (McMurray-Avila 2001).

Core Outreach Services

Outreach programs share the goal of establishing a meaningful connection with homeless people, whatever their location, and then linking them to services and supports that are critical for improvement. Core outreach services include activities that focus on engagement, information and referral, and direct services.

Engagement

Outreach programs target people who are unserved or underserved by the service delivery system. Engagement activities focus on developing a personal connection with these individuals; they are the linchpin of all outreach activities. For these persons, fear and mistrust of service providers is common and often based on previous negative experiences. Many are also isolated and have histories of

Outreach workers gather on Regent Street in London in July 2003 to discuss their plans before fanning out to offer assistance to homeless people.

Source: Karen Christensen; used with permission.

fragmented relationships. People who use alcohol and drugs are even more disconnected. In addition, human service programs can create barriers to access that make it especially difficult for homeless persons to get the help they need. These include rigid eligibility criteria, inflexible scheduling, long waiting lists, and negative attitudes among staff toward homeless clients (Interagency Council on the Homeless 1992).

Engagement activities seek to overcome these personal and programmatic barriers through persistent and respectful attempts to make contact. The goal is to establish a trusting relationship that will create the bridge to critical services and supports, and that will provide the foundation for all future treatment interventions (Morse and Calsyn et al. 1996). The elements most critical to engagement include a patient and persistent approach, respect for the person's perceived needs, good listening skills, and the capacity to provide concrete benefits such as food, clothing, or showers. Although the need for human connection is most apparent during initial contacts, outreach programs need to establish ongoing relationships, sometimes over extended periods of time. It may be necessary for outreach workers to spend many weeks, months, or even years in developing a relationship as part of the engagement process (Winarski 1998).

Information and Referral

Outreach programs serve as important sources of information about services and resources useful to homeless people. These include programs that provide financial assistance, basic supports, housing, health, and social services (McMurray-Avila 2001). Homeless people may not be aware that these resources are available or know how to access them. Outreach workers also play a critical role by linking homeless people to these resources. Rather than just scheduling appointments, the referral process includes an orientation to procedures such as intake forms and documenting eligibility requirements. They also provide follow-up support to ensure that a meaningful contact has taken place. Because people who are homeless often have multiple, complex needs, they often need linkages to multiple service providers and resources. Effective outreach programs need to establish durable linkages across systems, public and private, including those that serve both the homeless and the non-homeless, youth and adults (Erickson and Page, 1999).

Direct Services

Because homeless people have needs that require immediate attention, and because of the difficulties inherent in establishing multiple linkages, outreach programs themselves typically provide a broad range of direct services (Interagency Council on the Homeless 1992). These include screening and assessment for medical, psychiatric, and social problems, especially as these relate to the presence of life-threatening conditions. Outreach programs often include mobile treatment teams that can prescribe medication and provide basic primary, psychiatric, and chemical dependency services. Fixed-site programs also provide clinical services that require structured settings, such as individual and group interventions that provide education about symptoms of mental illness and the effects of medication, skills training, cognitive-behavioral therapies, and vocational counseling (McMurray-Avila 2001). Outreach programs that combine information and referral strategies with these direct services have been found to be the most cost-effective (Morse 1999).

IMPLICATIONS

Outreach services are the first and most critical step to help ensure the survival of people who are homeless. Outreach also develops important connections with people who have become disaffiliated from meaningful roles in their communities. However, to help homeless persons make the successful transition from a focus on survival to integration into community, enduring linkages with mainstream services and resources need to be established. Outreach programs need to be conducted as part of a comprehensive system of care that supports the transition of homeless individuals into the mainstream. An ideal system includes health care, income support, legal services, housing, and rehabilitation and employment services (Interagency Council on the Homeless 1992). The objectives of outreach cannot be fully realized unless they are part of a comprehensive and integrated network of care.

—*James T. Winarski*

Further Reading

Erickson, S., & Page, J. (1999). To dance with grace: Outreach and engagement to persons on the street. In L. B. Fosburg & D. L. Dennis (Eds.), *Practical lessons: The 1998 National Symposium on Homelessness Research*. Delmar, NY: National Resource Center on Homelessness and Mental Illness.

Interagency Council on the Homeless. (1991). *Reaching out: A guide for service providers*. Washington, DC: Department of Housing and Urban Development.

Interagency Council on the Homeless. (1992). *Outcasts on main street: Report of the federal task force on homelessness and severe mental illness*. Washington, DC: Department of Housing and Urban Development.

Interagency Council on the Homeless. (1994). *Priority: Home! The federal plan to break the cycle of homelessness*. Washington, DC: U.S. Department of Housing and Urban Development.

McMurray-Avila, M. (2001). *Organizing health services for homeless people: A practical guide*. Nashville, TN: National Health Care for the Homeless Council.

Morse, G. (1999). *Reaching out to homeless people with serious mental illnesses under managed care*. Prepared for the National Resource Center on Homelessness and Mental Illness under contract to the Center for Mental Health Services.

Morse, G. A., Calsyn, R. J., et al. (1996). Outreach to homeless mentally ill people: Conceptual and clinical consideration. *Community Mental Health Journal, 32*(3), 261–274.

Rog, D. J. (1988). *Engaging homeless persons with mental illness into treatment*. Alexandria, VA: National Mental Health Association.

Winarski, J. T. (1994). Providing outreach outside the shelter. In E. Bassuk, A. Birk, & J. Liftik (Eds.), *Community care for homeless clients with mental illness, substance abuse, and dual diagnosis* (pp. 10–1–10–18). Newton, MA: The Better Homes Fund.

Winarski, J. T. (1998). *Implementing interventions for homeless individuals with co-occurring mental health and substance use disorders: A PATH technical assistance package*. Sudbury, MA: Advocates for Human Potential under contract with the Substance Abuse and Mental Health Services Administration, Center for Mental Health Services. (Monograph SMA 98–3204).